*Bond Markets,
Analysis and Strategies*

FOURTH EDITION

Bond Markets, Analysis and Strategies

Frank J. Fabozzi, CFA

Adjunct Professor of Finance
School of Management
Yale University

Prentice Hall, Upper Saddle River, New Jersey 07458

Senior Editor: Paul Donnelly
Editorial Assistant: Cheryl Clayton
Vice President/Editorial Director: James Boyd
Assistant Editor: Gladys Soto
Marketing Manager: Patrick Lynch
Production Manager: Gail Steier de Acevedo
Production Coordinator: Maureen Wilson
Permissions Coordinator: Monica Stipanov
Manufacturing Buyer: Natacha St. Hill Moore
Senior Manufacturing Manager: Vincent Scelta
Cover Design: Bruce Kenselaar
Cover Art/Photo: John Nelson/Stock Illustration Source, Inc.
Full Service Composition: UG / GGS Information Services, Inc.

Copyright © 2000, 1996, 1993, 1989 by Prentice-Hall, Inc.
Upper Saddle River, New Jersey 07458

All rights reserved. No part of this book may be reproduced, in any form or
by any means, without written permission from the Publisher.

Library of Congress Cataloging-in-Publication Data
Fabozzi, Frank J.
   Bond markets, analysis and strategies / Frank J. Fabozzi. — 4th
ed.
     p.   cm.
   Includes bibliographical references and index.
   ISBN 0-13-040266-4
   1. Bonds.   2. Investment analysis.   3. Portfolio management.
4. Bond market. I. Title.
HG4651.F28   2000
332.63'23—dc21   99-22185
                                            CIP

Prentice-Hall International (UK) Limited, London
Prentice-Hall of Australia Pty. Limited, Sydney
Prentice-Hall Canada, Inc., Toronto
Prentice-Hall Hispanoamericana, S.A., Mexico
Prentice-Hall of India Private Limited, New Delhi
Prentice-Hall of Japan, Inc., Tokyo
Prentice-Hall (Singapore) Pte Ltd.
Editora Prentice-Hall do Brasil, Ltda., Rio de Janeiro

Printed in the United States of America

10 9 8 7 6 5 4 3 2

To the memory of two wonderful mothers,
Josephine Fabozzi
and
Patricia Marie Hieber

Brief Contents

Contents

Preface to the Fourth Edition

The first edition of *Bond Markets, Analysis and Strategies* was published in 1989. The objective was to provide coverage of the products, analytical techniques for valuing bonds and quantifying their exposure to changes in interest rates, and portfolio strategies for achieving a client's objectives. In the two editions subsequently published and in the current edition, the coverage of each of these areas has been updated. In the product area, the updating has been primarily for the latest developments in mortgage-backed securities and asset-backed securities. The updating of analytical techniques has been in the valuation of bonds with embedded options and measures for assessing the interest rate risk of complex instruments. Strategies for accomplishing investment objectives, particularly employing derivative instruments, have been updated in each edition.

Each edition has benefited from the feedback of readers, instructors using the book at universities and training programs, and CFA candidates who have used the book in their studies. Many discussions with portfolio managers and analysts, as well as my experiences serving on the board of directors of several funds and consulting assignments, have been invaluable in improving the content of the book. Moreover, my fixed income course at Yale's School of Management and various presentations to institutional investor groups throughout the world provided me with the testing ground for new material.

I am indebted to the following individuals who shared with me their views on various topics covered in this book: Scott Amero (BlackRock Financial Management), Anand Bhattacharya (Countrywide Securities), Douglas Bendt (Mortgage Risk Assessment Corporation), David Canuel (Charter Oak Capital Management), John Carlson (Fidelity Management and Research), Dwight Churchill (Fidelity Management and Research), Ravi Dattatreya (Sumitomo Bank Capital Markets), Mark Dunetz (Guardian Life), Sylvan Feldstein (Guardian Life), Michael Ferri (George Mason University), John Finnery (Fordham University), Gifford Fong (Gifford Fong Associates), Jack Francis (Baruch College, CUNY), Laurie Goodman (Paine Webber), Joseph Guagliardo (FNX), David Horowitz (Miller, Anderson & Sherrerd), Frank Jones (Guardian Life), Andrew Kalotay (Andrew Kalotay Associates), Dragomir Krgin (Merrill Lynch), Martin Leibowitz (CREF), Jack Malvey (Lehman Brothers), Steven Mann (University of South Carolina), Jan Mayle (TIPS), William McLelland, Franco Modigliani (MIT), Ed Murphy (Merchants Mutual Insurance), Scott Pinkus (White Oak Capital Management), Sharmin Mossavar-Rahmani

(Goldman Sachs Asset Management), Chuck Ramsey (Mortgage Risk Assessment Corporation), Scott Richard (Miller, Anderson & Sherrerd), Ron Ryan (Ryan Labs), Dexter Senft (Lehman Brothers), Richard Wilson (Fitch IBCA), Ben Wolkowitz (Morgan Stanley), David Yuen (Susquehanna Advisors Group), Paul Zhao (TIAA-CREF), and Yu Zhu (Merrill Lynch).

I also received extremely helpful comments from a number of colleagues using the text in an academic setting. These individuals helped me refine this edition and I am sincerely appreciative of their suggestions. They are:

Russell R. Wermers, University of Colorado at Boulder

John H. Spitzer, University of Iowa

John Edmunds, Babson College

I am confident that the fourth edition continues the tradition of providing up-to-date information about the bond market and the tools for managing bond portfolios.

Frank J. Fabozzi

CHAPTER 1

Introduction

Learning Objectives

After reading this chapter you will understand:

- the fundamental features of bonds

- the types of issuers

- the importance of the term to maturity of a bond

- floating-rate and inverse-floating-rate securities

- what is meant by a bond with an embedded option and the effect of an embedded option on a bond's cash flow

- the various types of embedded options

- convertible bonds

- the types of risks faced by investors in fixed-income securities

- the various ways of classifying financial innovation

A bond is a debt instrument requiring the issuer (also called the debtor or borrower) to repay to the lender/investor the amount borrowed plus interest over a specified period of time. A typical ("plain vanilla") bond issued in the United States specifies (1) a fixed date when the amount borrowed (the principal) is due, and (2) the contractual amount of interest, which typically is paid every six months. The date on which the principal is required to be repaid is called the maturity date. Assuming that the issuer does not default or redeem the issue prior to the maturity date, an investor holding this bond until the maturity date is assured of a known cash flow pattern.

For a variety of reasons to be discussed later in this chapter, the 1980s saw the development of a wide range of bond structures. In the residential mortgage market particularly, new types of mortgage designs were introduced. The practice of pooling of individual mortgages to form mortgage pass-through securities grew dramatically. Using the basic instruments in the mortgage market (mortgages and mortgage pass-through securities), issuers created derivative instruments such as collateralized mortgage obligations and stripped mortgage-backed securities that met specific investment needs of a broadening range of institutional investors.

SECTORS OF THE U.S. BOND MARKET

The U.S. bond market is the largest bond market in the world. The market is divided into six sectors: U.S. Treasury sector, agency sector, municipal sector, corporate sector, asset-backed securities, and mortgage sector. The *Treasury sector* includes securities issued by the U.S. government. These securities include Treasury bills, notes, and bonds. The U.S. Treasury is the largest issuer of securities in the world. This sector plays a key role in the valuation of securities and the determination of interest rates throughout the world.

The *agency sector* includes securities issued by federally related institutions and government sponsored enterprises. The distinction between these issuers is described in Chapter 6. The securities issued are not backed by any collateral and are referred to as *agency debenture securities.* This sector is the smallest sector of the bond market.

The *municipal sector* is where state and local governments and their authorities raise funds. The two major sectors within the municipal sector are general obligation sector and the revenue sector. Bonds issued in this sector typically are exempt from federal income taxes. Consequently, the municipal sector is commonly referred to as the *tax-exempt sector.*

The *corporate sector* includes securities issued by U.S. corporations and non-U.S. corporations issued in the United States. The latter securities are referred to as *Yankee bonds.* Issuers in the corporate sector issue bonds, medium-term notes, structured notes, and commercial paper. The corporate sector is divided into the investment grade and noninvestment grade sectors.

An alternative to the corporate sector where a corporate issuer can raise funds is in the *asset-backed securities sector.* In this sector, a corporate issuer pools loans or receivables and uses the pool of assets as collateral for the issuance of a security. The various types of asset-backed securities are described in Chapter 13.

The mortgage sector is the sector where securities are backed by mortgage loans. These are loans obtained by borrowers in order to purchase residential property or an entity to purchase commercial property. Organizations that have classified bond sectors have defined the mortgage sector in different ways. For example, the organizations that have created bond indexes include in the mortgage sector only mortgage-backed securities issued by a federally related institution or a government sponsored enterprise. Mortgage-backed securities issued by corporate entities are often classified as asset-backed securities. Mortgage loans and mortgage-backed securities are the subject of Chapters 11 and 12.

Non-U.S. bond markets include the Eurobond market and other national bond markets. We discuss these markets in Chapter 9.

OVERVIEW OF BOND FEATURES

In this section we provide an overview of some important features of bonds. A more detailed treatment of these features is presented in later chapters. The bond **indenture** is the contract between the issuer and the bondholder, which sets forth all the obligations of the issuer.

Type of Issuer

A key feature of a bond is the nature of the issuer. There are three issuers of bonds: the federal government and its agencies, municipal governments, and corporations (domestic and foreign). Within the municipal and corporate bond markets, there is a wide range of issuers, each with different abilities to satisfy their contractual obligation to lenders.

Term to Maturity

The term to maturity of a bond is the number of years over which the issuer has promised to meet the conditions of the obligation. The maturity of a bond refers to the date that the debt will cease to exist, at which time the issuer will redeem the bond by paying the principal. The practice in the bond market, however, is to refer to the **term to maturity** of a bond as simply its **maturity** or **term.** As we explain subsequently, there may be provisions in the indenture that allow either the issuer or bondholder to alter a bond's term to maturity.

Generally, bonds with a maturity of between one and five years are considered **short term.** Bonds with a maturity between five and 12 years are viewed as **intermediate-term,** and **long-term** bonds are those with a maturity of more than 12 years.

There are three reasons why the term to maturity of a bond is important. The most obvious is that it indicates the time period over which the holder of the bond can expect to receive the coupon payments and the number of years before the principal will be paid in full. The second reason that term to maturity is important is that the yield on a bond depends on it. As explained in Chapter 5, the shape of the yield curve determines how term to maturity affects the yield. Finally, the price of a bond will fluctuate over its life as yields in the market change. As demonstrated in Chapter 4, the volatility of a bond's price is dependent on its maturity. More specifically, with all other factors constant, the longer the maturity of a bond, the greater the price volatility resulting from a change in market yields.

Principal and Coupon Rate

The **principal value** (or simply **principal**) of a bond is the amount that the issuer agrees to repay the bondholder at the maturity date. This amount is also referred to as the **redemption value, maturity value, par value,** or **face value.**

The **coupon rate,** also called the **nominal rate,** is the interest rate that the issuer agrees to pay each year. The annual amount of the interest payment made to owners during the term of the bond is called the **coupon.** The coupon rate multiplied by the principal of the bond provides the dollar amount of the coupon. For example, a bond with an 8% coupon rate and a principal of $1,000 will pay annual interest of $80. In the United States and Japan, the usual practice is for the issuer to pay the coupon in two semiannual installments. For bonds issued in European bond markets or the Eurobond market, coupon payments are made only once per year.

Note that all bonds make periodic coupon payments, except for one type that makes none. These bonds, called **zero-coupon bonds,** made their debut in the U.S. bond market in the early 1980s. The holder of a zero-coupon bond realizes interest by buying the bond substantially below its principal value. Interest is then paid at the maturity date, with the exact amount being the difference between the principal value and the price paid for the bond. The reason behind the issuance of zero-coupon bonds is explained in Chapter 3.

Floating-rate bonds also exist. For these bonds coupon rates are reset periodically according to a predetermined benchmark. Although the coupon rate on most floating-rate bonds is reset on the basis of some financial index, there are some issues where the benchmark for the coupon rate is a nonfinancial index, such as the price of a commodity. While the coupon on floating-rate bonds benchmarked off an interest rate benchmark typically rises as the benchmark rises and falls as the benchmark falls, there are issues whose coupon interest rate moves in the opposite direction from the change in interest rates. Such issues are called **inverse floaters;** institutional investors use them as hedging vehicles.

In the 1980s, new structures in the high-yield (junk bond) sector of the corporate bond market have provided variations in the way in which coupon payments are made. One reason is that a leveraged buyout (LBO) or a recapitalization financed with high-yield bonds, with consequent heavy interest payment burdens, places severe cash flow constraints on the corporation. To reduce this burden, firms involved in LBOs and recapitalizations have issued **deferred-coupon bonds** that let the issuer avoid using cash to make interest payments for a specified number of years. There are three types of deferred-coupon structures: (1) deferred-interest bonds, (2) step-up bonds, and (3) payment-in-kind bonds. Another high-yield bond structure requires that the issuer reset the coupon rate so that the bond will trade at a predetermined price. High-yield bond structures are discussed in Chapter 7.

In addition to indicating the coupon payments that the investor should expect to receive over the term of the bond, the coupon rate also indicates the degree to which the bond's price will be affected by changes in interest rates. As illustrated in Chapter 4, all other factors constant, the higher the coupon rate, the less the price will change in response to a change in interest rates. Consequently, the coupon rate and the term to maturity have opposite effects on a bond's price volatility.

Amortization Feature

The principal repayment of a bond issue can call for either (1) the total principal to be repaid at maturity or (2) the principal repaid over the life of the bond. In the latter case, there is a schedule of principal repayments. This schedule is called an **amortization schedule.** Loans that have this feature are automobile loans and home mortgage loans.

As we will see in later chapters, there are securities that are created from loans that have an amortization schedule. These securities will then have a schedule of periodic principal repayments. Such securities are referred to as **amortizing securities.** Securities that do not have a schedule of periodic principal repayment are called **non-amortizing securities.**

For amortizing securities, investors do not talk in terms of a bond's maturity. This is because the stated maturity of such securities only identifies when the final principal payment will be made. The repayment of the principal is being made over time. For amortizing securities, a measure called the **weighted average life** or simply **average life** of a security is computed. This calculation will be explained later when we cover the two major types of amortizing securities, mortgage-backed securities and asset-backed securities.

Embedded Options

It is common for a bond issue to include a provision in the indenture that gives either the bondholder and/or the issuer an option to take some action against the other party. The most common type of option embedded in a bond is a **call feature.** This provision grants the issuer the right to retire the debt, fully or partially, before the scheduled maturity date. Inclusion of a call feature benefits bond issuers by allowing them to replace an old bond issue with a lower-interest cost issue if interest rates in the market decline. A call provision effectively allows the issuer to alter the maturity of a bond. For reasons explained in the next section, a call provision is detrimental to the bondholder's interests.

The right to call an obligation is also included in most loans and therefore in all securities created from such loans. This is because the borrower typically has the right to pay off a loan at any time, in whole or in part, prior to the stated maturity date of the loan. That is, the borrower has the right to alter the amortization schedule for amortizing securities.

An issue may also include a provision that allows the bondholder to change the maturity of a bond. An issue with a **put provision** included in the indenture grants the bondholder the right to sell the issue back to the issuer at par value on designated dates. Here the advantage to the investor is that if interest rates rise after the issue date, thereby reducing a bond's price, the investor can force the issuer to redeem the bond at par value.

A **convertible bond** is an issue giving the bondholder the right to exchange the bond for a specified number of shares of common stock. Such a feature allows the bondholder to take advantage of favorable movements in the price of the issuer's common stock. An **exchangeable bond** allows the bondholder to exchange the issue for a specified number of common stock shares of a corporation different from the issuer of the bond. These bonds are discussed and analyzed in Chapter 16.

Some issues allow either the issuer or the bondholder the right to select the currency in which a cash flow will be paid. This option effectively gives the party with the right to choose the currency the opportunity to benefit from a favorable exchange rate movement. Such issues are described in Chapter 9.

The presence of embedded options makes the valuation of bonds complex. It requires investors to have an understanding of the basic principles of options, a topic covered in Chapter 14 for callable and putable bonds and Chapter 15 for mortgage-backed securities and asset-backed securities. The valuation of bonds with embedded options frequently is complicated further by the presence of several options within a given issue. For example, an issue may include a call provision, a put provision, and a conversion provision, all of which have varying significance in different situations.

RISKS ASSOCIATED WITH INVESTING IN BONDS

Bonds may expose an investor to one or more of the following risks: (1) interest-rate risk; (2) reinvestment risk; (3) call risk; (4) default risk; (5) inflation risk; (6) exchange-rate risk; (7) liquidity risk; (8) volatility risk; and (9) risk risk. While each of these risks is discussed further in later chapters, we describe them briefly in the following sections. In later chapters, other risks, such as yield curve risk, event risk, and tax risk, are also introduced.

Interest-Rate Risk

The price of a typical bond will change in the opposite direction from a change in interest rates: As interest rates rise, the price of a bond will fall; as interest rates fall, the price of a bond will rise. This property is illustrated in Chapter 2. If an investor has to sell a bond prior to the maturity date, an increase in interest rates will mean the realization of a capital loss (i.e., selling the bond below the purchase price). This risk is referred to as **interest-rate risk** or **market risk.** This risk is by far the major risk faced by an investor in the bond market.

As noted earlier, the actual degree of sensitivity of a bond's price to changes in market interest rates depends on various characteristics of the issue, such as coupon and maturity. It will also depend on any options embedded in the issue (e.g., call and put provisions), because, as we explain in later chapters, these options are also affected by interest-rate movements.

Reinvestment Income or Reinvestment Risk

As explained in Chapter 3, calculation of the yield of a bond assumes that the cash flows received are reinvested. The additional income from such reinvestment, sometimes called **interest-on-interest,** depends on the prevailing interest-rate levels at the time of reinvestment, as well as on the reinvestment strategy. Variability in the reinvestment rate of a given strategy because of changes in market interest rates is called **reinvestment risk.** This risk is that the interest rate at which interim cash flows can be reinvested will fall. Reinvestment risk is greater for longer holding periods, as well as for bonds with large, early, cash flows, such as high-coupon bonds. This risk is analyzed in more detail in Chapter 3.

It should be noted that interest-rate risk and reinvestment risk have offsetting effects. That is, interest-rate risk is the risk that interest rates will rise, thereby reducing a bond's price. In contrast, reinvestment risk is the risk that interest rates will fall. A strategy based on these offsetting effects is called immunization, a topic covered in Chapter 19.

Call Risk

As explained earlier, many bonds include a provision that allows the issuer to retire or "call" all or part of the issue before the maturity date. The issuer usually retains this right in order to have flexibility to refinance the bond in the future if the market interest rate drops below the coupon rate.

From the investor's perspective, there are three disadvantages to call provisions. First, the cash flow pattern of a callable bond is not known with certainty. Second, because the issuer will call the bonds when interest rates have dropped, the investor is exposed to reinvestment risk (i.e., the investor will have to reinvest the proceeds when the bond is called at relatively lower interest rates). Finally, the capital appreciation potential of a bond will be reduced, because the price of a callable bond may not rise much above the price at which the issuer will call the bond.[1]

Even though the investor is usually compensated for taking call risk by means of a lower price or a higher yield, it is not easy to determine if this compensation is suffi-

---

[1]The reason for this is explained in Chapter 14.

cient. In any case the returns from a bond with call risk can be dramatically different from those obtainable from an otherwise comparable noncallable bond. The magnitude of this risk depends on various parameters of the call provision, as well as on market conditions. Call risk is so pervasive in bond portfolio management that many market participants consider it second only to interest-rate risk in importance. Techniques for analyzing callable bonds are presented in Chapter 14.

Default Risk

Default risk, also referred to as **credit risk,** refers to the risk that the issuer of a bond may default (i.e., will be unable to make timely principal and interest payments on the issue). Default risk is gauged by quality ratings assigned by four nationally recognized rating companies: Moody's Investors Service, Standard & Poor's Corporation, Duff & Phelps Credit Rating Company, and Fitch IBCA, as well as the credit research staffs of securities firms.

Because of this risk, bonds with default risk trade in the market at a price that is lower than comparable U.S. Treasury securities, which are considered free of default risk. In other words, a non–U.S. Treasury bond will trade in the market at a higher yield than a Treasury bond that is comparable otherwise.

Except in the case of the lowest-rated securities, known as **high-yield** or **junk bonds,** the investor is normally more concerned with the changes in the perceived default risk and/or the cost associated with a given level of default risk than with the actual event of default. Even though the actual default of an issuing corporation may be highly unlikely, they reason, the impact of a change in perceived default risk, or the spread demanded by the market for any given level of default risk, can have an immediate impact on the value of a bond.

Inflation Risk

Inflation risk or **purchasing-power risk** arises because of the variation in the value of cash flows from a security due to inflation, as measured in terms of purchasing power. For example, if investors purchase a bond on which they can realize a coupon rate of 7% but the rate of inflation is 8%, the purchasing power of the cash flow actually has declined. For all but floating-rate bonds, an investor is exposed to inflation risk because the interest rate the issuer promises to make is fixed for the life of the issue. To the extent that interest rates reflect the expected inflation rate, floating-rate bonds have a lower level of inflation risk.

Exchange-Rate Risk

A non–dollar-denominated bond (i.e., a bond whose payments occur in a foreign currency) has unknown U.S. dollar cash flows. The dollar cash flows are dependent on the exchange rate at the time the payments are received. For example, suppose that an investor purchases a bond whose payments are in Japanese yen. If the yen depreciates relative to the U.S. dollar, fewer dollars will be received. The risk of this occurring is referred to as **exchange-rate** or **currency risk.** Of course, should the yen appreciate relative to the U.S. dollar, the investor will benefit by receiving more dollars.

Liquidity Risk

Liquidity or **marketability risk** depends on the ease with which an issue can be sold at or near its value. The primary measure of liquidity is the size of the spread between the bid price and the ask price quoted by a dealer. The wider the dealer spread, the more the liquidity risk. For an investor who plans to hold the bond until the maturity date, liquidity risk is less important.

Volatility Risk

As explained in Chapter 14, the price of a bond with certain types of embedded options depends on the level of interest rates and factors that influence the value of the embedded option. One of these factors is the expected volatility of interest rates. Specifically, the value of an option rises when expected interest-rate volatility increases. In the case of a bond that is callable, or a mortgage-backed security, in which the investor has granted the borrower an option, the price of the security falls, because the investor has given away a more valuable option. The risk that a change in volatility will affect the price of a bond adversely is called **volatility risk.**

Risk Risk

There have been new and innovative structures introduced into the bond market. Unfortunately, the risk/return characteristics of these securities are not always understood by money managers. **Risk risk** is defined as not knowing what the risk of a security is. When financial calamities are reported in the press, it is not uncommon to hear a money manager or a board member of the affected organization say "we didn't know this could happen." Although a money manager or a board member may not be able to predict the future, there is no reason why the potential outcome of an investment or investment strategy is not known in advance.

There are two ways to mitigate or eliminate risk risk. The first approach is to keep up with the literature on the state-of-the art methodologies for analyzing securities. Your reading of this book is a step in that direction. The second approach is to avoid securities that are not clearly understood. Unfortunately, it is investments in more complex securities that offer opportunities and return enhancement. This brings us back to the first approach.

FINANCIAL INNOVATION AND THE BOND MARKET

Since the 1960s, there has been a surge of significant financial innovations, many of them in the bond market. Observers of financial markets have categorized these innovations in different ways. For example, the Economic Council of Canada classifies financial innovations into three broad categories[2]:

- **Market-broadening instruments,** which augment the liquidity of markets and the availability of funds by attracting new investors and offering new opportunities for borrowers.

---

[2]*Globalization and Canada's Financial Markets* (Ottawa, Ontario, Canada: Supply and Services Canada, 1989), p. 32.

- **Risk-management instruments,** which reallocate financial risks to those who are less averse to them, or who have offsetting exposure, and who are presumably better able to shoulder them.
- **Arbitraging instruments and processes,** which enable investors and borrowers to take advantage of differences in costs and returns between markets, and which reflect differences in the perception of risks as well as in information, taxation, and regulation.

Another classification system of financial innovations based on more specific functions has been suggested by the Bank for International Settlements: **price-risk-transferring innovations, credit-risk-transferring instruments, liquidity-generating innovations, credit-generating instruments,** and **equity-generating instruments.**[3] Price-risk-transferring innovations are those that provide market participants with more efficient means for dealing with price or exchange-rate risk. Credit-risk-transferring instruments reallocate the risk of default. Liquidity-generating innovations do three things: (1) they increase the liquidity of the market, (2) they allow borrowers to draw upon new sources of funds, and (3) they allow market participants to circumvent capital constraints imposed by regulations. Credit- and equity-generating innovations increase the amount of debt funds available to borrowers and increase the capital base of financial and nonfinancial institutions, respectively.

Stephen Ross suggests two classes of financial innovation: (1) new financial products (financial assets and derivative instruments) better suited to the circumstances of the time (e.g., to inflation and volatile interest rates) and to the markets in which they trade, and (2) strategies that primarily use these financial products.[4]

One of the objectives of this book is to explain the financial innovations that are taking place in the bond market. As you read the chapters on various bond sectors and various bond portfolio strategies, be sure you understand the factors behind the innovations.

OVERVIEW OF THE BOOK

The next four chapters of Section I set forth the basic analytical framework necessary to understand the pricing of bonds and their investment characteristics. How the price of a bond is determined is explained in Chapter 2. The various measures of a bond's return are illustrated and evaluated critically in Chapter 3, which is followed by an explanation of the price-volatility characteristics of bonds in Chapter 4. The factors that affect the yield of a bond are explained in Chapter 5, and the important role of the term structure of interest rates (i.e., the relationship between maturity and yield) is introduced.

In Section II the various sectors of the debt market are described. As Treasury securities provide the benchmark against which all bonds are valued, it is imperative to have a thorough understanding of the Treasury market. Treasury securities, Treasury derivative securities (zero-coupon Treasury securities or "stripped" Treasury securi-

---

[3]Bank for International Settlements, *Recent Innovations in International Banking* (Basel: BIS, April 1986).
[4]Stephen A. Ross, "Institutional Markets, Financial Marketing, and Financial Innovation," *Journal of Finance,* July 1989, p. 541.

ties), and federal agency securities are introduced in Chapter 6. In Chapters 7, 8, and 9 the investment characteristics and special features of U.S. corporate debt, municipal securities, and non–U.S. bonds, respectively, are explained.

Chapters 10, 11, and 12 focus on mortgage-backed securities. The various types of mortgage instruments are described in Chapter 10. Mortgage pass-through securities are discussed in Chapter 11 and derivative mortgage-backed securities (collateralized mortgage obligations and stripped mortgage-backed securities) in Chapter 12. Asset-backed securities are the subject of Chapter 13.

In Section III the methodologies for valuing bonds are explained: in Chapter 14, the binomial method for valuing bonds with embedded options, and in Chapter 15, the Monte Carlo simulation model for mortgage-backed securities. A by-product of these valuation models is the option-adjusted spread. The analysis of convertible bonds is covered in Chapter 16.

Portfolio strategies are discussed in Section IV. Chapter 17 explains the objectives of bond portfolio management and the various types of portfolio strategies, active and structured, the latter designed to achieve the performance of some predetermined benchmark. These strategies include indexing, the subject of Chapter 18, and liability funding strategies (immunization and cash flow matching), the subject of Chapter 19. Measuring and evaluating the investment performance of a fixed-income portfolio manager are explained in Chapter 20, together with the AIMR Performance Presentation Standards.

In the final section, Section V, the various instruments that can be used to control portfolio risk are explained. Chapter 21 covers interest-rate futures contracts; Chapter 22, interest-rate options; and Chapter 23, interest-rate swaps and interest-rate agreements (caps, floors, collars, and compound options). Coverage includes the pricing of these contracts and their role in bond portfolio management.

Questions

1. Which sector of the U.S. bond market is referred to as the tax-exempt sector?
2. What is the Yankee bond sector of the U.S. bond market?
3. Who are the major types of issuers of bonds in the United States?
4. What is the cash flow of a 10-year bond that pays coupon interest semiannually, has a coupon rate of 7%, and has a par value of $100,000?
5. What is the cash flow of a seven-year bond that pays no coupon interest and has a par value of $10,000?
6. Give three reasons why the maturity of a bond is important.
7. Generally, in terms of years, how does one classify bonds as short term, intermediate term, and long term?
8. a. What is a floating-rate bond?
   b. What is an inverse-floating-rate bond?
   c. Can you determine today what the cash flow of either a floating-rate bond or an inverse-floating-rate bond will be?
9. What is a deferred coupon bond?
10. a. What is meant by an amortizing security?
    b. Why is the maturity of an amortizing security not a useful measure?
11. What is a bond with an embedded option?

12. a. What does the call feature in a bond entitle the issuer to do?
    b. What is the advantage of a call feature for an issuer?
    c. What are the disadvantages of a call feature for the bondholder?
13. What does the put feature in a bond entitle the bondholder to do?
14. What are a convertible bond and an exchangeable bond?
15. Does an investor who purchases a zero-coupon bond face reinvestment risk?
16. What risks does an investor who purchases a French corporation's bond whose cash flows are denominated in French francs face?
17. Why may liquidity risk and interest-rate risk be unimportant to a person who invests in a three-year bond and plans to hold that bond to the maturity date?
18. What is risk risk?
19. What is a price-risk transferring innovation?

CHAPTER 2

Pricing of Bonds

Learning Objectives

After reading this chapter you will understand:

■ the time value of money

■ how to calculate the price of a bond

■ that to price a bond it is necessary to estimate the expected cash flows and determine the appropriate yield at which to discount the expected cash flows

■ why the price of a bond changes in the direction opposite to the change in required yield

■ that the relationship between price and yield of an option-free bond is convex

■ the relationship between coupon rate, required yield, and price

■ how the price of a bond changes as it approaches maturity

■ the reasons why the price of a bond changes

■ the complications of pricing bonds

■ the pricing of floating-rate and inverse-floating-rate securities

■ what accrued interest is and how bond prices are quoted

In this chapter we explain how the price of a bond is determined, and in the next we discuss how the yield on a bond is measured. Basic to understanding pricing models and yield measures is an understanding of the time value of money. Therefore, we begin this chapter with a review of this concept.

REVIEW OF TIME VALUE OF MONEY

The notion that money has a time value is one of the basic concepts in the analysis of any financial instrument. Money has time value because of the opportunity to invest it at some interest rate.

12

Future Value

To determine the future value of any sum of money invested today, equation (2.1) can be used:

$$P_n = P_0(1 + r)^n \qquad \textbf{(2.1)}$$

where:

n = number of periods
P_n = future value n periods from now (in dollars)
P_0 = original principal (in dollars)
r = interest rate per period (in decimal form)

The expression $(1 + r)^n$ represents the future value of $1 invested today for n periods at a compounding rate of r.

For example, suppose that a pension fund manager invests $10 million in a financial instrument that promises to pay 9.2% per year for six years. The future value of the $10 million investment is $16,956,500; that is,

$$
\begin{aligned}
P_6 &= \$10,000,000(1.092)^6 \\
&= \$10,000,000(1.69565) \\
&= \$16,956,500
\end{aligned}
$$

This example demonstrates how to compute the future value when interest is paid once per year (i.e., the period is equal to the number of years). When interest is paid more than one time per year, both the interest rate and the number of periods used to compute the future value must be adjusted as follows:

$$r = \frac{\text{annual interest rate}}{\text{number of times interest is paid per year}}$$

n = number of times interest is paid per year × number of years

For example, suppose that the portfolio manager in the first example invests $10 million in a financial instrument that promises to pay an annual interest rate of 9.2% for six years, but the interest is paid semiannually (i.e., twice per year). Then

$$r = \frac{0.092}{2} = 0.046$$

$$n = 2 \times 6 = 12$$

and

$$
\begin{aligned}
P_{12} &= \$10,000,000(1.046)^{12} \\
&= \$10,000,000(1.71546) \\
&= \$17,154,600
\end{aligned}
$$

Notice that the future value of $10 million when interest is paid semiannually ($17,154,600) is greater than when interest is paid annually ($16,956,500), even though the same annual rate is applied to both investments. The higher future value when interest is paid semiannually reflects the greater opportunity for reinvesting the interest paid.

Future Value of an Ordinary Annuity

When the same amount of money is invested periodically, it is referred to as an **annuity.** When the first investment occurs one period from now, it is referred to as an **ordinary annuity.** The future value of an ordinary annuity can be found by finding the future value of each investment at the end of the investment horizon and then adding these future values. However, it is easier to compute the future value of an ordinary annuity using the equation

$$P_n = A\left[\frac{(1 + r)^n - 1}{r}\right] \qquad\qquad (2.2)$$

where A is the amount of the annuity (in dollars). The term in brackets is the **future value of an ordinary annuity of $1** at the end of n periods.

To see how this formula can be applied, suppose that a portfolio manager purchases $20 million par value of a 15-year bond that promises to pay 10% interest per year. The issuer makes a payment once a year, with the first annual interest payment occurring one year from now. How much will the portfolio manager have if (1) the bond is held until it matures 15 years from now, and (2) annual payments are invested at an annual interest rate of 8%?

The amount that the portfolio manager will have at the end of 15 years will be equal to:

1. The $20 million when the bond matures.
2. 15 annual interest payments of $2,000,000 (0.10 × $20 million).
3. The interest earned by investing the annual interest payments at 8% per year.

We can determine the sum of the second and third items by applying equation (2.2). In this illustration the annuity is $2,000,000 per year. Therefore,

$$A = \$2,000,000$$
$$r = 0.08$$
$$n = 15$$

and

$$P_{15} = \$2,000,000\left[\frac{(1.08)^{15} - 1}{0.08}\right]$$

$$= \$2,000,000\left[\frac{3.17217 - 1}{0.08}\right]$$

$$= \$2,000,000[27.152125]$$

$$= \$54,304,250$$

The future value of the ordinary annuity of $2,000,000 per year for 15 years invested at 8% is $54,304,250. Because $30,000,000 (15 × $2,000,000) of this future value represents the total dollar amount of annual interest payments made by the issuer and invested by the portfolio manager, the balance of $24,304,250 ($54,304,250 − $30,000,000) is the interest earned by reinvesting these annual interest payments. Thus the total dollars that the portfolio manager will have at the end of 15 years by making the investment will be:

Par (maturity) value	$20,000,000
Interest payments	30,000,000
Interest on reinvestment of interest payments	24,304,250
Total future dollars	$74,304,250

As you shall see in Chapter 3, it is necessary to calculate these total future dollars at the end of a portfolio manager's investment horizon in order to assess the relative value of a bond.

Let's rework the analysis for this bond assuming that the interest is paid every six months (based on an annual rate), with the first six-month payment to be received and immediately invested six months from now. We shall assume that the semiannual interest payments can be reinvested at an annual interest rate of 8%.

Interest payments received every six months are $1,000,000. The future value of the 30 semiannual interest payments of $1,000,000 to be received plus the interest earned by investing the interest payments is found as follows:

$$A = \$1,000,000$$

$$r = \frac{0.08}{2} = 0.04$$

$$n = 15 \times 2 = 30$$

$$P_{30} = \$1,000,000 \left[\frac{(1.04)^{30} - 1}{0.04} \right]$$

$$= \$1,000,000 \left[\frac{3.2434 - 1}{0.04} \right]$$

$$= \$1,000,000[56.085]$$

$$= \$56,085,000$$

Because the interest payments are equal to $30,000,000, the interest earned on the interest payments reinvested is $26,085,000. The opportunity for more frequent reinvestment of interest payments received makes the interest earned of $26,085,000 from reinvesting the interest payments greater than the $24,304,250 interest earned when interest is paid only one time per year.

The total future dollars that the portfolio manager will have at the end of 15 years by making the investment are as follows:

Par (maturity) value	$20,000,000
Interest payments	30,000,000
Interest on reinvestment of interest payments	26,085,000
Total future dollars	$76,085,000

Present Value

We have explained how to compute the future value of an investment. Now we illustrate how to work the process in reverse; that is, we show how to determine the amount of money that must be invested today in order to realize a specific future value. This amount is called the **present value.** Because, as we explain later in this chapter, the price of *any* financial instrument is the present value of its expected cash flows, it is necessary to understand present value to be able to price fixed-income instruments.

What we are interested in is how to determine the amount of money that must be invested today at an interest rate of r per period for n periods to produce a specific future value. This can be done by solving the formula for the future value given by equation (2.1) for the original principal (P_0):

$$P_0 = P_n \left[\frac{1}{(1 + r)^n} \right]$$

Instead of using P_0, however, we denote the present value by PV. Therefore, the present value formula can be rewritten as

$$PV = P_n \left[\frac{1}{(1 + r)^n} \right] \tag{2.3}$$

The term in brackets is the present value of $1; that is, it indicates how much must be set aside today, earning an interest rate of r per period, in order to have $1 n periods from now.

The process of computing the present value is also referred to as **discounting.** Therefore, the present value is sometimes referred to as the **discounted value,** and the interest rate is referred to as the **discount rate.**

To illustrate how to apply equation (2.3), suppose that a portfolio manager has the opportunity to purchase a financial instrument that promises to pay $5 million seven years from now with no interim cash flows. Assuming that the portfolio manager wants to earn an annual interest rate of 10% on this investment, the present value of this investment is computed as follows:

$$r = 0.10$$
$$n = 7$$
$$P_7 = \$5,000,000$$
$$PV = \$5,000,000 \left[\frac{1}{(1.10)^7} \right]$$
$$= \$5,000,000 \left[\frac{1}{1.948717} \right]$$
$$= \$5,000,000 \, [0.513158]$$
$$= \$2,565,791$$

The equation shows that if $2,565,791 is invested today at 10% annual interest, the investment will grow to $5 million at the end of seven years. Suppose that this financial instrument is actually selling for more than $2,565,791. Then the portfolio manager would be earning less than 10% by investing in this financial instrument at a purchase price greater than $2,565,791. The reverse is true if the financial instrument is selling for less than $2,565,791. Then the portfolio manager would be earning more than 10%.

There are two properties of present value that you should recognize. First, for a given future value at a specified time in the future, the higher the interest rate (or discount rate), the lower the present value. The reason the present value decreases as the interest rate increases should be easy to understand: The higher the interest rate that can be earned on any sum invested today, the less has to be invested today to realize a specified future value.

The second property of present value is that for a given interest rate (discount rate), the further into the future the future value will be received, the lower its present value. The reason is that the further into the future a given future value is to be received, the more opportunity there is for interest to accumulate. Thus fewer dollars have to be invested.

Present Value of a Series of Future Values

In most applications in portfolio management a financial instrument will offer a series of future values. To determine the present value of a series of future values, the present value of each future value must first be computed. Then these present values are added together to obtain the present value of the entire series of future values.

Mathematically, this can be expressed as follows:

$$PV = \sum_{t=1}^{n} \frac{P_t}{(1 + r)^t} \tag{2.4}$$

For example, suppose that a portfolio manager is considering the purchase of a financial instrument that promises to make these payments:

Years from Now	Promised Payment by Issuer
1	$ 100
2	100
3	100
4	100
5	1,100

Assume that the portfolio manager wants a 6.25% annual interest rate on this investment. The present value of such an investment can be computed as follows:

Years from Now	Future Value of Payment	Present Value of $1 at 6.25%	Present Value of Payment
1	$ 100	0.9412	$ 94.12
2	100	0.8858	88.58
3	100	0.8337	83.37
4	100	0.7847	78.47
5	1,100	0.7385	$1812.35
		Present value =	$1,156.89

Present Value of an Ordinary Annuity

When the same dollar amount of money is received each period or paid each year, the series is referred to as an **annuity.** When the first payment is received one period from now, the annuity is called an **ordinary annuity.** When the first payment is immediate, the annuity is called an **annuity due.** In all the applications discussed in this book, we shall deal with ordinary annuities.

To compute the present value of an ordinary annuity, the present value of each future value can be computed and then summed. Alternatively, a formula for the present value of an ordinary annuity can be used:

$$PV = A \left[\frac{1 - \frac{1}{(1 + r)^n}}{r} \right] \tag{2.5}$$

where A is the amount of the annuity (in dollars). The term in brackets is the **present value of an ordinary annuity of \$1 for n periods.**

Suppose that an investor expects to receive \$100 at the end of each year for the next eight years from an investment and that the appropriate discount rate to be used for discounting is 9%. The present value of this ordinary annuity is

$$A = \$100$$
$$r = 0.09$$
$$n = 8$$

$$PV = \$100 \left[\frac{1 - \frac{1}{(1.09)^8}}{0.09} \right]$$

$$= \$100 \left[\frac{1 - \frac{1}{1.99256}}{0.09} \right]$$

$$= \$100 \left[\frac{1 - 0.501867}{0.09} \right]$$

$$= \$100[5.$$
$$= \$553.48$$

Present Value When Payments Occur More Than Once per Year

In our computations of the present value we have assumed that the future value to be received or paid occurs each year. In practice, the future value to be received may occur more than once per year. When that is the case, the formulas we have developed for determining the present value must be modified in two ways. First, the annual interest rate is divided by the frequency per year.[1] For example, if the future values are received semiannually, the annual interest rate is divided by 2; if they are paid

---

[1]Technically, this is not the proper way for adjusting the annual interest rate. The technically proper method of adjustment is discussed in Chapter 3.

or received quarterly, the annual interest rate is divided by 4. Second, the number of periods when the future value will be received must be adjusted by multiplying the number of years by the frequency per year.

PRICING A BOND

The price of any financial instrument is equal to the present value of the *expected* cash flows from the financial instrument. Therefore determining the price requires

1. An estimate of the expected cash flows
2. An estimate of the appropriate required yield

The expected cash flows for some financial instruments are simple to compute; for others, the task is more difficult. The required yield reflects the yield for financial instruments with **comparable** risk, or **alternative** (or **substitute**) **investments.**

The first step in determining the price of a bond is to determine its cash flows. The cash flows for a bond that the issuer cannot retire prior to its stated maturity date (i.e., a noncallable bond[2]) consist of

1. Periodic coupon interest payments to the maturity date
2. The par (or maturity) value at maturity

Our illustrations of bond pricing use three assumptions to simplify the analysis:

1. The coupon payments are made every six months. (For most domestic bond issues, coupon interest is in fact paid semiannually.)
2. The next coupon payment for the bond is received exactly six months from now.
3. The coupon interest is fixed for the term of the bond.

Consequently, the cash flow for a noncallable bond consists of an annuity of a fixed coupon interest payment paid semiannually and the par or maturity value. For example, a 20-year bond with a 10% coupon rate and a par or maturity value of $1,000 has the following cash flows from coupon interest:

$$\text{annual coupon interest} = \$1{,}000 \times 0.10$$
$$= \$100$$
$$\text{semiannual coupon interest} = \$100/2$$
$$= \$50$$

Therefore, there are 40 semiannual cash flows of $50, and a $1,000 cash flow 40 six-month periods from now. Notice the treatment of the par value. It is *not* treated as if it is received 20 years from now. Instead, it is treated on a basis consistent with the coupon payments, which are semiannual.

The required yield is determined by investigating the yields offered on comparable bonds in the market. By comparable, we mean noncallable bonds of the same credit quality and the same maturity.[3] The required yield typically is expressed as an

---

[2]In Chapter 14 we discuss the pricing of callable bonds.
[3]In Chapter 4 we introduce a measure of interest-rate risk known as duration. There, instead of talking in terms of bonds with the same maturity as being comparable, we recast the analysis in terms of duration.

annual interest rate. When the cash flows occur semiannually, the market convention is to use one-half the annual interest rate as the periodic interest rate with which to discount the cash flows.

Given the cash flows of a bond and the required yield, we have all the analytical tools to price a bond. As the price of a bond is the present value of the cash flows, it is determined by adding these two present values:

1. The present value of the semiannual coupon payments
2. The present value of the par or maturity value at the maturity date

In general, the price of a bond can be computed using the following formula:

$$P = \frac{C}{1 + r} + \frac{C}{(1 + r)^2} + \frac{C}{(1 + r)^3} + \cdots + \frac{C}{(1 + r)^n} + \frac{M}{(1 + r)^n}$$

or

$$P = \sum_{t=1}^{n} \frac{C}{(1 + r)^t} + \frac{M}{(1 + r)^n} \qquad (2.6)$$

where:

P = price (in dollars)
n = number of periods (number of years times 2)
C = semiannual coupon payment (in dollars)
r = periodic interest rate (required annual yield divided by 2)
M = maturity value
t = time period when the payment is to be received

Because the semiannual coupon payments are equivalent to an ordinary annuity, applying equation (2.5) for the present value of an ordinary annuity gives the present value of the coupon payments:

$$C\left[\frac{1 - \frac{1}{(1 + r)^n}}{r}\right] \qquad (2.7)$$

To illustrate how to compute the price of a bond, consider a 20-year 10% coupon bond with a par value of $1,000. Let's suppose that the required yield on this bond is 11%. The cash flows for this bond are as follows:

1. 40 semiannual coupon payments of $50
2. $1,000 to be received 40 six-month periods from now

The semiannual or periodic interest rate (or periodic required yield) is 5.5% (11% divided by 2).

The present value of the 40 semiannual coupon payments of $50 discounted at 5.5% is $802.31, calculated as

$$C = \$50$$
$$n = 40$$
$$r = 0.055$$

$$= \$50 \left[\frac{1 - \dfrac{1}{(1.055)^{40}}}{0.055} \right]$$

$$= \$50 \left[\frac{1 - \dfrac{1}{8.51332}}{0.055} \right]$$

$$= \$50 \left[\frac{1 - 0.117463}{0.055} \right]$$

$$= \$50[16.04613]$$

$$= \$802.31$$

The present value of the par or maturity value of $1,000 received *40 six-month periods from now,* discounted at 5.5%, is $117.46, as follows:

$$\frac{\$1,000}{(1.055)^{40}} = \frac{\$1,000}{8.51332}$$

$$= \$117.46$$

The price of the bond is then equal to the sum of the two present values:

	Present value of coupon payments	$802.31
+	Present value of par (maturity value)	117.46
	Price	$919.77

Suppose that, instead of an 11% required yield, the required yield is 6.8%. The price of the bond would then be $1,347.04, demonstrated as follows.

The present value of the coupon payments using a periodic interest rate of 3.4% (6.8%/2) is

$$\$50 \left[\frac{1 - \dfrac{1}{(1.034)^{40}}}{0.034} \right] = \$50[21.69029]$$

$$= \$1,084.51$$

The present value of the par or maturity value of $1,000 received *40 six-month periods from now* discounted at 3.4% is

$$\frac{\$1,000}{(1.034)^{40}} = \$262.53$$

The price of the bond is then as follows:

	Present value of coupon payments	$1,084.51
+	Present value of par (maturity value)	262.53
	Price	$1,347.04

If the required yield is equal to the coupon rate of 10%, the price of the bond would be its par value, $1,000, as the following calculations demonstrate.

Using a periodic interest rate of 5.0% (10%/2), the present value of the coupon payments is

$$\$50\left[\frac{1 - \frac{1}{(1.050)^{40}}}{0.050}\right] = \$50[17.15909]$$

$$= \$857.95$$

The present value of the par or maturity value of $1,000 received *40 six-month periods from now* discounted at 5% is

$$\frac{\$1,000}{(1.050)^{40}} = \$142.05$$

The price of the bond is then as follows:

	Present value of coupon payments	$ 857.95
+	Present value of par (maturity value)	142.05
	Price	$1,000.00

Pricing Zero-Coupon Bonds

Some bonds do not make any periodic coupon payments. Instead, the investor realizes interest as the difference between the maturity value and the purchase price. These bonds are called **zero-coupon bonds.** The price of a zero-coupon bond is calculated by substituting zero for C in equation (2.6):

$$P = \frac{M}{(1 + r)^n} \tag{2.8}$$

Equation (2.8) states that the price of a zero-coupon bond is simply the present value of the maturity value. In the present value computation, however, the number of periods used for discounting is not the number of years to maturity of the bond, but rather double the number of years. The discount rate is one-half the required annual yield. For example, the price of a zero-coupon bond that matures 15 years from now, if the maturity value is $1,000 and the required yield is 9.4%, is $252.12, as shown:

$$M = \$1,000$$

$$r = 0.047\left(= \frac{0.094}{2}\right)$$

$$n = 30(= 2 \times 15)$$

$$P = \frac{\$1,000}{(1.047)^{30}}$$

$$= \frac{\$1,000}{3.96644}$$

$$= \$252.12$$

Price-Yield Relationship

A fundamental property of a bond is that its price changes in the opposite direction from the change in the required yield. The reason is that the price of the bond is the present value of the cash flows. As the required yield increases, the present value of the cash flow decreases; hence the price decreases. The opposite is true when the required yield decreases: The present value of the cash flows increases, and therefore the price of the bond increases. This can be seen by examining the price for the 20-year 10% bond when the required yield is 11%, 10%, and 6.8%. Exhibit 2-1 shows the price of the 20-year 10% coupon bond for various required yields.

If we graph the price-yield relationship for any noncallable bond, we will find that it has the "bowed" shape shown in Exhibit 2-2. This shape is referred to as *convex*. The convexity of the price-yield relationship has important implications for the investment properties of a bond, as we explain in Chapter 4.

Relationship between Coupon Rate, Required Yield, and Price

As yields in the marketplace change, the only variable that can change to compensate an investor for the new required yield in the market is the price of the bond. When the coupon rate is equal to the required yield, the price of the bond will be equal to its par value, as we demonstrated for the 20-year 10% coupon bond.

When yields in the marketplace rise above the coupon rate at *a given point in time,* the price of the bond adjusts so that an investor contemplating the purchase of the bond can realize some additional interest. If it did not, investors would not buy the issue because it offers a below market yield; the resulting lack of demand would cause the price to fall and thus the yield on the bond to increase. This is how a bond's price falls below its par value.

The capital appreciation realized by holding the bond to maturity represents a form of interest to a new investor to compensate for a coupon rate that is lower than the required yield. When a bond sells below its par value, it is said to be selling at a **discount.** In our earlier calculation of bond price we saw that when the required yield

EXHIBIT 2-1	Price-Yield Relationship for a 20-Year 10% Coupon Bond		
Yield	*Price*	*Yield*	*Price*
0.045	$1,720.32	0.110	$919.77
0.050	1,627.57	0.115	883.50
0.055	1,541.76	0.120	849.54
0.060	1,462.30	0.125	817.70
0.065	1,388.65	0.130	787.82
0.070	1,320.33	0.135	759.75
0.075	1,256.89	0.140	733.37
0.080	1,197.93	0.145	708.53
0.085	1,143.08	0.150	685.14
0.090	1,092.01	0.155	663.08
0.095	1,044.41	0.160	642.26
0.100	1,000.00	0.165	622.59
0.105	958.53		

EXHIBIT 2-2 Shape of Price-Yield Relationship

is greater than the coupon rate, the price of the bond is always lower than the par value ($1,000).

When the required yield in the market is below the coupon rate, the bond must sell above its par value. This is because investors who have the opportunity to purchase the bond at par would be getting a coupon rate in excess of what the market requires. As a result, investors would bid up the price of the bond because its yield is so attractive. The price would eventually be bid up to a level where the bond offers the required yield in the market. A bond whose price is above its par value is said to be selling at a **premium.** The relationship between coupon rate, required yield, and price can be summarized as follows:

$$\text{coupon rate} < \text{required yield} \leftrightarrow \text{price} < \text{par (discount bond)}$$
$$\text{coupon rate} = \text{required yield} \leftrightarrow \text{price} = \text{par}$$
$$\text{coupon rate} > \text{required yield} \leftrightarrow \text{price} > \text{par (premium bond)}$$

Relationship between Bond Price and Time If Interest Rates Are Unchanged

If the required yield does not change between the time the bond is purchased and the maturity date, what will happen to the price of the bond? For a bond selling at par value, the coupon rate is equal to the required yield. As the bond moves closer to maturity, the bond will continue to sell at par value. Its price will remain constant as the bond moves toward the maturity date.

The price of a bond will *not* remain constant for a bond selling at a premium or a discount. Exhibit 2-3 shows the time path of a 20-year 10% coupon bond selling at a discount and the same bond selling at a premium as it approaches maturity. Notice that the discount bond increases in price as it approaches maturity, assuming that the

EXHIBIT 2-3	Time Path for the Price of a 20-Year 10% Bond Selling at a Discount and Premium As It Approaches Maturity	
Year	*Price of Discount Bond Selling to Yield 12%*	*Price of Premium Bond Selling to Yield 7.8%*
20.0	$849.54	$1,221.00
19.5	850.51	1,218.62
19.0	851.54	1,216.14
18.5	852.63	1,213.57
18.0	853.79	1,210.90
17.5	855.02	1,208.13
17.0	856.32	1,205.24
16.5	857.70	1,202.25
16.0	859.16	1,199.14
15.5	860.71	1,195.90
15.0	862.35	1,192.54
14.5	864.09	1,189.05
14.0	865.94	1,185.43
13.5	867.89	1,181.66
13.0	869.97	1,177.74
12.5	872.17	1,173.67
12.0	874.50	1,169.45
11.5	876.97	1,165.06
11.0	879.58	1,160.49
10.5	882.36	1,155.75
10.0	885.30	1,150.83
9.5	888.42	1,145.71
9.0	891.72	1,140.39
8.5	895.23	1,134.87
8.0	898.94	1,129.13
7.5	902.88	1,123.16
7.0	907.05	1,116.97
6.5	911.47	1,110.53
6.0	916.16	1,103.84
5.5	921.13	1,096.89
5.0	926.40	1,089.67
4.5	931.98	1,082.16
4.0	937.90	1,074.37
3.5	944.18	1,066.27
3.0	950.83	1,057.85
2.5	957.88	1,049.11
2.0	965.35	1,040.02
1.5	973.27	1,030.58
1.0	981.67	1,020.78
0.5	990.57	1,010.59
0.0	1,000.00	1,000.00

required yield does not change. For a premium bond, the opposite occurs. For both bonds, the price will equal par value at the maturity date.

Reasons for the Change in the Price of a Bond

The price of a bond will change for one or more of the following three reasons:

1. There is a change in the required yield owing to changes in the credit quality of the issuer.
2. There is a change in the price of the bond selling at a premium or a discount, without any change in the required yield, simply because the bond is moving toward maturity.
3. There is a change in the required yield owing to a change in the yield on comparable bonds (i.e., a change in the yield required by the market).

Reasons 2 and 3 for a change in price are discussed in this chapter. Predicting a change in an issue's credit quality (reason 1) before that change is recognized by the market is one of the challenges of investment management.

COMPLICATIONS

The framework for pricing a bond discussed in this chapter assumes that:

1. The next coupon payment is exactly six months away.
2. The cash flows are known.
3. The appropriate required yield can be determined.
4. One rate is used to discount all cash flows.

Let's look at the implications of each assumption for the pricing of a bond.

Next Coupon Payment Due in Less Than Six Months

When an investor purchases a bond whose next coupon payment is due in less than six months, the accepted method for computing the price of the bond is as follows:

$$P = \sum_{t=1}^{n} \frac{C}{(1 + r)^v(1 + r)^{t-1}} + \frac{M}{(1 + r)^v(1 + r)^{n-1}} \tag{2.9}$$

where:

$$v = \frac{\text{days between settlement and next coupon}}{\text{days in six-month period}}$$

Note that when v is 1 (i.e., when the next coupon payment is six months away, equation (2.9) reduces to equation (2.6).

Cash Flows May Not Be Known

For noncallable bonds, assuming that the issuer does not default, the cash flows are known. For most bonds, however, the cash flows are not known with certainty. This is because an issuer may call a bond before the stated maturity date. With callable bonds, the cash flow will, in fact, depend on the level of current interest rates relative to the coupon rate. For example, the issuer will typically call a bond when interest rates drop far enough below the coupon rate so that it is economical to retire the bond issue prior to maturity and issue new bonds at a lower coupon rate.[4] Consequently, the cash flows of bonds that may be called prior to maturity are dependent on current interest rates in the marketplace.

Determining the Appropriate Required Yield

All required yields are benchmarked off yields offered by Treasury securities, the subject of Chapter 5. The analytical framework that we develop in this book is one of decomposing the required yield for a bond into its component parts, as we discuss in later chapters.

One Discount Rate Applicable to All Cash Flows

Our pricing analysis has assumed that it is appropriate to discount each cash flow using the same discount rate. As explained in Chapter 5, a bond can be viewed as a package of zero-coupon bonds, in which case a unique discount rate should be used to determine the present value of each cash flow.

PRICING FLOATING-RATE AND INVERSE-FLOATING-RATE SECURITIES

The cash flow is not known for either a floating-rate or an inverse-floating-rate security; it will depend on the reference rate in the future.

Price of a Floater

The coupon rate of a floating-rate security (or **floater**) is equal to a reference rate plus some spread or margin. For example, the coupon rate of a floater can reset at the rate on a three-month Treasury bill (the reference rate) plus 50 basis points (the spread).

The price of a floater depends on two factors: (1) the spread over the reference rate and (2) any restrictions that may be imposed on the resetting of the coupon rate. For example, a floater may have a maximum coupon rate called a **cap** or a minimum coupon rate called a **floor.** The price of a floater will trade close to its par value as long as (1) the spread above the reference rate that the market requires is unchanged and (2) neither the cap nor the floor is reached.[5]

If the market requires a larger (smaller) spread, the price of a floater will trade below (above) par. If the coupon rate is restricted from changing to the reference rate plus the spread because of the cap, then the price of a floater will trade below par.

---

[4]Mortgage-backed securities, discussed in Chapters 11 and 12, are another example; the individual borrowers have the right to prepay all or part of the mortgage obligation prior to the scheduled due date.
[5]In between coupon reset dates, the floater can trade above or below par.

Price of an Inverse Floater

In general, an inverse floater is created from a fixed-rate security.[6] The security from which the inverse floater is created is called the **collateral.** From the collateral two bonds are created: a floater and an inverse floater. This is depicted in Exhibit 2-4.

The two bonds are created such that (1) the total coupon interest paid to the two bonds in each period is less than or equal to the collateral's coupon interest in each period, and (2) the total par value of the two bonds is less than or equal to the collateral's total par value. Equivalently, the floater and inverse floater are structured so that the cash flow from the collateral will be sufficient to satisfy the obligation of the two bonds.

For example, consider a 10-year 7.5% coupon semiannual-pay bond. Suppose that $100 million of the bond is used as collateral to create a floater with a par value of $50 million and an inverse floater with a par value of $50 million. Suppose that the coupon rate is reset every six months based on the following formula:

> Floater coupon: reference rate + 1%
>
> Inverse floater coupon: 14% − reference rate

Notice that the total par value of the floater and inverse floater equals the par value of the collateral, $100 million. The weighted average of the coupon rate of the combination of the two bonds is

$$0.5(\text{reference rate} + 1\%) + 0.5(14\% - \text{reference rate}) = 7.5\%$$

Thus, regardless of the level of the reference rate, the combined coupon rate for the two bonds is equal to the coupon rate of the collateral, 7.5%.

There is one problem with the coupon formulas given here. Suppose that the reference rate exceeds 14%. Then the formula for the coupon rate for the inverse floater will be negative. To prevent this from happening, a floor is placed on the coupon rate for the inverse floater. Typically, the floor is set at zero. Because of the floor, the coupon rate on the floater must be restricted so that the coupon interest paid to the two bonds does not exceed the collateral's coupon interest. In our hypothetical struc-

EXHIBIT 2-4 Creation of an Inverse Floater

---

[6]Inverse floaters are also created using interest-rate swaps without the need to create a floater.

ture, the maximum coupon rate that must be imposed on the floater is 15%. Thus, when a floater and an inverse floater are created from the collateral, a floor is imposed on the inverse and a cap is imposed on the floater.

The valuation of the cap and the floor is beyond our discussion at this point. Here it is sufficient to point out that the price of an inverse floater is found by determining the price of the collateral and the price of the floater. This can be seen as follows:

$$\text{collateral's price} = \text{floater's price} + \text{inverse's price}$$

Therefore,

$$\text{inverse's price} = \text{collateral's price} - \text{floater's price}$$

Notice that the factors that affect the price of an inverse floater are affected by the reference rate only to the extent that it affects the restrictions on the floater's rate. This is quite an important result. Some investors mistakenly believe that because the coupon rate rises, the price of an inverse floater should increase if the reference rate decreases. This is not true. The key in pricing an inverse floater is how changes in interest rates affect the price of the collateral. The reference rate is important only to the extent that it restricts the coupon rate of the floater.

PRICE QUOTES AND ACCRUED INTEREST

Price Quotes

Throughout this chapter we have assumed that the maturity or par value of a bond is $1,000. A bond may have a maturity or par value greater or less than $1,000. Consequently, when quoting bond prices, traders quote the price as a percentage of par value.

A bond selling at par is quoted as 100, meaning 100% of its par value. A bond selling at a discount will be selling for less than 100; a bond selling at a premium will be selling for more than 100. The following examples illustrate how a price quote is converted into a dollar price.

(1) Price Quote	(2) Converted to a Decimal [= (1)/100]	(3) Par Value	(4) Dollar Price [= (2) × (3)]
97	0.9700000	$ 10,000	$ 9,700.00
85½	0.8550000	100,000	85,500.00
90¼	0.9025000	5,000	4,512.50
80⅛	0.8012500	10,000	8,012.50
76⁵⁄₃₂	0.7615625	1,000,000	761,562.50
86¹¹⁄₆₄	0.8617188	100,000	86,171.88
100	1.0000000	50,000	50,000.00
109	1.0900000	1,000	1,090.00
103¾	1.0375000	100,000	103,750.00
105⅜	1.0537500	25,000	26,343.75
103¹⁹⁄₃₂	1.0359375	1,000,000	1,035,937.50

Accrued Interest

When an investor purchases a bond between coupon payments, the investor must compensate the seller of the bond for the coupon interest earned from the time of the last coupon payment to the settlement date of the bond.[7] This amount is called **accrued interest.** The computation of accrued interest depends on the type of bond. For a Treasury coupon security (discussed in Chapter 6), accrued interest is based on the actual number of days the bond is held by the seller. For corporate and municipal bonds, accrued interest is based on a 360-day year, with each month having 30 days.

The amount that the buyer pays the seller is the agreed-upon price plus accrued interest. This is often referred to as the **full price** or **dirty price.** The price of a bond without accrued interest is called the **clean price.**

SUMMARY

In this chapter we have shown how to determine the price of a noncallable bond. The price is simply the present value of the bond's expected cash flows, the discount rate being equal to the yield offered on comparable bonds. For a noncallable bond, the cash flows are the coupon payments and the par value or maturity value. For a zero-coupon bond, there are no coupon payments. The price is equal to the present value of the maturity value, where the number of periods used to compute the present value is double the number of years and the discount rate is a semiannual yield.

The higher (lower) the required yield, the lower (higher) the price of a bond. Therefore, a bond's price changes in the opposite direction from the change in the required yield. When the coupon rate is equal to the required yield, the bond will sell at its par value. When the coupon rate is less (greater) than the required yield, the bond will sell for less (more) than its par value and is said to be selling at a discount (premium).

Over time, the price of a premium or discount bond will change even if the required yield does not change. Assuming that the credit quality of the issuer is unchanged, the price change on any bond can be decomposed into a portion attributable to a change in the required yield and a portion attributable to the time path of the bond.

The price of a floating-rate bond will trade close to par value if the spread required by the market does not change and there are no restrictions on the coupon rate. The price of an inverse floater depends on the price of the collateral from which it is created and the price of the floater.

Questions

1. A pension fund manager invests $10 million in a debt obligation that promises to pay 7.3% per year for four years. What is the future value of the $10 million?
2. Suppose that a life insurance company has guaranteed a payment of $14 million to a pension fund 4.5 years from now. If the life insurance company receives a premium of $10.4 million from the pension fund and can invest the entire premium

---

[7]The exceptions are bonds that are in default. Such bonds are said to be quoted **flat,** that is, without accrued interest.

for 4.5 years at an annual interest rate of 6.25%, will it have sufficient funds from this investment to meet the $14 million obligation?

3. a. The portfolio manager of a tax-exempt fund is considering investing $500,000 in a debt instrument that pays an annual interest rate of 5.7% for four years. At the end of four years, the portfolio manager plans to reinvest the proceeds for three more years and expects that for the three-year period, an annual interest rate of 7.2% can be earned. What is the future value of this investment?

   b. Suppose that the portfolio manager in Question 3, part a, has the opportunity to invest the $500,000 for seven years in a debt obligation that promises to pay an annual interest rate of 6.1% compounded semiannually. Is this investment alternative more attractive than the one in Question 3, part a?

4. Suppose that a portfolio manager purchases $10 million of par value of an eight-year bond that has a coupon rate of 7% and pays interest once per year. The first annual coupon payment will be made one year from now. How much will the portfolio manager have if she (1) holds the bond until it matures eight years from now, and (2) can reinvest all the annual interest payments at an annual interest rate of 6.2%?

5. a. If the discount rate that is used to calculate the present value of a debt obligation's cash flow is increased, what happens to the price of that debt obligation?

   b. Suppose that the discount rate used to calculate the present value of a debt obligation's cash flow is x%. Suppose also that the only cash flow for this debt obligation is $200,000 four years from now and $200,000 five years from now. For which of these cash flows will the present value be greater?

6. The pension fund obligation of a corporation is calculated as the present value of the actuarially projected benefits that will have to be paid to beneficiaries. Why is the interest rate used to discount the projected benefits important?

7. A pension fund manager knows that the following liabilities must be satisfied:

Years from Now	Liability (in millions)
1	$2.0
2	3.0
3	5.4
4	5.8

Suppose that the pension fund manager wants to invest a sum of money that will satisfy this liability stream. Assuming that any amount that can be invested today can earn an annual interest rate of 7.6%, how much must be invested today to satisfy this liability stream?

8. Calculate for each of the following bonds the price per $1,000 of par value assuming semiannual coupon payments.

Bond	Coupon Rate (%)	Years to Maturity	Required Yield (%)
A	8	9	7
B	9	20	9
C	6	15	10
D	0	14	8

9. Consider a bond selling at par ($100) with a coupon rate of 6% and 10 years to maturity.
   a. What is the price of this bond if the required yield is 15%?
   b. What is the price of this bond if the required yield increases from 15% to 16%, and by what percentage did the price of this bond change?
   c. What is the price of this bond if the required yield is 5%?

    d. What is the price of this bond if the required yield increases from 5% to 6%, and by what percentage did the price of this bond change?

    e. From your answers to Question 9, parts b and d, what can you say about the relative price volatility of a bond in high- compared with low-interest-rate environments?

10. Suppose that you purchased a debt obligation three years ago at its par value of $100,000 and nine years remaining to maturity. The market price of this debt obligation today is $90,000. What are some reasons why the price of this debt obligation could have declined since you purchased it three years ago?

11. Suppose that you are reviewing a price sheet for bonds and see the following prices (per $100 par value) reported. You observe what seem to be several errors. Without calculating the price of each bond, indicate which bonds seem to be reported incorrectly, and explain why.

Bond	Price	Coupon Rate (%)	Required Yield (%)
U	90	6	9
V	96	9	8
W	110	8	6
X	105	0	5
Y	107	7	9
Z	100	6	6

12. What is the maximum price of a bond?

13. What is the "dirty" price of a bond?

14. Explain why you agree or disagree with the following statement: "The price of a floater will always trade at its par value."

15. Explain why you agree or disagree with the following statement: "The price of an inverse floater will increase when the reference rate decreases."

CHAPTER 3

Measuring Yield

Learning Objectives

After reading this chapter you will understand:

- how to calculate the yield on any investment

- how to calculate the current yield, yield to maturity, yield to call, yield to put, and cash flow yield

- how to calculate the yield of a portfolio

- how to calculate the effective margin for a floating-rate security

- the three potential sources of a bond's return

- what reinvestment risk is

- the limitations of conventional yield measures

- how to calculate the total return for a bond

- why the total return is superior to conventional yield measures

- how to use horizon analysis to assess the potential return performance of a bond

In Chapter 2 we showed how to determine the price of a bond, and we described the relationship between price and yield. In this chapter we discuss various yield measures and their meaning for evaluating the relative attractiveness of a bond. We begin with an explanation of how to compute the yield on any investment.

COMPUTING THE YIELD OR INTERNAL RATE OF RETURN ON ANY INVESTMENT

The yield on any investment is the interest rate that will make the present value of the cash flows from the investment equal to the price (or cost) of the investment. Mathematically, the yield on any investment, y, is the interest rate that satisfies the equation

$$P = \frac{CF_1}{1 + y} + \frac{CF_2}{(1 + y)^2} + \frac{CF_3}{(1 + y)^3} + \cdots + \frac{CF_N}{(1 + y)^N}$$

This expression can be rewritten in shorthand notation as

$$P = \sum_{t=1}^{N} \frac{CF_t}{(1 + y)^t}$$ (3.1)

where:

CF_t = cash flow in year t
  P = price of the investment
  N = number of years

The yield calculated from this relationship is also called the **internal rate of return.**

Solving for the yield (y) requires a trial-and-error (iterative) procedure. The objective is to find the interest rate that will make the present value of the cash flows equal to the price. An example demonstrates how this is done.

Suppose that a financial instrument selling for $903.10 promises to make the following annual payments:

Years from Now	Promised Annual Payments (Cash Flow to Investor)
1	$ 100
2	100
3	100
4	1,000

To compute yield, different interest rates must be tried until the present value of the cash flows is equal to $903.10 (the price of the financial instrument). Trying an annual interest rate of 10% gives the following present value:

Years from Now	Promised Annual Payments (Cash Flow to Investor)	Present Value of Cash Flow at 10%
1	$ 100	$ 90.91
2	100	82.64
3	100	75.13
4	1,000	683.01
		Present value = $931.69

Because the present value computed using a 10% interest rate exceeds the price of $903.10, a higher interest rate must be used, to reduce the present value. If a 12% interest rate is used, the present value is $875.71, computed as follows:

Years from Now	Promised Annual Payments (Cash Flow to Investor)	Present Value of Cash Flow at 12%
1	$ 100	$ 89.29
2	100	79.72
3	100	71.18
4	1,000	635.52
		Present value = $875.71

Using 12%, the present value of the cash flow is less than the price of the financial instrument. Therefore, a lower interest rate must be tried, to increase the present value. Using an 11% interest rate:

Years from Now	Promised Annual Payments (Cash Flow to Investor)	Present Value of Cash Flow at 11%
1	$ 100	$ 90.09
2	100	81.16
3	100	73.12
4	1,000	658.73
		Present value = $903.10

Using 11%, the present value of the cash flow is equal to the price of the financial instrument. Therefore, the yield is 11%.

Although the formula for the yield is based on annual cash flows, it can be generalized to any number of periodic payments in a year. The generalized formula for determining the yield is

$$P = \sum_{t=1}^{n} \frac{CF_t}{(1 + y)^t} \tag{3.2}$$

where:

CF_t = cash flow in period t
  n = number of periods

Keep in mind that the yield computed is now the yield for the period. That is, if the cash flows are semiannual, the yield is a semiannual yield. If the cash flows are monthly, the yield is a monthly yield. To compute the *simple* annual interest rate, the yield for the period is multiplied by the number of periods in the year.

Special Case: Investment with Only One Future Cash Flow

In one special case it is not necessary to go through the time-consuming trial-and-error procedure to determine the yield. This is where there is only one future cash flow from the investment. When an investment has only one future cash flow at period n (CF_n), equation (3.2) reduces to

$$P = \frac{CF_n}{(1 + y)^n}$$

Solving for yield, y, we obtain

$$y = \left[\frac{CF_n}{P} \right]^{1/n} - 1 \tag{3.3}$$

To illustrate how to use equation (3.3), suppose that a financial instrument currently selling for $62,321.30 promises to pay $100,000 six years from now. The yield for this investment is 8.20%, as follows:

$$y = \left[\frac{100{,}000.00}{62{,}321.30} \right]^{1/6} - 1$$
$$= (1.60459)^{1/6} - 1$$
$$= 1.082 - 1$$
$$= 0.082 \text{ or } 8.2\%$$

Note in equation (3.3) that the ratio of the future cash flow in period n to the price of the financial instrument (i.e., CF_n/P) is equal to the future value per \$1 invested.

Annualizing Yields

In Chapter 2 we annualized interest rates by multiplying by the number of periods in a year, and we called the resulting value the **simple annual interest rate.** For example, a semiannual yield is annualized by multiplying by 2. Alternatively, an annual interest rate is converted to a semiannual interest rate by dividing by 2.

This simplified procedure for computing the annual interest rate given a periodic (weekly, monthly, quarterly, semiannually, and so on) interest rate is not accurate. To obtain an effective annual yield associated with a periodic interest rate, the following formula is used:

$$\text{effective annual yield} = (1 + \text{periodic interest rate})^m - 1$$

where m is the frequency of payments per year. For example, suppose that the periodic interest rate is 4% and the frequency of payments is twice per year. Then

$$\text{effective annual yield} = (1.04)^2 - 1 = 1.0816 - 1$$
$$= 0.0816 \text{ or } 8.16\%$$

If interest is paid quarterly, the periodic interest rate is 2% (8%/4), and the effective annual yield is 8.24%, as follows:

$$\text{effective annual yield} = (1.02)^4 - 1 = 1.0824 - 1$$
$$= 0.0824 \text{ or } 8.24\%$$

We can also determine the periodic interest rate that will produce a given annual interest rate by solving the effective annual yield equation for the periodic interest rate. Solving, we find that

$$\text{periodic interest rate} = (1 + \text{effective annual yield})^{1/m} - 1$$

For example, the periodic quarterly interest rate that would produce an effective annual yield of 12% is

$$\text{periodic interest rate} = (1.12)^{1/4} - 1 = 1.0287 - 1$$
$$= 0.0287 \text{ or } 2.87\%$$

CONVENTIONAL YIELD MEASURES

There are several bond yield measures commonly quoted by dealers and used by portfolio managers. In this section we discuss each yield measure and show how it is computed. In the next section we critically evaluate yield measures in terms of their usefulness in identifying the relative value of a bond.

Current Yield

Current yield relates the annual coupon interest to the market price. The formula for the current yield is

$$\text{current yield} = \frac{\text{annual dollar coupon interest}}{\text{price}}$$

For example, the current yield for a 15-year 7% coupon bond with a par value of $1,000 selling for $769.40 is 9.10%:

$$\text{current yield} = \frac{\$70}{\$769.40} = 0.0910 \text{ or } 9.10\%$$

The current yield calculation takes into account only the coupon interest and no other source of return that will affect an investor's yield. No consideration is given to the capital gain that the investor will realize when a bond is purchased at a discount and held to maturity; nor is there any recognition of the capital loss that the investor will realize if a bond purchased at a premium is held to maturity. The time value of money is also ignored.

Yield to Maturity

In the first section of this chapter we explained how to compute the yield or internal rate of return on any investment. The yield is the interest rate that will make the present value of the cash flows equal to the price (or initial investment). The **yield to maturity** is computed in the same way as the yield (internal rate of return); the cash flows are those that the investor would realize by holding the bond to maturity. For a semiannual pay bond, the yield to maturity is found by first computing the periodic interest rate, y, that satisfies the relationship

$$P = \frac{C}{1 + y} + \frac{C}{(1 + y)^2} + \frac{C}{(1 + y)^3} + \cdots + \frac{C}{(1 + y)^n} + \frac{M}{(1 + y)^n}$$

$$P = \sum_{t=1}^{n} \frac{C}{(1 + y)^t} + \frac{M}{(1 + y)^n} \tag{3.4}$$

where:

P = price of the bond
C = *semiannual* coupon interest (in dollars)
M = maturity value (in dollars)
n = number of periods (number of years × 2)

For a semiannual pay bond, doubling the periodic interest rate or discount rate (y) gives the yield to maturity. However, recall from our discussion of annualizing yields that doubling the periodic interest rate understates the effective annual yield. Despite this, the market convention is to compute the yield to maturity by doubling the periodic interest rate, y, that satisfies equation (3.4). The yield to maturity computed on the basis of this market convention is called the **bond-equivalent yield.**

The computation of the yield to maturity requires a trial-and-error procedure. To illustrate the computation, consider the bond that we used to compute the current yield. The cash flow for this bond is (1) 30 coupon payments of $35 every six months and (2) $1,000 to be paid 30 six-month periods from now.

To get y in equation (3.4), different interest rates must be tried until the present value of the cash flows is equal to the price of $769.42. The present value of the cash flows of the bond for several periodic interest rates is as follows:

Annual Interest Rate (%)	Semiannual Rate y (%)	Present Value of 30 Payments of $35[a]	Present Value of $1,000 30 Periods from Now[b]	Present Value of Cash Flows
9.00	4.50	$570.11	$267.00	$837.11
9.50	4.75	553.71	248.53	802.24
10.00	5.00	538.04	231.38	769.42
10.50	5.25	532.04	215.45	738.49
11.00	5.50	508.68	200.64	709.32

[a]The present value of the coupon payments is found using the formula

$$\$35\left[\frac{1 - \frac{1}{(1 + y)^{30}}}{y}\right]$$

[b]The present value of the maturity value is found using the formula

$$\$1,000\left[\frac{1}{(1 + y)^{30}}\right]$$

When a 5% semiannual interest rate is used, the present value of the cash flows is $769.42. Therefore, y is 5%, and the yield to maturity on a bond-equivalent basis is 10%.

It is much easier to compute the yield to maturity for a zero-coupon bond because equation (3.3) can be used. As the cash flow in period n is the maturity value M, equation (3.3) can be rewritten as[1]

$$y = \left[\frac{M}{P}\right]^{1/n} - 1 \tag{3.5}$$

For example, for a 10-year zero-coupon bond with a maturity value of $1,000, selling for $439.18, y is 4.2%:

$$y = \left[\frac{\$1,000}{\$439.18}\right]^{1/20} - 1 = (2.27697)^{0.05} - 1$$
$$= 1.042 - 1$$
$$= 0.042$$

Note that the number of periods is equal to 20 semiannual periods, which is double the number of years. The number of years is not used because we want a yield value

---

[1]That is, M is substituted for CF_n.

that may be compared with alternative coupon bonds. To get the bond-equivalent annual yield, we must double y, which gives us 8.4%.

The yield-to-maturity calculation takes into account not only the current coupon income but also any capital gain or loss that the investor will realize by *holding the bond to maturity*. In addition, the yield to maturity considers the timing of the cash flows. The relationship among the coupon rate, current yield, and yield to maturity looks like this:

Bond Selling at:	*Relationship*
Par	Coupon rate = current yield = yield to maturity
Discount	Coupon rate < current yield < yield to maturity
Premium	Coupon rate > current yield > yield to maturity

Yield to Call

As explained in Chapter 1, the issuer may be entitled to call a bond prior to the stated maturity date. When the bond may be called and at what price are specified at the time the bond is issued. The price at which the bond may be called is referred to as the **call price.** For some issues, the call price is the same regardless of when the issue is called. For other callable issues, the call price depends on when the issue is called. That is, there is a **call schedule** that specifies a call price for each call date.

For callable issues, the practice has been to calculate a **yield to call** as well as a yield to maturity. The yield to call assumes that the issuer will call the bond at some assumed call date and the call price is then the call price specified in the call schedule. Typically, investors calculate a **yield to first call** and a **yield to par call.** The former yield measure assumes that the issue will be called on the first call date. The latter yield measure assumes that the issue will be called the first time on the call schedule when the issuer is entitled to call the bond at par value.

The procedure for calculating the yield to any assumed call date is the same as for any yield calculation: Determine the interest rate that will make the present value of the expected cash flows equal to the bond's price. In the case of yield to first call, the expected cash flows are the coupon payments to the first call date and the call price as specified in the call schedule. For the yield to first par call, the expected cash flows are the coupon payments to the first date at which the issuer may call the bond at par value plus the last cash flow of par value.

Mathematically, the yield to call can be expressed as follows:

$$P = \frac{C}{1+y} + \frac{C}{(1+y)^2} + \frac{C}{(1+y)^3} + \cdots \frac{C}{(1+y)^{n^*}} + \frac{M^*}{(1+y)^{n^*}}$$

$$P = \sum_{t=1}^{n^*} \frac{C}{(1+y)^t} + \frac{M^*}{(1+y)^{n^*}} \qquad (3.6)$$

where:

M^* = call price (in dollars)
n^* = number of periods until the assumed call date (number of years × 2)

For a semiannual pay bond, doubling the periodic interest rate (y) gives the yield to call on a bond-equivalent basis.

To illustrate the computation, consider an 18-year 11% coupon bond with a maturity value of $1,000 selling for $1,169. Suppose that the first call date is 8 years from now and that the call price is $1,055. The cash flows for this bond if it is called in 13 years are (1) 26 coupon payments of $55 every six months, and (2) $1,055 due in 16 six-month periods from now.

The value for y in equation (3.6) is the one that will make the present value of the cash flows to the first call date equal to the bond's price of $1,169. The process of finding the yield to first call is the same as that for finding the yield to maturity. The present value at several periodic interest rates is as follows:

Annual Interest Rate (%)	Semiannual Rate y (%)	Present Value of 16 Payments of $55[a]	Present Value of $1,055 16 Periods from Now[b]	Present Value of Cash Flows
8.000	4.0000	$640.88	$563.27	$1,204.15
8.250	4.1250	635.01	552.55	1,187.56
8.500	4.2500	629.22	542.05	1,171.26
8.535	4.2675	628.41	540.59	1,169.00
8.600	4.3000	626.92	537.90	1,164.83

[a]The present value of the coupon payments is found using the formula

$$\$55\left[\frac{1 - \frac{1}{(1 + y)^{16}}}{y}\right]$$

[b]The present value of the call price is found using the formula

$$\$1,055\left[\frac{1}{(1 + y)^{16}}\right]$$

Because a periodic interest rate of 4.2675% makes the present value of the cash flows equal to the price, 4.2675% is y, the yield to first call. Therefore, the yield to first call on a bond-equivalent basis is 8.535%.

Suppose that the first par call date for this bond is 13 years from now. Then the yield to first par call is the interest rate that will make the present value of $55 every six months for the next 26 six-month periods plus the par value of $1,000 26 six-month periods from now equal to the price of $1,169. It is left as an exercise for the reader to show that the semiannual interest rate that equates the present value of the cash flows to the price is 4.3965%. Therefore, 8.793% is the yield to first par call.

Yield to Put

As explained in Chapter 1, an issue can be putable. This means that the bondholder can force the issuer to buy the issue at a specified price. As with a callable issue, a putable issue can have a put schedule. The schedule specifies when the issue can be put and the price, called the put price.

When an issue is putable, a **yield to put** is calculated. The yield to put is the interest rate that makes the present value of the cash flows to the assumed put date plus the put price on that date as set forth in the put schedule equal to the bond's price. The formula is the same as equation (3.6), but M^* is now defined as the put price and

n^* is the number of periods until the assumed put date. The procedure is the same as calculating yield to maturity and yield to call.

For example, consider again the 11% coupon 18-year issue selling for $1,169. Assume that the issue is putable at par ($1,000) in five years. The yield to put is the interest rate that makes the present value of $55 per period for 10 six-month periods plus the put price of $1,000 equal to the $1,169. It is left to the reader to demonstrate that a discount rate of 3.471% will result in this equality. Doubling this rate gives 6.942% and is the yield to put.

Yield to Worst

A practice in the industry is for an investor to calculate the yield to maturity, the yield to every possible call date, and the yield to every possible put date. The minimum of all of these yields is called the **yield to worst.**

Cash Flow Yield

In later chapters we will cover fixed income securities whose cash flows include scheduled principal repayments prior to maturity. That is, the cash flow in each period includes interest plus principal repayment. Such securities are called **amortizing securities.** Mortgage-backed securities and asset-backed securities are examples. In addition, the amount that the borrower can repay in principal may exceed the scheduled amount. This excess amount of principal repayment over the amount scheduled is called a **prepayment.** Thus, for amortizing securities, the cash flow each period consists of three components: (1) coupon interest, (2) scheduled principal repayment, and (3) prepayments.

For amortizing securities, market participants calculate a **cash flow yield.** It is the interest rate that will make the present value of the projected cash flows equal to the market price. The difficulty is projecting what the prepayment will be in each period. We will illustrate this calculation in Chapter 11.

Yield (Internal Rate of Return) for a Portfolio

The yield for a portfolio of bonds is not simply the average or weighted average of the yield to maturity of the individual bond issues in the portfolio. It is computed by determining the cash flows for the portfolio and determining the interest rate that will make the present value of the cash flows equal to the market value of the portfolio.[2]

Consider a three-bond portfolio as follows:

Bond	Coupon Rate (%)	Maturity (years)	Par Value	Price	Yield to Maturity (%)
A	7.0	5	$10,000,000	$ 9,209,000	9.0
B	10.5	7	20,000,000	20,000,000	10.5
C	6.0	3	30,000,000	28,050,000	8.5

---

[2] In Chapter 4 we discuss the concept of duration. A good approximation to the yield for a portfolio can be obtained by using duration to weight the yield to maturity of the individual bonds in the portfolio.

To simplify the illustration, it is assumed that the coupon payment date is the same for each bond. The portfolio's total market value is $57,259,000. The cash flow for each bond in the portfolio and for the entire portfolio follows:

Period Cash Flow Received	Bond A	Bond B	Bond C	Portfolio
1	$ 350,000	$ 1,050,000	$ 900,000	$ 2,300,000
2	350,000	1,050,000	900,000	2,300,000
3	350,000	1,050,000	900,000	2,300,000
4	350,000	1,050,000	900,000	2,300,000
5	350,000	1,050,000	900,000	2,300,000
6	350,000	1,050,000	30,900,000	32,300,000
7	350,000	1,050,000	—	1,400,000
8	350,000	1,050,000	—	1,400,000
9	350,000	1,050,000	—	1,400,000
10	10,350,000	1,050,000	—	11,400,000
11	—	1,050,000	—	1,050,000
12	—	1,050,000	—	1,050,000
13	—	1,050,000	—	1,050,000
14	—	21,050,000	—	21,050,000

To determine the yield (internal rate of return) for this three-bond portfolio, the interest rate must be found that makes the present value of the cash flows shown in the last column of the preceding table equal to $57,259,000 (the total market value of the portfolio). If an interest rate of 4.77% is used, the present value of the cash flows will equal $57,259,000. Doubling 4.77% gives 9.54%, which is the yield on the portfolio on a bond-equivalent basis.

Yield Measure for Floating-Rate Securities

The coupon rate for a floating-rate security changes periodically according to some reference rate. Because the value for the reference rate in the future is not known, it is not possible to determine the cash flows. This means that a yield to maturity cannot be calculated for a floating-rate bond.

A conventional measure used to estimate the potential return for a floating-rate security is the security's **effective margin.** This measure estimates the average spread or margin over the reference rate that the investor can expect to earn over the life of the security. The procedure for calculating the effective margin is as follows:

Step 1: Determine the cash flows assuming that the reference rate does not change over the life of the security.

Step 2: Select a margin (spread).

Step 3: Discount the cash flows found in step 1 by the current value of the reference rate plus the margin selected in step 2.

Step 4: Compare the present value of the cash flows as calculated in step 3 with the price. If the present value is equal to the security's price, the effective margin is the margin assumed in step 2. If the present value is not equal to the security's price, go back to step 2 and try a different margin.

For a security selling at par, the effective margin is simply the spread over the reference rate.

To illustrate the calculation, suppose that a six-year floating-rate security selling for 99.3098 pays a rate based on some reference rate plus 80 basis points. The coupon rate is reset every six months. Assume that the current value of the reference rate is 10%. Exhibit 3-1 shows the calculation of the effective margin for this security. The first column shows the current value of the reference rate. The second column sets forth the cash flows for the security. The cash flow for the first 11 periods is equal to one-half the current value of the reference rate (5%) plus the semiannual spread of 40 basis points multiplied by 100. In the twelfth six-month period, the cash flow is 5.4 plus the maturity value of 100. The top row of the last five columns shows the assumed margin. The rows below the assumed margin show the present value of each cash flow. The last row gives the total present value of the cash flows.

For the five assumed yield spreads, the present value is equal to the price of the floating-rate security (99.3098) when the assumed margin is 96 basis points. Therefore, the effective margin on a semiannual basis is 48 basis points and 96 basis points on an annual basis. (Notice that the effective margin is 80 basis points, the same as the spread over the reference rate when the security is selling at par.)

A drawback of the effective margin as a measure of the potential return from investing in a floating-rate security is that the effective margin approach assumes that the reference rate will not change over the life of the security. Second, if the floating-rate security has a cap or floor, this is not taken into consideration.

EXHIBIT 3-1   Calculation of the Effective Margin for a Floating-Rate Security

Floating-rate security: Maturity: six years
Coupon rate: reference rate + 80 basis points
Reset every six months

Period	Index	Cash Flow[a]	Present Value of Cash Flow at Assumed Annual Yield Spread (basis points)				
			80	84	88	96	100
1	10%	5.4	5.1233	5.1224	5.1214	5.1195	5.1185
2	10	5.4	4.8609	4.8590	4.8572	4.8535	4.8516
3	10	5.4	4.6118	4.6092	4.6066	4.6013	4.5987
4	10	5.4	4.3755	4.3722	4.3689	4.3623	4.3590
5	10	5.4	4.1514	4.1474	4.1435	4.1356	4.1317
6	10	5.4	3.9387	3.9342	3.9297	3.9208	3.9163
7	10	5.4	3.7369	3.7319	3.7270	3.7171	3.7122
8	10	5.4	3.5454	3.5401	3.5347	3.5240	3.5186
9	10	5.4	3.3638	3.3580	3.3523	3.3409	3.3352
10	10	5.4	3.1914	3.1854	3.1794	3.1673	3.1613
11	10	5.4	3.0279	3.0216	3.0153	3.0028	2.9965
12	10	105.4	56.0729	55.9454	55.8182	55.5647	55.4385
		Present value =	100.0000	99.8269	99.6541	99.3098	99.1381

[a]For periods 1–11: cash flow = 100 (reference rate + assumed margin) (0.5); for period 12: cash flow = 100 (reference rate + assumed margin) (0.5) + 100.

POTENTIAL SOURCES OF A BOND'S DOLLAR RETURN

An investor who purchases a bond can expect to receive a dollar return from one or more of these sources:

1. The periodic coupon interest payments made by the issuer
2. Any capital gain (or capital loss—negative dollar return) when the bond matures, is called, or is sold
3. Interest income generated from reinvestment of the periodic cash flows

The last component of the potential dollar return is referred to as **reinvestment income.** For a standard bond that makes only coupon payments and no periodic principal payments prior to the maturity date, the interim cash flows are simply the coupon payments. Consequently, for such bonds the reinvestment income is simply interest earned from reinvesting the coupon interest payments. For these bonds, the third component of the potential source of dollar return is referred to as the **interest-on-interest component.** For amortizing securities, the reinvestment income is the interest income from reinvesting both the coupon interest payments and periodic principal repayments prior to the maturity date. In our subsequent discussion, we will look at the sources of return for nonamortizing securities (that is, bonds in which no periodic principal is repaid prior to the maturity date).

Any measure of a bond's potential yield should take into consideration each of these three potential sources of return. The current yield considers only the coupon interest payments. No consideration is given to any capital gain (or loss) or interest on interest. The yield to maturity takes into account coupon interest and any capital gain (or loss). It also considers the interest-on-interest component. However, as will be demonstrated later, implicit in the yield-to-maturity computation is the assumption that the coupon payments can be reinvested at the computed yield to maturity. The yield to maturity, therefore, is a *promised* yield—that is, it will be realized only if (1) the bond is held to maturity, and (2) the coupon interest payments are reinvested at the yield to maturity. If neither (1) nor (2) occurs, the actual yield realized by an investor can be greater than or less than the yield to maturity.

The yield to call also takes into account all three potential sources of return. In this case, the assumption is that the coupon payments can be reinvested at the yield to call. Therefore, the yield-to-call measure suffers from the same drawback as the yield to maturity in that it assumes coupon interest payments are reinvested at the computed yield to call. Also, it assumes that the bond will be called by the issuer on the assumed call date.

The cash flow yield, which will be more fully discussed in Chapter 11, also takes into consideration all three sources as is the case with yield to maturity, but it makes two additional assumptions. First, it assumes that the periodic principal repayments are reinvested at the computed cash flow yield. Second, it assumes that the prepayments projected to obtain the cash flows are actually realized.

Determining the Interest-on-Interest Dollar Return

Let's focus on nonamortizing securities. The interest-on-interest component can represent a substantial portion of a bond's potential return. The potential total dollar return from coupon interest and interest on interest can be computed by applying the future value of an annuity formula given in Chapter 2. Letting r denote the semiannual reinvestment rate, the interest on interest plus the total coupon payments can be found from the equation

$$\begin{matrix} \text{coupon interest} \\ + \\ \text{interest on interest} \end{matrix} = C\left[\frac{(1 + r)^n - 1}{r}\right] \qquad (3.7)$$

The total dollar amount of coupon interest is found by multiplying the semiannual coupon interest by the number of periods:

$$\text{total coupon interest} = nC$$

The interest-on-interest component is then the difference between the coupon interest plus interest on interest and the total dollar coupon interest, as expressed by the formula

$$\text{interest on interest} = C\left[\frac{(1 + r)^n - 1}{r}\right] - nC \qquad (3.8)$$

The yield-to-maturity measure assumes that the reinvestment rate is the yield to maturity.

For example, let's consider the 15-year 7% bond that we have used to illustrate how to compute current yield and yield to maturity. If the price of this bond per $1,000 of par value is $769.40, the yield to maturity for this bond is 10%. Assuming an annual reinvestment rate of 10% or a semiannual reinvestment rate of 5%, the interest on interest plus total coupon payments using equation (3.7) is

$$\begin{matrix} \text{coupon interest} \\ + \\ \text{interest on interest} \end{matrix} = \$35\left[\frac{(1.05)^{30} - 1}{0.05}\right]$$

$$= \$2,325.36$$

Using equation (3.8), the interest-on-interest component is

$$\text{interest on interest} = \$2,325.36 - 30\,(\$35)$$
$$= \$1,275.36$$

Yield to Maturity and Reinvestment Risk

Let's look at the potential total dollar return from holding this bond to maturity. As mentioned earlier, the total dollar return comes from three sources:

1. Total coupon interest of $1,050 (coupon interest of $35 every six months for 15 years)
2. Interest on interest of $1,275.36 earned from reinvesting the semiannual coupon interest payments at 5% every six months
3. A capital gain of $230.60 ($1,000 minus $769.40)

The potential total dollar return if the coupons can be reinvested at the yield to maturity of 10% is then $2,555.96.

Notice that if an investor places the money that would have been used to purchase this bond, $769.40, in a savings account earning 5% semiannually for 15 years, the future value of the savings account would be

$$\$769.40(1.05)^{30} = \$3,325.30$$

For the initial investment of $769.40, the total dollar return is $2,555.90.

So, an investor who invests $769.40 for 15 years at 10% per year (5% semiannually) expects to receive at the end of 15 years the initial investment of $769.40 plus $2,555.90. Ignoring rounding errors, this is what we found by breaking down the dollar return on the bond assuming a reinvestment rate equal to the yield to maturity of 10%. Thus it can be seen that for the bond to yield 10%, the investor must generate $1,275.36 by reinvesting the coupon payments. This means that to generate a yield to maturity of 10%, approximately half ($1,275.36/$2,555.96) of this bond's total dollar return must come from the reinvestment of the coupon payments.

The investor will realize the yield to maturity at the time of purchase only if the bond is held to maturity and the coupon payments can be reinvested at the computed yield to maturity. The risk that the investor faces is that future reinvestment rates will be less than the yield to maturity at the time the bond is purchased. This risk is referred to as **reinvestment risk.**

There are two characteristics of a bond that determine the importance of the interest-on-interest component and therefore the degree of reinvestment risk: maturity and coupon. For a given yield to maturity and a given coupon rate, the longer the maturity, the more dependent the bond's total dollar return is on the interest-on-interest component in order to realize the yield to maturity at the time of purchase. In other words, the longer the maturity, the greater the reinvestment risk. The implication is that the yield-to-maturity measure for long-term coupon bonds tells little about the potential yield that an investor may realize if the bond is held to maturity. For long-term bonds, the interest-on-interest component may be as high as 80% of the bond's potential total dollar return.

Turning to the coupon rate, for a given maturity and a given yield to maturity, the higher the coupon rate, the more dependent the bond's total dollar return will be on the reinvestment of the coupon payments in order to produce the yield to maturity anticipated at the time of purchase. This means that when maturity and yield to maturity are held constant, premium bonds are more dependent on the interest-on-interest component than are bonds selling at par. Discount bonds are less dependent on the interest-on-interest component than are bonds selling at par. For zero-coupon bonds, none of the bond's total dollar return is dependent on the interest-on-interest component, so a zero-coupon bond has zero reinvestment risk if held to maturity. Thus the yield earned on a zero-coupon bond held to maturity is equal to the promised yield to maturity.

Cash Flow Yield and Reinvestment Risk

For amortizing securities, reinvestment risk is even greater than for nonamortizing securities. The reason is that the investor must now reinvest the periodic principal repayments in addition to the periodic coupon interest payments. Moreover, as explained later in this book when we cover the two major types of amortizing securities—mortgage-backed securities and asset-backed securities—the cash flows are monthly, not semiannually as with nonamortizing securities. Consequently, the investor must not only reinvest periodic coupon interest payments and principal, but must do it more often. This increases reinvestment risk.

There is one more aspect of nonamortizing securities that adds to their reinvestment risk. Typically, for nonamortizing securities the borrower can accelerate the periodic principal repayment. That is, the borrower can prepay. But a borrower will typically prepay when interest rates decline. Consequently, if a borrower prepays when interest rates decline, the investor faces greater reinvestment risk because he or she must reinvest the prepaid principal at a lower interest rate.

TOTAL RETURN

In the preceding section we explain that the yield to maturity is a **promised** yield. At the time of purchase an investor is promised a yield, as measured by the yield to maturity, if both of the following conditions are satisfied:

1. The bond is held to maturity.
2. All coupon interest payments are reinvested at the yield to maturity.

We focused on the second assumption, and we showed that the interest-on-interest component for a bond may constitute a substantial portion of the bond's total dollar return. Therefore, reinvesting the coupon interest payments at a rate of interest less than the yield to maturity will produce a lower yield than the yield to maturity.

Rather than assuming that the coupon interest payments are reinvested at the yield to maturity, an investor can make an explicit assumption about the reinvestment rate based on personal expectations. The **total return** is a measure of yield that incorporates an explicit assumption about the reinvestment rate.

Let's take a careful look at the first assumption—that a bond will be held to maturity. Suppose, for example, that an investor who has a five-year investment horizon is considering the following four bonds:

Bond	Coupon (%)	Maturity (years)	Yield to Maturity (%)
A	5	3	9.0
B	6	20	8.6
C	11	15	9.2
D	8	5	8.0

Assuming that all four bonds are of the same credit quality, which is most attractive to this investor? An investor who selects bond C because it offers the highest yield to maturity is failing to recognize that the investment horizon calls for selling the bond after five years, at a price that depends on the yield required in the market for 10-year 11% coupon bonds at the time. Hence there could be a capital gain or capital loss that will make the return higher or lower than the yield to maturity promised now. Moreover, the higher coupon on bond C relative to the other three bonds means that more of this bond's return will be dependent on the reinvestment of coupon interest payments.

Bond A offers the second highest yield to maturity. On the surface, it seems to be particularly attractive because it eliminates the problem of realizing a possible capital loss when the bond must be sold prior to the maturity date. Moreover, the reinvestment risk seems to be less than for the other three bonds because the coupon rate is the lowest. However, the investor would not be eliminating the reinvestment risk because after three years the proceeds received at maturity must be reinvested for two more years. The yield that the investor will realize depends on interest rates three years from now on two-year bonds when the proceeds must be rolled over.

The yield to maturity does not seem to be helping us to identify the best bond. How, then, do we find out which is the best bond? The answer depends on the investor's expectations. Specifically, it depends on the interest rate at which the coupon interest payments can be reinvested until the end of the investor's planned investment horizon. Also, for bonds with a maturity longer than the investment horizon, it depends on the investor's expectations about required yields in the market at the end of the planned investment horizon. Consequently, any of these bonds can be the best alternative, depending on some reinvestment rate and some future required yield at the end of the planned investment horizon. The total return measure takes these expectations into account and will determine the best investment for the investor, depending on personal expectations.

The yield-to-call measure is subject to the same problems as the yield to maturity. First, it assumes that the bond will be held until the first call date. Second, it assumes that the coupon interest payments will be reinvested at the yield to call. If an investor's planned investment horizon is shorter than the time to the first call date, the bond may have to be sold for less than its acquisition cost. If, on the other hand, the investment horizon is longer than the time to the first call date, there is the problem of reinvesting the proceeds from the time the bond is called until the end of the planned investment horizon. Consequently, the yield to call does not tell us very much. The total return, however, can accommodate the analysis of callable bonds.

Computing the Total Return for a Bond

The idea underlying total return is simple. The objective is first to compute the total future dollars that will result from investing in a bond assuming a particular reinvestment rate. The total return is then computed as the interest rate that will make the initial investment in the bond grow to the computed total future dollars.

The procedure for computing the total return for a bond held over some investment horizon can be summarized as follows. For an assumed reinvestment rate, the dollar return that will be available at the end of the investment horizon can be computed for both the coupon interest payments and the interest-on-interest component. In addition, at the end of the planned investment horizon the investor will receive either the par value or some other value (based on the market yield on the bond when it is sold). The total return is then the interest rate that will make the amount invested in the bond (i.e., the current market price plus accrued interest) grow to the future dollars available at the end of the planned investment horizon.

More formally, the steps for computing the total return for a bond held over some investment horizon are as follows:

Step 1: Compute the total coupon payments plus the interest on interest based on the assumed reinvestment rate. The coupon payments plus the interest on interest can be computed using equation (3.7). The reinvestment rate in this case is one-half the annual interest rate that the investor assumes can be earned on the reinvestment of coupon interest payments.

Step 2: Determine the projected sale price at the end of the planned investment horizon. The projected sale price will depend on the projected required yield at the end of the planned investment horizon. The projected sale price will be equal to the present value of the remaining
cash flows of the bond discounted at the projected required yield.

Step 3: Sum the values computed in steps 1 and 2. The sum is the total future
dollars that will be received from the investment, given the assumed
reinvestment rate and the projected required yield at the end of the investment horizon.[3]

Step 4: To obtain the semiannual total return, use the formula

$$\left[\frac{\text{total future dollars}}{\text{purchase price of bond}} \right]^{1/h} - 1 \qquad (3.9)$$

where h is the number of six-month periods in the investment horizon.
Notice that this formula is simply an application of equation (3.3), the
yield for an investment with just one future cash flow.

Step 5: As interest is assumed to be paid semiannually, double the interest rate
found in step 4. The resulting interest rate is the total return.

To illustrate computation of the total return, suppose that an investor with a
three-year investment horizon is considering purchasing a 20-year 8% coupon
bond for $828.40. The yield to maturity for this bond is 10%. The investor expects
to be able to reinvest the coupon interest payments at an annual interest rate of 6%
and that at the end of the planned investment horizon the then-17-year bond will
be selling to offer a yield to maturity of 7%. The total return for this bond is found
as follows:

Step 1: Compute the total coupon payments plus the interest on interest,
assuming an annual reinvestment rate of 6%, or 3% every six months.
The coupon payments are $40 every six months for three years or six
periods (the planned investment horizon). Applying equation (3.7), the
total coupon interest plus interest on interest is

$$\begin{array}{c} \text{coupon interest} \\ + \\ \text{interest on interest} \end{array} = \$40\left[\frac{(1.03)^6 - 1}{0.03} \right] = \$40\left[\frac{1.1941 - 1}{0.03} \right]$$

$$= \$40[6.4684]$$

$$= \$258.74$$

Step 2: Determining the projected sale price at the end of three years, assuming that the required yield to maturity for 17-year bonds is 7%, is accomplished by calculating the present value of 34 coupon payments of

---

[3]The total future dollars computed here differ from the total dollar return that we used in showing the importance of the interest-on-interest component in the preceding section. The total dollar return there includes only the capital gain (or capital loss if there was one), not the purchase price, which is included in
calculating the total future dollars; that is,

total dollar return = total future dollars − purchase price of bond

$40 plus the present value of the maturity value of $1,000, discounted at 3.5%. The projected sale price is $1,098.51.[4]

Step 3: Adding the amounts in steps 1 and 2 gives total future dollars of $1,357.25.

Step 4: To obtain the semiannual total return, compute the following:

$$\left[\frac{\$1,375.25}{\$828.40}\right]^{1/6} - 1 = (1.63840)^{0.16667} - 1 = 1.0858 - 1$$

$$= 0.0858 \text{ or } 8.58\%$$

Step 5: Double 8.58%, for a total return of 17.16%.

There is no need in this case to assume that the reinvestment rate will be constant for the entire investment horizon. An example will show how the total return measure can accommodate multiple reinvestment rates.

Suppose that an investor has a six-year investment horizon. The investor is considering a 13-year 9% coupon bond selling at par. The investor's expectations are as follows:

1. The first four semiannual coupon payments can be reinvested from the time of receipt to the end of the investment horizon at a simple annual interest rate of 8%.
2. The last eight semiannual coupon payments can be reinvested from the time of receipt to the end of the investment horizon at a 10% simple annual interest rate.
3. The required yield to maturity on seven-year bonds at the end of the investment horizon will be 10.6%.

Using these three assumptions, the total return is computed as follows:

Step 1: Coupon payments of $45 every six months for six years (the investment horizon) will be received. The coupon interest plus interest on interest for the first four coupon payments, assuming a semiannual reinvestment rate of 4%, is

$$\begin{array}{c} \text{coupon interest} \\ + \\ \text{interest on interest} \end{array} = \$45\left[\frac{(1.04)^4 - 1}{0.04}\right]$$

$$= \$191.09$$

---

[4]The present value of the 34 coupon payments discounted at 3.5% is

$$\$40\left[\frac{1 - \frac{1}{(1.035)^{34}}}{0.035}\right] = \$788.03$$

The present value of the maturity value discounted at 3.5% is

$$\frac{\$1,000}{(1.035)^{34}} = \$310.48$$

The projected sale price is $788.03 plus $310.48, or $1,098.51.

This gives the coupon plus interest on interest as of the end of the second year (four periods). Reinvested at 4% until the end of the planned investment horizon, four years or eight periods later, $191.09 will grow to

$$\$191.09(1.04)^8 = \$261.52$$

The coupon interest plus interest on interest for the last eight coupon payments, assuming a semiannual reinvestment rate of 5%, is

$$
\begin{array}{c}
\text{coupon interest} \\
+ \\
\text{interest on interest}
\end{array}
= \$45\left[\frac{(1.05)^8 - 1}{0.05}\right]
$$

$$= \$429.71$$

The coupon interest plus interest on interest from all 12 coupon interest payments is $691.23 ($261.52 + $429.71).

Step 2: The projected sale price of the bond, assuming that the required yield is 10.6%, is $922.31.[5]

Step 3: The total future dollars are $1,613.54 ($691.23 + $922.31).

Step 4: Compute the following:

$$\left[\frac{\$1,613.54}{\$1,000.00}\right]^{1/12} - 1 = (1.61354)^{0.08333} - 1$$

$$= 1.0407 - 1$$

$$= 0.0407 \text{ or } 4.07\%$$

Step 5: Doubling 4.07% gives a total return of 8.14%.

Applications of the Total Return (Horizon Analysis)

The total return measure allows a portfolio manager to project the performance of a bond on the basis of the planned investment horizon and expectations concerning reinvestment rates and future market yields. This permits the portfolio manager to evaluate which of several potential bonds considered for acquisition will perform best over the planned investment horizon. As we have emphasized, this cannot be done using the yield to maturity as a measure of relative value.

Using total return to assess performance over some investment horizon is called **horizon analysis.** When a total return is calculated over an investment horizon, it is referred to as a **horizon return.** In this book we use the terms **horizon return** and **total return** interchangeably.

---

[5]The present value of the coupon payments discounted at 5.3% is

$$\$45\left[\frac{1 - \frac{1}{(1.053)^{14}}}{0.053}\right] = \$437.02$$

The present value of the maturity value discounted at 5.3% is

$$\frac{\$1,000}{(1.053)^{14}} = \$485.29$$

The projected sale price is $437.02 plus $485.29, or $922.31.

Horizon analysis is also used to evaluate bond swaps. In a bond swap the portfolio manager considers exchanging a bond held in the portfolio for another bond. When the objective of the bond swap is to enhance the return of the portfolio over the planned investment horizon, the total return for the bond being considered for purchase can be computed and compared with the total return for the bond held in the portfolio to determine if the bond being held should be replaced. We discuss several bond swap strategies in Chapter 20.

An often-cited objection to the total return measure is that it requires the portfolio manager to formulate assumptions about reinvestment rates and future yields as well as to think in terms of an investment horizon. Unfortunately, some portfolio managers find comfort in measures such as the yield to maturity and yield to call simply because they do not require incorporating any particular expectations. The horizon analysis framework, however, enables the portfolio manager to analyze the performance of a bond under different interest-rate scenarios for reinvestment rates and future market yields. Only by investigating multiple scenarios can the portfolio manager see how sensitive the bond's performance will be to each scenario. Chapter 12 explains a framework for incorporating the market's expectation of future interest rates.

SUMMARY

In this chapter we have explained the conventional yield measures commonly used by bond market participants: current yield, yield to maturity, yield to call, yield to put, yield to worst, and cash flow yield. We then reviewed the three potential sources of dollar return from investing in a bond—coupon interest, reinvestment income, and capital gain (or loss)—and showed that none of the conventional yield measures deals satisfactorily with all of these sources. The current yield measure fails to consider both reinvestment income and capital gain (or loss). The yield to maturity considers all three sources but is deficient in assuming that all coupon interest can be reinvested at the yield to maturity. The risk that the coupon payments will be reinvested at a rate less than the yield to maturity is called reinvestment risk. The yield to call has the same shortcoming; it assumes that the coupon interest can be reinvested at the yield to call. The cash flow yield makes the same assumptions as the yield to maturity, plus it assumes that periodic principal payments can be reinvested at the computed cash flow yield and that the prepayments are actually realized. We then presented a yield measure, the total return, that is a more meaningful measure for assessing the relative attractiveness of a bond given the investor's or the portfolio manager's expectations and planned investment horizon.

Questions

1. A debt obligation offers the following payments:

Years from Now	Cash Flow to Investor
1	$2,000
2	2,000
3	2,500
4	4,000

Suppose that the price of this debt obligation is $7,704. What is the yield or internal rate of return offered by this debt obligation?

2. What is the effective annual yield if the semiannual periodic interest rate is 4.3%?
3. What is the yield to maturity of a bond?
4. What is the yield to maturity calculated on a bond-equivalent basis?
5. a. Show the cash flows for the following four bonds, each of which has a par value of $1,000 and pays interest semiannually:

Bond	Coupon Rate (%)	Number of Years to Maturity	Price
W	7	5	$884.20
X	8	7	948.90
Y	9	4	967.70
Z	0	10	456.39

  b. Calculate the yield to maturity for the four bonds.
6. A portfolio manager is considering buying two bonds. Bond A matures in three years and has a coupon rate of 10% payable semiannually. Bond B, of the same credit quality, matures in 10 years and has a coupon rate of 12% payable semiannually. Both bonds are priced at par.
  a. Suppose that the portfolio manager plans to hold the bond that is purchased for three years. Which would be the best bond for the portfolio manager to purchase?
  b. Suppose that the portfolio manager plans to hold the bond that is purchased for six years instead of three years. In this case, which would be the best bond for the portfolio manager to purchase?
  c. Suppose that the portfolio manager is managing the assets of a life insurance company that has issued a five-year guaranteed investment contract (GIC). The interest rate that the life insurance company has agreed to pay is 9% on a semiannual basis. Which of the two bonds should the portfolio manager purchase to ensure that the GIC payments will be satisfied and that a profit will be generated by the life insurance company?
7. Consider the following bond:

Coupon rate = 11%
Maturity = 18 years
Par value = $1,000
First par call in 13 years
Only put date in five years and putable at par value

Suppose that the market price for this bond $1,169.
  a. Show that the yield to maturity for this bond is 9.077%.
  b. Show that the yield to first par call is 8.793%.
  c. Show that the yield to put is 6.942%.
  d. Suppose that the call schedule for this bond is as follows:
      Can be called in eight years at $1,055
      Can be called in 13 years at $1,000
And suppose this bond can only be put in five years and assume that the yield to first par call is 8.535%. What is the yield to worst for this bond?
8. a. What is meant by an amortizing security?
  b. What are the three components of the cash flow for an amortizing security?
  c. What is meant by a cash flow yield?
9. How is the internal rate of return of a portfolio calculated?

10. What is the limitation of using the internal rate of return of a portfolio as a measure of the portfolio's yield?

11. Suppose that the coupon rate of a floating-rate security resets every six months at a spread of 70 basis points over the reference rate. If the bond is trading at below par value, explain whether the effective margin is greater than or less than 70 basis points.

12. An investor is considering the purchase of a 20-year 7% coupon bond selling for $816 and a par value of $1,000. The yield to maturity for this bond is 9%.
    a. What would be the total future dollars if this investor invested $816 for 20 years earning 9% compounded semiannually?
    b. What are the total coupon payments over the life of this bond?
    c. What would be the total future dollars from the coupon payments and the repayment of principal at the end of 20 years?
    d. For the bond to produce the same total future dollars as in part a, how much must the interest on interest be?
    e. Calculate the interest on interest from the bond assuming that the semiannual coupon payments can be reinvested at 4.5% every six months and demonstrate that the resulting amount is the same as in part d.

13. What is the total return for a 20-year zero-coupon bond that is offering a yield to maturity of 8% if the bond is held to maturity?

14. Explain why the total return from holding a bond to maturity will be between the yield to maturity and the reinvestment rate.

15. For a long-term high-yield coupon bond, do you think that the total return from holding a bond to maturity will be closer to the yield to maturity or the reinvestment rate?

16. Suppose that an investor with a five-year investment horizon is considering purchasing a seven-year 9% coupon bond selling at par. The investor expects that he can reinvest the coupon payments at an annual interest rate of 9.4% and that at the end of the investment horizon two-year bonds will be selling to offer a yield to maturity of 11.2%. What is the total return for this bond?

17. Two portfolio managers are discussing the investment characteristics of amortizing securities. Manager A believes that the advantage of these securities relative to nonamortizing securities is that because the periodic cash flows include principal repayments as well as coupon payments, the manager can generate greater reinvestment income. In addition, the payments are typically monthly so even greater reinvestment income can be generated. Manager B believes that the need to reinvest monthly and the need to invest larger amounts than just coupon interest payments make amortizing securities less attractive. Whom do you agree with and why?

CHAPTER 4

Bond Price Volatility

Learning Objectives

After reading this chapter you will understand:

■ the price–yield relationship of an option-free bond

■ the factors that affect the price volatility of a bond when yields change

■ the price-volatility properties of an option-free bond

■ how to calculate the price value of a basis point

■ how to calculate and interpret the Macaulay duration, modified duration, and dollar duration of a bond

■ why duration is a measure of a bond's price sensitivity to yield changes

■ how to compute the duration of a portfolio

■ limitations of using duration as a measure of price volatility

■ how price change estimated by duration can be adjusted for a bond's convexity

■ how to approximate the duration and convexity of a bond

■ the duration of an inverse floater

■ how to measure a portfolio's sensitivity to a nonparallel shift in interest rates (key rate duration)

To employ effective bond portfolio strategies, it is necessary to understand the price volatility of bonds resulting from changes in interest rates. The purpose of this chapter is to explain the price volatility characteristics of a bond and to present several measures to quantify price volatility.

REVIEW OF THE PRICE–YIELD RELATIONSHIP FOR OPTION-FREE BONDS

As we explain in Chapter 2, a fundamental principle of an option-free bond (i.e., a bond that does not have an embedded option) is that the price of the bond changes in the direction opposite to that of a change in the required yield for the bond. This prin-

55

ciple follows from the fact that the price of a bond is equal to the present value of its expected cash flows. An increase (decrease) in the required yield decreases (increases) the present value of its expected cash flows and therefore decreases (increases) the bond's price. Exhibit 4-1 illustrates this property for the following six hypothetical bonds, where the bond prices are shown assuming a par value of $100 and pay interest semiannually:

1. A 9% coupon bond with 5 years to maturity
2. A 9% coupon bond with 25 years to maturity
3. A 6% coupon bond with 5 years to maturity
4. A 6% coupon bond with 25 years to maturity
5. A zero-coupon bond with 5 years to maturity
6. A zero-coupon bond with 25 years to maturity

When the price–yield relationship for any option-free bond is graphed, it exhibits the shape shown in Exhibit 4-2. Notice that as the required yield rises, the price of the option-free bond declines. This relationship is not linear, however (i.e., it is not a straight line). The shape of the price–yield relationship for any option-free bond is referred to as **convex.**

The price–yield relationship that we have discussed refers to an instantaneous change in the required yield. As we explain in Chapter 2, the price of a bond will change over time as a result of (1) a change in the perceived credit risk of the issuer, (2) a discount or premium bond approaching the maturity date, and (3) a change in market interest rates.

EXHIBIT 4-1 Price–Yield Relationship for Six Hypothetical Bonds

Required Yield (%)	Price at Required Yield (coupon/maturity in years)					
	9%/5	**9%/25**	**6%/5**	**6%/25**	**0%/5**	**0%/25**
6.00	112.7953	138.5946	100.0000	100.0000	74.4094	22.8107
7.00	108.3166	123.4556	95.8417	88.2722	70.8919	17.9053
8.00	104.0554	110.7410	91.8891	78.5178	67.5564	14.0713
8.50	102.0027	105.1482	89.9864	74.2587	65.9537	12.4795
8.90	100.3966	100.9961	88.4983	71.1105	64.7017	11.3391
8.99	100.0395	100.0988	88.1676	70.4318	64.4236	11.0975
9.00	100.0000	100.0000	88.1309	70.3570	64.3928	11.0710
9.01	99.9604	99.9013	88.0943	70.2824	64.3620	11.0445
9.10	99.6053	99.0199	87.7654	69.6164	64.0855	10.8093
9.50	98.0459	95.2539	86.3214	66.7773	62.8723	9.8242
10.00	96.1391	90.8720	84.5565	63.4881	61.3913	8.7204
11.00	92.4624	83.0685	81.1559	57.6712	58.5431	6.8767
12.00	88.9599	76.3572	77.9197	52.7144	55.8395	5.4288

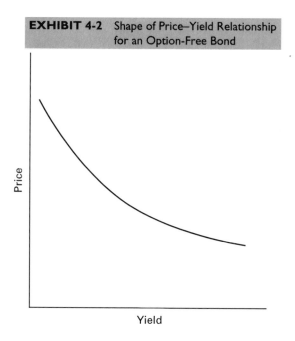

EXHIBIT 4-2 Shape of Price–Yield Relationship for an Option-Free Bond

PRICE VOLATILITY CHARACTERISTICS OF OPTION-FREE BONDS

Exhibit 4-3 shows for the six hypothetical bonds in Exhibit 4-1 the percentage change in the bond's price for various changes in the required yield, assuming that the initial yield for all six bonds is 9%. An examination of Exhibit 4–3 reveals several properties concerning the price volatility of an option-free bond.

Property 1: Although the prices of all option-free bonds move in the opposite direction from the change in yield required, the percentage price change is not the same for all bonds.

Property 2: For very small changes in the yield required, the percentage price change for a given bond is roughly the same, whether the yield required increases or decreases.

Property 3: For large changes in the required yield, the percentage price change is not the same for an increase in the required yield as it is for a decrease in the required yield.

Property 4: For a given large change in basis points, the percentage price increase is greater than the percentage price decrease.

The implication of property 4 is that if an investor owns a bond (i.e., is "long" a bond), the price appreciation that will be realized if the required yield decreases is greater than the capital loss that will be realized if the required yield rises by the same number of basis points. For an investor who is "short" a bond, the reverse is true: The potential capital loss is greater than the potential capital gain if the required yield changes by a given number of basis points.

EXHIBIT 4-3 Instantaneous Percentage Price Change for Six Hypothetical Bonds

Six hypothetical bonds, priced initially to yield 9%:

    9% coupon, 5 years to maturity, price = $100.0000
    9% coupon, 25 years to maturity, price =   100.0000
    6% coupon, 5 years to maturity, price =   88.1309
    6% coupon, 25 years to maturity, price =   70.3570
    0% coupon, 5 years to maturity, price =   64.3928
    0% coupon, 25 years to maturity, price =   11.0710

Yield (%) Changes to:	Change in Basis Points	Percentage Price Change (coupon/maturity in years)					
		9%/5	9%/25	6%/5	6%/25	0%/5	0%/25
6.00	−300	12.80	38.59	13.47	42.13	15.56	106.04
7.00	−200	8.32	23.46	8.75	25.46	10.09	61.73
8.00	−100	4.06	10.74	4.26	11.60	4.91	27.10
8.50	−50	2.00	5.15	2.11	5.55	2.42	12.72
8.90	−10	0.40	1.00	0.42	1.07	0.48	2.42
8.99	−1	0.04	0.10	0.04	0.11	0.05	0.24
9.01	1	−0.04	−0.10	−0.04	−0.11	−0.05	−0.24
9.10	10	−0.39	−0.98	−0.41	−1.05	−0.48	−2.36
9.50	50	−1.95	−4.75	−2.05	−5.09	−2.36	−11.26
10.00	100	−3.86	−9.13	−4.06	−9.76	−4.66	−21.23
11.00	200	−7.54	−16.93	−7.91	−18.03	−9.08	−37.89
12.00	300	−11.04	−23.64	−11.59	−25.08	−13.28	−50.96

An explanation for these four properties of bond price volatility lies in the convex shape of the price–yield relationship. We will investigate this in more detail later in the chapter.

Characteristics of a Bond That Affect Its Price Volatility

There are two characteristics of an option-free bond that determine its price volatility: coupon and term to maturity.

Characteristic 1:   For a given term to maturity and initial yield, the price volatility of a bond is greater, the lower the coupon rate. This characteristic can be seen by comparing the 9%, 6%, and zero-coupon bonds with the same maturity.

Characteristic 2:   For a given coupon rate and initial yield, the longer the term to maturity, the greater the price volatility. This can be seen in Exhibit 4-3 by comparing the five-year bonds with the 25-year bonds with the same coupon.

An implication of the second characteristic is that investors who want to increase a portfolio's price volatility because they expect interest rates to fall, all other factors being constant, should hold bonds with long maturities in the portfolio. To reduce a portfolio's price volatility in anticipation of a rise in interest rates, bonds with shorter-term maturities should be held in the portfolio.

EXHIBIT 4-4	Price Change for a 100-Basis-Point Change in Yield for a 9% 25-Year Bond Trading at Different Yield Levels			
Yield Level (%)	*Initial Price*	*New Price[a]*	*Price Decline*	*Percent Decline*
7	$123.46	$110.74	$12.72	10.30
8	110.74	100.00	10.74	9.70
9	100.00	90.87	9.13	9.13
10	90.87	83.07	7.80	8.58
11	83.07	76.36	6.71	8.08
12	76.36	70.55	5.81	7.61
13	70.55	65.50	5.05	7.16
14	65.50	61.08	4.42	6.75

[a]As a result of a 100-basis-point increase in yield.

Effects of Yield to Maturity

We cannot ignore the fact that credit considerations cause different bonds to trade at different yields, even if they have the same coupon and maturity. How, then, holding other factors constant, does the yield to maturity affect a bond's price volatility? As it turns out, the higher the yield to maturity at which a bond trades, the lower the price volatility.

To see this, compare the 9% 25-year bond trading at various yield levels in Exhibit 4-4. The first column shows the yield level the bond is trading at, and the second column gives the initial price. The third column indicates the bond's price if yields change by 100 basis points. The fourth and fifth columns show the dollar price change and the percentage price change. Note in these last two columns that the higher the initial yield, the lower the price volatility. An implication of this is that for a given change in yields, price volatility is greater when yield levels in the market are low, and price volatility is lower when yield levels are high.

MEASURES OF BOND PRICE VOLATILITY

Money managers, arbitrageurs, and traders need to have a way to measure a bond's price volatility to implement hedging and trading strategies. Three measures that are commonly employed are (1) price value of a basis point, (2) yield value of a price change, and (3) duration.

Price Value of a Basis Point

The **price value of a basis point,** also referred to as the **dollar value of an 01,** is the change in the price of the bond if the required yield changes by 1 basis point. Note that this measure of price volatility indicates **dollar price volatility** as opposed to percentage price volatility (price change as a percent of the initial price). Typically, the price value of a basis point is expressed as the absolute value of the change in price. Owing to property 2 of the price–yield relationship, price volatility is the same for an increase or a decrease of 1 basis point in required yield.

We can illustrate how to calculate the price value of a basis point by using the six bonds in Exhibit 4-1. For each bond, the initial price, the price after increasing the required yield by 1 basis point (from 9% to 9.01%), and the price value of a basis point (the difference between the two prices) are as follows:

Bond	Initial Price (9% yield)	Price at 9.01%	Price Value of a Basis Point[a]
5-year 9% coupon	100.0000	99.9604	0.0396
25-year 9% coupon	100.0000	99.9013	0.0987
5-year 6% coupon	88.1309	88.0945	0.0364
25-year 6% coupon	70.3570	70.2824	0.0746
5-year zero-coupon	64.3928	64.3620	0.0308
25-year zero-coupon	11.0710	11.0445	0.0265

[a]Absolute value per $100 of par value.

Because this measure of price volatility is in terms of dollar price change, dividing the price value of a basis point by the initial price gives the percentage price change for a 1-basis-point change in yield.

Yield Value of a Price Change

Another measure of the price volatility of a bond used by investors is the change in the yield for a specified price change. This is estimated by first calculating the bond's yield to maturity if the bond's price is decreased by, say, X dollars. Then the difference between the initial yield and the new yield is the yield value of an X dollar price change. The smaller this value, the greater the dollar price volatility, because it would take a smaller change in yield to produce a price change of X dollars.

As we explain in Chapter 5, Treasury notes and bonds are quoted in 32nds of a percentage point of par. Consequently, in the Treasury market investors compute the yield value of a 32nd. The yield value of a 32nd for our two hypothetical 9% coupon bonds is computed as follows, assuming that the price is decreased by a 32nd:

Bond	Initial Price Minus a 32nd[a]	Yield at New Price	Initial Yield	Yield Value of a 32nd
5-year 9% coupon	99.96875	9.008	9.000	0.008
25-year 9% coupon	99.96875	9.003	9.000	0.003

[a]Initial price of 100 minus 1/32 of 1%.

Corporate bonds and municipal bonds, the subject of Chapters 6 and 7, are traded in 8ths of a point. Consequently, investors in these markets compute the yield value of an 8th. The calculation of the yield value of an 8th for our two hypothetical 9% coupon bonds is as follows, assuming that price is decreased by an 8th:

Bond	Initial Price Minus an 8th[a]	Yield at New Price	Initial Yield	Yield Value of an 8th
5-year 9% coupon	99.8750	9.032	9.000	0.032
25-year 9% coupon	99.8750	9.013	9.000	0.013

[a]Initial price of 100 minus 1/8 of 1%.

Duration

In Chapter 2 we explained that the price of an option-free bond can be expressed mathematically as follows[1]:

$$P = \frac{C}{1 + y} + \frac{C}{(1 + y)^2} + \cdots + \frac{C}{(1 + y)^n} + \frac{M}{(1 + y)^n} \qquad (4.1)$$

where:

P = price of the bond
C = semiannual coupon interest (in dollars)
y = one-half the yield to maturity or required yield
n = number of semiannual periods (number of years $\times$ 2)
M = maturity value (in dollars)

To determine the approximate change in price for a small change in yield, the first derivative of equation (4.1) with respect to the required yield can be computed as

$$\frac{dP}{dy} = \frac{(-1)C}{(1 + y)^2} + \frac{(-2)C}{(1 + y)^3} + \cdots + \frac{(-n)C}{(1 + y)^{n+1}} + \frac{(-n)M}{(1 + y)^{n+1}} \qquad (4.2)$$

Rearranging equation (4.2), we obtain

$$\frac{dP}{dy} = -\frac{1}{1 + y}\left[\frac{1C}{1 + y} + \frac{2C}{(1 + y)^2} + \cdots + \frac{nC}{(1 + y)^n} + \frac{nM}{(1 + y)^n}\right] \qquad (4.3)$$

The term in brackets is the weighted average term to maturity of the cash flows from the bond, where the weights are the present value of the cash flow.

Equation (4.3) indicates the approximate dollar price change for a small change in the required yield. Dividing both sides of equation (4.3) by P gives the approximate percentage price change:

$$\frac{dP}{dy}\frac{1}{P} = -\frac{1}{1 + y}\left[\frac{1C}{1 + y} + \frac{2C}{(1 + y)^2} + \cdots + \frac{nC}{(1 + y)^n} + \frac{nM}{(1 + y)^n}\right]\frac{1}{P} \qquad (4.4)$$

---

[1]Equation (4.1) assumes that the next coupon payment is exactly six months from now and that there is no accrued interest. As we explain at the end of Chapter 2, it is not difficult to extend the model to account for the first coupon payment occurring less than six months from the valuation date and to adjust the price to include accrued interest.

The expression in brackets divided by the price (or here multiplied by the reciprocal of the price) is commonly referred to as **Macaulay duration**[2]; that is,

$$\text{Macaulay duration} = \frac{\dfrac{1C}{1 + y} + \dfrac{2C}{(1 + y)^2} + \cdots + \dfrac{nC}{(1 + y)^n} + \dfrac{nM}{(1 + y)^n}}{P}$$

which can be rewritten as

$$\text{Macaulay duration} = \frac{\displaystyle\sum_{t=1}^{n} \frac{tC}{(1 + y)^t} + \frac{nM}{(1 + y)^n}}{P} \tag{4.5}$$

Substituting Macaulay duration into equation (4.4) for the approximate percentage price change gives

$$\frac{dP}{dy}\frac{1}{P} = -\frac{1}{1 + y} \ \text{Macaulay duration} \tag{4.6}$$

Investors commonly refer to the ratio of Macaulay duration to $1 + y$ as **modified duration;** that is,

$$\text{modified duration} = \frac{\text{Macaulay duration}}{1 + y} \tag{4.7}$$

Substituting equation (4.7) into equation (4.6) gives

$$\frac{dP}{dy}\frac{1}{P} = -\text{modified duration} \tag{4.8}$$

Equation (4.8) states that modified duration is related to the approximate percentage change in price for a given change in yield. Because for all option-free bonds modified duration is positive, equation (4.8) states that there is an inverse relationship between modified duration and the approximate percentage change in price for a given yield change. This is to be expected from the fundamental principle that bond prices move in the opposite direction of the change in interest rates.

Exhibits 4-5 and 4-6 show the computation of the Macaulay duration and modified duration of two five-year coupon bonds. The durations computed in these exhibits are in terms of duration per period. Consequently, the durations are in half-years because the cash flows of the bonds occur every six months. To adjust the durations to an annual figure, the durations must be divided by 2, as shown at the bottom of Exhibits 4-5 and 4-6. In general, if the cash flows occur m times per year, the durations are adjusted by dividing by m; that is,

---

[2]In a 1938 National Bureau of Economic Research study on bond yields, Frederick Macaulay coined this term and used this measure rather than maturity as a proxy for the average length of time that a bond investment is outstanding. [See Frederick Macaulay, *Some Theoretical Problems Suggested by the Movement of Interest Rates, Bond Yields, and Stock Prices in the U.S. Since 1856* (New York: National Bureau of Economic Research, 1938).] In examining the interest rate sensitivity of financial institutions, Redington and Samuelson independently developed the duration concept. (See F. M. Redington, "Review of the Principle of Life Office Valuation," *Journal of the Institute of Actuaries,* 1952, pp. 286–340; and Paul A. Samuelson, "The Effect of Interest Rate Increases on the Banking System," *American Economic Review,* March 1945, pp. 16–27.)

$$\text{duration in years} = \frac{\text{duration in } m \text{ periods per year}}{m}$$

Macaulay duration in years and modified duration for the six hypothetical bonds are as follows:

Bond	Macaulay Duration (years)	Modified Duration
9%/5-year	4.13	3.96
9%/25-year	10.33	9.88
6%/5-year	4.35	4.16
6%/25-year	11.10	10.62
0%/5-year	5.00	4.78
0%/25-year	25.00	23.92

Rather than use equation (4.5) to calculate Macaulay duration and then equation (4.7) to obtain modified duration, we can derive an alternative formula that does not require the extensive calculations required by equation (4.5). This is done by rewriting the price of a bond in terms of its two components: (1) the present value of an annuity,

EXHIBIT 4-5   Calculation of Macaulay Duration and Modified Duration for 5-Year 9% Bond Selling to Yield 9%

Coupon rate: 9.00%
Term (years):   5
Initial yield: 9.00%

Period, t	Cash Flow[a]	PV of $1 at 4.5%	PV of CF	t × PVCF
1	$ 4.50	0.956937	4.306220	4.30622
2	4.50	0.915729	4.120785	8.24156
3	4.50	0.876296	3.943335	11.83000
4	4.50	0.838561	3.773526	15.09410
5	4.50	0.802451	3.611030	18.05514
6	4.50	0.767895	3.455531	20.73318
7	4.50	0.734828	3.306728	23.14709
8	4.50	0.703185	3.164333	25.31466
9	4.50	0.672904	3.028070	27.25262
10	104.50	0.643927	67.290443	672.90442
			100.000000	826.87899

[a]Cash flow per $100 of par value.

$$\text{Macaulay duration (in half-years)} = \frac{826.87899}{100.000000} = 8.27$$

$$\text{Macaulay duration (in years)} = \frac{8.27}{2} = 4.13$$

$$\text{Macaulay duration} = \frac{4.13}{1.0450} = 3.96$$

EXHIBIT 4-6   Calculation of Macaulay Duration and Modified Duration for 5-Year 6% Bond Selling to Yield 9%

Coupon rate: 6.00%
Term (years):   5
Initial yield: 9.00%

Period, t	Cash Flow[a]	PV of $1 at 4.5%	PV of CF	t × PVCF
1	$ 3.00	0.956937	2.870813	2.87081
2	3.00	0.915729	2.747190	5.49437
3	3.00	0.876296	2.628890	7.88666
4	3.00	0.838561	2.515684	10.06273
5	3.00	0.802451	2.407353	12.03676
6	3.00	0.767895	2.303687	13.82212
7	3.00	0.734828	2.204485	15.43139
8	3.00	0.703185	2.109555	16.87644
9	3.00	0.672904	2.018713	18.16841
10	103.00	0.643927	66.324551	663.24551
Total			88.130923	765.89520

[a]Cash flow per $100 of par value.

$$\text{Macaulay duration (in half–years)} = \frac{765.89520}{88.130923} = 8.69$$

$$\text{Macaulay duration (in years)} = \frac{8.69}{2} = 4.35$$

$$\text{Modified duration} = \frac{4.35}{1.0450} = 4.16$$

where the annuity is the sum of the coupon payments, and (2) the present value of the par value. That is, the price of a bond per $100 of par value can be written as follows[3]:

$$P = C\left[\frac{1 - \frac{1}{(1 + y)^n}}{y}\right] + \frac{100}{(1 + y)^n} \tag{4.9}$$

By taking the first derivative of equation (4.9) and dividing by P, we obtain another formula for modified duration:

$$\text{modified duration} = \frac{\frac{C}{y^2}\left[1 - \frac{1}{(1 + y)^n}\right] + \frac{n(100 - C/y)}{(1 + y)^{n+1}}}{P} \tag{4.10}$$

where the price is expressed as a percentage of par value. Macaulay duration can be expressed by multiplying equation (4.10) by $(1 + y)$. To illustrate how to apply equation (4.10), consider the 25-year 6% bond selling at 70.357 to yield 9%. Then

$C = 3(0.06 \times 100 \times 1/2)$
$y = 0.045(0.09 \times 1/2)$

---

[3]The first term in equation (4.9) is the present value of the coupon payments from equation (2.7) discounting at y.

$n = 50$

$P = 70.357$

Substituting into equation (4.10) yields

$$\text{modified duration} = \frac{\dfrac{3}{(0.045)^2}\left[1 - \dfrac{1}{(1.045)^{50}}\right] + \dfrac{50(100 - 3/0.045)}{(1.045)^{51}}}{70.357}$$

$$= \frac{1,481.481(0.88929) + 176.5704}{70.357}$$

$$= 21.23508$$

Converting to an annual number by dividing by 2 gives a modified duration of 10.62. Multiplying by 1.045 gives 11.10, which is Macaulay duration.

Properties of Duration   As can be seen from the various durations computed for the six hypothetical bonds, the modified duration and Macaulay duration of a coupon bond are less than the maturity. It should be obvious from the formula that the Macaulay duration of a zero-coupon bond is equal to its maturity; a zero-coupon bond's modified duration, however, is less than its maturity. Also, the lower the coupon, generally the greater the modified and Macaulay duration of the bond.[4]

There is a consistency between the properties of bond price volatility we discussed earlier and the properties of modified duration. We showed earlier that when all other factors are constant, the longer the maturity, the greater the price volatility. A property of modified duration is that when all other factors are constant, the longer the maturity, the greater the modified duration. We also showed that the lower the coupon rate, all other factors being constant, the greater the bond price volatility. As we have just seen, generally the lower the coupon rate, the greater the modified duration. Thus the greater the modified duration, the greater the price volatility.

Finally, as we noted earlier, another factor that will influence the price volatility is the yield to maturity. All other factors constant, the higher the yield level, the lower the price volatility. The same property holds for modified duration, as can be seen in the following table, which shows the modified duration of a 25-year 9% coupon bond at various yield levels:

Yield (%)	Modified Duration
7	11.21
8	10.53
9	9.88
10	9.27
11	8.70
12	8.16
13	7.66
14	7.21

---

[4]This property does not hold for long-maturity deep-discount bonds.

Approximating the Percentage Price Change   If we multiply both sides of equation (4.8) by the change in the required yield (dy), we have the following relationship:

$$\frac{dP}{P} = -\text{modified duration} \times dy \tag{4.11}$$

Equation (4.11) can be used to approximate the percentage price change for a given change in required yield.

To illustrate the relationship, consider the 25-year 6% bond selling at 70.3570 to yield 9%. The modified duration for this bond is 10.62. If yields increase instantaneously from 9% to 9.10%, a yield change of +0.0010 (10 basis points), the *approximate* percentage change in price using equation (4.11) is

$$-10.62(+0.0010) = -0.0106 \text{ or } -1.06\%$$

Notice from Exhibit 4-3 that the actual percentage change in price is −1.05%. Similarly, if yields decrease instantaneously from 9% to 8.90% (a 10-basis-point decrease), the approximate percentage change in price using equation (4.11) would be +1.06%. According to Exhibit 4-3, the actual percentage price change would be +1.07%. This example illustrates that for small changes in the required yield, modified duration gives a good approximation of the percentage change in price.

Instead of a small change in required yield, let's assume that yields increase by 200 basis points, from 9% to 11% (a yield change of +0.02). The approximate percentage change in price using equation (4.11) is

$$-10.62(+0.02) = -0.2124 = -21.24\%$$

How good is this approximation? As can be seen from Exhibit 4-3, the actual percentage change in price is only −18.03%. Moreover, if the required yield decreased by 200 basis points, from 9% to 7%, the approximate percentage change in price based on duration would be +21.24%, compared with an actual percentage change in price of +25.46%. Modified duration provides not only a flawed approximation but also a symmetric percentage price change, which, as we point out earlier in this chapter, is not a property of the price–yield relationship for bonds when there are large changes in yield.

We can use equation (4.11) to provide an interpretation of modified duration. Suppose that the yield on any bond changes by 100 basis points. Then, substituting 100 basis points (0.01) into equation (4.11), the following is obtained:

$$\frac{dP}{P} = -\text{modified duration} (0.01) = -\text{modified duration} (\%)$$

Thus, *modified duration can be interpreted as the approximate percentage change in price for a 100-basis-point change in yield.*

Approximating the Dollar Price Change   Modified duration is a proxy for the percentage change in price. Investors also like to know the dollar price volatility of a bond. Of course, equation (4.2) can be used to compute the dollar price volatility. Alternatively, multiplying both sides of equation (4.8) by P gives

$$\frac{dP}{dy} = (-\text{modified duration})P \tag{4.12}$$

The expression on the right-hand side is called **dollar duration:**

$$\text{dollar duration} = -(\text{modified duration})P \tag{4.13}$$

When we know the percentage price change and the initial price, the estimated dollar price change using modified duration can be determined. Alternatively, the estimated dollar price change can be obtained by multiplying both sides of equation (4.11) by P, giving

$$dP = -(\text{modified duration})P(dy)$$

From equation (4.13) we can substitute dollar duration for the product of modified duration and P. Thus

$$dP = -(\text{dollar duration})(dy) \qquad \textbf{(4.14)}$$

For small changes in the required yield, equation (4.14) does a good job in estimating the change in price. For example, consider the 6% 25-year bond selling at 70.3570 to yield 9%. The dollar duration is 747.2009. For a 1-basis-point (0.0001) increase in the required yield, the estimated price change per $100 of face value is

$$dP = -(\$747.2009)(0.0001)$$
$$= -\$0.0747$$

From Exhibit 4-1 we see that the actual price is 70.2824. The actual price change would therefore be 0.0746 (70.2824 − 70.3570). Notice that the dollar duration for a 1-basis-point change is the same as the price value of a basis point.

Now let's see what happens when there is a large change in the required yield for the same bond. If the required yield increases from 9% to 11% (or 200 basis points), the approximate dollar price change per $100 par value is

$$dP = -(\$747.2009)(0.02)$$
$$= -\$14.94$$

From Exhibit 4-1 we see that the actual price for this bond if the required yield is 11% is 57.6712. Thus the actual price decline is 12.6858 (57.6712 − 70.3570). The estimated dollar price change is more than the actual price change. The reverse is true for a decrease in the required yield. This result is consistent with what we illustrated earlier. When there are large movements in the required yield, dollar duration or modified duration is not adequate to approximate the price reaction. Duration will overestimate the price change when the required yield rises, thereby underestimating the new price. When the required yield falls, duration will underestimate the price change and thereby underestimate the new price.

Portfolio Duration

Thus far we have looked at the duration of an individual bond. The duration of a portfolio is simply the weighted average duration of the bonds in the portfolios. That is, the duration of each bond in the portfolio is weighted by its percentage within the portfolio. For example, consider the following four-bond portfolio with a total market value of $100 million:

Bond	Market Value	Portfolio Weight	Duration
A	$10 million	0.10	4
B	$40 million	0.40	7
C	$30 million	0.30	6
D	$20 million	0.20	2

The portfolio weight for a bond is simply the market value of the bond divided by the total market value of $100 million. The portfolio duration is then

$$0.1 \times 4 + 0.4 \times 7 + 0.3 \times 6 + 0.2 \times 2 = 5.4$$

The portfolio's duration is 5.4 and interpreted as follows: If all the yields affecting the four bonds in the portfolio change by 100 basis points, the portfolio's value will change by approximately 5.4%.

CONVEXITY

The three measures for price volatility that we describe in the preceding section are good measures for small changes in yield or price. We have explained how these measures are related. Exhibit 4-7 does this more formally.

Because all the duration measures are only approximations for small changes in yield, they do not capture the effect of the convexity of a bond on its price performance when yields change by more than a small amount. The duration measure can be supplemented with additional measure to capture the curvature or convexity of a bond. In this section we tie together the convex price–yield relationship for a bond and several of the properties of bond price volatility discussed earlier.

EXHIBIT 4-7 Measures of Bond Price Volatility and Their Relationships to One Another

Notation:
D = Macaulay duration
D^* = modified duration
PVBP = price value of a basis point
YV32 = yield value of a 32nd
y = yield to maturity in decimal form
Y = yield to maturity in percentage terms ($Y = 100 \times y$)
P = price of bond
m = number of coupons per year

Relationships:

$D^* = \dfrac{D}{1 + y/m}$	by definition
$\dfrac{\mathrm{D}P/P}{\mathrm{D}y} \approx D^*$	to a close approximation for a small Δy
$\Delta P/\Delta Y \approx$ slope of price–yield curve	to a close approximation for a small ΔY
$\text{PVBP} \approx \dfrac{D^* \times P}{10000}$	to a close approximation
$\text{YV32} \approx \dfrac{1}{3200 \times \text{PVBP}}$	to a close approximation (when the yield is in percentage terms)
$\text{PVBP} \approx \dfrac{1}{3200 \times \text{YV32}}$	to a close approximation (when the yield is in percentage terms)

For bonds at or near par:
$\text{PVBP} \approx D^*/100$	to a close approximation
$D^* \approx \Delta P/\Delta Y$	to a close approximation for a small ΔY

EXHIBIT 4-8   Line Tangent to the Price–Yield Relationship

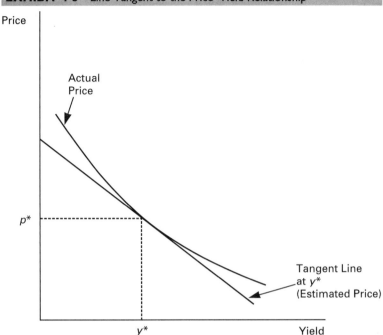

In Exhibit 4-8 a tangent line is drawn to the price–yield relationship at yield y^*. The tangent shows the rate of change of price with respect to a change in interest rates at that point (yield level). The slope of the tangent line is closely related to the price value of a basis point. Consequently, for a given starting price, the tangent (which tells the rate of absolute price changes) is closely related to the duration of the bond (which tells about the rate of percentage of price changes). The steeper the tangent line, the greater the duration; the flatter the tangent line, the lower the duration. Thus for a given starting price, the tangent line and the duration can be used interchangeably and can be thought of as one and the same method of estimating the rate of price changes.

Notice what happens to duration (steepness of the tangent line) as yield changes: As yield increases (decreases), duration decreases (increases). This property holds for all option-free bonds, as we noted earlier.

If we draw a vertical line from any yield (on the horizontal axis), as in Exhibit 4-9, the distance between the horizontal axis and the tangent line represents the price approximated by using duration starting with the initial yield y^*. The approximation will always understate the actual price. This agrees with what we demonstrated earlier about the relationship between duration (and the tangent line) and the approximate price change. When yields decrease, the estimated price change will be less than the actual price change, thereby underestimating the actual price. On the other hand, when yields increase, the estimated price change will be greater than the actual price change, resulting in an underestimate of the actual price.

For small changes in yield, the tangent line and duration do a good job in estimating the actual price. However, the farther away from the initial yield y^*, the worse the

EXHIBIT 4-9 Price Approximation Using Duration

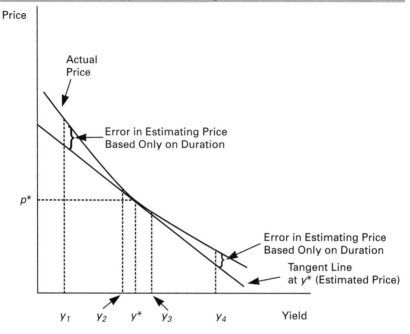

approximation. It should be apparent that the accuracy of the approximation depends on the convexity of the price–yield relationship for the bond.

Measuring Convexity

Duration (modified or dollar) attempts to estimate a convex relationship with a straight line (the tangent line). Is it possible to specify a mathematical relationship that provides a better approximation to the price change of the bond if the required yield changes?

We can use the first two terms of a Taylor series to approximate the price change as follows[5]:

$$dP = \frac{dP}{dy}dy + \frac{1}{2}\frac{d^2P}{dy^2}(dy)^2 + \text{error} \qquad (4.15)$$

Dividing both sides of equation (4.15) by P to get the percentage price change gives us

$$\frac{dP}{P} = \frac{dP}{dy}\frac{1}{P}dy + \frac{1}{2}\frac{d^2P}{dy^2}\frac{1}{P}(dy)^2 + \frac{\text{error}}{P} \qquad (4.16)$$

The first term on the right-hand side of equation (4.15) is equation (4.14); that is, it is the dollar price change based on dollar duration. Thus the first term in equation (4.15) is our approximation of the price change based on duration. In equation (4.16),

---

[5]A Taylor series, discussed in calculus textbooks, can be used to approximate a mathematical function. Here, the mathematical function to be approximated is the price function.

the first term on the right-hand side is the approximate percentage change in price based on modified duration.

The second term in equations (4.15) and (4.16) includes the second derivative of the price function [equation (4.1)]. It is the second derivative that is used as a proxy measure to correct for the convexity of the price–yield relationship. Market participants refer to the second derivative of price [equation (4.1)] as the **dollar convexity measure** of the bond; that is,

$$\text{dollar convexity measure} = \frac{d^2P}{dy^2} \tag{4.17}$$

The product of the dollar convexity measure and the square of the change in the required yield indicates the estimated price change due to convexity. That is, the approximate change in price due to convexity is

$$dP = (\text{dollar convexity measure})(dy)^2 \tag{4.18}$$

The second derivative divided by price is a measure of the percentage change in the price of the bond due to convexity and is referred to simply as the **convexity measure;** that is,

$$\text{convexity measure} = \frac{d^2P}{dy^2} \frac{1}{P} \tag{4.19}$$

and the percentage price change due to convexity is

$$\frac{dP}{P} = \frac{1}{2}(\text{convexity measure})(dy)^2 \tag{4.20}$$

The second derivative of the price equation (4.1) is

$$\frac{d^2P}{dy^2} = \sum_{t=1}^{n} \frac{t(t+1)C}{(1+y)^{t+2}} + \frac{n(n+1)M}{(1+y)^{n+2}} \tag{4.21}$$

Exhibits 4-10 and 4-11 demonstrate how to calculate the second derivative [equation (4.21)], annualized dollar convexity measure, and annualized convexity measure for the two five-year coupon bonds. The convexity measure is in terms of periods squared. To convert the convexity measures to an annual figure, equations (4.17) and (4.19) must be divided by 4 (which is 2 squared). In general, if the cash flows occur m times per year, convexity is adjusted to an annual figure as follows:

$$\text{convexity measure in years} = \frac{\text{convexity measure in } m \text{ periods per year}}{m^2}$$

Annualized convexity measure and annualized dollar convexity measure for our six hypothetical bonds can be summarized as follows:

Bond (per $100 par)	Second Derivative	Annualized Convexity Measure (per $100 par)	Annualized Dollar Convexity Measure
9%/5-year	7,781.02	19.45	$ 1,945.26
9%/25-year	64,288.42	160.72	16,072.00
6%/5-year	7,349.45	20.85	1,837.36
6%/25-year	51,476.26	182.92	12,869.70
0%/5-year	6,486.30	25.18	1,621.42
0%/25-year	25,851.93	583.78	6,463.02

EXHIBIT 4-10 Calculation of Convexity Measure and Dollar Convexity Measure for Five-Year 9% Bond Selling to Yield 9%

Coupon rate: **9.00%**
Term (years): **5**
Initial yield: **9.00%**
Price: **100**

Period, t	Cash Flow[a]	$\dfrac{1}{(1.045)^{t+2}}$	$t(t+1)CF$	$\dfrac{t(t+1)CF}{(1.045)^{t+2}}$
1	$ 4.50	0.876296	9	7.886
2	4.50	0.838561	27	22.641
3	4.50	0.802451	54	43.332
4	4.50	0.767895	90	69.110
5	4.50	0.734828	135	99.201
6	4.50	0.703185	189	132.901
7	4.50	0.672904	252	169.571
8	4.50	0.643927	324	208.632
9	4.50	0.616198	405	249.560
10	104.50	0.589663	11,495	6,778.186
			12,980	7,781.020

[a]Cash flow per $100 of par value.

$$\text{Second derivative} = 7,781.02$$

$$\text{Convexity measure (half} - \text{years)} = \frac{7,781.020}{100.0000} = 77.8102$$

$$\text{Convexity measure (years)} = \frac{77.8102}{4} = 19.4526$$

$$\text{Dollar convexity measure} = 100 \times 19.4526 = 1,945.26$$

Alternatively, the second derivative can be determined by taking the second derivative of equation (4.9). By doing so, we can simplify equation (4.21) as follows:

$$\frac{d^2P}{dy^2} = \frac{2C}{y^3}\left[1 - \frac{1}{(1+y)^n}\right] - \frac{2Cn}{y^2(1+y)^{n+1}} + \frac{n(n+1)(100 - C/y)}{(1+y)^{n+2}} \quad \textbf{(4.22)}$$

To illustrate how to use equation (4.22), consider the 25-year 6% bond selling at 70.357 to yield 9%. The second derivative is

$$\frac{2(3)}{(0.045)^3}\left[1 - \frac{1}{(1.045)^{50}}\right] - \frac{2(3)(50)}{(0.045)^2(1.045)^{51}} + \frac{50(51)(100 - 3/0.045)}{(1.045)^{52}}$$

$$= 65,843.62(0.88929) - 15,695.14 + 8,617.31$$

$$= 51,476.26$$

This agrees with the value reported earlier.

Approximating Percentage Price Change Using Duration and Convexity Measures

Equation (4.16) tells us that the percentage price change of a bond can be estimated using both duration and convexity measure. To illustrate how this is done, consider the 25-year 6% bond selling to yield 9%. The modified duration for this bond is

EXHIBIT 4-11   Calculation of Convexity Measure and Dollar Convexity
Measure for Five-Year 6% Bond Selling to Yield 9%

Coupon rate: **6.00%**
Term (years): **5**
Initial yield: **9.00%**
Price: **88.1309**

Period, t	Cash Flow[a]	$\frac{1}{(1.045)^{t+2}}$	$t(t+1)CF$	$\frac{t(t+1)CF}{(1.045)^{t+2}}$
1	$ 3.00	0.876296	6	5.257
2	3.00	0.838561	18	15.094
3	3.00	0.802451	36	28,888
4	3.00	0.767895	60	46.073
5	3.00	0.734828	90	66.134
6	3.00	0.703185	126	88.601
7	3.00	0.672904	168	113.047
8	3.00	0.643927	216	139.088
9	3.00	0.616198	270	166.373
10	103.00	0.589663	11,330	6,680.891
			12,320	7,349.446

[a]Cash flow per $100 of par value.

Second derivative = 7,349.45

$$\text{Convexity measure (half}-\text{years)} = \frac{7,349.45}{88.1309} = 83.3924$$

$$\text{Convexity measure (years)} = \frac{83.3924}{4} = 20.8481$$

$$\text{Dollar convexity measure} = 88.1309 \times 20.8481 = 1,837.36$$

10.62, and the convexity measure is 182.92. If the required yield increases by 200 basis points, from 9% to 11%, the approximate percentage change in the price of the bond is

percentage change in price due to duration from equation (4.11)

$$= -(\text{modified duration})(dy)$$
$$= -(10.62)(0.02) = -0.2124 = -21.24\%$$
plus

percentage change in price due to convexity from equation (4.20)

$$= \frac{1}{2}(\text{convexity measure})(dy)^2$$
$$= \frac{1}{2}(182.92)(0.02)^2 = 0.0366 = 3.66\%$$

The estimated percentage price change due to duration and convexity is

$$-21.24\% + 3.66\% = -17.58\%$$

From Exhibit 4-3 we see that the actual change is −18.03%. Using duration and convexity measures together gives a better approximation of the actual price change for a large movement in the required yield. Suppose, instead, that the required yield **decreases** by 200 basis points. Then the approximate percentage change in the price of the bond using modified duration and convexity is

percentage change in price due to duration from equation (4.11)

$$= -(\text{modified duration})(dy)$$
$$= -(10.62)(-0.02) = +0.2124 = +21.24\%$$

plus

percentage change in price due to convexity from equation (4.20)

$$= \frac{1}{2}(\text{convexity measure})(dy)^2$$

$$= \frac{1}{2}(182.92)(-0.02)^2 = 0.0366 = 3.66\%$$

The estimated percentage price change due to duration and convexity is

$$+21.24\% + 3.66\% = 24.90\%$$

From Exhibit 4-3 we see that the actual change is +25.46%. Once again, using both duration and convexity measure provides a good approximation of the actual price change for a large movement in the required yield.

Some Notes on Convexity

There are three points that should be kept in mind regarding a bond's convexity and convexity measure. First, it is important to understand the distinction between the use of the term *convexity,* which refers to the general shape of the price–yield relationship, and the term *convexity measure,* which is related to the quantification of how the price of the bond will change when interest rates change.

The second point has to do with how to interpret the convexity measure. Recall that for duration, the interpretation of this measure is straightforward. A duration of 4, for example, is interpreted as the approximate percentage change in the price of the bond for a 100-basis-point change in interest rates. How do we interpret a convexity measure? It's not that simple because the approximate percentage change in price due to convexity is affected by the square of the change in rates, as shown in equation (4.20). In that equation, the approximate percentage change in price due to convexity is the product of three numbers: (1) ½, (2) convexity measure, and (3) the square of the change in yield.

The final point is that in practice different vendors of analytical systems and different writers compute the convexity measure in different ways. To see why, look back at equation (4.16) and focus on the second term on the right-hand side of the equation. In equation (4.19), we used part of that equation to define the convexity measure. Specifically, the convexity measure is the product of the second derivative and the reciprocal of the price. Suppose instead that we defined the convexity measure from the second term of equation (4.16) to be

$$\text{convexity measure} = \frac{1}{2}\frac{d^2P}{dy^2}\frac{1}{P}$$

That is, the convexity measure shown is just one-half the convexity measure given by equation (4.19). Does it make a difference? Not at all. We must just make sure that we make the adjustment to the relationship between the approximate percentage price change due to convexity and the convexity measure accordingly. Specifically, in equation (4.20), the relationship would be changed as follows:

$$\frac{dP}{P} = (\text{convexity measure}) \times (dy)^2$$

The bottom line is that the approximate percentage price change due to convexity is the same regardless of whether the preceding equation or equation (4.20) is used. This relates to our second point. The interpretation of the convexity measure on a stand-alone basis is not meaningful because different vendors and writers may scale the measure in different ways. What is important is relating the convexity measure and the change in yield (squared).

Value of Convexity

Up to this point, we have focused on how taking convexity into account can improve the approximation of a bond's price change for a given yield change. The convexity of a bond, however, has another important investment implication, which is illustrated in Exhibit 4-12. The exhibit shows two bonds, A and B. The two bonds have the same duration and are offering the same yield; they have different convexities, however. Bond B is more convex (bowed) than bond A.

What is the implication of the greater convexity for B? Whether the market yield rises or falls, B will have a higher price. That is, if the required yield rises, the capital loss on bond B will be less than it will be on bond A. A fall in the required yield will generate greater price appreciation for B than for A.

Generally, the market will take the greater convexity of B compared with A into account in pricing the two bonds. That is, the market will price convexity. Consequently, although there may be times when a situation such as that depicted in Exhibit 4-12 will exist, generally the market will require investors to "pay up" (accept a lower yield) for the greater convexity offered by bond B.

The question is: How much should the market want investors to pay up for convexity? Look again at Exhibit 4-12. Notice that if investors expect that market yields will change by very little—that is, they expect low interest rate volatility—the advantage of owning bond B over bond A is insignificant because both bonds will offer approximately the same price for small changes in yield. In this case, investors should not be willing to pay much for convexity. In fact, if the market is pricing convexity high, which means that A will be offering a higher yield than B, investors with expectations of low interest rate volatility would probably be willing to "sell convexity"—that is, to sell B if they own it and buy A. In contrast, if investors expect substantial interest rate volatility, bond B would probably sell at a much lower yield than A.

Properties of Convexity

All option-free bonds have the following convexity properties.

Property 1: As the required yield increases (decreases), the convexity of a bond decreases (increases). This property is referred to as **positive convexity.**

An implication of positive convexity is that the duration of an option-free bond moves in the right direction as market yields change. That is, if market yields rise, the

EXHIBIT 4-12 Comparison of Convexity of Two Bonds

price of a bond will fall. The price decline is slowed down by a decline in the duration of the bond as market yields rise. In contrast, should market yields fall, duration increases so that percentage price change accelerates. With an option-free bond, both these changes in duration occur.

This is portrayed graphically in Exhibit 4-13. The slope of the tangent line in the exhibit gets flatter as the required yield increases. A flatter tangent line means a smaller

EXHIBIT 4-13 Change in Duration as the Required Yield Changes

duration as the required yield rises. In contrast, the tangent line gets steeper as the required yield decreases, implying that the duration gets larger. This property will hold for all option-free bonds. Also, from this graphical presentation we can see that the convexity is actually measuring the rate of change of the dollar duration as market yields change.

Property 2:   For a given yield and maturity, the lower the coupon, the greater the convexity of a bond.

This can be seen from the computed convexity of our hypothetical bonds. Of the three five-year bonds, the zero-coupon bond has the highest convexity, and the 9% coupon bond has the lowest convexity. The same is true of the 25-year bonds.

Property 3:   For a given yield and modified duration, the lower the coupon, the smaller the convexity.

The investment implication of property 3 is that zero-coupon bonds have the lowest convexity for a given modified duration.

ADDITIONAL CONCERNS WHEN USING DURATION

Our illustrations have demonstrated that relying on duration as the sole measure of the price volatility of a bond may mislead investors. There are two other concerns about using duration that we should point out.

First, in the derivation of the relationship between modified duration and bond price volatility, we started with the price equation (4.1). This price equation assumes that all cash flows for the bond are discounted at the same discount rate. The appropriateness of this assumption is examined in Chapter 5, where we analyze the yield curve. Essentially, the derivation of equation (4.3) assumes that the yield curve is flat and all shifts are parallel. In Chapter 17 we show the limitations of applying duration when this assumption does not hold, and the yield curve does not shift in a parallel fashion. This is extremely important when we try to use a portfolio's duration to quantify the responsiveness of a portfolio's value to a change in interest rates. If a portfolio has bonds with different maturities, the duration measure may not provide a good estimate for unequal changes in interest rates of different maturities. At the end of this chapter, we'll look at one approach to measuring the sensitivity of a portfolio when interest rates for all maturities do not change by the same number of basis points.

Our second concern is misapplication of duration to bonds with embedded options. The principles we have illustrated apply only to option-free bonds. When changes in yields result in a change in the expected cash flow for a bond, which is the case for bonds with embedded options, the duration and convexity measures are appropriate only in certain circumstances. We discuss the price volatility of bonds with embedded options in Chapters 14 and 15.

The duration measure introduced in those chapters that takes into account any embedded options is called **effective duration.**

DON'T THINK OF DURATION AS A MEASURE OF TIME

Unfortunately, market participants often confuse the main purpose of duration by constantly referring to it as some measure of the weighted average life of a bond. This is because of the original use of duration by Macaulay. If you rely on this interpretation of duration, it will be difficult for you to understand why a bond with a maturity of 20 years can have a duration greater than 20 years. For example, in Chapter 12 we discuss collateralized mortgage obligation (CMO) bond classes. Certain CMO bond classes have a greater duration than the underlying mortgage loans. That is, a CMO bond class can have a duration of 40 although the underlying mortgage loans from which the CMO is created can have a maturity of 30 years. Also, some CMO bond classes have a negative duration. How can this happen?

The answer to this puzzle is that duration is the approximate percentage change in price for a small change in interest rates. In fact, as explained earlier, a good way to remember duration is that it is the approximate percentage change in price for a 100-basis-point change in interest rates.

Certain CMO bond classes are leveraged instruments whose price sensitivity or duration, as a result, are a multiple of the underlying mortgage loans from which they were created. Thus, a CMO bond class with a duration of 40 does not mean that it has some type of weighted average life of 40 years. Instead, it means that for a 100-basis-point change in yield, that bond's price will change by roughly 40%.

Similarly, we interpret the duration of an option in the same way. A call option can have a duration of 20 when the time to expiration of the option is one year.[6] This is confusing to someone who interprets duration as some measure of the life of an option. What it means is that if yields change by 100 basis points for the bond underlying the option, the value of the option will change by approximately 20%.

APPROXIMATING A BOND'S DURATION AND CONVEXITY MEASURE

When we understand that duration is related to percentage price change, a simple formula can be used to calculate the approximate duration of a bond or any other more complex derivative securities or options described throughout this book. All we are interested in is the percentage price change of a bond when interest rates change by a small amount. This can be found quite easily by the following procedure:

Step 1: Increase the yield on the bond by a small number of basis points and determine the new price at this higher yield level. We denote this new price by P_+.

Step 2: Decrease the yield on the bond by the same number of basis points and calculate the new price. We will denote this new price by P_-.

Step 3: Letting P_0 be the initial price, duration can be approximated using the following formula:

$$\text{approximate duration} = \frac{P_- - P_+}{2(P_0)(\Delta y)} \qquad (4.23)$$

where Δy is the change in yield used to calculate the new prices (in decimal form). What the formula is measuring is the average percentage price change (relative to the initial price) per 1-basis-point change in yield.

---

[6]We see how to measure the duration of an option in Chapter 22.

To see how good this approximation is, let's apply it to the 25-year 6% coupon bond trading at 9%. All the necessary information is provided in Exhibit 4-2. The initial price (P_0) is 70.3570. The steps are as follows:

Step 1:   Increase the yield on the bond by 10 basis points from 9% to 9.1%. Thus, Δy is 0.001. The new price (P_+) is 69.6164.

Step 2:   Decrease the yield on the bond by 10 basis points from 9% to 8.9%. The new price (P_-) is 71.1105.

Step 3:   Because the initial price, P_0, is 70.3570, the duration can be approximated as follows:

$$\text{approximate duration} = \frac{71.1105 - 69.6164}{2(70.3570)(0.001)} = 10.62$$

How good is the approximation? The modified duration as calculated by using equations (4.5) and (4.7) is 10.62.

If an investor is interested in the duration of any financial instrument, equation (4.23) can be used. However, to use the equation, it is necessary to have a good pricing model to get the new prices in steps 1 and 2. These models are discussed in later chapters. *It is important to emphasize here that duration is a by-product of a pricing model. If the pricing model is poor, the resulting duration estimate is poor.*

Similarly, the convexity measure of any bond can be approximated using the following formula:

$$\text{approximate convexity measure} = \frac{P_+ + P_- - 2P_0}{P_0(\mathbf{D}y)^2} \qquad \textbf{(4.24)}$$

Using our previous illustration, the approximate convexity measure is

$$\text{approximate convexity measure} = \frac{71.1105 + 69.6164 - 2(70.3570)}{70.3570(0.001)^2} = 183.3$$

As reported previously, the convexity measure calculated by formula is 182.92. Thus, equation (4.24) does a fine job.

As we noted earlier, the convexity measure can be measured in a different way. Equation (4.24) can be rewritten to include 2 in the denominator. All this means is that when the percentage change in price due to convexity is computed using equation (4.20), the ½ should be eliminated.

Duration of an Inverse Floater

In Chapter 2 we discussed how an inverse floater is created and how it is priced. Here we will look at the duration of an inverse floater. The duration of the inverse floater is related to the duration of the collateral and the duration of the floater. Assuming that the duration of the floater is close to zero, it can be shown that the duration of an inverse floater is as follows[7]:

$$\text{duration of inverse floater} = (1 + L)(\text{duration of collateral}) \times \frac{\text{collateral price}}{\text{inverse price}}$$

---

[7]William R. Leach, "A Portfolio Manager's Perspective of Inverses and Inverse IOs," Chapter 9 in Frank J. Fabozzi (ed.), *Advances in the Valuation and Management of Mortgage-Backed Securities* (New Hope, PA: Frank J. Fabozzi Associates, 1998).

where L is the ratio of the par value of the floater to the par value of the inverse floater. For example, if collateral with a par value of $100 million is used to create a floater with a par value of $80 million and an inverse floater with a par value of $20 million, L is 4 ($80 million/$20 million).

It is easy to see why an inverse's duration is a multiple of the collateral. Suppose that the par value of the collateral of $100 million is split as follows: $80 million for the floater and $20 million for the inverse floater. Suppose also that the collateral and inverse are trading at par so that the ratio of the prices is 1 and that the duration for the collateral is 8. For a 100-basis-point change in interest rates, the collateral's price will decline by 8% or $8 million (8% × $100 million). Assuming that the floater's price does not change when interest rates increase, the $8 million decline must come from the inverse floater. For the inverse floater to realize a decline in value of $8 million when its value is $20 million, the duration must be 40. That is, a duration of 40 will produce a 40% change in value or $8 million (40% times $20 million). Thus, the duration is five times the collateral's duration of 8. Or equivalently, because L is 4, it is $(1 + 4)$ times the collateral's duration.

Notice that even if the maturity of the collateral is 30 years, the duration of the inverse is greater than the maturity of the collateral. Investors who interpret duration as some time of weighted life of a security would be surprised by this result.

MEASURING A BOND PORTFOLIO'S RESPONSIVENESS TO NONPARALLEL CHANGES IN INTEREST RATES

We noted earlier in this chapter when we identified the shortcoming of duration that this measure may be inadequate in measuring how a security's price or a portfolio's value will change when interest rates do not change in a parallel manner. (We will discuss how yield curve shifts in Chapter 5.) This is particularly the case for a bond portfolio. As a result, it is necessary to be able to measure the exposure of a bond or bond portfolio to shifts in the yield curve. There have been several approaches that have been suggested for measuring this exposure. We will discuss only one in this chapter, **key rate duration**.[8]

The basic principle of key rate duration is to change the yield for a particular maturity of the yield curve and determine the sensitivity of a security or portfolio to that change holding all other yields constant. The sensitivity of the change in value to a particular change in yield is called **rate duration.** There is a rate duration for every point on the yield curve. Consequently, there is not one rate duration, but a vector of durations representing each maturity on the yield curve. The total change in value of a bond or a portfolio if all rates change by the same number of basis points is simply the duration of a security or portfolio we discussed earlier in this chapter.

The notion of using multiple durations was first suggested in 1988 by Donald Chambers and Willard Carleton; they called it **duration vectors.**[9] Robert Reitano sug-

---

[8]The other measures are yield curve reshaping duration and yield curve specific duration. These measures are discussed in Chapter 7 of Frank J. Fabozzi, *Duration, Convexity, and Other Bond Risk Measures* (New Hope, PA: Frank J. Fabozzi Associates, 1999). The discussion in this section on key rate duration is adapted from that chapter.

[9]Donald Chambers and Willard Carleton, "A Generalized Approach to Duration," *Research in Finance* 7(1988).

gested a similar approach in a series of papers and called the durations **partial durations.**[10] The most popular version of this approach is that developed by Thomas Ho in 1992, who called it rate duration.[11]

Ho's approach focuses on 11 key maturities of a Treasury curve, which we will describe in Chapter 5. The specific curve used in the analysis is called the Treasury spot rate curve; this important curve shows the relationship between maturity and yields on Treasury zero-coupon securities (see Chapter 5 for a detailed discussion). The rate durations are called **key rate durations.** The specific maturities on the spot rate curve for which a key rate duration is measured are 3 months, 1 year, 2 years, 3 years, 5 years, 7 years, 10 years, 15 years, 20 years, 25 years, and 30 years. Changes in rates between any two key rates are calculated using a linear approximation.

A key rate duration for a particular portfolio maturity should be interpreted as follows: Holding the yield for all other maturities constant, the key rate duration is the approximate percentage change in the value of a portfolio (or bond) for a 100 basis point change in the yield for the maturity whose rate has been changed. Thus, a key rate duration is quantified by changing the yield of the maturity of interest and determining how the value or price changes. In fact, equation (4.23) is used. The prices denoted by P_- and P_+ in the equation are the prices in the case of a bond and the portfolio values in the case of a bond portfolio found by holding all other interest rates constant and changing the yield for the maturity whose key rate duration is sought.

Let's look at three actual portfolios to make the concept of key rate duration more concrete. Exhibit 4-14 shows three portfolios consisting of different maturity Treasury securities as of April 23, 1997. The duration for each portfolio is the same, 4.7.[12] The exhibit shows the key rate durations for each security and the key rate durations for each portfolio. The key rate durations differ for each portfolio. Look at the 30-year key rate duration for each portfolio. For the first portfolio in the exhibit, the 30-year duration is 0.5. This means that if the 30-year Treasury spot rate changes by 100 basis points and the spot rate for all other maturities does not change, the portfolio's value will change by approximately 0.5%. For the second portfolio, the 30-year key rate duration is zero; thus, for a 100-basis-point change in the 30-year Treasury spot rate and holding the spot rate for all other maturities the same, the second portfolio's value will not change. The third portfolio's 30-year key rate duration is 0.10, so its value will change by 0.1% for a 100-basis-point change assuming no change in the spot rate for other maturities.

From this illustration it can be seen that despite the same portfolio duration for all three portfolios (4.7), they will each be expected to react in a different way if the 30-year spot rate changes. Exhibit 4-14 indicates that each portfolio will have quite different reactions to changes in the interest rate for different maturities.

---

[10]See, for example, Robert R. Reitano, "Non-Parallel Yield Curve Shifts and Durational Leverage," *Journal of Portfolio Management,* Summer 1990, pp. 62–67, and "A Multivariate Approach to Duration Analysis," *ARCH* 2 (1989).

[11]Thomas S. Y. Ho, "Key Rate Durations: Measure of Interest Rate Risk," *Journal of Fixed Income,* September 1992, pp. 29–44.

[12]Note that the exhibit indicates "Eff duration," which stands for effective duration. We'll discuss this measure in Chapter 14. Because the portfolio consists of Treasury securities that are option-free securities, as explained in Chapter 14, effective duration is the same as modified duration. Also note that the three portfolios are labeled "ladder portfolio," "barbell portfolio," and "bullet portfolio." We'll see why in Chapter 17.

EXHIBIT 4-14 Key Rate Durations for Three Treasury Portfolios (April 23, 1997)

Bond	Code	Cusip	Coupon	Maturity	Description			Size
1	TB	912810EW	6.000	2/15/26	TB	2/26	6.000	4,057,595
2	TN	912827X4	6.375	3/31/01	TN	3/01	6.375	11,679,547
3	TB	912810ET	7.625	2/15/25	TB	2/25	7.625	11,124,914
4	TC	912810BR	8.500	5/15/99	TC	599	8.500	2,987,478
5	TB	912810EG	8.750	8/15/20	TB	8/20	8.750	5,348,333
6	TB	912810DS	10.625	8/15/15	TB	8/15	10.625	1,944,533
7	TC	912810CM	11.750	2/15/10	TC	2/10	11.750	7,323,250
8	TC	912810DL	12.500	8/15/14	TC	8/14	12.500	1,212,780
9	TN	912820AQ	0.000	5/15/99	TN	599	0.000	37,154,780
10	TN	912820AT	0.000	5/15/99	TN	5/99	0.000	10,840,357
11	TN	912820BA	0.000	5/15/99	TN	5/99	0.000	8,472,702
Total Portfolio								

Bond	Code	Cusip	Coupon	Maturity	Description			Size
1	TN	9128272P	6.625	3/31/02	TN	3/02	6.625	86,528,320
2	TC	912810BR	8.500	5/15/99	TC	5/99	8.500	69,852,088
3	TB	912810DY	8.750	5/15/17	TB	5/17	8.750	63,761,372
Total Portfolio								

Bond	Code	Cusip	Coupon	Maturity	Description			Size
1	TN	9128272H	5.875	2/15/00	TN	2/00	5.875	2,388,518
2	TN	912827V4	6.125	9/30/00	TN	9/00	6.125	3,949,212
3	TN	9128272J	6.250	2/15/07	TN	2/07	6.250	26,670,542
4	TB	912810EQ	6.250	8/25/23	TB	8/23	6.250	7,015,242
5	TN	9128272J	7.125	9/30/99	TN	9/99	7.125	1,146,557
6	TB	912810EM	7.250	8/15/22	TB	8/22	7.250	1,059,479
7	TB	912810DX	7.500	11/15/16	TB	11/16	7.500	2,360,381
8	TC	912810BR	8.500	5/15/99	TC	5/99	8.500	33,741,656
9	TB	222655P9	8.750	11/15/08	TB	11/08	8.750	10,540,286
Total Portfolio								

Source: Global Advanced Technology (now BARRA)

EXHIBIT 4-14 *(cont.)*

LADDER PORTFOLIO

Key Rate Durations

3Mo	1yr	2yr	3yr	5yr	7yr	10yr	15yr	20yr	25yr	30yr	Eff Dur
0.02	0.06	0.12	0.26	0.47	0.73	1.33	1.69	1.57	1.45	4.60	12.31
0.01	0.06	0.11	1.79	1.45	0.00	0.00	0.00	0.00	0.00	0.00	3.42
0.02	0.06	0.12	0.27	0.49	0.76	1.38	1.76	1.62	2.32	2.81	11.63
0.06	0.00	0.00	0.00	0.00	0.00	0.00	0.00	0.00	0.00	0.00	0.06
0.02	0.06	0.12	0.28	0.50	0.78	1.42	1.81	2.80	2.74	0.00	10.56
0.02	0.07	0.13	0.30	0.53	0.83	1.50	1.01	2.77	0.00	0.00	9.16
0.02	0.08	0.15	0.36	0.62	3.10	1.03	0.01	0.00	0.00	0.00	5.36
0.02	0.07	0.14	0.33	0.59	0.91	3.19	1.86	0.01	0.00	0.00	7.13
0.00	0.66	0.86	0.00	0.00	0.00	0.00	0.00	0.00	0.00	0.00	1.52
0.00	0.00	1.54	0.70	0.00	0.00	0.00	0.00	0.00	0.00	0.00	2.24
0.00	0.00	0.00	1.84	2.09	0.00	0.00	0.00	0.00	0.00	0.00	3.93
0.01	0.25	0.49	0.50	0.49	0.50	0.50	0.50	0.50	0.50	0.50	4.75

BARBELL PORTFOLIO

Key Rate Durations

3Mo	1yr	2yr	3yr	5yr	7yr	10yr	15yr	20yr	25yr	30yr	Eff Dur
0.12	0.06	0.12	0.34	3.62	0.00	0.00	0.00	0.00	0.00	0.00	4.14
0.07	0.00	0.00	0.00	0.00	0.00	0.00	0.00	0.00	0.00	0.00	0.07
0.01	0.06	0.12	0.28	0.50	0.78	1.41	1.80	4.69	0.06	0.00	9.73
0.03	0.04	0.08	0.22	1.49	0.25	0.46	0.59	1.53	0.02	0.00	4.71

BULLET PORTFOLIO

Key Rate Durations

3Mo	1yr	2yr	3yr	5yr	7yr	10yr	15yr	20yr	25yr	30yr	Eff Dur
0.01	0.05	0.52	1.94	0.00	0.00	0.00	0.00	0.00	0.00	0.00	2.82
0.02	0.05	0.11	2.26	0.61	0.00	0.00	0.00	0.00	0.00	0.00	3.04
0.02	0.06	0.11	0.25	0.45	1.00	5.20	0.00	0.00	0.00	0.00	7.08
0.02	0.06	0.12	0.27	0.48	0.74	1.34	1.71	1.58	3.99	1.51	11.82
0.01	0.06	1.23	0.90	0.00	0.00	0.00	0.00	0.00	0.00	0.00	2.20
0.02	0.06	0.12	0.27	0.49	0.76	1.37	1.75	1.62	4.51	0.32	11.30
0.01	0.06	0.12	0.27	0.48	0.75	1.36	2.12	4.74	0.00	0.00	9.93
0.06	0.00	0.00	0.00	0.00	0.00	0.00	0.00	0.00	0.00	0.00	0.06
0.01	0.06	0.13	0.29	0.51	0.80	3.98	1.45	0.00	0.00	0.00	7.24
0.03	0.04	0.10	0.20	0.30	0.51	2.24	0.50	0.24	0.30	0.10	4.75

SUMMARY

The price–yield relationship for all option-free bonds is convex. There are three properties of the price volatility of an option-free bond: (1) for small changes in yield, the percentage price change is symmetric; (2) for large changes in yield, the percentage price change is asymmetric; and (3) for large changes in yield the price appreciation is greater than the price depreciation for a given change in yield.

The price volatility of an option-free bond is affected by two characteristics of a bond (maturity and coupon) and the yield level at which a bond trades. For a given maturity and yield, the lower the coupon rate, the greater the price volatility. For a given coupon rate and yield, the longer the maturity, the greater the price volatility. For a given coupon rate and maturity, the price volatility is greater the lower the yield.

There are three measures of bond price volatility: price value of a basis point, the yield value of a price change, and duration. We focused on the various duration measures—Macaulay duration, modified duration, and dollar duration—showing the relationship between bond price volatility and each of these measures. Modified duration is the approximate percentage change in price for a 100-basis-point change in yield. The dollar duration is the approximate dollar price change.

Duration does a good job of estimating a bond's percentage price change for a small change in yield. However, it does not do as good a job for a large change in yield. The percentage price change due to convexity can be used to supplement the approximate price change using duration. Together, the duration and convexity measures provide an excellent approximation of the price change when yields change.

Duration is an approximation of price change assuming a parallel shift in the yield curve. Duration should not be interpreted as a measure of the weighted life of a bond. For certain bonds, the modified duration can be greater than the maturity of a bond. Duration and convexity can be approximated by looking at how the price of a bond changes when the yield is changed up and down by a small number of basis points. The duration of an inverse floater is a multiple of the duration of the collateral from which it is created.

The duration of a portfolio is the weighted average duration of the bonds constituting the portfolio. When a manager attempts to gauge the sensitivity of a bond portfolio to changes in interest rates by computing a portfolio's duration, it is assumed that the interest rate for all maturities changes by the same number of basis points. To estimate the sensitivity of a bond portfolio to unequal changes in interest rates, rate duration can be computed. A rate duration is the approximate change in the value of a portfolio (or bond) to a change in the interest rate of a particular maturity assuming that the interest rate for all other maturities is held constant. Practitioners compute a key rate duration, which is simply the rate duration for key maturities.

Questions

1. The price value of a basis point will be the same regardless if the yield is increased or decreased by 1 basis point. However, the price value of 100 basis points (i.e., the change in price for a 100-basis-point change in interest rates) will not be the same if the yield is increased or decreased by 100 basis points. Why?

2. Calculate the requested measures for bonds A and B (assume that each bond pays interest semiannually):

	A	B
Coupon	8%	9%
Yield to maturity	8%	8%
Maturity (years)	2	5
Par	$100.00	$100.00
Price	$100.000	$104.055

a. Price value of a basis point
b. Macaulay duration
c. Modified duration
d. The approximate duration using the shortcut formula by changing yields by 20 basis points and compare your answer with the convexity measure calculated in part (c).
e. Convexity measure
f. The approximate convexity measure using the shortcut formula by changing yields by 20 basis points and compare your answer to the convexity measure calculated in part (e).

3. Can you tell from the following information which of the following three bonds will have the greatest price volatility, assuming that each is trading to offer the same yield to maturity?

Bond	Coupon Rate (%)	Maturity (years)
X	8	9
Y	10	11
Z	11	12

4. For bonds A and B in Question 2:
a. Calculate the actual price of the bonds for a 100-basis-point increase in interest rates.
b. Using duration, estimate the price of the bonds for a 100-basis-point increase in interest rates.
c. Using both duration and convexity measure, estimate the price of the bonds for a 100-basis-point increase in interest rates.
d. Comment on the accuracy of your results in parts (b) and (c), and state why one approximation is closer to the actual price than the other.
e. Without working through calculations, indicate whether the duration of the two bonds would be higher or lower if the yield to maturity is 10% rather than 8%.

5. State why you would agree or disagree with the following statement: As the duration of a zero-coupon bond is equal to its maturity, the price responsiveness of a zero-coupon bond to yield changes is the same regardless of the level of interest rates.

6. State why you would agree or disagree with the following statement: When interest rates are low, there will be little difference between the Macaulay duration and modified duration measures.

7. State why you would agree or disagree with the following statement: If two bonds have the same dollar duration, yield, and price, their dollar price sensitivity will be the same for a given change in interest rates.

8. State why you would agree or disagree with the following statement: For a 1-basis-point change in yield, the price value of a basis point is equal to the dollar duration.

9. The November 26, 1990, issue of *BondWeek* includes an article, "Van Kampen Merritt Shortens." The article begins as follows: "Peter Hegel, first v.p. at Van Kampen Merritt Investment Advisory, is shortening his $3 billion portfolio from 110% of his normal duration of 6½ years to 103–105% because he thinks that in the short run the bond rally is near an end." Explain Hegel's strategy and the use of the duration measure in this context.

10. Consider the following two Treasury securities:

Bond	Price	Modified Duration (years)
A	$100	6
B	80	7

Which bond will have the greater dollar price volatility for a 25-basis-point change in interest rates?

11. What are the limitations of using duration as a measure of a bond's price sensitivity to interest-rate changes?

12. The following excerpt is taken from an article titled "Denver Investment to Make $800 Million Treasury Move," which appeared in the December 9, 1991 issue of *BondWeek*, p. 1: "Denver Investment Advisors will swap $800 million of long zero-coupon Treasuries for intermediate Treasuries. . . . The move would shorten the duration of its $2.5 billion fixed-income portfolio. . . ."
Why would the swap described here shorten the duration of the portfolio?

13. You are a portfolio manager who has presented a report to a client. The report indicates the duration of each security in the portfolio. One of the securities has a maturity of 15 years but a duration of 25. The client believes that there is an error in the report because he believes that the duration cannot be greater than the security's maturity. What would be your response to this client?

14. Explain why the duration of an inverse floater is a multiple of the duration of the collateral from which the inverse floater is created.

15. Consider the following portfolio:

Bond	Market Value	Duration
A	$13 million	2
B	$27 million	7
C	$60 million	8
D	$40 million	14

a. What is the portfolio's duration?
b. If interest rates for all maturities change by 50 basis points, what is the approximate percentage change in the value of the portfolio?

16. "If two portfolios have the same duration, the change in their value when interest rates change will be the same." Explain why you agree or disagree with this statement.

17. In the fifth edition of *The Handbook of Fixed Income Securities* (Irwin Professional Publishing, 1997), page 104 gives the following formula for the approximate convexity measure:

$$\frac{P_+ + P_- - 2(P_0)}{2(P_0)(Dy)^2}$$

where the variables are defined as in equation (4.24) of this chapter. Compare this formula with the approximate convexity measure given by equation (4.24). Which formula is correct?

18. a. Explain what a 10-year key rate duration of 0.35 means?
    b. How is a key rate duration computed?

CHAPTER 5

Factors Affecting Bond Yields and the Term Structure of Interest Rates

Learning Objectives

After reading this chapter you will understand:

■ why the yield on a Treasury security is the base interest rate

■ the factors that affect the yield spread between two bonds

■ what a yield curve is

■ a spot rate and a spot rate curve

■ how theoretical spot rates are derived using arbitrage arguments from the Treasury yield curve

■ what the term structure of interest rates is

■ why the price of a Treasury bond should be based on theoretical spot rates

■ a forward rate and how a forward rate is derived

■ how long-term rates are related to the current short-term rate and short-term forward rates

■ why forward rates should be viewed as hedgeable rates

■ the various theories about the determinants of the shape of the term structure: pure expectations theory, the liquidity theory, the preferred habitat theory, and the market segmentation theory

In all financial markets throughout the world, there is not one yield offered on all bonds. The yield offered on a particular bond depends on a myriad of factors having to do with the type of issuer, the characteristics of the bond issue, and the state of the economy. In this chapter we look at the factors that affect the yield offered in the bond market. We begin with the minimum interest rate that an investor wants from investing in a bond, the yield on U.S. Treasury securities. Then we describe why the yield on a non–U.S. Treasury security will differ from that of a U.S. Treasury security. Finally, we focus on one particular factor that affects the yield offered on a security: maturity. The pattern of interest rates on securities of the same issuer but with different maturities is called the term structure of interest rates. The importance of analyzing the term structure of interest rates for U.S. Treasury securities is explained.

BASE INTEREST RATE

The securities issued by the U.S. Department of the Treasury are backed by the full faith and credit of the U.S. government. Consequently, market participants throughout the world view them as having no credit risk. As such, interest rates on Treasury securities are the key interest rates in the U.S. economy as well as in international capital markets. The large size of any single issue has contributed to making the Treasury market the most active and hence the most liquid market in the world.

The minimum interest rate that investors want is referred to as the **base interest rate** or **benchmark interest rate** that investors will demand for investing in a non-Treasury security. This rate is the yield to maturity (hereafter referred to as simply **yield**) offered on a comparable maturity Treasury security that was most recently issued ("on the run"). So, for example, if an investor wanted to purchase a 10-year bond on September 19, 1997, the minimum yield the investor would seek is 6.086%, the yield on the most recently issued 10-year Treasury (see Exhibit 5-1).

RISK PREMIUM

Market participants talk of interest rates on non-Treasury securities as **trading at a spread** to a particular on-the-run Treasury security. For example, on September 19, 1997, the yield on the Wal-Mart Stores bonds (rated AA) with 10 years to maturity was 6.476%. From Exhibit 5-1 it can be seen that on that same date, the yield on the 10-year on-the-run Treasury was 6.086%. The yield spread is then 6.476% minus 6.086%, or 0.39%, which is equal to 39 basis points. This spread, called a **risk premium,** reflects the additional risks the investor faces by acquiring a security that is not

EXHIBIT 5-1   Yields for On-the-Run Treasuries on September 19, 1997

Maturity	Yield
3 months	5.054%
6 months	5.262
1 year	5.465
2 years	5.800
3 years	5.872
5 years	5.999
10 years	6.086
30 years	6.372

Source: Lehman Brothers, *Global Relative Value,* September 22, 1997, Table T-2.

issued by the U.S. government. Thus we can express the interest rate offered on a non-Treasury security as

$$\text{base interest rate} + \text{spread}$$

or, equivalently,

$$\text{base interest rate} + \text{risk premium}$$

Yield spreads can be measured in terms of the difference between the yield on two bonds. The difference is measured in basis points. Unless otherwise stated, yield spreads are typically measured in this way. Yield spreads can also be measured on a relative basis by taking the ratio of the yield spread to the yield level. This is called a **relative yield spread:**

$$\text{relative yield spread} = \frac{\text{yield on bond A} - \text{yield on bond B}}{\text{yield on bond B}}$$

Sometimes bonds are compared in terms of a yield ratio, the quotient of two bond yields:

$$\text{yield ratio} = \frac{\text{yield on bond A}}{\text{yield on bond B}}$$

The factors that affect the yield spread include (1) the type of issuer, (2) the issuer's perceived creditworthiness, (3) the term or maturity of the instrument, (4) provisions that grant either the issuer or the investor the option to do something, (5) the taxability of the interest received by investors, and (6) the expected liquidity of the security.

Types of Issuers

The bond market is classified by the type of issuer, including the U.S. government, U.S. government agencies, municipal governments, corporations (domestic and foreign), and foreign governments. These classifications are referred to as **market sectors.** Different sectors are generally perceived to represent different risks and rewards. Some market sectors are further subdivided into categories intended to reflect common economic characteristics. For example, within the corporate market sector, issuers are classified as follows: (1) industrial companies, (2) utility companies, (3) finance companies, (4) banks, and (5) Yankee issuers.[1] Excluding the Treasury market sector, the other market sectors have a wide range of issuers, each with different abilities to satisfy their contractual obligations. Therefore, a key feature of a debt obligation is the nature of the issuer.

The spread between the interest rate offered in two sectors of the bond market with the same maturity is referred to as an **intermarket sector spread.** The most common intermarket sector spread calculated is the spread between Treasury securities and some sector of the non-Treasury market with the same maturity. For example, on September 19, 1997, BBB rated industrial bonds with a maturity of 10 years were trading at 76 basis points higher than the 10-year Treasury security. Thus, this intermarket sector spread was 76 basis points. Exhibit 5-2 shows the benchmark spread be-

---

[1] Yankee issues are bonds issued by non–U.S. entities in the U.S. bond market.

EXHIBIT 5-2	Benchmark Spreads of the 25 Largest Issuers in the Lehman Brothers Corporate Index				
	2 Year	*5 Year*	*7 Year*	*10 Year*	*30 Year*
Ford/Ford Motor Credit (A1/A+)	30	41	47	60	72
GM/GMAC (A3/A−)	32	43	48	59	73
Quebec (A2/A+)	30	45	52	63	83
Associates Corp. NA (Aa3/AA−)	27	40	48	57	NA
Ontario (Aa3/AA−)	20	25	30	45	50
Korea (A1/AA−)	80	102	115	125	160
Philip Morris (A2/A)	50	67	87	94	110
JCPenney (A2/A)	29	38	52	64	85
Chase Manhattan (A1/A)	25	44	49	65	87
News Corp (Baa3/BBB)	50	53	87	98	140
Lockheed Martin (A3/BBB+)	30	39	45	53	71
BankAmerica (A1/A+)	25	43	48	63	84
BellSouth (Aaa/AAA)	20	26	31	35	45
IBM (A1/A)	22	32	39	49	66
Merrill Lynch & Co. (Aa3/AA−)	28	41	44	56	NA
Nationsbank (A2/A)	27	46	55	68	85
Commercial Credit (A1/A+)	25	43	50	63	NA
GE/GECC (Aaa/AAA)	20	28	32	42	53
Italy, Republic of (A1/AA)	10	14	22	26	55
Wal-Mart Stores (Aa1/AA)	20	32	36	39	54
AT&T (Aa3/AA−)	23	35	39	48	55
Manitoba (A1/A+)	20	31	34	42	55
Norfolk Southern (Baa1/BBB+)	30	40	48	60	76
Salomon Inc. (Baa1/BBB+)	50	69	79	90	NA
Canada (Aa2/AA+)	4	8	12	20	33

Source: Lehman Brothers, *Global Relative Value,* Fixed Income Research, September 22, 1997, Table T-6.

tween the largest issuers in the corporate bond index created by Lehman Brothers[2] and Treasury securities with approximately the same maturity.

The spread between two issues within is a market sector is called an **intramarket sector spread.** For example, on September 19, 1997, the spread between 10-year AA rated bonds of banks and industrials (both sectors of the corporate bond market) was 13 basis points. That is, 10-year AA rated banks were selling to yield 13 basis points more than 10-year AA rated industrials. Exhibit 5-3 provides the information for determining intramarket sector spreads. Shown in the table is the intermarket sector spread between a sector of the corporate market and Treasuries by maturity and credit quality. From this information, the intramarket sector spread can be determined. For example, look at 10-year AA rated industrial bonds and 10-year AA rated bank bonds. The intermarket sector spreads are 41 basis points and 54 basis points, respectively. From this information we can determine that banks are trading at 13 basis points higher than industrials.

---

[2]Bond indexes are covered in Chapter 18.

EXHIBIT 5-3 Intermarket Sector Spreads between Sectors of the Corporate Bond Market and Treasuries

	AAA				AA				A				BBB			
	Sprd/	90-DAY			Sprd/	90-DAY			Sprd/	90-DAY			Sprd/	90-DAY		
Maturity	1-Wk Chg	High	Low	Avg	1-Wk Chg	High	Low	Avg	1-Wk Chg	High	Low	Avg	1-Wk Chg	High	Low	Avg
Industrials																
2	20/+1	20	19	19	21/+1	21	20	20	26/+1	26	25	25	43/+1	43	42	42
3	23/+1	23	22	22	24/+1	24	23	23	30/+1	30	29	29	50/+1	50	49	49
5	25/0	25	25	25	30/+1	30	29	29	35/+1	35	34	34	56/+1	56	54	54
10	35/0	35	34	35	41/+1	41	38	39	48/0	48	44	46	76/−1	77	71	74
30	41/0	42	40	41	47/+1	49	44	47	55/0	62	52	56	81/−1	89	78	83
Utilities																
2	20/0	20	20	20	22/0	22	22	22	27/0	28	27	27	40/0	40	40	40
3	23/0	23	23	23	27/0	27	27	27	34/0	35	34	34	48/0	48	48	48
5	27/0	27	27	27	35/0	35	35	35	39/0	40	39	39	55/0	55	55	55
10	36/0	36	35	36	50/0	50	48	49	54/0	55	53	54	75/0	75	74	75
30	44/0	46	44	45	54/0	56	54	55	64/0	68	64	66	86/0	90	86	88
Finance																
2	18/0	18	18	18	20/0	20	20	20	27/0	27	27	27	42/0	42	42	42
3	23/0	23	23	23	25/0	25	25	25	34/0	34	33	34	49/0	49	48	49
5	27/0	27	27	27	35/0	35	33	34	41/0	41	38	40	57/0	57	52	54
10	45/0	45	43	43	53/0	53	49	52	61/0	61	55	58	77/0	77	68	72
Banks																
2	21/0	21	21	21	22/0	22	22	22	30/0	30	29	30	44/0	44	43	44
3	24/0	24	24	24	25/0	25	24	25	39/0	39	37	39	52/0	52	50	52
5	34/0	34	33	34	37/0	37	37	37	49/0	49	45	47	63/0	63	59	61
10	49/0	50	49	49	54/0	54	52	53	69/0	69	61	65	89/0	89	82	85

Source: Lehman Brothers, *Global Relative Value*, Fixed Income Research, September 22, 1997, Table T-6.

Perceived Credit Worthiness of Issuer

Default risk or credit risk refers to the risk that the issuer of a bond may be unable to make timely principal and/or interest payments. Most market participants rely primarily on commercial rating companies to assess the default risk of an issuer. We discuss these rating companies in Chapter 7.

The spread between Treasury securities and non-Treasury securities that are identical in all respects except for quality is referred to as a **quality spread** or **credit spread.** It is important to keep in mind by what is meant by "identical in all respects except for quality." As explained in Chapters 4 and 7 and discussed further subsequently, issues may have provisions that can be beneficial or detrimental to a bondholder. If these provisions are absent in a Treasury issue but present in a non-Treasury under examination, the quality spread would be distorted because it reflects the value of these other provisions.

To the extent that the intermarket sector spreads shown in Exhibits 5-2 and 5-3 are for non-Treasury issues that do not have these provisions, these spreads would be quality spreads.

Inclusion of Options

It is not uncommon for a bond issue to include a provision that gives either the bondholder and/or the issuer an option to take some action against the other party. Such embedded options are discussed throughout this book. The most common type of option in a bond issue is the call provision that grants the issuer the right to retire the debt, fully or partially, before the scheduled maturity date. The inclusion of a call feature benefits issuers by allowing them to replace an old bond issue with a lower-interest-cost issue should interest rates in the market decline. Effectively, a call provision allows the issuer to alter the maturity of a bond. A call provision is detrimental to the bondholder because the bondholder must reinvest the proceeds received at a lower interest rate.

The presence of an embedded option has an effect on the spread of an issue relative to a Treasury security and the spread relative to otherwise comparable issues that do not have an embedded option. In general, market participants will require a larger spread to a comparable Treasury security for an issue with an embedded option that is favorable to the issuer (e.g., a call option) than for an issue without such an option. In contrast, market participants will require a smaller spread to a comparable Treasury security for an issue with an embedded option that is favorable to the investor (e.g., put option or conversion option). In fact, for a bond with an option that is favorable to an investor, the interest rate on an issue may be less than that on a comparable Treasury security!

Taxability of Interest

Unless exempted under the federal income tax code, interest income is taxable at the federal level. In addition to federal income taxes, there may be state and local taxes on interest income.

The federal tax code specifically exempts the interest income from qualified municipal bond issues from taxation at the federal level. Because of the tax-exempt feature of municipal bonds, the yield on municipal bonds is less than that on Treasuries with the same maturity. Exhibit 5-4 shows this relationship on September 12, 1996

EXHIBIT 5-4 Yield on High-Grade, Tax-Exempt Securities on September 13, 1996

Maturity	Yield (%)	Yield as a Percentage of Treasury Yield
1 year	3.95%	67.0%
3 years	4.45	69.0
5 years	4.65	70.1
10 years	5.10	74.2
30 years	5.75	81.3

Source: Adapted from Goldman, Sachs & Co., "Fixed Income Research," *Weekly Market Update*, September 13, 1996, p. A-5, Exhibit 19.

high-grade tax-exempt securities. The difference in yield between tax-exempt securities and Treasury securities is typically measured not in basis points but in percentage terms. More specifically, it is measured as the percentage of the yield on a tax-exempt security relative to a comparable Treasury security. This is reported in Exhibit 5-4.

The yield on a taxable bond issue after federal income taxes are paid is called the **after-tax yield:**

$$\text{after-tax yield} = \text{pretax yield} \times (1 - \text{marginal tax rate})$$

Of course, the marginal tax rate varies among investors. For example, suppose that a taxable bond issue offers a yield of 9% and is acquired by an investor facing a marginal tax rate of 31%. The after-tax yield would then be

$$\text{after-tax yield} = 0.09 \times (1 - 0.31) = 0.0621 = 6.21\%$$

Alternatively, we can determine the yield that must be offered on a taxable bond issue to give the same after-tax yield as a tax-exempt issue. This yield, called the **equivalent taxable yield,** is determined as follows:

$$\text{equivalent taxable yield} = \frac{\text{tax-exempt yield}}{1 - \text{marginal tax rate}}$$

For example, consider an investor facing a 31% marginal tax rate who purchases a tax-exempt issue with a yield of 6.21%. The equivalent taxable yield is then

$$\text{equivalent taxable yield} = \frac{0.0621}{1 - 0.31} = 0.09 = 9\%$$

Notice that the higher the marginal tax rate, the higher the equivalent taxable yield. For example, in our previous example, if the marginal tax rate is 36% rather than 31%, the equivalent taxable yield would be 9.7% rather than 9%:

$$\text{equivalent taxable yield} = \frac{0.0621}{1 - 0.36} = 0.097 = 9.7\%$$

The municipal bond market is divided into two major sectors: general obligations and revenue bonds. The revenue bond sector is further decomposed into the follow-

EXHIBIT 5-5	Spreads between Tax-Exempt Revenue Sectors and AAA Rated General Obligation Bonds (September 12, 1996)		
Sector	*Yield*	*Spread*	*12-Month Average*
Housing	6.20%	45 bp	50 bp
Power	6.13	38	33
Hospital	6.13	38	47
Insured	5.98	23	25
New York Revenue	5.90	15	23
California Revenue	5.95	20	30

Source: Adapted from Exhibit 21 in Goldman Sachs & Co., *Weekly Market Update,* Fixed Income Research, September 13, 1996, A-5.

ing sectors: (1) housing, (2) power, (3) hospitals, and (4) insured. For the tax-exempt bond market, the benchmark for calculating spreads is not Treasuries. Rather, it is a generic AAA general obligation bond with a specified maturity. Exhibit 5-5 shows the spread to a AAA general obligation bond for various sectors in the tax-exempt bond market. The 12-month average spread is also shown.

State and local governments may tax interest income on bond issues that are exempt from federal income taxes. Some municipalities exempt interest income from all municipal issues from taxation; others do not. Some states exempt interest income from bonds issued by municipalities within the state but tax the interest income from bonds issued by municipalities outside the state. The implication is that two municipal securities of the same quality rating and the same maturity may trade at some spread because of the relative demand for bonds of municipalities in different states. For example, in a high-income-tax state such as New York, the demand for bonds of municipalities will drive down their yield relative to municipalities in a low-income-tax state such as Florida. In Exhibit 5-5 the spread relative to AAA general obligations bonds between revenue bonds for issuers in New York and California is shown. Notice that the spread is even less than that of insured revenue bonds because of the bidding up of these bonds by residents in New York and California.

Municipalities are not permitted to tax the interest income from securities issued by the U.S. Treasury. Thus, part of the spread between Treasury securities and taxable non-Treasury securities of the same maturity reflects the value of the exemption from state and local taxes.

Expected Liquidity of an Issue

Bonds trade with different degrees of liquidity. The greater the expected liquidity, the lower the yield that investors would require. As noted earlier, Treasury securities are the most liquid securities in the world. The lower yield offered on Treasury securities relative to non-Treasury securities reflects the difference in liquidity. Even within the Treasury market, on-the-run issues have greater liquidity than off-the-run issues.

Financeability of an Issue

A portfolio manager can use an issue as collateral for borrowing funds. By borrowing funds, a portfolio manager can create leverage. We will discuss this strategy in Chapter 17. The typical market used by portfolio managers to borrow funds using a security as collateral for a loan is the repurchase agreement market or "repo" market. We will discuss this market and the repo agreement in Chapter 17.

Basically, when a portfolio manager wants to borrow funds via a repo agreement, a dealer provides the funds. The interest rate the dealer charges is called the repo rate. There is not one repo rate but a structure of rates depending on the maturity of the loan and the specific issue being financed. With respect to the latter, there are times when dealers are in need of particular issues to cover a short position. When a dealer needs a particular issue, that dealer will be willing to offer to lend funds at a lower repo rate than the general repo rate in the market. The dealer is willing to offer attractive financing because it can use the collateral (i.e., the particular issue it needs) to cover a short position for the life of the repo agreement. Because such issues offer below-market financing opportunities, the price of such issues will be bid up, and therefore their yield is less than otherwise comparable issues. The spread between the yield on such issues and issues that do not offer a below-market repo rate reflects the financing advantage.

This spread is commonly observed in the Treasury market between on-the-run and off-the-run issues. Consequently, the spread between on-the-run and off-the-run issues of approximately the same maturity reflects not only differences in liquidity but any financing advantage. This spread not only occurs between on-the-run and off-the-run issues. There are times in the market when particular off-the-run issues are needed by dealers for various activities that they perform.

Term to Maturity

As we explained in Chapter 2, the price of a bond will fluctuate over its life as yields in the market change. The time remaining on a bond's life is referred to its **term to maturity** or simply **maturity.** As demonstrated in Chapter 4, the volatility of a bond's price is dependent on its term to maturity. More specifically, with all other factors constant, the longer the term to maturity of a bond, the greater the price volatility resulting from a change in market yields. Generally, bonds are classified into three **maturity sectors:** Bonds with a term to maturity of between one to five years are considered **short term;** bonds with a term to maturity between five and 12 years are viewed as **intermediate term;** and **long-term** bonds are those with a term to maturity greater than 12 years. The spread between any two maturity sectors of the market is called a **maturity spread.** The relationship between the yields on otherwise comparable securities with different maturities is called the **term structure of interest rates.**

TERM STRUCTURE OF INTEREST RATES

The term structure of interest rates plays a key role in the valuation of bonds. For this reason, we devote a good deal of space to this important topic.

Yield Curve

The graphical depiction of the relationship between the yield on bonds of the same credit quality but different maturities is known as the **yield curve.** In the past, most investors have constructed yield curves from observations of prices and yields in the Treasury market. Two factors account for this tendency. First, Treasury securities are free of default risk, and differences in credit worthiness do not affect yields. Therefore, these instruments are directly comparable. Second, as the largest and most active bond market, the Treasury market offers the fewest problems of illiquidity or infrequent trading. The disadvantage, as noted previously, is that the yields may be biased downward because they reflect favorable financing opportunities.

Exhibit 5-6 shows three actual yield curves on three separate dates—3/3/89, 12/28/89, and 10/24/94. The data used to construct these three yield curves were the on-the-run issues at the time. Notice the greater number of data points for the two yield curves in 1989. This is because at that time the Treasury issued coupon bonds with more maturities than it presently does.

From a practical viewpoint, as we explained earlier in this chapter, a key function of the Treasury yield curve is to serve as a benchmark for pricing bonds and to set yields in all other sectors of the debt market: bank loans, mortgages, corporate debt, and international bonds. However, market participants are coming to realize that the traditionally constructed Treasury yield curve is an unsatisfactory measure of the relation between required yield and maturity. The key reason is that securities with the same maturity may actually carry different yields. As we explain in the next section, this phenomenon reflects the role and impact of differences in the bonds' coupon rates. Hence, it is necessary to develop more accurate and reliable estimates of the Treasury yield curve. In what follows we show the problems posed by traditional approaches to the Treasury yield curve and offer the correct approach to building a yield curve. This approach consists of identifying yields that apply to zero-coupon bonds and therefore eliminates the problem of coupon rate differences in the yield–maturity relationship.

Why the Yield Curve Should Not Be Used to Price a Bond

The price of a bond is the present value of its cash flow. However, in our illustrations and our discussion of the pricing of a bond in Chapter 2, we assume that one interest rate should be used to discount all the bond's cash flows. The appropriate interest rate is the yield on a Treasury security, with the same maturity as the bond, plus an appropriate risk premium.

As noted previously, however, there is a problem with using the Treasury yield curve to determine the appropriate yield at which to discount the cash flow of a bond. To illustrate this problem, consider the following two hypothetical five-year Treasury bonds, A and B. The difference between these two Treasury bonds is the coupon rate, which is 12% for A and 3% for B. The cash flow for these two bonds per $100 of par value for the 10 six-month periods (five years) to maturity would be:

Period	Cash Flow for A	Cash Flow for B
1–9	$ 6.00	$ 1.50
10	106.00	101.50

Because of the different cash flow patterns, it is not appropriate to use the same interest rate to discount all cash flows. Instead, each cash flow should be discounted at a unique interest rate that is appropriate for the time period in which the cash flow will be received. But what should be the interest rate for each period?

The correct way to think about bonds A and B is not as bonds but as packages of cash flows. More specifically, they are packages of zero-coupon instruments. Thus, the interest earned is the difference between the maturity value and the price paid. For example, bond A can be viewed as 10 zero-coupon instruments: one with a maturity value

EXHIBIT 5-6 Treasury Yield Curve Shape on 3 Days

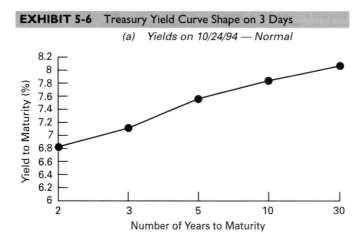

(a) Yields on 10/24/94 — Normal

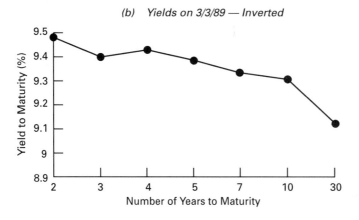

(b) Yields on 3/3/89 — Inverted

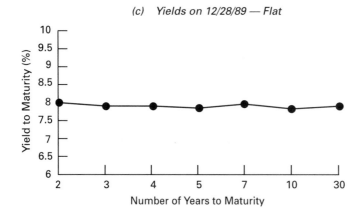

(c) Yields on 12/28/89 — Flat

of $6 maturing six months from now, a second with a maturity value of $6 maturing one year from now, a third with a maturity value of $6 maturing 1.5 years from now, and so on. The final zero-coupon instrument matures 10 six-month periods from now and has a maturity value of $106. Similarly, bond B can be viewed as 10 zero-coupon instruments with maturity values of $1.50 for the first nine six-month periods and $101.50 for the last six-month period. Obviously, in the case of each coupon bond (A or B), the value or price of the bond is equal to the total value of its component zero-coupon instruments.

In general, any bond can be viewed as a package of zero-coupon instruments. That is, each zero-coupon instrument in the package has a maturity equal to its coupon payment date or, in the case of the principal, the maturity date. The value of the bond should equal the value of all the component zero-coupon instruments. If this does not hold, it is possible for a market participant to generate riskless profits by stripping off the coupon payments and creating stripped securities (see Chapter 6).

To determine the value of each zero-coupon instrument, it is necessary to know the yield on a zero-coupon Treasury with that same maturity. This yield is called the **spot rate,** and the graphical depiction of the relationship between the spot rate and maturity is called the **spot rate curve.** Because there are no zero-coupon Treasury debt issues with a maturity greater than one year, it is not possible to construct such a curve solely from observations of market activity on Treasury securities. Rather, it is necessary to derive this curve from theoretical considerations as applied to the yields of the actually traded Treasury debt securities. Such a curve is called a **theoretical spot rate curve** and is the graphical depiction of the **term structure of interest rate.**

Constructing the Theoretical Spot Rate Curve for Treasuries[3]

A default-free theoretical spot rate curve can be constructed from the yield on Treasury securities. The Treasury issues that are candidates for inclusion are

1. on-the-run Treasury issues
2. on-the-run Treasury issues and selected off-the-run Treasury issues
3. all Treasury coupon securities and bills
4. Treasury coupon strips

Each type of Treasury is explained in the next chapter. After the securities that are to be included in the construction of the theoretical spot rate curve are selected, the methodology for constructing the curve must be determined. The methodology depends on the securities included. If Treasury coupon strips are used, the procedure is simple, because the observed yields are the spot rates. If the on-the-run Treasury issues with or without selected off-the-run Treasury issues are used, a methodology called **bootstrapping** is used. When all Treasury coupon securities and bills are used, then elaborate statistical techniques are used.

On-the-Run Treasury Issues   The **on-the-run Treasury issues** are the most recently auctioned issue of a given maturity. These issues include the three-month, six-month, and one-year Treasury bills, the two-year, five-year, and 10-year Treasury notes, and the 30-year Treasury bond. Treasury bills are zero-coupon instruments; the notes and the bond are coupon securities.

---

[3]This discussion draws from Chapter 2 in Frank J. Fabozzi, *Valuation of Fixed Income Securities and Derivatives: Third Edition* (New Hope, PA: Frank J. Fabozzi Associates, 1998).

There is an observed yield for each of the on-the-run issues (see, for example, Exhibit 5-1). (The three-year issue is no longer issued.) For the coupon issues, these yields are not the yields used in the analysis when the issue is not trading at par. Instead, for each on-the-run coupon issue, the estimated yield necessary to make the issue trade at par is used. The resulting on-the-run yield curve is called the **par coupon curve.**

The goal is to construct a theoretical spot rate curve with 60 semiannual spot rates: six-month rate to 30-year rate. Excluding the three-month bill, there are only six maturity points available when only on-the-run issues are used. The 54 missing maturity points are extrapolated from the surrounding maturity points on the par yield curve. The simplest extrapolation method, and the one most commonly used, is linear extrapolation. Specifically, given the yield on the par coupon curve at two maturity points, the following is calculated:

$$\frac{\text{yield at higher maturity} - \text{yield at lower maturity}}{\text{number of semiannual period between the two maturity points}}$$

Then, the yield for all intermediate semiannual maturity points is found by adding to the yield at the lower maturity the amount computed here.

For example, suppose that the yield from the par yield curve for the two-year and five-year on-the-run issues is 6% and 6.6%, respectively. There are six semiannual periods between these two maturity points. The extrapolated yield for the 2.0, 2.5, 3.0, 3.5, 4.0, and 4.5 maturity points is found as follows. Calculate

$$\frac{6.6\% - 6\%}{4} = 0.10\%$$

Then

$$2.5\text{-year yield} = 6.00\% + 0.10\% = 6.10\%$$

$$3.0\text{-year yield} = 6.10\% + 0.10\% = 6.20\%$$

$$3.5\text{-year yield} = 6.20\% + 0.10\% = 6.30\%$$

$$4.0\text{-year yield} = 6.30\% + 0.10\% = 6.40\%$$

$$4.5\text{-year yield} = 6.40\% + 0.10\% = 6.50\%$$

There are two problems with using just the on-the-run issues. First, there is a large gap between some of the maturities points, which may result in misleading yields for those maturity points when estimated using the linear extrapolation method. Specifically, the concern is with the large gap between the five-year and 10-year maturity points and the 10-year and 30-year maturity points. The second problem is that the yields for the on-the-run issues themselves may be misleading because most offer the favorable financing opportunity in the repo market mentioned earlier. This means that the true yield is greater than the quoted (observed) yield.

Now let's look at how the par yield curve is converted into the theoretical spot rate curve using bootstrapping. For simplicity, we will illustrate this methodology to calculate the theoretical spot rate curve for only 10 years. That is, 20 semiannual spot rates will be computed. Suppose that the par yield curve is the one shown in Exhibit 5-7.[4]

---

[4]Note that the intermediate maturity points in Exhibit 5-7 were not calculated using the linear extrapolation procedure.

Period	Years	Yield to Maturity/ Coupon Rate (%)
EXHIBIT 5-7		Maturity and Yield to Maturity for 20 Hypothetical Treasury Securities[a]
1	0.5	5.25
2	1.0	5.50
3	1.5	5.75
4	2.0	6.00
5	2.5	6.25
6	3.0	6.50
7	3.5	6.75
8	4.0	6.80
9	4.5	7.00
10	5.0	7.10
11	5.5	7.15
12	6.0	7.20
13	6.5	7.30
14	7.0	7.35
15	7.5	7.40
16	8.0	7.50
17	8.5	7.60
18	9.0	7.60
19	9.5	7.70
20	10.0	7.80

[a]All bonds with the exception of the six-month and one-year issues are at par (100). For these issues the coupon rate is equal to the yield to maturity. The six-month and one-year issues are zero-coupon instruments and the price is less than par.

To explain the process of estimating the theoretical spot rate curve from observed yields on Treasury securities, we use the data for the price, annualized yield (yield to maturity), and maturity of the 20 hypothetical Treasury securities shown in Exhibit 5-7. Each security is assumed to have a market price equal to its par value, so that the yield to maturity and the coupon rate are equal.

Throughout the analysis and illustrations to come, it is important to remember that the basic principle is that the value of the Treasury coupon security should be equal to the value of the package of zero-coupon Treasury securities that duplicates the coupon bond's cash flow.

Consider the six-month Treasury bill in Exhibit 5-7. As explained in Chapter 6, a Treasury bill is a zero-coupon instrument; hence, its annualized yield of 5.25% is equal to the spot rate. Similarly, for the one-year Treasury, the cited yield of 5.5% is the one-year spot rate. Given these two spot rates, we can compute the spot rate for a theoretical 1.5-year zero-coupon Treasury. The price of a theoretical 1.5-year zero-coupon Treasury should equal the present value of three cash flows from an actual

1.5-year coupon Treasury, where the yield used for discounting is the spot rate corresponding to the cash flow. Exhibit 5-7 shows the coupon rate for a 1.5-year Treasury as 5.75%. Using $100 as par, the cash flow for this Treasury security is

$$
\begin{array}{lll}
0.5 \text{ year:} & 0.0575 \times \$100 \times 0.5 & = \$ 2.875 \\
1.0 \text{ year:} & 0.0575 \times \$100 \times 0.5 & = 2.875 \\
1.5 \text{ years:} & 0.0575 \times \$100 \times 0.5 + 100 = & 102.875
\end{array}
$$

The present value of the cash flow is then

$$
\frac{2.875}{1 + z_1} + \frac{2.875}{(1 + z_2)^2} + \frac{102.875}{(1 + z_3)^3}
$$

where:

z_1 = one-half the annualized six-month theoretical spot rate
z_2 = one-half the one-year theoretical spot rate
z_3 = one-half the annual value of the 1.5-year theoretical spot rate

Because the six-month spot rate and one-year spot rate are 5.25% and 5.50%, respectively, we know these facts:

$$
z_1 = 0.02625 \quad \text{and} \quad z_2 = 0.0275
$$

We can compute the present value of the 1.5-year coupon Treasury security as

$$
\frac{2.875}{1.02625} + \frac{2.875}{(1.0275)^2} + \frac{102.875}{(1 + z_3)^3}
$$

Because the price of the 1.5-year coupon Treasury security is $100, the following relationship must hold:

$$
100 = \frac{2.875}{1.02625} + \frac{2.875}{(1.0275)^2} + \frac{102.875}{(1 + z_3)^3}
$$

We can solve for the theoretical 1.5-year spot rate as follows:

$$
100 = 2.801461 + 2.723166 + \frac{102.875}{(1 + z_3)^3}
$$

$$
94.47537 = \frac{102.875}{(1 + z_3)^3}
$$

$$
(1 + z_3)^3 = 1.028798
$$

$$
z_3 = 0.028798
$$

Doubling this yield, we obtain the bond-equivalent yield of 0.0576 or 5.76%, which is the theoretical 1.5-year spot rate. That rate is the rate that the market would apply to a 1.5-year zero-coupon Treasury security if, in fact, such a security existed.

Given the theoretical 1.5-year spot rate, we can obtain the theoretical two-year spot rate. The cash flow for the two-year coupon Treasury in Exhibit 5-7 is

$$
\begin{array}{lll}
0.5 \text{ year:} & 0.060 \times \$100 \times 0.5 & = \$ 3.00 \\
1.0 \text{ year:} & 0.060 \times \$100 \times 0.5 & = 3.00 \\
1.5 \text{ years:} & 0.060 \times \$100 \times 0.5 & = 3.00 \\
2.0 \text{ years:} & 0.060 \times \$100 \times 0.5 + 100 = & 103.00
\end{array}
$$

The present value of the cash flow is then

$$\frac{3.00}{1 + z_1} + \frac{3.00}{(1 + z_2)^2} + \frac{3.00}{(1 + z_3)^3} + \frac{103.00}{(1 + z_4)^4}$$

where z_4 is one-half the two-year theoretical spot rate. Because the six-month spot rate, one-year spot rate, and 1.5-year spot rate are 5.25%, 5.50%, and 5.76%, respectively, then

$$z_1 = 0.02625 \qquad z_2 = 0.0275 \qquad z_3 = 0.028798$$

Therefore, the present value of the two-year coupon Treasury security is

$$\frac{3.00}{1.002625} + \frac{3.00}{(1.0275)^2} + \frac{3.00}{(1.028798)^3} + \frac{103.00}{(1 + z_4)^4}$$

Because the price of the two-year coupon Treasury security is $100, the following relationship must hold:

$$100 = \frac{3.00}{1.002625} + \frac{3.00}{(1.0275)^2} + \frac{3.00}{(1.028798)^3} + \frac{103.00}{(1 + z_4)^4}$$

We can solve for the theoretical two-year spot rate as follows:

$$100 = 2.92326 + 2.84156 + 2.75506 + \frac{103.00}{(1 + z_4)^4}$$

$$91.48011 = \frac{103.00}{(1 + z_4)^4}$$

$$(1 + z_4)^4 = 1.125927$$

$$z_4 = 0.030095$$

Doubling this yield, we obtain the theoretical two-year spot rate bond-equivalent yield of 6.02%.

One can follow this approach sequentially to derive the theoretical 2.5-year spot rate from the calculated values of z_1, z_2, z_3, z_4 (the six-month, one-year, 1.5-year, and two-year rates), and the price and coupon of the bond with a maturity of 2.5 years. Further, one could derive theoretical spot rates for the remaining 15 half-yearly rates.

The spot rates using this process are shown in Exhibit 5-8. They represent the term structure of interest rates for maturities up to 10 years at the particular time to which the bond price quotations refer.

Exhibit 5-9 shows the theoretical spot rate curve estimated on August 13, 1996, by applying the bootstrapping methodology to on-the-run issues. Also shown in the exhibit are the rates based on the coupon strips. Note the significant divergence between the coupon strips and the rates generated from bootstrapping after the six-year maturity point.

EXHIBIT 5-8 Theoretical Spot Rates

Period	Years	Spot Rate (%)
1	0.5	5.25
2	1.0	5.50
3	1.5	5.76
4	2.0	6.02
5	2.5	6.28
6	3.0	6.55
7	3.5	6.82
8	4.0	6.87
9	4.5	7.09
10	5.0	7.20
11	5.5	7.26
12	6.0	7.31
13	6.5	7.43
14	7.0	7.48
15	7.5	7.54
16	8.0	7.67
17	8.5	7.80
18	9.0	7.79
19	9.5	7.93
20	10.0	8.07

On-the-Run Treasury Issues and Selected Off-the-Run Treasury Issues   As noted previously, one of the problems with using just the on-the-run issues is the large gaps between maturities, particularly after five years. To mitigate this problem, some dealers and vendors use selected off-the-run Treasury issues. Typically, the issues used are the 20-year issue and 25-year issue. Given the par coupon curve including any off-the-run selected issues, the linear extrapolation method is used to fill in the gaps for the other maturities. The bootstrapping method is then used to construct the theoretical spot rate curve.

Exhibit 5-9 compares the theoretical annual spot rates on August 13, 1996, using the bootstrapping methodology applied to (1) the on-run-issues and (2) the on-the-run issues plus the 20-year and 25-year off-the-run issues. The table also includes the coupon strip rates. Notice how much closer the theoretical spot rate curve comes to the coupon strips curve when the on-the-run issues are supplemented with the 20-year and 25-year off-the-run issues.

All Treasury Coupon Securities and Bills   Using only on-the-run issues, even when extended to include a few off-the-run issues, fails to recognize the information embodied in Treasury prices that are not included in the analysis. Thus, it is argued that it is more appropriate to use all Treasury coupon securities and bills to construct the theoretical spot rate curve. Some practitioners do not use callable Treasury bonds.[5]

---

[5]A common practice is to filter the Treasury securities universe to eliminate securities that offer advantageous financing in the repo market.

EXHIBIT 5-9 Comparison of Theoretical Annual Spot Rates Using Bootstrapping Methodology, Merrill Lynch Exponential Spline Methodology, and Coupon Strips on August 13, 1996

	Bootstrapping Using On-the-Run Issues	*Bootstrapping Using On-the-Run Issues + 20-Year and 25-Year Issues*	*Exponential Spline*	*Coupon Strip*
1	5.62	5.62	5.69	5.60
2	5.98	5.98	6.00	5.98
3	6.17	6.17	6.18	6.17
4	6.27	6.27	6.29	6.27
5	6.36	6.36	6.37	6.35
6	6.42	6.42	6.44	6.42
7	6.47	6.47	6.51	6.51
8	6.53	6.53	6.58	6.60
9	6.59	6.59	6.65	6.68
10	6.66	6.66	6.71	6.74
11	6.66	6.68	6.77	6.79
12	6.67	6.72	6.83	6.84
13	6.68	6.75	6.89	6.90
14	6.69	6.78	6.94	6.94
15	6.71	6.82	6.98	6.98
16	6.72	6.86	7.02	7.03
17	6.73	6.89	7.06	7.06
18	6.75	6.94	7.09	7.07
19	6.77	6.98	7.12	7.10
20	6.78	7.02	7.14	7.11
21	6.80	7.04	7.16	7.13
22	6.82	7.04	7.16	7.14
23	6.84	7.05	7.16	7.14
24	6.86	7.05	7.15	7.13
25	6.88	7.06	7.12	7.10
26	6.90	7.01	7.08	7.06
27	6.92	6.96	7.02	6.98
28	6.95	6.91	6.95	6.95
29	6.98	6.86	6.85	6.88
30	7.00	6.81	6.74	6.85[a]

[a]29.5 yrs

Source: The data points were provided by Philip H. Galdi, Analyst at Merrill Lynch, and Shenglin Lu, Analyst at Merrill Lynch. These data were used to construct the spot rate curves in Philip H. Galdi and Shenglin Lu, *Analyzing Risk and Relative Value of Corporate and Government Securities,* Merrill Lynch & Co., Global Securities Research & Economics Group, Fixed Income Analytics, 1997. Copyright ©1997 Merrill Lynch, Pierce, Fenner & Smith Incorporated.

When all coupon securities and bills are used, statistical methodologies must be employed to construct the theoretical spot rate curve rather than bootstrapping because there may be more than one yield for each maturity. Several statistical methodologies have been proposed to estimate the spot rate curve. The most common methodology used is "exponential spline fitting."[6] An adjustment for the effect of taxes and for call features on U.S. Treasury bonds can be incorporated into the statistical model. A discussion of this statistical methodology is beyond the scope this book.[7]

Exhibit 5-9 provides a comparison of the theoretical spot rate constructed on August 13, 1996 using coupon strips with those of the exponential spline methodology as developed by Merrill Lynch and the bootstrapping methodology. Notice how close the spot rates based on the spline methodology are to the coupon strips, particularly after the six-year maturity point.

Treasury Coupon Strips   As explained in the next chapter, Treasury coupon strips are zero-coupon Treasury securities. It would seem logical that the observed yield on strips could be used to construct an actual spot rate curve rather than go through the procedure we describe here. There are three problems with using the observed rates on strips. First, the liquidity of the strips market is not as great as that of the Treasury coupon market. Thus, the observed rates on strips reflect a premium for liquidity.

Second, the tax treatment of strips is different from that of Treasury coupon securities. Specifically, the accrued interest on strips is taxed even though no cash is received by the investor. Thus they are negative cash flow securities to taxable entities, and as a result, their yield reflects this tax disadvantage.

Finally, there are maturity sectors in which non–U.S. investors find it advantageous to trade off yield for tax advantages associated with a strip. Specifically, certain foreign tax authorities allow their citizens to treat the difference between the maturity value and the purchase price as a capital gain and tax this gain at a favorable tax rate. Some will grant this favorable treatment only when the strip is created from the principal rather than the coupon. For this reason, those who use Treasury strips to represent theoretical spot rates restrict the issues included to coupon strips.

Using the Theoretical Spot Rate Curve

We can now apply the spot rates to price a bond. In Chapter 2 we showed how to price a bond assuming that each cash flow is discounted at one discount rate. Exhibit 5-10 shows how to value a Treasury bond properly using the theoretical spot rates. The bond in the illustration is a hypothetical 10-year Treasury security with a coupon rate of 10%.

---

[6]Willard R. Carleton and Ian Cooper, "Estimation and Uses of the Term Structure of Interest Rates," *Journal of Finance,* September 1976, pp. 1067–83; J. Huston McCulloch, "Measuring the Term Structure of Interest Rates," *Journal of Business,* January 1971, pp. 19–31; and McCulloch, "The Tax Adjusted Yield Curve," *Journal of Finance,* June 1975, pp. 811–830.
[7]See Oldrich A. Vasicek and H. Gifford Fong, "Term Structure Modeling Using Exponential Splines," *Journal of Finance,* May 1982, pp. 339–58. For an example of a dealer model, see Arnold Shapiro *et al., Merrill Lynch Exponential Spline Model,* Merrill Lynch & Co., Global Securities Research & Economics Group, Fixed Income Analytics, August 8, 1994.

EXHIBIT 5-10	Determining the Theoretical Value of a 10% 10-Year Treasury Security Using the Theoretical Spot Rates				
Period	*Year*	*Cash Flow*	*Spot Rate (%)*	*PV of $1 at Spot Rate*	*PV of Cash Flow*
1	0.5	5	5.25	0.974421	4.872107
2	1.0	5	5.50	0.947188	4.735942
3	1.5	5	5.76	0.918351	4.591756
4	2.0	5	6.02	0.888156	4.440782
5	2.5	5	6.28	0.856724	4.283619
6	3.0	5	6.55	0.824206	4.12103
7	3.5	5	6.82	0.790757	3.953783
8	4.0	5	6.87	0.763256	3.81628
9	4.5	5	7.09	0.730718	3.653589
10	5.0	5	7.20	0.701952	3.509758
11	5.5	5	7.26	0.675697	3.378483
12	6.0	5	7.31	0.650028	3.250138
13	6.5	5	7.43	0.622448	3.112238
14	7.0	5	7.48	0.597889	2.989446
15	7.5	5	7.54	0.573919	2.869594
16	8.0	5	7.67	0.547625	2.738125
17	8.5	5	7.80	0.521766	2.608831
18	9.0	5	7.79	0.502665	2.513325
19	9.5	5	7.93	0.477729	2.388643
20	10.0	105	8.07	0.453268	47.593170
				Theoretical value = 115.4206	

The third column of the exhibit shows the cash flow per $100 of par value for each of the 20 six-month periods. The fourth column shows the theoretical spot rate for each maturity given in Exhibit 5-8. The fifth column gives the present value of $1 when discounted at the theoretical spot rate shown in the fourth column. The last column gives the present value of the cash flow, found by multiplying the third column by the fifth column. The theoretical price of this bond is the sum of the present values in the last column, $115.4206.

Although we have stated that the price of a Treasury security should be equal to the present value of its cash flow where each cash flow is discounted at the theoretical spot rates, the question is: What forces a Treasury to be priced based on the spot rates? The answer is that arbitrage forces this. For example, the theoretical price of $115.4206 can be viewed as the value of a package of zero-coupon instruments. That is, if this 10% 10-year Treasury security is purchased and then stripped, it will generate proceeds of $115.4206. The stripped Treasury securities created are the securities we describe in Chapter 6.

Now suppose, instead, that the market priced the 10% 10-year Treasury security based on the yield to maturity of 10-year Treasury securities as indicated by the yield curve. As can be seen in Exhibit 5-7, the yield to maturity for 10-year Treasury securities is 7.8%. If the 10% 10-year Treasury security is priced using a discount rate of

7.8%, its price would be $115.0826, a price that is less than its theoretical value. A government securities dealer who had the opportunity to buy this Treasury security for $115.0826 would buy it, then strip it and sell the zero-coupon securities created. As we just noted, the total proceeds from this process would be $115.4206. Thus, the dealer would realize an arbitrage profit of $0.338 per $100 of par value purchased. The actions of dealers to capture this arbitrage profit would drive up the price of this Treasury security. Only when the price reaches $115.4206—the theoretical value when the cash flows are discounted at the theoretical spot rates—will the arbitrage disappear. It is this action that forces Treasury securities to be priced based on the theoretical spot rates.

Spot Rates and the Base Interest Rate

We can now modify our earlier statement about the base interest rate for a given maturity. It is not simply the yield on the on-the-run Treasury security for that maturity, but the theoretical Treasury spot rate for that maturity. It is to the theoretical Treasury spot rates that a risk premium must be added in order to value a non-Treasury security.

Forward Rates

Thus we have seen that from the yield curve we can extrapolate the theoretical spot rates. In addition, we can extrapolate what some market participants refer to as the market's consensus of future interest rates. To see the importance of knowing the market's consensus for future interest rates, consider the following two investment alternatives for an investor who has a one-year investment horizon.

Alternative 1   Buy a one-year instrument.
Alternative 2   Buy a six-month instrument and when it matures in six months, buy another six-month instrument.

With alternative 1, the investor will realize the one-year spot rate and that rate is known with certainty. In contrast, with alternative 2, the investor will realize the six-month spot rate, but the six-month rate six months from now is unknown. Therefore, for alternative 2, the rate that will be earned over one year is not known with certainty. This is illustrated in Exhibit 5-11.

Suppose that this investor expected that six months from now the six-month rate will be higher than it is today. The investor might then feel that alternative 2 would be

EXHIBIT 5-11   Two Alternative One-Year Investments

Total Dollars at End
of One Year per $100
Investment

$$\xleftarrow{\hspace{2cm}} (1 + z_2^2) \xrightarrow{\hspace{2cm}} \qquad \$100(1 + z_2^2)$$

$$\xleftarrow{} 1 + z_1 \xrightarrow{} \xleftarrow{} 1 + f \xrightarrow{} \qquad \$100(1 + z_1)(1 + f)$$

| Today | 6 Months | 1 Year |

the better investment. However, this is not necessarily true. To understand why and to appreciate the need to understand why it is necessary to know what the market's consensus of future interest rates is, let's continue with our illustration.

The investor will be indifferent to the two alternatives if they produce the same total dollars over the one-year investment horizon. Given the one-year spot rate, there is some rate on a six-month instrument six months from now that will make the investor indifferent between the two alternatives. We denote that rate by f.

The value of f can be readily determined given the theoretical one-year spot rate and the six-month spot rate. If an investor placed $100 in a one-year instrument (alternative 1), the total dollars that will be generated at the end of one year is

$$\text{total dollars at end of year for alternative 1} = \$100(1 + z_2)^2 \qquad \textbf{(5.1)}$$

where z_2 is the one-year spot rate. (Remember that we are working in six-month periods, so the subscript 2 represents two six-month periods, or one year.)

The proceeds from investing at the six-month spot rate will generate the following total dollars at the end of six months:

$$\text{total dollars at end of six months for alternative 2} = \$100(1 + z_1) \qquad \textbf{(5.2)}$$

where z_1 is the six-month spot rate. If the amount in equation (5.2) is reinvested at the six-month rate six months from now, which we denoted f, the total dollars at the end of one year would be

$$\text{total dollars at end of year for alternative 2} = \$100(1 + z_1)(1 + f) \qquad \textbf{(5.3)}$$

The investor will be indifferent between the two alternatives if the total dollars are the same. This will occur if equation (5.1) is equal to equation (5.3). Setting these two equations equal we get the following:

$$\$100(1 + z_2)^2 = \$100(1 + z_1)(1 + f) \qquad \textbf{(5.4)}$$

Solving equation (5.4) for f, we get

$$f = \frac{(1 + z_2)^2}{1 + z_1} - 1 \qquad \textbf{(5.5)}$$

Doubling f gives the bond-equivalent yield for the six-month rate six months from now in which we are interested.

We can illustrate the use of equation (5.5) with the theoretical spot rates shown in Exhibit 5-8. From that exhibit we know that

$$\text{six-month spot rate} = 0.0525; \text{ therefore, } z_1 = 0.2625$$
$$\text{one-year spot rate} = 0.0550; \text{ therefore, } z_2 = 0.2750$$

Substituting into equation (5.5), we have

$$f = \frac{(1.02750)^2}{1.02625} - 1$$
$$= 0.028752$$

Therefore, the annual rate for f on a bond-equivalent basis is 5.75% (2.8752% $\times$ 2).

Here is how we use this rate of 5.75%. If the six-month rate six months from now is less than 5.75%, the total dollars at the end of one year would be higher by investing in the one-year instrument (alternative 1). If the six-month rate six months from now is greater than 5.75%, the total dollars at the end of one year would be higher by investing in the six-month instrument and reinvesting the proceeds six months from now at the six-month rate at the time (alternative 2). Of course, if the six-month rate six months from now is 5.75%, the two alternatives give the same total number of dollars at the end of one year.

Now that we have the rate for f that we are interested in and we know how that rate can be used, let's return to the question we posed at the outset. From Exhibit 5-8 the six-month spot rate is 5.25%. Suppose that the investor expects that six months from now, the six-month rate will be 5.60%. That is, the investor expects that the six-month rate will be higher than its current level. Should the investor select alternative 2 because the six-month rate six months from now is expected to be higher? The answer is no. As we explained earlier, if the rate is less than 5.75%, alternative 1 is the better alternative. Because this investor expects a rate of 5.60%, he should select alternative 1 despite the fact that he expects the six-month rate to be higher than it is today.

This is a somewhat surprising result for some investors. But the reason for this is that the market prices its expectations of future interest rates into the rates offered on investments with different maturities. This is why knowing the market's consensus of future interest rates is critical. The rate that we determined for f is the market's consensus for the six-month rate six months from now. A future interest rate calculated from either the spot rates or the yield curve is called a **forward rate.**

Relationship between Six-Month Forward Rates and Spot Rates   In general, the relationship between a t-period spot rate, the current six-month spot rate, and the six-month forward rates is as follows:

$$z_t = [(1 + z_1)(1 + f_1)(1 + f_2)(1 + f_3) \cdots (1 + f_{t-1})]^{1/t} - 1 \qquad \textbf{(5.6)}$$

where f_t is the six-month forward rate beginning t six-month periods from now.

To illustrate how to use equation (5.6), let's look at how the five-year (10-year) spot rate is related to the six-month forward rates. Six-month forward rates were calculated for the spot rate given in Exhibit 5-8. The values for f_1 through f_9 are as follows:

$f_1 = 0.02875$	$f_2 = 0.03140$	$f_3 = 0.03670$	$f_4 = 0.03945$
$f_5 = 0.04320$	$f_6 = 0.03605$	$f_7 = 0.04455$	$f_8 = 0.04100$
$f_9 = 0.03885$			

The six-month spot rate is 2.625% (5.25% on a bond-equivalent basis). Substituting these values into equation (5.6) we have

$$z_{10} = [(1.02875)(1.02625)(1.03140)(1.03670)(1.03945)(1.04320)$$
$$\cdot(1.03605)(1.04455)(1.04100)(1.03855)]^{1/10} - 1 = 0.036 = 3.6\%$$

Note that when doubled this value agrees with the five-year (10-period) spot rate shown in Exhibit 5-8.

Other Forward Rates   We can take this sort of analysis much further. It is not necessary to limit ourselves to six-month forward rates. The spot rates can be used to calculate the forward rate for any time in the future for any investment horizon. As examples, the following can be calculated:

- The two-year forward rate five years from now
- The six-year forward rate 10 years from now
- The seven-year forward rate three years from now

Forward Rate as a Hedgeable Rate   A natural question about forward rates is how well they do at predicting future interest rates. Studies have demonstrated that forward rates do not do a good job in predicting future interest rates.[8] Then why the big deal about understanding forward rates? As we demonstrated in our illustration of how to select between two alternative investments, the reason is that the forward rates indicate how an investor's expectations must differ from the market's consensus in order to make the correct decision.

In our illustration the six-month forward rate may not be realized. That is irrelevant. The fact is that the six-month forward rate indicated to the investor that if his expectation about the six-month rate six months from now is less than 5.75%, he would be better off with alternative 1.

For this reason, as well as others explained later, some market participants prefer not to talk about forward rates as being market consensus rates. Instead, they refer to forward rates as being **hedgeable rates.** For example, by buying the one-year security, the investor was able to hedge the six-month rate six months from now.

Determinants of the Shape of the Term Structure

If we plot the term structure—the yield to maturity, or the spot rate, at successive maturities against maturity—what is it likely to look like? Exhibit 5-12 shows three shapes that have appeared with some frequency over time. Part (a) shows an upward-sloping yield curve; that is, yield rises steadily as maturity increases. This shape is commonly referred to as a **normal** or **positive yield curve.** Part (b) shows a downward-sloping or **inverted** yield curve, where yields decline as maturity increases. Finally, part (c) shows **a flat** yield curve.

Two major theories have evolved to account for these observed shapes of the yield curve: **expectations theories** and **market segmentation theory.**

There are several forms of the **expectations theory: pure expectations theory, liquidity theory,** and **preferred habitat theory.** Expectations theories share a hypothesis about the behavior of short-term forward rates and also assume that the forward rates in current long-term bonds are closely related to the market's expectations about future short-term rates. These three theories differ, however, as to whether other factors also affect forward rates, and how. The pure expectations theory postulates that no systematic factors other than expected future short-term rates affect forward rates; the liquidity theory and the preferred habitat theory assert that there are other factors. Accordingly, the last two forms of the expectations theory are sometimes referred to as **biased expectations theories.** Exhibit 5-13 depicts the relationships among these three theories.

Pure Expectations Theory   According to the pure expectations theory, the forward rates exclusively represent the expected future rates. Thus, the entire term structure at

---

EXHIBIT 5-12 Four Shapes That Have Been Observed for the Yield Curve

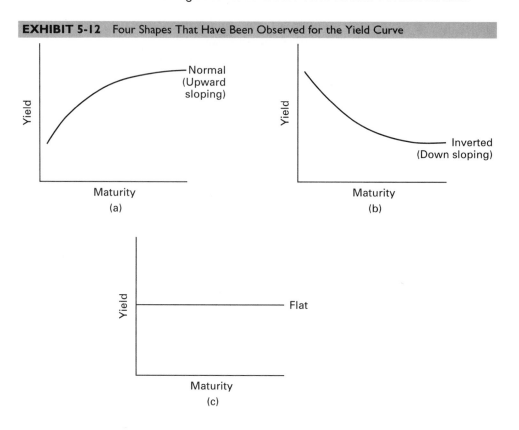

EXHIBIT 5-13 Term Structure Theories

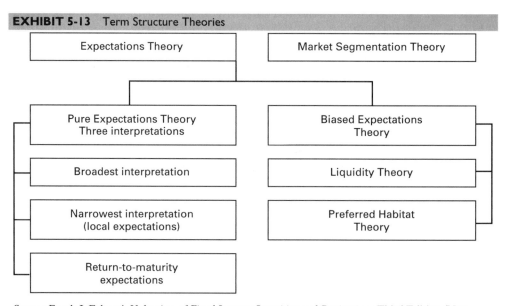

Source: Frank J. Fabozzi, *Valuation of Fixed Income Securities and Derivatives,* Third Edition (New Hope, PA: Frank J. Fabozzi Associates, 1998), p. 53.

a given time reflects the market's current expectations of the family of future short-term rates. Under this view, a rising term structure, as in part (a) of Exhibit 5-12, must indicate that the market expects short-term rates to rise throughout the relevant future. Similarly, a flat term structure reflects an expectation that future short-term rates will be mostly constant, and a falling term structure must reflect an expectation that future short rates will decline steadily.

We can illustrate this theory by considering how the expectation of a rising short-term future rate would affect the behavior of various market participants so as to result in a rising yield curve. Assume an initially flat term structure, and suppose that subsequent economic news leads market participants to expect interest rates to rise.

1. Those market participants interested in a long-term investment would not want to buy long-term bonds because they would expect the yield structure to rise sooner or later, resulting in a price decline for the bonds and a capital loss on the long-term bonds purchased. Instead, they would want to invest in short-term debt obligations until the rise in yield had occurred, permitting them to reinvest their funds at the higher yield.
2. Speculators expecting rising rates would anticipate a decline in the price of long-term bonds and therefore would want to sell any long-term bonds they own and possibly to "sell-short" some they do not now own. (Should interest rates rise as expected, the price of longer-term bonds will fall. Because the speculator sold these bonds short and can then purchase them at a lower price to cover the short sale, a profit will be earned.) Speculators will reinvest in short-term debt obligations.
3. Borrowers wishing to acquire long-term funds would be pulled toward borrowing now in the long end of the market by the expectation that borrowing at a later time would be more expensive.

All these responses would tend either to lower the net demand for, or to increase the supply of, long-maturity bonds, and all three responses would increase demand for short-term debt obligations. This would require a rise in long-term yields in relation to short-term yields; that is, these actions by investors, speculators, and borrowers would tilt the term structure upward until it is consistent with expectations of higher future interest rates. By analogous reasoning, an unexpected event leading to the expectation of lower future rates will result in the yield curve sloping down.

Unfortunately, the pure expectations theory suffers from one shortcoming, which, qualitatively, is quite serious. It neglects the risks inherent in investing in bonds and similar instruments. If forward rates were perfect predictors of future interest rates, the future prices of bonds would be known with certainty. The return over any investment period would be certain and independent of the maturity of the instrument initially acquired and of the time at which the investor needed to liquidate the instrument. However, with uncertainty about future interest rates and hence about future prices of bonds, these instruments become risky investments in the sense that the return over some investment horizon is unknown.

There are two risks that cause uncertainty about the return over some investment horizon: price risk and reinvestment risk. The first is the uncertainty about the price of the bond at the end of the investment horizon. For example, an investor who plans to invest for five years might consider the following three investment alternatives:

(1) invest in a five-year bond and hold it for five years, (2) invest in a 12-year bond and sell it at the end of five years, and (3) invest in a 30-year bond and sell it at the end of five years. The return that will be realized for the second and third alternatives is not known because the price of each long-term bond at the end of five years is not known. In the case of the 12-year bond, the price will depend on the yield on seven-year debt securities five years from now; and the price of the 30-year bond will depend on the yield on 25-year bonds five years from now. Because forward rates implied in the current term structure for a future 12-year bond and a future 25-year bond are not perfect predictors of the actual future rates, there is uncertainty about the price for both bonds five years from now. Thus, there is price risk, that is, the risk that the price of the bond will be lower than currently expected at the end of the investment horizon. As explained in Chapter 4, an important feature of price risk is that it is greater the longer the maturity of the bond.

The second risk has to do with the uncertainty about the rate at which the proceeds from a bond can be reinvested until the expected maturity date: that is, reinvestment risk. For example, an investor who plans to invest for five years might consider the following three alternative investments: (1) invest in a five-year bond and hold it for five years, (2) invest in a six-month instrument and when it matures, reinvest the proceeds in six-month instruments over the entire five-year investment horizon, and (3) invest in a two-year bond and when it matures, reinvest the proceeds in a three-year bond. The risk in the second and third alternatives is that the return over the five-year investment horizon is unknown because rates at which the proceeds can be reinvested until maturity are unknown.

There are several interpretations of the pure expectations theory that have been put forth by economists. These interpretations are not exact equivalents nor are they consistent with each other, in large part because they offer different treatments of the two risks associated with realizing a return that we have just explained.[9]

The broadest interpretation of the pure expectations theory suggests that investors expect the return for any investment horizon to be the same, regardless of the maturity strategy selected.[10] For example, consider an investor who has a five-year investment horizon. According to this theory, it makes no difference if a five-year, 12-year, or 30-year bond is purchased and held for five years because the investor expects the return from all three bonds to be the same over five years. A major criticism of this very broad interpretation of the theory is that, because of price risk associated with investing in bonds with a maturity greater than the investment horizon, the expected returns from these three very different bond investments should differ in significant ways.[11]

A second interpretation, referred to as the **local expectations theory,** a form of pure expectations theory, suggests that the returns on bonds of different maturities will be the same over a short-term investment horizon. For example, if an investor has a six-month investment horizon, buying a five-year, 10-year, or 20-year bond will pro-

---

[9]These formulations are summarized by John Cox, Jonathan Ingersoll, Jr., and Stephen Ross, "A Reexamination of Traditional Hypotheses about the Term Structure of Interest Rates," *Journal of Finance,* September 1981, pp. 769–799.

[10]F. Lutz, "The Structure of Interest Rates," *Quarterly Journal of Economics,* 1940–41, pp. 36–63.

[11]Cox, Ingersoll, and Ross, "A Reexamination of Traditional Hypotheses about the Term Structure of Interest Rates," pp. 774–775.

duce the same six-month return. It has been demonstrated that the local expectations formulation, which is narrow in scope, is the only one of the interpretations of the pure expectations theory that can be sustained in equilibrium.[12]

The third and final interpretation of the pure expectations theory suggests that the return that an investor will realize by rolling over short-term bonds to some investment horizon will be the same as holding a zero-coupon bond with a maturity that is the same as that investment horizon. (Because a zero-coupon bond has no reinvestment risk, future interest rates over the investment horizon do not affect the return.) This variant is called the **return-to-maturity expectations interpretation.** For example, let's assume that an investor has a five-year investment horizon. By buying a five-year zero-coupon bond and holding it to maturity, the investor's return is the difference between the maturity value and the price of the bond, all divided by the price of the bond. According to return-to-maturity expectations, the same return will be realized by buying a six-month instrument and rolling it over for five years. The validity of this interpretation is currently subject to considerable doubt.

Liquidity Theory   We have explained that the drawback of the pure expectations theory is that it does not consider the risks associated with investing in bonds. There is the risk in holding a long-term bond for one period, and that risk increases with the bond's maturity because maturity and price volatility are directly related.

Given this uncertainty and the reasonable consideration that investors typically do not like uncertainty, some economists and financial analysts have suggested a different theory. This theory states that investors will hold longer-term maturities if they are offered a long-term rate higher than the average of expected future rates by a risk premium that is positively related to the term to maturity.[13] Put differently, the forward rates should reflect both interest-rate expectations and a "liquidity" premium (really a risk premium), and the premium should be higher for longer maturities.

According to this theory, which is called the **liquidity theory of the term structure,** the implied forward rates will not be an unbiased estimate of the market's expectations of future interest rates because they embody a liquidity premium. Thus, an upward-sloping yield curve may reflect expectations that future interest rates either (1) will rise, or (2) will be flat or even fall, but with a liquidity premium increasing fast enough with maturity so as to produce an upward-sloping yield curve.

Preferred Habitat Theory   Another theory, the preferred habitat theory, also adopts the view that the term structure reflects the expectation of the future path of interest rates as well as a risk premium. However, the preferred habitat theory rejects the assertion that the risk premium must rise uniformly with maturity.[14] Proponents of the preferred habitat theory say that the risk premium would rise uniformly with maturity only if all investors intend to liquidate their investment at the shortest possible date while all borrowers are anxious to borrow long. This assumption can be rejected since institutions have holding periods dictated by the nature of their liabilities.

---

[12]Ibid.

[13]John R. Hicks, *Value and Capital,* 2nd ed. (London: Oxford University Press, 1946), pp. 141–145.

[14]Franco Modigliani and Richard Sutch, "Innovations in Interest Rate Policy," *American Economic Review,* May 1966, pp. 178–197.

The preferred habitat theory asserts that to the extent that the demand and supply of funds in a given maturity range do not match, some lenders and borrowers will be induced to shift to maturities showing the opposite imbalances. However, they will need to be compensated by an appropriate risk premium whose magnitude will reflect the extent of aversion to either price or reinvestment risk.

Thus, this theory proposes that the shape of the yield curve is determined by both expectations of future interest rates and a risk premium, positive or negative, to induce market participants to shift out of their preferred habitat. Clearly, according to this theory, yield curves sloping up, down, flat, or humped are all possible.

Market Segmentation Theory The market segmentation theory also recognizes that investors have preferred habitats dictated by the nature of their liabilities. This theory also proposes that the major reason for the shape of the yield curve lies in asset–liability management constraints (either regulatory or self-imposed) and/or creditors (borrowers) restricting their lending (financing) to specific maturity sectors.[15] However, the market segmentation theory differs from the preferred habitat theory in that it assumes that neither investors nor borrowers are willing to shift from one maturity sector to another to take advantage of opportunities arising from differences between expectations and forward rates. Thus, for the segmentation theory, the shape of the yield curve is determined by supply of and demand for securities within each maturity sector.

SUMMARY

In all economies, there is not just one interest rate but a structure of interest rates. The difference between the yield on any two bonds is called the yield spread. The base interest rate is the yield on a Treasury security. The yield spread between a non-Treasury security and a comparable on-the-run Treasury security is called a risk premium. The factors that affect the spread include (1) the type of issuer (e.g., agency, corporate, municipality), (2) the issuer's perceived credit worthiness as measured by the rating system of commercial rating companies, (3) the term or maturity of the instrument, (4) the embedded options in a bond issue (e.g., call, put, or conversion provisions), (5) the taxability of interest income at the federal and municipal levels, (6) the expected liquidity of the issue, and (7) the financeability of an issue.

The relationship between yield and maturity is referred to as the term structure of interest rates. The graphical depiction of the relationship between the yield on bonds of the same credit quality but different maturities is known as the yield curve.

There is a problem with using the Treasury yield curve to determine the one yield at which to discount all the cash payments of any bond. Each cash flow should be discounted at a unique interest rate that is applicable to the time period when the cash flow is to be received. Because any bond can be viewed as a package of zero-coupon instruments, its value should equal the value of all the component zero-coupon instru-

---

[15]This theory was suggested in J.M. Culbertson, "The Term Structure of Interest Rates," *Quarterly Journal of Economics,* November 1957, pp. 489–504.

ments. The rate on a zero-coupon bond is called the spot rate. The relationship between the spot rate and maturity is called the term structure of interest rates.

A default-free theoretical spot rate curve can be constructed from the yield on Treasury securities using either (1) only on-the-run Treasury issues, (2) on-the-run Treasury issues and selected off-the-run Treasury issues, (3) all Treasury coupon securities and bills, and (4) Treasury coupon strips. When the securities used are either (1) or (2) a method known as bootstrapping is used. More complex statistical techniques are used when all Treasury coupon securities and bills are used.

Under certain assumptions, the market's expectation of future interest rates can be extrapolated from the theoretical Treasury spot rate curve. The resulting forward rate is called the implied forward rate. The spot rate is related to the current six-month spot rate and the implied six-month forward rates.

Several theories have been proposed about the determination of the term structure: pure expectations theory, the biased expectations theory (the liquidity theory and preferred habitat theory), and the market segmentation theory. All the expectation theories hypothesize that the one-period forward rates represent the market's expectations of future actual rates. The pure expectations theory asserts that it is the only factor. The biased expectations theories assert that there are other factors.

Questions

1. In the September 13, 1996, *Weekly Market Update* published by Goldman, Sachs & Co., the following information was reported in various exhibits for the Treasury market as of the close of business Thursday, September 12, 1996:

On-the-Run Treasuries

Maturity	Yield (%)
3 months	5.29
6 months	5.49
1 year	5.90
2 years	6.27
3 years	6.45
5 years	6.63
10 years	6.87
30 years	7.08

Key Off-the-Run Treasuries

Issue	Yield (%)
Old 5-year	6.65%
Old 10-year	6.89
Old 30-year	7.12

a. What is the credit risk associated with a Treasury security?
b. Why is the Treasury yield considered the base interest rate?
c. What is meant by on-the-run Treasuries?
d. What is meant by off-the-run Treasuries?
e. What is the yield spread between (1) the off-the-run 10-year Treasury issue and the on-the-run 10-year Treasury issue, and (2) the off-the-run 30-year Treasury issue and the on-the-run 30-year Treasury issue?

f. What does the yield spread between the off-the-run Treasury issue and the on-the-run Treasury issue reflect?

2. In the May 29, 1992, *Weekly Market Update* published by Goldman, Sachs & Co., the following information was reported in various exhibits for certain corporate bonds as of the close of business Thursday, May 28, 1992:

Issuer	Rating	Yield (%)	Spread (basis points)	Treasury Benchmark (years)
General Electric Capital Co	Triple A	7.87	50	10
Mobil Corp	Double A	7.77	40	10
Southern Bell Tel & Teleg	Triple A	8.60	72	30
Bell Tel Co Pa	Double A	8.66	78	30
AMR Corp	Triple B	9.43	155	30

a. What does rating mean?
b. Which of the five bonds has the greatest credit risk?
c. What is meant by spread?
d. What is meant by Treasury benchmark?
e. Why do each of the spreads reported above reflect a risk premium?

3. For the corporate bond issues reported in Question 2, answer the following questions:
a. What is the yield spread between the Southern Bell Telephone and Telegraph bond issue and the Bell Telephone Company (Pennsylvania) bond issue?
b. The Southern Bell Telephone and Telegraph bond issue is not callable, but the Bell Telephone Company (Pennsylvania) bond issue is callable. What does the yield spread in part a reflect?
c. AMR Corp. is the parent company of American Airlines and is therefore classified in the transportation industry. The issue is not callable. What is the yield spread between AMR Corp. and Southern Bell Telephone and Telegraph bond issue, and what does this spread reflect?
d. What is the spread between the General Electric Capital Co. issue and the Mobil Corp. issue?
e. The Mobil Corp. issue is not callable. However, the General Electric Capital Co. issue is callable. How does this information help you in understanding the spread between these two issues?

4. The yield spread between two corporate bond issues reflects more than just differences in their credit risk. What other factors would the spread reflect?

5. In the May 29, 1992, *Weekly Market Update* published by Goldman, Sachs & Co., the following information was reported in an exhibit for high-grade, tax-exempt securities as of the close of business Thursday, May 28, 1992:

Maturity (years)	Yield (%)	Yield (%) as a Percentage of Treasury Yield
1	3.20	76.5
3	4.65	80.4
5	5.10	76.4
10	5.80	78.7
30	6.50	82.5

a. What is meant by a tax-exempt security?
b. What is meant by high-grade issue?

    c. Why is the yield on a tax-exempt security less than the yield on a Treasury security of the same maturity?

    d. What is the equivalent taxable yield?

    e. Also reported in the same issue of the Goldman, Sachs report is information on intramarket yield spreads. What are these?

6. a. What is an embedded option in a bond?

    b. Give three examples of an embedded option that might be included in a bond issue.

    c. Does an embedded option increase or decrease the risk premium relative to the base interest rate?

7. a. What is a yield curve?

    b. Why is the Treasury yield curve the one that is most closely watched by market participants?

8. What is a spot rate?

9. Explain why it is inappropriate to use one yield to discount all the cash flows of a financial asset.

10. Explain why a financial asset can be viewed as a package of zero-coupon instruments.

11. How are spot rates related to forward rates?

12. You are a financial consultant. At various times you have heard comments on interest rates from one of your clients. How would you respond to each comment?

    a. "The yield curve is upward-sloping today. This suggests that the market consensus is that interest rates are expected to increase in the future."

    b. "I can't make any sense out of today's term structure. For short-term yields (up to three years) the spot rates increase with maturity; for maturities greater than three years but less than eight years, the spot rates decline with maturity; and for maturities greater than eight years the spot rates are virtually the same for each maturity. There is simply no theory that explains a term structure with this shape."

    c. "When I want to determine the market's consensus of future interest rates, I calculate the forward rates."

13. You observe the yields of the following Treasury securities (all yields are shown on a bond-equivalent basis):

Year	Yield to Maturity (%)	Spot Rate (%)	Year	Yield to Maturity (%)	Spot Rate (%)
0.5	5.25	5.25	5.5	7.75	7.97
1.0	5.50	5.50	6.0	8.00	8.27
1.5	5.75	5.76	6.5	8.25	8.59
2.0	6.00	?	7.0	8.50	8.92
2.5	6.25	?	7.5	8.75	9.25
3.0	6.50	?	8.0	9.00	9.61
3.5	6.75	?	8.5	9.25	9.97
4.0	7.00	?	9.0	9.50	10.36
4.5	7.25	?	9.5	9.75	10.77
5.0	7.50	?	10.0	10.00	11.20

All the securities maturing from 1.5 years on are selling at par. The 0.5 and one-year securities are zero-coupon instruments.

    a. Calculate the missing spot rates.

    b. What should the price of a 6% six-year Treasury security be?

    c. What is the six-month forward rate starting in the sixth year?

14. You observe the following Treasury yields (all yields are shown on a bond-equivalent basis):

Year	Yield to Maturity (%)	Spot Rate (%)
0.5	10.00	10.00
1.0	9.75	9.75
1.5	9.50	9.48
2.0	9.25	9.22
2.5	9.00	8.95
3.0	8.75	8.68
3.5	8.50	8.41
4.0	8.25	8.14
4.5	8.00	7.86
5.0	7.75	7.58
5.5	7.50	7.30
6.0	7.25	7.02
6.5	7.00	6.74
7.0	6.75	6.46
7.5	6.50	6.18
8.0	6.25	5.90
8.5	6.00	5.62
9.0	5.75	5.35
9.5	5.50	?
10.0	5.25	?

All the securities maturing from 1.5 years on are selling at par. The 0.5 and one-year securities are zero-coupon instruments.
a. Calculate the missing spot rates.
b. What should the price of a 5% four-year Treasury security be?
15. What Treasury issues can be used to construct the theoretical spot rate curve?
16. What are the problems with using only on-the-run Treasury issues to construct the theoretical spot rate curve?
17. When all Treasury issues are used to construct the theoretical spot rate curve, what methodology is used to construct the curve?
18. a. What are the limitations of using Treasury strips to construct the theoretical spot rate curve?
   b. When Treasury strips are used to construct the curve, why are only coupon strips used?
19. What actions force a Treasury's bond price to be valued in the market at the present value of the cash flows discounted at the Treasury spot rates?
20. Explain the role that forward rates play in making investment decisions.
21. "Forward rates are poor predictors of the actual future rates that are realized. Consequently, they are of little value to an investor." Explain why you agree or disagree with this statement.
22. Bart Simpson is considering two alternative investments. The first alternative is to invest in an instrument that matures in two years. The second alternative is to invest in an instrument that matures in one year and at the end of one year, reinvest the proceeds in a one-year instrument. He believes that one-year interest rates one year from now will be higher than they are today and therefore is leaning in favor of the second alternative. What would you recommend to Bart Simpson?
23. a. What is the common hypothesis about the behavior of short-term forward rates shared by the various forms of the expectations theory?

    b. What is price risk and reinvestment risk and how do these two risks affect the pure expectations theory?

    c. Give three interpretations of the pure expectations theory.

24. a. What are the two biased expectations theories about the term structure of interest rates?

    b. What are the underlying hypotheses of these two theories?

CHAPTER 6

Treasury and Agency Securities Markets

Learning Objectives

After reading this chapter you will understand:

■ the different types of securities issued by the Treasury

■ the operation of the primary market for Treasury securities

■ the role of government dealers and government brokers

■ the secondary market for Treasury securities

■ how Treasury securities are quoted in the secondary market

■ the zero-coupon Treasury securities market

■ the difference between government-sponsored enterprises and federally related institutions

The second largest sector of the bond market (after the mortgage market) is the market for U.S. Treasury securities; the smallest sector is the U.S. government agency securities market. We discuss them together in this chapter. As explained in Chapter 11, a majority of the securities backed by a pool of mortgages are guaranteed by a federally sponsored agency of the U.S. government. These securities are classified as part of the mortgage-backed securities market rather than as U.S. government agency securities.

TREASURY SECURITIES[1]

Treasury securities are issued by the U.S. Department of the Treasury and are backed by the full faith and credit of the U.S. government. Consequently, market participants view them as having no credit risk. Interest rates on Treasury securities are the benchmark interest rates throughout the U.S. economy as well as in international capital markets. In Chapter 5 we described this important role played by Treasury securities.

---

[1]The discussion in this section draws from Chapter 1 in Frank J. Fabozzi, *Treasury Securities and Derivatives* (New Hope, PA: Frank J. Fabozzi Associates, 1997).

Two factors account for the prominent role of U.S. Treasury securities: volume (in terms of dollars outstanding) and liquidity. The Department of the Treasury is the largest single issuer of debt in the world. As of early 1997, the amount of marketable Treasury securities outstanding was $3.4 trillion, represented by less than 260 issues. By contrast, the U.S. corporate bond market, the subject of Chapter 7, is about $1.4 trillion with more than 10,000 issues; the U.S. municipal bond market, the subject of Chapter 8, is about $1.3 trillion, with more than 70,000 separate issuers and millions of individual issues. The large volume of total debt and the large size of any single issue have contributed to making the Treasury market the most active and hence the most liquid market in the world. The dealer spread between bid and ask price is considerably narrower than in other sectors of the bond market.

Treasury securities are available in book-entry form at the Federal Reserve Bank. This means that the investor receives only a receipt as evidence of ownership instead of an engraved certificate. An advantage of book entry is ease in transferring ownership of the security. Interest income from Treasury securities is subject to federal income taxes but is exempt from state and local income taxes.

Types of Treasury Securities

There are two types of Treasury securities: discount and coupon securities. Treasury coupon securities come in two forms: fixed-rate and variable-rate securities. As explained subsequently, the reference rate for variable-rate securities is the Consumer Price Index.

Treasury Bills   Discount Treasuries are issued at a discount to par value, have no coupon rate, and mature at par value. The current practice of the Treasury is to issue all securities with maturities of one year or less as discount securities. These securities are called **bills.** As discussed in the next section, Treasury bills are issued on a regular basis with initial maturities of 91 days, 182 days, and 364 days. Because of holidays, these days may be either lower or higher by one day. In addition, cash management bills of varying maturities less than 364 days are occasionally issued on a discount basis.

Treasury Notes and Bonds   All securities with initial maturities of two years or more are issued as coupon securities. Coupon securities are issued at approximately par, have a coupon rate, and mature at par value. Treasury coupon securities issued with original maturities between two and 10 years are called **notes.** Treasury coupon securities with original maturities greater than 10 years are called **bonds.** Treasury notes and bonds are referred to as **Treasury coupon securities.** Treasury coupon securities are currently issued on a regular basis with initial maturities of two years, five years, 10 years, and 30 years.[2] On quote sheets, an *n* is used to denote a Treasury note. No notation typically follows an issue to identify it as a bond.

None of the currently issued Treasury coupon securities are callable. The 30-year bonds issued through November 1984 were callable but since then have been noncallable. Outstanding callable Treasury bonds are callable five years prior to their

---

[2]The Treasury also issues Series EE and Series HH bonds. Neither of these bonds are marketable. Therefore, we exclude these Treasury debt obligations from discussions in this chapter. The Treasury issues other nonmarketable securities to state and local governments that acquire them to reinvest proceeds for advanced refundings of the debt that they issued. These nonmarketable securities that are sold to state and local governments are known as SLUGS.

maturity date and identified by two dates: when the bond is first callable and the maturity date. The call price is **par value.**

Treasury Inflation Protection Securities   On January 29, 1997, the U.S. Department of the Treasury issued for the first time Treasury securities that adjust for inflation. These securities are popularly referred to as **Treasury inflation protection securities,** or TIPS. The first issue was a 10-year note. Subsequently, the Treasury issued a five-year note in July 1997 and a 30-year bond in 1998.

Here is how TIPS work: The coupon rate on an issue is set at a fixed rate. That rate is determined via the auction process described later in the chapter. The coupon rate is called the real rate because it is the rate that the investor earns above the inflation rate. The adjustment for inflation is as follows. The principal that the Treasury Department will base both the dollar amount of the coupon payment and the maturity value will be adjusted semiannually. This is called the **inflation-adjusted principal.** For example, suppose that the coupon rate for a TIPS is 3.5% and the annual inflation rate is 3%. Suppose further that an investor purchases $100,000 of par value (principal) of this issue and that the semiannual inflation rate is 1.5%. Multiplying 1.5% by the initial principal of $100,000 gives the inflation-adjusted principal of $101,500. The dollar amount of the coupon payment for the period is found by multiplying the inflation-adjusted principal times the semiannual coupon rate. In our example, it is $1,776.25, which is found by multiplying $101,500 (the inflation-adjusted principal) by 1.75% (the semiannual coupon rate). Suppose that in the subsequent semiannual period, the inflation rate is 2%. Then the inflation-adjusted principal is found by multiplying the prior inflation-adjusted principal of $101,500 by the semiannual inflation rate of 1%. The new inflation-adjusted principal would then be $102,515. The dollar amount of the coupon payment would be the semiannual coupon rate of 1.75% multiplied by the new inflation-adjusted principal of $102,515, or $1,794.01.

As can be seen, part of the adjustment for inflation comes in the coupon payment because it is based on the inflation-adjusted principal. The majority of the compensation for inflation comes in the form of the adjustment to the principal that is paid at the maturity date. However, the U.S. government has decided to tax the adjustment each year. This feature reduces the attractiveness of TIPS as investments in accounts of tax-paying entities.

Because of the possibility of disinflation (i.e., price declines), the inflation-adjusted principal at maturity may turn out to be less than the initial par value. The Treasury has structured TIPS so that they are redeemed at the greater of the inflation-adjusted principal and the initial par value.

Now let's look at the inflation index that the government has decided to use for the inflation adjustment. The index is the nonseasonally adjusted U.S. City Average All Items Consumer Price Index for All Urban Consumers (CPI-U). The CPI is published by the U.S. government and measures the average change in the prices paid by urban consumers for a fixed basket of more than 360 categories of goods and services. The product groups (or categories) covered are housing, food and beverage, apparel and upkeep, medical care, entertainment, transportation, and "other goods and services." There are two versions of the CPI—the Urban Wage Earners and Clerical Workers Price Index (CPI-W) and the All Urban Consumers Price Index (CPI-U). The latter is a broader index; it is the one selected by the Treasury to adjust the principal for inflation and is referred to as the reference CPI. If the CPI-U is discontinued or altered by law, the U.S. Department of the Treasury will determine an alternative reference inflation index to use.

An inflation-adjusted principal must be calculated for a settlement date. The inflation-adjusted principal will be defined in terms of an index ratio, which is the ratio of the reference CPI for the settlement date to the reference CPI for the issue date. The reference CPI will be calculated with a three-month lag. For example, the reference CPI for May 1 will be the CPI-U reported in February. The U.S. Department of the Treasury will publish a daily index ratio for an issue each month.

The Treasury Auction Process

The Public Debt Act of 1942 grants the Department of the Treasury considerable discretion in deciding on the terms for a marketable security. An issue may be sold on an interest-bearing or discount basis and may be sold on a competitive basis or other basis, at whatever prices the Secretary of the Treasury may establish. However, Congress imposes a restriction on the total amount of bonds outstanding. Although Congress has granted an exemption to this restriction, there have been times when the failure of Congress to extend the exemption has resulted in the delay or cancellation of a Treasury bond offering.

Treasury securities are all issued on an auction basis. Until 1991, in the auction primary dealers and large commercial banks that were not primary dealers would submit bids for their own account and for their customers. Others who wished to participate in the auction process could only submit competitive bids for their own account, not their customers. Consequently, a broker–dealer in government securities that was not a primary dealer could not submit a competitive bid on behalf of its customers. Moreover, unlike primary dealers, nonprimary dealers had to make large cash deposits or provide guarantees to assure that they could fulfill their obligation to purchase the securities for which they bid.

In the early 1990s, the Treasury announced that it would allow qualified broker–dealers to bid for their customers at Treasury auctions. If a qualified broker–dealer establishes a payment link with the Federal Reserve System, no deposit or guaranty would be required. Moreover, the auction is no longer handled by the submission of hand-delivered sealed bids to the Federal Reserve. The new auction process is a computerized auction system that can be electronically accessed by qualified broker–dealers.

Auction Cycles   The Treasury believes its borrowing costs will be less if it provides buyers of Treasury securities stable expectations regarding new issues of its debt, so it has regularized its auction cycles. However, there have been occasional changes in its auction cycles.

The current auction cycles are as follows. There are weekly three-month and six-month bill auctions; "year-bill" auctions are every fourth week. The three-month and six-month bills are auctioned on a Monday. The year-bill is auctioned on a Thursday. If the scheduled auction date is a nonbusiness day, the Treasury typically moves the auction to the next business day.

For coupon securities, there are monthly two-year note and five-year note auctions and quarterly auctions for the 10-year note and 30-year bond (the "refunding" auction). The three current auction cycles for coupon securities are summarized as follows:

2-year and 5-year	Monthly (issued on the last day of each month)
10-year and 30-year	Quarterly (issued on the 15th of February, May, August, and November)
TIPS	Quarterly (January, April, July, and October)

On the announcement day, the Treasury announces the amount of each issue to be auctioned. It also announces the auction date, settlement date, and maturities to be issued. Due to the regularization of the auction cycles, however, these aspects of the auction are usually correctly anticipated. Occasionally an outstanding issue is "reopened" (that is, the amount of an outstanding note is increased) at an auction instead of a new issue auctioned. In recent years, the Department of the Treasury has reopened the 10-year note several times.

Determination of the Results of an Auction   The auction for Treasury securities is conducted on a competitive bid basis. Competitive bids must be submitted on a yield basis. Noncompetitive tenders may also be submitted for up to a $1 million face amount for bills and $5 million face amount for notes and bonds. Such tenders are based only on quantity, not yield.

The auction results are determined by first deducting the total noncompetitive tenders and nonpublic purchases (such as purchases by the Federal Reserve itself) from the total securities being auctioned. The remainder is the amount to be awarded to the competitive bidders. For example, in April 1996 there was an auction for the two-year Treasury note. The amount auctioned by the Treasury was $19.946 billion. The noncompetitive bids totaled $1.169 billion. This meant that there was $18.777 billion to be distributed to competitive bidders. For this auction, there were bids for $47.604 billion.

The bids are then arranged from the lowest yield bid to the highest yield bid. This is equivalent to arranging the bids from the highest price to the lowest price. Starting from the lowest yield bid, all competitive bids are accepted until the amount to be distributed to the competitive bidders is completely allocated. The highest yield accepted by the Treasury is referred to as the "stop yield," and bidders at that yield are awarded a percentage of their total tender offer. For the two-year Treasury auction in April 1996, the stop yield was 5.939%. Bidders higher in yield than the stop yield were not distributed any of the new issue.

At what yield is a winning bidder awarded the auctioned security? At the time of this writing, there are two types of auctions held to determine the yield winning bidders will pay for the auctioned security: multiple-price auctions and single-price auctions. **Single-price auctions** are held for the two-year and five-year notes and the TIPS. In a single-price auction, all bidders are awarded securities at the highest yield of accepted competitive tenders (i.e., the stop yield). For example, in the two-year auction of April 1996, the stop yield was 5.939%.

All other Treasury securities are issued using a multiple-price auction. Here the lowest-yield (i.e., highest price) bidders are awarded securities at their bid price. Successively higher-yielding bidders are awarded securities at their bid price until the total amount offered (less noncompetitive tenders) is awarded. The price paid by noncompetitive bidders is the average price of the competitive bids. For example, the auction result for an actual 364-day Treasury bill offering was as follows:

Total issue	= $9.00 billion
Less noncompetitive bids	= 0.64 billion
Less Federal Reserve	= 2.80 billion
Left for competitive bidders	= $5.56 billion

Total competitive bids might have been received as follows:

Amount (in Billions)	Bid (%)
$0.20	7.55% (lowest yield/highest price)
0.26	7.56
0.33	7.57
0.57	7.58 (average yield/average price)
0.79	7.59
0.96	7.60
1.25	7.61
1.52	7.62 (stop yield/lowest price)

The Treasury allocated bills to competitive bidders from the low-yield bid to the high-yield bid until $5.56 billion was distributed. Those who bid 7.55% to 7.61% were awarded the entire amount for which they bid. The total that was awarded to these bidders was $4.36 billion, leaving $1.2 billion to be awarded, less than the $1.52 billion bid at 7.62%. Each of the bidders at 7.62% was awarded 79% ($1.2/$1.52) of the amount they bid. For example, if a financial institution bid for $100 million at 7.62%, it would be awarded $79 million. The results of the auction would show 7.55% low, 7.58% average, and 7.62% the stop yield, with 79% awarded at the stop. Bidders higher in yield than 7.62% were shut out.

The difference between the average yield of all the bids accepted by the Treasury and the stop yield is called the **tail.** Market participants use the tail as a measure of the success of the auction. The larger the tail, the less successful the auction. This is because the average price at which accepted bidders realized securities was considerably lower than the highest price paid. The 364-day Treasury bill auction had a tail of 4 basis points—the stop yield of 7.62% less the average yield of 7.58%.

The **bid-to-cover ratio** is the ratio of the amount of bids submitted relative to the auction size.

The Secondary Market

The secondary market for Treasury securities is an over-the-counter market in which a group of U.S. government securities dealers offer continuous bid and ask prices on outstanding Treasuries. There is virtual 24-hour trading of Treasury securities. The three primary trading locations are New York, London, and Tokyo. Trading begins at 8:30 A.M. Tokyo time (7:30 P.M. New York time) and continues to about 4:00 P.M. Tokyo time (3:00 A.M. New York time).[3] Trading then goes on to London, where trading begins at 8:00 A.M. London time and then on to New York at 12:30 P.M. London time (7:30 A.M. New York time). In New York trading begins at 7:30 A.M. and continues until 5:30 P.M.[4]

The secondary market is the most liquid financial market in the world. The most recently auctioned Treasury issue for a maturity is referred to as the **on-the-run issue** or **current coupon issue.** Issues auctioned prior to the current coupon issues typically are referred to as **off-the-run issues.** They are not as liquid as an on-the-run issue for a given maturity; that is, the bid–ask spread is larger for off-the-run issues relative to an on-the-run issue.

All Treasury bills and all Treasury coupon securities issued since January 1, 1983 are available only in book-entry registered form at the Federal Reserve System. The normal settlement period for Treasury securities is the business day after the transaction day (next day settlement). By prior agreement, transactions may be made for settlement on the same day as the transaction day (same day or spot settlement), or for settlement on the fifth business day after the transaction day (corporate settlement).

When-Issued Market   Treasury securities are traded prior to the time they are issued by the Treasury. This component of the Treasury secondary market is called the **when-issued market,** or **wi market.** When-issued trading for both bills and coupon securities extends from the day the auction is announced until the issue day. All deliveries on when-issued trades occur on the issue day of the security traded.

Treasury Dealers and Interdealer Brokers   Any firm can deal in government securities, but in implementing its open market operations, the Federal Reserve will deal directly only with dealers that it designates as primary or recognized dealers. Basically, the Federal Reserve wants to be sure that firms requesting status as primary dealers have adequate capital relative to positions assumed in Treasury securities and do a reasonable amount of volume in Treasury securities. Exhibit 6-1 lists the primary dealers as of May 18, 1999. Primary dealers include diversified and specialized securities firms, money center banks, and foreign-owned financial entities.

Treasury dealers trade with the investing public and with other dealer firms. When they trade with each other, it is through intermediaries known as interdealer brokers. Dealers leave firm bids and offers with interdealer brokers who display the highest bid and lowest offer in a computer network tied to each trading desk and displayed on a monitor. The dealer responding to a bid or offer by "hitting" or "taking" pays a commission to the interdealer broker. The size and prices of these transactions are visible to all dealers at once. The fees charged are negotiable and vary depending

---

[3]These are the trading hours when New York is on daylight savings time. The main difference when New York is on standard time is that Tokyo starts an hour earlier relative to New York (6:30 P.M. New York time).

[4]Michael J. Fleming, "The Round-the-Clock Market for U.S. Treasury Securities," *Economic Policy Review,* Federal Reserve Bank of New York, July 1997, pp. 9–32.

EXHIBIT 6-1   Primary Government Securities Dealers

ABN AMRO Incorporated
Aubrey G. Lanston & Co., Inc.
Banc of America Securities LLC
Banc One Capital Markets, Inc.
Bear, Stearns & Co., Inc.
BT Alex. Brown Incorporated
Barclays Capital Inc.
Chase Securities Inc.
CIBC Oppenheimer Corp.
Credit Suisse First Boston Corporation
Daiwa Securities America Inc.
Deutsche Bank Securities Inc.
Donaldson, Lufkin & Jenrette Securities Corporation
Dresdner Kleinwort Benson North America LLC.
Fuji Securities Inc.
Goldman, Sachs & Co.
Greenwich Capital Markets, Inc.
HSBC Securities, Inc.
J. P. Morgan Securities, Inc.
Lehman Brothers Inc.
Merrill Lynch Government Securities Inc.
Morgan Stanley & Co. Incorporated
Nesbitt Burns Securities Inc.
Nomura Securities International, Inc.
Paine Webber Incorporated
Paribas Corporation
Prudential Securities Incorporated
Salomon Smith Barney Inc.
Warburg Dillon Read LLC.
Zions First National Bank

Source: Market Reports Division, Federal Reserve Bank of New York, May 18, 1999

on transaction volume. Typically the fee is as follows: for a three-month bill, 1/4 of a hundredth of a point ($12.50 per $1 million); for a six-month bill, 1/2 of a hundredth of a point ($25 per $1 million); for a one-year bill, 1/4 of a hundredth of a point ($25 per $1 million); and, for coupon securities, 1/8 of a 32nd of a point ($39.06 per $1 million).

Six interdealer brokers handle the bulk of daily trading volume. They include Cantor, Fitzgerald Securities Inc.; Garban Ltd.; Liberty Brokerage Inc.; RMJ Securities Corp.; Hilliard Farber & Co. Inc. (Treasury bills only); and Tullett and Tokyo Securities Inc. These six firms service the primary government dealers and a dozen or so other large government dealers aspiring to be primary dealers.

Dealers use interdealer brokers because of the speed and efficiency with which trades can be accomplished. With the exception of Cantor, Fitzgerald Securities Inc., interdealer brokers do not trade for their own account, and they keep the names of the dealers involved in trades confidential. The quotes provided on the government dealer screens represent prices in the "inside" or "interdealer" market. Historically, primary dealers have resisted attempts to allow the general public to have access to them. However, as a result of government pressure, GovPX Inc. was formed to provide greater public disclosure. GovPX is a joint venture of five of the six interdealer brokers and the primary dealers in which information on best bids and offers, size, and trade price are distributed via Bloomberg, Reuters, and Knight-Ridder. In addition, some dealers have developed an electronic trading system that allows trading between them and investors via Bloomberg. One example is Deutsche Morgan Grenfell's AutoBond System.

One study of trading volume in the interdealer market for the on-the-run issues found that about 43% of the trading volume takes place for the five-year and 10-year notes.[5] It has been suggested that the high volume of trading for these intermediate term notes is due to hedging activity. Specifically, it is driven by the hedging of dealer swap transactions.[6]

Price Quotes for Treasury Bills   The convention for quoting bids and offers is different for Treasury bills and Treasury coupon securities. Bids and offers on Treasury bills are quoted in a special way. Unlike bonds that pay coupon interest, Treasury bill values are quoted on a **bank discount basis,** not on a price basis. The yield on a bank discount basis is computed as follows:

$$Y_d = \frac{D}{F} \times \frac{360}{t}$$

where:

Y_d = annualized yield on a bank discount basis (expressed as a decimal)
D = dollar discount, which is equal to the difference between the face value and the price
F = face value
t = number of days remaining to maturity

As an example, a Treasury bill with 100 days to maturity, a face value of $100,000, and selling for $97,569 would be quoted at 8.75% on a bank discount basis:

$$D = \$100,000 - \$97,569$$
$$= \$2,431$$

Therefore,

$$Y_d = \frac{\$2,431}{\$100,000} \times \frac{360}{100}$$
$$= 8.75\%$$

---

[5]Fleming, "The Round-the-Clock Market for U.S. Treasury Securities."
[6]Brian Madigan and Jeff Stehm, "An Overview of the Secondary Market for U.S. Treasury Securities in London and Tokyo," Board of Governors of the Federal Reserve System, *Finance and Economics Discussion Series* 94-17, July 1994.

Given the yield on a bank discount basis, the price of a Treasury bill is found by first solving the formula for Y_d for the dollar discount (D), as follows:

$$D = Y_d \times F \times t / 360$$

The price is then

$$\text{price} = F - D$$

For the 100-day Treasury bill with a face value of $100,000, if the yield on a bank discount basis is quoted as 8.75%, D is equal to

$$D = 0.0875 \times \$100,000 \times 100/360$$
$$= \$2,431$$

Therefore,

$$\text{price} = \$100,000 - \$2,431$$
$$= \$97,569$$

The quoted yield on a bank discount basis is not a meaningful measure of the return from holding a Treasury bill, for two reasons. First, the measure is based on a face-value investment rather than on the actual dollar amount invested. Second, the yield is annualized according to a 360-day rather than a 365-day year, making it difficult to compare Treasury bill yields with Treasury notes and bonds, which pay interest on a 365-day basis. The use of 360 days for a year is a money market convention for some money market instruments, however. Despite its shortcomings as a measure of return, this is the method that dealers have adopted to quote Treasury bills. Many dealer quote sheets, and some reporting services provide two other yield measures that attempt to make the quoted yield comparable to that for a coupon bond and other money market instruments.

The measure that seeks to make the Treasury bill quote comparable to Treasury notes and bonds is called the **bond equivalent yield,** which we explained in Chapter 3. The **CD equivalent yield** (also called the **money market equivalent yield**) makes the quoted yield on a Treasury bill more comparable to yield quotations on other money market instruments that pay interest on a 360-day basis. It does this by taking into consideration the price of the Treasury bill rather than its face value. The formula for the CD equivalent yield is

$$\text{CD equivalent yield} = \frac{360Y_d}{360 - t(Y_d)}$$

As an illustration, consider once again the hypothetical 100-day Treasury bill with a face value of $100,000, selling for $97,569, and offering a yield on a bank discount basis of 8.75%. The

$$\text{CD equivalent yield} = \frac{360(0.0875)}{360 - 100(0.0875)}$$
$$= 8.97\%$$

Quotes on Treasury Coupon Securities   Treasury coupon securities are quoted in a different manner than Treasury bills. They trade on a dollar price basis in price units of 1/32 of 1% of par (par is taken to be $100). For example, a quote of 92-14 refers to a price of 92 and 14/32. On the basis of $100,000 par value, a change in price of 1% equates to $1,000, and 1/32 equates to $31.25. A plus sign following the number of 32nds means that a 64th is added to the price. For example, 92-14+ refers to a price of 92 and 29/64 or 92.453125% of par value.

On quote sheets and screens, the price quote is followed by some yield-to-maturity measure. Yield quotes can be based on the Street or the Treasury method. The difference between the two yield measures is the procedure used to discount the first coupon payment when it is not exactly six months away.[7] This occurs for two reasons. First, for certain securities, the first coupon payment may be more or less than six months away. This situation is referred to as an **odd** or **irregular** first coupon payment. When the first coupon payment is more than six months away, it is said to have a **long** first coupon. When the first coupon payment is less than six months from the date of issuance, the Treasury security is said to have a **short** first coupon.[8] The second circumstance when the first coupon payment may come in less than six months is when a security is purchased between coupon dates. From a practical point of view, once a security is issued and traded in the secondary market, investors and traders use the Street method.

When an investor purchases a bond between coupon payments, if the issuer is not in default, the investor must compensate the seller of the bond for the coupon interest earned from the time of the last coupon payment to the settlement date of the bond. This amount is called **accrued interest.**

When calculating accrued interest, three pieces of information are needed: (1) the number of days in the accrued interest period, (2) the number of days in the coupon period, and (3) the dollar amount of the coupon payment. The number of days in the accrued interest period represents the number of days over which the investor has earned interest. Given these values, the accrued interest (AI) assuming semiannual payments is calculated as follows:

---

[7]The difference between the Street and Treasury practices for computing yield is the procedure for discounting over a long first coupon period and over a fractional six-month period. The **Treasury method** (also called the **Fed method**) assumes simple interest over the period from the valuation date to the next coupon payment. The **Street method** (also called the **Securities Industry Association** or **SIA method**) assumes compound interest over the period from the valuation date to the next coupon payment. For example, suppose that the next coupon payment is X days from the valuation date (or previous coupon date) and W is the number of days between the issuance date (or previous coupon date) and the first coupon date (or next coupon date). Letting K denote the ratio of X to W, the discounting of a coupon payment, $C/2$, for both methods for a semiannual yield to maturity, y, is simple interest over period (Treasury method):

$$\frac{C/2}{1 + Ky}$$

compound interest over period (Street method):

$$\frac{C/2}{(1 + y)^K}$$

[8]The Treasury issues a security with a short first coupon when the auction date is the 15th or the end of the month but that day falls on a weekend or holiday. In such cases the Treasury issues the security on the next business day but pays the first coupon on the 15th or at the end of the month six months later. Thus, the first coupon payment is less than six months away.

$$AI = \frac{\text{Annual dollar coupon}}{2} \times \frac{\text{Days in AI period}}{\text{Days in coupon period}}$$

For example, suppose that (1) there are 50 days in the accrued interest period, (2) there are 183 days in a coupon period, and (3) the annual dollar coupon per $100 of par value is $8. Then the accrued interest is

$$AI = \frac{\$8}{2} \times \frac{50}{183} = \$1.0929$$

The calculation of the number days in the accrued interest period and the number of days in the coupon period begins with the determination of three key dates: trade date, settlement date, and date of previous coupon payment. The **trade date** is the date on which the transaction is executed. The **settlement date** is the date a transaction is completed. For Treasury securities, settlement is the next business day after the trade date. Interest accrues on a Treasury coupon security from and including the date of the previous coupon payment up to but excluding the settlement date.

The number of days in the accrued interest period and the number of days in the coupon period may not be simply the actual number of calendar days between two dates. The reason is that there is a market convention for each type of security that specifies how to determine the number of days between two dates. These conventions are called day count conventions. There are different day count conventions for Treasury securities than for government agency securities, municipal bonds, and corporate bonds.

For Treasury coupon securities, the day count convention used is to determine the actual number of days between two dates. This is referred to as the **actual/actual day count convention.** For example, consider a Treasury coupon security whose previous coupon payment was May 15. The next coupon payment would be on November 15. Suppose this Treasury security is purchased with a settlement date of September 10. First, the number of days of accrued interest is calculated. The actual number of days between May 15 (the previous coupon date) and September 10 (the settlement date) is 118 days, as follows:

May 15 to May 31	17 days
June	30 days
July	31 days
August	31 days
September 1 to September 10	9 days
	118 days

The number of days in the coupon period is the actual number of days between May 15 and November 15, which is 184 days. The number of days between the settlement date (September 10) and the next coupon date (November 15) is therefore 66 days (184 days – 118 days). Notice that in computing the number of days from May 15 to May 31, May 15 is counted in determining the number of days in the accrued interest period; however, the settlement date (September 10) is not included for purposes of determining the number of days in the accrued interest period.

STRIPPED TREASURY SECURITIES

The Treasury does not issue zero-coupon notes or bonds. However, because of the demand for zero-coupon instruments with no credit risk, the private sector has created such securities.

The profit potential for a government dealer who strips a Treasury security lies in arbitrage resulting from the mispricing of the security. We explained the reason for this in Chapter 5.

Trademark Products

In August 1982 both Merrill Lynch and Salomon Brothers created synthetic zero-coupon Treasury receipts. Merrill Lynch marketed its Treasury receipts as **Treasury Income Growth Receipts** (TIGRs), and Salomon Brothers marketed its as **Certificates of Accrual on Treasury Securities** (CATS). The procedure was to purchase Treasury bonds and deposit them in a bank custody account. The firms then issued receipts representing an ownership interest in each coupon payment on the underlying Treasury bond in the account and a receipt for ownership of the underlying Treasury bond's maturity value. This process of separating each coupon payment, as well as the principal (called the **corpus**), and selling securities against them is referred to as **coupon stripping.** Although the receipts created from the coupon stripping process are not issued by the U.S. Treasury, the underlying bond deposited in the bank custody account is a debt obligation of the U.S. Treasury, so the cash flow from the underlying security is certain.

To illustrate the process, suppose that $100 million of a Treasury bond with a 20-year maturity and a coupon rate of 10% is purchased to create zero-coupon Treasury securities. The cash flow from this Treasury bond is 40 semiannual payments of $5 million each ($100 million times 0.10 divided by 2) and the repayment of principal (corpus) of $100 million 20 years from now. This Treasury bond is deposited in a bank custody account. Receipts are then issued, each with a different single payment claim on the bank custody account. As there are 41 different payments to be made by the Treasury, a receipt representing a single payment claim on each payment is issued, which is effectively a zero-coupon bond. The amount of the maturity value for a receipt on a particular payment, whether coupon or corpus, depends on the amount of the payment to be made by the Treasury on the underlying Treasury bond. In our example, 40 coupon receipts each have a maturity value of $5 million, and one receipt, the corpus, has a maturity value of $100 million. The maturity dates for the receipts coincide with the corresponding payment dates by the Treasury.

Other investment banking firms followed suit by creating their own receipts.[9] They all are referred to as **trademark** zero-coupon Treasury securities because they are associated with particular firms.[10] Receipts of one firm were rarely traded by competing dealers, so the secondary market was not liquid for any one trademark. More-

---

[9]Lehman Brothers offered Lehman Investment Opportunities Notes (LIONs); E.F. Hutton offered Treasury Bond Receipts (TBRs); and Dean Witter Reynolds offered Easy Growth Treasury Receipts (ETRs). There were also GATORs, COUGARs, and—you'll like this one—DOGS (Dibs on Government Securities).

[10]They are also called "animal products," for obvious reasons.

over, the investor was exposed to the risk—as small as it may be—that the custodian bank may go bankrupt.

Treasury Receipts

To broaden the market and improve liquidity of these receipts, a group of primary dealers in the government market agreed to issue generic receipts that would not be associated directly with any of the participating dealers. These generic receipts are referred to as **Treasury receipts** (TRs). Rather than representing a share of the trust as the trademarks do, TRs represent ownership of a Treasury security. A common problem with both trademark and generic receipts was that settlement required physical delivery, which is often cumbersome and inefficient.

Strips

In February 1985, the Treasury announced its **Separate Trading of Registered Interest and Principal of Securities (STRIPS)** program to facilitate the stripping of designated Treasury securities. Specifically, all new Treasury bonds and all new Treasury notes with maturities of 10 years and longer are eligible. The zero-coupon Treasury securities created under the STRIPS program are direct obligations of the U.S. government. Moreover, the securities clear through the Federal Reserve's book-entry system.[11] Creation of the STRIPS program ended the origination of trademarks and generic receipts.

There may be confusion when a market participant refers to a "stripped Treasury." Today, a stripped Treasury typically means a STRIPS product. However, because there are trademark products and TRs still traded in the market, an investor should clarify what product is the subject of the discussion. In the chapters that follow, we will refer to stripped Treasury securities as simply "strips."

On dealer quote sheets and vendor screens STRIPS are identified by whether the cash flow is created from the coupon (denoted ci), principal from a Treasury bond (denoted bp), or principal from a Treasury note (denoted np). The reason why a distinction is made between the STRIPS created from the coupon and the principal has to do with the tax treatment by non–U.S. entities, as discussed in the next section.

Tax Treatment

A disadvantage of a taxable entity investing in stripped Treasury securities is that accrued interest is taxed each year even though interest is not paid. Thus, these instruments are negative cash flow instruments until the maturity date. They have negative cash flow because tax payments on interest earned but not received in cash must be made.

One reason for distinguishing between STRIPS created from the principal and interest is that some foreign buyers have a preference for the STRIPS created from the principal. This preference is due to the tax treatment of the interest in their home country. The tax laws of some countries treat the interest as a capital gain, which

---

[11]In 1987, the Treasury permitted the conversion of stripped coupons into book-entry form under its **Coupons Under Book-Entry Safekeeping (CUBES)** program.

receives a preferential tax treatment (i.e., lower tax rate) compared with ordinary interest income if the stripped security was created from the principal.

Reconstituting a Bond

In our illustration of coupon stripping in Chapter 5, the price of the Treasury security is less than its theoretical price. Suppose, instead, that the Treasury security is greater than its theoretical price. In such cases, investors can purchase in the market a package of zero-coupon Treasury securities such that the cash flow of the package of securities replicates the cash flow of the mispriced coupon Treasury security. By doing so, the investor will realize a yield higher than the yield on the coupon Treasury security. This process is called **reconstitution.**

It is the process of coupon stripping and reconstituting that will prevent the actual spot rate curve observed on zero-coupon Treasuries from departing significantly from the theoretical spot rate curve. As more stripping and reconstituting occurs, forces of demand and supply will cause rates to return to their theoretical spot rate levels. This is, in fact, what has happened in the Treasury market and in other government bond markets.

FEDERAL AGENCY SECURITIES[12]

Federal agency securities can be classified by the type of issuer, those issued by federally related institutions and those issued by government sponsored enterprises. Those federal agencies that provide credit for the housing market issue two types of securities: debentures and mortgage-backed securities. Our focus here is on the former securities. We discuss mortgage-backed securities in Chapters 11 and 12.

Federally Related Institutions

Federally related institutions are arms of the federal government and generally do not issue securities directly in the marketplace. Federally related institutions include the Export-Import Bank of the United States, Tennessee Valley Authority (TVA), Commodity Credit Corporation, Farmers Housing Administration, General Services Administration, Government National Mortgage Association, Maritime Administration, the Private Export Funding Corporation, the Rural Electrification Administration, Rural Telephone Bank, Small Business Administration, and Washington Metropolitan Area Transit Authority.

All federally related institutions are exempt from SEC registration. With the exception of securities of the TVA and the Private Export Funding Corporation, the securities are backed by the full faith and credit of the United States government. In recent years, the major issuer of these securities has been the TVA; most federally related institutions do not issue securities.

Interest income on securities issued by federally related institutions is exempt from state and local income taxes.

---

[12]The discussion in this section is adapted from Chapter 4 in Frank J. Fabozzi, *Fixed Income Securities* (New Hope, PA: Frank J. Fabozzi Associates, 1997).

Government Sponsored Enterprises

Government sponsored enterprises (GSEs) are privately owned, publicly chartered entities. They were created by Congress to reduce the cost of capital for certain borrowing sectors of the economy deemed to be important enough to warrant assistance. The entities in these privileged sectors include farmers, homeowners, and students. The enabling legislation dealing with a GSE is amended periodically. Government sponsored enterprises issue securities directly in the marketplace. The market for these securities, though smaller than that of Treasury securities, has in recent years become an active and important sector of the bond market. Government sponsored enterprises are also issuers of global bonds.

Today there are five GSEs that issue debentures: **Federal Farm Credit Bank System, Federal Home Loan Bank System (FHLBS), Federal National Mortgage Association, Federal Home Loan Mortgage Corporation,** and **Student Loan Marketing Association.** The **Federal Farm Credit Bank System (FFCBS)** is responsible for the credit market in the agricultural sector of the economy. The Federal Home Loan Bank, Federal Home Loan Mortgage Corporation, and Federal National Mortgage Association are responsible for providing credit to the housing sectors. The Student Loan Marketing Association provides funds to support higher education.

In general, GSEs issue two types of debentures: discount notes and bonds. Discount notes are short-term obligations, with maturities ranging from overnight to 360 days. As with Treasury bills, no coupon interest is paid. Instead, the investor earns interest by buying the note at a discount. Bonds have maturities greater than two years. There are issues with bullet maturities and those with call provisions—long and short calls. GSEs also issue structured notes.

In the following sections we briefly describe the five GSEs that currently issue securities and the three GSEs that have outstanding issues.

Federal Home Loan Bank System   The FHLBS consists of the 12 district Federal Home Loan Banks and their member banks. The Federal Home Loan Bank Board was originally responsible for regulating all federally chartered savings and loan associations and savings banks, as well as state-chartered institutions insured by the Federal Savings and Loan Insurance Corporation. These responsibilities have been curtailed since 1989. The major source of debt funding for the Federal Home Loan Banks is the issuance of consolidated debt obligations, which are joint and several obligations of the 12 Federal Home Loan Banks. As noted earlier, FHLBS is the largest issuer of federal agency debt. Consolidated FHLBS discount notes are issued on a daily basis. Six or seven deals are issued by the FHLBS in a typical day. Bonds of this GSE are issued monthly.

Financing Corporation   The deposits of savings and loans were once insured by the Federal Savings and Loan Insurance Corporation (FSLIC), overseen by the Federal Home Loan Bank Board. When difficulties encountered in the savings and loan industry raised concerns about FSLIC's ability to meet its responsibility to insure deposits, Congress passed the Competitive Equality and Banking Act in 1987. This legislation included provisions to recapitalize FSLIC and establish a new government sponsored agency, the Financing Corporation (FICO), to issue debt in order to provide funding for FICO. FICO issued its first bonds in September 1987—a 30-year noncallable $500 million issue. The principal of these bonds is backed by zero-coupon

Treasury securities. The legislation permitted FICO to issue up to $10.825 billion but not more than $3.75 billion in any one year. FICO was legislated to be dismantled in 2026, or after all securities have matured, whichever came sooner.

Resolution Trust Corporation   The 1987 legislation that created FICO did not go far enough to resolve the problems facing the beleaguered savings and loan industry. In 1989, Congress passed more comprehensive legislation, the Financial Institutions Reform, Recovery and Enforcement Act (FIRREA). This legislation has three key elements. First, it transfers supervision of savings and loans to a newly created Office of Thrift Supervision. Second, it shifts the FSLIC insurance function to a Savings Association Insurance Fund, placed under the supervision of the Federal Deposit Insurance Corporation. Third, it establishes the Resolution Trust Corporation (RTC) as a GSE charged with the responsibility of liquidating or bailing out insolvent savings and loan institutions. The RTC obtained its funding from the Resolution Funding Corporation (REFCORP), which was authorized to issue up to $40 billion of long-term bonds. The principal of this debt is backed by zero-coupon Treasury bonds. REFCORP has issued both 30-year and 40-year bonds.

Federal National Mortgage Association   The residential mortgage debt market in the United States represents the largest debt market in the world. The problem the U.S. government faces is to attract investors to invest in residential mortgages. At one time, savings and loan associations were the primary investors, especially with special inducements the government provided. But because there was not an active market where these debt instruments traded, they were illiquid and financial institutions that invested in them were exposed to liquidity risk. In the 1930s, Congress figured out a way to handle this problem. It created a federally related institution, the Federal National Mortgage Association, popularly known as "Fannie Mae," which was charged with the responsibility to create a liquid secondary market for mortgages. Fannie Mae was to accomplish this objective by buying and selling mortgages. Fannie Mae needed a funding source in case it faced a liquidity squeeze. Congress provided this by giving Fannie Mae a credit line with the Treasury. Despite the presence of Fannie Mae, the secondary mortgage market did not develop to any significant extent. During periods of tight money, Fannie Mae could do little to mitigate a housing crisis. In 1968, Congress divided Fannie Mae into two entities: (1) the current Fannie Mae and (2) the Government National Mortgage Association (popularly known as "Ginnie Mae"). Ginnie Mae's function is to use the "full faith and credit of the U.S. government" to support the market for government insured mortgages. (The mortgage-backed securities guaranteed by Ginnie Mae will be discussed in Chapter 11.) Although it started out as a federally related institution, today Fannie Mae is a GSE.

Fannie Mae funds its portfolio purchase of mortgages through the sale of securities. It issues discount notes on the first Monday of each month. The discount notes have a maturity at issuance of six months, one year, or two years. Each month Fannie Mae issues debentures with a maturity typically less than 10 years through a selling group composed of more than 50 members. These are called notes. However, sometimes notes with a maturity of up to 30 years are issued. Typically, the issues are callable. The notes are often structured notes designed at the time based on investor demand.

Federal Home Loan Mortgage Corporation   In 1970—two years after Congress divided Fannie Mae into the now current Fannie Mae and Ginnie Mae—Congress created the Federal Home Loan Mortgage Corporation. The reason for the creation of Freddie Mac, the nickname for this GSE, was to provide support for conventional mortgages. These are mortgages not guaranteed by the U.S. government. As with Fannie Mae, Freddie Mac borrows funds to finance its purchase of mortgages. Typically, the debentures issued are long-term callable securities.

Federal Farm Credit Bank System   The purpose of the FFCBS is to facilitate adequate, dependable credit and related services to the agricultural sector of the economy. The Farm Credit System consists of three entities: the Federal Land Banks, Federal Intermediate Credit Banks, and Banks for Cooperatives. Before 1979, each entity issued securities in its own name. Starting in 1979, they began to issue debt on a consolidated basis as "joint and several obligations" of the FFCBS. All financing for the FFCBS is arranged through the Federal Farm Credit Banks Funding Corporation, which issues consolidated obligations.

FFCBS issues two types of short-term notes daily: discount notes and coupon notes. The discount notes are issued with a maturity of three months and six months. The coupon notes are issued with a maturity of one year and pay interest semiannually. There are debentures issued quarterly with maturities up to 10 years that pay interest semiannually. There are floating-rate debentures with various reference rates.

Farm Credit Financial Assistance Corporation   In the 1980s, the FFCBS faced financial difficulties because of defaults on loans made to farmers. The defaults were caused largely by high interest rates in the late 1970s and early 1980s and by depressed prices on agricultural products. To recapitalize the Federal Farm Credit Bank System, Congress created the Farm Credit Financial Assistance Corporation (FACO) in 1987. This federally sponsored agency was authorized to issue debt to assist the FFCBS. FACO bonds, unlike the debt of other GSEs, are backed by the Treasury.

Student Loan Marketing Association   Popularly known as "Sallie Mae," the Student Loan Marketing Association provides liquidity for private lenders participating in the Federal Guaranteed Student Loan Program, the Health Education Assistance Loan Program, and the PLUS loan program (a program that provides loans to the parents of undergraduate students).

Sallie Mae issues monthly floating-rate notes that mature in six months. In addition, it issues longer-term floating-rate bonds. In 1995, Sallie Mae began issuing floating-rate notes backed by student loans. These securities are called asset-backed securities. (In Chapter 13, we describe the general characteristics of asset-backed securities.)

Credit Risk

With the exception of the securities issued by the Farm Credit Financial Assistance Corporation, GSE securities are not backed by the full faith and credit of the U.S. government, as is the case with Treasury securities. Consequently, investors purchasing GSEs are exposed to credit risk. The yield spread between these securities and Treasury securities of comparable maturity reflects differences in perceived credit risk and liquidity. The spread attributable to credit risk reflects financial problems faced by the issuing GSE and the likelihood that the federal government will allow the GSE to default on its outstanding obligations.

Two examples will illustrate this point. In late 1981 and early 1982, the net income of the Federal National Mortgage Association weakened, causing analysts to report that the securities of this GSE carried greater credit risk than previously perceived. As a result, the yield spread over Treasuries on its debt rose from 91 basis points (on average) in 1981 to as high as 150 basis points. In subsequent years, the Federal National Mortgage Association's net income improved, and its yield spread to Treasuries narrowed. As another example, in 1985 the yield spread on securities of the Farm Credit Bank System rose substantially above those on comparable-maturity Treasuries because of the agency's financial difficulties. The spread between 1985 and 1986 varied with the prospects of Congressional approval of a bailout measure for the system.

Secondary Market

The price quotation convention for GSE securities is the same as that for Treasury securities. That is, the bid and ask price quotations are expressed as a percentage of par plus fractional 32nds of a point. There are some GSE issues that trade with almost the same liquidity as Treasury securities. Other issues that are supported only by a few dealers trade much like off-the-run corporate bonds.

SUMMARY

The U.S. Treasury market is closely watched by all participants in the financial markets because interest rates on Treasury securities are the benchmark interest rates throughout the world. The Treasury issues three types of securities: bills, notes, and bonds. Treasury bills have a maturity of one year or less, are sold at a discount from par, and do not make periodic interest payments. Treasury notes and bonds are coupon securities. The Treasury issues coupon securities whose coupon payment is tied to the Consumer Price Index. These securities are popularly referred to as Treasury Inflation Protection Securities, or TIPS.

Treasury securities are issued on a competitive bid auction basis, according to a regular auction cycle. The auction process relies on the participation of the primary government securities dealers, with which the Federal Reserve deals directly. The secondary market for Treasury securities is an over-the-counter market, where dealers trade with the general investing public and with other dealers. In the secondary market, Treasury bills are quoted on a bank discount basis; Treasury coupon securities are quoted on a price basis.

Although the Treasury does not issue zero-coupon Treasury securities, government dealers have created these instruments synthetically by a process called coupon stripping. Zero-coupon Treasury securities include trademarks, Treasury receipts, and STRIPS. Creation of the first two types of zero-coupon Treasury securities has ceased; STRIPS now dominate the market. The motivation for government dealers to create these securities is the arbitrage opportunities available.

Government-sponsored enterprises securities and federally related institution securities constitute the federal agency securities market. The former are privately owned, publicly chartered entities created to reduce the cost of borrowing for certain sectors of the economy. Federally related institutions are arms of the federal government whose debt is generally guaranteed by the U.S. government.

Questions

1. What are the differences among a Treasury bill, Treasury note, and Treasury bond?
2. The following questions are about the Treasury Inflation Protected Security (TIPS).
   a. What is meant by the "real rate."
   b. What is meant by the "inflation-adjusted principal."
   c. Suppose that the coupon rate for a TIPS is 3%. Suppose further that an investor purchases $10,000 of par value (initial principal) of this issue today and that the semiannual inflation rate is 1%. (i) What is the dollar coupon interest that will be paid in cash at the end of the first six months? (ii) What is the inflation-adjusted principal at the end of six months?
   d. Suppose that an investor buys a five-year TIPS and there is deflation for the entire period. What is the principal that will be paid by the Department of the Treasury at the maturity date?
   e. How is interest income on TIPS treated at the federal income tax level?
3. What is the when-issued market?
4. Why do government dealers use government brokers?
5. Suppose that the price of a Treasury bill with 90 days to maturity and a $1 million face value is $980,000. What is the yield on a bank discount basis?
6. The bid and ask yields for a Treasury bill were quoted by a dealer as 5.91% and 5.89%, respectively. Shouldn't the bid yield be less than the ask yield, because the bid yield indicates how much the dealer is willing to pay and the ask yield is what the dealer is willing to sell the Treasury bill for?
7. Calculate the dollar price for the following Treasury coupon securities:

	Price Quoted	*Par*
(1)	95–4	$ 100,000
(2)	87–16	1,000,000
(3)	102–10	10,000,000
(4)	116–30	10,000
(5)	102–4+	100,000

8. a. In a Treasury auction, how is the price that a competitive bidder must pay determined in a single-price auction format?
   b. In a Treasury auction, how is the price that a noncompetitive bidder must pay determined in a single-price auction format?
9. a. In a Treasury auction, how is the price that a competitive bidder must pay determined in a multiple-price auction format?
   b. In a Treasury auction, how is the price that a noncompetitive bidder must pay determined in a multiple-price auction format?
10. Suppose that a Treasury coupon security is purchased on April 8 and that the last coupon payment was on February 15. Assume that the year in which this security is purchased is not a leap year.
   a. How many days in the accrued interest period?
   b. If the coupon rate for this Treasury security is 7% and the par value of the issue purchased is $1 million, what is the accrued interest?

11. The following is from the March 1991 monthly report published by Blackstone Financial Management:

    The Treasury also brought $34.5 billion in new securities to the market in February as part of the normal quarterly refunding. . . . the auctions went slightly better than expected given the significant size and the uncertainties surrounding the duration of the war. The 3-year was issued at a 6.98% average yield, the 10-year at a 7.85% average yield, and the 30-year at a 7.98% average yield. All bids were accepted at the average yield or better (i.e., with no tail), indicating ample demand for the securities.

    What is the average yield and the tail? Why does the absence of a tail indicate ample demand for the Treasuries auctioned?

12. The following questions relate to stripped Treasury securities:
    a. What are the differences among a STRIP, a trademark Treasury zero-coupon security, and a Treasury receipt?
    b. What is the only type of stripped Treasury security issued today?
    c. Why is a stripped Treasury security identified by whether it is created from the coupon or the principal?
    d. What is the federal income tax treatment of accrued interest income on stripped Treasury securities?

13. What is the difference between a government sponsored enterprise and a federally related institution?

14. Why is there credit risk for certain issuers of federal agency securities?

CHAPTER 7

Corporate Debt Instruments

Learning Objectives

After reading this chapter you will understand:

- the key provisions of a corporate bond issue

- provisions for paying off a bond issue prior to the stated maturity date

- corporate bond ratings and what investment-grade bonds and non-investment-grade (or high yield) bonds are

- event risk

- bond structures that have been used in the high-yield bond market

- the general characteristics of the secondary market for corporate bonds

- empirical evidence concerning the historical risk and return pattern in the corporate bond market

- a medium-term note

- the difference between the primary offering of a medium-term note and a corporate bond

- what a structured medium-term note is and the flexibility it affords issuers

- what commercial paper is and why it is issued

- the credit ratings of commercial paper

- the difference between directly placed and dealer-placed commercial paper

- the basic provisions in the Bankruptcy Reform Act of 1978

- the difference between a liquidation and a reorganization

- the principle of absolute priority in a bankruptcy and the different hypotheses as to why there is a violation of absolute priority

Corporate debt instruments are financial obligations of a corporation that have priority over its common stock and preferred stock in the case of bankruptcy. Corporate debt instruments can be classified as follows: (1) corporate bonds, (2) medium-term notes, (3) commercial paper, and (4) asset-backed securities.

In this chapter we discuss these instruments. We postpone the discussion of convertible corporate bonds to Chapter 16 and asset-backed securities until Chapter 13.

CORPORATE BONDS

Corporate bonds are classified by the type of issuer. The four general classifications used by bond information services are: (1) utilities, (2) transportations, (3) industrials, and (4) banks and finance companies. Finer breakdowns are often made to create more homogeneous groupings. For example, utilities are subdivided into electric power companies, gas distribution companies, water companies, and communication companies. Transportations are divided further into airlines, railroads, and trucking companies. Industrials are the catchall class and the most heterogeneous of the groupings with respect to investment characteristics. Industrials include all kinds of manufacturing, merchandising, and service companies.

Features of a Corporate Bond Issue

The essential features of a corporate bond are relatively simple. The corporate issuer promises to pay a specified percentage of par value on designated dates (the coupon payments) and to repay par or principal value of the bond at maturity. Failure to pay either the principal or interest when due constitutes legal default, and investors can go to court to enforce the contract. Bondholders, as creditors, have a prior legal claim over common and preferred stockholders as to both income and assets of the corporation for the principal and interest due them.

The promises of corporate bond issuers and the rights of investors who buy them are set forth in great detail in contracts called **bond indentures.** If bondholders were handed the complete indenture, they would have trouble understanding the language and even greater difficulty in determining from time to time whether the corporate issuer were keeping all the promises made. These problems are solved for the most part by bringing in a corporate trustee as a third party to the contract. The indenture is made out to the corporate trustee as a representative of the interests of bondholders; that is, a trustee acts in a fiduciary capacity for investors who own the bond issue. A corporate trustee is a bond or trust company with a corporate trust department whose officers are experts in performing the functions of a trustee.

Most corporate bonds are **term bonds;** that is, they run for a term of years, then become due and payable. Any amount of the liability that has not been paid off prior to maturity must be paid off at that time. The term may be long or short. Generally, obligations due in under 10 years from the date of issue are called **notes.** (However, the word *notes* has been used to describe particular types of securities that can have maturities considerably longer than 10 years.) Most corporate borrowings take the form of **bonds** due in 20 to 30 years. Term bonds may be retired by payment at final maturity or retired prior to maturity if provided for in the indenture. Some corporate bond issues are arranged so that specified principal amounts become due on specified dates. Such issues are called **serial bonds.** Equipment trust certificates (discussed later) are structured as serial bonds.

Security for Bonds   Either real property (using a mortgage) or personal property may be pledged to offer security beyond the issuer's general credit standing. A mortgage bond grants the bondholders a lien against the pledged assets, that is, a legal right to sell the mortgaged property to satisfy unpaid obligations to the bondholders. In practice, foreclosure and sale of mortgaged property is unusual. Usually in the case of default, a financial reorganization of the issuer provides for settlement of the debt to bondholders. The mortgage lien is important, though, because it gives the mortgage bondholders a strong bargaining position relative to other creditors in determining the terms of any reorganization.

Some companies do not own fixed assets or other real property and so have nothing on which they can give a mortgage lien to secure bondholders. Instead, they own securities of other companies; they are holding companies, and the other companies are subsidiaries. To satisfy the desire of bondholders for security, they will pledge stocks, notes, bonds or whatever other kind of obligations they own. These assets are termed **collateral** (or personal property); bonds secured by such assets are called **collateral trust bonds.**

Many years ago the railway companies developed a way of financing purchase of cars and locomotives **(rolling stock)** in a way that enabled them to borrow at just about the lowest rates in the corporate bond market. Railway rolling stock has for a long time been seen as excellent security for debt. The equipment is sufficiently standardized that it can be used by one railroad as well as another. It can be readily moved from the tracks of one railroad to another's, and there is generally a good market for lease or sale of cars and locomotives. The railroads have taken advantage of these characteristics of rolling stock by developing a legal arrangement for giving investors a legal claim on it that is different from, and generally superior to, a mortgage lien. The legal arrangement vests legal title to railway equipment in a trustee.

The procedure works like this. A railway company orders some cars and locomotives from a manufacturer. The manufacturer then transfers legal title to the equipment to a trustee, who in turn leases it to the railroad, and at the same time sells equipment trust certificates to obtain the funds to pay the manufacturer. The trustee collects lease payments from the railroad and uses the money to pay interest and principal on the certificates. The principal is therefore paid off on specified dates. Although the railway companies developed the equipment trust arrangement, it has been used since by companies engaged in providing other kinds of transportation. For example, trucking companies finance the purchase of huge fleets of trucks in the same manner; airlines use this kind of financing to purchase transport planes; and international oil companies use it to buy huge tankers.

Debenture bonds are debt securities not secured by a specific pledge of property, but that does not mean that they have no claim on property of issuers or on their earnings. Debenture bondholders have the claim of general creditors on all assets of the issuer not pledged specifically to secure other debt. And they have a claim on pledged assets even to the extent that these assets have more value than necessary to satisfy secured creditors. Subordinated debenture bonds rank after secured debt, after debenture bonds, and often after some general creditors in their claim on assets and earnings.

The type of security issued determines the cost to the corporation. For a given corporation, mortgage bonds will cost less than debenture bonds, and debenture bonds will cost less than subordinated debenture bonds.

Guaranteed bonds are obligations guaranteed by another entity. The safety of a guaranteed bond depends upon the guarantor's financial capability as well as the financial capability of the issuer. The terms of the guarantee may call for the guarantor to guarantee the payment of interest and/or repayment of the principal.

It is important to recognize that the superior legal status of any debt security will not prevent bondholders from suffering financial loss when the issuer's ability to generate cash flow adequate to pay its obligations is seriously eroded.

Provisions for Paying Off Bonds   Most corporate issues have a call provision allowing the issuer an option to buy back all or part of the issue prior to the stated maturity date. Some issues specify that the issuer must retire a predetermined amount of the issue periodically. Various types of corporate call provisions are discussed in the following sections.[1]

(1) Call and refund provisions.   An important question in negotiating the terms of a new bond issue is whether the issuer shall have the right to redeem the entire amount of bonds outstanding on a date before maturity. Issuers generally want this right because they recognize that at some time in the future the general level of interest rates may fall sufficiently below the issue's coupon rate that redeeming the issue and replacing it with another issue with a lower coupon rate would be attractive. This right is a disadvantage to the bondholder.

A company wanting to retire a debt issue prior to maturity usually must pay a premium over the par value for the privilege. The initial call premium on long-term debt traditionally has been the interest coupon plus par or the initial reoffering price (in some cases it is the higher of the two). Thus a 30-year bond initially priced at 100 with a 10% coupon may have a call price of 110% for the first year, scaled down in relatively equal amounts to par starting in year 21 to maturity.

Anheuser-Busch Companies, Inc. offered $200 million of 10% debentures in mid-1988 at 100% of par; the maturity is July 1, 2018. Exhibit 7-1 shows the redemption schedule for the bonds. Note that the initial call price is equal to the coupon plus the reoffering price. Subsequent redemption prices are in decrements of 50 basis points (0.5 of 1%) to par starting July 1, 2008. Some issues only show the call premium, such as 8.583%, 8.154%, 7.725%, instead of the whole price.

The prices shown in Exhibit 7-1 are called the **regular** or **general redemption prices.** There are also **special redemption prices** for debt redeemed through the sinking fund (discussed next) and through other provisions, and the proceeds from the confiscation of property through the right of eminent domain. The special redemption price is usually par, but in the case of some utility issues it initially may be the public offering price, which is amortized down to par (if a premium) over the life of the bonds.

The Anheuser-Busch debentures are currently callable; that is, the company may redeem the bonds at any time at the general redemption prices cited previously sub-

---

[1]For a more detailed explanation of corporate call provisions, see Richard S. Wilson and Frank J. Fabozzi, *Corporate Bonds: Structures and Analysis* (Buckingham, PA: Frank J. Fabozzi Associates, 1995).

EXHIBIT 7-1   Redemption Schedule for Anheuser-Busch Companies, Inc.
10% Sinking Fund Debentures Due July 1, 2018

Redemption

The Debentures will be redeemable at the option of the Company at any time in whole or in part, upon not fewer than 30 nor more than 60 days' notice, at the following redemption prices (which are expressed in percentages of principal amount) in each case together with accrued interest to the date fixed for redemption:

If redeemed during the 12 months beginning July 1,

1988	110.0%
1989	109.5%
1990	109.0%
1991	108.5%
1992	108.0%
1993	107.5%
1994	107.0%
1995	106.5%
1996	106.0%
1997	105.5%
1998	105.0%
1999	104.5%
2000	104.0%
2001	103.5%
2002	103.0%
2003	102.5%
2004	102.0%
2005	101.5%
2006	101.0%
2007	100.5%
2008 and thereafter	100.0%

Provided, however, that prior to July 1, 1998, the Company may not redeem any of the Debentures pursuant to such option, directly or indirectly, from or in anticipation of the proceeds of the issuance of any indebtedness for money borrowed having an interest cost of less than 10% per annum.

Source: Prospectus dated June 23, 1988.

ject only to the 10-year prohibition against lower-cost refunding. Other issues may not be called for any reason for a certain number of years.

If a debt does not have any protection against early call, it is said to be a currently callable issue, as is the Anheuser issue. But most new bond issues, even if currently callable, usually have some restrictions against certain types of early redemption. The most common restriction is that prohibiting the refunding of the bonds for a certain number of years. Bonds that are noncallable for the issue's life are more common than bonds that are nonrefundable for life but otherwise callable.

Many investors are confused by the terms **noncallable** and **nonrefundable.** Hess and Winn said: "The terms **noncallable** and **nonrefundable** are often used rather loosely as interchangeable entities, although from a technical standpoint they have different meanings."[2] Call protection is much more absolute than refunding protection. Although there may be certain exceptions to absolute or complete call protection in some cases (such as sinking funds and the redemption of debt under certain mandatory provisions), it still provides greater assurance against premature and unwanted redemption than does refunding protection. Refunding prohibition merely prevents redemption only from certain sources, namely the proceeds of other debt issues sold at a lower cost of money. The holder is protected only if interest rates decline, and the borrower can obtain lower-cost money to pay off the debt. The Anheuser bonds cannot be redeemed prior to July 2, 1998, if the company raises the funds from a new issue with an interest cost lower than 10%. There is nothing to prevent the company from calling the bonds within the 10-year refunding protected period from debt sold at a higher rate (although it normally wouldn't do so) or from funds obtained through other means.

Refunding means to replace an old bond issue with a new one, often at a lower interest cost. In the *Florida Power & Light* case the judge said:

> The terms *redemption* and *refunding* are not synonymous. A *redemption* is
> simply a call of bonds. A *refunding* occurs when the issuer sells bonds in
> order to use the proceeds to redeem an earlier series of bonds. The refunding
> bond issue being sold is closely linked to the one being redeemed by contrac-
> tual language and proximity in time so that the proceeds will be available to
> pay for the redemption. Otherwise, the issuer would be taking an inordinate
> risk that market conditions would change between the redemption of the ear-
> lier issue and the sale of the later issue.[3]

Beginning in early 1986 a number of industrial companies issued long-term debt with extended call protection, not refunding protection. A number are noncallable for the issue's life, such as Dow Chemical Company's 8⅝% debentures due in 2006 and Atlantic Richfield's 9⅞% debentures due in 2016. The prospectuses for both issues expressly prohibit redemption prior to maturity. In Wall Street, these noncallable-for-life issues are referred to as **bullet bonds.** Other issues carry 15 years of call protection, such as Eastman Kodak's 9.95% Debentures due July 1, 2018, and not callable prior to July 1, 2003.

Bonds can be called in whole (the entire issue) or in part (only a portion). When less than the entire issue is called, the specific bonds to be called are selected randomly or on a pro rata basis. When bonds are selected randomly, the serial number of the certificates is published in the *Wall Street Journal* and major metropolitan dailies.

(2) Sinking fund provision. Corporate bond indentures may require the issuer to retire a specified portion of an issue each year. This is referred to as a **sinking fund requirement.** This kind of provision for repayment of corporate debt may be designed to liquidate all of a bond issue by the maturity date, or it may be arranged to pay only

[2]Arleigh P. Hess, Jr., and Willis J. Winn, *The Value of the Call Privilege* (Philadelphia: University of Pennsylvania, 1962), p. 24.
[3]*Lucas et al.* v. *Florida Power & Light Company,* Final Judgment, paragraph 77.

a part of the total by the end of the term. If only a part is paid, the remainder is called a **balloon maturity.** The purpose of the sinking fund provision is to reduce credit risk.

Generally, the issuer may satisfy the sinking fund requirement by either (1) making a cash payment of the face amount of the bonds to be retired to the corporate trustee, who then calls the bonds for redemption using a lottery, or (2) delivering to the trustee bonds purchased in the open market that have a total face value equal to the amount that must be retired. If the bonds are retired using the first method, interest payments stop at the redemption date.

Usually, the periodic payments required for sinking fund purposes will be the same for each period. A few indentures might permit variable periodic payments, where payments change according to certain prescribed conditions set forth in the indenture. Many corporate bond indentures include a provision that grants the issuer the option to retire more than the amount stipulated for sinking fund retirement. This is referred to as an **accelerated sinking fund provision.**

Usually, the sinking fund call price is the par value if the bonds were originally sold at par. When issued at a price in excess of par, the call price generally starts at the issuance price and scales down to par as the issue approaches maturity.

Accrued Interest

As explained in Chapter 2, in addition to the agreed-upon price, the buyer must pay the seller accrued interest. Market convention for determining the number of days in a corporate bond coupon period and the number of days from the last coupon payment to settlement date differs from that for a Treasury coupon security. Whereas a calendar year has 365 days (366 days in the case of a leap year), corporate bond interest is computed as if the year were 360 days. Each month in a corporate bond year is 30 days, whether it is February, April, or August. A 12% coupon corporate bond pays $120 per year per $1,000 par value, accruing interest at $10 per month or $0.33333 per day. The accrued interest on a 12% corporate bond for three months is $30; for three months and 25 days, $38.33, and so on. The corporate calendar is referred to as "30/360."

Corporate Bond Ratings

Professional money managers use various techniques to analyze information on companies and bond issues in order to estimate the ability of the issuer to live up to its future contractual obligations.[4] This activity is known as **credit analysis.**

Some large institutional investors and many investment banking firms have their own credit analysis departments. Few individual investors and institutional bond investors, though, do their own analysis. Instead, they rely primarily on nationally recognized rating companies that perform credit analysis and issue their conclusions in the form of ratings. The four commercial rating companies are (1) Duff and Phelps Credit Rating Co., (2) Fitch Investors Service, (3) Moody's Investors Service, and (4) Standard & Poor's Corporation. The rating systems use similar symbols, as shown in Exhibit 7-2.

---

[4]For an in-depth discussion of credit analysis, see Jane Tripp Howe, "Credit Analysis for Corporate Bonds," Chapter 15 in Frank J. Fabozzi (ed.), *The Handbook of Corporate Debt Instruments* (New Hope, PA: Frank J. Fabozzi Associates, 1998).

EXHIBIT 7-2 Summary of Corporate Bond Ratings Systems and Symbols

Moody's	S&P	Fitch	D&P	Brief Definition
			Investment Grade: High Creditworthiness	
Aaa	AAA	AAA	AAA	Gilt edge, prime, maximum safety
Aa1	AA+	AA+	AA+	
Aa2	AA	AA	AA	Very high grade, high quality
Aa3	AA−	AA−	AA−	
A1	A+	A+	A+	
A2	A	A	A	Upper medium grade
A3	A−	A−	A−	
Baa1	BBB+	BBB+	BBB+	
Baa2	BBB	BBB	BBB	Lower medium grade
Baa3	BBB−	BBB−	BBB−	
			Distinctly Speculative: Low Creditworthiness	
Ba1	BB+	BB+	BB+	
Ba2	BB	BB	BB	Low grade, speculative
Ba3	BB−	BB−	BB−	
B1	B+	B+	B+	
B2	B	B	B	Highly speculative
B3	B−	B−	B−	
			Predominantly Speculative: Substantial Risk or in Default	
	CCC+			
Caa	CCC	CCC	CCC	Substantial risk, in poor standing
	CCC−			
Ca	CC	CC		May be in default, extremely speculative
C	C	C		Even more speculative than those above
	CI			CI = Income bonds; no interest is being paid
		DDD		Default
		DD	DD	
	D	D		

The two most widely used systems of bond ratings are those of Moody's and Standard & Poor's. In both systems the term **high grade** means low credit risk, or conversely, high probability of future payments. The highest-grade bonds are designated by Moody's by the letters Aaa, and by Standard & Poor's by AAA. The next-highest grade is Aa or AA; for the third grade both rating agencies use A. The next three grades are Baa or BBB, Ba or BB, and B, respectively. There are also C grades. Standard & Poor's uses plus or minus signs to provide a narrower credit quality breakdown within each class, and Moody's uses 1, 2, or 3 for the same purpose. Bonds rated triple A (AAA or Aaa) are said to be **prime;** double A (AA or Aa) are of **high quality;** single A issues are called **upper medium grade,** and triple B are **medium grade.** Lower-rated bonds are said to have speculative elements or to be distinctly speculative.

Bond issues that are assigned a rating in the top four categories are referred to as **investment-grade bonds.** Issues that carry a rating below the top four categories are referred to as **non–investment-grade bonds,** or more popularly as **high-yield bonds** or **junk bonds.** Thus, the corporate bond market can be divided into two sectors: the investment-grade and non–investment-grade markets.

The rating agencies accumulate statistics on how ratings change over various periods of time. A table that specifies this information is called a **rating transition matrix.**

EXHIBIT 7-3	One Year Rating Transition Matrix							
	Rating at End of Year							
Rating at Start of Year	*Aaa*	*Aa*	*A*	*Baa*	*Ba*	*B*	*C or D*	*Total*
Aaa	91.90	7.38	0.72	0.00	0.00	0.00	0.00	100.00
Aa	1.13	91.26	7.09	0.31	0.21	0.00	0.00	100.00
A	0.10	2.56	91.20	5.33	0.61	0.20	0.00	100.00
Baa	0.00	0.21	5.36	87.94	5.46	0.82	0.21	100.00

Source: Exhibit 1 in Leland E. Crabbe, "A Framework for Corporate Bond Strategy," *Journal of Fixed Income,* June 1995, p. 16. Reprinted by permission of Institutional Investor.

Exhibit 7-3 shows a one-year rating transition matrix based on a Moody's study for the period 1970–1993. Here is how to interpret the table. The rows indicate the rating at the beginning of a year. The columns show the rating at the end of the year. For example, look at the second row. This row shows the transition for double-A rated bonds at the beginning of a year. The number 91.26 in the second row means that on average 91.26% of double-A rated bonds at the beginning of the year remained double-A rated at year end. The value 1.13 means that on average 1.13% of double-A rated bonds at the beginning of the year were upgraded to triple A. The value 0.31 means that on average 0.31% of double-A rated bonds at the beginning of the year were downgraded to a triple-B rating. From Exhibit 7-3 it should be clear that the probability of a downgrade is much higher than an upgrade for investment grade bonds.

Default Rates

As explained later in this chapter, there are several methodologies that have been used to compute the default rate for corporate bonds. Exhibit 7-4 shows the default rate for all U.S. corporate bonds by year from 1971 to 1997 as compiled by Edward Altman and Vellore Kishore.[5] The annual default rate reported in the exhibit is measured by the par value of all corporate bonds that defaulted in a given calendar year divided by the total par value outstanding during the year. The average default rate for the entire period was 0.53%. When the default rates were weighted by the par value outstanding in each year, the default rate was higher, 0.66%. Later in this chapter we will see how this default rate for all domestic corporate bonds contrasts with the default rate for just high-yield corporate bonds.

Event Risk

In Chapter 5 we described various types of risk. Occasionally, the ability of an issuer to make interest and principal payments changes seriously and unexpectedly because of (1) a natural or industrial accident or some regulatory change, or (2) a takeover or corporate restructuring. These risks are referred to generically as **event risk.** Examples of the first type of event risk would be a change in the accounting treatment of loan losses for commercial banks or cancellation of nuclear plants by public utilities.

---

[5]Edward I. Altman and Vellore M. Kishore, "Defaults and Returns on High Yield Bonds," Chapter 14 in Frank J. Fabozzi (ed.), *The Handbook of Corporate Debt Instruments* (New Hope, PA: Frank J. Fabozzi Associates, 1998).

EXHIBIT 7-4 Corporate Bond Default Rates 1971–1997 (All Domestic Corporate U.S. Bonds)

Year	Amount Outstanding Beginning of Year ($ Billions)	Default Amount— Straight Debt Only ($ Billions)	Default Amount— Converts Only ($ Billions)	Par Value of all Public Bond Defaults ($ Billions)	Default Rate (%)
1997	1,684.59	4.20	0.74	4.94	0.29
1996	1,430.01	3.34	0.35	3.68	0.26
1995	1,238.90	4.55	0.33	4.88	0.39
1994	1,093.69	3.42	0.37	3.78	0.35
1993	982.48	2.29	0.29	2.57	0.26
1992	864.32	5.55	0.33	5.87	0.68
1991	762.27	18.86	0.78	19.64	2.58
1990	711.11	18.35	0.95	19.31	2.72
1989	645.94	8.11	1.00	9.11	1.41
1988	580.31	3.94	0.57	4.51	0.78
1987	528.94	7.49	1.75	9.24	1.75
1986	458.13	3.16	0.30	3.46	0.75
1985	413.20	0.99	0.31	1.30	0.32
1984	372.90	0.34	0.28	0.62	0.17
1983	352.30	0.30	0.11	0.41	0.12
1982	331.40	0.75	0.42	1.17	0.35
1981	311.90	0.03	0.05	0.08	0.03
1980	281.70	0.22	0.03	0.26	0.09
1979	258.60	0.02	0.01	0.03	0.01
1978	248.30	0.12	0.07	0.19	0.08
1977	229.10	0.38	0.07	0.45	0.20
1976	209.90	0.03	0.08	0.11	0.05
1975	183.50	0.20	0.12	0.32	0.17
1974	162.90	0.12	0.17	0.29	0.18
1973	154.40	0.05	0.15	0.20	0.13
1972	143.00	0.19	0.08	0.27	0.19
1971	125.50	0.08	0.04	0.12	0.10

Average default rate— 1971 to 1997: 0.53
Average default rate— 1978 to 1997: 0.67
Weighted average default rate— 1971 to 1997: 0.66
Weighted average default rate— 1978 to 1997: 0.70
Median default rate— 1971 to 1997: 0.26

Source: Exhibit 5 in Edward I. Altman and Vellore M. Kishore, "Defaults and Returns on High Yield Bonds," Chapter 14 in Frank J. Fabozzi (ed.), *The Handbook of Corporate Debt Instruments* (New Hope, PA: Frank J. Fabozzi Associates, 1998).

A good example of the second type of event risk is the 1988 takeover of RJR Nabisco for $25 billion through a financing technique known as a **leveraged buyout** (LBO). The new company took on a substantial amount of debt incurred to finance the acquisition of the firm.[6] In the case of RJR Nabisco, the debt and equity after

---

[6]For a discussion of event risk associated with takeovers, see N. R. Vijayarghavan and Randy Snook, "Takeover Event Risk and Corporate Bond Portfolio Management," in Frank J. Fabozzi (ed.), *Advances and Innovations in Bond and Mortgage Markets* (Chicago: Probus Publishing, 1989).

the leveraged buyout were $29.9 and $1.2 billion, respectively. Because the corporation must service a larger amount of debt, its bond quality rating was reduced; RJR Nabisco's quality rating as assigned by Moody's dropped from A1 to B3. To see how much more investors demanded because of the company's new capital structure with a greater proportion of debt, look at Exhibit 7-5. The exhibit shows the impact of the initial LBO bid announcement on yield spreads for RJR Nabisco's debt. The yield spread to a benchmark Treasury increased from about 100 basis points to 350 basis points.

Event risk can have spillover effects on other firms. A nuclear accident, for example, will affect all utilities producing nuclear power. And in the case of takeovers, consider once again the RJR Nabisco LBO. An LBO of $25 billion was considered impractical prior to the RJR Nabisco LBO, but the RJR transaction showed that size was not an obstacle, and other large firms previously thought to be unlikely candidates for an LBO became fair game. To see the spillover effect, look at Exhibit 7-6, which shows how event risk fears caused yield spreads to widen for three large firms.

High-Yield Corporate Bond Sector

As we have noted, high-yield bonds, commonly called junk bonds, are issues with quality ratings below triple B. Bond issues in this sector of the market may have been rated investment grade at the time of issuance and have been downgraded subsequently to non–investment grade, or they may have been rated non–investment grade at the time of issuance, called **original-issue high-yield bonds.** Bonds that have been downgraded fall into two groups: (1) issues that have been downgraded because the

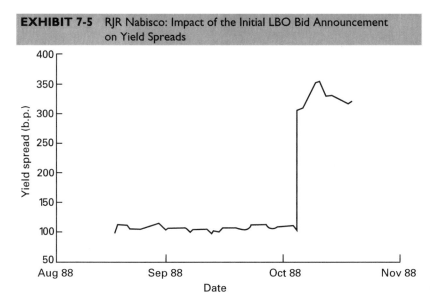

EXHIBIT 7-5   RJR Nabisco: Impact of the Initial LBO Bid Announcement on Yield Spreads

RJR Nabisco 9 3/8 due April 2016–U.S. Treasury 8 7/8 due August 2017.

Source: N. R. Vijayarghavan and Randy Snook, "Takeover Event Risk and Corporate Bond Portfolio Management," in Frank J. Fabozzi (ed.), *Advances and Innovations in Bond and Mortgage Markets* (Chicago: Probus Publishing, 1989), p. 55.

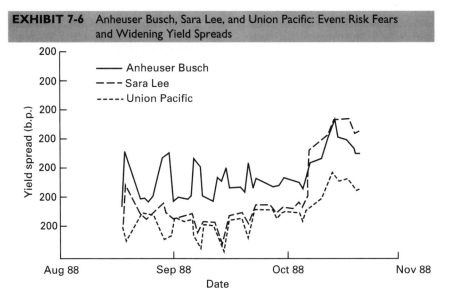

EXHIBIT 7-6 Anheuser Busch, Sara Lee, and Union Pacific: Event Risk Fears and Widening Yield Spreads

Corporates are spread to the U.S. Treasury 8 7/8 due August 2017.

Source: N. R. Vijayarghavan and Randy Snook, "Takeover Event Risk and Corporate Bond Portfolio Management," in Frank J. Fabozzi (ed.), *Advances and Innovations in Bond and Mortgage Markets* (Chicago: Probus Publishing, 1989), p. 56.

issuer voluntarily significantly increased their debt as a result of a leveraged buyout or a recapitalization, and (2) issues that have been downgraded for other reasons. The latter issues are commonly referred to as "fallen angels."

In the early years of the high-yield market, all the issues had a conventional structure; that is, the issues paid a fixed coupon rate and were term bonds. Today, however, there are more complex bond structures in the high-yield corporate bond sector, particularly for bonds issued for LBO financing and recapitalizations producing higher debt. The structures we describe next have features that are more attractive to issuers.

In an LBO or a recapitalization, the heavy interest payment burden that the corporation assumes places severe cash flow constraints on the firm. To reduce this burden, firms involved in LBOs and recapitalizations have issued bonds with **deferred coupon structures** that permit the issuer to avoid using cash to make interest payments for a period of three to seven years. There are three types of deferred coupon structures: (1) deferred-interest bonds, (2) step-up bonds, and (3) payment-in-kind bonds.

Deferred-interest bonds are the most common type of deferred coupon structure. These bonds sell at a deep discount and do not pay interest for an initial period, typically from three to seven years. (Because no interest is paid for the initial period, these bonds are sometimes referred to as zero-coupon bonds.) **Step-up bonds** do pay coupon interest, but the coupon rate is low for an initial period and then increases ("steps up") to a higher coupon rate. Finally, **payment-in-kind (PIK) bonds** give the issuer an option to pay cash at a coupon payment date or give the bondholder a similar bond (i.e., a bond with the same coupon rate and a par value equal to the amount of the coupon payment that would have been paid). The period during which the issuer can make this choice varies from five to 10 years.

In late 1987, a junk bond came to market with a structure allowing the issuer to reset the coupon rate so that the bond will trade at a predetermined price.[7] The coupon rate may reset annually or even more frequently, or reset only one time over the life of the bond. Generally, the coupon rate at reset time will be the average of rates suggested by two investment banking firms. The new rate will then reflect (1) the level of interest rates at the reset date, and (2) the credit spread the market wants on the issue at the reset date. This structure is called an **extendable reset.**

Notice the difference between an extendable reset bond and a floating-rate issue as described earlier. In a floating-rate issue, the coupon rate resets according to a fixed spread over some benchmark, with the spread specified in the indenture. The amount of the spread reflects market conditions at the time the issue is offered. The coupon rate on an extendable reset bond by contrast is reset based on market conditions (as suggested by several investment banking firms) at the time of the reset date. Moreover, the new coupon rate reflects the new level of interest rates and the new spread that investors seek.

The advantage to issuers of extendable reset bonds is again that they can be assured of a long-term source of funds based on short-term rates. For investors, the advantage of these bonds is that the coupon rate will reset to the market rate—both the level of interest rates and the credit spread, in principle keeping the issue at par. In fact, experience with reset bonds has not been favorable during the recent period of difficulties in the high-yield bond market. The sudden substantial increase in default risk has meant that the rise in the rate needed to keep the issue at par was so large that it would have insured the bankruptcy of the firm. As a result, the rise in the coupon rate has been insufficient to keep the issue at the stipulated price.

Secondary Market

As with all bonds, the principal secondary market for corporate bonds is the over-the-counter market. There is some trading on exchanges. Several trading facilities have developed such as BondNet. However, the share of exchanges and other trading facilities is still minor relative to all of corporate bond trading.

The Securities and Exchange Commission (SEC) has been concerned with the transparency of the market with respect to quotes and last-trade information. Encouraged by the SEC, the Nasdaq Stock Market developed an electronic reporting facility for trades and quotes for high-yield corporate bonds that are actively traded. This system, called the Fixed Income Pricing System (FIPS), provides some transparency to the market. Nevertheless, FIPS and other vendor quote systems are still far from the

---

[7]Most of the bonds have a coupon reset formula that requires the issuer to reset the coupon so that the bond will trade at a price of $101.

ideal market information regarding trades and quotes expected by corporate bond investors.[8] In late 1998, Congress was conducting hearings on improving the reporting systems for all corporate bonds.

Private-Placement Market for Corporate Bonds

Securities privately placed are exempt from the registration with the SEC because they are issued in transactions that do not involve a public offering. The private-placement market has undergone a major change since the adoption of SEC Rule 144A in 1990, which allows the trading of privately placed securities among qualified institutional buyers. Not all private placements are Rule 144A private placement. Consequently, the private-placement market can be divided into two sectors. First is the traditional private-placement market, which includes non-144A securities. Second is the market for 144A securities.

Rule 144A private placements are now underwritten by investment bankers on a firm commitment basis, just as with publicly issued bonds. The features in these issues are similar to those of publicly issued bonds described at the outset of this chapter. For example, the restrictions imposed on the borrower are less onerous than for traditional private-placement issues. For underwritten issues, the size of the offering is comparable to that of publicly offered bonds.

Unlike publicly issued bonds, the issuers of privately placed issues tend to be less well known. In this way, the private placement market shares a common characteristic with the bank loan market that we will discuss later in this chapter. Borrowers in the publicly issued bond market are typically large corporations. Issuers of privately placed bonds tend to be medium-sized corporations. Those corporations that borrow from banks tend to be small corporations.

Although the liquidity of issues has increased since Rule 144A became effective, it is still not comparable to that of publicly offered issues. Yields on privately placed debt issues are still higher than those on publicly offered bonds. However, one market observer reports that the premium that must be paid by borrowers in the private-placement market has decreased as investment banking firms have committed capital and trading personnel to making markets for securities issued under Rule 144A.[9]

Risk and Return in the Corporate Bond Market

Because of the credit risk associated with corporate bonds, it is expected that the performance of this sector of the market would outperform Treasury securities. Moreover, within the corporate bond market, because of the greater credit risk associated with high-yield bonds compared to investment-grade bonds, it is expected that the former would outperform the latter.

Exhibit 7-7 provides statistics for various sectors of the bond market and the equity market as reported by Sam DeRosa-Farag.[10] The sectors of the bond market

---

[8]For a discussion of FIPS and empirical evidence on trading volume and liquidity, see Gordon J. Alexander, Amy K. Edwards, and Michael G. Ferri, "Trading Volume and Liquidity in Nasdaq's High-Yield Bond Market," unpublished SEC paper, September 1998.

[9]Victoria Keefe, "Underwritten 144A Deals Surge," *Corporate Financing Week,* August 31, 1992, pp. 1 and 10.

[10]Sam DeRosa-Farag, "High Yield as an Asset Class," Chapter 5 in *The Handbook of Corporate Debt Instruments.*

EXHIBIT 7-7 Summary Statistics for Various Assets: 1980–1987

Asset: 1980–1997	Return	Arithmetic Return	Volatility	Serial Correlation	Highest Return	Lowest Return	Median	N Positive Periods	N Negative Periods
U.S. 30-Day T-Bill	7.13	7.13	0.91	0.94	1.35	0.21	6.43	216	0
U.S. Intermediate Treasury	10.16	10.39	7.19	0.24	11.98	−6.41	10.69	150	66
ML Corp Master	11.31	11.65	8.88	0.21	11.97	−7.36	12.29	150	66
DLJ HY Bonds	13.71	14.07	9.19	0.31	11.67	−8.25	13.36	163	53
S&P 500	17.13	18.39	17.24	−0.02	13.43	−21.52	21.13	144	72
U.S. Inflation	4.23	4.23	1.08	0.60	1.44	−0.46	3.67	197	12

Source: Adapted from Exhibit 1 in Sam DeRosa-Farag, "High Yield as an Asset Class," Chapter 5 in Frank J. Fabozzi (ed.), *The Handbook of Corporate Debt Instruments* (New Hope, PA: Frank J. Fabozzi Associates, 1998).

reported in the exhibit are (1) 30-day U.S. Treasury bills, (2) U.S. intermediate Treasuries, (3) investment grade corporate bonds (as measured by the Merrill Lynch Corporate Master Index[11]) and (4) high-yield corporate bonds (as measured by the Donaldson, Lufkin, Jenrette High Yield Bond Index). The S&P 500 is used to gauge the performance of the equity market. Also shown is the rate of inflation for the period. For each sector shown, the following is reported for the period 1980–1997: (1) the return for the period, (2) the volatility of the return (as measured by the standard deviation of returns), (3) the highest and lowest monthly (annualized) return, and (4) the number of months with positive and negative returns. All the sectors shown in the exhibit beat the rate of inflation.

Focusing on the first two statistics reported in Exhibit 7-7, return and volatility (which measures risk), it can be seen that all the sectors had a higher return than 30-day Treasury bills but had a greater return volatility. The two corporate bond indices had a higher return than intermediate Treasuries, but with a greater return volatility. Investment grade corporate bonds had a lower return than high-yield corporate bonds, but the former also had lower return volatility than the latter. Finally, the equity market generated a higher return than all sectors of the bond market but had a greater return volatility. In summary, the results reported in Exhibit 7-7 are consistent with what is expected in an efficient capital market: Higher returns can only be realized by accepting greater risk (as measured by return volatility). Moreover, the findings in Exhibit 7-7 are consistent with the findings of other studies that cover other periods and use other indices to represent sectors of the market.

The implication is that investors who are willing to accept credit risk have been compensated for that risk in the form of a higher return. In addition, investors who have been willing to accept greater credit risk by investing in high-yield corporate bonds rather than investment grade corporate bonds have realized a higher return. There is further empirical evidence for both the investment-grade and high-yield sectors that we discuss in the next sections.

Performance of Investment-Grade Corporate Bonds   A study by Thomas Bennett, Stephen Esser, and Christian Roth reported the risk and reward relationship in the corporate bond market.[12] Exhibit 7-8 shows for the four investment-grade ratings and the first two non-investment-grading ratings the actual yield spread over U.S. Treasuries for the 10 years ending 1992. Also shown in the figure is the yield spread required to offset credit losses for each quality rating. As indicated in Exhibit 7-8, investors have been rewarded for accepting corporate credit risk.

Exhibit 7-9 shows the annualized total returns and return spreads versus U.S. Treasuries for investment-grade corporates and the Standard & Poor's 500 for various periods ending in 1992. The two key findings as reported in Exhibit 7-9 are that (1) corporate bonds outperformed Treasuries, and (2) the lower the credit rating, the better the performance relative to Treasuries. Thus, the ratings appear to do a good job of differentiating the credit risk associated with investing in corporate bonds.

---

[11]Bond indexes are discussed in Chapter 18.
[12]Thomas L. Bennett, Stephen F. Esser, and Christian G. Roth, *Corporate Credit Risk and Reward* (West Conshohocken, PA: Miller, Anderson & Sherrerd, 1993).

EXHIBIT 7-8   Actual versus Required Corporate Bond Yield Premium, 1983–1992

Source: Data from Salomon Brothers, Moody's Investors Service, and Miller, Anderson & Sherrerd, as reported in Thomas L. Bennett, Stephen F. Esser, and Christian G. Roth, *Corporate Credit Risk and Reward* (West Conshohocken, PA: Miller, Anderson & Sherrerd, 1993). Reprinted by permission.

EXHIBIT 7-9   Annualized Total Returns and Return Spreads: U.S. Treasuries, Investment-Grade Corporates, and S&P 500, Periods Ended December 1992

	20 Years	*10 Years*	*5 Years*
Treasuries	9.13%	11.63%	10.85%
Corporates	9.64%	12.53%	11.46%
Spread vs. Treasuries	+51 basis points	+90 basis points	+61 basis points
AAA	9.20%	11.89%	11.04%
Spread vs. Treasuries	+7 basis points	+27 basis points	+27 basis points
AA	9.35%	12.18%	11.33%
Spread vs. Treasuries	+23 basis points	+55 basis points	+48 basis points
A	9.63%	12.58%	11.54%
Spread vs. Treasuries	+50 basis points	+95 basis points	+69 basis points
BBB	10.37%	13.45%	11.68%
Spread vs. Treasuries	+124 basis points	+182 basis points	+83 basis points
S&P 500	11.33%	16.18%	15.88%

Source: Data from Lehman Brothers and Miller, Anderson & Sherrerd, as reported in Thomas L. Bennett, Stephen F. Esser, and Christian G. Roth, *Corporate Credit Risk and Reward* (West Conshohocken, PA: Miller, Anderson & Sherrerd, 1993). Reprinted by permission.

Performance of High-Yield Bonds   There have been several studies of the risk and return in the high-yield bond market. Historically, the promised yields offered on high-yield bonds have been substantial. The last column in Exhibit 7-10 shows the

EXHIBIT 7-10 Annual Returns, Yields, and Spreads on 10-Year Treasury and High-Yield Bonds (1978–1997)

	Return (%)			Promised Yield (%)*		
Year	High Yield	Treasury	Spread	High Yield	Treasury	Spread
1997	12.83	11.16	1.67	8.86	5.75	3.11
1996	11.06	0.04	11.02	9.41	6.44	2.97
1995	19.91	23.58	−3.67	9.70	5.58	4.12
1994	−1.17	−8.29	7.13	11.27	7.83	3.44
1993	17.18	12.08	5.11	9.61	5.80	3.81
1992	18.16	6.50	11.66	11.28	6.69	4.59
1991	34.58	17.18	17.40	13.11	6.70	6.41
1990	−4.36	6.88	−11.24	17.58	8.83	8.75
1989	1.62	15.99	−14.37	15.41	7.93	7.48
1988	13.47	9.20	4.27	13.95	9.00	4.95
1987	4.67	−2.67	7.34	12.66	8.75	3.91
1986	16.09	24.08	−7.99	14.45	9.55	4.90
1985	22.51	31.54	−9.03	15.40	11.65	3.75
1984	8.50	14.82	−6.32	14.97	11.87	3.10
1983	21.80	2.23	19.57	15.74	10.70	5.04
1982	32.45	42.08	−9.63	17.84	13.86	3.98
1981	7.56	0.48	7.08	15.97	12.08	3.89
1980	−1.00	−2.96	1.96	13.46	10.23	3.23
1979	3.69	−0.86	4.55	12.07	9.13	2.94
1978	7.57	−1.11	8.68	10.92	8.11	2.81

Arithmetical Annual Average:

1978–1997	12.36	10.10	2.26	13.18	8.82	4.36

Compound Annual Average:

1978–1997	11.88	9.41	2.47			

*End of year yields.

Source: Exhibit 15 in Edward I. Altman and Vellore M. Kishore, "Defaults and Returns on High Yield Bonds," Chapter 14 in Frank J. Fabozzi (ed.), *The Handbook of Corporate Debt Instruments* (New Hope, PA: Frank J. Fabozzi Associates, 1998).

promised yield spread of high-yield bonds over 10-Year Treasury securities for the period 1978–1997 as reported by Altman and Kishore. (As explained in Chapter 3, the yield to maturity is a measure of the promised yield because it assumes that the security is held to maturity, coupon payments can be reinvested at the computed yield to maturity, and the issue does not default. Thus, the difference between two promised yields is a promised yield spread.) As can be seen in the last column of the exhibit, the promised yield spread varied by year. It ranged from a low of 281 basis points in 1978 to a high of 875 basis points in 1990. The annual average promised yield spread for the 20-year period was 436 basis points. Are the promised yield spreads justified by the higher potential default rate for high-yield corporate bonds? This important question has been investigated extensively.

Most of the research on the high-yield-bond sector focuses on default rates.[13] From an investment perspective, default rates by themselves are not of paramount significance: It is perfectly possible for a portfolio of high-yield bonds to suffer defaults and to outperform Treasuries at the same time, provided that the yield spread of the portfolio is sufficiently high to offset the losses from default. Furthermore, because holders of defaulted bonds typically recover a portion of the par amount of their investment, the default loss rate is lower than the default rate. Therefore, focusing exclusively on default rates merely highlights the worst possible outcome that a diversified portfolio of high-yield bonds would suffer, assuming that all defaulted bonds would be totally worthless. Assessing the potential rewards from investing in this market sector requires understanding not only default and default loss rates, but also total returns offered over various investment horizons.

First, let's look at what research has found for the default rate experience of low-quality corporate bonds. In their 1987 study, Altman and Nammacher found that the annual default rate for low-rated corporate debt was 2.15%, a figure that Altman has since updated upward. Drexel Burnham Lambert's (DBL) estimates have also shown default rates of about 2.40% per year. Asquith, Mullins, and Wolff, however, found that nearly one out of every three junk bonds defaults. The large discrepancy arises because the researchers use three different definitions of "default rate"; even if applied to the same universe of bonds (which they are not), all three results could be valid simultaneously.[14]

Altman and Nammacher define the default rate as the par value of all high-yield bonds that defaulted in a given calendar year, divided by the total par value outstanding during the year. Their estimates are simple averages of the annual default rates over a number of years. In contrast, DBL takes the cumulative dollar value of all defaulted high-yield bonds, divides by the cumulative dollar value of all high-yield issuance, and further divides by the weighted average number of years outstanding to obtain an average annual default rate. Asquith, Mullins, and Wolff use a cumulative default statistic. For all bonds issued in a given year, the default rate is the total par

[13]See, for example, Edward I. Altman, "Measuring Corporate Bond Mortality and Performance," *Journal of Finance,* September 1989, pp. 909–922; Edward I. Altman and Scott A. Nammacher, *Investing in Junk Bonds* (New York: Wiley, 1987); Paul Asquith, David W. Mullins, Jr., and Eric D. Wolff, "Original Issue High Yield Bonds: Aging Analysis of Defaults, Exchanges, and Calls," *Journal of Finance,* September 1989, pp. 923–952; Marshall Blume and Donald Keim, "Risk and Return Characteristics of Lower-Grade Bonds 1977–1987," Working Paper (8-89), Rodney L. White Center for Financial Research, Wharton School, University of Pennsylvania, 1989; Marshall Blume and Donald Keim, "Realized Returns and Defaults on Lower-Grade Bonds," Rodney L. White Center for Financial Research, Wharton School, University of Pennsylvania, 1989; Bond Investors Association, "Bond Investors Association Issues Definitive Corporate Default Statistics," press release dated August 15, 1989; Gregory T. Hradsky and Robert D. Long, "High Yield Default Losses and the Return Performance of Bankrupt Debt," *Financial Analysts Journal,* July–August 1989, pp. 38–49; "Historical Default Rates of Corporate Bond Issuers 1970–1988," *Moody's Special Report,* July 1989 (New York: Moody's Investors Service); "High-Yield Bond Default Rates," *Standard & Poor's Creditweek,* August 7, 1989, pp. 21–23; David Wyss, Christopher Probyn, and Robert de Angelis, "The Impact of Recession on High-Yield Bonds," DRI–McGraw-Hill (Washington, DC: Alliance for Capital Access, 1989); and the 1984–1989 issues of *High Yield Market Report: Financing America's Futures* (New York and Beverly Hills: Drexel Burnham Lambert, Incorporated).
[14]As a parallel, we know that the mortality rate in the United States is currently less than 1% per year, but we also know that 100% of all human beings (eventually) die.

value of defaulted issues as of the date of their study, divided by the total par amount originally issued to obtain a cumulative default rate. Their result (that about one in three high-yield bonds default) is not normalized by the number of years outstanding.

Although all three measures are useful indicators of bond default propensity, they are not directly comparable. Even when restated on an annualized basis, they do not all measure the same quantity. The default statistics from all studies, however, are surprisingly similar when cumulative rates have been annualized. Exhibit 7-11 shows the default rates by year for the period 1971–1997 as reported in the most recent study by Altman and Kishore.[15] The bottom of the exhibit reports that the arithmetic average default rate for the entire period was 2.6% and the weighted average default rate (i.e., weighted by the par value of the amount outstanding for each year) was 3.3%. For a more recent time period, 1985 to 1997, the arithmetic average default rate was higher, 3.7%.

Next let's look at the historical loss rate realized by investors in high-yield corporate bonds. This rate, referred to as a **default loss rate,** is reported in the last column of Exhibit 7-11. The methodology for computing the default loss rate by Altman and Kishore is as follows. First, the **default loss of principal** is computed by multiplying the default rate for the year by the average loss of principal. The average loss of principal is computed by first determining the recovery per $100 of par value. They quantify the recovery per $100 of par value using the weighted average price of all issues after default. The difference between par value of $100 and the recovery of principal is the default loss of principal. For example, in 1997, the weighted average price after default per $100 par value was $54.2, as reported in the fifth column of Exhibit 7-11. The recovery of principal was therefore $54.2 and the default loss of principal for 1997 was therefore $45.8. The default loss from principal for 1997 is then the product of the default rate for 1997 of 1.25% (fourth column of Exhibit 7-11) and the default loss of principal of $45.8. The product is 0.573%. Next the default loss of coupon interest is computed. This is found by multiplying the default rate by the weighted average coupon rate divided by 2 (because the coupon payments are semiannual). Again, looking at 1997, the weighted average coupon is shown in the next-to-the-last column in the exhibit to be 11.87%. The default loss of coupon is then the product of the default rate of 1.25% and one-half of 11.87%, or 0.074%. The default loss rate is then the sum of the default loss rate of principal and the default loss rate of principal. For 1997, it is 0.65%.

Now let's look at the total return of the high-yield corporate bond sector because, as we noted earlier, default rates do not tell us how a sector has performed. There have been several such total return studies published that cover different time periods.[16,17,18,19] These studies make different assumptions about factors such as default rate computations, recovery rates, reinvestment rates, and the treatment of default.

---

[15]Altman and Kishore, "Defaults and Returns on High Yield Bonds."

[16]The Altman and Nammacher and Hradsky and Long studies cite significantly lower default rates but they employ a definition of default rate that ignores the effect of aging on the propensity to default.

[17]Rayner Cheung, Joseph C. Bencivenga, and Frank J. Fabozzi, "Original Issue High-Yield Bonds: Historical Return and Default Experiences 1977–1989," *Journal of Fixed Income,* September 1992, pp. 58–76.

[18]Marshall E. Blume, Donald B. Keim, and Sandeep A. Patel, "Returns and Volatility of Low-Grade Bonds 1977–1989," *Journal of Finance,* March 1991, pp. 49–74.

[19]Bradford Cornell and K. Green, "The Investment Performance of Low-Grade Bond Funds," *Journal of Finance,* March 1991, pp. 29–48.

EXHIBIT 7-11 Default Rates and Default Losses for High-Yield Corporate Bonds: 1978–1997

Year	Par Value Outstanding* ($ MM)	Par Value of Default ($ MM)	Default Rate (%)	Weighted Price After Default ($)	Weighted Coupon (%)	Default Loss (%)
1997	$335,400	$4,200	1.25	$54.2	11.87	0.65
1996	271,000	3,336	1.23	51.9	8.92	0.65
1995	240,000	4,551	1.90	40.6	11.83	1.24
1994	235,000	3,418	1.45	39.4	10.25	0.96
1993	206,907	2,287	1.11	56.6	12.98	0.56
1992	163,000	5,545	3.40	50.1	12.32	1.91
1991	183,600	18,862	10.27	36.0	11.59	7.16
1990	181,000	18,354	10.14	23.4	12.94	8.42
1989	189,258	8,110	4.29	38.3	13.40	2.93
1988	148,187	3,944	2.66	43.6	11.91	1.66
1987	129,557	7,486	5.78	75.9	12.07	1.74
1986	90,243	3,156	3.50	34.5	10.61	2.48
1985	58,088	992	1.71	45.9	13.69	1.04
1984	40,939	344	0.84	48.6	12.23	0.48
1983	27,492	301	1.09	55.7	10.11	0.54
1982	18,109	577	3.19	38.6	9.61	2.11
1981	17,115	27	0.16	12.0	15.75	0.15
1980	14,935	224	1.50	21.1	8.43	1.25
1979	10,356	20	0.19	31	10.63	0.14
1978	8,946	119	1.33	60	8.38	0.59

Default Rate Summary

		Default Rates (%)	Standard Deviation
Arithmetic Average Default Rate	1971 to 1997	2.613	2.554
	1978 to 1997	2.849	2.808
	1985 to 1997	3.745	3.059
Weighted Average Default Rate**	1971 to 1997	3.311	3.452
	1978 to 1997	3.342	3.066
Median Annual Default Rate	1971 to 1997	1.500	

*As of mid-year.
**Weighted by par value of amount outstanding for each year.

Default Loss Rate Summary

	Default Rate (%)	Weighted Price After Default ($)	Weighted Coupon (%)	Default Loss (%)
Arithmetic Average 1978–1997:	2.85	42.9	11.48	1.83
Weighted Average 1978–1997:	3.34			2.18

Sources: Adapted from Exhibits 5 and 6 in Edward I. Altman and Vellore M. Kishore, "Defaults and Returns on High Yield Bonds," Chapter 14 in Frank J. Fabozzi (ed.), *The Handbook of Corporate Debt Instruments* (New Hope, PA: Frank J. Fabozzi Associates, 1998).

Despite the differences in time periods and methodologies, none of the studies seems to suggest that investing in high-yield corporate bonds offers exceptional value. Rather, the findings are consistent with what we stated at the outset of this section: In the long run, high-yield corporate bonds have outperformed both investment grade corporate bonds and Treasuries but have been outperformed by common stock. Therefore, any claim of superior or inferior performance by advocates and critics of this sector of the bond market must be taken with the greatest caution.

Exhibit 7-10 provides a summary of the return on high-yield corporate bonds versus 10-year Treasuries for the years 1978 to 1997 as reported by Altman and Kishore. As expected, there are some years in which 10-year Treasuries have outperformed the high-yield corporate bond market. However, over the entire 20-year period, the arithmetic annual return and the compounded annual return of high-yield corporate bonds exceeded that of 10-year Treasuries by 226 and 247 basis points, respectively.

MEDIUM-TERM NOTES

A **medium-term note** (MTN) is a corporate debt instrument, with the unique characteristic that notes are offered continuously to investors by an agent of the issuer. Investors can select from several maturity ranges: nine months to one year, more than one year to 18 months, more than 18 months to two years, and so on up to 30 years. Medium-term notes are registered with the SEC under Rule 415 (the shelf registration rule), which gives a corporation the maximum flexibility for issuing securities on a continuous basis.

The term *medium-term note* to describe this corporate debt instrument is misleading. Traditionally, the term *note* or *medium-term note* was used to refer to debt issues with a maturity greater than one year but less than 15 years. Certainly, this is not a characteristic of MTNs because they have been sold with maturities from nine months to 30 years and even longer. For example, in July 1993, Walt Disney Corporation issued a security with a 100-year maturity off its MTN shelf registration.

General Motors Acceptance Corporation first used MTNs in 1972 to fund automobile loans with maturities of five years and less. The purpose of the MTN was to fill the funding gap between commercial paper and long-term bonds. It is for this reason that they are referred to as "medium term." The MTNs were issued directly to investors without the use of an agent. Only a few corporations issued MTNs in the 1970s. About $800 million of MTNs were outstanding by 1981. The market was hampered from developing for two reasons. First, because the issues must be registered with the SEC, registration costs made the issuance of MTNs expensive relative to other funding sources. This cost could be avoided by placing MTNs privately. However, as we explained earlier in this chapter, private placements carry a higher interest cost. Second, there was no secondary market for MTNs.

The modern-day MTN was pioneered by Merrill Lynch in 1981. The first MTN issuer was Ford Motor Credit company. By 1983, GMAC and Chrysler Financial used Merrill Lynch as an agent to issue MTNs. Merrill Lynch and other investment banking firms committed funds to make a secondary market for MTNs, thereby improving liquidity. In 1982, Rule 415 was adopted, making it easier for issuers to sell registered securities on a continuous basis.

Although we elected to discuss MTNs in our discussion of domestic corporate debt, they are also issued by foreign corporations, federal agencies, supranational institutions, and sovereign countries.

Borrowers have flexibility in designing MTNs to satisfy their own needs. They can issue fixed- or floating-rate debt.[20] The coupon payments can be denominated in U.S. dollars or in a foreign currency. Earlier in this chapter we described the various security structures; MTNs have been designed with the same features. For example, there are MTNs backed by equipment trust certificates issued by railways and subordinated notes issued by bank holding companies. In Chapter 13 we discuss asset-backed securities. There are asset-backed MTNs.

When the treasurer of a corporation is contemplating an offering of either an MTN or corporate bonds, there are two factors that affect the decision. The most obvious is the cost of the funds raised after consideration of registration and distribution costs. This cost is referred to as the **all-in-cost of funds.** The second is the flexibility afforded to the issuer in structuring the offering. The tremendous growth in the MTN market is evidence of the relative advantage of MTNs with respect to cost and flexibility for some offerings. However, the fact that there are corporations that raise funds by issuing both bonds and MTNs is evidence that there is no absolute advantage in all instances and market environments.

Primary Market

Medium-term notes differ from corporate bonds in the manner in which they are distributed to investors when they are initially sold. Although some investment-grade corporate bond issues are sold on a best-efforts basis, typically they are underwritten by investment bankers. Traditionally, MTNs have been distributed on a best-efforts basis by either an investment banking firm or other broker/dealers acting as agents. Another difference between corporate bond and MTNs when they are offered is that MTNs are usually sold in relatively small amounts on a continuous or an intermittent basis, whereas corporate bonds are sold in large, discrete offerings.

A corporation that wants an MTN program will file a shelf registration with the SEC for the offering of securities. Although the SEC registration for MTN offerings are between $100 and $1 billion, after the total is sold, the issuer can file another shelf registration.[21] The registration will include a list of the investment banking firms, usually two to four, that the corporation has arranged to act as agents to distribute the MTNs. The large New York–based investment banking firms dominate the distribution market for MTNs.

The issuer then posts rates over a range of maturities: for example, nine months to one year, one year to 18 months, 18 months to two years, and annually thereafter. Exhibit 7-12 provides an example of an offering rate schedule for an MTN program. Usually, an issuer will post rates as a spread over a Treasury security of comparable maturity. For example, in the two- to three-year maturity range, the offering rate is 35 basis points over the two-year Treasury. Because the two-year Treasury is shown in the table at 4%, the offering rate is 4.35%. Rates will not be posted for maturity

---

[20]Leland E. Crabbe, "Medium-Term Notes and Structured Notes," Chapter 3 in *The Handbook of Corporate Debt Instruments.*
[21]Crabbe, "Medium Term Notes and Structured Notes."

EXHIBIT 7-12 Offering Rate Schedule for a Medium-Term Note Program

Medium-Term Notes		Yield Spread of MTN over Treasury Securities (basis points)	Treasury Securities	
Maturity Range	Yield (%)		Maturity	Yield (%)
9 months to 12 months	a	a	9 months	3.35
12 months to 18 month	a	a	12 months	3.50
18 months to 2 years	a	a	18 months	3.80
2 years to 3 years	4.35	35	2 years	4.00
3 years to 4 years	5.05	55	3 years	4.50
4 years to 5 years	5.60	60	4 years	5.00
5 years to 6 years	6.05	60	5 years	5.45
6 years to 7 years	6.10	40	6 years	5.70
7 years to 8 years	6.30	40	7 years	5.90
8 years to 9 years	6.45	40	8 years	6.05
9 years to 10 years	6.60	40	9 years	6.20
10 years	6.70	40	10 years	6.30

[a]No rate posted.

Source: Exhibit 1 in Leland E. Crabbe, "Medium-Term Notes and Structured Notes," Chapter 3 in Frank J. Fabozzi (ed.), *The Handbook of Corporate Debt Instruments* (New Hope, PA: Frank J. Fabozzi Associates, 1998).

ranges that the issuer does not desire to sell. For example, in Exhibit 7-12 the issuer does not wish to sell MTNs with a maturity of less than two years.

The agents will then make the offering rate schedule available to their investor base interested in MTNs. An investor who is interested in the offering will contact the agent. In turn, the agent contacts the issuer to confirm the terms of the transaction. Because the maturity range in the offering rate schedule does not specify a specific maturity date, the investor can choose the final maturity subject to approval by the issuer. The minimum size that an investor can purchase of an MTN offering typically ranges from $1 million to $25 million.

The rate offering schedule can be changed at any time by the issuer either in response to changing market conditions or because the issuer has raised the desired amount of funds at a given maturity. In the latter case, the issuer can either not post a rate for that maturity range or lower the rate.

Structured MTNs

At one time the typical MTN was a fixed-rate debenture that was noncallable. It is common today for issuers of MTNs to couple their offerings with transactions in the derivative markets (options, futures/forwards, swaps, caps, and floors) so as to create debt obligations with more interesting risk–return features than are available in the corporate bond market. Specifically, an issue can be floating-rate over all or part of the life of the security, and the coupon reset formula can be based on a benchmark interest rate, equity index or individual stock price, a foreign exchange rate, or a commodity index. Inverse floaters are created in the structured MTN market. MTNs can have various embedded options included.

MTNs created when the issuer simultaneously transacts in the derivative markets are called **structured notes.** The most common derivative instrument used in creating structured notes is a swap. The development of the MTN market has been fostered by commercial banks involved in the swap market. By using the derivative markets in combination with an offering, borrowers are able to create investment vehicles that are more customized for institutional investors to satisfy their investment objectives, even though they are forbidden from using swaps for hedging. Moreover, it allows institutional investors who are restricted to investing in investment-grade debt issues the opportunity to participate in other asset classes to make a market play. For example, an investor who buys an MTN whose coupon rate is tied to the performance of the S&P 500 is participating in the equity market without owning common stock. If the coupon rate is tied to a foreign stock index, the investor is participating in the equity market of a foreign country without owning foreign common stock. In exchange for creating a structured note product, borrowers can reduce their funding costs.

How do borrowers or their agents find investors who are willing to buy structured notes? In a typical offering of a corporate bond, the sales force of the underwriting firm will solicit interest in the offering from its customer base. That is, the sales forces will make an inquiry. In the structured note market, the process is often quite different. Because of the small size of an offering and the flexibility to customize the offering in the swap market, investors can approach an issuer through its agent about designing a security for their needs. This process of customers inquiring of issuers or their agents to design a security is called a **reverse inquiry.** Transactions that originate from reverse inquiries account for a significant share of MTN transactions.[22]

COMMERCIAL PAPER

Commercial paper is a short-term unsecured promissory note that is issued in the open market and that represents the obligation of the issuing corporation. The types of corporate issuers of commercial paper have changed since 1980. In the 1970s, large high–credit-quality corporations were the principal issuers of commercial paper. In the 1980s, medium- and low-quality corporate issuers were able to raise funds via the commercial paper market; however, since 1989 such issuers have not found a receptive market for their issues and therefore have withdrawn from the market. The issuance of commercial paper is an alternative to bank borrowing for large corporations (nonfinancial and financial) with strong credit ratings.

The original purpose of commercial paper was to provide short-term funds for seasonal and working capital needs. Basically, it provided high–credit-quality corporations a less expensive form of short-term borrowing than bank borrowing. As the U.S. economy expanded in the 1980s, corporations sought to increase their short-term borrowing to finance high production levels. Commercial paper became even more attractive to those who could access the market because the cost of borrowing by issuing commercial paper was considerably cheaper than bank borrowing in the early 1980s. For example, using the 30-day London interbank offered rate (LIBOR) as a gauge for

---

[22]Crabbe, "Medium-Term Notes and Structured Notes."

the cost of borrowing by high-quality corporations, the spread between LIBOR and commercial paper rates ranged between 0 and 60 basis points from 1975 to 1980. Between 1980 and 1985 that spread widened, exceeding 150 points at times. This encouraged medium- and low-quality corporate issuers into the market.

In the 1980s, corporations began to use commercial paper for other purposes. It has been used quite often for **bridge financing.** For example, suppose that a corporation needs long-term funds to build a plant or acquire equipment. Rather than raising long-term funds immediately, the corporation may elect to postpone the offering until more favorable capital market conditions prevail. The funds raised by issuing commercial paper are used until longer-term securities are sold. As merger and acquisition activity increased in the 1980s, commercial paper was sometimes used as bridge financing to finance corporate takeovers. Moreover, the interest-rate-swaps market encouraged the use of the commercial paper market. In an interest-rate swap, one party exchanges a fixed rate for a floating rate. Corporate issuers would issue commercial paper and use the interest-rate swap to convert the floating interest rate on commercial paper into a fixed interest rate.

The minimum round-lot transaction is $100,000, although some issuers will sell commercial paper in denominations of $25,000. There is very little secondary trading of commercial paper. Typically, an investor in commercial paper is an entity that plans to hold it until maturity. This is understandable because an investor can purchase commercial paper in a direct transaction with the issuer that will issue paper with the specific maturity the investor desires.

Characteristics of Commercial Paper

In the United States, the maturity of commercial paper is typically less than 270 days, and the most common maturity range is 30 to 50 days or less.[23] There are reasons for this. First, the Securities Act of 1933 requires that securities be registered with the SEC. Special provisions in the 1933 act exempt commercial paper from registration as long as the maturity does not exceed 270 days. Hence, to avoid the costs associated with registering issues with the SEC, firms rarely issue commercial paper with maturities exceeding 270 days. Another consideration in determining the maturity is whether the commercial paper would be eligible collateral for a bank that wanted to borrow from the Federal Reserve Bank's discount window. To be eligible, the maturity of the paper may not exceed 90 days. Because eligible paper trades at lower cost than paper that is not eligible, issuers prefer to issue paper whose maturity does not exceed 90 days.

To pay off holders of maturing paper, issuers generally use the proceeds obtained by selling new commercial paper. This process is often described as **rolling over** short-term paper. The risk that the investor in commercial paper faces is that the issuer will be unable to issue new paper at maturity. As a safeguard against this **rollover risk,** commercial paper is typically backed by unused bank credit lines. Because there is a commitment fee charged by a bank for providing a credit line, this safeguard increases the effective cost of issuing commercial paper.

---

[23]*Money Market Instruments* (New York: Merrill Lynch Money Markets Inc., 1989), p. 16.

Issuers of Commercial Paper

Corporate issuers of commercial paper can be divided into financial companies and nonfinancial companies. There are three types of financial companies: captive finance companies, bank-related finance companies, and independent finance companies. Captive finance companies are subsidiaries of equipment manufacturing companies. Their primary purpose is to secure financing for the customers of the parent company. For example, the three major U.S. automobile manufacturers have captive finance companies: General Motors Acceptance Corporation (GMAC), Ford Credit, and Chrysler Financial. GMAC is by the far the largest issuer of commercial paper in the United States. A bank holding company may have a subsidiary that is a finance company which provides loans to enable individuals and businesses to acquire a wide range of products. Independent finance companies are those that are not subsidiaries of equipment manufacturing firms or bank holding companies.

While the issuers of commercial paper typically have high credit ratings, smaller and less-well-known companies with lower credit ratings were able to issue paper in the 1980s. They have been able to do so by means of credit support from a firm with a high credit rating or by collateralizing the issue with high-quality assets. The latter type of commercial paper is called **asset-backed commercial paper** and the former type is called **credit-supported commercial paper.** An example of credit-supported commercial paper is one supported by a letter of credit. The terms of a letter of credit specify that the bank issuing the letter guarantees that if the issuer fails to pay off the paper when it comes due, the bank will do so. The bank will charge a fee for the letter of credit. From the issuer's perspective, the fee enables it to enter the commercial paper market and obtain funding at a lower cost than that of bank borrowing. Commercial paper issued with this credit enhancement is referred to as **LOC paper.** The credit enhancement may also take the form of a surety bond from an insurance company.[24] The key innovation that gave lower and lesser known corporations access to the commercial paper market is the asset-backed structure described in Chapter 13. Both domestic and foreign corporations issue commercial paper in the United States. Commercial paper issued by foreign entities is called **Yankee commercial paper.**

Default Risk and Credit Ratings

With one exception, between 1971 and mid-1989 there were no defaults on commercial paper.[25] With the weakening economy in the late 1980s, three defaults occurred in 1989 and four in 1990. This and two other factors caused corporate medium- and lower-quality-rated issuers out of the commercial paper. The first factor was that banks became reluctant to provide backup facilities for these issuers. The introduction of the risk-based capital requirements for commercial banks made these commitments less attractive. Second, the demand for medium-grade commercial paper by money market mutual funds, the major buyer of commercial paper, was reduced by several SEC rulings in 1991. Specifically, at one time there was no restriction on

---

[24]A surety bond is a policy written by an insurance company to protect another party against loss or violation of a contract.

[25]Mitchell A. Post, "The Evolution of the U.S. Commercial Paper Market Since 1980," *Federal Reserve Bulletin,* December 1992, p. 888. The one exception was Manville Corporation in August 1982, which defaulted after filing in bankruptcy court for protection against potential liability from lawsuits related to injuries and deaths from asbestos.

medium-grade commercial paper that money market mutual funds could hold. Now there are.

The four companies that rate corporate bonds and medium-term notes also rate commercial paper. The ratings assigned by these four rating companies is shown in Exhibit 7-13. As with the ratings on other securities, commercial paper ratings are categorized as either **investment grade** and **noninvestment grade.** These ratings are used by money market mutual funds in determining the amount of commercial paper that they are permitted to hold. The SEC requirements establish two categories of eligible commercial paper: first-tier paper and second-tier paper. In general, to be categorized as first-tier paper the SEC requires that two of the rating companies rate the issue as 1 (see Exhibit 7-13). To be categorized as two-tier paper requires that one rating company rate the issue as "1" and at least one other rate it as 2 or two companies rate it at "2". It is the second-tier paper that is considered medium grade and for which there are restrictions on the amount that can be held by money market mutual funds.

Directly Placed versus Dealer-Placed Paper

Commercial paper is classified as either direct paper or dealer paper. **Direct paper** is sold by the issuing firm directly to investors without the help of an agent or an intermediary. A large majority of the issuers of direct paper are financial companies. These entities require continuous funds in order to provide loans to customers. As a result, they find it cost-effective to establish a sales force to sell their commercial paper directly to investors. With **dealer-placed** commercial paper, the issuer uses the services of an agent to sell its paper. The agent distributes the paper on a "best efforts" underwriting basis.

Secondary Market

Despite the fact that the commercial paper market is larger than markets for other money market instruments, secondary trading activity is much smaller. The typical investor in commercial paper is an entity that plans to hold it until maturity, given that

EXHIBIT 7-13 Commercial Paper Ratings[a]

| | *Commercial Rating Company* | | | |
Category	*Duff & Phelps*	*Fitch*	*Moody's*	*S&P*
Investment grade	Duff 1+	F-1+		A-1+
	Duff 1	F-1	P-1	A-1
	Duff 1−			
	Duff 2	F-2	P-2	A-2
	Duff 3	F-3	P-3	A-3
Noninvestment grade	Duff 4	F-S	NP (not prime)	B
				C
In default	Duff 5	D		D

[a]The definition of ratings varies by rating agency.

Source: Mitchell A. Post, "The Evolution of the U.S. Commercial Paper Market Since 1980," *Federal Reserve Bulletin,* December 1992, p. 882.

an investor can purchase commercial paper with the specific maturity desired. Should an investor's economic circumstances change so that there is a need to sell the paper, it can be sold back to the dealer or, in the case of directly placed paper, the issuer will repurchase it.

Yields on Commercial Paper

Like Treasury bills, commercial paper is a discount instrument. That is, it is sold at a price that is less than its maturity value. The difference between the maturity value and the price paid is the interest earned by the investor, although there is some commercial paper that is issued as an interest-bearing instrument. For commercial paper, a year is treated as having 360 days.

The yield offered on commercial paper tracks that of other money market instruments. The commercial paper rate is higher than that on Treasury bills for the same maturity. There are three reasons for this. First, the investor in commercial paper is exposed to credit risk. Second, interest earned from investing in Treasury bills is exempt from state and local income taxes. As a result, commercial paper has to offer a higher yield to offset this tax advantage. Finally, commercial paper is less liquid than Treasury bills. The liquidity premium demanded is probably small, however, because investors typically follow a buy-and-hold strategy with commercial paper and so are less concerned with liquidity.

The yield on commercial paper is higher by a few basis points than the yield on certificates of deposit for the same maturity. The higher yield available on commercial paper is attributable to the poorer liquidity relative to certificates of deposit.

BANKRUPTCY AND CREDITOR RIGHTS

The holder of a corporate debt instrument has priority over the equity owners in the case of bankruptcy of a corporation, and as we have explained, there are creditors who have priority over other creditors. In this section we provide an overview of the bankruptcy process and then look at what actually happens to creditors in bankruptcies.

Bankruptcy Process

The law governing bankruptcy in the United States is the Bankruptcy Reform Act of 1978.[26] One purpose of the act is to set forth the rules for a corporation to be either liquidated or reorganized. The **liquidation** of a corporation means that all the assets will be distributed to the holders of claims of the corporation and no corporate entity will survive. In a **reorganization,** a new corporate entity will result. Some holders of the claim of the bankrupt corporation will receive cash in exchange for their claims, others may receive new securities in the corporation that results from the reorganization, and others may receive a combination of both cash and new securities in the resulting corporation.

---

[26]For a discussion of the Bankruptcy Report Act of 1978 and a nontechnical description of its principal features, see Jane Tripp Howe, "Investing in Chapter 11 and Other Distressed Companies," Chapter 20 in Fabozzi and Fabozzi (eds.), *The Handbook of Fixed Income Securities,* 4th ed.

Another purpose of the bankruptcy act is to give a corporation time to decide whether to reorganize or liquidate and then the necessary time to formulate a plan to accomplish either a reorganization or liquidation. This is achieved because when a corporation files for bankruptcy, the act grants the corporation protection from creditors who seek to collect their claims.[27] A company that files for protection under the bankruptcy act generally becomes a **debtor in possession,** and continues to operate its business under the supervision of the court.

The bankruptcy act is composed of 15 chapters, each chapter covering a particular type of bankruptcy. Of particular interest to us are two of the chapters, Chapter 7 and Chapter 11. Chapter 7 deals with the liquidation of a company; Chapter 11 deals with the reorganization of a company.

Absolute Priority: Theory and Practice

When a company is liquidated, creditors receive distributions based on the **absolute priority rule** to the extent that assets are available. The absolute priority rule is the principle that senior creditors are paid in full before junior creditors are paid anything. For secured creditors and unsecured creditors, the absolute priority rule guarantees their seniority to equity holders.

In liquidations, the absolute priority rule generally holds. In contrast, there is a good body of literature that argues that strict absolute priority has not been upheld by the courts or the SEC.[28] Studies of actual reorganizations under Chapter 11 have found that the violation of absolute priority is the rule rather the exception.[29]

There are several hypotheses that have been suggested as to why in a reorganization the distribution made to claimholders will diverge from that required by the absolute priority principle. The **incentive hypothesis** argues that the longer the negotiation process among the parties, the greater the bankruptcy costs and the smaller the amount to be distributed to all parties. This is because in a reorganization, a committee representing the various claimholders is appointed with the purpose of formulating a plan of reorganization. To be accepted, a plan of reorganization must be approved by at least two-thirds of the amount and a majority of the number of claims voting and at least two-thirds of the outstanding shares of each class of interests. Consequently, a long-lasting bargaining process is expected. The longer the negotiation process among the parties, the more likely that the company will be operated in a manner that is not in the best interest of the creditors and, as a result, the smaller the amount to be distributed to all parties. Because all impaired classes, including equity

---

[27]The petition for bankruptcy can be filed either by the company itself, in which case it is called a **voluntary bankruptcy,** or be filed by its creditors, in which case it is called an **involuntary bankruptcy.**

[28]See, for example, William H. Meckling, "Financial Markets, Default, and Bankruptcy," *Law and Contemporary Problems,* Vol. 41, 1977, pp. 124–177; Merton H. Miller, "The Wealth Transfers of Bankruptcy: Some Illustrative Examples," *Law and Contemporary Problems,* Vol. 41, 1977, pp. 39–46; Jerome B. Warner, "Bankruptcy, Absolute Priority, and the Pricing of Risky Debt Claims," *Journal of Financial Economics,* Vol. 4, 1977, pp. 239–276; and, Thomas H. Jackson, "Of Liquidation, Continuation, and Delay: An Analysis of Bankruptcy Policy and Nonbankruptcy Rules," *American Bankruptcy Law Journal,* Vol. 60, 1986, pp. 399–428.

[29]See Julian R. Franks and Walter N. Torous, "An Empirical Investigation of U.S. Firms in Reorganization," *Journal of Finance,* July 1989, pp. 747–769; Lawrence A. Weiss, "Bankruptcy Resolution: Direct Costs and Violation of Priority of Claims," *Journal of Financial Economics,* 1990, pp. 285–314; and Frank J. Fabozzi, Jane Tripp Howe, Takashi Makabe, and Toshihide Sudo, "Recent Evidence on the Distribution Patterns in Chapter 11 Reorganizations," *Journal of Fixed Income,* Spring 1993, pp. 6–23.

holders, generally must approve the plan of reorganization, creditors often convince equity holders to accept the plan by offering to distribute some value to them.

The **recontracting process hypothesis** argues that the violation of absolute priority reflects a recontracting process between stockholders and senior creditors that gives recognition to the ability of management to preserve value on behalf of stockholders.[30] According to the **stockholders' influence on the reorganization plan hypothesis,** creditors are less informed about the true economic operating conditions of the firm than management. As the distribution to creditors in the plan of reorganization is based on the valuation by the firm, creditors without perfect information easily suffer the loss.[31] According to Wruck, managers generally have a better understanding than creditors or stockholders about a firm's internal operations while creditors and stockholders can have better information about industry trends. Management may therefore use its superior knowledge to present the data in a manner that reinforces its position.[32]

The essence of the **strategic bargaining process hypothesis** is that the increasing complexity of firms that declare bankruptcy will accentuate the negotiating process and result in an even higher incidence of violation of the absolute priority rule. The probable outcome is further supported by the increased number of official committees in the reorganization process, as well as the increased number of financial and legal advisors.

There are some who argue that creditors will receive a higher value in reorganization than they would in liquidation, in part because of the costs associated with liquidation.[33] Finally, the lack of symmetry in the tax system (negative taxes are not permitted, although loss deductions may be carried forward) results in situations in which the only way to use all current loss deductions is to merge.[34] The tax system may encourage continuance or merger and discourage bankruptcy.

Consequently, although investors in the debt of a corporation may feel that they have priority over the equity owners and priority over other classes of debtors, the actual outcome of a bankruptcy may be far different from what the terms of the debt agreement state.

One study examined the extent of violation of the absolute priority rule among three broad groups: secured creditors, unsecured creditors, and equity holders, and also among various types of debt and equity securities.[35] They also provided evidence on which asset class bears the cost of violations of absolute priority and an initial estimate of total distributed value relative to liquidation value. Their findings suggest that unsecured creditors bear a disproportionate cost of reorganization and that more senior unsecured creditors may bear a disproportionate cost relative to the junior

---

[30]Douglas G. Baird and Thomas H. Jackson, "Bargaining after the Fall and the Contours of the Absolute Priority Rule," *University of Chicago Law Review,* Vol. 55, 1988, pp. 738–789.

[31]L. A. Bebchuk, "A New Approach to Corporate Reorganizations," *Harvard Law Review,* Vol. 101, 1988, pp. 775–804.

[32]Karen Hooper Wruck, "Financial Distress, Reorganization, and Organizational Efficiency," *Journal of Financial Economics,* Vol. 27, 1990, pp. 419–444.

[33]Michael C. Jensen, "Eclipse of the Public Corporation," *Harvard Business Review,* Vol. 89, 1989, pp. 61–62, and Wruck, "Financial Distress, Reorganization, and Organizational Efficiency."

[34]J. I. Bulow and J. B. Shoven, "The Bankruptcy Decision," *Bell Journal of Economics,* 1978. For a further discussion of the importance of NOLs and the current tax law, see Fabozzi et al., "Recent Evidence on the Distribution Patterns in Chapter 11 Reorganizations."

[35]Fabozzi et al., "Recent Evidence on the Distribution Patterns in Chapter 11 Reorganizations."

unsecured creditors, whereas equity holders often benefit from violations of absolute priority.

SUMMARY

Corporate bonds are debts obligating a corporation to pay periodic interest with full repayment at maturity. The promises of the corporate bond issuer and the rights of the investors are set forth in the bond indenture. Provisions to be specified include call and sinking fund provisions, as well as limitations on further debt and on management powers.

Security for bonds may be real or personal property. A mortgage bond grants the bondholders a lien against the pledged assets. Collateral trust bonds are secured by securities owned by the issuer. Debenture bonds are not secured by a specific pledge of property; bondholders have the claim of general creditors on all assets of the issuer not pledged specifically to secure other debt. Subordinated debenture bonds are issues that rank after secured debt, after debenture bonds, and often after some general creditors in their claim on assets and earnings.

The credit risk of a corporate borrower can be gauged by the quality rating assigned by the four nationally recognized rating companies. Issues rated in the top ratings of both raters are referred to as investment-grade bonds; those below the top four ratings are called non–investment-grade bonds, high-yield bonds, or junk bonds.

Event risk refers to the possibility of an event that leads investors to doubt the ability of an issuer to make interest and principal payments. Event risk can occur because of a natural or industrial accident, or a takeover or corporate restructuring.

The high-yield sector of the corporate bond market is the market for non–investment-grade corporate bonds. Several complex bond structures are issued in the high-yield sector of the corporate bond market. These include deferred-coupon bonds (deferred-interest bonds, step-up bonds, and payment-in-kind bonds) and extendable reset bonds.

Studies of the historical risk and return of the corporate bond market indicate that long-run returns are in line with what capital market theory would suggest. That is, in the long run, investment-grade corporate bonds have outperformed Treasury securities, and high-yield bonds have outperformed both investment-grade corporate bonds and Treasuries but have been outperformed by common stock.

Medium-term notes are corporate debt obligations offered on a continuous basis. They are registered with the SEC under the shelf registration rule and are offered through agents. The rates posted are for various maturity ranges, with maturities as short as nine months to as long as 30 years. Medium-term notes have been issued simultaneously with transactions in the derivatives market, particularly the swap market, to create structured MTNs. These products allow issuers greater flexibility in creating MTNs that are attractive to investors who seek to hedge or undertake a market play that they might otherwise be prohibited from doing.

Commercial paper is a short-term unsecured promissory note issued in the open market that represents the obligation of the issuing entity. It is sold on a discount basis. To avoid SEC registration, the maturity of commercial paper is less than 270 days. Generally, commercial paper maturity is less than 90 days so that it will qualify as eligible collateral for the bank to borrow from the Federal Reserve Bank's discount window. Financial and nonfinancial corporations issue commercial paper, with the majority issued by the former. The commercial paper market was limited to entities with strong credit ratings, but lower-rated issuers have used credit enhancements to enter the market. Direct paper is sold by the issuing firm directly to investors without using a securities dealer as an intermediary; with dealer-placed commercial paper, the issuer uses the services of a securities firm to sell its paper. There is little liquidity in the commercial paper market.

The Bankruptcy Reform Act of 1978 governs the bankruptcy process in the United States. Chapter 7 of the bankruptcy act deals with the liquidation of a company. Chapter 11 deals with the reorganization of a company. Creditors receive distributions based on the absolute priority rule to the extent assets are available. This means that senior creditors are paid in full before junior creditors are paid anything. Generally, this rule holds in the case of liquidations. In contrast, the absolute priority rule is typically violated in a reorganization.

Questions

1. What is an industrial bond?
2. a. What is the difference between refunding protection and call protection?
   b. Which protection provides the investor with greater protection that the bonds will be acquired by the issuer prior to the stated maturity date?
3. a. What is a bullet bond?
   b. Can a bullet bond be redeemed prior to the stated maturity date?
4. a. What is a sinking fund requirement in a bond issue?
   b. "A sinking fund provision in a bond issue benefits the investor." Do you agree with this statement?
5. Who are the companies that assign ratings to debt obligations?
6. What is the difference between a fallen angel and an original-issue high-yield bond?
7. a. What is event risk?
   b. Give two examples of event risk.
8. "A floating-rate note and an extendable reset bond both have coupon rates readjusted periodically. Therefore, they are basically the same instrument." Do you agree with this statement?
9. a. What is a payment-in-kind bond?
   b. An investor who purchases a payment-in-kind bond will find that increased interest rate volatility will have an adverse economic impact. If interest rates rise substantially, there will be an adverse consequence. So too will a substantial decline in interest rates have adverse consequences. Why?
10. What is a rating transition matrix?
11. Indicate why you agree or disagree with the following statements pertaining to the private-placement corporate debt market:
    a. "Since Rule 144A became effective, all privately placed issues can be bought and sold in the market."
    b. "Traditionally privately placed issues are now similar to publicly offered securities."
12. Indicate why you agree or disagree with the following statement: "Investing in the junk bond market offers the opportunity to realize superior investment returns compared with other debt instruments and common stock."

13. a. Explain the various ways in which default rates are quoted.
    b. Show how the default loss rate reported in Exhibit 7-11 for 1995 is computed.
14. In what ways does an MTN differ from a corporate bond?
15. What derivative instrument is commonly used in creating a structured MTN?
16. Indicate why you agree or disagree with the following statements:
    a. "Most MTN issues are rated non–investment grade at the time of offering."
    b. "Typically, a corporate issuer with an MTN program will post rates for every maturity range."
    c. "An offering rate schedule for an MTN program is fixed for two years after the securities are registered."
17. What is reverse inquiry?
18. Why is commercial paper an alternative to short-term bank borrowing for a corporation?
19. What is the difference between directly placed paper and dealer-placed paper?
20. What does the yield spread between commercial paper and Treasury bills of the same maturity reflect?
21. a. What is the difference between a liquidation and a reorganization?
    b. What is the difference between a Chapter 7 and Chapter 11 bankruptcy filing?
22. What is a debtor in possession?
23. What is the principle of absolute priority?
24. Comment on the following statement: "An investor who purchases the mortgage bonds of a corporation knows that should the corporation become bankrupt, mortgage bondholders will be paid in full before the common stockholders receive any proceeds."
25. Give three reasons to explain why absolute priority might be violated in a reorganization.

CHAPTER 8

Municipal Securities

Learning Objectives

After reading this chapter you will understand:

- who buys municipal securities and why the securities are attractive investments to these buyers

- the two basic security structures: general obligation bonds and revenue bonds

- the flow of funds structure for revenue bonds

- municipal bonds with hybrid structures and special bond security structures such as refunded bonds and insured municipal bonds

- the different types of tax-exempt short-term municipal securities

- what municipal derivative securities are

- how municipal inverse floaters are created

- the tax risk that investors face when investing in municipal securities

- yield spreads within the municipal market

- the shape of the municipal yield curve

- the primary and secondary markets for municipal securities

Municipal securities are issued by state and local governments and by governmental entities such as "authorities" or special districts. There are both tax-exempt and taxable municipal bonds. "Tax-exempt" means that interest on municipal bonds is exempt from federal income taxation, and it may or may not be taxable at the state and local levels. Most municipal bonds outstanding are tax-exempt. Municipal securities come in a variety of types, with different redemption features, credit risks, and liquidity.

Municipal securities are issued for various purposes. Short-term notes typically are sold in anticipation of the receipt of funds from taxes or receipt of proceeds from the sale of a bond issue, for example. Proceeds from the sale of short-term notes permit the issuing municipality to cover seasonal and temporary imbalances between outlays for expenditures and inflows from taxes. Municipalities issue long-term bonds as the principal means for financing both

(1) long-term capital projects such as schools, bridges, roads, and airports, and
(2) long-term budget deficits that arise from current operations.

INVESTORS IN MUNICIPAL SECURITIES

The single most important advantage of municipal securities to investors is the exemption of interest income from federal taxation, and the investor groups that have purchased these securities not surprisingly are those that benefit most from this exemption. Investors dominating the municipal securities market are households (retail investors), commercial banks, and property and casualty insurance companies. Although these three groups have dominated the market since the mid-1950s, their relative participation has shifted as the tax code has changed the relative demand for municipal securities.

Retail investor participation in the municipal securities market has fluctuated considerably since 1972. Retail investor market share had been trending downward, with some interruptions, but in 1981 the trend was reversed, and individual investors are now the largest holders of municipal securities. Individual investors may purchase municipal securities directly or through mutual funds and unit trusts. Recent legislation that has influenced the demand for municipal securities includes the Tax Reform Act of 1986, the Tax Act of 1990, and the Tax Act of 1992.

Two particular provisions of the Tax Reform Act of 1986 tend to offset one another, but on balance, make municipal securities more attractive to individual investors. First, the maximum marginal tax rate for individuals was reduced from 50% before tax revision to 28%. Some previously tax-exempt municipal interest income is now subject to an alternative minimum tax. Both the reduction in maximum marginal tax rates and the potential for taxation of municipal interest income under the alternative minimum tax reduce the value of the tax exemption feature. At the same time, however, the Tax Reform Act of 1986 eliminates or reduces the attractiveness of alternative investment vehicles that individual investors had been using to shelter investment income from taxation.

Then in 1990 the Tax Act served to increase the attractiveness of municipal securities by raising the maximum marginal tax rate to 33%. In fact, the effective tax rate is higher than 33% because of various limitations on deductions that households may take. The 1992 Tax Act increased the maximum tax rate to just under 40%.

Although individual investors are not entitled to deduct any interest cost that they incur to purchase municipal securities, commercial banks (before the Tax Reform Act of 1986) had been entitled to deduct 80% of the interest cost of funds used to purchase municipal bonds.[1] The 1986 act repealed this special exemption for banks for securities purchased after August 7, 1986. As a result, bank demand for municipal securities has declined dramatically.

Commercial banks hold the obligations of state and local governments for a variety of reasons in addition to shielding income from federal taxation. Most state and local governments mandate that public deposits at a bank be collateralized. Although

---

[1]Specifically, the Internal Revenue Code specifies that interest paid or accrued on "indebtedness incurred or continued to purchase or carry obligations, the interest on which is wholly exempt from taxes," is not tax-deductible.

Treasury or federal agency securities can serve as collateral, in fact the use of municipal securities is favored. Obligations of state and local governments may also be used as collateral when commercial banks borrow at the discount window of the Federal Reserve. Furthermore, banks frequently serve as underwriters or market makers for municipal securities, and these functions require maintaining inventories of these securities.

Purchases of municipal securities by property and casualty companies are primarily a function of their underwriting profit and investment income. Company profitability depends primarily upon the difference between the cost of claims filed and the revenues generated from insurance premiums and investment income, and claims on property and casualty companies are difficult to anticipate. Varying court awards for liability suits, the effect of inflation upon replacement and repair costs, and the unpredictability of weather are the chief factors that affect the level of claims experienced. Premiums for various types of insurance also are subject to competitive pressures and to approval from state insurance commissioners.

As can be expected, then, the profitability of property and casualty companies is cyclical. Normally, intense price competition follows highly profitable years. During these high-income periods, property and casualty companies typically step up their purchases of municipal securities in order to shield income from taxation. Lower rate increases for premiums are usually granted by state insurance commissioners during this time. Underwriting losses traditionally begin to exact a toll, as premium and investment income fail to keep pace with claims settlement costs. As underwriting losses mount, property and casualty insurance companies curtail their investment in municipal securities. The profitability cycle is completed when a company wins rate increases from state commissioners after sustaining continued underwriting losses. The 1986 act includes several provisions that reduce, but do not eliminate, the demand for municipal securities by property and casualty insurance companies.

TYPES AND FEATURES OF MUNICIPAL SECURITIES

There are basically two different types of municipal bond security structures: general obligation bonds and revenue bonds. There are also securities that share characteristics of both general obligation and revenue bonds.

General Obligation Bonds

General obligation bonds are debt instruments issued by states, counties, special districts, cities, towns, and school districts. Usually, a general obligation bond is secured by the issuer's unlimited taxing power. Some general obligations bonds are backed by taxes that are limited as to revenue sources and maximum property-tax millage amounts.[2] Such bonds are known as **limited-tax general obligation bonds.** For smaller governmental entities such as school districts and towns, the only available unlimited taxing power is on property. For larger general obligation bond issuers such as states and big cities, tax revenue sources are more diverse and may include corporate and individual income taxes, sales taxes, and property taxes. The security pledges for these

---

[2]Tax rates are assessed based on a millage, where 1 mill is equal to 0.001. So if a municipality has a millage rate of 5 mills and a property has an assessed value of $80,000, the tax would be 0.005 times $80,000, or $400.

larger issuers, such as states, are sometimes referred to as being **full faith and credit obligations.**

Additionally, certain general obligation bonds are secured not only by the issuer's general taxing powers to create revenues accumulated in a general fund, but also by certain identified fees, grants, and special charges, which provide additional revenues from outside the general fund. Such bonds are known as **double-barreled** in security because of the dual nature of the revenue sources.

Revenue Bonds

The second basic type of security structure is found in a revenue bond. Such bonds are issued for either project or enterprise financings in which the bond issuers pledge to the bondholders the revenues generated by the operating projects financed. A feasibility study is performed before the endeavor is undertaken to determine whether it can be self-supporting.

Flow of Funds Structure   For a revenue bond, the revenue of the enterprise is pledged to service the debt of the issue. The details of how revenue received by the enterprise will be disbursed are set forth in the trust indenture. Typically, the flow of funds for a revenue bond is as follows. First, all revenues from the enterprise are put into a revenue fund. It is from the revenue fund that disbursements for expenses are made to the following funds: **operation and maintenance fund, sinking fund, debt service reserve fund, renewal and replacement fund, reserve maintenance fund,** and **surplus fund.**[3]

Operations of the enterprise have priority over the servicing of the issue's debt, and cash needed to operate the enterprise is deposited from the revenue fund into the operation and maintenance fund. The pledge of revenue to the bondholders is a net revenue pledge, net meaning after operation expenses, so cash required to service the debt is deposited next in the sinking fund. Disbursements are then made to bondholders as specified in the trust indenture. Any remaining cash is then distributed to the reserve funds. The purpose of the debt service reserve fund is to accumulate cash to cover any shortfall of future revenue to service the issue's debt. The specific amount that must be deposited is stated in the trust indenture. The function of the renewal and replacement fund is to accumulate cash for regularly scheduled major repairs and equipment replacement. The function of the reserve maintenance fund is to accumulate cash for extraordinary maintenance or replacement costs that might arise. Finally, if any cash remains after disbursement for operations, debt servicing, and reserves, it is deposited in the surplus fund. The issuer can use the cash in this fund in any way it deems appropriate.

There are various restrictive covenants included in the trust indenture for a revenue bond to protect the bondholders. A rate, or user charge, covenant dictates how charges will be set on the product or service sold by the enterprise. The covenant could specify that the minimum charges be set so as to satisfy both expenses and debt servicing, or to yield a higher rate to provide for a certain amount of reserves. An ad-

---

[3]There are structures in which it is legally permissible for others to tap the revenues of the enterprise prior to the disbursement set forth in the flow of funds structure described next. For example, it is possible that the revenue bond could be structured such that the revenue is first applied to the general obligation of the municipality that has issued the bond.

ditional bonds' covenant indicates whether additional bonds with the same lien may be issued. If additional bonds with the same lien may be issued, conditions that must first be satisfied are specified. Other covenants specify that the facility may not be sold, the amount of insurance to be maintained, requirements for recordkeeping and for the auditing of the enterprise's financial statements by an independent accounting firm, and requirements for maintaining the facilities in good order.

Following are examples of revenue bonds.[4]

Airport Revenue Bonds   The revenues securing these bonds usually come from either traffic-generated sources—such as landing fees, concession fees, and airline fueling fees—or lease revenues from one or more airlines for the use of a specific facility such as a terminal or hangar.

College and University Revenue Bonds   The revenues securing these bonds usually include dormitory room rental fees, tuition payments, and sometimes the general assets of the college or university as well.

Hospital Revenue Bonds   The security for hospital revenue bonds usually depends on federal and state reimbursement programs (such as Medicaid and Medicare), third-party commercial payers (such as Blue Cross, health maintenance organizations, and private insurance), and individual patient payments.

Single-Family Mortgage Revenue Bonds   These bonds are usually secured by the mortgages and loan repayments on single-family homes. Security features vary but can include Federal Housing Administration (FHA), Veterans Administration (VA), or private mortgage insurance.[5]

Multifamily Revenue Bonds   These revenue bonds are usually issued for multifamily housing projects for senior citizens and low-income families. Some housing revenue bonds are secured by mortgages that are federally insured; others receive federal government operating subsidies or interest-cost subsidies; still others receive only local property tax reductions as subsidies.

Industrial Revenue Bonds   Generally, industrial revenue bonds are issued by state and local governments on behalf of individual corporations and businesses. The security for these bonds usually depends on the economic soundness of the particular corporation or business involved.

Public Power Revenue Bonds   These bonds are secured by revenues to be produced from electrical operating plants. Some bonds are for a single issuer, who constructs and operates power plants and then sells the electricity. Other public power revenue bonds are issued by groups of public and private investor-owned utilities for the joint financing of the construction of one or more power plants.

Resource Recovery Revenue Bonds   A resource recovery facility converts refuse (solid waste) into commercially salable energy, recoverable products, and a residue to be landfilled. The major revenues securing these bonds usually are (1) fees paid by

---

[4]The descriptions are adapted from various writings coauthored with Sylvan G. Feldstein of The Guardian Life.
[5]Mortgage insurance is discussed in Chapter 10.

those who deliver the waste to the facility for disposal; (2) revenues from steam, electricity, or refuse-derived fuel sold to either an electric power company or another energy user; and (3) revenues from the sale of recoverable materials such as aluminum and steel scrap.

Seaport Revenue Bonds   The security for these bonds can include specific lease agreements with the benefiting companies, or pledged marine terminal and cargo tonnage fees.

Sports Complex and Convention Center Revenue Bonds   These bonds usually receive revenues from sporting or convention events held at the facilities and, in some instances, from specific outside revenues such as local motel and hotel room taxes.

Student Loan Revenue Bonds   Student loan repayments under student loan revenue bond programs are sometimes 100% guaranteed either directly by the federal government or by a state guaranty agency.

Toll Road and Gas Tax Revenue Bonds   There are generally two types of highway revenue bonds. Bond proceeds of the first type are used to build such specific revenue-producing facilities as toll roads, bridges, and tunnels. For these pure enterprise-type revenue bonds, the revenues pledged usually are the monies collected through tolls. The second type of highway revenue bond is one in which bondholders are paid by earmarked revenues outside of toll collections, such as gasoline taxes, automobile registration payments, and driver's license fees.

Water Revenue Bonds   Water revenue bonds are issued to finance the construction of water treatment plants, pumping stations, collection facilities, and distribution systems. Revenues usually come from connection fees and charges paid by users of the water systems.

Hybrid and Special Bond Securities

Some municipal bonds that have the basic characteristics of general obligation bonds and revenue bonds have more issue-specific structures as well. Some examples are insured bonds, bank-backed municipal bonds, refunded bonds, moral obligation bonds, and "troubled city" bailout bonds.

Insured Bonds   Insured bonds, in addition to being secured by the issuer's revenue, are also backed by insurance policies written by commercial insurance companies. Insurance on a municipal bond is an agreement by an insurance company to pay the bondholder any bond principal and/or coupon interest that is due on a stated maturity date but that has not been paid by the bond issuer. When issued, this municipal bond insurance usually extends for the term of the bond issue, and it cannot be canceled by the insurance company.

Because municipal bond insurance reduces credit risk for the investor, the marketability of certain municipal bonds can be greatly expanded. Municipal bonds that benefit most from the insurance would include lower-quality bonds, bonds issued by smaller governmental units not widely known in the financial community, bonds that have a sound though complex and difficult-to-understand security structure, and bonds issued by infrequent local-government borrowers who do not have a general market following among investors.

Of course, a major factor for an issuer to obtain bond insurance is that its credit-worthiness without the insurance is substantially lower than what it would be with the insurance. That is, the interest cost savings are only of sufficient magnitude to offset the cost of the insurance premium when the underlying creditworthiness of the issuer is lower. In general, although insured municipal bonds sell at yields lower than they would without the insurance, they tend to have yields higher than other triple A–rated bonds.

Most insured municipal bonds are insured by one of the following insurance companies that are primarily in the business of insuring municipal bonds: AMBAC Indemnity Corporation; Capital Guaranty Insurance Company; Connie Lee Insurance Company; Financial Guaranty Insurance Company; Financial Security Assurance, Inc.; and Municipal Bond Investors Insurance Corporation.

Bank-Backed Municipal Bonds   Since the 1980s, municipal obligations have been increasingly supported by various types of credit facilities provided by commercial banks. The support is in addition to the issuer's cash flow revenues.

There are three basic types of bank support: letter of credit, irrevocable line of credit, and revolving line of credit. A **letter-of-credit agreement** is the strongest type of support available from a commercial bank. Under this arrangement, the bank is required to advance funds to the trustee if a default has occurred. An **irrevocable line of credit** is not a guarantee of the bond issue, although it does provide a level of security. A **revolving line of credit** is a liquidity-type credit facility that provides a source of liquidity for payment of maturing debt in the event that no other funds of the issuer are currently available. Because a bank can cancel a revolving line of credit without notice if the issuer fails to meet certain covenants, bond security depends entirely on the creditworthiness of the municipal issuer.

Refunded Bonds   Although originally issued as either revenue or general obligation bonds, municipals are sometimes refunded. A refunding usually occurs when the original bonds are escrowed or collateralized by direct obligations guaranteed by the U.S. government. By this it is meant that a portfolio of securities guaranteed by the U.S. government are placed in trust. The portfolio of securities is assembled such that the cash flow from all the securities matches the obligations that the issuer must pay. For example, suppose that a municipality has a 7% $100 million issue with 12 years remaining to maturity. The municipality's obligation is to make payments of $3.5 million every six months for the next 12 years and $100 million 12 years from now. If the issuer wants to refund this issue, a portfolio of U.S. government obligations can be purchased that has a cash flow of $3.5 million every six months for the next 12 years and $100 million 12 years from now.

When this portfolio of securities whose cash flow matches that of the municipality's obligation is in place, the refunded bonds are no longer secured as either general obligation or revenue bonds. The bonds are now supported by the portfolio of securities held in an escrow fund. Such bonds, if escrowed with securities guaranteed by the U.S. government, have little if any credit risk. They are the safest municipal bond investments available.

The escrow fund for a refunded municipal bond can be structured so that the refunded bonds are to be called at the first possible call date or a subsequent call date established in the original bond indenture. Such bonds are known as **prerefunded municipal bonds.** Although refunded bonds are usually retired at their first or subsequent call date, some are structured to match the debt obligation to the retirement date. Such bonds are known as **escrowed-to-maturity** bonds.

There are three reasons why a municipal issuer may refund an issue by creating an escrow fund. First, many refunded issues were originally issued as revenue bonds. Included in revenue issues are restrictive-bond covenants. The municipality may wish to eliminate these restrictions. The creation of an escrow fund to pay the bondholders legally eliminates any restrictive-bond covenants. This is the motivation for the escrowed-to-maturity bonds. Second, some issues are refunded in order to alter the maturity schedule of the obligation. Finally, when interest rates have declined after a municipal security has been issued, there is a tax arbitrage opportunity available to the issuer by paying existing bondholders a lower interest rate and using the proceeds to create a portfolio of U.S. government securities paying a higher interest rate.[6] This is the motivation for the prerefunded bonds.

Moral Obligation Bonds   A moral obligation bond is a security structure for state-issued bonds legally authorizing but not requiring the state legislature to make an appropriation out of general state tax revenues.

Troubled City Bailout Bonds   Troubled city bailout bonds are structured to appear as pure revenue bonds, but in essence they are not. Revenues come from general-purpose taxes and revenues that otherwise would have gone to the state's or the city's general fund. These bond structures were created to bail out underlying general obligation bond issuers from severe budget deficits. Examples are the New York State Municipal Assistance Corporation of the City of New York Bonds (MAC) and the State of Illinois Chicago School Finance Authority Bonds.

Redemption Features

Municipal bonds are issued with one of two debt retirement structures, or a combination. Either a bond has a serial maturity structure or it has a term maturity structure. A **serial maturity structure** requires a portion of the debt obligation to be retired each year. A **term maturity structure** provides for the debt obligation to be repaid on a final date.

Usually, term bonds have maturities ranging from 20 to 40 years and retirement schedules (sinking fund provisions) that begin five to 10 years before the final term maturity. Municipal bonds may be called prior to the stated maturity date, either according to a mandatory sinking fund or at the option of the issuer. In revenue bonds there is a catastrophe call provision that requires the issuer to call the entire issue if the facility is destroyed.

---

[6]Because the interest rate that a municipality must pay on borrowed funds is less than the interest rate paid by the U.S. government, in the absence of any restrictions in the tax code, a municipal issuer can realize a tax arbitrage. This can be done by issuing a bond and immediately investing the proceeds in a U.S. government security. There are tax rules that prevent such arbitrage. Should a municipal issuer violate the tax-arbitrage rules, the Internal Revenue Service will rule the issue to be taxable. However, if subsequent to the issuance of a bond interest rates decline so that the issuer will find it advantageous to call the bond, the establishment of the escrow fund will not violate the tax-arbitrage rules.

Special Investment Features

In Chapter 7 we described zero-coupon bonds, floating-rate bonds, and putable bonds in the corporate bond market. The municipal market also has securities with these features.

In the municipal bond market there are two types of zero-coupon bonds. One type is issued at a very deep discount and matures at par. The difference between the par value and the purchase price represents a predetermined compound yield. These zero-coupon bonds are similar to those issued in the taxable bond market for Treasuries and corporates. The second type is called a **municipal multiplier,** or **compound interest bond.** This is a bond issued at par that has interest payments. The interest payments are not distributed to the holder of the bond until maturity, but the issuer agrees to reinvest the undistributed interest payments at the bond's yield to maturity when it was issued. For example, suppose that a 10% 10-year coupon bond with a par value of $5,000 is sold at par to yield 10%. Every six months the maturity value of this bond is increased by 5% of the maturity value of the previous six months. At the end of 10 years, the maturity value of the bond will be equal to $13,266.[7] In the case of a 10-year zero-coupon bond priced to yield 10%, the bond would have a maturity value of $5,000 but sell for $1,884 when issued.[8]

MUNICIPAL MONEY MARKET PRODUCTS

Tax-exempt money market products include notes, commercial paper, variable-rate demand obligations, and a hybrid of the last two products.

Municipal Notes

Municipal notes include tax anticipation notes (TANs), revenue anticipation notes (RANs), grant anticipation notes (GANs), and bond anticipation notes (BANs). These are temporary borrowings by states, local governments, and special jurisdictions. Usually, notes are issued for a period of 12 months, although it is not uncommon for notes to be issued for periods as short as three months and for as long as three years. TANs and RANs (also known as TRANs) are issued in anticipation of the collection of taxes or other expected revenues. These are borrowings to even out irregular flows into the treasuries of the issuing entity. BANs are issued in anticipation of the sale of long-term bonds.

Tax-Exempt Commercial Paper

As with commercial paper issued by corporations, tax-exempt commercial paper is used by municipalities to raise funds on a short-term basis ranging from one to 270 days. The dealer sets interest rates for various maturity dates and the investor then selects the desired date. Provisions in the 1986 tax act have restricted the issuance of

---

[7]This is found by computing the future value of $5,000 twenty periods from now using a 5% interest rate. That is,

$$\$5,000 \times (1.05)^{20} = \$13,266$$

[8]This is found by computing the present value of $5,000 twenty periods from now by using a 5% interest rate. That is,

$$\$5,000 \times \frac{1}{(1.05)^{20}} = \$1,884$$

tax-exempt commercial paper. Specifically, the act limits the new issuance of municipal obligations that is tax exempt, and as a result, every maturity of a tax-exempt municipal issuance is considered a new debt issuance. Consequently, very limited issuance of tax-exempt commercial paper exists. Instead, issuers use one of the next two products to raise short-term funds.

Variable-Rate Demand Obligations

Variable-rate demand obligations (VRDOs) are floating-rate obligations that have a nominal long-term maturity but have a coupon rate that is reset either daily or every seven days. The investor has an option to put the issue back to the trustee at any time with seven days' notice. The put price is par plus accrued interest.

Commercial Paper/VRDO Hybrid

The commercial paper/VRDO hybrid is customized to meet the cash flow needs of an investor. As with tax-exempt commercial paper, there is flexibility in structuring the maturity, because the remarketing agent establishes interest rates for a range of maturities. Although the instrument may have a long nominal maturity, there is a put provision, as with a VRDO. Put periods can range from one day to more than 360 days. On the put date, the investor can put back the bonds, receiving principal and interest, or the investor can elect to extend the maturity at the new interest rate and put date posted by the remarketing agent at that time. Thus, the investor has two choices when initially purchasing this instrument: the interest rate and the put date. Interest is generally paid on the put date if the date is within 180 days. If the put date is more than 180 days forward, interest is paid semiannually.

Commercial paper dealers market these products under a proprietary name. For example, the Merrill Lynch product is called unit priced demand adjustable tax-exempt securities, or UPDATES. Lehman Brothers markets these simply as money market municipals. Goldman Sachs refers to these securities as flexible rate notes and Smith Barney Shearson markets them as BITS (bond interest term series).

MUNICIPAL DERIVATIVE SECURITIES

In recent years, a number of municipal products have been created from the basic fixed-rate municipal bond. This has been done by splitting up cash flows of newly issued bonds as well as bonds existing in the secondary markets. These products have been created by dividing the coupon interest payments and principal payments into two or more bond classes, or **tranches.** The resulting bond classes may have far different yield and price volatility characteristics than the underlying fixed-rate municipal bond from which they were created. By expanding the risk/return profile available in the municipal marketplace, institutional investors have more flexibility in structuring municipal bond portfolios either to satisfy a specific asset–liability objective or to make an interest rate or yield curve bet. In exchange for such benefits, municipal issuers benefit by being able to issue securities at a lower interest cost.

The name *derivative securities* has been attributed to these bond classes because they derive their value from the underlying fixed-rate municipal bond. Much of the development in this market has paralleled that of the taxable (specifically, the mortgage-backed securities) market discussed in Chapter 11. The ability of investment bankers to create these securities has been enhanced by the development of the municipal swap market. Next we give two examples of municipal derivative securities.

Floaters/Inverse Floaters

A common type of derivative security is one in which two classes of securities, a **floating-rate security** and an **inverse-floating-rate bond,** are created from a fixed-rate bond. The coupon rate on the floating-rate security is reset based on the results of a Dutch auction. The auction can take place anywhere between seven and 35 days. The coupon rate on the floating-rate security changes in the same direction as market rates. The inverse-floating-rate bond receives the residual interest; that is, the coupon interest paid on this bond is the difference between the fixed rate on the underlying bond and the rate on the floating-rate security. Thus the coupon rate on the inverse-floating-rate bond changes in the opposite direction of interest rates.

The sum of the interest paid on the floater and inverse floater (plus fees associated with the auction) must always equal the sum of the fixed-rate bond from which they were created. A floor (a minimum interest rate) is established on the inverse floater. Typically, the floor is zero. As a result, a cap (maximum interest rate) will be imposed on the floater such that the combined floor of zero on the inverse floater and the cap on the floater is equal to the total interest rate on the fixed-rate bond from which they were created.

Inverse floaters can be created in one of three ways. First, a municipal dealer can buy in the secondary market a fixed-rate municipal bond and place it in a trust. The trust then issues a floater and an inverse floater. The second method is similar to the first except that the municipal dealer uses a newly issued municipal bond to create a floater and an inverse floater. These two methods are illustrated in Exhibit 8-1. The third method is to create an inverse floater without the need to create a floater. This is done using the municipal swaps market and is discussed in Chapter 23.

The dealer determines the ratio of floaters to inverse floaters. For example, an investment banking firm may purchase $100 million of the underlying bond in the secondary market and issue $50 million of floaters and $50 million of inverse floaters. The dealer may opt for a 60/40 or any other split. The split of floaters/inverse floaters determines the leverage of the inverse floaters and thus affects its price volatility when interest rates change. In Chapter 4, we explained that the duration of an inverse floater is a multiple of the underlying fixed-rate issue from which it was created. The multiple is determined by the leverage. To date, the most popular split of floaters and

EXHIBIT 8-1   Creation of a Municipal Inverse Floater

Fixed-rate municipal bond (newly issued or seasoned)

Municipal floating-rate bond

Municipal inverse-floating-rate bond

inverse floaters has been 50/50. In such instances, the inverse floater will have double the duration of the fixed-rate bond from which it is created. Determination of the leverage will be set based on the desires of investors at the time of the transaction.

The investor in the inverse floater can purchase the corresponding floater at auction and combine her two positions to effectively own the underlying fixed-rate bond. This can be done if interest rates are rising and the investor wishes to close out her inverse floater position. Because the market for inverse floaters is not highly liquid at this time, this represents an easy way to convert her position into a synthetic fixed-rate bond. In the future, the investor may opt to split the issue again, retaining the inverse floater. This is a valuable option for investors. As a result, the yield on this bond will generally be less than the yield on a comparable fixed-rate bond that does not have this option.

Several investment banking firms active in the municipal bond market have developed proprietary products. Merrill Lynch's institutional floaters are called FLOATS and its inverse floaters are called RITES (residual interest tax-exempt securities). Goldman Sachs' proprietary products are called PARS (periodic auction reset securities), which are floaters, and INFLOS, which are inverse floaters. Lehman Brothers' proprietary products are called RIBS (residual interest bonds) and SAVRS (select auction variable-rate securities).

Strips and Partial Strips

Municipal strip obligations are created when a municipal bond's cash flows are used to back zero-coupon instruments. The maturity value of each zero-coupon bond represents a cash flow on the underlying security. These are similar to the strips that are created in the Treasury market that we described in Chapter 6. One example of this in the municipal bond market is Merrill Lynch's M-TIGRS.

Partial strips have also been created from cash bonds, which are zero-coupon instruments to a particular date, such as a call date, and then converted into coupon-paying instruments. These are called **convertibles** or **step-up bonds.** Merrill Lynch markets these as LIMOS. Goldman Sachs uses the name GAINS for these instruments.

Other products can be created by allocating the interest payments and principal of a fixed-coupon-rate municipal bond to more than two bond classes. For example, consider a noncallable/nonputable $100 million par value issue with a coupon rate of 6%. From this fixed-rate issue, it would be possible to create three bond classes: (1) $60 million par value of a 4% fixed-rate coupon bond, (2) a floating-rate bond with a par value of $20 million and a coupon rate that floats based on the J. J. Kenny index plus 200 basis points, and (3) an inverse floating rate with a par value of $20 million, which receives the residual interest from the difference between the underlying issue and the coupon on the floating-rate class. Notice that the total par value of the collateral is distributed among the three bond classes, as is the fixed coupon interest on the underlying issue. In addition to creating a floater and an inverse floater, a synthetic fixed-rate municipal bond selling at a discount has also been created. This is because in this illustration the required coupon rate on the underlying municipal bond would be 6% for it to sell at par, but the fixed-rate bond class created has the same maturity and only a 4% coupon rate. Thus, it will sell at a discount. An investor who prefers a discount security (which has higher volatility than a similar bond selling at par, as explained in Chapter 4) because of an anticipated decline in interest rates but finds it difficult to obtain such bonds in the marketplace will be attracted to this synthetic bond.

These types of structure were introduced by Lehman Brothers in February 1993 as part of a $95.6 million offering of the Pennsylvania Housing Agency and again a month later in a $740 million offering of the Puerto Rico Telephone Agency.[9] These are collectively called **pieces and strips.**

CREDIT RISK

Although municipal bonds at one time were considered second in safety only to U.S. Treasury securities, today there are new concerns about the credit risks of municipal securities.[10] The first concern came out of the New York City billion-dollar financial crisis in 1975. On February 25, 1975, the State of New York's Urban Development Corporation defaulted on a $100 million note issue that was the obligation of New York City; many market participants had been convinced that the State of New York would not allow the issue to default. Although New York City was later able to obtain a $140 million revolving credit from banks to cure the default, lenders became concerned that the city would face difficulties in repaying its accumulated debt, which stood at $14 billion on March 31, 1975. This financial crisis sent a loud and clear warning to market participants in general—regardless of supposedly ironclad protection for the bondholder, when issuers such as large cities have severe financial difficulties, the financial stakes of public employee unions, vendors, and community groups may be dominant forces in balancing budgets. This reality was reinforced by the federal bankruptcy law that took effect in October 1979, which made it easier for the issuer of a municipal security to go into bankruptcy.

The second reason for concern about municipal securities credit risk is the proliferation in this market of innovative financing techniques to secure new bond issues. In addition to the established general obligation bonds and revenue bonds, there are now more non–voter-approved, innovative, and legally untested security mechanisms. These innovative financing mechanisms include "moral obligation" bonds and commercial bank-backed letters of credit bonds, to name a few. What distinguishes these newer bonds from the more traditional general obligation and revenue bonds is that there is no history of court decisions or other case law that firmly establishes the rights of the bondholders and the obligations of the issuers. It is not possible to determine in advance the probable legal outcome if the newer financing mechanisms were to be challenged in court. This is illustrated most dramatically by the bonds of the Washington Public Power Supply System (WPPSS), where bondholder rights to certain revenues were not upheld by the highest court in the state of Washington.

As with corporate bonds, some institutional investors in the municipal bond market rely on their own in-house municipal credit analysts for determining the creditworthiness of a municipal issue; other investors rely on the nationally recognized rating companies. The two leading rating companies are Moody's and Standard &

---

[9]Aaron Pressman, "Lehman's 'Strips and Pieces' Allow Investors Multitude of Options in Structuring Portfolios," *The Bond Buyer,* March 26, 1993.
[10]For a history of defaults of municipal bonds, see Chapter 2 in Sylvan G. Feldstein and Frank J. Fabozzi, *The Dow Jones–Irwin Guide to Municipal Bonds* (Homewood, IL: Dow Jones–Irwin, 1987).

Poor's, and the assigned rating system is essentially the same as that used for corporate bonds.

In evaluating general obligation bonds, the commercial rating companies assess information in four basic categories.[11] The first category includes information on the issuer's debt structure to determine the overall debt burden. The second category relates to the issuer's ability and political discipline to maintain sound budgetary policy. The focus of attention here usually is on the issuer's general operating funds and whether it has maintained at least balanced budgets over three to five years. The third category involves determining the specific local taxes and intergovernmental revenues available to the issuer as well as obtaining historical information both on tax collection rates, which are important when looking at property tax levies, and on the dependence of local budgets on specific revenue sources. The fourth and last category of information necessary to the credit analysis is an assessment of the issuer's overall socioeconomic environment. The determinations that have to be made here include trends of local employment distribution and composition, population growth, real estate property valuation, and personal income, among other economic factors.

Although there are numerous security structures for revenue bonds, the underlying principle in rating is whether the project being financed will generate sufficient cash flow to satisfy the obligations due bondholders.[12] A natural question to ask is: How good are the ratings? Of the municipal securities that were rated by a commercial rating company in 1929 and plunged into default in 1932, 78% had been rated double A or better, and 48% had been rated triple A. Since then the ability of rating agencies to assess the creditworthiness of municipal securities has evolved to a level of general industry acceptance and respectability. In most instances, ratings adequately describe the financial condition of the issuers and identify the credit risk factors. A small but significant number of recent instances still have caused market participants to reexamine their reliance on the opinions of the rating companies. One example is the bonds of the WPPSS mentioned previously. The two major commercial rating companies gave their highest ratings to these bonds in the early 1980s. While these high-quality ratings were in effect, WPPSS sold more than $8 billion in long-term bonds. By 1986 more than $2 billion of these bonds were in default.

RISKS ASSOCIATED WITH INVESTING IN MUNICIPAL SECURITIES

The investor in municipal securities is exposed to the same risks affecting corporate bonds plus an additional one that may be labeled **tax risk.** There are two types of tax risk to which tax-exempt municipal securities buyers are exposed. The first is the risk that the federal income tax rate will be reduced. The higher the marginal tax rate, the greater the value of the tax exemption feature. As the marginal tax rate declines, the

---

[11]Although there are many similarities in how Moody's and Standard & Poor's approach the credit rating of general obligation bonds, there are differences in their approaches as well. For a discussion of these differences, see Feldstein and Fabozzi, *The Dow Jones–Irwin Guide to Municipal Bonds.*

[12]A comprehensive discussion of the analysis of various revenue bond structures is found in Sylvan G. Feldstein, Frank J. Fabozzi, and Irving M. Pollack (eds.), *The Municipal Bond Handbook,* Vol. II (Homewood, IL: Dow Jones–Irwin, 1983); and Feldstein and Fabozzi, *The Dow Jones–Irwin Guide to Municipal Bonds.*

price of a tax-exempt municipal security will decline. When in 1995 there were Congressional proposals regarding the introduction of a flat tax with a low tax rate, tax-exempt municipal bonds began trading at lower prices.

The second type of tax risk is that a municipal bond issued as a tax-exempt issue may eventually be declared to be taxable by the Internal Revenue Service. This may occur because many municipal revenue bonds have elaborate security structures that could be subject to future adverse congressional action and IRS interpretation. A loss of the tax exemption feature will cause the municipal bond to decline in value in order to provide a yield comparable to similar taxable bonds. As an example, in June 1980, the Battery Park City Authority sold $97.315 million in notes, which at the time of issuance legal counsel advised were exempt from federal income taxation. In November 1980, however, the IRS held that interest on these notes was not exempt. The issue was not settled until September 1981, when the Authority and the IRS signed a formal agreement resolving the matter so as to make the interest on the notes tax-exempt.

YIELDS ON MUNICIPAL BONDS

As explained in Chapter 5, a common yield measure used to compare the yield on a tax-exempt municipal bond with a comparable taxable bond is the equivalent taxable yield. The equivalent taxable yield is computed as follows:

$$\text{equivalent taxable yield} = \frac{\text{tax-exempt yield}}{1 - \text{marginal tax rate}}$$

For example, suppose that an investor in the 40% marginal tax bracket is considering the acquisition of a tax-exempt municipal bond that offers a yield of 6.5%. The equivalent taxable yield is 10.83%, as follows:

$$\text{equivalent taxable yield} = \frac{0.065}{1 - 0.40} = 0.1083$$

When computing the equivalent taxable yield, the traditionally computed yield to maturity is not the tax-exempt yield if the issue is selling at a discount because only the coupon interest is exempt from federal income taxes. Instead, the yield to maturity after an assumed tax rate on the capital gain is computed and used in the numerator of the formula shown here. The yield to maturity after an assumed tax on the capital gain is calculated in the same manner as the traditional yield to maturity as explained in Chapter 3.

Yield Spreads

Because of the tax-exempt feature of municipal bonds, the yield on municipal bonds is less than that on Treasuries with the same maturity. Exhibit 8-2 shows this ratio on January 1, 1998 and January 1, 1999. The ratio of municipal yields to Treasury yields varies over time, as can be seen in Exhibit 8-2, which graphs the triple A municipal yields as a percentage of U.S. Treasury yields. Yield spreads within the municipal bond market are attributable to differences between credit ratings (i.e., quality spreads), sectors within markets (intramarket spreads), and differences between maturities (maturity spreads).

EXHIBIT 8-2

As of 1-1-98

(Yield)

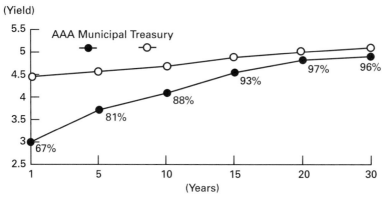

As of 1-1-99

Source: Goldman, Sachs & Co., "Fixed Income Research," *Weekly Market Update*, November 18, 1994, p. A-5. Reprinted by permission.

Quality Spreads

Our statement in Chapter 5 about quality spreads between credit ratings for corporate bonds over the interest-rate cycle is true for municipal bonds: Quality spreads widen during recessionary periods but narrow during periods of economic prosperity. Another factor that can cause changes in the quality spread is a temporary oversupply of issues within a market sector. For example, a substantial new-issue volume of high-grade state general obligation bonds may tend to decrease the spread between high-grade and lower-grade revenue bonds. In a weak market environment, it is easier for high-grade municipal bonds to come to market than weaker ones. Therefore, it is not uncommon for high grades to flood weak markets at the same time there is a relative scarcity of medium- and lower-grade municipal bond issues.

Maturity Spreads

In the municipal bond market, several benchmark curves exist. In general, a benchmark yield curve is constructed for AAA-quality-rated state general obligation bonds. Exhibit 8-3 shows such a yield curve.

EXHIBIT 8-3 AAA State General Obligation Yield Curve and
U.S. Treasury Yield Curve after 40% Tax

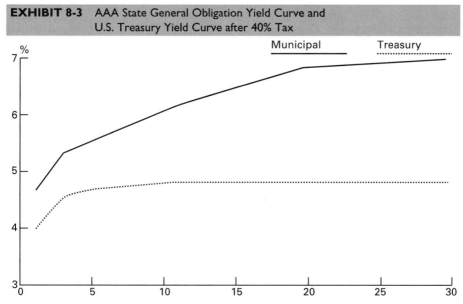

Source: Goldman, Sachs & Co., "Fixed Income Research," *Weekly Market Update,* November 18,
1994, p. A-5. Reprinted by permission.

In the Treasury and corporate bond markets, it is not unusual to find at different
times all four shapes for the yield curve described in Chapter 5. In general, the municipal yield curve is positively sloped. There was a brief period where the municipal
yield curve became inverted. In fact, during the period when the Treasury yield curve
was inverted, the municipal yield curve maintained its upward-sloping shape. Prior to
1986 the municipal yield curve was consistently steeper than the Treasury yield curve
as measured by the spread between the 30-year and one-year issue. Between 1986 and
1990, the steepness was comparable. In 1991, the municipal yield curve became
steeper than the Treasury yield curve. Exhibit 8-3 compares the two yield curves assuming a 40% tax rate on Treasury coupon interest.

Intramarket Spreads

There are spreads between different sectors within the revenue market. Exhibit 8-4
shows the spread between different revenue bonds. Each revenue bond category is
measured against a triple A general obligation benchmark.

Spreads between General Market and In-State Issues

There is another reason for spreads between municipal issues. Bonds of municipal issuers located in certain states yield considerably less than issues of identical credit
quality that come from other states that trade in the general market. One reason for
this is that states often exempt interest from in-state issues from state and local personal income taxes, whereas interest from out-of-state issues is generally not exempt.
Consequently, in states with high income taxes, such as New York and California,
strong investor demand for in-state issues will reduce their yields relative to bonds of

EXHIBIT 8-4 Spreads within the Revenue Bond Market (Intramarket Spreads)[a]

Type of Revenue Bond	Yield (%)	Spread to Benchmark (basis points)
Housing	7.41	46
Public power	7.34	39
Hospital	7.86	91

[a]Benchmark: AAA general obligation bonds

Source: Goldman, Sachs & Co., "Fixed Income Research," *Weekly Market Update,* November 18, 1994, p. A-5. Reprinted by permission.

issuers located in states where state and local income taxes are not important considerations (e.g., Florida).

MUNICIPAL BOND MARKET

Primary Market

A substantial number of municipal obligations are brought to market each week. A state or local government can market its new issue by offering bonds publicly to the investing community or by placing them privately with a small group of investors. When a public offering is selected, the issue usually is underwritten by investment bankers and/or municipal bond departments of commercial banks. Public offerings may be marketed by either competitive bidding or direct negotiations with underwriters. When an issue is marketed via competitive bidding, the issue is awarded to the bidder submitting the best bid.

Usually, state and local governments require a competitive sale to be announced in a recognized financial publication, such as the *Bond Buyer,* which is a trade publication for the municipal bond industry. The *Bond Buyer* also provides information on upcoming competitive sales and most negotiated sales, as well as the results of previous weeks.

Most states mandate that general obligation issues be marketed through competitive bidding, but generally this is not required for revenue bonds. Recent scandals involving financial contributions of underwriters to elected officials have made some municipalities concerned with whether they are receiving the lowest-cost funding possible. Consequently, more municipalities are requiring competitive bidding for both general obligation and revenue issues.

An **official statement** describing the issue and the issuer is prepared for new offerings. Municipal bonds have legal opinions that are summarized in the official statement. The relationship of the legal opinion to the safety of the bond is twofold. First, bond counsel determines if the issuer is indeed legally able to issue the bonds. Second, bond counsel verifies that the issuer has prepared for the bond sale properly by having enacted various required ordinances, resolutions, and trust indentures and without violating any other laws and regulations.

Secondary Market

Municipal bonds are traded in the over-the-counter market supported by municipal bond dealers across the country. Markets are maintained on smaller issuers (referred to as **local general credits**) by regional brokerage firms, local banks, and by some of the larger Wall Street firms. Larger issuers (referred to as **general names**) are supported by the larger brokerage firms and banks, many of whom have investment banking relationships with these issuers. There are brokers who serve as intermediaries in the sale of large blocks of municipal bonds among dealers and large institutional investors. In addition to these brokers and the daily offerings sent out over the *Bond Buyer's* "munifacts" teletype system, many dealers advertise their municipal bond offering for the retail market in what is known as *The Blue List.* This is a 100-plus-page booklet published every weekday by the Standard & Poor's Corporation that gives municipal securities offerings and prices.

In the municipal bond markets, an odd lot of bonds is $25,000 or less in par value for retail investors. For institutions, anything below $100,000 in par value is considered an odd lot. Dealer spreads depend on several factors. For the retail investor, the spread can range from as low as one-fourth of one point ($12.50 per $5,000 par value) on large blocks of actively traded bonds to four points ($200 per $5,000 of par value) for odd-lot sales of an inactive issue. For institutional investors, the dealer spread rarely exceeds one-half of one point ($25 per $5,000 of par value).

The convention for both corporate and Treasury bonds is to quote prices as a percentage of par value with 100 equal to par. Municipal bonds, however, generally are traded and quoted in terms of yield (yield to maturity or yield to call). The price of the bond in this case is called a **basis price.** The exception is certain long-maturity revenue bonds. A bond traded and quoted in dollar prices (actually, as a percentage of par value) is called a **dollar bond.**

SUMMARY

Municipal securities are issued by state and local governments and their authorities, with the coupon interest on most issues being exempt from federal income taxes. The primary investors in these securities are households (which includes mutual funds), commercial banks, and property and casualty insurance companies. Changes in the tax law have an effect on the relative attractiveness of municipal securities for these three groups of investors.

The two basic security structures are general obligation bonds and revenue bonds. The former are secured by the issuer's generally taxing power. Revenue bonds are used to finance specific projects and are dependent on revenues from those projects to satisfy the obligations. There are also hybrid securities that have certain characteristics of both general obligation and revenue bonds, and some securities that have unique structures. Municipal money market products include notes, commercial paper, variable-rate demand notes, and a hybrid of commercial paper and variable-rate demand notes. Derivative securities have been created from the basic fixed-rate municipal bond, the most popular being inverse floaters.

Municipal bonds may be retired with a serial maturity structure, a term maturity structure, or a combination. As in the case of corporate bonds, there are zero-coupon bonds and floating-rate bonds. Investing in municipal securities exposes investors to the same qualitative risks as investing in corporate bonds, with the additional risk that a change in the tax law may affect the price of municipal securities adversely.

Because of the tax-exempt feature, yields on municipal securities are lower than those on comparably rated taxable securities. Within the municipal bond market, there are quality spreads and maturity spread. Typically, the municipal yield curve is upward sloping. Moreover, there are yield spreads related to differences between in-state issues and general market issues.

Questions

1. Explain why you agree or disagree with the following statements:
   a. "All municipal bonds are exempt from federal income taxes."
   b. "All municipal bonds are exempt from state and local taxes."
2. If Congress changes the tax law so as to increase marginal tax rates, what will happen to the price of municipal bonds?
3. Why would a property and casualty insurance company shift its allocation of funds from corporate bonds to municipal bonds?
4. What is the difference between a general obligation bond and a revenue bond?
5. Which type of municipal bond would an investor analyze using an approach similar to that for analyzing a corporate bond?
6. a. In a revenue bond, which fund has priority when funds are disbursed from the reserve fund, the operation and maintenance fund or the debt service reserve fund?
   b. In a revenue bond, what is a catastrophe call provision?
7. What is the tax risk associated with investing in a municipal bond?
8. "An insured municipal bond is safer than an uninsured municipal bond." Indicate whether you agree or disagree with this statement.
9. In your view, would the typical AAA- or AA-rated municipal bond be insured?
10. Explain the different types of refunded bonds.
11. Give two reasons why an issuing municipality would want to refund an outstanding bond issue.
12. a. What are the three basic types of bank support for a bank-backed municipal security?
    b. Which is the strongest type of support available from a commercial bank?
13. What are TAN, RAN, GAN, and BAN?
14. Why has there been a decline in the issuance of tax-exempt commercial paper?
15. a. Explain how an inverse-floating-rate municipal bond can be created.
    b. Who determines the leverage of an inverse floater?
    c. What is the duration of an inverse floater?
16. For years, observers and analysts of the debt market believed that municipal securities were free of any risk of default. Why do most people now believe that municipal debt can carry a substantial amount of credit or default risk?
17. a. What is the equivalent taxable yield for an investor facing a 40% marginal tax rate, and who can purchase a tax-exempt municipal bond with a yield of 7.2?
    b. What are the limitations of using the equivalent taxable yield as a measure of relative value of a tax-exempt bond versus a taxable bond?
18. a. What is typically the benchmark yield curve in the municipal bond market?
    b. What can you say about the typical relationship between the yield on short- and long-term municipal bonds?
19. How does the steepness of the Treasury yield curve compare with that of the municipal yield curve?

CHAPTER 9

Non–U.S. Bonds

Learning Objectives

After reading this chapter you will understand:

- the reasons for the globalization of financial markets

- the classification of global financial markets

- what the foreign bond market is

- what a Eurobond is and the different types of Eurobond structures

- factors considered in the rating of sovereign bonds

- how to compare yields on U.S. bonds and Eurobonds

- what a global bond is

- the foreign exchange risk exposure of an investor who invests in nondollar-denominated bonds

- the motivation for investing in nondollar bonds

- the methods of distribution of new government bonds

- the government bond markets of Japan, Germany, the United Kingdom, France, Canada, the Netherlands, and Australia

- the emerging bond markets

- the two clearing systems to handle international transactions: Euroclear and Cedel

Prior to the 1980s, U.S. bond investors invested exclusively in U.S. domestic bonds. Among the reasons for their lack of participation in the non–U.S. bond markets were lack of familiarity with the structure of these markets, lack of familiarity with interest rate movements in these markets, concern about the liquidity of these markets, unfamiliarity with and concern about foreign sovereign and private credit risk, and foreign withholding taxes on U.S. investors.

In recent years, however, U.S. investors have become increasingly aware of non–U.S. interest-rate movements and their relationship to U.S. interest rates. In addition, foreign countries have liberalized their bond markets, making them more liquid and more accessible to international investors. In many cases, withholding taxes have been eliminated or reduced. Futures and options markets have been developed on government bonds in several major countries, permitting more effective implementation of hedging and arbitrage strategies. And in general, there is an increased awareness of the non–U.S. bond markets as potential sources of return enhancement and/or risk reduction. As a result, U.S. bond managers—mainly money managers who manage pension funds or other institutional monies, and mutual fund managers or others who manage retail monies—have increasingly adopted a global approach and invested in bonds from several countries.

Many global investors participate only in the foreign government bond markets rather than the nongovernment bond markets, because of the low credit risk, the liquidity, and the simplicity of the government markets. While nongovernment markets ("semigovernment," local government, corporate, and mortgage bond markets) provide higher yields, they also have greater credit risks, and foreign investors may not be ready to accept alien credit risks and less liquidity. In this chapter we look at the Eurobond market and several non–U.S. government bond markets.

CLASSIFICATION OF GLOBAL BOND MARKETS

There is no uniform system for classifying the sectors of the global bond market, although one possible classification is as follows. From the perspective of a given country, the global bond market can be classified into two markets: an internal bond market and an external bond market. The **internal bond market** is also called the **national bond market.** It can be decomposed into two parts: the domestic bond market and the foreign bond market. The **domestic bond market** is where issuers domiciled in the country issue bonds and where those bonds are subsequently traded. Exhibit 9-1 provides a schematic presentation of this classification system.

The **foreign bond market** of a country is where bonds of issuers not domiciled in the country are issued and traded. For example, in the U.S. the foreign bond market is the market where bonds are issued by non–U.S. entities and then subsequently traded. Bonds traded in the U.S. foreign bond market are nicknamed **Yankee bonds.** In Japan, a yen-denominated bond issued by a British corporation and subsequently traded in Japan's bond market is part of the Japanese foreign bond market. Yen-denominated bonds issued by non-Japanese entities are nicknamed **Samurai bonds.**

EXHIBIT 9-1 Classification of Global Financial Markets

Foreign bonds in the United Kingdom are referred to as **bulldog bonds,** in the Netherlands as **Rembrandt bonds,** and in Spain as **matador bonds.**

Regulatory authorities in the country where the bond is issued impose certain rules governing the issuance of foreign bonds. These may include (1) restrictions on the bond structures that may be issued (e.g., unsecured debt, zero-coupon bonds, convertible bonds, and so on), (2) restrictions on the minimum or maximum size of an issue and/or the frequency with which an issuer may come to market, (3) a waiting period before an issuer can bring the issue to market (imposed to avoid an oversupply of issues), (4) a minimum quality standard (credit rating) for the issue or issuer, (5) disclosure and periodic reporting requirements, and (6) restrictions on the types of financial institutions permitted to underwrite issues. The 1980s have been characterized by general government relaxation or abolition of these restrictions so as to open up their bond markets to issuers.

The **external bond market,** also called the **international bond market,** includes bonds with the following distinguishing features: (1) they are underwritten by an international syndicate; (2) at issuance they are offered simultaneously to investors in a number of countries; (3) they are issued outside the jurisdiction of any single country; and (4) they are in unregistered form. The external bond market is commonly referred to as the **offshore bond market,** or, more popularly, the **Eurobond market.** The classification used here is by no means universally accepted. Some market observers refer to the external bond market as consisting of the foreign bond market and the Eurobond market.

In September 1989 the first true **global bond** was issued. This was a 10-year $1.5 billion offering of the World Bank. What makes this issue a global bond is its simultaneous offering in the U.S. Yankee bond market and in the Eurobond market. It represents the first attempt to surmount the fragmented market for U.S. dollar-denominated bonds. A few corporations have since begun to issue global bonds. Since June 1990, Citicorp has had several global bond issues, ranging from $1 billion to $1.5 billion. Each issue was backed by credit-card receivables and denominated in U.S. dollars. Two Canadian utility companies, Ontario-Hydro and Hydro-Quebec, have had several global bond offerings. The first global non–U.S. dollar issue was done by Ontario-Hydro in December 1990, denominated in Canadian dollars. In more recent years, global bonds have been issued by financial institutions in the form of asset-backed securities, particularly credit card receivable asset-backed securities.

In general, it is felt that the following three characteristics must be met for an entity to issue global bonds: (1) the issuer must have a consistent demand for funds, (2) the amount of funds needed on a regular basis must be around $1 billion, and (3) the issuer must have a high credit rating.[1]

FOREIGN EXCHANGE RISK AND BOND RETURNS

The return to U.S. investors from investments in non–U.S. bonds that are denominated in a foreign currency consists of two components: (1) the return on the security measured in the currency in which the bond is denominated (called **local currency**

---

[1] These three characteristics were suggested by Dan Roth, then-Treasurer of the World Bank (Desmond Dodd, "New Currencies Seen as Next Test for Global Issues," *Corporate Financing Week,* Special Supplement, November 25, 1991, p. 9.)

return), which results from coupon payments, reinvestment income, and capital gains/losses; and (2) changes in the foreign exchange rate.

An **exchange rate** is the amount of one currency that can be exchanged for another currency, or the price of one currency in terms of another currency. Since the early 1970s, exchange rates between currencies have been free to float, with market forces determining the relative value of a currency.[2] Thus, each day a currency's value may stay the same, increase, or decrease relative to that of another currency. When a currency declines in value relative to another currency, it is said to have **depreciated** relative to the other currency. Alternatively, this is the same as saying that the other currency has **appreciated.**

From the perspective of a U.S. investor, the cash flows of assets denominated in a foreign currency expose the investor to uncertainty as to the cash flow in U.S. dollars. The actual U.S. dollars that the investor gets depend on the exchange rate between the U.S. dollar and the foreign currency at the time the nondollar cash flow is received and exchanged for U.S. dollars. If the foreign currency depreciates (declines in value) relative to the U.S. dollar, the dollar value of the cash flows will be proportionately less. This risk is referred to as **foreign exchange risk.** This risk can be hedged with foreign exchange spot, forwards, futures, or options instruments (although there is a cost of hedging).

Several reasons have been offered for why U.S. investors should allocate a portion of their fixed income portfolio to nondollar bonds. The party line is that diversifying bond investments across countries—particularly with the currency hedged—may provide diversification resulting in a reduction in risk. This is generally demonstrated using modern portfolio theory by showing that investors can realize a higher expected return for a given level of risk (as measured by the standard deviation of return) by adding nondollar bonds in a portfolio containing U.S. bonds. Although there was ample evidence in the 1980s and early 1990s that this might have been true, recent evidence suggests that the reduction in risk may not be that great.[3]

One study suggests that while the diversification benefits may not be that great, a powerful reason for a U.S. investor to invest in nondollar bonds is "the increased opportunities to find value that multiple markets provide" but it is hard to quantify such a benefit because it depends on the investor's talents.[4] That is, nondollar bond investments—with the currency hedged—permits investment strategies based on interest-rate changes in various countries, thereby providing additional dimensions to the actual investment decision or a broader range of investment choices. Another reason given for nondollar bond investing is that the decision not to hedge the currency component can then be regarded as an active currency play.

---

[2] In practice, national monetary authorities can intervene in the foreign exchange market for their currency for a variety of economic reasons, so the current foreign exchange system is sometimes referred to as a *managed* floating rate system.

[3] See Robert Litterman, "Nondollar Bond Markets: Opportunities for U.S. Portfolio Managers," *Fixed Income Research* (New York: Goldman, Sachs & Co., April 1992), and Michael R. Rosenberg, "International Fixed Income Investing: Theory and Practice," Chapter 49 in Frank J. Fabozzi and T. Dessa Fabozzi (eds.), *The Handbook of Fixed Income Securities* (Burr Ridge, IL: Irwin Professional Publishing, 1995).

[4] Litterman, "Nondollar Bond Markets," pp. 2–3.

SIZE OF THE WORLD BOND MARKET

Exhibit 9-2 summarizes the size in U.S. dollars of the major bond markets at year end 1997. The values reported are in nominal dollars outstanding, not market value. The U.S. bond market is by far the largest bond market in the world. It is more than double the size of the second largest bond market, Japan. For the 21 countries shown, information for the following sectors are shown in Exhibit 9-2: central government, central government agency and government guaranty, state and local governments, corporate issues (including convertible issues), noncorporate domestic issues, foreign bonds, Eurobonds, and private placements. For each country the largest sector is the central government sector.

EUROBOND MARKET

The Eurobond market is divided into sectors depending on the currency in which the issue is denominated. For example, when Eurobonds are denominated in U.S. dollars, they are referred to as **Eurodollar bonds.** Eurobonds denominated in Japanese yen are referred to as **Euroyen bonds.**

In recent years it has become increasingly difficult to classify a bond issue as a foreign bond or a Eurobond based on the distinguishing characteristics that we cited earlier.[5] We noted that the most important characteristic of a Eurobond offering is the composition of the underwriting syndicate. Yet "bought deals"—when there is only one underwriter—are becoming increasingly common. A bond offering in which there is only one underwriter and in which the issue is placed primarily outside the national market of both the issuer and underwriter would not traditionally be classified as a Eurobond offering. Another characteristic of a Eurobond is that it is not regulated by the single country whose currency is used to pay bondholders. In practice, however, only the United States and Canada do not place restrictions on U.S. dollar– or Canadian dollar–denominated issues sold outside their two countries. Regulators of other countries whose currencies are used in Eurobond issues have closely supervised such offerings. Their power to regulate Eurobond offerings comes from their ability to impose foreign exchange and/or capital restrictions.

Although Eurobonds are typically registered on a national stock exchange, the most common being the Luxembourg, London, or Zurich exchanges, the bulk of all trading is in the over-the-counter market. Listing is purely to circumvent restrictions imposed on some institutional investors who are prohibited from purchasing securities that are not listed on an exchange. Some of the stronger issuers privately place issues with international institutional investors.

Issuers of foreign bonds include national governments and their subdivisions, corporations (financial and nonfinancial), and supranationals. A **supranational** is an entity that is formed by two or more central governments through international treaties. The purpose for creating a supranational is to promote economic development for the member countries. Two examples of supranational institutions are the International Bank for Reconstruction and Development, popularly referred to as the World Bank,

---

[5]Michael Bowe, *Eurobonds* (Kent, U.K.: Square Mile Books, 1988), pp. 16–17.

EXHIBIT 9-2 Size of Major Bond Markets at Year-End 1996 (Nominal Value Outstanding; Billions of U.S. Dollars or Equivalent)

Bond Market	Total Publicly Issued	As a Pct of Public Issues in All Markets	Central Govt.	Central Govt. Agency & Govt. Guaranty	State & Local Govt.	Corp. (Incl. Cvts.)	Other Domestic Publicly Issued	Foreign Bonds	Intl. Bonds[b]	Euro Bonds	Private Place Unclass.
U.S. Dollar	$9,583.4	44.5%	$2,682.3	$2,634.5	$1,049.6	$1,910.0	$346.9	$175.9		$784.3	$717.4
Japanese Yen	3,655.9	17.0	1,951.5	197.4	96.6	410.0	655.2	105.9		239.3	552.5
Deutschemark	2,303.1	10.7	699.8	55.8	83.0	2.1	1,158.7	—	$303.7[c]	—	—
Italian Lira	1,274.4	5.9	978.4	20.4	—	4.6	182.5	3.3		85.0	—
French Franc	1,044.0	4.8	509.7	219.3	2.8	152.7	—	6.5		153.0	—
U.K. Sterling	661.8	3.1	446.5	—	0.1	32.7	—	6.7		175.9	—
Canadian Dollar	446.3	2.1	202.8	—	110.3	61.2	0.7	0.4		71.0	—
Dutch Guilder	400.8	1.9	196.8	—	—	119.9	—	5.0		76.4	82.6
Belgian Franc	386.9	1.8	216.9	5.7	2.7	16.2	110.4	36.6		1.2	—
Danish Krone	288.0	1.3	104.2	—	—	—	175.1	—		8.7	—
Swedish Krona	253.4	1.2	117.4	—	1.0	7.4	123.9	—		3.7	—
Swiss Franc	241.4	1.1	26.3	—	22.5	27.9	64.8	99.8		—	68.3
Spanish Peseta	234.4	1.1	171.8	—	13.4	17.6	16.2	15.4		—	—
Australian Dollar	163.6	0.8	74.4	37.0	—	13.9	—	0.4		37.8	—
Austrian Schilling	132.5	0.6	57.0	1.8	0.5	4.5	66.4	2.4		—	5.3
European Currency Unit	130.0	0.6	65.6	—	—	—	—	—		64.4	—
South African Rand	74.4	0.3	57.4	13.4	1.9	—	—	—		1.7	—
Portuguese Escudo	58.7	0.3	35.2	—	1.3	6.3	7.7	8.2		—	—
Greek Drachma	57.6	0.3	55.7	—	—	—	—	1.4		0.5	—
Finnish Markka	56.4	0.3	38.6	—	0.9	5.4	9.6	—		1.8	—
Norwegian Krone	49.0	0.2	19.1	2.3	6.8	3.3	16.8	0.4		0.3	—
Irish Pound	30.0	0.1	27.5	0.9	—	1.0	—	0.2		0.3	—
New Zealand Dollar	21.5	0.1	12.9	1.3	—	3.0	—	0.2		4.2	—
Total	$21,547.4	100.0%	$8,747.9	$3,189.8	$1,393.3	$2,799.8	$2,934.9	$468.5	$2,481.6[d]	$2,013.1	$1,426.1[e]
Sector as a Pct. of Public Issues in All Markets		100.0%	40.6%	14.8%	6.5%	13.0%	13.6%		11.5%		

[a]Exchange rates prevailing as of December 31, 1996: ¥116.0/US$; DM1.5548/US$; Lit1,530.6/US$; C$1.3696/US$; £0.5889/US$; Dfl1.6859/US$; Bfr32.005/US$; Dkr5.945/US$; Skr6.871/US$; Sfr1.3464/US$; Pta131.28/US$; A$1.2555/US$; Ffr5.237/US$; Ecu0.7988/US$; R4.6825/US$; Esc156.38/US$; Dr247.02/US$; Fmk4.6439/US$; Nkr6.4425/US$; Ir£0.5948/US$; and NZ$1.4156/US$. [b]Includes both Foreign and Eurobond totals. [c]The German bond market does not distinguish between Euro and Foreign international issues. [d]Includes straight, convertible and floating-rate debt. [e]In addition, an unspecified amount of privately placed issues of the private sectors exists.

Source: How Big is the World Bond Market?—1997 Update, Salomon Brothers Inc., September 1997.

and the Inter-American Development Bank. The general objective of the former is to improve the efficiency of the international financial and trading markets. The objective of the latter supranational is to promote economic growth in the developing countries of the Americas.

Securities Issued in the Eurobond Market

The Eurobond market has been characterized by new and innovative bond structures to accommodate particular needs of issuers and investors. There are, of course, the "plain vanilla," fixed-rate coupon bonds, referred to as **Euro straights.** Because these are issued on an unsecured basis, they are usually issued by high-quality entities.

Coupon payments are made annually, rather than semiannually, because of the higher cost of distributing interest to geographically dispersed bondholders. There are also zero-coupon bond issues, deferred-coupon issues, and step-up issues, all of which were described in earlier chapters.

Dual-Currency Bonds   There are issues that pay coupon interest in one currency but pay the principal in a different currency. Such issues are called **dual-currency issues.** For the first type of dual-currency bond, the exchange rate that is used to convert the principal and coupon payments into a specific currency is specified at the time the bond is issued. The second type differs from the first in that the applicable exchange rate is the rate that prevails at the time a cash flow is made (i.e., at the spot exchange rate at the time a payment is made). The third type is one that offers to either the investor or the issuer the choice of currency. These bonds are commonly referred to as **option currency bonds.** A specific example is the index currency option note (ICON) introduced by the Long-Term Credit Bank of Japan in 1985.

Convertible Bonds and Bonds with Warrants   A convertible Eurobond is one that can be converted into another asset. Bonds with attached warrants represent a large part of the Eurobond market. A warrant grants the owner of the warrant the right to enter into another financial transaction with the issuer if the owner will benefit as a result of exercising. Most warrants are detachable from the host bond; that is, the bondholder may detach the warrant from the bond and sell it.

There are a wide array of bonds with warrants: equity warrants, debt warrants, and currency warrants. An **equity warrant** permits the warrant owner to buy the common stock of the issuer at a specified price. A **debt warrant** entitles the warrant owner to buy additional bonds from the issuer at the same price and yield as the host bond. The debt warrant owner will benefit if interest rates decline because a bond with a higher coupon can be purchased from the same issuer. A **currency warrant** permits the warrant owner to exchange one currency for another at a set price (i.e., a fixed exchange rate). This feature protects the bondholder against a depreciation of the foreign currency in which the bond's cash flows are denominated. There are also **gold warrants,** which allow the warrant holder to purchase gold from the issuer of the bond.

Floating-Rate Notes   There are a wide variety of floating-rate Eurobond notes. In the Eurobond market, almost all floating-rate notes are denominated in U.S. dollars, with non–U.S. banks being the major issuers. The coupon rate on a Eurodollar floating-rate note is some stated margin over the London interbank offered rate (LIBOR), the bid on LIBOR (referred to as LIBID), or the arithmetic average of LIBOR and LIBID (referred to as LIMEAN). The size of the spread reflects the perceived credit risk of the issuer, margins available in the syndicated loan market, and the liquidity of the issue. Typical reset periods for the coupon rate are either every six months or every quarter, with the rate tied to six-month or three-month LIBOR, respectively; that is, the length of the reset period and the maturity of the index used to establish the rate for the period are matched.

Many issues have either a minimum coupon rate (or floor) that the coupon rate cannot fall below and a maximum coupon rate (or cap) that the coupon rate cannot rise above. An issue that has both a floor and a cap is said to be **collared.** There are some issues that grant the borrower the right to convert the floating coupon rate into a fixed coupon rate at some time. There are some issues referred to as **drop-lock bonds,** which automatically change the floating coupon rate into a fixed coupon rate under certain circumstances.

A floating-rate note issue will either have a stated maturity date, or it may be a **perpetual** (also called **undated**) **issue** (i.e., with no stated maturity date). The perpetual issue was introduced into the Eurobond market in 1984. For floating-rate notes that do mature, the term is usually greater than five years, with the typical maturity being between seven and 12 years. There are callable and putable floating-rate notes; some issues are both callable and putable.

Comparing Yields on U.S. Bonds and Eurodollar Bonds

Because Eurodollar bonds pay annually rather than semiannually, an adjustment is required to make a direct comparison between the yield to maturity on a U.S. fixed-rate bond and that on a Eurodollar fixed-rate bond. Given the yield to maturity on a Eurodollar fixed-rate bond, its bond-equivalent yield is computed as follows:

bond-equivalent yield of Eurodollar bond

$$= 2[(1 + \text{yield to maturity on Eurodollar bond})^{1/2} - 1]$$

For example, suppose that the yield to maturity on a Eurodollar bond is 10%. Then the bond-equivalent yield is

$$2[(1.10)^{1/2} - 1] = 0.09762 = 9.762\%$$

Notice that the bond-equivalent yield will always be less than the Eurodollar bond's yield to maturity.

To convert the bond-equivalent yield of a U.S. bond issue to an annual-pay basis so that it can be compared to the yield to maturity of a Eurodollar bond, the following formula can be used:

yield to maturity on annual-pay basis

$$= \left(1 + \frac{\text{yield to maturity on bond-equivalent basis}}{2}\right)^2 - 1$$

For example, suppose that the yield to maturity of a U.S. bond issue quoted on a bond-equivalent yield basis is 10%. The yield to maturity on an annual-pay basis would be

$$[(1.05)^2 - 1] = 0.1025 = 10.25\%$$

The yield to maturity on an annual basis is always greater than the yield to maturity on a bond-equivalent basis.

SOVEREIGN BOND RATINGS

Sovereign debt is the obligation of a country's central government. Whereas U.S. government debt is not rated by any nationally recognized statistical rating organization, the debt of other national governments is rated. For the reasons discussed subsequently, there are two sovereign debt ratings assigned by rating agencies: a local currency debt rating and a foreign currency debt rating.

The categories used by Standard & Poor's in deriving their ratings are listed in Exhibit 9-3. The two general categories are economic risk and political risk. The former category is an assessment of the ability of a government to satisfy its obligations. Both quantitative and qualitative analyses are used in assessing economic risk. Political risk is an assessment of the willingness of a government to satisfy its obligations. A government may have the ability to pay but may be unwilling to pay. Political risk is assessed based on qualitative analysis of the economic and political factors that influence a government's economic policies.

The reason for distinguishing between local debt ratings and foreign currency debt ratings is that historically, the default frequency differs by the currency denomination of the debt. Specifically, defaults have been greater on foreign currency-denominated debt. For example, an S&P survey of 113 countries found that since 1970 there were eight defaults by sovereigns on their local currency debt but 69 on foreign currency debt.

The reason for the difference in default rates for local currency debt and foreign currency debt is that if a government is willing to raise taxes and control its domestic financial system, it can generate sufficient local currency to meet its local currency debt obligation. This is not the case with foreign currency-denominated debt. A national government must purchase foreign currency to meet a debt obligation in that foreign currency and therefore has less control with respect to its exchange rate. Thus, a significant depreciation of the local currency relative to a foreign currency in which a debt obligation is denominated will impair a national government's ability to satisfy such obligation.

The implication of this is that the factors S&P analyzes in assessing the creditworthiness of a national government's local currency debt and foreign currency debt will differ to some extent. In assessing the credit quality of local currency debt, for example, S&P emphasizes domestic government policies that foster or impede timely debt service. The key factors looked at by S&P are as follows:

"• Stability of political institutions and degree of popular participation in the political process.
 • Economic system and structure.
 • Living standards and degree of social and economic cohesion.

EXHIBIT 9-3 Sovereign Ratings Methodology Profile

Political Risk
- Form of government and adaptability of political institutions
- Extent of popular participation
- Orderliness of leadership succession
- Degree of consensus on economic policy objectives
- Integration in global trade and financial system
- Internal and external security risks

Income and Economic Structure
- Living standards, income, and wealth distribution
- Market, non-market economy
- Resource endowments, degree of diversification

Economic Growth Prospects
- Size, composition of savings, and investment
- Rate, pattern of economic growth

Fiscal Flexibility
- General government operating and total budget balances
- Tax competitiveness and tax-raising flexibility
- Spending pressures

Public Debt Burden
- General government financial assets
- Public debt and interest burden
- Currency composition, structure of public debt
- Pension liabilities
- Contingent liabilities

Price Stability
- Trends in price inflation
- Rates of money and credit growth
- Exchange rate policy
- Degree of central bank autonomy

Balance of Payments Flexibility
- Impact on external accounts of fiscal and monetary policies
- Structure of the current account
- Composition of capital flows

External Debt and Liquidity
- Size and currency composition of public external debt
- Importance of banks and other public and private entities as contingent liabilities of the sovereign
- Maturity structure and debt service burden
- Debt service track record
- Level, composition of reserves and other public external assets

---

Source: Exhibit 1 in David T. Beers and Marie Cavanaugh, "Sovereign Credit Ratings: A Primer," Chapter 6 in Frank J. Fabozzi and Alberto Franco (eds.), *Handbook of Emerging Fixed Income and Currency Markets* (New Hope, PA: Frank J. Fabozzi Associates, 1997).

- Fiscal policy and budgetary flexibility.
- Public debt burden and debt service track record.
- Monetary policy and inflation pressures."

The single most important leading indicator according to S&P is the rate of inflation.

For foreign currency debt, credit analysis by S&P focuses on the interaction of domestic and foreign government policies. S&P analyzes a country's balance of payments and the structure of its external balance sheet. The area of analysis with respect to its external balance sheet are the net public debt, total net external debt, and net external liabilities.

OVERVIEW OF SEVERAL NON–U.S. GOVERNMENT BOND MARKETS

The institutional settings for government bond markets throughout the world vary considerably, and these variations may affect liquidity and the ways in which strategies are implemented, or, more precisely, affect the tactics of investment strategies. For example, in the government bond market different primary market issuance practices may affect the liquidity and the price behavior of specific government bonds in a country. The nature of the secondary market affects the ease and cost of trading. The importance of the benchmark effect in various countries may influence which bonds to trade and hold. In addition, yields are calculated according to different methods in various countries, and these differences will affect the interpretation of yield spreads. Withholding and transfer tax practices also affect global investment strategies.

Although the cash flows of a government bond issue are typically in the currency of the issuing country, in recent years there have been an increasing number of issues denominated in **European currency units** (ECUs). An ECU is a composite currency created by the European Economic Community. The currencies in ECUs are those that are included in the European Monetary System (EMS). The weight of each country's currency is figured according to the relative importance of a country's economic trade and financial sector within the European Economic Community. With the introduction of the Euro in 1998, future issues will be denominated in this currency.

We review next the Japanese, German, U.K., French, Canadian, Dutch, and Australian government bond markets in order to provide a flavor of the variety of government bonds available.[6] Short-term government issues, referred to as Treasury bills, are not stressed, although, just as in the United States, the Treasury bill is often the largest sector of the government debt market. Before describing these government bond markets, we describe the various methods that can be used to issue government bonds.

Methods of Distribution of New Government Securities

We described the primary market for distribution of U.S. Treasury securities in Chapter 6. There are four methods that have been used in distributing new securities of central governments: the regular calendar auction/Dutch style system, the regular calendar auction/minimum-price offering, the ad hoc auction system, and the tap system.

---

[6]The brief description of each market is drawn from Frank J. Jones and Frank J. Fabozzi, *Major Government Bond Markets* (Chicago: Probus Publishing, 1991).

In the **regular calendar auction/Dutch style auction system,** there is a regular calendar auction and winning bidders are allocated securities at the yield (price) they bid. As we explained in Chapter 6, this is a multiple-price auction and the U.S. Department of the Treasury currently uses this method when issuing all U.S. Treasury securities except the two-year and five-year notes.

In the **regular calendar auction/minimum-price offering system,** there is a regular calendar of offering. The price (yield) at which winning bidders are awarded the securities is different from the Dutch style auction. Rather than awarding a winning bidder at the yield (price) they bid, all winning bidders are awarded securities at the highest yield accepted by the government (i.e., the stop-out yield). For example, if the highest yield or stop-out yield for a government issue at auction is 7.14% and someone bids 7.12%, that bidder would be awarded the securities at 7.12%. In contrast, with the minimum-price offering method, that bidder would be awarded securities at 7.14% which means a lower price than at the bid price of 7.12%. In Chapter 6, we referred to this auction method as a single-price auction. The regular calendar auction/minimum-price offering method is used in Germany and France. In the United States it is currently used in the issuance of the two-year and five-year notes.

In the **ad hoc auction system,** governments announce auctions when prevailing market conditions appear favorable. It is only at the time of the auction that the amount to be auctioned and the maturity of the security to be offered are announced. This is one of the methods used by the Bank of England in distributing British government bonds. From the issuing government's perspective, there are two advantages of an ad hoc auction system over a regular calendar auction. First, a regular calendar auction introduces greater market volatility than an ad hoc auction does because yields tend to rise as the announced auction date approaches and then fall afterward. Second, there is reduced flexibility in raising funds with a regular calendar auction. After the election of the Conservative Party in England in 1992, there was a significant drop in the yields on British government bonds. The Bank of England used that window to obtain almost a third of the government's funding needs for fiscal year 1992–1993 in just the first two months of its fiscal year.

In a **tap system** additional bonds of a previously outstanding bond issue are auctioned. The government announces periodically that it is adding this new supply. The tap system has been used in the United Kingdom and the Netherlands.

Japanese Government Bonds

There are four types of Japanese government securities issued publicly: (1) short-term Treasury bills, (2) medium-term bonds, (3) long-term bonds, and (4) super-long-term bonds.

There are two types of medium-term bonds: bonds with coupons and zero-coupon bonds. Bonds with coupons have maturities of two, three, and four years. The market for medium-term bonds tends to be illiquid because such bonds are typically purchased by individuals and investment trust funds, which tend to be buy-and-hold investors. The other type of medium-term bond is the five-year zero-coupon bond. These are sold primarily to individual investors; consequently, the market for these securities tends to be illiquid.

Ten-year bonds are coupon bearing and are referred to as **long-term bonds.** During October 1986, 20-year fixed-rate bonds, referred to as **super-long-term bonds,** were issued publicly for the first time. There were three subsequent issues during 1987 and additional issues during 1988. As a rule, 10-year bonds are issued each month; 20-year bonds recently have been issued at the rate of three times per year; and five-year discount bonds recently have been issued at a rate of once a quarter. Auctions of coupon-bearing medium-term bonds are held nearly every month, although in recent years only two-year bonds have been issued.

Long-term bonds and super-long-term bonds are noncallable, but the government can repurchase bonds in the secondary market. Both long-term bonds and super-long-term bonds are numbered serially and referred to by number rather than maturity and coupon. For example, the No. 129 10-year is the 6.4% of 03/20/00, and the No. 16 super-long is the 6.8% of 09/20/11. All coupon bonds pay semiannual interest, just as in the U.S. Treasury coupon market.

In recent years, the Japanese government has cut back sharply on the issuance of medium-term and super-long-term bonds. Issuance of long-term (10-year) bonds has been reduced somewhat, although the issuance of Treasury bills has been increased substantially. Additional information about the primary and secondary markets for Japanese government bonds is provided at the end of this chapter.

German Government Bonds

The Federal Republic of Germany issues four types of securities: (1) Treasury discount paper (**Unverzinsliche Schätzungsweisungen,** often abbreviated as U-Schatze); (2) federal government notes, **Bundeskassenobligationen** (also called Kassens); (3) **Bundesobligationen** (often called OBLEs); and (4) federal government bonds **Bundesanleihen,** also referred to as Bunds). With the unification of West and East Germany in October 1990, the German Unity Fund began to issue Unity Fund bonds (Unities), which are fully guaranteed by the federal government. Government agency bonds are also issued by the Federal Railway **(Bundesbahn)** and the Post Office **(Bundespost)** with the full faith and credit of the federal government.

U-Schatze are discounted money market instruments with maturities of up to two years. Kassens are notes issued to satisfy the short- and medium-term needs of the German government and its agencies. Maturities range from two to six years. They are bullet issues with no call features. Kassens are issued irregularly several times a year by tender; OBLEs are five-year federal government debt issues.

Bunds have original maturities from six to 30 years, although recently no issues have been longer than 10 years. Ten-year Bunds are the largest sector of the German government securities market in terms of amount outstanding and secondary market turnover. Although 10-year Bunds typically have been issued on a monthly basis, this schedule has not been rigid.

All coupon payments are annual rather than semiannual as in the United States and Japan; this is the convention followed in the European bond market overall. Additional information about the German government bond market follows at the end of the chapter.

U.K. Government Bonds

Gilts (gilt-edged stock) are bonds issued and guaranteed by the British government. Four types of gilts are available: (1) straights (most are bullet bonds but some are callable), (2) convertibles, (3) index-linked, and (4) irredeemables (perpetuals also called "undateds").

Generally, **convertibles** have short maturities that give the holder the option to convert into a specified amount of a longer-maturity gilt (or more than one gilt) for a number of years. Convertibles have a series of conversion dates with varying (decreasing) conversion values. For example, convertibles may offer conversion dates every half-year for two and a half years, with the conversion value decreasing from £102 to £98. Thus, every convertible bond has a conversion schedule (or more than one) indicating the issues into which it can be converted, with conversion dates and corresponding conversion prices for each bond into which it can be converted. Index-linked gilts have coupons and final redemption amounts linked to the General Index of Retail Price (RPI), an index that is released each month by the Central Statistical Office. **Index-linked gilts** have low coupons, 2% to 2½%, which, in effect, reflect the real rate of return. Maturities of index-linked gilts vary from short term to the year 2024. **Irredeemable gilts** are issued without a final maturity but are redeemable after a specified date on three months' notice from the government. The largest of these is the War Loan 3½% or after. Twenty-five years ago, this was the largest of all gilt issues, with £1.9 billion outstanding. These gilts were issued when yields were low and have coupons in the range 2½% to 4%. There are currently six irredeemable issues outstanding.

There are more types of gilts than there are types of issues in other government bond markets. More than 100 gilt-edged bond issues are outstanding. Each gilt is specified by name, coupon, redemption (maturity) date (if any; irredeemables have no maturity date), and callability (callable gilts are also called "double-dated"). Gilts have nine different names: Exchequer, Treasury, Funding, Redemption, Transport, Gas, Conversion, Consols, and War Loan (redemptions have reduced War Loans to only one outstanding issue). Each name refers specifically to the government department that issued the bond or the reason for the issue. For example, "Conversion" indicates that the gilts are converted gilts resulting from the conversion of previously issued convertible gilts; "Transport" and "Gas" refer to bonds issued upon nationalization of these industries. The names have no practical significance, however, and do not affect value. Recently, all new issues have been either Treasury or Exchequer. There is no distinction between these two types of issues.

Maturities range from one to 30 years. Recently, the government has issued less long-term debt. Typical categories for gilts by maturity are (1) short-dated gilts: zero to seven years; (2) medium-dated gilts: seven to 15 years; (3) long-dated gilts: greater than 15 years; and (4) undated gilts: no redemption date (e.g., the War Loan).

French Government Bonds

The French Treasury issues instruments with maturities of three months to 30 years. Treasury bills, in general, are called BTNs **(bons du Trésor négociables)** and include discount Treasury bills [Bons Taux Fixe (BTF)], which have maturities of 13, 26, and 52 weeks, and interest-bearing Treasury bills [Treasury notes: **bons taux fixe et a in-**

térêts annuels (BTAN)] that have a fixed-coupon rate and are currently issued with two- and five-year maturities.

The market for French government bonds, the **obligation assimilables du Trésor** (OAT), has been reformed significantly since May 1985. This reform has increased the liquidity of the market, making it more attractive to foreign investors. OATs are fungible Treasury bonds with both fixed rates and floating rates.[7] OATs are not callable. They were first issued (via auction) during May 1985, and all government bond issues since have been OATs. Beginning in 1987, the French Treasury harmonized its auction cycle by issuing five types of OATs on a monthly basis.

There are two types of floaters: one based on bond yields and the other on bill yields. OAT TME (**taux moyen d'emprunts d'état,** or, more explicitly, **taux mensuel de rendement d'emprunts d'état à long terme**) are floating-rate bonds based on bond yields. The coupon is fixed annually based on an index of government bond yields on issues with maturities of seven years or more. Coupon is paid annually. OAT TRB (**taux révisable des bons du Trésor,** floating-rate bonds based on Treasury bill yields.

Since 1985, OATs have been the only type of bonds issued. Before 1985, however, French government bonds had no standard form, and several types of bonds were issued, some of them still outstanding. For example, exchangeable bonds (**emprunts exchangeables)** allowed either a fixed-rate bond to be converted to a floating-rate bond or a floating-rate bond to be converted to a fixed-rate bond during prespecified time periods. Bonds with exchange warrants (**emprunts bon d'enchange)** were a type of exchangeable bond with a detachable warrant that can be sold separately in the secondary market for TME-type variable-rate bonds (as indicated above). Extendable bonds (**emprunts prorogeables)** granted the owner the right to extend the maturity to a prespecified date. Renewable bonds [**obligations renouvelables du Trésor** (ORTs)] have been issued with six-year maturities and the right to renew within a three-year period (interest is capitalized and paid either at maturity or time of renewal). In this case the owner may exchange the old ORT for a new six-year ORT with a new interest rate determined at time of renewal.

Canadian Government Bonds

The Canadian government bond has been closely related to the U.S. government debt market and has a similar structure, including types of issues. The Canadian government bond market has a wide variety of issues. Government bonds with maturities of two to 30 years are issued. The long maturity ranges have become increasingly important in recent years. Treasury bills with maturities of three, six, and 12 months are issued weekly.

Coupons on Canadian government bonds range from 3% to 18%, and all bonds have fixed coupons. All new Canadian bonds are in "bullet" form; that is, they are not callable or putable. Some previous issues, however, have had purchase funds that permit the government periodically to buy a small proportion (precisely 0.5% per quarter) if the issue is trading below the original issue price.

In 1991, the Canadian government issued its first issue of real return bonds ($700 million, due in 2021). The issue was priced to yield a real return equal to 4.25%.

---

[7]The word *assimilables* means *assimilations* or *fungible,* which, in practice, means that within a year new bonds of a given maturity are issued as new tranches of existing bonds.

Dutch Government Bonds

There are two basic Dutch government bond instruments outstanding. The first type is sinking fund issues. The second type is three- to 15-year bullet issues. Until mid-1988 the Dutch government market was dominated by sinking fund bonds ("sinkers"), but since then the market has been dominated by bullets, specifically 10-year bullets. Dutch investors have preferred sinkers, but international investors did not, so reorientation of the Dutch market toward sinkers is consistent with growing internationalization of the market. All sinking fund bonds are now quite illiquid. Ten-year Dutch guilders are issued approximately eight times per year.

Australian Government Bonds

The Australian bond market often experiences substantial foreign participation because it has been regarded as a high-yield market and is a stable country. Commonwealth Government Securities are guaranteed with respect to principal and interest by the Commonwealth Government of Australia. The two major types of Australian government securities are Treasury notes and Treasury bonds. There are also small amounts of index-linked Treasury bonds and retail-oriented Australian savings bonds. Treasury notes are discount securities up to 26 weeks in maturity. Treasury bonds have fixed maturities (up to about 20 years) and pay coupons semiannually. Indexed-linked Treasury bonds have either interest payments or capital linked to the Australian Consumer Price Index. Interest-indexed securities pay a fixed coupon every six months plus an arrears adjustment that amounts to the increase in the CPI. Capital-indexed securities also pay a fixed coupon (usually 4%), with the increase in the CPI added to the capital value of the bond and paid on maturity. Interest-indexed bonds rarely trade.

EMERGING MARKET BONDS

The financial markets of Latin America, Asia with the exception of Japan, and Eastern Europe are viewed as emerging markets. Investing in the government bonds of emerging market countries entails considerably more credit risk than investing in the government bonds of major industrialized countries. Standard & Poor's and Moody's rate emerging market sovereign debt. Although there are exceptions, the securities issued by governments of emerging market countries are denominated in U.S. dollars. Some governments of emerging market countries have been able to issue Eurobonds.

A good amount of secondary trading of government debt of emerging markets is in **Brady bonds.** Basically, these bonds represent a restructuring of nonperforming bank loans of governments into marketable securities. An agreement for the restructuring of nonperforming bank loans was first worked out between Mexico and the United States by the then Secretary of the Treasury Nicholas Brady—hence, nicknamed Brady bonds. The agreement called for U.S. government and multilateral support to provide relief for principal and interest payments owed to banks outside Mexico if Mexico successfully implemented certain structural reforms. This U.S. government program was then extended to the government debt of other emerging markets.

Countries that issue Brady bonds are referred to as "Brady countries." As of August 1996, there were 13 Brady countries—eight from Latin America (Argentina,

Brazil, Costa Rica, the Dominican Republic, Ecuador, Mexico, Uruguay, and Venezuela) and five outside of Latin America (Bulgaria, Jordan, Nigeria, Philippines, and Poland). The Brady bonds issued by Argentina, Brazil, Mexico, and Venezuela represent more than 75% of Brady bonds issued.

There are two types of Brady bonds. The first type covers the interest due on these loans ("past-due interest bonds"). The second type covers the principal amount owed on the bank loans ("principal bonds"). Principal bonds have maturities at issuance from 25 to 30 years and are bullet bonds. They are more frequently traded than the past-due interest bonds and therefore have better liquidity. The principal bonds fall into two categories: par and discount bonds. Par principal bonds have a fixed rate; discount principal bonds have a floating rate.

Generally, principal bonds are partially collateralized by U.S. Treasury zero-coupon securities. As a result, for many Brady bonds the next two to three coupon payments following a default by the underlying government are guaranteed.

CLEARING SYSTEMS

Global financial markets require an effective system for the settlement of transactions. That is, buyers must receive the securities purchased, and sellers must receive cash payment, which is complicated when buyer and seller may be in two different countries. Moreover, the broker or dealer firms involved in a transaction may also be in different countries from the buyer and seller. Geographical separation of parties increases the potential for fails (i.e., the failure of the seller to deliver securities or of the buyer to make cash payment).

In response to such problems, two clearing systems have developed to handle international transactions: Euroclear, started in December 1968 by Morgan Guaranty Trust Company of New York, and Cedel, started in Luxembourg in September 1970. Their original objective was to handle Eurobond transactions, but now they handle a wide variety of securities and settle international primary and secondary equity transactions. They also provide important services for the effective functioning of global market transactions beyond the settlement of transactions. First, they offer financing services for dealers to finance their positions. Second, they provide a securities borrowing service so that dealers who are short securities can borrow them to cover their positions.

SUMMARY

In this chapter the Eurobond market and the non–U.S. government bond markets are discussed. The global bond market can be classified into two markets: the internal or national bond market, which consists of a domestic bond market and a foreign bond market, and the external or international bond market (or Eurobond market).

The Eurobond market is divided into sectors based on the currency in which the issue is denominated. Many innovative bond structures have been introduced in the Eurobond market, such as dual-currency issues and various types of convertible bonds and bonds with warrants. The floating-rate sector of the Eurobond market is dominated by U.S. dollar-denominated issues.

When a U.S. investor purchases non–U.S. bonds that are denominated in a foreign currency, the return to be realized will consist of two components. The first component is the local currency return, which results from coupon payments, reinvestment income, and capital gains/losses. The second component is any foreign exchange gain or loss resulting from converting the nondollar cash flows to U.S. dollars. Foreign exchange risk is the risk that the foreign currency depreciates (declines in value) relative to the U.S. dollar, resulting in the U.S. dollar value of the cash flows being lower.

Although it is often stated that the primary motivation to investing in non–U.S. bonds is that it provides diversification benefits, such benefits may not be significant. Rather, investing in non–U.S. bonds gives a money manager the opportunity to capitalize on factors that affect bond prices in non–U.S. markets and permits a currency play.

Sovereign debt is the obligation of a country's central government. Ratings are assigned separately for local currency denominated debt and foreign currency denominated debt. The two general categories analyzed by rating companies in assigning ratings are economic risk and political risk.

Many investors who have made the decision to invest in non–U.S. bonds participate only in the foreign government bond markets rather than the nongovernment bond markets. This is because of the low credit risk, liquidity, and simplicity of the government markets. In this chapter we reviewed the Japanese, German, United Kingdom, French, Canadian, Dutch, and Australian government bond markets.

Investors in the debt of governments of emerging countries are exposed to credit risk. Brady bonds are an important part of the bond market of emerging countries that are part of the Brady Plan. Euroclear and Cedel are two clearing systems that handle Eurobond transactions as well as provide dealer financing and a securities borrowing service.

Questions

1. What risk is faced by a U.S. life insurance company that buys British government bonds?
2. Why do U.S. investors who invest in non–U.S. bonds prefer foreign government bonds?
3. What institutional factors of a foreign government bond market affect the tactics of investment strategies?
4. "The strongest argument for investing in nondollar bonds is that there are diversification benefits." Explain why you agree or disagree with this statement.
5. What arguments are offered for investing in nondollar bonds?
6. What is the difference between LIBID and LIMEAN?
7. What is the foreign bond market of a country?
8. What is a global bond?
9. What are the general characteristics that must be met for an entity to issue global bonds?
10. What is a Eurobond?
11. What are the different types of warrants that have been included in Eurobond offerings?

12. This excerpt, which discusses dual currency bonds, is taken from the *International Capital Market,* published in 1989 by the European Investment Bank:

> The generic name of dual-currency bonds hides many different variations which are difficult to characterize in detail. These variations on the same basic concept have given birth to specific names like Index Currency Option notes (ICON), foreign interest payment bonds (FIPS), forex-linked bonds, heaven and hell bonds, to name but a few. Despite this diversity it is, however, possible to attempt a broad-brush classification of the various types of dual-currency bonds.
>
> The first category covers bond issues denominated in one currency but for which coupon and repayment of the principal are made in another designated currency at an exchange rate fixed at the time of issue. A second category comprises dual-currency bonds in which coupon payments and redemption proceeds are made in a currency different from the currency of denomination at the spot exchange rate that will prevail at the time of payment.
>
> Within this category, one finds the forex-linked bonds, foreign currency bonds and heaven and hell bonds. A final category includes bonds which offer to issuers or the holder the choice of the currency in which payments and/or redemptions are to be made at the future spot exchange rate. ICONs fall into this latter category because there is an implicit option due to the exchange rate revision formula. Usually, these bonds are referred to as option currency bonds.
>
> Irrespective of the above-mentioned categories, all dual-currency bonds expose the issuers and the holders to some form of foreign exchange risk. . . . Pricing dual-currency bonds is therefore an application of option pricing, as the bonds can be looked at as a combination of a straight bond and a currency option. The value of the straight bond component is obtained according to traditional fixed-rate bond valuation models. The pricing of the option component is, ex post, equal to the difference between the dual currency bond price and its straight bond component. . . .

   a. Why do all currency bonds "expose the issuers and the holders to some form of foreign exchange risk" regardless of the category of bond?

   b. Do you agree that the pricing of all dual-currency bonds is an application of option pricing?

   c. Why should the price of the option component be "equal to the difference between the dual currency bond price and its bond component"?

13. a. Why do rating agencies assign a different rating to the debt of a sovereign entity based on whether the debt is denominated in a local currency or a foreign currency?

   b. What is the single most important leading indicator according to Standard & Poor's in assessing a sovereign entities debt?

14. a. What are the four types of securities issued by the Japanese government?

   b. How is the benchmark government issue determined in the Japanese bond market?

15. What is a gilt?

16. Suppose that the yield to maturity on a Eurodollar bond is 7.8%. What is the bond-equivalent yield?

17. What are the different methods for the issuance of government securities?
18. The quotation following is from an article titled "Spanish Bonds to Be Tops" that appeared in the March 4, 1991, issue of *BondWeek:*

> The Spanish bond market will be one of the best performing European markets this year due to its relatively high yields, a strong peseta [the Spanish currency] and moves by the Spanish government to liberalize the market, according to analysts. The Spanish government's recent move to lower short-term rates from 14.7% to 14.5%, hold monthly auctions and abolish the 25% withholding tax on bonos (government bonds) for non-residents has also helped increase liquidity in the market, they said.

Explain why the relatively high yields, a strong peseta, and the government's liberalization policies will contribute to the projected favorable performance of the Spanish bond market cited in this quotation.

19. A withholding tax is a tax imposed by a country on interest or dividends to be paid to foreign (i.e., nonresident) investors who have purchased securities in that country. Foreign investors, of course, want to avoid withholding taxes. The excerpt below discussing withholding taxes is taken from the *International Capital Market* in 1989 published by the European Investment Bank:

> During 1989 changes in withholding tax regimes—actual and proposed— made for additional gyrations in securities prices. Speculation as to the permanence of the 10% withholding tax on coupon income of all domestically issued bonds in Germany was already alive when it was introduced on January 1, 1989. When the decision was finally taken in May to abolish the tax as from July 1, yield relations between the Euro-deutschemark and the domestic markets had already begun to change. Yields on Euro-deutschemark bonds by supranational borrowers, for instance, which had traded below German government bonds (Bunds), started to rise in early April and returned to their traditional level above those of Bunds. Issuing patterns also fell back to those of the pre-withholding tax period: German entities reduced sharply their issuing activity in the Euromarket. The heavy outflow of long-term funds from Germany that had preceded the introduction of the withholding tax was also partly reversed.

   a. What is a Euro-deutschemark bond?
   b. Why would proposed withholding taxes cause gyrations in securities prices?
   c. Explain why imposition of the German 10% withholding tax in January 1989 caused yields on Euro-deutschemark bonds issued by supranational borrowers to trade at a lower yield than German government bonds.
   d. Why did issuing patterns fall back to those of the pre-withholding tax period?
20. What risk associated with the government bonds of emerging countries is not viewed as being present in industrialized countries?
21. a. What are Brady bonds?
    b. What are the two types of Brady bonds?
22. Describe the role of Cedel and Euroclear.

CHAPTER 10

Mortgage Loans

Learning Objectives

After reading this chapter you will understand:

- what a mortgage is

- who the major originators of mortgages are and what they do with mortgage loans after origination

- the factors that mortgage originators consider when granting a mortgage loan

- what mortgage servicing involves

- the various types of mortgage insurance

- the alternative mortgage instruments available to borrowers

- the fixed-rate, level-payment, fully amortized mortgage instrument and its cash flow characteristics

- the cash flow components of all mortgage loans

- what prepayments are and their impact on the cash flow

- the risks associated with investing in mortgages

- the factors that affect defaults on mortgage loans

Although the American dream may be to own a home, the major portion of the funds to purchase one must be borrowed. The market where these funds are borrowed is called the mortgage market. This chapter and the two that follow describe mortgage loans and the various securities created by using mortgage loans as collateral. In this chapter we focus on individual mortgage loans: the characteristics of mortgage loans, the participants (mortgage originators and investors) in this market, the more popular mortgage loan designs, and the market for mortgage loans.

WHAT IS A MORTGAGE?

A **mortgage** is a loan secured by the collateral of specified real estate property, which obliges the borrower to make a predetermined series of payments. The mortgage gives the lender (the mortgagee) the right of foreclosure on the loan if the borrower (the mortgagor) defaults. That is, if the borrower fails to make the contracted payments, the lender can seize the property to ensure that the debt is paid off.

When the lender makes the loan based on the credit of the borrower and on the collateral for the mortgage, the mortgage is said to be a **conventional mortgage.** The lender also may take out mortgage insurance to provide a guarantee for the fulfillment of the borrower's obligations. There are three forms of mortgage insurance that are guaranteed by the U.S. government if the borrower can qualify: Federal Housing Administration (FHA), Veterans Administration (VA), and Federal Farmers Administration (FmHA) insurance. There are also private mortgage insurers. The cost of mortgage insurance is paid to the guarantor by the mortgage originator but passed along to the borrower in the form of higher mortgage payments.

The types of real estate properties that can be mortgaged are divided into two broad categories: *residential* and *nonresidential* properties. The former category includes houses, condominiums, cooperatives, and apartments. Residential real estate can be subdivided into single-family (one-to-four-family) structures and multifamily structures (apartment buildings in which more than four families reside). Nonresidential property includes commercial and farm properties. Our focus in this chapter and the next two is on residential mortgage loans.

PARTICIPANTS IN THE MORTGAGE MARKET

In addition to the ultimate lenders of funds and the government agencies described in the next chapter, there are three groups involved in the market: mortgage originators, mortgage servicers, and mortgage insurers.

Mortgage Originators

The original lender is called the **mortgage originator.** Mortgage originators include thrifts, commercial banks, mortgage bankers, life insurance companies, and pension funds. The three largest originators for all types of residential mortgages are thrifts, commercial banks, and mortgage bankers. Originators may generate income for themselves in one or more ways. First, they typically charge an origination fee. This fee is expressed in terms of points, where each point represents 1% of the borrowed funds. For example, an origination fee of two points on a $100,000 mortgage represents $2,000. Originators also charge application fees and certain processing fees.

The second source of revenue is the profit that might be generated from selling a mortgage at a higher price than it originally cost. This profit is called **secondary marketing profit.** Of course, if mortgage rates rise, an originator will realize a loss when the mortgages are sold in the secondary market. Finally, the mortgage originator may hold the mortgage in its investment portfolio.

A potential homeowner who wants to borrow funds to purchase a home will apply for a loan from a mortgage originator. Upon completion of the application form, which provides financial information about the applicant, and payment of an application fee, the mortgage originator will perform a credit evaluation of the applicant. The two primary factors in determining whether the funds will be lent are the **payment-to-income** (PTI) ratio and the **loan-to-value** (LTV) ratio. The PTI, the ratio of monthly payments (both mortgage and real estate tax payments) to monthly income, is a measure of the ability of the applicant to make monthly payments. The lower this ratio, the greater the likelihood that the applicant will be able to meet the required payments. The difference between the purchase price of the property and the amount borrowed is the borrower's down payment. The LTV is the ratio of the amount of the loan to the market (or appraised) value of the property. The lower this ratio, the more protection the lender has if the applicant defaults and the property must be repossessed and sold.

Mortgage originators can either (1) hold the mortgage in their portfolio, (2) sell the mortgage to an investor who wishes to hold the mortgage or who will place the mortgage in a pool of mortgages to be used as collateral for the issuance of a security, or (3) use the mortgage themselves as collateral for the issuance of a security. When a mortgage is used as collateral for the issuance of a security, the mortgage is said to be **securitized.** In Chapter 11 we discuss the process of securitizing mortgages.

When a mortgage originator intends to sell the mortgage, it will obtain a commitment from the potential investor (buyer). Two federally sponsored credit agencies and several private companies buy mortgages. As these agencies and private companies pool these mortgages and sell them to investors, they are called **conduits.**

The two agencies, the Federal Home Loan Mortgage Corporation and the Federal National Mortgage Association (discussed further), purchase only conforming mortgages. A **conforming mortgage** is one that meets the underwriting standards established by these agencies for being in a pool of mortgages underlying a security that they guarantee. Three underwriting standards established by these agencies in order to qualify as a conforming mortgage are (1) a maximum PTI, (2) a maximum LTV, and (3) a maximum loan amount. If an applicant does not satisfy the underwriting standards, the mortgage is called a **nonconforming mortgage.**[1] Mortgages acquired by the agency may be held as investments in their portfolio or securitized. The securities offered are discussed in Chapter 11.

Examples of private conduits are Residential Funding Corporation, GE Capital Mortgage Services, Norwest Asset Securities, Prudential Home Mortgage, Chase Mortgage Finance, and Capstead Capital Corp. Private conduits typically will securitize the mortgages purchased rather than hold them as an investment. Both conforming and nonconforming mortgages are purchased. Nonconforming mortgages do not necessarily have greater credit risk. For example, a person with an annual income of $500,000 may apply for a mortgage loan of $300,000 on real estate that she wants to purchase for $1 million. This would be a nonconforming mortgage because the amount of the mortgage exceeds the limit currently established for a conforming mortgage. The person's income, however, can easily accommodate the monthly mortgage payments. Moreover, the lender's risk exposure is minimal, for it has lent $300,000 backed by collateral of $1 million.

Mortgage Servicers

Every mortgage loan must be serviced. Servicing of a mortgage loan involves collecting monthly payments and forwarding proceeds to owners of the loan, sending payment notices to mortgagors; reminding mortgagors when payments are overdue,

---

[1]Loans that exceed the maximum loan amount and thus do not qualify as conforming mortgages are called **jumbo** loans.

maintaining records of principal balances; administering an escrow balance for real estate taxes and insurance purposes, initiating foreclosure proceedings if necessary, and furnishing tax information to mortgagors when applicable.

Mortgage servicers include bank-related entities, thrift-related entities, and mortgage bankers. There are five sources of revenue from mortgage servicing. The primary source is the **servicing fee.** This fee is a fixed percentage of the outstanding mortgage balance. Consequently, the revenue from servicing declines over time as the mortgage balance amortizes. The second source of servicing income arises from the interest that can be earned by the servicer from the escrow balance that the borrower often maintains with the servicer. The third source of revenue is the float earned on the monthly mortgage payment. This opportunity arises because of the delay permitted between the time the servicer receives the payment and the time that the payment must be sent to the investor. Fourth, there are several sources of ancillary income. First, a late fee is charged by the servicer if the payment is not made on time. Second, many servicers receive commissions from cross-selling their borrowers credit life and other insurance products. Third, fees can also be generated from selling mailing lists.

Finally, there are other benefits of servicing rights for servicers who are also lenders. Their portfolio of borrowers is a potential source for other loans, such as second mortgages, automobile loans, and credit cards.

Mortgage Insurers

There are two types of mortgage-related insurance. The first type, originated by the lender to insure against default by the borrower, is called **mortgage insurance** or **private mortgage insurance.** It is usually required by lenders on loans with LTV ratios greater than 80%. The amount insured will be some percentage of the loan and may decline as the LTV ratio declines. Although the insurance is required by the lender, its cost is borne by the borrower, usually through a higher contract rate. Mortgage insurance can be obtained from a private mortgage insurance company or, if the borrower qualifies, from the FHA, VA, or FmHA.

The second type of mortgage-related insurance is acquired by the borrower, usually with a life insurance company, and is typically called **credit life.** Unlike mortgage insurance, this type of insurance is not required by the lender. The policy provides for a continuation of mortgage payments after the death of the insured person, which allows the survivors to continue living in the house. Because the insurance coverage decreases as the mortgage balance declines, this type of mortgage insurance is simply a term policy.

Although both types of insurance have a beneficial effect on the creditworthiness of the borrower, the first type is more important from the lender's perspective. Mortgage insurance is sought by the lender when the borrower is viewed as being capable of meeting the monthly mortgage payments but does not have enough funds for a large down payment. For example, suppose that a borrower seeks financing of $100,000 to purchase a single-family residence for $110,000, thus making a down payment of $10,000. The LTV ratio is 90.9%, exceeding the uninsured maximum LTV of 80%. Even if the lender's credit analysis indicates that the borrower's PTI ratio is acceptable, the mortgage loan cannot be extended. However, if a private mortgage insurance company insures a portion of the loan, the lender is afforded protection. Mortgage insurance companies will write policies to insure a maximum of 20% of loans with an LTV ranging from 80 to 90%, and a maximum of 25% of loans with an LTV ranging from 90 to 95%. The lender is still exposed to default by the borrower on the noninsured portion of the mortgage loan, and in the case of private mortgage insurers, exposed as well to the risk that the insurer will default.

ALTERNATIVE MORTGAGE INSTRUMENTS

There are many types of mortgage loans from which a borrower can select. We review several of the more popular mortgage designs here.

The interest rate on a mortgage loan (called the **contract rate**) is greater than the risk-free interest rate, in particular the yield on a Treasury security of comparable maturity. The spread reflects the higher costs of collection, the costs associated with default, which are not eliminated despite the collateral, poorer liquidity, and uncertainty concerning the timing of the cash flow (which we explain later). The frequency of payment is typically monthly, and the prevailing term of the mortgage is 20 to 30 years, although in recent years an increasing number of 15-year mortgages have been originated.

Level-Payment Fixed-Rate Mortgage

The basic idea behind the design of the level-payment fixed-rate mortgage, or simply level-payment mortgage, is that the borrower pays interest and repays principal in equal installments over an agreed-upon period of time, called the maturity or term of the mortgage. Thus at the end of the term the loan has been fully amortized.

Each monthly mortgage payment for a level-payment mortgage is due on the first of each month and consists of

1. Interest of one-twelfth of the fixed annual interest rate times the amount of the outstanding mortgage balance at the beginning of the previous month.
2. A repayment of a portion of the outstanding mortgage balance (principal).

The difference between the monthly mortgage payment and the portion of the payment that represents interest equals the amount that is applied to reduce the outstanding mortgage balance. The monthly mortgage payment is designed so that after the last scheduled monthly payment of the loan is made, the amount of the outstanding mortgage balance is zero (i.e., the mortgage is fully repaid).

To illustrate a level-payment fixed-rate mortgage, consider a 30-year (360-month) $100,000 mortgage with an 8.125% mortgage rate. The monthly mortgage payment would be $742.50. (The formula for calculating the monthly mortgage payment is given later.)

Exhibit 10-1 shows for selected months how each monthly mortgage payment is divided between interest and repayment of principal. At the beginning of month 1, the mortgage balance is $100,000, the amount of the original loan. The mortgage payment for month 1 includes interest on the $100,000 borrowed for the month. Because the interest rate is 8.125%, the monthly interest rate is 0.0067708 (0.08125 divided by 12). Interest for month 1 is therefore $677.08 ($100,000 times 0.0067708). The $65.41 difference between the monthly mortgage payment of $742.50 and the interest of $677.08 is the portion of the monthly mortgage payment that represents repayment of principal. This $65.41 in month 1 reduces the mortgage balance.

EXHIBIT 10-1 Amortization Schedule for a Level-Payment Fixed-Rate Mortgage

Mortgage loan: $100,000
Mortgage rate: 8.125%
Monthly payment: $742.50
Term of loan: 30 years (360 months)

Month	Beginning Mortgage Balance	Monthly Payment	Monthly Interest	Sch. Princ. Repay.	Ending Mortgage Balance
1	100,000.00	742.50	677.08	65.41	99,934.59
2	99,934.59	742.50	676.64	65.86	99,868.73
3	99,868.73	742.50	676.19	66.30	99,802.43
4	99,802.43	742.50	675.75	66.75	99,735.68
25	98,301.53	742.50	665.58	76.91	98,224.62
26	98,224.62	742.50	665.06	77.43	98,147.19
27	98,147.19	742.50	664.54	77.96	98,069.23
74	93,849.98	742.50	635.44	107.05	93,742.93
75	93,742.93	742.50	634.72	107.78	93,635.15
76	93,635.15	742.50	633.99	108.51	93,526.64
141	84,811.77	742.50	574.25	168.25	84,643.52
142	84,643.52	742.50	573.11	169.39	84,474.13
143	84,474.13	742.50	571.96	170.54	84,303.59
184	76,446.29	742.50	517.61	224.89	76,221.40
185	76,221.40	742.50	516.08	226.41	75,994.99
186	75,994.99	742.50	514.55	227.95	75,767.04
233	63,430.19	742.50	429.48	313.02	63,117.17
234	63,117.17	742.50	427.36	315.14	62,802.03
235	62,802.03	742.50	425.22	317.28	62,484.75
289	42,200.92	742.50	285.74	456.76	41,744.15
290	41,744.15	742.50	282.64	459.85	41,284.30
291	41,284.30	742.50	279.53	462.97	40,821.33
321	25,941.42	742.50	175.65	566.85	25,374.57
322	25,374.57	742.50	171.81	570.69	24,803.88
323	24,803.88	742.50	167.94	574.55	24,229.32
358	2,197.66	742.50	14.88	727.62	1,470.05
359	1,470.05	742.50	9.95	732.54	737.50
360	737.50	742.50	4.99	737.50	0.00

The mortgage balance at the end of month 1 (beginning of month 2) is then $99,934.59 ($100,000 minus $65.41). The interest for the second monthly mortgage payment is $676.64, the monthly interest rate (0.0066708) times the mortgage balance at the beginning of month 2 ($99,934.59). The difference between the $742.50 monthly mortgage payment and the $676.64 interest is $65.86, representing the amount of the mortgage balance paid off with that monthly mortgage payment. Notice that the last mortgage payment in month 360 is sufficient to pay off the remaining mortgage balance. When a loan repayment schedule is structured in this way, so that the payments made by the borrower will completely pay off the interest and principal, the loan is said to be **fully amortizing.** Exhibit 10-1 is then referred to as an **amortization schedule.**

As Exhibit 10-1 clearly shows, **the portion of the monthly mortgage payment applied to interest declines each month and the portion applied to reducing the mortgage balance increases.** The reason for this is that as the mortgage balance is reduced with each monthly mortgage payment, the interest on the mortgage balance declines. Because the monthly mortgage payment is fixed, an increasingly larger portion of the monthly payment is applied to reduce the principal in each subsequent month.

Servicing Fee   What was ignored in the amortization is the portion of the cash flow that must be paid to the servicer of the mortgage. The servicing fee is a specified portion of the mortgage rate. The monthly cash flow from a mortgage loan, regardless of the mortgage design, can therefore be decomposed into three parts: (1) the servicing fee, (2) the interest payment net of the servicing fee, and (3) the scheduled principal repayment.

Determining the Monthly Mortgage Payment   To compute the monthly mortgage payment for a level-payment mortgage requires the application of the formula for the present value of an ordinary annuity formula presented in Chapter 2. The formula is

$$PV = A\left[\frac{1 - (1 + i)^{-n}}{i}\right]$$

where:

A = amount of the annuity ($)
n = number of periods
PV = present value of an annuity ($)
i = periodic interest rate

We can redefine the terms in the foregoing formula for a level-payment mortgage as follows:

$$MB_0 = MP\left[\frac{1 - (1 + i)^{-n}}{i}\right]$$

where:

MP = monthly mortgage payment ($)
n = number of months
MB_0 = original mortgage balance ($)
i = simple monthly interest rate (annual interest rate/12)

Solving for the monthly mortgage payment (MP) gives

$$MP = \frac{MB_0}{\dfrac{1 - (1 + i)^{-n}}{i}}$$

Alternatively, this can be expressed in a simplified form as follows:

$$MP = MB_0\left[\frac{i(1 + i)^n}{(1 + i)^n - 1}\right]$$

The term in brackets is called the **payment factor** or **annuity factor.** It is the monthly payment for a $1 mortgage loan with an interest rate of i and a term of n months.

To illustrate how the formula is applied, we'll use the $100,000 30-year 8.125% mortgage that we discussed previously. Thus, $n = 360$, $MB_0 = \$100,000$, and $i = 0.0067708 \, (= 0.08125/12)$. The monthly mortgage payment is then

$$MP = \$100,000\left[\frac{0.0067708(1.0067708)^{360}}{(1.0067708)^{360} - 1}\right]$$

$$= \$100,000\left[\frac{0.0067708(11.35063)}{11.35063 - 1}\right]$$

$$= \$100,000[0.007425]$$

$$= \$742.50$$

This agrees with the monthly mortgage payment we used in Exhibit 10-1. The payment factor or annuity factor is 0.007425.

Adjustable-Rate Mortgage

An **adjustable-rate mortgage** (ARM) is a loan in which the contract rate is reset periodically in accordance with some appropriately chosen reference rate, typically one based on a short-term interest rate. Outstanding ARMs call for resetting the contract rate either every month, six months, year, two years, three years, or five years. The contract rate at the reset date is equal to a reference rate plus a spread. The amount of the spread reflects market conditions, the features of the ARM, and the increased cost of servicing an ARM compared with a fixed-rate mortgage.

Reference Rates   Two categories of reference rates have been used in ARMs: (1) market-determined rates, and (2) calculated rates based on the cost of funds for thrifts. Market-determined rates have been limited to Treasury-based rates. The reference rate will have an important impact on the performance of an ARM and how they are priced.

   Cost of funds for thrifts indexes are calculated based on the monthly weighted-average interest cost for liabilities of thrifts. The two most popular are the Eleventh Federal Home Loan Bank Board District Cost of Funds Index (COFI) and the National Cost of Funds Index, the former being the most popular.

   The Eleventh District includes the states of California, Arizona, and Nevada. The cost of funds is calculated by first computing the monthly interest expenses for all thrifts included in the Eleventh District. The interest expenses are summed and then divided by the average of the beginning and ending monthly balance. The index value is reported with a one-month lag. For example, June's Eleventh District COFI is reported in July. The contract rate for a mortgage based on the Eleventh District COFI is usually reset based on the previous month's reported index rate. For example, if the reset date is August, the index rate reported in July will be used to set the contract rate. Consequently, there is a two-month lag by the time the average cost of funds is reflected in the contract rate. This obviously is an advantage to the borrower when interest rates are rising and a disadvantage to the investor. The opposite is true when interest rates are falling.

   The National Cost of Funds Index is calculated based on all federally insured S&Ls. A median cost of funds is calculated rather than an average. This index is reported with about a 1.5-month delay. The contract rate is typically reset based on the most recently reported index value.

Features of Adjustable-Rate Mortgages   To encourage borrowers to accept ARMs rather than fixed-rate mortgages, mortgage originators generally offer an initial contract rate that is less than the prevailing market mortgage rate. This below-market initial contract rate, set by the mortgage originator based on competitive market conditions, is commonly referred to as a **teaser rate.** At the reset date, the reference rate plus the spread determines the new contract rate. For example, suppose that one-year ARMs are typically offering a 175-basis-point spread over the reference rate. Suppose also that the reference rate is 5.0%, so that the initial contract rate should be 6.75%. The mortgage originator might set an initial contract rate of 6.05%, a rate 70 basis points below the current value of the reference rate plus the spread.

A pure ARM is one that resets periodically and has no other terms that affect the monthly mortgage payment. However, the monthly mortgage payment, and hence the investor's cash flow, are affected by other terms. These are due to (1) periodic caps, and (2) lifetime rate caps and floors. Rate caps limit the amount that the contract rate may increase or decrease at the reset date. A lifetime cap sets the maximum contract rate over the term of the loan.

Balloon Mortgages

In a **balloon mortgage,** the borrower is given long-term financing by the lender, but at specified future dates the contract rate is renegotiated. Thus, the lender is providing long-term funds for what is effectively short-term borrowing, how short depending on the frequency of the renegotiation period. Effectively, it is a short-term balloon loan in which the lender agrees to provide financing for the remainder of the term of the mortgage. The balloon payment is the original amount borrowed less the amount amortized. Thus, in a balloon mortgage, the actual maturity is shorter than the stated maturity.

This mortgage design, though much discussed in the late 1970s and throughout the 1980s, did not catch on until 1990. Two government-sponsored enterprises, discussed in Chapter 11, the Federal National Mortgage Association (Fannie Mae) and the Federal Home Loan Mortgage Corporation (Freddie Mac) have programs for the purchase of these mortgages. Freddie Mac's 30-year balloon, for example, can have either a rene-gotiation period of five-years ("30-due-in-5") or seven-years ("30-due-in-7"). If certain conditions are met, Freddie Mac guarantees the extension of the loan.

Two-Step Mortgages

Akin to the idea of a balloon loan with a refinancing option for the borrower is a fixed-rate mortgage with a single rate reset at some point prior to maturity. Unlike a refinancing option, this rate reset occurs without specific action on the part of the borrower.

One example of this structure is the **two-step loan** structure, in which a loan car-ries a fixed rate for some period, usually seven years, and then resets once. The rate reset can be based on any rate; currently, Fannie Mae's two-step mortgage purchase program specifies that the new rate be calculated by adding 250 basis points to a weekly average of the 10-year constant maturity Treasury yield. Fannie Mae also lim-its any increase in the mortgage rate to no more than 600 basis points over the initial mortgage rate; other cap levels may become popular as well.

Unlike in balloon mortgages, the rate reset on the two-step mortgage does not consist of a repayment of the initial loan and the origination of a new one; thus, a

30-year two-step mortgage has a 30-year final maturity rather than the shorter final maturity of a balloon mortgage. Essentially, then, the two-step mortgage is an adjustable-rate mortgage with a single reset.

Growing Equity Mortgages

A **growing equity mortgage** (GEM) is a fixed-rate mortgage whose monthly mortgage payments increase over time. The initial monthly mortgage payment is the same as for a level-payment mortgage. The higher monthly mortgage payments are applied to paying off the principal. As a result, the principal of a GEM is repaid faster. For example, a 30-year $100,000 GEM loan with a contract rate of 8.125% might call for an initial monthly payment of $742.50 (the same as a level-payment 8.125% 30-year mortgage loan). However, the GEM payment would gradually increase, and the GEM might be fully paid in only 15 years. Pools of GEMs have been securitized.

Tiered Payment Mortgages

A **tiered payment mortgage** is a mortgage design with a fixed rate but a monthly mortgage payment that increases over time. The initial monthly mortgage payment is below that of a fixed-rate level payment mortgage. As a result, there will be a shortfall in the interest payment necessary to fully amortize the mortgage. This interest shortfall is paid to the lender from a subsidized account called a "buydown account." This account is established at the time the loan is originated by the borrower, lender, or a third party such as a relative or business associate.

Fixed/Adjustable-Rate Mortgage Hybrids

Another type of mortgage loan structure that has experienced growing popularity is the **fixed/adjustable-rate mortgage hybrid.** Typically, these mortgages are originated with fixed rates for their first five, seven, or 10 years, after which the interest rate on the loan begins floating with contractual characteristics similar to those of current ARM structures. For instance, one popular hybrid structure carries a fixed rate for five years, and thereafter has a floating rate that resets every six months at a margin over the six-month CD index. Like many other ARMs, the coupon is subject to both periodic and lifetime limitations on the rate change. Other fixed/ARM hybrids turn into one-year Treasury ARMs, or monthly Eleventh District COFI ARMs after their fixed period. In many cases, the first coupon reset is not subject to any periodic caps that may apply to later coupon resets, and instead, is subject only to the lifetime cap.

RISKS ASSOCIATED WITH INVESTING IN MORTGAGES

Investors are exposed to four main risks by investing in mortgage loans: (1) default risk, (2) liquidity risk, (3) interest-rate risk, and (4) prepayment risk.

Default Risk

The default or credit risk is the risk that the homeowner/borrower will default. For FHA-, VA-, and FmHA-insured mortgages, this risk is minimal. For privately insured mortgages, the risk can be gauged by the credit rating of the private insurance company that has insured the mortgage. For conventional mortgages, the credit risk depends on the borrower. In recent years the market for securities backed by a pool of nonconforming mortgage loans that are not backed by an agency-guaranteed government has grown dramatically; an understanding of default risk is critical to investors in such securities.

Default Studies[2]   There are several studies of mortgage loan defaults. The measure of default used in these studies is the **conditional default rate,** which is the probability that a mortgage loan will default this year. Alternatively, the conditional default rate is the percentage of mortgage loans that start the year and default sometime during the year. It is a conditional measure because it is the probability of default given that a mortgage loan has survived to this year.[3] Measuring default in this way is better than measuring it in terms of the percentage of mortgage loans that were originated and subsequently defaulted, because the conditional default rate relates defaults to a particular point in time and to a particular set of economic conditions.

One of the first extensive statistical studies of conditional default rates was by Peters, Pinkus, and Askin.[4] Their database included 503,000 conventional fixed-rate one- to four-family owner-occupied mortgage loans sold to Freddie Mac between 1973 and 1980. Of the sample mortgage loans, only about 1,000 (0.2%) defaulted during the study period. In a more recent study, Van Order examined 725,000 conventional fixed-rate single-family mortgage loans originated from 1973 to 1983 purchased by Freddie Mac.[5] The default experience of these mortgage loans was investigated through the middle of 1990.

One of the key characteristics of a mortgage loan that affects defaults is the LTV ratio at origination (called **original LTV**). The higher the original LTV or, equivalently, the less equity the borrower has in the property, the higher the probability of default. This finding was supported by Van Order's findings for the default rate by original LTV.[6] In addition, Van Order found that the origination year was significant in explaining defaults, with 1976 and 1981 being the worst years.

Unfortunately, many default models using original LTV have underestimated the level of deliquencies in recent years. Mismeasurement of the amount of equity borrowers have in their home is the chief cause. Such mismeasurement is due to two factors: declining home prices and removal of equity via second mortgages or home equity lines of credit.

A study by Bendt, Ramsey, and Fabozzi examined not just the original LTV and its impact on default rates, but also the current LTV.[7] The **current LTV** considers the loan value to the estimated current market price. Exhibit 10-2 shows the effects of

---

[2]This discussion draws from Chapter 8 in Frank J. Fabozzi, Chuck Ramsey, and Frank Ramirez, *Collateralized Mortgage Obligations: Structures and Analysis* (Buckingham, PA: Frank J. Fabozzi Associates, 1994).
[3]In other fields, conditional rates or probabilities are referred to as hazard rates.
[4]Helen F. Peters, Scott M. Pinkus, and David J. Askin, "Default: The Last Resort," *Secondary Mortgage Markets,* August 1984, pp. 16–22.
[5]Robert Van Order, "The Hazards of Default," *Secondary Mortgage Markets,* Fall 1990, pp. 29–32.
[6]This was also found by Peters, Pinkus, and Askin, "Default: The Last Resort," and by Scott Brown et al. for FHA/VA loans as well as conventional loans [*Analysis of Mortgage Servicing Portfolios* (New York: Financial Strategies Group, Prudential-Bache Capital Funding, December 1990)].
[7]Doulas L. Bendt, Chuck Ramsey, and Frank J. Fabozzi, "The Rating Agencies' Approach: New Evidence," Chapter 6 in Frank J. Fabozzi, Chuck Ramsey, and Frank Ramirez (eds.), *Whole-Loan CMOs* (Buckingham, PA: Frank J. Fabozzi Associates, 1995).

EXHIBIT 10-2 Percentage of Loans without Second Mortgages within LTV Ranges

Source: Data from Mortgage Risk Assessment Corporation, reported in Frank J. Fabozzi, Chuck Ramsey, and Frank Ramirez, *Collateralized Mortgage Obligations: Structures and Analysis* (Buckingham, PA: Frank J. Fabozzi Associates, 1994).

changing property values on the distribution of LTVs. Almost all original LTVs fall under 80% in a large pool of nonconforming mortgage loans (100,000 plus) analyzed and none above 90%. Adjusted for declines in property values, however, nearly 40% have current LTVs above 80% and about 15% have current LTVs above 90%.

The Bendt–Ramsey–Fabozzi study also examined defaults taking into consideration second mortgages. Exhibit 10-3 shows that borrowers with second mortgages behind their first mortgage become delinquent twice as often as borrowers without second mortgages. As Exhibit 10-4 shows, even adjusting for the higher LTVs that take into account second mortgages, borrowers with second mortgages have higher deliquency rates compared with borrowers with the same LTV without seconds. On average, deliquency rates are about 25% higher—possibly because the combined monthly payments on a first and second mortgage would be higher than the same-sized first mortgage.

Empirical studies also suggest that there is a seasoning effect for default rates. That is, default rates tend to decline as mortgage loans become seasoned.[8] The reason for the seasoning effect on default rates is twofold. First, because a borrower typically knows shortly after moving into a home whether he or she can afford to make the mortgage payments, default rates are higher in the earlier years. Second, the longer a borrower remains in a home, the lower the LTV ratio (i.e., the greater the equity in the home), and therefore the incentive to default declines.

Van Order also examined several characteristics of the borrower that he hypothesized would affect default rates. For example, as explained earlier in this chapter, the PTI ratio is a measure of the burden of the mortgage payments. It is expected that the higher this ratio at origination, the greater the probability of default. Van Order found that the probability of default increased only slightly the higher this burden. As

---

[8]For conventional mortgage loans, the maximum default rate appears to be three to four years after origination. For FHA/VA mortgage loans, it seems to be two to three years after origination.

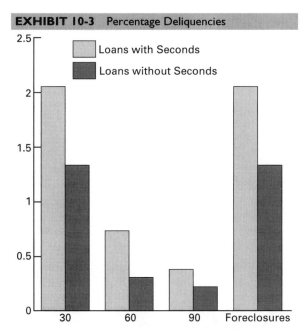

EXHIBIT 10-3   Percentage Deliquencies

Source: Data from Mortgage Risk Assessment Corporation, reported in Frank J. Fabozzi, Chuck Ramsey, and Frank Ramirez, *Collateralized Mortgage Obligations: Structures and Analysis* (Buckingham, PA: Frank J. Fabozzi Associates, 1994).

he notes, this conclusion is only tentative because his sample did not include many observations with high PTIs. None of the other borrower characteristics appeared to affect default rates significantly.

State Foreclosure Laws and Default Losses   State foreclosure laws affect default losses significantly. These state laws differ in three primary ways: (1) foreclosure procedures, (2) statutory right of redemption, and (3) deficiency judgment.[9] Foreclosure procedures can be either judicial or nonjudicial. The former is done under court supervision, resulting in a lengthening of the time to sell the property. This delay increases the losses associated with a foreclosure because of the opportunity loss on funds that could be reinvested, additional taxes and insurance that must be paid, and legal expenses. Moreover, the property value might decline in the interim due to lack of maintenance or downturn in property values. In a nonjudicial foreclosure,[10] a sale can be made faster because there is no court proceeding; therefore, the costs

[9]Terrence M. Clauretie and Thomas N. Herzog, "How State Laws Affect Foreclosure Costs," *Secondary Mortgage Markets,* Spring 1989, pp. 26–27.
[10]Such foreclosure procedures are also called power-of-sale procedures, foreclosures by advertisement, or a trustee's sale.

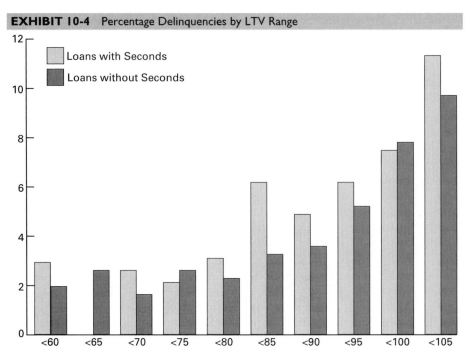

EXHIBIT 10-4 Percentage Delinquencies by LTV Range

Source: Data from Mortgage Risk Assessment Corporation, reported in Frank J. Fabozzi, Chuck Ramsey, and Frank Ramirez, *Collateralized Mortgage Obligations: Structures and Analysis* (Buckingham, PA: Frank J. Fabozzi Associates, 1994).

associated with foreclosure are reduced. There are 23 states that permit only judicial foreclosure.[11]

A statutory right of redemption is a right granted to the borrower to redeem the property by paying any deficiencies, including legal expenses, for a specified period *after* a foreclosure[12]; 29 states grant this right to borrowers.[13] If this right allows the borrower the right to occupy the property after foreclosure, there is the standard moral hazard problem, which could result in deterioration of the property, as well as reluctance of potential buyers to bid on property where moral hazard exists. This will result in lower bid prices being received.

A deficiency judgment allows the lender to recover any deficiencies from the borrower's personal assets. Although the costs of recovery and the limited personal assets of the borrower may make pursuit of this right by the lender uneconomical, its existence may discourage a default in some instances. This would occur in cases in which the borrower has the capacity to pay and sufficient personal assets to satisfy any judgment, but whose property value has declined so that no equity remains in the property (i.e., the LTV is 1 or higher). Only six states do not allow deficiency judgments.[14]

---

[11]Clauretie and Herzog, "How State Laws Affect Foreclosure Costs," p. 26.
[12]An equitable right of redemption gives the borrower the right to redeem the property by paying all deficiencies and legal costs *before* a foreclosure. This right is granted to borrowers in all states.
[13]Clauretie and Herzog, "How State Laws Affect Foreclosure Costs," p. 26.
[14]Ibid., p. 27.

An empirical study by Clauretie and Herzog, based on data from private mortgage insurance and FHA claims, investigated the effect of state laws on losses.[15] A statistical analysis of the data found that losses are significantly lower in states with nonjudicial foreclosure procedures and a deficiency judgment right[16]; losses are greater where states grant a statutory right of redemption. These researchers found that on a $100,000 loan, lenders are exposed to potential additional losses of $500 to $1,000 if a property is located in a state with only a judicial foreclosure process and statutory right of redemption.

Liquidity Risk

Although there is an active secondary market for mortgage loans, the fact is that bid–ask spreads are large compared with other debt instruments (i.e., mortgage loans tend to be rather illiquid because they are large and indivisible).

The bid–ask spread on mortgage loans varies. Typical spreads are around ten 32nds, with aggressive bidding reducing spreads to eight 32nds when collateral is needed to create mortgage-backed securities. For mortgage loans with unusual collateral, spreads are much wider—the odder the collateral, the higher the spread.

Interest-Rate Risk

Because a mortgage loan is a debt instrument, and long-term on the average—indeed, one of the longest—its price will move in the direction opposite to market interest rates. Moreover, because the borrower can repay the loan at any time, the investor faces the same problem of negative convexity when rates decline as that of the holder of any callable bond. This is discussed further in Chapter 14.

Prepayment Risk

In our illustration of the cash flow from a level-payment fixed-rate mortgage, we assumed that the homeowner would not pay any portion of the mortgage balance off prior to the scheduled due date. But homeowners do pay off all or part of their mortgage balance prior to the maturity date. Payments made in excess of the scheduled principal repayments are called **prepayments.**

Prepayments occur for one of several reasons. First, homeowners prepay the entire mortgage when they sell their home. The sale of a home may be due to (1) a change of employment that necessitates moving, (2) the purchase of a more expensive home ("trading up"), or (3) a divorce in which the settlement requires sale of the marital residence. Second, as we explained earlier in this chapter, the borrower has the right to pay off all or part of the mortgage balance at any time. Effectively, someone who invests in a mortgage has granted the borrower an option to prepay the mortgage and the debtor will have an incentive to do so as market rates fall below the contract rate. Third, in the case of homeowners who cannot meet their mortgage obligations, the property is repossessed and sold. The proceeds from the sale are used to pay off

---

[15]Ibid., pp. 27–28.

[16]The deficiency judgment was not found to be statistically significant for the FHA data. The low default rates in California in the study period and the fact that California was one of only six states that did not have a deficiency judgment may have caused this result.

the mortgage in the case of a conventional mortgage. For an insured mortgage, the insurer will pay off the mortgage balance. Finally, if property is destroyed by fire or another insured catastrophe occurs, the insurance proceeds are used to pay off the mortgage. The effect of prepayments is that the cash flow from a mortgage is not known with certainty. This is true for all mortgage loans, not just level-payment fixed-rate mortgages.

In the next chapter, securities backed by a pool of mortgage loans that overcomes many of the drawbacks of investing directly in mortgage loans are described.

SUMMARY

A mortgage is a loan secured by the collateral of some specified real estate property which obliges the borrower to make a predetermined series of payments. Because of the nature of mortgage loans, there are three groups involved in the market: mortgage originators, mortgage servicers, and mortgage insurers. The original lender is called the mortgage originator.

The interest rate on a mortgage loan is generally above the risk-free interest rate, in particular the yield on a Treasury security of comparable maturity, with the spread reflecting the costs of servicing the loan, the costs associated with default which are not eliminated despite the collateral, poorer liquidity, and the uncertainty concerning the timing of the cash flow.

There is a wide range of mortgage designs. These include the level-payment fixed-rate mortgage, the adjustable-rate mortgage, the balloon mortgage, the growing equity mortgage, the tiered payment mortgage, and the fixed/adjustable-rate mortgage hybrids.

The monthly cash flow from a mortgage loan, regardless of the mortgage design, can be decomposed into three parts: (1) the servicing fee, (2) the interest payment, and (3) the scheduled principal repayment. There is uncertainty associated with investing in a mortgage because of prepayments; that is, the cash flow is not known with certainty. This uncertainty is called prepayment risk Those investing in mortgages also face liquidity risk and price risk and may be exposed to credit risk.

Questions

1. a. What are the sources of revenue arising from mortgage origination?
   b. What are the risks associated with the mortgage origination process?
2. What are the two primary factors in determining whether funds will be lent to an applicant for a mortgage loan?
3. What is a conventional mortgage?
4. What can mortgage originators do with a loan after originating it?
5. What are a conforming mortgage and a nonconforming mortgage?
6. What are the sources of revenue from mortgage servicing?
7. Why is the interest rate on a mortgage loan not necessarily the same as the interest rate that the investor receives?
8. a. What are the two types of mortgage insurance?
   b. Which is the more important type of insurance from the lender's perspective?
9. a. What are the components of the cash flow of a mortgage loan?
   b. Why is the cash flow of a mortgage unknown?
10. What is a prepayment?

11. In what sense has the investor in a mortgage granted the borrower (homeowner) a call option?
12. a. What are the two categories of reference rates used in adjustable-rate mortgages?
    b. Which category of reference rate would you expect to increase faster when interest rates are rising? Why?
13. What types of features are included in an adjustable-rate mortgage to restrict how the contract rate may change at the reset date?
14. a. What is a balloon mortgage?
    b. What is the actual final maturity of a balloon mortgage?
15. Explain why in a fixed-rate level-payment mortgage the amount of the mortgage payment applied to interest declines over time while the amount applied to the repayment of principal increases.
16. Consider the following fixed-rate level-payment mortgage:

$$\text{maturity} = 360 \text{ months}$$
$$\text{amount borrowed} = \$150,000$$
$$\text{annual mortgage rate} = 8\%$$

What is the monthly mortgage payment?
17. For the following fixed-rate level-payment mortgage, construct an amortization schedule for the first 10 months:

$$\text{maturity} = 360 \text{ months}$$
$$\text{amount borrowed} = \$100,000$$
$$\text{annual mortgage rate} = 10\%$$
$$\text{monthly mortgage payment} = \$877.57$$

18. What is the most important factor that has been found to gauge the risk that a borrower will default?
19. a. What is the original LTV of a mortgage loan?
    b. What is the current LTV of a mortgage loan?
    c. hat is the problem with using the original LTV to assess the likelihood that a seasoned mortgage will default?
20. Indicate three ways in which state foreclosure laws can affect default losses.

CHAPTER 11

Mortgage Pass-Through Securities

Learning Objectives

After reading this chapter you will understand:

- what a mortgage pass-through security is

- the cash flow characteristics of mortgage pass-through securities

- the importance of prepayments projections in estimating the cash flow of a mortgage pass-through security

- the WAC and WAM of a pass-through security

- the different types of agency pass-through securities

- what nonagency pass-through securities are and the different ways in which they can be credit enhanced

- what the PSA prepayment benchmark is and how it is used for determining the cash flow of a pass-through security

- the factors that affect prepayments

- what the PSA standard default assumption curve is

- what the cash flow yield is and its limitations

- how the average life of a mortgage pass-through security is calculated

- why prepayment risk can be divided into contraction risk and extension risk

- the market trading conventions of mortgage pass-through securities

A mortgage pass-through security, or simply a pass-through, is created when one or more mortgage holders form a collection (pool) of mortgages and sell shares or participation certificates in the pool. From the pass-through, two further derivative mortgage-backed securities are created: collateralized mortgage obligations and stripped mortgage-backed securities, which we discuss in Chapter 12. The pass-through is the subject of this chapter.

CASH FLOW CHARACTERISTICS

The cash flow of a mortgage pass-through security depends on the cash flow of the underlying mortgages. As we explained in Chapter 10, the cash flow consists of monthly mortgage payments representing interest, the scheduled repayment of principal, and any prepayments. The creation of a pass-through and its cash flow are diagrammed in Exhibit 11-1.

Payments are made to security holders each month. Neither the amount nor the timing, however, of the cash flow from the pool of mortgages is identical to that of the cash flow passed through to investors. The monthly cash flow for a pass-through is less

EXHIBIT 11-1   Creation of a Pass-Through and Its Cash Flow

Each loan is for $100,000

Total loans: $1 million

than the monthly cash flow of the underlying mortgages by an amount equal to servicing and other fees. The other fees are those charged by the issuer or guarantor of the pass-through for guaranteeing the issue. The coupon rate on a pass-through, called the **pass-through coupon rate,** is less than the mortgage rate on the underlying pool of mortgage loans by an amount equal to the servicing and guaranteeing fees.

The timing of the cash flow is also different. The monthly mortgage payment is due from each mortgagor on the first day of each month, but there is a delay in passing through the corresponding monthly cash flow to the securityholders. The length of the delay varies by the type of pass-through security.

Because of prepayments, the cash flow of a pass-through is also not known with certainty. The various conventions for estimating the cash flow are discussed later in the chapter.

WAC AND WAM

Not all of the mortgages that are included in a pool of mortgages that are securitized have the same mortgage rate and the same maturity. Consequently, when describing a pass-through security, a weighted average coupon rate and a weighted-average maturity are determined.

A **weighted-average coupon rate (WAC)** is found by weighting the mortgage rate of each mortgage loan in the pool by the amount of the mortgage outstanding. A **weighted-average maturity (WAM)** is found by weighting the remaining number of months to maturity for each mortgage loan in the pool by the amount of the mortgage outstanding.

AGENCY PASS-THROUGHS

There are three major types of pass-throughs, guaranteed by three organizations: Government National Mortgage Association (Ginnie Mae), Federal Home Loan Mortgage Corporation (Freddie Mac), and Federal National Mortgage Association (Fannie Mae). These are called **agency pass-throughs.**

An agency can provide one of two types of guarantees. One type of guarantee is the timely payment of both interest and principal, meaning that interest and principal will be paid when due, even if some of the mortgagors fail to make their monthly mortgage payments. Pass-throughs with this type of guarantee are referred to as **fully modified pass-throughs.** The second type also guarantees both interest and principal payments, but it guarantees only the timely payment of interest. The scheduled principal is passed through as it is collected, with a guarantee that the scheduled payment will be made no later than a specified date. Pass-throughs with this type of guarantee are called **modified pass-throughs.**

Ginnie Mae pass-throughs are guaranteed by the full faith and credit of the U.S. government. For this reason, Ginnie Mae pass-throughs are viewed as risk-free in terms of default risk, just like Treasury securities. The security guaranteed by Ginnie Mae is called a **mortgage-backed security (MBS).** All Ginnie Mae MBS are fully modified pass-throughs. Only mortgage loans insured or guaranteed by either the Rural Housing Service, the Veterans Administration, or the Farmers Home Administration can be included in a mortgage pool guaranteed by Ginnie Mae.

Freddie Mac issues a pass-through called a **participation certificate (PC).** Although a guarantee of Freddie Mac is not a guarantee by the U.S. government, most market participants view Freddie Mac PCs as similar, although not identical, in creditworthiness to Ginnie Mae pass-throughs. In 1990, Freddie Mac introduced its **Gold PC,** which has stronger guarantees than other PCs it issues and will be the only type of PC issued in the future. Specifically, non-Gold PCs that have been issued are modified pass-throughs. All Gold PCs issued are fully modified pass-throughs. For modified PCs issued by Freddie Mac, the scheduled principal is passed through as it is collected, with Freddie Mac guaranteeing only that the scheduled payment will be made no later than one year after it is due.

The pass-throughs issued by Fannie Mae are called **mortgage-backed securities (MBSs).** Like a Freddie Mac PC, a Fannie Mae MBS is not an obligation of the federal government. All Fannie Mae MBSs are fully modified pass-throughs.

NONAGENCY PASS-THROUGHS

Nonagency pass-through securities are issued by commercial banks, thrifts, and private conduits. Private conduits purchase nonconforming mortgages, pool them, and then sell pass-throughs in which the collateral is the underlying pool of nonconforming mortgages. The private conduits that issue pass-throughs are doing what the government created the agency conduits to do, without any guarantees (implicit or explicit) from the U.S. government. Nonagency mortgage pass-throughs must be registered with the Securities and Exchange Commission. They are rated by the same four nationally recognized companies that rate debt obligations. The development of credit enhancement has been the key to the success of this market.

Credit Enhancement[1]

The primary factors considered by the nationally recognized rating companies in assigning a rating are the type of property (single-family residences, condominiums), the type of loan (fixed-rate level payment, adjustable rate, balloon), the term of the loans, the geographical dispersion of the loans, the loan size (conforming loans, jumbo loans), the amount of seasoning of the loans, and the purpose of the loans (purchase or refinancing). Typically, a double A or triple A rating is sought. The amount of credit enhancement necessary depends on what the rating agency requires to bring the attributes of a particular pool of mortgages to the credit rating sought.

There are two general types of credit enhancement structures: external and internal. We describe each type in the next sections.

External Credit Enhancements   External credit enhancements come in the form of third-party guarantees that provide for first-loss protection against losses up to a

---

[1]This discussion draws from Chapter 8 of Frank J. Fabozzi, Chuck Ramsey, and Frank Ramirez, *Collateralized Mortgage Obligations: Structures and Analysis* (Buckingham, PA: Frank J. Fabozzi Associates, 1994).

specified level, for example, 10%. The most common forms of external enhancements are (1) a corporate guarantee, (2) a letter of credit, (3) pool insurance, and (4) bond insurance.

Pool insurance policies cover losses resulting from defaults and foreclosures. Policies are typically written for a dollar amount of coverage that continues in force throughout the life of the pool. However, some policies are written so that the dollar amount of coverage declines as the pool seasons as long as two conditions are met: (1) the credit performance is better than expected, and (2) the rating agencies that rated the issue approve. Because only defaults and foreclosures are covered, additional insurance must be obtained to cover losses resulting from bankruptcy (i.e., court-mandated modification of mortgage debt), fraud arising in the origination process, and special hazards (i.e., losses resulting from events not covered by a standard homeowner's insurance policy).

Bond insurance provides the same function as in the municipal bond structures. Typically, bond insurance is not used as the primary protection but to supplement other forms of credit enhancement.

The rating of the third-party guarantor must be at least as high as the rating sought. Thus, if the third-party guarantor has a single A rating, a triple A rating for the asset-backed security cannot be obtained by using only this guarantee. The disadvantage of a third-party guarantee is that the rating agencies take a "weak link approach" when assigning ratings. If the rating of the third-party guarantor is downgraded, the security's rating will be downgraded even if the collateral is performing as expected. Therefore, it is imperative that an investor perform credit analysis on both the collateral (the loans) and the third-party guarantor.

Internal Credit Enhancements   Internal credit enhancements come in more complicated forms than external credit enhancements and may alter the cash flow characteristics of the loans even in the absence of default. The most common forms of internal credit enhancement are reserve funds, overcollateralization, and senior/subordinated structures.

Reserve funds.   **Reserve funds** come in two forms, cash reserve funds and excess servicing spread. **Cash reserve funds** are straight deposits of cash generated from issuance proceeds. In this case, part of the underwriting profits from the deal are deposited into a hypothecated fund that typically invests in money market instruments. Cash reserve funds are typically used in conjunction with letters of credit or other kinds of external credit enhancements.

Excess servicing spread accounts involve the allocation of excess spread or cash into a separate reserve account after paying out the net coupon, servicing fee, and all other expenses on a monthly basis. For example, suppose that the gross WAC is 7.75%, the servicing and other fees are 0.25%, and the net WAC is 7.25%. This means that there is excess servicing of 0.25%. The amount in the reserve account will gradually increase and can be used to pay for possible future losses.

Overcollateralization.   **Overcollateralization** involves establishing a pool of assets with a greater principal amount than the principal amount of the pool of mortgage loans. For example, the principal amount of an issue may be $300 million, but the principal amount of the pool of mortgages is $305 million.

Senior/subordinated structure. The most widely used internal credit support structure by far is the senior/subordinated structure. The subordinated class is the first-loss piece absorbing all losses on the underlying collateral, thus protecting the senior class. For example, a $100 million deal can be divided into two classes: a $92.25 million senior class and a $7.75 million subordinated class. The subordination level in this hypothetical structure is 7.75%. The subordinated class will absorb all losses up to $7.75 million and the senior class will start to experience losses thereafter. So if there is $5 million of losses, the subordinated class will realize this loss. Thus, it would realize a 64.5% loss ($5/$7.75). If, instead, there is $10 million of losses, the subordinated class will experience $7.75 million of losses or a 100% loss and the senior class will experience a loss of $2.25 million ($10 million minus $7.75 million) or a 2.4% loss ($2.4/$92.25).

The subordinated class holder obviously would require a yield premium to take on the greater default risk exposure relative to the senior class. This setup is another form of self-insurance in which the senior class holder is giving up yield spread to the subordinated class holder. This form of credit enhancement still does not affect cash flow characteristics of the senior class except in the form of prepayment. To the extent that losses are within the subordination level, the senior class holder will receive principal as if a prepayment has occurred.

Almost all existing senior/subordinated structures also incorporate a **shifting interest structure.** A shifting interest structure redirects prepayments disproportionally from the subordinated class to the senior class according to a specified schedule. An example of such a schedule would be as follows:

Months	*Percentage of Prepayments Directed to Senior Class*
1–60	70
61–72	60
73–84	40
85–96	20
97–108	12
109+	pro rata

The rationale for the shifting interest structure is to have enough insurance outstanding to cover future losses. Because of the shifting interest structure, the subordination amount may actually grow in time, especially in a low-default fast-prepayment environment. This is sometimes referred to as "riding up the credit curve." Using the same example of our previous $100 million deal with 7.75% initial subordination and assuming a cumulative paydown (prepayments and regular repayments) of $20 million by year 3, the subordination will actually increase to 10.7% [$7.75 / ($92.25 − $20)] without any net losses. Even if the subordinated class has experienced some losses, say, $1 million, the subordination will still increase to 9.3% [($7.75 − $1) / ($92.25 − $20)].

PREPAYMENT CONVENTIONS AND CASH FLOW[2]

To value a pass-through security, it is necessary to project its cash flow. The difficulty is that the cash flow is unknown because of prepayments. The only way to project a cash flow is to make some assumption about the prepayment rate over the life of the underlying mortgage pool. The prepayment rate assumed is called the **prepayment speed** or, simply, **speed.** The yield calculated based on the projected cash flow is called a **cash flow yield.**

Estimating the cash flow from a pass-through requires making an assumption about future prepayments. Several conventions have been used as a benchmark for prepayment rates: (1) Federal Housing Administration (FHA) experience, (2) the conditional prepayment rate, and (3) the Public Securities Association (PSA) prepayment benchmark. Although the first convention is no longer used, we discuss it because of its historical significance.

In the early stages of the development of the pass-through market, cash flows were calculated assuming no prepayments for the first 12 years, at which time all the mortgages in the pool were assumed to prepay. This naive approach was replaced by the **FHA prepayment experience** approach, which also is no longer in use. This prepayment assumption, based on the prepayment experience for 30-year mortgages derived from an FHA table on mortgage survival factors, was once the most commonly used benchmark for prepayment rates. It calls for the projection of the cash flow for a mortgage pool on the assumption that the prepayment rate will be the same as the FHA experience with 30-year mortgage loans.

Despite the method's past popularity, prepayments based on FHA experience are not necessarily indicative of the prepayment rate for a particular pool, mainly because FHA prepayments are for mortgages originated over all sorts of interest-rate periods. Prepayment rates are tied to interest-rate cycles, however, so an average prepayment rate over various cycles is not very useful in estimating prepayments. Moreover, new FHA tables are published periodically, causing confusion about the FHA table on which prepayments should be based. Finally, because FHA mortgages are assumable, unlike FNMA, FHLMC, and most nonconforming mortgages that have due-on-sale provisions, FHA statistics underestimate prepayments for non-FHA mortgages. Because estimated prepayments using FHA experience may be misleading, the resulting cash flow is not meaningful for valuing pass-throughs.

Conditional Prepayment Rate

Another benchmark for projecting prepayments and the cash flow of a pass-through requires assuming that some fraction of the remaining principal in the pool is prepaid each month for the remaining term of the mortgage. The prepayment rate assumed for a pool, called the **conditional prepayment rate (CPR),** is based on the characteristics of the pool (including its historical prepayment experience) and the current and

---

[2]This section and the one to follow are adapted from Chapter 3 of Fabozzi, Ramsey, and Ramirez, *Collateralized Mortgage Obligations: Structures and Analysis.*

expected future economic environment. It is referred to as a conditional rate because it is conditional on the remaining mortgage balance.

Single-Monthly Mortality Rate   The CPR is an annual prepayment rate. To estimate monthly prepayments, the CPR must be converted into a monthly prepayment rate, commonly referred to as the **single-monthly mortality rate (SMM).** A formula can be used to determine the SMM for a given CPR:

$$SMM = 1 - (1 - CPR)^{1/12} \tag{11.1}$$

Suppose that the CPR used to estimate prepayments is 6%. The corresponding SMM is

$$SMM = 1 - (1 - 0.06)^{1/12}$$

$$= 1 - (0.94)^{0.08333} = 0.005143$$

SMM Rate and Monthly Prepayment   An SMM of $w\%$ means that approximately $w\%$ of the remaining mortgage balance at the beginning of the month, less the scheduled principal payment, will prepay that month. That is,
prepayment for month t

$$= SMM \times (\text{beginning mortgage balance for month } t \tag{11.2}$$
$$- \text{scheduled principal payment for month } t)$$

For example, suppose that an investor owns a pass-through in which the remaining mortgage balance at the beginning of some month is $290 million. Assuming that the SMM is 0.5143% and the scheduled principal payment is $3 million, the estimated prepayment for the month is

$$0.005143(\$290,000,000 - \$3,000,000) = \$1,476,041$$

PSA Prepayment Benchmark

The Public Securities Association (PSA) prepayment benchmark is expressed as a monthly series of annual prepayment rates.[3] The PSA benchmark assumes that prepayment rates are low for newly originated mortgages and then will speed up as the mortgages become seasoned.

The PSA benchmark assumes the following CPRs for 30-year mortgages: (1) a CPR of 0.2% for the first month, increased by 0.2% per year per month for the next 30 months when it reaches 6% per year, and (2) a 6% CPR for the remaining years. This benchmark, referred to as "100% PSA" or simply "100 PSA," is depicted graphically in Exhibit 11-2. Mathematically, 100 PSA can be expressed as follows:

---

[3]This benchmark is commonly referred to as a *prepayment model,* suggesting that it can be used to estimate prepayments. Characterization of this benchmark as a prepayment model is inappropriate. It is simply a market convention of prepayment behavior.

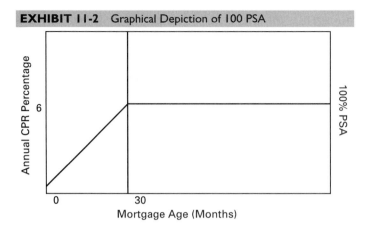

EXHIBIT 11-2 Graphical Depiction of 100 PSA

- If $t \leq 30$:   CPR $= 6\%\,(t/30)$
- If $t > 30$:   CPR $= 6\%$

where t is the number of months since the mortgage originated.

Slower or faster speeds are then referred to as some percentage of PSA. For example, 50 PSA means one-half the CPR of the PSA benchmark prepayment rate; 150 PSA means 1.5 times the CPR of the PSA benchmark prepayment rate; 300 PSA means three times the CPR of the benchmark prepayment rate. A prepayment rate of 0 PSA means that no prepayments are assumed.

The **average time to move** implied by various PSA assumptions is shown in Exhibit 11-3. For example, 100 PSA means that for newly originated mortgages, homeowners prepay on average after 17.4 years. If an investor believes that housing turnover is about eight years (i.e., homeowners prepay on average after eight years), then as shown in Exhibit 11-3, 275 PSA is the appropriate speed for newly originated mortgages.

EXHIBIT 11-3 Average Time to Move Implied by PSA (Years)

Mortgage Age (months)	PSA									
	75%	100%	125%	150%	175%	200%	225%	250%	275%	300%
0	22.9	17.4	14.1	11.8	10.3	9.1	8.1	7.4	6.8	6.3
6	22.5	17.0	13.6	11.4	9.8	8.6	7.7	7.0	6.4	5.6
12	22.2	16.6	13.3	11.1	9.5	8.3	7.4	6.6	6.0	5.5
24	21.8	16.2	12.8	10.7	9.1	7.9	7.0	6.2	5.8	5.1

Source: Karen Auld Wagner and Evan B. Firestone, "Homeowner Mobility and Mortgage Prepayment Forecasting," Chapter 11 in Frank J. Fabozzi (ed.), *Handbook of Mortgage-Backed Securities* (Chicago: Probus Publishing, 1995), Exhibit 2.

The CPR is converted to an SMM using equation (11.1). For example, the SMMs for month 5, month 20, and months 31 through 360 assuming 100 PSA are calculated as follows:

For month 5:
$$\text{CPR} = 6\%(5/30) = 1\% = 0.01$$
$$\text{SMM} = 1 - (1 - 0.01)^{1/12}$$
$$= 1 - (0.99)^{0.083333} = 0.000837$$

For month 20:
$$\text{CPR} = 6\%(20/30) = 4\% = 0.04$$
$$\text{SMM} = 1 - (1 - 0.04)^{1/12}$$
$$= 1 - (0.96)^{0.083333} = 0.003396$$

For months 31–360:
$$\text{CPR} = 6\%$$
$$\text{SMM} = 1 - (1 - 0.06)^{1/12}$$
$$= 1 - (0.94)^{0.083333} = 0.005143$$

The SMMs for month 5, month 20, and months 31 through 360 assuming 165 PSA are computed as follows:

For month 5:
$$\text{CPR} = 6\%(5/30) = 1\% = 0.01$$
$$165\ \text{PSA} = 1.65(0.01) = 0.0165$$
$$\text{SMM} = 1 - (1 - 0.0165)^{1/12}$$
$$= 1 - (0.9835)^{0.083333} = 0.001386$$

For month 20:
$$\text{CPR} = 6\%(20/30) = 4\% = 0.04$$
$$165\ \text{PSA} = 1.65(.04) = 0.066$$
$$\text{SMM} = 1 - (1 - 0.066)^{1/12}$$
$$= 1 - (0.934)^{0.083333} = 0.005674$$

For months 31–360:
$$\text{CPR} = 6\%$$
$$165\ \text{PSA} = 1.65(0.06) = 0.099$$
$$\text{SMM} = 1 - (1 - 0.099)^{1/12}$$
$$= 1 - (0.901)^{0.083333} = 0.007828$$

Notice that the SMM assuming 165 PSA is not just 1.65 times the SMM assuming 100 PSA. It is the CPR that is a multiple of the CPR assuming 100 PSA.

Monthly Cash Flow Construction   We now show how to construct a monthly cash flow for a hypothetical pass-through given a PSA assumption. For the purpose of this illustration, the underlying mortgages for this hypothetical pass-through are assumed to be fixed-rate level-payment mortgages with a WAC rate of 8.125%. It will be assumed that the pass-through rate is 7.5%, with a WAM of 357 months.

Exhibit 11-4 shows the cash flow for selected months assuming 100 PSA. The cash flow is broken down into three components: (1) interest (based on the pass-through rate), (2) the regularly scheduled principal repayment, and (3) prepayments based on 100 PSA.

Let's walk through Exhibit 11-4 column by column.

EXHIBIT 11-4 Monthly Cash Flow for a $400 Million 7.5% Pass-Through Rate with a WAC of 8.125% and a WAM of 357 Months Assuming 100 PSA

(1) Month	(2) Outstanding Balance	(3) SMM	(4) Mortgage Payment	(5) Interest	(6) Scheduled Principal	(7) Prepayment	(8) Total Principal	(9) Cash Flow
1	400,000,000	0.00067	2,975,868	2,500,000	267,535	267,470	535,005	3,035,005
2	399,464,995	0.00084	2,973,877	2,496,656	269,166	334,198	603,364	3,100,020
3	398,861,631	0.00101	2,971,387	2,492,885	270,762	400,800	671,562	3,164,447
4	398,190,069	0.00117	2,968,399	2,488,688	272,321	467,243	739,564	3,228,252
5	397,450,505	0.00134	2,964,914	2,484,066	273,843	533,493	807,335	3,291,401
6	396,643,170	0.00151	2,960,931	2,479,020	275,327	599,514	874,841	3,353,860
7	395,768,329	0.00168	2,956,453	2,473,552	276,772	665,273	942,045	3,415,597
8	394,826,284	0.00185	2,951,480	2,467,664	278,177	730,736	1,008,913	3,476,577
9	393,817,371	0.00202	2,946,013	2,461,359	279,542	795,869	1,075,410	3,536,769
10	392,741,961	0.00219	2,940,056	2,454,637	280,865	860,637	1,141,502	3,596,140
11	391,600,459	0.00236	2,933,608	2,447,503	282,147	925,008	1,207,155	3,654,658
12	390,393,304	0.00254	2,926,674	2,439,958	283,386	988,948	1,272,333	3,712,291
13	389,120,971	0.00271	2,919,254	2,432,006	284,581	1,052,423	1,337,004	3,769,010
14	387,783,966	0.00288	2,911,353	2,423,650	285,733	1,115,402	1,401,134	3,824,784
15	386,382,832	0.00305	2,902,973	2,414,893	286,839	1,177,851	1,464,690	3,879,583
16	384,918,142	0.00322	2,894,117	2,405,738	287,900	1,239,739	1,527,639	3,933,378
17	383,390,502	0.00340	2,884,789	2,396,191	288,915	1,301,033	1,589,949	3,986,139
18	381,800,553	0.00357	2,874,992	2,386,253	289,884	1,361,703	1,651,587	4,037,840
19	380,148,966	0.00374	2,864,730	2,375,931	290,805	1,421,717	1,712,522	4,088,453
20	378,436,444	0.00392	2,854,008	2,365,228	291,678	1,481,046	1,772,724	4,137,952
21	376,663,720	0.00409	2,842,830	2,354,148	292,503	1,539,658	1,832,161	4,186,309
22	374,831,559	0.00427	2,831,201	2,342,697	293,279	1,597,525	1,890,804	4,233,501
23	372,940,755	0.00444	2,819,125	2,330,880	294,005	1,654,618	1,948,623	4,279,503
24	370,992,132	0.00462	2,806,607	2,318,701	294,681	1,710,908	2,005,589	4,324,290
25	368,986,543	0.00479	2,793,654	2,306,166	295,307	1,766,368	2,061,675	4,367,841
26	366,924,868	0.00497	2,780,270	2,293,280	295,883	1,820,970	2,116,852	4,410,133
27	364,808,016	0.00514	2,766,461	2,280,050	296,406	1,874,688	2,171,094	4,451,144
28	362,636,921	0.00514	2,752,233	2,266,481	296,879	1,863,519	2,160,398	4,426,879
29	360,476,523	0.00514	2,738,078	2,252,978	297,351	1,852,406	2,149,758	4,402,736
30	358,326,766	0.00514	2,723,996	2,239,542	297,825	1,841,347	2,139,173	4,378,715
100	231,249,776	0.00514	1,898,682	1,445,311	332,928	1,187,608	1,520,537	2,965,848
101	229,729,239	0.00514	1,888,917	1,435,808	333,459	1,179,785	1,513,244	2,949,052
102	228,215,995	0.00514	1,879,202	1,426,350	333,990	1,172,000	1,505,990	2,932,340
103	226,710,004	0.00514	1,869,538	1,416,938	334,522	1,164,252	1,498,774	2,915,712
104	225,211,230	0.00514	1,859,923	1,407,570	335,055	1,156,541	1,491,596	2,899,166
105	223,719,634	0.00514	1,850,357	1,398,248	335,589	1,148,867	1,484,456	2,882,703
200	109,791,339	0.00514	1,133,751	686,196	390,372	562,651	953,023	1,639,219
201	108,838,316	0.00514	1,127,920	680,239	390,994	557,746	948,740	1,628,980
202	107,889,576	0.00514	1,122,119	674,310	391,617	552,863	944,480	1,618,790
203	106,945,096	0.00514	1,116,348	668,407	392,241	548,003	940,243	1,608,650
204	106,004,852	0.00514	1,110,607	662,530	392,866	543,164	936,029	1,598,560
205	105,068,823	0.00514	1,104,895	656,680	393,491	538,347	931,838	1,588,518
300	32,383,611	0.00514	676,991	202,398	457,727	164,195	621,923	824,320
301	31,761,689	0.00514	673,510	198,511	458,457	160,993	619,449	817,960
302	31,142,239	0.00514	670,046	194,639	459,187	157,803	616,990	811,629
303	30,525,249	0.00514	666,600	190,783	459,918	154,626	614,545	805,328
304	29,910,704	0.00514	663,171	186,942	460,651	151,462	612,113	799,055
305	29,298,591	0.00514	659,761	183,116	461,385	148,310	609,695	792,811
350	4,060,411	0.00514	523,138	25,378	495,645	18,334	513,979	539,356
351	3,546,432	0.00514	520,447	22,165	496,435	15,686	512,121	534,286
352	3,034,311	0.00514	517,770	18,964	497,226	13,048	510,274	529,238
353	2,524,037	0.00514	515,107	15,775	498,018	10,420	508,437	524,213
354	2,015,600	0.00514	512,458	12,597	498,811	7,801	506,612	519,209
355	1,508,988	0.00514	509,823	9,431	499,606	5,191	504,797	514,228
356	1,004,191	0.00514	507,201	6,276	500,401	2,591	502,992	509,269
357	501,199	0.00514	504,592	3,132	501,199	0	501,199	504,331

Column 1.   This is the month.

Column 2.   This column gives the outstanding mortgage balance at the beginning of the month. It is equal to the outstanding balance at the beginning of the preceding month reduced by the total principal payment in the preceding month.

Column 3.   This column shows the SMM for 100 PSA. Two things should be noted in this column. First, for month 1, the SMM is for a pass-through that has been seasoned three months. That is, the CPR is 0.8%. This is because the WAM is 357. Second, from month 27 on, the SMM is 0.00514, which corresponds to a CPR of 6%.

Column 4.   The total monthly mortgage payment is shown in this column. Notice that the total monthly mortgage payment declines over time as prepayments reduce the mortgage balance outstanding. There is a formula to determine what the monthly mortgage balance will be for each month given prepayments.[4]

Column 5.   The monthly interest paid to the pass-through investor is found in this column. This value is determined by multiplying the outstanding mortgage balance at the beginning of the month by the pass-through rate of 7.5% and dividing by 12.

Column 6.   This column gives the regularly scheduled principal repayment. This is the difference between the total monthly mortgage payment (the amount shown in column 4) and the gross coupon interest for the month. The gross coupon interest is 8.125% multiplied by the outstanding mortgage balance at the beginning of the month, then divided by 12.

Column 7.   The prepayment for the month is reported in this column. The prepayment is found by using equation (11.2). So, for example, in month 100, the beginning mortgage balance is $231,249,776, the scheduled principal payment is $332,298, and the SMM at 100 PSA is 0.00514301 (only 0.00514 is shown in the table, to save space), so the prepayment is

$$0.00514301(\$231,249,776 - \$332,928) = \$1,187,608$$

Column 8.   The total principal payment, which is the sum of columns 6 and 7, is shown in this column.

Column 9.   The projected monthly cash flow for this pass-through is shown in this last column. The monthly cash flow is the sum of the interest paid to the pass-through investor (column 5) and the total principal payments for the month (column 8).

Exhibit 11-5 shows selected monthly cash flows for the same pass-through assuming 165 PSA.

Beware of Conventions

The PSA prepayment benchmark is simply a market convention. It is the product of a study by the PSA based on FHA prepayment experience. Data that the PSA committee examined seemed to suggest that mortgages became seasoned (i.e., prepayment rates tended to level off) after 30 months and the CPR tended to be 6%. How,

---

[4]The formula is presented in Chapter 20 of Frank J. Fabozzi, *Fixed Income Mathematics: Analytical and Statistical Techniques* (Chicago: Probus Publishing, 1993).

EXHIBIT 11–5 Monthly Cash Flow for a $400 Million 7.5% Pass-Through Rate with a WAC of 8.125% and a WAM of 357 Months Assuming 165 PSA

(1) Month	(2) Outstanding Balance	(3) SMM	(4) Mortgage Payment	(5) Interest	(6) Scheduled Principal	(7) Prepayment	(8) Total Principal	(9) Total Cash Flow
1	400,000,000	0.00111	2,975,868	2,500,000	267,535	442,389	709,923	3,209,923
2	399,290,077	0.00139	2,972,575	2,495,563	269,048	552,847	821,896	3,317,459
3	398,468,181	0.00167	2,968,456	2,490,426	270,495	663,065	933,560	3,423,986
4	397,534,621	0.00195	2,963,513	2,484,591	271,873	772,949	1,044,822	3,529,413
5	396,489,799	0.00223	2,957,747	2,478,061	273,181	882,405	1,155,586	3,633,647
6	395,334,213	0.00251	2,951,160	2,470,839	274,418	991,341	1,265,759	3,736,598
7	394,068,454	0.00279	2,943,755	2,462,928	275,583	1,099,664	1,375,246	3,838,174
8	392,693,208	0.00308	2,935,534	2,454,333	276,674	1,207,280	1,483,954	3,938,287
9	391,209,254	0.00336	2,926,503	2,445,058	277,690	1,314,099	1,591,789	4,036,847
10	389,617,464	0.00365	2,916,666	2,435,109	278,631	1,420,029	1,698,659	4,133,769
11	387,918,805	0.00393	2,906,028	2,424,493	279,494	1,524,979	1,804,473	4,228,965
12	386,114,332	0.00422	2,894,595	2,413,215	280,280	1,628,859	1,909,139	4,322,353
13	384,205,194	0.00451	2,882,375	2,401,282	280,986	1,731,581	2,012,567	4,413,850
14	382,192,626	0.00480	2,869,375	2,388,704	281,613	1,833,058	2,114,670	4,503,374
15	380,077,956	0.00509	2,855,603	2,375,487	282,159	1,933,203	2,215,361	4,590,848
16	377,862,595	0.00538	2,841,068	2,361,641	282,623	2,031,931	2,314,554	4,676,195
17	375,548,041	0.00567	2,825,779	2,347,175	283,006	2,129,159	2,412,164	4,759,339
18	373,135,877	0.00597	2,809,746	2,332,099	283,305	2,224,805	2,508,110	4,840,210
19	370,627,766	0.00626	2,792,980	2,316,424	283,521	2,318,790	2,602,312	4,918,735
20	368,025,455	0.00656	2,775,493	2,300,159	283,654	2,411,036	2,694,690	4,994,849
21	365,330,765	0.00685	2,757,296	2,283,317	283,702	2,501,466	2,785,169	5,068,486
22	362,545,596	0.00715	2,738,402	2,265,910	283,666	2,590,008	2,873,674	5,139,584
23	359,671,922	0.00745	2,718,823	2,247,950	283,545	2,676,588	2,960,133	5,208,083
24	356,711,789	0.00775	2,698,575	2,229,449	283,338	2,761,139	3,044,477	5,273,926
25	353,667,312	0.00805	2,677,670	2,210,421	283,047	2,843,593	3,126,640	5,337,061
26	350,540,672	0.00835	2,656,123	2,190,879	282,671	2,923,885	3,206,556	5,397,435
27	347,334,116	0.00865	2,633,950	2,170,838	282,209	3,001,955	3,284,164	5,455,002
28	344,049,952	0.00865	2,611,167	2,150,312	281,662	2,973,553	3,255,215	5,405,527
29	340,794,737	0.00865	2,588,581	2,129,967	281,116	2,945,400	3,226,516	5,356,483
30	337,568,221	0.00865	2,566,190	2,109,801	280,572	2,917,496	3,198,067	5,307,869
100	170,142,350	0.00865	1,396,958	1,063,390	244,953	1,469,591	1,714,544	2,777,933
101	168,427,806	0.00865	1,384,875	1,052,674	244,478	1,454,765	1,699,243	2,751,916
102	166,728,563	0.00865	1,372,896	1,042,054	244,004	1,440,071	1,684,075	2,726,128
103	165,044,489	0.00865	1,361,020	1,031,528	243,531	1,425,508	1,669,039	2,700,567
104	163,375,450	0.00865	1,349,248	1,021,097	243,060	1,411,075	1,654,134	2,675,231
105	161,721,315	0.00865	1,337,577	1,010,758	242,589	1,396,771	1,639,359	2,650,118
200	56,746,664	0.00865	585,990	354,667	201,767	489,106	690,874	1,045,540
201	56,055,790	0.00865	580,921	350,349	201,377	483,134	684,510	1,034,859
202	55,371,280	0.00865	575,896	346,070	200,986	477,216	678,202	1,024,273
203	54,693,077	0.00865	570,915	341,832	200,597	471,353	671,950	1,013,782
204	54,021,127	0.00865	565,976	337,632	200,208	465,544	665,752	1,003,384
205	53,355,375	0.00865	561,081	333,471	199,820	459,789	659,609	993,080
300	11,758,141	0.00865	245,808	73,488	166,196	100,269	266,465	339,953
301	11,491,677	0.00865	243,682	71,823	165,874	97,967	263,841	335,664
302	11,227,836	0.00865	241,574	70,174	165,552	95,687	261,240	331,414
303	10,966,596	0.00865	239,485	68,541	165,232	93,430	258,662	327,203
304	10,707,934	0.00865	237,413	66,925	164,912	91,196	256,107	323,032
305	10,451,827	0.00865	235,360	65,324	164,592	88,983	253,575	318,899
350	1,235,674	0.00865	159,202	7,723	150,836	9,384	160,220	167,943
351	1,075,454	0.00865	157,825	6,722	150,544	8,000	158,544	165,266
352	916,910	0.00865	156,460	5,731	150,252	6,631	156,883	162,614
353	760,027	0.00865	155,107	4,750	149,961	5,277	155,238	159,988
354	604,789	0.00865	153,765	3,780	149,670	3,937	153,607	157,387
355	451,182	0.00865	152,435	2,820	149,380	2,611	151,991	154,811
356	299,191	0.00865	151,117	1,870	149,091	1,298	150,389	152,259
357	148,802	0.00865	149,809	930	148,802	0	148,802	149,732

though, did the PSA come up with the CPRs used for months 1 through 29? In fact, these numbers are not based on empirical evidence but on a linear increase from month 1 to month 30 so that at month 30 the CPR is 6%. Moreover, the same benchmark or seasoning process is used in quoting pass-throughs regardless of the collateral: 30- and 15-year loans, fixed- or adjustable-rate loans, and conventional or VA/FHA-insured loans.

Astute money managers recognize that the CPR is a convenient shorthand enabling market participants to quote yield and/or price, but that as a convention in determining value it has many limitations.

FACTORS AFFECTING PREPAYMENT BEHAVIOR

In this section we review the factors that have been observed to affect prepayments. The factors that affect prepayment behavior are (1) prevailing mortgage rate, (2) characteristics of the underlying mortgage pool, (3) seasonal factors, and (4) general economic activity.

Prevailing Mortgage Rate

The current mortgage rate affects prepayments in three ways. First, the spread between the prevailing mortgage rate and the contract rate paid by the homeowner affects the incentive to refinance. (By **contract rate** we mean the rate on the mortgage loan.) Second, the path of mortgage rates since the loan was originated affects prepayments through a phenomenon referred to as **refinancing burnout.** Both the spread and path of mortgage rates affect prepayments that are the product of refinancing. The third way in which the prevailing mortgage rate affects prepayments is through its effect on the affordability of housing and housing turnover. We discuss each in the following sections.

Spread between Contract Rate and Prevailing Mortgage Rate   The single most important factor affecting prepayments because of refinancing is the current level of mortgage rates relative to the borrower's contract rate. The greater the difference between the two, the greater the incentive to refinance the mortgage loan. For refinancing to make economic sense, the interest savings must be greater than the costs associated with refinancing the mortgage. These costs include legal expenses, origination fees, title insurance, and the value of the time associated with obtaining another mortgage loan. Some of these costs—such as title insurance and origination points—will vary proportionately with the amount to be financed. Other costs, such as the application fee and legal expenses, are typically fixed.

Historically, it has been observed that when mortgage rates fall to more than 200 basis points below the contract rate, prepayment rates increase. However, the creativity of mortgage originators in designing mortgage loans such that the refinancing costs are folded into the amount borrowed has changed the view that mortgage rates must drop dramatically below the contract rate to make refinancing economic. Moreover, mortgage originators now do an effective job of advertising to make homeowners cognizant of the economic benefits of refinancing.

Path of Mortgage Rates   The historical pattern of prepayments and economic theory suggests that it is not only the level of mortgage rates that affects prepayment behavior but also the path that mortgage rates take to get to the current level.

To illustrate why, suppose that the underlying contract rate for a pool of mortgage loans is 11% and that three years after origination, the prevailing mortgage rate declines to 8%. Let's consider two possible paths of the mortgage rate in getting to the 8% level. In the first path, the mortgage rate declines to 8% at the end of the first year, then rises to 13% at the end of the second year, and then falls to 8% at the end of the third year. In the second path, the mortgage rate rises to 12% at the end of the first year, continues its rise to 13% at the end of the second year, and then falls to 8% at the end of the third year.

If the mortgage rate follows the first path, those who can benefit from refinancing will more than likely take advantage of this opportunity when the mortgage rate drops to 8% in the first year. When the mortgage rate drops again to 8% at the end of the third year, the likelihood is that prepayments because of refinancing will not surge; those who can benefit by taking advantage of the refinancing opportunity will have done so already when the mortgage rate declined for the first time. This is the prepayment behavior referred to as the refinancing burnout (or simply, burnout) phenomenon.

In contrast, the expected prepayment behavior when the mortgage rate follows the second path is quite different. Prepayment rates are expected to be low in the first two years. When the mortgage rate declines to 8% in the third year, refinancing activity and therefore prepayments are expected to surge. Consequently, the burnout phenomenon is related to the path of mortgage rates.

Level of Mortgage Rates   As we discussed earlier, prepayments occur because of housing turnover and refinancing. Our focus so far has been on the factors that affect prepayments caused by refinancing. The level of mortgage rates affects housing turnover to the extent that a lower rate increases the affordability of homes.

Characteristics of the Underlying Mortgage Loans

The following characteristics of the underlying mortgage loans affect prepayments: (1) the contract rate, (2) whether the loans are FHA/VA-guaranteed or conventional, (3) the amount of seasoning, (4) the type of loan (e.g., a 30-year level-payment mortgage, five-year balloon mortgage, and so on), and (5) the geographical location of the underlying properties.

Seasonal Factors

There is a well-documented seasonal pattern in prepayments. This pattern is related to activity in the primary housing market, with home buying increasing in the spring and gradually reaching a peak in late summer. Home buying declines in the fall and winter. Mirroring this activity are the prepayments that result from the turnover of housing as home buyers sell their existing homes and purchase new ones. Prepayments are low in the winter months and begin to rise in the spring, reaching a peak in the summer months. However, probably because of delays in passing through prepayments, the peak may not be observed until early fall.

General Economic Activity

Economic theory would suggest that general economic activity affects prepayment behavior through its effect on housing turnover. The link is as follows: A growing economy results in a rise in personal income and in opportunities for worker migration; this increases family mobility and as a result, increases housing turnover. The opposite holds for a weak economy. Some researchers suggest that prepayments can be projected by identifying and forecasting the turnover rate of the single-family housing stock.[5]

Although some modelers of prepayment behavior may incorporate macroeconomic measures of economic activity such as gross domestic product, industrial production, or housing starts, the trend has been to ignore them or limit their use to specific applications. There are two reasons why macroeconomic measures have been ignored by some modelers. First, empirical tests suggest that the inclusion of macroeconomic measures does not significantly improve the forecasting ability of a prepayment model.[6] Second, as explained earlier, prepayment models are based on a projection of a path for future mortgage rates. The inclusion of macroeconomic variables in a prepayment model would require the forecasting of the value of these variables over long time periods.

Macroeconomic variables, however, have been used by some researchers in prepayment models to capture the effect of housing turnover on prepayments by specifying a relationship between interest rates and housing turnover. This is the approach used, for example, in the Prudential Securities Model.[7]

Prepayment Models

A prepayment model is a statistical model that is used to forecast prepayments. It begins by modeling the statistical relationships among the factors that are expected to affect prepayments. One study suggests that four factors discussed previously explain about 95% of the variation in prepayment rates: refinancing incentives, burnout, seasoning, and seasonality.[8] These factors are then combined into one model. For example, in the Goldman, Sachs prepayment model the effects interact proportionally through the following multiplicative function, which is used to project prepayments:

$$\text{monthly prepayment rate} = (\text{refinancing incentive}) \times (\text{seasoning multiplier})$$
$$\times (\text{month multiplier}) \times (\text{burnout multiplier})$$

where the various multipliers are adjustments for the effects we discussed earlier in this chapter.

---

[5]See, for example, Joseph C. Hu, "An Alternative Prepayment Projection Based on Housing Activity," in Frank J. Fabozzi (ed.), *The Handbook of Mortgage-Backed Securities* (Chicago: Probus Publishing, 1988), pp. 639–648.

[6]Scott F. Richard and Richard Roll, "Prepayments on Fixed-Rate Mortgage-Backed Securities," *Journal of Portfolio Management*, Spring 1989, pp. 78–79.

[7]Lakbhir S. Hayre, Kenneth Lauterbach, and Cyrus Mohebbi, "Prepayment Models and Methodologies," in Frank J. Fabozzi (ed.), *Advances and Innovations in the Bond and Mortgage Markets* (Chicago: Probus Publishing, 1989), p. 338.

[8]Scott F. Richard, "Relative Prepayment Rates on Thirty-Year FNMA, FHLMC and GNMA Fixed Rate Mortgage-Backed Securities," in Fabozzi (ed.), *Advances and Innovations in the Bond and Mortgage Markets,* pp. 351–369.

The product of a prepayment forecast is not one prepayment rate but a set of prepayment rates for each month of the remaining term of a mortgage pool. The set of monthly prepayment rates, however, is not reported by Wall Street firms or vendors. Instead, a single prepayment rate is reported. One way to convert a set of monthly prepayment rates into a single prepayment rate is to calculate a simple average of the prepayment rates. The obvious drawback to this approach is that it does not take into consideration the outstanding balance each month. An alternative approach is to use some type of weighted average, selecting the weights to reflect the amount of the monthly cash flow corresponding to a monthly prepayment rate. This is done by first computing the cash flow yield for a pass-through given its market price and the set of monthly prepayment rates. Then a single prepayment rate (CPR or PSA multiple) that gives the same cash flow yield is found.

CASH FLOW FOR NONAGENCY PASS-THROUGHS

In agency pass-through securities, the cash flow is not affected by defaults and delinquencies. For nonagency pass-throughs, the effect of defaults and delinquencies must be considered. With the increase in the issuance of nonagency pass-through securities (as well as nonagency CMOs, described in Chapter 12), a standardized benchmark for default rates has been introduced by the Public Securities Association (PSA). The PSA standard default assumption (SDA) benchmark gives the annual default rate for a mortgage pool as a function of the seasoning of the mortgages. The PSA SDA benchmark, or 100 SDA, specifies the following:

1. The default rate in month 1 is 0.02% and increases by 0.02% up to month 30, so that in month 30, the default rate is 0.60%.
2. From month 30 to month 60, the default rate remains at 0.60%.
3. From month 61 to month 120, the default rate declines from 0.60% to 0.03%.
4. From month 120 on, the default rate remains constant at 0.03%.

This pattern is illustrated in Exhibit 11-6.

EXHIBIT 11-6 PSA Standard Default Assumption Benchmark (100 SDA)

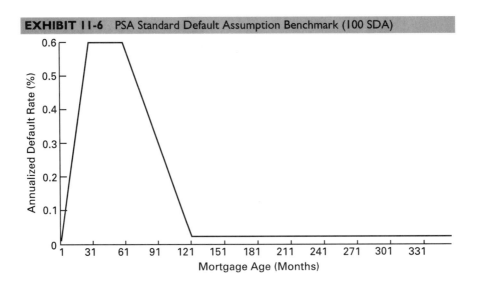

As with the PSA prepayment benchmark, multiples of the benchmark are found by multiplying the default rate by the assumed multiple. For example, 200 SDA means the following pattern:

1. The default rate in month 1 is 0.04% and increases by 0.04% up to month 30, so that in month 30, the default rate is 1.20%.
2. From month 30 to month 60, the default rate remains at 1.20%.
3. From month 61 to month 120, the default rate declines from 1.20% to 0.06%.
4. From month 120 on, the default rate remains constant at 0.06%.

A 0 SDA means that no defaults are assumed.

CASH FLOW YIELD

Given the projected cash flow and the price of a pass-through, its yield can be calculated. The yield is the interest rate that will make the present value of the expected cash flow equal to the price. A yield computed in this manner is known as a **cash flow yield.**

Bond-Equivalent Yield

For a pass-through, the yield that makes the present value of the cash flow equal to the price is a monthly interest rate. The next step is to annualize the monthly yield. According to market convention, to compare the yield for a pass-through to that of a Treasury or corporate bond, the monthly yield should not be annualized just by multiplying the monthly yield by 12. The reason is that a Treasury bond and a corporate bond pay interest semiannually, whereas a pass-through has a monthly cash flow. By reinvesting monthly cash flows, the pass-through holder has the opportunity to generate greater interest than can be earned by a bond holder who has only semiannual coupon payments to reinvest. Therefore, the yield on a pass-through must be calculated so as to make it comparable to the yield to maturity for a bond.

This is accomplished by computing the **bond-equivalent yield.** As explained in Chapter 3, this is simply a market convention for annualizing any fixed-income instrument that pays interest more than once a year. The bond-equivalent yield is found by doubling a semiannual yield. For a pass-through security, the semiannual yield is

$$\text{semiannual cash flow yield} = (1 + y_M)^6 - 1$$

where y_M is the monthly interest rate that will equate the present value of the projected monthly cash flow to the price of the pass-through. The bond-equivalent yield is found by doubling the semiannual cash flow yield; that is,

$$\text{bond-equivalent yield} = 2[(1 + y_M)^6 - 1]$$

Limitations of Cash Flow Yield Measure

The yield corresponding to a price must be qualified by an assumption concerning prepayments. Although yields are frequently quoted, remember that the yield is based on some underlying prepayment assumption. Consequently, a yield of 9% based on 150% PSA means that it is assumed that the underlying mortgages will prepay at a rate equal to 150% PSA. A yield number without qualification as to the prepayment assumption is meaningless.

In fact, even with specification of the prepayment assumption, the yield number is meaningless in terms of the relative value of a pass-through. For an investor to realize the yield based on some PSA assumption, a number of conditions must be met: (1) the investor must reinvest all the cash flows at the calculated yield, (2) the investor must hold the pass-through security until all the mortgages have been paid off, and (3) the assumed prepayment rate must actually occur over the life of the pass-through. Moreover, in the case of private-label pass-throughs, the assumed default and delinquencies must actually occur. Now, if all this is likely, we can trust the yield numbers. Otherwise, investors must be cautious in using yield numbers to evaluate pass-through securities.

Yield Spread to Treasuries

Although we have explained that it is not possible to calculate a yield with certainty, it has been stated that pass-through securities offer a higher yield than Treasury securities. Typically, the comparison is between Ginnie Mae pass-through securities and Treasuries, for both are free of default risk. Presumably, the difference between the two yields primarily represents prepayment risk. The question should be whether the premium the investor receives in terms of higher yield for bearing prepayment risk is adequate. This is where option-pricing models applied to pass-through securities have been used. Option-pricing models let us determine if the pass-through security is offering the proper compensation for accepting prepayment risk.

The yield spread between private-label pass-through securities and agency pass-through securities reflects both credit risk and prepayment risk. The reason for the difference in prepayment risk lies in the nature of the underlying mortgages. For example, in the case of Ginnie Mae pass-through securities, the underlying mortgages are FHA- or VA-insured mortgages. Borrowers who obtain such government guarantees have different prepayment characteristics than those of holders of non–government-insured mortgages. Specifically, when interest rates decline, prepayments on FHA/VA-insured mortgages do not increase as fast as those for non–FHA/VA-insured mortgages. This reflects the fact that borrowers who obtain government-guaranteed mortgages typically do not have the ability to take on refinancing costs as rates decline. There are similar differences between the prepayment patterns of Ginnie Mae pass-through securities and the two other agency pass-through securities.

When we speak of comparing the yield of a mortgage pass-through security to a comparable Treasury, what does "comparable" mean? The stated maturity of a mortgage pass-through security is an inappropriate measure because of prepayments. Instead, market participants have used two measures: Macaulay duration and average life. As we explain in Chapter 4, Macaulay duration is a weighted-average term to maturity where the weights are the present value of the cash flows. The more commonly used measure is the average life.

Average Life

The **average life** of a mortgage-backed security is the average time to receipt of principal payments (scheduled principal payments and projected prepayments), weighted by the amount of principal expected. Mathematically, the average life is expressed as follows:

EXHIBIT 11-7 Average Life of a Pass-Through Based on Different PSA Prepayment Assumptions

PSA speed	50	100	165	200	300	400	500	600	700
Average life	15.11	11.66	8.76	7.68	5.63	4.44	3.68	3.16	2.78

$$\text{average life} = \sum_{t=1}^{T} \frac{t \times \text{principal received at time } t}{12(\text{total principal})}$$

where T is the number of months. The average life of a pass-through depends on the PSA prepayment assumption. To see this, the average life is shown in Exhibit 11-7 for different prepayment speeds for the pass-through we used to illustrate the cash flow for 100 PSA and 165 PSA in Exhibits 11-2 and 11-3.

PREPAYMENT RISK AND ASSET/LIABILITY MANAGEMENT

An investor who owns pass-through securities does not know what the cash flow will be because that depends on prepayments. The risk associated with prepayments is called **prepayment risk.** To understand prepayment risk, suppose that an investor buys a 10% coupon Ginnie Mae at a time when mortgage rates are 10%. Let's consider what will happen to prepayments if mortgage rates decline to, say, 6%. There will be two adverse consequences. First, we know from the basic property of fixed-income securities that the price of an option-free bond will rise. But in the case of a pass-through security, the rise in price will not be as large as that of an option-free bond because a fall in interest rates increases the borrower's incentive to prepay the loan and refinance the debt at a lower rate. This results in the same adverse consequence faced by holders of callable corporate and municipal bonds. As in the case of those instruments, the upside price potential of a pass-through security is truncated because of prepayments. This characteristic, as we explain in Chapter 14, is referred to as **negative convexity.** This should not be surprising, because a mortgage loan effectively grants the borrower the right to call the loan at par value. The second adverse consequence is that the cash flow must be reinvested at a lower rate. These two adverse consequences when mortgage rates decline are referred to as **contraction risk.**

Now let's look at what happens if mortgage rates rise to 15%. The price of the pass-through, like the price of any bond, will decline. But again it will decline more because the higher rates will tend to slow down the rate of prepayment, in effect increasing the amount invested at the coupon rate, which is lower than the market rate. Prepayments will slow down because homeowners will not refinance or partially prepay their mortgages when mortgage rates are higher than the contract rate of 10%. Of course, this is just the time when investors want prepayments to speed up so that they can reinvest the prepayments at the higher market interest rate. This adverse consequence of rising mortgage rates is called **extension risk.**

Therefore, prepayment risk encompasses contraction risk and extension risk. Prepayment risk makes pass-through securities unattractive for certain financial institutions to hold from an asset–liability perspective. Let's look at why particular institutional investors may find pass-throughs unattractive:

1. Thrifts and commercial banks want to lock in a spread over their cost of funds. Their funds are raised on a short-term basis. If they invest in fixed-

rate pass-through securities, they will be mismatched because a pass-through is a longer-term security. In particular, depository institutions are exposed to extension risk when they invest in pass-through securities.

2. To satisfy certain obligations of insurance companies, pass-through securities may be unattractive. More specifically, consider a life insurance company that has issued a four-year GIC. The uncertainty about the cash flow from a pass-through security and the likelihood that slow prepayments will result in the instrument being long term make it an unappealing investment vehicle for such accounts. In such instances, a pass-through security exposes the insurance company to extension risk.

3. Consider a pension fund that wants to satisfy long-term liabilities by locking in prevailing interest rates. Buying a pass-through security exposes the pension fund to the risk that prepayments will speed up and the maturity of the investment will shorten considerably. Prepayments will speed up when interest rates decline, thereby forcing reinvestment of prepayments at a lower interest rate. In this case the pension fund is exposed to contraction risk.

We can see that some institutional investors are concerned with extension risk and others with contraction risk when they purchase a pass-through security. Is it possible to alter the cash flow of a pass-through so as to reduce the contraction risk and extension risk for institutional investors? This can be done, as we shall see later in Chapter 12.

It should be understood that prepayments are not necessarily an adverse event for an investor. The effect on investment performance will depend upon whether the pass-through is purchased at a discount or at a premium. Prepayments enhance the return from holding a pass-through if it is purchased at a discount, for two reasons. First, the investor realizes a capital gain equal to the difference between the par value and the price paid. Second, a pass-through will trade at a discount because the pass-through's coupon rate is lower than the current coupon rate for newly issued pass-throughs. Consequently, prepayments allow the investor to reinvest the proceeds at a higher coupon rate. For a pass-through purchased at a premium to par, prepayments reduce investment returns for two reasons: (1) the investor realizes a capital loss equal to the difference between the price paid and par, and (2) the proceeds must be reinvested at a lower coupon rate.

SECONDARY MARKET TRADING

Pass-throughs are quoted in the same manner as U.S. Treasury coupon securities. A quote of 94-05 means 94 and 5/32nds of par value, or 94.15625% of par value. As we explain in our discussion of prepayments, the yield corresponding to a price must be qualified by an assumption concerning prepayments.

Pass-throughs are identified by a pool prefix and pool number provided by the agency. The prefix indicates the type of pass-through. For example, a pool prefix of 20 for a Freddie Mac PC means that the underlying pool consists of conventional mortgages with an original maturity of 15 years. A pool prefix of AR for a Ginnie Mae

MBS means that the underlying pool consists of adjustable-rate mortgages. The pool number indicates the specific mortgages underlying the pass-through and the issuer of the pass-through.

Many trades occur while a pool is still unspecified, and therefore no pool information is known at the time of the trade. This kind of trade is known as a "TBA" (to be announced) trade. When an investor purchases, say, $1 million GNMA 8s on a TBA basis, the investor can receive up to three pools, with pool numbers being announced shortly before the settlement date. Three pools can be delivered because the PSA has established guidelines for standards of delivery and settlement of mortgage-backed securities,[9] under which our hypothetical TBA trade permits three possible pools to be delivered. The option of what pools to deliver is left to the seller, as long as selection and delivery satisfy the PSA guidelines. In contrast to TBA trades, a pool number may be specified. In this case the transaction will involve delivery of the pool specifically designated.[10]

There are many seasoned issues of the same agency with the same coupon rate outstanding at a given point in time. For example, there are more than 30,000 pools of 30-year Ginnie Mae MBSs outstanding with a coupon rate of 9%. One pass-through may be backed by a pool of mortgage loans in which all the properties are located in California, whereas another may be backed by a pool of mortgage loans in which all the properties are in Minnesota. Yet another may be backed by a pool of mortgage loans in which the properties are from several regions in the country. So which pool are dealers referring to when they talk about Ginnie Mae 9s? They do not refer to any specific pool but instead to a generic security, although the prepayment characteristics of pass-throughs with underlying pools from different parts of the country are different. Thus, the projected prepayment rates for pass-throughs reported by dealer firms are for generic pass-throughs. A particular pool purchased may have a materially different prepayment speed from the generic. Moreover, when an investor purchases a pass-through without specifying a pool number, the seller can deliver the worst-paying pools as long as the pools delivered satisfy good delivery requirements.

Prior to March 1999, the PSA delivery standards allowed the seller in a TBA trade to under- or over-deliver by 1% per $1 million traded. So, if $1 million of par value is sold at par, the seller could deliver as little as $990,000 or as much as $1,010,000. The seller would select the amount to deliver based on prevailing prices. This was a valuable option to sellers in a TBA trade and a disadvantage to buyers. In March 1999, the PSA changed its delivery standards so that the seller in a TBA trade may only under- or over-delivery by 0.1%. Consequently, the value of this delivery option to the seller is now minimal.

---

[9] Public Securities Association, *Uniform Practices for the Clearance and Settlement of Mortgage-Backed Securities.* More specifically, the requirement for good delivery permits a maximum of three pools per $1 million traded, or a maximum of four pools per $1 million for coupons of 12% or more.

[10] For a further discussion of specified pools, see Chuck Ramsey and J. Michael Henderson, "Specified Pools," Chapter 5 in Frank J. Fabozzi (ed.), *The Handbook of Mortgage-Backed Securities,* 3rd ed. (Chicago: Probus Publishing, 1992).

SUMMARY

A mortgage pass-through security is created when one or more mortgage holders form a collection (pool) of mortgages and sell shares or participation certificates in the pool. The monthly cash flow of a pass-through depends on the cash flow of the underlying mortgages and therefore consists of monthly mortgage payments representing interest, the scheduled repayment of principal, and any prepayments. The cash flow is less than that of the underlying mortgages by an amount equal to servicing and any guarantor fees. As with individual mortgage loans, because of prepayments the cash flow of a pass-through is not known with certainty.

The major types of pass-throughs are agency pass-throughs issued by Ginnie Mae, Freddie Mac, and Fannie Mae. There are two types of guarantees that may be provided by an agency: (1) timely payment of both interest and principal, and (2) timely payment of interest and eventual payment of the scheduled principal when it is collected but no later than a specified date. Ginnie Mae pass-throughs are guaranteed by the full faith and credit of the U.S. government and consequently are viewed as risk-free in terms of default risk. Freddie Mac and Fannie Mae are government-sponsored enterprises, and therefore their guarantee does not carry the full faith and credit of the U.S. government.

Nonagency pass-throughs are issued by entities such as commercial banks, thrifts, and private conduits. Unlike agency pass-throughs, these pass-throughs are rated by the nationally recognized rating companies and require some form of credit enhancement to obtain a high credit rating. Credit enhancement may be internal or external, or a combination of both.

Estimating the cash flow from a pass-through requires forecasting prepayments. The current convention is to use the PSA prepayment benchmark, which is a series of conditional prepayment rates, to obtain the cash flow.

There are four factors that affect prepayment behavior: (1) prevailing mortgage rate, (2) characteristics of the underlying mortgage pool, (3) seasonal factors, and (4) general economic activity. A prepayment model begins by modeling the statistical relationships among the factors that are expected to affect prepayments. The product of a prepayment forecast is a set of prepayment rates for each month of the remaining term of a mortgage pool, which are then converted into a PSA speed.

For nonagency pass-throughs, the effect of defaults and delinquencies on the cash flow must be considered. A standardized benchmark for default rates has been introduced by the PSA. The PSA SDA benchmark gives the annual default rate for a mortgage pool as a function of the seasoning of the mortgages.

Given the projected cash flow and the market price of a pass-through, a cash flow yield can be calculated. Investors must recognize that the PSA prepayment benchmark is a convention enabling market participants to quote yield and/or price but that it has many limitations for determining the value of a pass-through. The yield spread is quoted as the difference between the cash flow yield and the yield to maturity of a comparable Treasury. A measure commonly used to estimate the life of a pass-through is its average life.

The prepayment risk associated with investing in mortgage pass-through securities can be decomposed into contraction risk and extension risk. Prepayment risk makes pass-through securities unattractive for certain financial institutions to hold from an asset–liability perspective.

Pass-throughs are quoted in the same manner as U.S. Treasury coupon securities. They are identified by a pool prefix and pool number. A TBA trade occurs while a pool is still unspecified, and therefore no pool information is known at the time of the trade. The seller has the right in this case to deliver pass-throughs backed by pools that satisfy the PSA requirements for good delivery.

Questions

1. What is a mortgage pass-through security?
2. Describe the cash flow of a mortgage pass-through security.
3. What are the WAC and WAM of a pass-through security?
4. a. What are the different types of agency pass-through securities?
   b. Which type of agency pass-through carries the full faith and credit of the U.S. government?
5. Explain whether all agency pass-through securities guarantee timely payment of interest and scheduled principal.
6. What is a nonagency pass-through security?
7. What is the disadvantage of a nonagency pass-through that is credit enhanced with a corporate guarantee?
8. a. What is a senior-subordinated structure?
   b. What is a shifting interest-rate structure, and what is the rationale for its inclusion in a nonagency pass-through security?
   c. To what extent does a shifting interest structure alter the cash flows?
9. Why is overcollateralization a form of credit enhancement for a nonagency pass-through security?
10. Does the presence of a third-party guarantor alter the cash flows of a nonagency pass-through security?
11. Why is an assumed prepayment speed necessary to project the cash flow of a pass-through?
12. What does a conditional prepayment rate of 8% mean?
13. Indicate whether you agree or disagree with the following statement: "The PSA prepayment benchmark is a model for forecasting prepayments for a pass-through security."
14. a. Complete the following table:

CPR Assuming:			
Month	*100% PSA*	*70% PSA*	*320% PSA*
1			
4			
9			
27			
40			
120			
340			

   b. Complete the following table:

SMM Assuming:

Month	100% PSA	70% PSA	320% PSA
1			
4			
9			
27			
40			
120			
340			

15. Complete the following table (in thousands of dollars) assuming a prepayment rate of 165 PSA:

Original balance: $100,000,000
Pass-through rate: 9.0%
WAM: 360 months

Month	Out. Bal.	SMM	Mort. Pay.	Interest	Sch. Prin.	Pre- pay.	Tot. Prin.	Cash Flow	Total CF
1	100,000		841						
2	99,934		841						

16. a. How does the spread between prevailing mortgage rates and the contract rate affect prepayments?
    b. Why is the path that mortgage rates followed in the past important in predicting future prepayments?
    c. Why is there a seasonal effect in prepayments?
17. Why was the PSA Standard Default curve introduced?
18. a. What is the cash flow yield of a mortgage pass-through security?
    b. What are the limitations of cash flow yield measures for a mortgage pass-through security?
    c. What is the bond-equivalent yield if the monthly cash flow yield is 0.7%?
19. What is the average life of a pass-through, and what does it depend on?
20. a. What are contraction risk and extension risk?
    b. Why would a pass-through with a WAM of 350 months be an unattractive investment for a savings and loan association?
21. a. Distinguish between a TBA and specified pool trade.
    b. What delivery options are granted to the seller in a TBA trade?

CHAPTER 12

Collateralized Mortgage Obligations and Stripped Mortgage-Backed Securities

Learning Objectives

After reading this chapter you will understand:

■ why and how a collateralized mortgage obligation is created

■ what a sequential-pay CMO is

■ how the average life of a sequential-pay CMO compares to that of the collateral from which it is created

■ what an accrual tranche is and its effect on the average life of sequential-pay tranches in the CMO structure

■ how a floater and an inverse floater are created from a CMO tranche

■ what a planned amortization class tranche is and how it is created

■ how the prepayment protection for a planned amortization class changes over time

■ what a support tranche is and the substantial prepayment risk to which it exposes investors

■ what a support bond with a schedule is

■ what a notional IO is and how it is created

■ what a REMIC is

■ the difference between an agency CMO, a private-label CMO, and a whole loan CMO

■ how stripped mortgage-backed securities are created

■ the various types of stripped mortgage-backed securities

■ the investment characteristics of stripped mortgage-backed securities

In this chapter we discuss collateralized mortgage obligations and stripped mortgage-backed securities. Because these securities derive their cash flow

259

from underlying mortgage collateral such as pass-throughs or a pool of whole loans, they are referred to as derivative mortgage-backed securities products.

COLLATERALIZED MORTGAGE OBLIGATIONS[1]

At the close of Chapter 11, we discussed the prepayment risks associated with investing in pass-throughs: contraction risk and extension risk. We note there that some institutional investors are concerned with extension risk when they invest in a pass-through, whereas others are more concerned with contraction risk. Fortunately, redirecting cash flows from a pass-through to various bond classes makes it possible to redistribute prepayment risk for investors who want to reduce their exposure to prepayment risk. Because the total prepayment risk of a pass-through will not be changed by altering the cash flows, other investors must be found who are willing to accept the unwanted prepayment risk.

Collateralized mortgage obligations (CMOs) are bond classes created by redirecting the cash flows of mortgage-related products so as to mitigate prepayment risk. The mere creation of a CMO cannot eliminate prepayment risk; it can only transfer the various forms of this risk among different classes of bondholders. The technique of redistributing the coupon interest and principal from the underlying mortgage-related products to different classes, so that a CMO class has a different coupon rate from that for the underlying collateral, results in instruments that have varying risk-return characteristics that may be more suitable to the needs and expectations of investors, thereby broadening the appeal of mortgage-backed products to various traditional fixed-income investors.

CMO Structure

A CMO is a security backed by a pool of pass-throughs, whole loans, or stripped mortgage-backed securities (explained later in the chapter). CMOs are structured so that there are several classes of bondholders with varying stated maturities. When there is more than one class of bondholders with the same level of credit priority, the structure is called a **pay-through structure,** as opposed to a **pass-through structure** in which there is only one class of bondholders at a given level of credit priority.

The bond classes created are commonly referred to as **tranches.** The principal payments from the underlying collateral are used to retire the tranches on a priority basis according to terms specified in the prospectus. In the following sections we describe the various types of CMO tranches.

Sequential-Pay Tranches

The first CMO was created in 1983 and was structured so that each class of bond would be retired sequentially. Such structures are referred to as **sequential-pay CMOs.** To illustrate a sequential-pay CMO, we discuss FJF-01,[2] a hypothetical deal

---

[1]This section is adapted from Chapters 1 to 7 of Frank J. Fabozzi and Charles Ramsey, *Collateralized Mortgage Obligations: Structures and Analysis,* 3rd ed. (New Hope, PA: Frank J. Fabozzi Associates, 1999).
[2]All CMO structures are given a name. In our illustration we use FJF, the initials of the author of this book.

made up to illustrate the basic features of the structure. The collateral for this hypothetical CMO is a hypothetical pass-through with a total par value of $400 million and the following characteristics: (1) the pass-through coupon rate is 7.5%, (2) the weighted average coupon (WAC) is 8.125%, and (3) the weighted-average maturity (WAM) is 357 months. This is the same pass-through that we used in Chapter 11 to describe the cash flow of a pass-through based on some PSA assumption.

From this $400 million of collateral, four bond classes or tranches are created. Their characteristics are summarized in Exhibit 12-1. The total par value of the four tranches is equal to the par value of the collateral (i.e., the pass-through security). In this simple structure, the coupon rate is the same for each tranche and also the same as the coupon rate on the collateral. There is no reason why this must be so, and in fact, typically the coupon rate varies by tranche.

Now remember that a CMO is created by redistributing the cash flow—interest and principal—to the different tranches based on a set of payment rules. The payment rules at the bottom of Exhibit 12-1 describe how the cash flow from the pass-through (i.e., collateral) is to be distributed to the four tranches. There are separate rules for the payment of the coupon interest and the payment of principal, the principal being the total of the regularly scheduled principal payment and any prepayments.

In FJF-01, each tranche receives periodic coupon interest payments based on the amount of the outstanding balance at the beginning of the month. The disbursement of the principal, however, is made in a special way. A tranche is not entitled to receive principal until the entire principal of the tranche before it has been paid off. More specifically, tranche A receives all the principal payments until the entire principal amount owed to that bond class, $194,500,000, is paid off; then tranche B begins to receive principal and continues to do so until it is paid the entire $36,000,000. Tranche C

EXHIBIT 12-1   FJF-01: Hypothetical Four-Tranche Sequential-Pay Structure[a]

Tranche	Par Amount	Coupon Rate (%)
A	$194,500,000	7.5
B	36,000,000	7.5
C	96,500,000	7.5
D	73,000,000	7.5
	$400,000,000	

[a]*Payment rules:*

1. *For payment of periodic coupon interest:* Disburse periodic coupon interest to each tranche on the basis of the amount of principal outstanding at the beginning of the period.
2. *For disbursement of principal payments:* Disburse principal payments to tranche A until it is paid off completely. After tranche A is paid off completely, disburse principal payments to tranche B until it is paid off completely. After tranche B is paid off completely, disburse principal payments to tranche C until it is paid off completely. After tranche C is paid off completely, disburse principal payments to tranche D until it is paid off completely.

then receives principal, and when it is paid off, tranche D starts receiving principal payments.

Although the priority rules for the disbursement of the principal payments are known, the precise amount of the principal in each period is not. This will depend on the cash flow, and therefore principal payments, of the collateral, which depends on the actual prepayment rate of the collateral. An assumed PSA speed allows the cash flow to be projected. Exhibit 11-4 shows the cash flow (interest, regularly scheduled principal repayment, and prepayments) assuming 165 PSA. Assuming that the collateral does prepay at 165 PSA, the cash flow available to all four tranches of FJF-01 will be precisely the cash flow shown in Exhibit 12-2.

To demonstrate how the priority rules for FJF-01 work, Exhibit 12-2 shows the cash flow for selected months assuming that the collateral prepays at 165 PSA. For each tranche, the exhibit shows (1) the balance at the end of the month, (2) the principal paid down (regularly scheduled principal repayment plus prepayments), and (3) interest. In month 1, the cash flow for the collateral consists of principal payment of $709,923 and interest of $2.5 million (0.075 times $400 million divided by 12). The interest payment is distributed to the four tranches based on the amount of the par value outstanding. So, for example, tranche A receives $1,215,625 (0.075 times $194,500,000 divided by 12) of the $2.5 million. The principal, however, is all distributed to tranche A. Therefore, the cash flow for tranche A in month 1 is $1,925,548. The principal balance at the end of month 1 for tranche A is $193,790,076 (the original principal balance of $194,500,000 less the principal payment of $709,923). No principal payment is distributed to the three other tranches because there is still a principal balance outstanding for tranche A. This will be true for months 2 through 80.

After month 81, the principal balance will be zero for tranche A. For the collateral, the cash flow in month 81 is $3,318,521, consisting of a principal payment of $2,032,196 and interest of $1,286,325. At the beginning of month 81 (end of month 80), the principal balance for tranche A is $311,926. Therefore, $311,926 of the $2,032,196 of the principal payment from the collateral will be disbursed to tranche A. After this payment is made, no additional principal payments are made to this tranche as the principal balance is zero. The remaining principal payment from the collateral, $1,720,271, is disbursed to tranche B. According to the assumed prepayment speed of 165 PSA, tranche B then begins receiving principal payments in month 81.

Exhibit 12-2 shows that tranche B is fully paid off by month 100, when tranche C now begins to receive principal payments. Tranche C is not fully paid off until month 178, at which time bond class D begins receiving the remaining principal payments. The maturity (i.e., the time until the principal is fully paid off) for these four tranches assuming 165 PSA would be 81 months for tranche A, 100 months for tranche B, 178 months for tranche C, and 357 months for tranche D.

The **principal pay-down window** for a tranche is the time period between the beginning and the ending of the principal payments to that tranche. So, for example, for tranche A, the principal pay-down window would be month 1 to month 81 assuming 165 PSA. For tranche B it is from month 82 to month 100. The window is also specified in terms of the length of the time from the beginning of the principal pay-down window to the end of the principal pay-down window. For tranche A, the window would be stated as 80 months, for tranche B, 19 months.

EXHIBIT 12-2   Monthly Cash Flow for Selected Months
for FJF-0I Assuming 165 PSA

	Tranche A			Tranche B		
Mo.	Balance	Principal	Interest	Balance	Principal	Interest
1	194,500,000	709,923	1,215,625	36,000,000	0	225,000
2	193,790,077	821,896	1,211,188	36,000,000	0	225,000
3	192,968,181	933,560	1,206,051	36,000,000	0	225,000
4	192,034,621	1,044,822	1,200,216	36,000,000	0	225,000
5	190,989,799	1,155,586	1,193,686	36,000,000	0	225,000
6	189,834,213	1,265,759	1,186,464	36,000,000	0	225,000
7	188,568,454	1,375,246	1,178,553	36,000,000	0	225,000
8	187,193,208	1,483,954	1,169,958	36,000,000	0	225,000
9	185,709,254	1,591,789	1,160,683	36,000,000	0	225,000
10	184,117,464	1,698,659	1,150,734	36,000,000	0	225,000
11	182,418,805	1,804,473	1,140,118	36,000,000	0	225,000
12	180,614,332	1,909,139	1,128,840	36,000,000	0	225,000
75	12,893,479	2,143,974	80,584	36,000,000	0	225,000
76	10,749,504	2,124,935	67,184	36,000,000	0	225,000
77	8,624,569	2,106,062	53,904	36,000,000	0	225,000
78	6,518,507	2,087,353	40,741	36,000,000	0	225,000
79	4,431,154	2,068,807	27,695	36,000,000	0	225,000
80	2,362,347	2,050,422	14,765	36,000,000	0	225,000
81	311,926	311,926	1,950	36,000,000	1,720,271	225,000
82	0	0	0	34,279,729	2,014,130	214,248
83	0	0	0	32,265,599	1,996,221	201,660
84	0	0	0	30,269,378	1,978,468	189,184
85	0	0	0	28,290,911	1,960,869	176,818
95	0	0	0	9,449,331	1,793,089	59,058
96	0	0	0	7,656,242	1,777,104	47,852
97	0	0	0	5,879,138	1,761,258	36,745
98	0	0	0	4,117,880	1,745,550	25,737
99	0	0	0	2,372,329	1,729,979	14,827
100	0	0	0	642,350	642,350	4,015
101	0	0	0	0	0	0
102	0	0	0	0	0	0
103	0	0	0	0	0	0
104	0	0	0	0	0	0
105	0	0	0	0	0	0

Let's look at what has been accomplished by creating the CMO. First, in Chapter 11 we indicated that the average life of the pass-through is 8.76 years, assuming a prepayment speed of 165 PSA. Exhibit 12-3 reports the average life of the collateral and the four tranches assuming different prepayment speeds. Notice that the four tranches

EXHIBIT 12-2 (*cont.*)

	Tranche C			Tranche D		
Mo.	**Balance**	**Principal**	**Interest**	**Balance**	**Principal**	**Interest**
1	96,500,000	0	603,125	73,000,000	0	456,250
2	96,500,000	0	603,125	73,000,000	0	456,250
3	96,500,000	0	603,125	73,000,000	0	456,250
4	96,500,000	0	603,125	73,000,000	0	456,250
5	96,500,000	0	603,125	73,000,000	0	456,250
6	96,500,000	0	603,125	73,000,000	0	456,250
7	96,500,000	0	603,125	73,000,000	0	456,250
8	96,500,000	0	603,125	73,000,000	0	456,250
9	96,500,000	0	603,125	73,000,000	0	456,250
10	96,500,000	0	603,125	73,000,000	0	456,250
11	96,500,000	0	603,125	73,000,000	0	456,250
12	96,500,000	0	603,125	73,000,000	0	456,250
95	96,500,000	0	603,125	73,000,000	0	456,250
96	96,500,000	0	603,125	73,000,000	0	456,250
97	96,500,000	0	603,125	73,000,000	0	456,250
98	96,500,000	0	603,125	73,000,000	0	456,250
99	96,500,000	0	603,125	73,000,000	0	456,250
100	96,500,000	1,072,194	603,125	73,000,000	0	456,250
101	95,427,806	1,699,243	596,424	73,000,000	0	456,250
102	93,728,563	1,684,075	585,804	73,000,000	0	456,250
103	92,044,489	1,669,039	575,278	73,000,000	0	456,250
104	90,375,450	1,654,134	564,847	73,000,000	0	456,250
105	88,721,315	1,639,359	554,508	73,000,000	0	456,250
175	3,260,287	869,602	20,377	73,000,000	0	456,250
176	2,390,685	861,673	14,942	73,000,000	0	456,250
177	1,529,013	853,813	9,556	73,000,000	0	456,250
178	675,199	675,199	4,220	73,000,000	170,824	456,250
179	0	0	0	72,829,176	838,300	455,182
180	0	0	0	71,990,876	830,646	449,943
181	0	0	0	71,160,230	823,058	444,751
182	0	0	0	70,337,173	815,536	439,607
183	0	0	0	69,521,637	808,081	434,510
184	0	0	0	68,713,556	800,690	429,460
185	0	0	0	67,912,866	793,365	424,455
350	0	0	0	1,235,674	160,220	7,723
351	0	0	0	1,075,454	158,544	6,722
352	0	0	0	916,910	156,883	5,731
353	0	0	0	760,027	155,238	4,750
354	0	0	0	604,789	153,607	3,780
355	0	0	0	451,182	151,991	2,820
356	0	0	0	299,191	150,389	1,870
357	0	0	0	148,802	148,802	930

EXHIBIT 12-3 Average Life for the Collateral and the Four Tranches of FJF-01

Prepayment Speed (PSA)	Average Life for				
	Collateral	Tranche A	Tranche B	Tranche C	Tranche D
50	15.11	7.48	15.98	21.02	27.24
100	11.66	4.90	10.86	15.78	24.58
165	8.76	3.48	7.49	11.19	20.27
200	7.68	3.05	6.42	9.60	18.11
300	5.63	2.32	4.64	6.81	13.36
400	4.44	1.94	3.70	5.31	10.34
500	3.68	1.69	3.12	4.38	8.35
600	3.16	1.51	2.74	3.75	6.96
700	2.78	1.38	2.47	3.30	5.95

have average lives that are both shorter and longer than the collateral, thereby attracting investors who have a preference for an average life different from that of the collateral.

There is still a major problem: There is considerable variability of the average life for the tranches. We'll see later how this can be tackled. However, there is some protection provided for each tranche against prepayment risk. This is because prioritizing the distribution of principal (i.e., establishing the payment rules for principal) effectively protects the shorter-term tranche A in this structure against extension risk. This protection must come from somewhere, so it comes from the three other tranches. Similarly, tranches C and D provide protection against extension risk for tranches A and B. At the same time, tranches C and D benefit because they are provided protection against contraction risk, the protection coming from tranches A and B.

Accrual Bonds

In FJF-01, the payment rules for interest provide for all tranches to be paid interest each month. In many sequential-pay CMO structures, at least one tranche does not receive current interest. Instead, the interest for that tranche would accrue and be added to the principal balance. Such a bond class is commonly referred to as an **accrual tranche,** or a **Z bond** (because the bond is similar to a zero-coupon bond). The interest that would have been paid to the accrual bond class is then used to speed up pay down of the principal balance of earlier bond classes.

To see this, consider FJF-02, a hypothetical CMO structure with the same collateral as FJF-01 and with four tranches, each with a coupon rate of 7.5%. The difference is in the last tranche, Z, which is an accrual. The structure for FJF-02 is shown in Exhibit 12-4.

Exhibit 12-5 shows cash flows for selected months for tranches A and B. Let's look at month 1 and compare it with month 1 in Exhibit 12-2. Both cash flows are based on 165 PSA. The principal payment from the collateral is $709,923. In FJF-01, this is the principal paydown for tranche A. In FJF-02, the interest for tranche Z, $456,250, is not paid to that tranche but instead is used to pay down the principal of tranche A. So the principal payment to tranche A in Exhibit 12-5 is $1,166,173, the

EXHIBIT 12-4 FJF-02: Hypothetical Four-Tranche Sequential-Pay Structure with an Accrual Bond Class[a]

Tranche	Par Amount	Coupon Rate (%)
A	$194,500,000	7.5
B	36,000,000	7.5
C	96,500,000	7.5
Z (accrual)	73,000,000	7.5
	$400,000,000	

[a]*Payment rules:*

1. *For payment of periodic coupon interest:* Disburse periodic coupon interest to tranches A, B, and C on the basis of the amount of principal outstanding at the beginning of the period. For tranche Z, accrue the interest based on the principal plus accrued interest in the preceding period. The interest for tranche Z is to be paid to the earlier tranches as a principal pay down.
2. *For disbursement of principal payments:* Disburse principal payments to tranche A until it is completely paid off. After tranche A is paid off completely, disburse principal payments to tranche B until it is paid off completely. After tranche B is paid off completely, disburse principal payments to tranche C until it is paid off completely. After tranche C is paid off completely, disburse principal payments to tranche Z until the original principal balance plus accrued interest is paid off completely.

collateral's principal payment of $709,923 plus the interest of $456,250 that was diverted from tranche Z.

The expected final maturity for tranches A, B, and C has shortened as a result of the inclusion of tranche Z. The final payout for tranche A is 64 months rather than 81 months; for tranche B it is 77 months rather than 100 months; and for tranche C it is 112 rather than 178 months.

The average lives for tranches A, B, and C are shorter in FJF-02 than in FJF-01 because of the inclusion of the accrual bond. For example, at 165 PSA, the average lives are as follows:

Structure	Tranche A	Tranche B	Tranche C
FJF-02	2.90	5.86	7.87
FJF-01	3.48	7.49	11.19

The reason for the shortening of the nonaccrual tranches is that the interest that would be paid to the accrual bond is being allocated to the other tranches. Tranche Z in FJF-02 will have a longer average life than that of tranche D in FJF-01.

Thus, shorter-term tranches and a longer-term tranche are created by including an accrual bond. The accrual bond has appeal to investors who are concerned with reinvestment risk. Because there are no coupon payments to reinvest, reinvestment risk is eliminated until all the other tranches are paid off.

EXHIBIT 12-5   Monthly Cash Flow for Selected Month
for Tranches A and B of FJF-02 Assuming 165 PSA

	Tranche A			Tranche B		
Month	Balance	Principal	Interest	Balance	Principal	Interest
1	194,500,000	1,166,173	1,215,625	36,000,000	0	225,000
2	193,333,827	1,280,997	1,208,336	36,000,000	0	225,000
3	192,052,829	1,395,531	1,200,330	36,000,000	0	225,000
4	190,657,298	1,509,680	1,191,608	36,000,000	0	225,000
5	189,147,619	1,623,350	1,182,173	36,000,000	0	225,000
6	187,524,269	1,736,446	1,172,027	36,000,000	0	225,000
7	185,787,823	1,848,875	1,161,174	36,000,000	0	225,000
8	183,938,947	1,960,543	1,149,618	36,000,000	0	225,000
9	181,978,404	2,071,357	1,137,365	36,000,000	0	225,000
10	179,907,047	2,181,225	1,124,419	36,000,000	0	225,000
11	177,725,822	2,290,054	1,110,786	36,000,000	0	225,000
12	175,435,768	2,397,755	1,096,474	36,000,000	0	225,000
⋮						
60	15,023,406	3,109,398	93,896	36,000,000	0	225,000
61	11,914,007	3,091,812	74,463	36,000,000	0	225,000
62	8,822,195	3,074,441	55,139	36,000,000	0	225,000
63	5,747,754	3,057,282	35,923	36,000,000	0	225,000
64	2,690,472	2,690,472	16,815	36,000,000	349,863	225,000
65	0	0	0	35,650,137	3,023,598	222,813
66	0	0	0	32,626,540	3,007,069	203,916
67	0	0	0	29,619,470	2,990,748	185,122
68	0	0	0	26,628,722	2,974,633	166,430
69	0	0	0	23,654,089	2,958,722	147,838
70	0	0	0	20,695,367	2,943,014	129,346
71	0	0	0	17,752,353	2,927,508	110,952
72	0	0	0	14,824,845	2,912,203	92,655
73	0	0	0	11,912,642	2,897,096	74,454
74	0	0	0	9,015,546	2,882,187	56,347
75	0	0	0	6,133,358	2,867,475	38,333
76	0	0	0	3,265,883	2,852,958	20,412
77	0	0	0	412,925	412,925	2,581
78	0	0	0	0	0	0

Floating-Rate Tranches

The CMO structures discussed previously offer a fixed coupon rate on all tranches. If CMO classes could be created only with fixed-rate coupons, the market for CMOs would be limited. Many financial institutions prefer floating-rate assets, which provide a better match for their liabilities.

Floating-rate tranches can be created from fixed-rate tranches by creating a floater and an inverse floater. We illustrate the creation of a floating-rate and an inverse-floating-rate bond class using the hypothetical CMO structure FJF-02, which is a four-tranche sequential-pay structure with an accrual bond. We can select any of the tranches from which to create a floating-rate and an inverse-floating-rate tranche. In fact, we can create these two securities for more than one of the four tranches or for only a portion of one tranche.

In this case we create a floater and an inverse floater from tranche C. The par value for this tranche is $96.5 million, and we create two tranches that have a combined par value of $96.5 million. We refer to this CMO structure with a floater and an inverse floater as FJF-03. It has five tranches, designated A, B, FL, IFL, and Z, where FL is the floating-rate tranche and IFL is the inverse floating-rate tranche. Exhibit 12-6 describes FJF-03. Any reference rate can be used to create a floater and the corresponding inverse floater. The reference rate for setting the coupon rate for FL and IFL in FJF-03 is taken as one-month LIBOR.

The amount of the par value of the floating-rate tranche will be some portion of the $96.5 million. There is an infinite number of ways to cut up the $96.5 million between the floater and inverse floater, and final partitioning will be driven by the demands of investors. In the FJF-03 structure, we made the floater from $72,375,000 or 75% of the $96.5 million. The coupon rate on the floater is set at one-month LIBOR plus 50 basis points. So, for example, if LIBOR is 3.75% at the reset date, the coupon rate on the floater is 3.75% + 0.5%, or 4.25%. There is a cap on the coupon rate for the floater (discussed later).

Unlike a floating-rate note in the corporate bond market, whose principal is unchanged over the life of the instrument, the floater's principal balance declines over

EXHIBIT 12-6 FJF-03: Hypothetical Five-Tranche Sequential-Pay Structure with Floater, Inverse Floater, and Accrual Bond Classes[a]

Tranche	Par Amount	Coupon Rate (%)
A	$194,500,000	7.50
B	36,000,000	7.50
FL	72,375,000	1-month LIBOR + 0.50
IFL	24,125,000	$28.50 - 3 \times$ (1-month LIBOR)
Z (accrual)	73,000,000	7.50
	$400,000,000	

[a]*Payment rules:*

1. *For payment of periodic coupon interest:* Disburse periodic coupon interest to tranches A, B, FL, and IFL on the basis of the amount of principal outstanding at the beginning of the period. For tranche Z, accrue the interest based on the principal plus accrued interest in the preceding period. The interest for tranche Z is to be paid to the earlier tranches as a principal paydown. The maximum coupon rate for FL is 10%; the minimum coupon rate for IFL is 0%.

2. *For disbursement of principal payments:* Disburse principal payments to tranche A until it is paid off completely. After tranche A is paid off completely, disburse principal payments to tranche B until it is paid off completely. After tranche B is paid off completely, disburse principal payments to tranches FL and IFL until they are paid off completely. The principal payments between tranches FL and IFL should be made in the following way: 75% to tranche FL and 25% to tranche IFL. After tranches FL and IFL are paid off completely, disburse principal payments to tranche Z until the original principal balance plus accrued interest is paid off completely.

time as principal payments are made. The principal payments to the floater are determined by the principal payments from the tranche from which the floater is created. In our CMO structure, this is tranche C.

Because the floater's par value is $72,375,000 of the $96.5 million, the balance is the inverse floater. Assuming that one-month LIBOR is the reference rate, the coupon rate on the inverse floater takes the following form:

$$K - L \times \text{(one-month LIBOR)}$$

In FJF-03, K is set at 28.50% and L at 3. Thus, if one-month LIBOR is 3.75%, the coupon rate for the month is

$$28.50\% - 3(3.75\%) = 17.25\%$$

K is the cap or maximum coupon rate for the inverse floater. In FJF-03, the cap for the inverse floater is 28.50%.

The L or multiple in the formula to determine the coupon rate for the inverse floater is called the **coupon leverage.** The higher the coupon leverage, the more the inverse floater's coupon rate changes for a given change in one-month LIBOR. For example, a coupon leverage of 3.0 means that a 100-basis point change in one-month LIBOR will change the coupon rate on the inverse floater by 300 basis points; a coupon leverage of 0.7 means that the coupon rate will change by 70 basis points for a 100-basis point change in one-month LIBOR. Inverse floaters with a wide variety of coupon leverages are available in the market. Participants refer to low-leverage inverse floaters as those with a coupon leverage between 0.5 and 2.1; medium-leverage as those with a coupon leverage higher than 2.1 but not exceeding 4.5; and high-leverage as those with a coupon leverage higher than 4.5. At the time of issuance, the issuer determines the coupon leverage according to investor desire. In FJF-03 the coupon leverage is set at 3.

Let's see how the total interest paid on the floater and inverse floater can be supported by the bond class with a coupon rate of 7.5% from which they are created. The coupon rate for the floating-rate class is

$$\text{one-month LIBOR} + 0.50$$

For the inverse floater the coupon rate is

$$28.50 - 3 \times \text{(one-month LIBOR)}$$

Because the floater is 75% of the $96.5 million and the inverse floater is 25%, the weighted-average coupon rate is

$$0.75 \text{ (floater coupon rate)} + 0.25 \text{ (inverse floater coupon rate)}$$

The weighted average coupon rate is 7.5%, regardless of the level of LIBOR. For example, if one-month LIBOR is 9%, then

$$\text{floater coupon rate} = 9.0\% + 0.5\% = 9.5\%$$
$$\text{inverse floater coupon rate} = 28.5 - 3(9.0\%) = 1.5\%$$

The weighted-average coupon rate is

$$0.75(9.5\%) + 0.25(1.5\%) = 7.5\%$$

Consequently, the 7.5% coupon rate on the bond class from which these two classes were created can support the aggregate interest payments that must be made to them. As in the case of the floater, the principal paydown of an inverse floater will be a proportionate amount of the principal paydown of bond class C.

Because one-month LIBOR is always positive, the coupon rate paid to the floating-rate bond class cannot be negative. If there are no restrictions placed on the coupon rate for the inverse floater, however, it is possible for the coupon rate for that bond class to be negative. To prevent this, a floor, or minimum, can be placed on the coupon rate. In many structures, the floor is set at zero. Once a floor is set for the inverse floater, a cap or ceiling is imposed on the floater. In FJF-03, a floor of zero is set for the inverse floater. The floor results in a cap or maximum coupon rate for the floater of 10%. This is found by substituting zero for the coupon rate of the inverse floater in the formula for the weighted-average coupon rate, and then setting the formula equal to 7.5%.

The cap for the floater and the inverse floater, the floor for the inverse floater, the coupon leverage, and the margin spread are not determined independently. Given four of these variables, the fifth will be determined.

Planned Amortization Class Tranches

The CMO innovations discussed previously attracted many institutional investors who had previously either avoided investing in mortgage-backed securities or allocated only a nominal portion of their portfolio to this sector of the fixed-income market. Although some traditional corporate bond buyers shifted their allocation to CMOs, a majority of institutional investors remained on the sidelines, concerned about investing in an instrument that they continued to perceive as posing significant prepayment risk because of the substantial average life variability, despite the innovations designed to reduce prepayment risk.

Potential demand for a CMO product with less uncertainty about the cash flow increased in the mid-1980s because of two trends in the corporate bond market. First was the increased event risk faced by investors, highlighted by the RJR Nabisco leveraged buyout in 1988. The second trend was a decline in the number of triple A–rated corporate issues. Traditional corporate bond buyers sought a structure with both the characteristics of a corporate bond (either a bullet maturity or a sinking fund type of schedule of principal repayment) and high credit quality. Although CMOs satisfied the second condition, they did not satisfy the first.

In March 1987, the M.D.C. Mortgage Funding Corporation CMO Series 0 included a class of bonds referred to as **stabilized mortgage reduction term (SMRT) bonds;** another class in its CMO Series P was referred to as **planned amortization class (PAC) bonds.** The Oxford Acceptance Corporation III Series C CMOs included a class of bonds referred to as a **planned redemption obligation (PRO) bonds.** The characteristic common to these three bonds is that if the prepayments are within a specified range, the cash flow pattern is known.

The greater predictability of the cash flow for these classes of bonds, now referred to exclusively as PAC bonds, occurs because there is a principal repayment schedule that must be satisfied. PAC bondholders have priority over all other classes in the CMO issue in receiving principal payments from the underlying collateral. The greater certainty of the cash flow for the PAC bonds comes at the expense of the non-PAC classes, called **support** or **companion bonds.** It is these bonds that absorb the prepayment risk. Because PAC bonds have protection against both extension risk and contraction risk, they are said to provide **two-sided prepayment protection.**

To illustrate how to create a PAC bond, we will use as collateral the $400 million pass-through with a coupon rate of 7.5%, an 8.125% WAC, and a WAM of 357 months. The second column of Exhibit 12-7 shows the principal payment (regularly scheduled principal repayment plus prepayments) for selected months assuming a prepayment speed of 90 PSA, and the next column shows the principal payments for selected months assuming that the pass-through prepays at 300 PSA.

The last column of Exhibit 12-7 gives the *minimum* principal payment if the collateral speed is 90 PSA or 300 PSA for months 1 to 349. (After month 346, the outstanding principal balance will be paid off if the prepayment speed is between 90 PSA and 300 PSA.) For example, in the first month, the principal payment would be $508,169.52 if the collateral prepays at 90 PSA and $1,075,931.20 if the collateral prepays at 300 PSA. Thus, the minimum principal payment is $508,169.52, as reported in the last column of Exhibit 12-7. In month 103, the minimum principal payment is also the amount if the prepayment speed is 90 PSA, $1,446,761, compared with $1,458,618.04 for 300 PSA. In month 104, however, a prepayment speed of 300 PSA would produce a principal payment of $1,433,539.23, which is less than the principal payment of $1,440,825.55 assuming 90 PSA. So $1,433,539.23 is reported in the last column of Exhibit 12-7. In fact, from month 104 on, the minimum principal payment is the one that would result assuming a prepayment speed of 300 PSA.

In fact, if the collateral prepays at *any* speed between 90 PSA and 300 PSA, the minimum principal payment would be the amount reported in the last column of Exhibit 12-7. For example, if we had included principal payment figures assuming a prepayment speed of 200 PSA, the minimum principal payment would not change: from month 11 through month 103, the minimum principal payment is that generated from 90 PSA, but from month 104 on, the minimum principal payment is that generated from 300 PSA.

This characteristic of the collateral allows for the creation of a PAC bond, assuming that the collateral prepays over its life at a speed between 90 PSA to 300 PSA. A schedule of principal repayments that the PAC bondholders are entitled to receive before any other bond class in the CMO is specified. The monthly schedule of principal repayments is as specified in the last column of Exhibit 12-7, which shows the minimum principal payment. Although there is no assurance that the collateral will prepay between these two speeds, a PAC bond can be structured to assume that it will.

Exhibit 12-8 shows a CMO structure, FJF-04, created from the $400 million, 7.5% coupon pass-through with a WAC of 8.125% and a WAM of 357 months. There are just two bond classes in this structure: a 7.5% coupon PAC bond created assuming 90 to 300 PSA with a par value of $243.8 million, and a support bond with a par value of $156.2 million. The two speeds used to create a PAC bond are called the **initial PAC collars** (or **initial PAC bands**); in our case 90 PSA is the lower collar and 300 PSA the upper collar.

Exhibit 12-9 reports the average life for the PAC bond and the support bond in FJF-04 assuming various *actual* prepayment speeds. Notice that between 90 PSA and 300 PSA, the average life for the PAC bond is stable at 7.26 years. However, at slower

EXHIBIT 12-7 Monthly Principal Payment for $400 Million 7.5% Coupon Pass-Through with an 8.125% WAC and a 357 WAM Assuming Prepayment Rates of 90 PSA and 300 PSA

Month	At 90% PSA	At 300% PSA	Minimum Principal Payment—the PAC Schedule
1	508,169.52	1,075,931.20	508,169.52
2	569,843.43	1,279,412.11	569,843.43
3	631,377.11	1,482,194.45	631,377.11
4	692,741.89	1,683,966.17	692,741.89
5	753,909.12	1,884,414.62	753,909.12
6	814,850.22	2,083,227.31	814,850.22
7	875,536.68	2,280,092.68	875,536.68
8	935,940.10	2,474,700.92	935,940.10
9	996,032.19	2,666,744.77	996,032.19
10	1,055,784.82	2,855,920.32	1,055,784.82
11	1,115,170.01	3,041,927.81	1,115,170.01
12	1,174,160.00	3,224,472.44	1,174,160.00
13	1,232,727.22	3,403,265.17	1,232,727.22
14	1,290,844.32	3,578,023.49	1,290,844.32
15	1,348,484.24	3,748,472.23	1,348,484.24
16	1,405,620.17	3,914,344.26	1,405,620.17
17	1,462,225.60	4,075,381.29	1,462,225.60
18	1,518,274.36	4,231,334.57	1,518,274.36
101	1,458,719.34	1,510,072.17	1,458,719.34
102	1,452,725.55	1,484,126.59	1,452,725.55
103	1,446,761.00	1,458,618.04	1,446,761.00
104	1,440,825.55	1,433,539.23	1,433,539.23
105	1,434,919.07	1,408,883.01	1,408,883.01
211	949,482.58	213,309.00	213,309.00
212	946,033.34	209,409.09	209,409.09
213	942,601.99	205,577.05	205,577.05
346	618,684.59	13,269.17	13,269.17
347	617,071.58	12,944.51	12,944.51
348	615,468.65	12,626.21	12,626.21
349	613,875.77	12,314.16	3,432.32
350	612,292.88	12,008.25	0
351	610,719.96	11,708.38	0
352	609,156.96	11,414.42	0
353	607,603.84	11,126.28	0
354	606,060.57	10,843.85	0
355	604,527.09	10,567.02	0
356	603,003.38	10,295.70	0
357	601,489.39	10,029.78	0

EXHIBIT 12-8   FJF-04 CMO Structure with One PAC Bond
and One Support Bond[a]

Tranche	Par Amount	Coupon Rate (%)
P (PAC)	$243,800,000	7.5
S (support)	156,200,000	7.5
	$400,000,000	

[a]*Payment rules:*

1. *For payment of periodic coupon interest:* Disburse periodic coupon interest to each tranche on the basis of the amount of principal outstanding at the beginning of the period.
2. *For disbursement of principal payments:* Disburse principal payments to tranche P based on its schedule of principal repayments. Tranche P has priority with respect to current and future principal payments to satisfy the schedule. Any excess principal payments in a month over the amount necessary to satisfy the schedule for tranche P are paid to tranche S. When tranche S is paid off completely, all principal payments are to be made to tranche P regardless of the schedule.

EXHIBIT 12-9   Average Life for PAC Bond and Support
Bond in FJF-04 Assuming Various
Prepayment Speeds

Prepayment Rate (PSA)	PAC Bond (P)	Support Bond (S)
0	15.97	27.26
50	9.44	24.00
90	7.26	18.56
100	7.26	18.56
150	7.26	12.57
165	7.26	11.16
200	7.26	8.38
250	7.26	5.37
300	7.26	3.13
350	6.56	2.51
400	5.92	2.17
450	5.38	1.94
500	4.93	1.77
700	3.70	1.37

or faster PSA speeds, the schedule is broken, and the average life changes, lengthening when the prepayment speed is less than 90 PSA and shortening when it is greater than 300 PSA. Even so, there is much greater variability for the average life of the support bond.

Creating a Series of PAC Bonds   Most CMO PAC structures have more than one class of PAC bonds. We created six PAC bonds from FJF-04, which we call FJF-05.

EXHIBIT 12-10 FJF-05 CMO Structure with Six PAC Bonds and One Support Bond[a]

Tranche	Par Amount	Coupon Rate (%)
P-A	$ 85,000,000	7.5
P-B	8,000,000	7.5
P-C	35,000,000	7.5
P-D	45,000,000	7.5
P-E	40,000,000	7.5
P-F	30,800,000	7.5
S	156,200,000	7.5
	$400,000,000	

[a]*Payment rules:*

1. *For payment of periodic coupon interest:* Disburse periodic coupon interest to each tranche on the basis of the amount of principal outstanding at the beginning of the period.
2. *For disbursement of principal payments:* Disburse principal payments to tranches P-A to P-F based on their respective schedules of principal repayments. Tranche P-A has priority with respect to current and future principal payments to satisfy the schedule. Any excess principal payments in a month over the amount necessary to satisfy the schedule for tranche P-A are paid to tranche S. When tranche P-A is paid off completely, tranche P-B has priority, then tranche P-C, and so on. When tranche S is paid off completely, all principal payments are to be made to the remaining PAC tranches in order of priority regardless of the schedule.

Information about this CMO structure is reported in Exhibit 12-10. The total par value of the six PAC bonds is equal to $243.8 million, which is the amount of the single PAC bond in FJF-04.

Exhibit 12-11 shows the average life for the six PAC bonds and the support bond in FJF-05 at various prepayment speeds. From a PAC bond in FJF-04 with an average life of 7.26, we have created six bonds with an average life as short as 2.58 years (P-A) and as long as 16.92 years (P-F) if prepayments stay within 90 PSA and 300 PSA.

As expected, the average lives are stable if the prepayment speed is between 90 PSA and 300 PSA. Notice that even outside this range the average life is stable for several of the PAC bonds. For example, the PAC P-A bond is stable even if prepayment speeds are as high as 400 PSA. For the PAC P-B, the average life does not vary when prepayments are in the initial collar until prepayments are greater than 350 PSA. Why is it that the shorter the PAC, the more protection it has against faster prepayments?

To understand why this is so, remember that there are $156.2 million in support bonds that are protecting the $85 million of PAC P-A. Thus, even if prepayments are faster than the initial upper collar, there may be sufficient support bonds to assure the satisfaction of the schedule. In fact, as can be seen from Exhibit 12-11, even if prepayments are at 400 PSA over the life of the collateral, the average life is unchanged.

EXHIBIT 12-11   Average Life for the Six PAC Bonds in FJF-05
Assuming Various Prepayment Speeds

Prepayment Rate (PSA)	PAC Bonds					
	P-A	*P-B*	*P-C*	*P-D*	*P-E*	*P-F*
0	8.46	14.61	16.49	19.41	21.91	23.76
50	3.58	6.82	8.36	11.30	14.50	18.20
90	2.58	4.72	5.78	7.89	10.83	16.92
100	2.58	4.72	5.78	7.89	10.83	16.92
150	2.58	4.72	5.78	7.89	10.83	16.92
165	2.58	4.72	5.78	7.89	10.83	16.92
200	2.58	4.72	5.78	7.89	10.83	16.92
250	2.58	4.72	5.78	7.89	10.83	16.92
300	2.58	4.72	5.78	7.89	10.83	16.92
350	2.58	4.72	5.49	6.95	9.24	14.91
400	2.57	4.37	4.91	6.17	8.33	13.21
450	2.50	3.97	4.44	5.56	7.45	11.81
500	2.40	3.65	4.07	5.06	6.74	10.65
700	2.06	2.82	3.10	3.75	4.88	7.51

Now consider PAC P-B. The support bonds are providing protection for both the $85 million of PAC P-A and $93 million of PAC P-B. As can be seen from Exhibit 12-11, prepayments could be 350 PSA and the average life is still unchanged. From Exhibit 12-11 it can be seen that the degree of protection against extension risk increases the shorter the PAC. Thus, whereas the initial collar may be 90 to 300 PSA, the **effective collar** is wider for the shorter PAC tranches. Exhibit 12-12 shows the effective collar for the six PAC tranches in FJF-04.

PAC Window   As we explained earlier, the length of time over which scheduled principal repayments are made is referred to as the window. A PAC window can be wide or narrow. The narrower a PAC window, the more it resembles a corporate bond with a bullet payment. PAC buyers appear to prefer tight windows, although institutional investors facing a liability schedule are generally better off with a window

EXHIBIT 12-12   Effective Collars for Each PAC Tranche in FJF-04

Amount of support bonds: $156.2 million	
Tranche	*Effective Collar*
P-A	90–450 PSA
P-B	90–350 PSA
P-C	90–300 PSA
P-D	90–300 PSA
P-E	90–300 PSA
P-F	90–300 PSA

that more closely matches the liabilities. Investor demand dictates the PAC windows that issuers will create. Investor demand in turn is governed by the nature of investor liabilities.

Effective Collars and Actual Prepayments   As we have emphasized several times, the creation of a mortgage-backed security cannot make prepayment risk disappear. This is true for both a pass-through and a CMO. Thus, the reduction in prepayment risk (both extension risk and contraction risk) that a PAC offers must come from somewhere.

Where does the prepayment protection come from? It comes from the support bonds. It is the support bonds that forego principal payments if the collateral prepayments are slow; support bonds do not receive any principal until the PAC bonds receive the scheduled principal repayment. This reduces the risk that the PAC bonds will extend. Similarly, it is the support bonds that absorb any principal payments in excess of the scheduled principal payment that are made. This reduces the contraction risk of the PAC bonds. *Thus the key to the prepayment protection offered by a PAC bond is the amount of support bonds outstanding. If the support bonds are paid off quickly because of faster-than-expected prepayments, there is no longer any protection for the PAC bonds.* In fact, in FJF-05, if the support bond is paid off, the structure is effectively reduced to a sequential-pay CMO.

The support bonds can be thought of as bodyguards for the PAC bondholders. When the bullets fly (i.e., prepayments occur) it is the bodyguards that get killed off first. The bodyguards are there to absorb the bullets. When all the bodyguards are killed off (i.e., the support bonds paid off with faster-than-expected prepayments), the PAC bonds must fend for themselves: they are exposed to all the bullets.

The top panel of Exhibit 12-13 shows what happens to the average life for all PAC tranches of FJF-05 one year from now if prepayments for the first 12 months are the speed shown and the future speed is the same as the first 12 months. For example, if the collateral prepays at 165 PSA for the first 12 months and then prepays at the same speed thereafter, the average life one year from now will be 1.81 years. Notice that for all the PAC tranches the average life is still stable for the initial collar. In contrast, the second panel shows what will happen to the average life one year from now if the collateral pays at 42 CPR for the first 12 months and prepays at the indicated speed thereafter. We selected 42 CPR so that the support bonds will be paid off by the end of the first year. The structure is now effectively a sequential-pay structure and, as indicated by the average lives reported in the exhibit, there is substantial average life variability for the original PAC tranches. A comparison of the lower and upper panel clearly demonstrates the role of the support bonds.

With the bodyguard metaphor for the support bonds in mind, let's consider two questions asked by CMO buyers:

1. Will the schedule of principal repayments be satisfied if prepayments are faster than the initial upper collar?
2. Will the schedule of principal repayments be satisfied as long as prepayments stay within the initial collar?

Let's address the first question. The initial upper collar for FJF-05 is 300 PSA. Suppose that actual prepayments are 500 PSA for seven consecutive months; will this disrupt the schedule of principal repayments? The answer is: It depends!

EXHIBIT 12-13   Average Life for PAC Tranches of FJF-05 One Year from Now Assuming Various Prepayment Speeds for the First 12 Months

Speed for:		*PAC*					
First 12 Months	**Thereafter**	**P-A**	**P-B**	**P-C**	**P-D**	**P-E**	**P-F**
90 PSA	90 PSA	1.81	3.72	4.77	6.89	9.82	15.91
100 PSA	100 PSA	1.81	3.72	4.77	6.89	9.82	15.91
165 PSA	165 PSA	1.81	3.72	4.77	6.89	9.82	15.91
200 PSA	200 PSA	1.81	3.72	4.77	6.89	9.82	15.91
300 PSA	300 PSA	1.81	3.72	4.77	6.89	9.82	15.91
400 PSA	400 PSA	1.80	3.37	3.90	5.17	7.32	12.21
600 PSA	600 PSA	1.41	2.16	2.50	3.29	4.65	7.83
800 PSA	800 PSA	1.09	1.56	1.79	2.34	3.28	5.48
Speed for:		*PAC*					
First 12 Months	**Thereafter**	**P-A**	**P-B**	**P-C**	**P-D**	**P-E**	**P-F**
42 CPR	90 PSA	2.73	6.17	8.26	12.78	18.86	25.42
42 CPR	100 PSA	2.52	5.69	7.63	11.92	17.93	24.92
42 CPR	165 PSA	1.70	3.77	5.06	8.08	12.91	21.07
42 CPR	200 PSA	1.46	3.19	4.28	6.83	11.03	18.94
42 CPR	300 PSA	1.05	2.24	2.96	4.69	7.61	13.97
42 CPR	400 PSA	0.84	1.74	2.28	3.55	5.72	10.67
42 CPR	600 PSA	0.60	1.23	1.57	2.37	3.73	6.92
42 CPR	800 PSA	0.47	0.97	1.22	1.77	2.71	4.92

To answer this question we need two pieces of information. First, when does the 500 PSA occur? Second, what has been the actual prepayment experience up to the time that prepayments are 500 PSA? For example, suppose that six years from now is when the prepayments reach 500 PSA and also suppose that for the past six years the actual prepayment speed has been 90 PSA every month. This means that there are more bodyguards (i.e., support bonds) around than was expected when the PAC was structured at the initial collar. In establishing the schedule of principal repayments, it was assumed that the bodyguards would be killed off at 300 PSA. But the actual prepayment experience results in them being killed off at only 90 PSA. Thus, six years from now when the 500 PSA is assumed to occur, there are more bodyguards than expected. Thus, a 500 PSA for seven consecutive months may have no effect on the ability of the schedule of principal repayments to be met.

In contrast, suppose that the actual prepayment experience for the first six years is 300 PSA (the upper collar of the initial PAC collar). In this case, there are no extra bodyguards around. As a result, any prepayment speeds faster than 300 PSA, such as 500 PSA in our example, jeopardize satisfaction of the principal repayment schedule and increase extension risk. This does not mean that the schedule will be **busted**—the term used in the CMO market when a PAC schedule is broken. It does mean that the prepayment protection is reduced.

It should be clear from these observations that the initial collars are not particularly useful in assessing the prepayment protection for a seasoned PAC bond. This is most important to understand, as it is common for CMO buyers to compare prepayment protection of PACs in different CMO structures, and conclude that the greater protection is offered by the one with the wider collar. This approach is inadequate because it is actual prepayment experience that determines the degree of prepayment protection as well as the expected future prepayment behavior of the collateral.

The way to determine this protection is to calculate the effective collar for a seasoned PAC bond. An effective collar for a seasoned PAC is the lower and the upper PSA that can occur in the future and still allow maintenance of the schedule of principal repayments.

The effective collar changes every month. An extended period over which actual prepayments are below the upper range of the initial PAC collar will result in an increase in the upper range of the effective collar. This is because there will be more bodyguards around than anticipated. An extended period of prepayments slower than the lower range of the initial PAC collar will raise the lower range of the effective collar. This is because it will take faster prepayments to make up the shortfall of the scheduled principal payments not made plus the scheduled future principal payments.

The PAC schedule may not be satisfied even if the actual prepayments never fall outside the initial collar. This may seem surprising because our previous analysis indicated that the average life would not change if prepayments are at either extreme of the initial collar. However, recall that all of our previous analysis has been based on a single PSA speed for the life of the structure.

Let's use vector analysis to see what happens to the effective collar if the prepayments are at the initial upper collar for a certain number of months. Exhibit 12-14 shows the average life two years from now for the PAC bond in FJF-04 assuming that prepayments are 300 PSA for the first 24 months. Notice that the average life is stable at six years if the prepayments for the following months are between 115 PSA and 300 PSA. That is, the effective PAC collar is no longer the initial collar. Instead, the lower collar has shifted upward. This means that the protection from year 2 on is for 115 to 300 PSA, a narrower band than initially even though the earlier prepayments did not exceed the initial upper collar.

EXHIBIT 12-14 Average Life Two Years from Now for PAC Bond of FJF-04 Assuming Prepayments of 300 PSA for First 24 Months

PSA from Year 2 on	Average Life (years)
95	6.43
105	6.11
115	6.01
120	6.00
125	6.00
300	6.00
305	5.62

Providing Greater Prepayment Protection for PACs   There are two ways to provide greater protection for PAC bonds: lockouts and reverse PAC structures. One obvious way to provide greater protection for PAC bonds is to issue fewer PAC bonds relative to support bonds. In FJF-05, for example, rather than creating the six PAC bonds with a total par value of $243.8 million, we could use only $158.8 million of the $400 million of collateral to create these bonds, by reducing the amount of each of the six PAC bonds. An alternative is not to issue one of the PAC bonds, typically the shorter-term one. For example, suppose that we create only the last five of the six PAC bonds in FJF-05. The $85 million for PAC P-A is then used to create more support bonds. Such a CMO structure with no principal payments to a PAC bond class in the earlier years is referred to as a **lockout structure.**

A lockout structure provides greater prepayment protection to all PAC bonds in the CMO structure. One way to provide greater prepayment protection to only some PAC bonds is to alter the principal payment rules for distributing principal when all the support bonds have been paid off. In FJF-05, for example, when the support bond in this structure is paid off, the structure effectively becomes a sequential-pay structure. For PAC P-A this means that although there is protection against extension risk, as this tranche receives principal payments before the other five PAC bonds, there is no protection against contraction.

To provide greater protection to PAC P-A, the payment rules after all support bonds have been paid off can be specified so that any principal payments in excess of the scheduled amount will be paid to the last PAC bond, P-F. Thus, PAC P-F is exposed to greater contraction risk, which provides the other five PAC bonds with more protection against contraction risk. The principal payment rules would also specify that when the support bond and PAC P-F bond are paid off, all principal payments in excess of the scheduled amounts to earlier tranches are to be paid to the next-to-last PAC bond, PAC P-E in our example.

A CMO structure requiring any excess principal payments to be made to the longer PAC bonds after all support bonds are paid off is called a **reverse PAC structure.**

Other PAC Tranches   Earlier we described how the collateral can be used to create a CMO with accrual bonds, floaters, and inverse floaters bonds. In addition, interest-only and principal-only tranches (described later) can be created. These same types of bond classes can be created from a PAC bond. The difference between the bond classes described and those created from a PAC bond is simply the prepayment protection offered by the PAC structure.

Targeted Amortization Class Bonds

A **targeted amortization class (TAC) bond** resembles a PAC bond in that both have a schedule of principal repayment. The difference between a PAC bond and a TAC bond is that the former has a wide PSA range over which the schedule of principal repayment is protected against contraction risk and extension risk. A TAC bond, in contrast, has a single PSA rate from which the schedule of principal repayment is protected. As a result, the prepayment protection afforded the TAC bond is less than that for a PAC bond.

The creation of a bond with a schedule of principal repayments based on a single prepayment rate results in protection against contraction risk but not extension risk.

Thus, whereas PAC bonds are said to have two-sided prepayment protection, TAC bonds have one-sided prepayment protection. Such a bond is acceptable to institutional investors who are not overly concerned with some extension risk but greatly concerned with contraction risk.

Some institutional investors are interested in protection against extension risk but are willing to accept contraction risk. This is the opposite protection from that sought by the buyers of TAC bonds. The structures created to provide such protection are referred to as **reverse TAC bonds.**

Very Accurately Determined Maturity Bonds

Accrual or Z bonds have been used in CMO structures as support for bonds called **very accurately determined maturity (VADM)** or **guaranteed final maturity bonds.** In this case the interest accruing (i.e., not being paid out) on a Z bond is used to pay the interest and principal on a VADM bond. This effectively provides protection against extension risk even if prepayments slow down, because the interest accruing on the Z bond will be sufficient to pay off the scheduled principal and interest on the VADM bond. Thus, the maximum final maturity can be determined with a high degree of certainty. If prepayments are high, resulting in the supporting Z bond being paid off faster, however, a VADM bond can shorten.

A VADM is similar in character to a reverse TAC. For structures with similar collateral, however, a VADM bond offers greater protection against extension risk. Moreover, most VADMs will not shorten significantly if prepayments speed up. Thus, they offer greater protection against contraction risk compared with a reverse TAC with the same underlying collateral. Compared with PACs, VADM bonds have greater absolute protection against extension risk, and though VADM bonds do not have as much protection against contraction risk, as noted previously, the structures that have included these bonds are such that contraction risk is generally not significant.

Interest-Only and Principal-Only Tranches

As we explain later in this chapter, stripped mortgage-backed securities are created by paying all the principal to one bond class and all the interest to another bond class. These two classes are referred to as the **principal-only (PO) bond class** and the **interest-only (IO) bond class.** We discuss the investment characteristics of these securities later.

CMO structures can be created so that a tranche can receive only the principal or only the interest. For example, consider FJF-01. Tranche B in this structure can be divided into two tranches, a principal-only tranche and an interest-only tranche.

Notional IOs

In our previous illustrations, we used a CMO structure in which all the tranches have the same coupon rate (7.5%) and that coupon rate is the same as the collateral. In practice, the same coupon rate would not be given to each tranche. Instead, the coupon rate would depend on the term structure of interest rates and the average life of the tranche, among other things.

In the earlier CMO deals, all of the excess interest between the coupon rate on the tranches and the coupon interest on the collateral was paid to an equity class referred to as the **CMO residual.** This is no longer the practice today. Instead, a tranche is created that receives the excess coupon interest. This tranche is called a **notional interest-only (IO) class** and also referred to as a **structured IO.**

To see how a notional IO is created, consider the CMO structure shown in Exhibit 12-15, FJF-06. This is the same structure as FJF-02 except that the coupon rate varies by tranche and there is a class denoted IO, which is the class of interest to us.

Notice that for this structure the par amount for the IO class is shown as $52,566,667 and the coupon rate is 7.5%. This is an IO class, so there is no par amount. The amount shown is the amount on which the interest payments will be determined, not the amount that will be paid to the holder of this bond. Therefore, it is called a **notional amount.**

Let's look at how the notional amount is determined. Consider first tranche A. The par value is $194.5 million and the coupon rate is 6%. Because the collateral's coupon rate is 7.5%, the excess interest is 150 basis points (1.5%). Therefore, an IO with a 1.5% coupon rate and a notional amount of $194.5 million can be created from tranche A. But this is equivalent to an IO with a notional amount of $38.9 million and a coupon rate of 7.5%. Mathematically, this notional amount is found as follows:

$$\text{notional amount for 7.5\% IO} = \frac{\text{tranche's par value} \times \text{excess interest}}{0.075}$$

EXHIBIT 12-15   FJF-06: Hypothetical Five Tranche Sequential Pay with an Accrual Tranche and an Interest-Only Tranche[a]

Tranche	Par Amount	Coupon Rate (%)
A	$194,500,000	6.00
B	36,000,000	6.50
C	96,500,000	7.00
Z	73,000,000	7.25
IO	52,566,667 (notional)	7.50
	$400,000,000	

[a]*Payment rules:*

1. *For payment of periodic coupon interest:* Disburse periodic coupon interest to tranches A, B, and C on the basis of the amount of principal outstanding at the beginning of the period. For tranche Z, accrue the interest based on the principal plus accrued interest in the preceding period. The interest for tranche Z is to be paid to the earlier tranches as a principal pay down. Disburse periodic interest to the IO tranche based on the notional amount at the beginning of the period.
2. *For disbursement of principal payments:* Disburse principal payments to tranche A until it is paid off completely. After tranche A is paid off completely, disburse principal payments to tranche B until it is paid off completely. After tranche B is paid off completely, disburse principal payments to tranche C until it is paid off completely. After tranche C is paid off completely, disburse principal payments to tranche Z until the original principal balance plus accrued interest is paid off completely.

where:

$$\text{excess interest} = \text{collateral coupon rate} - \text{tranche coupon rate}$$

For example, for tranche A,

$$\text{excess interest} = 0.075 - 0.060 = 0.015$$
$$\text{tranche's par value} = \$194,500,000$$
$$\text{notional amount for 7.5\% IO} = \frac{\$194,500,000 \times 0.015}{0.075}$$
$$= \$38,900,000$$

Similarly, from tranche B with a par value of $36 million, the excess interest is 100 basis points (1%), and therefore an IO with a coupon rate of 1% and a notional amount of $36 million can be created. But this is equivalent to creating an IO with a notional amount of $4.8 million and a coupon rate of 7.5%. This procedure is shown in the following table for all four tranches.

Tranche	Par Amount	Excess Interest (%)	Notional Amount for a 7.5% Coupon Rate IO
A	$194,500,000	1.50	$38,900,000
B	36,000,000	1.00	4,800,000
C	96,500,000	0.50	6,433,333
Z	73,000,000	0.25	2,433,333
		Notional amount for 7.5% IO	$52,566,667

Support Bonds

The support bonds—or bodyguards—are the bonds that provide prepayment protection for the PAC tranches. Consequently, they are exposed to the greatest level of prepayment risk. Because of this, investors must be particularly careful in assessing the cash flow characteristics of support bonds to reduce the likelihood of adverse portfolio consequences due to prepayments.

The support bond typically is divided into different bond classes. All the bond classes we have discussed earlier in this section are available, including sequential-pay support bond classes, floater and inverse floater support bond classes, and accrual support bond classes.

The support bond can even be partitioned so as to create support bond classes with a schedule of principal repayments. That is, support bond classes that are PAC bonds can be created. In a structure with a PAC bond and a support bond with a PAC schedule of principal repayments, the former is called a PAC I bond or level I PAC bond and the latter a PAC II bond or level II PAC bond. Although PAC II bonds have greater prepayment protection than the support bond classes without a schedule of principal repayments, the prepayment protection is less than that provided PAC I bonds.

Credit Risk

A CMO can be viewed as a business entity. The assets of this business are the collateral; that is, the pass-through securities or pool of mortgage loans backing the deal. The collateral for a CMO is held in trust for the exclusive benefit of all the bondholders. The liabilities are the payments due to the CMO bond classes. The liability obligation consists of the par value and periodic interest payment that is owed to each class of bond. The CMO or, equivalently, the business, is structured so that even under the worst possible consequences concerning prepayments, all the liabilities will be satisfied.

Credit risk exposure depends on who has issued the CMO. An issuer is either (1) Freddie Mac, Fannie Mae, or Ginnie Mae, or (2) a private entity. Those CMOs issued by the former are referred to as **agency CMOs.** Those issued by a private entity are called **nonagency CMOs** and can be divided into two types. A private entity that issues a CMO but whose underlying collateral is a pool of pass-throughs guaranteed by an agency is called a **private-label CMO.** If the collateral for a CMO is a pool of unsecuritized mortgages loans, the structure is referred to as a **whole loan CMO.** Today, the most common type of nonagency CMO is a whole loan CMO. Consequently, market participants use the terms **nonagency CMO** and **whole loan CMO** interchangeably.

As we noted in Chapter 11, the guarantee of a government-sponsored enterprise depends on the financial capacity of the agency. CMOs issued by private entities are rated by commercial rating agencies. There are various ways that such issues can be credit enhanced, as described in Chapter 13 when we discuss asset-backed securities.

Tax Considerations

The issuer of a CMO wants to be sure that the trust created to pass through the interest and principal payments is not treated as a taxable entity. A provision of the Tax Reform Act of 1986, called the Real Estate Mortgage Investment Conduit (REMIC), specifies the requirements that an issuer must fulfill so that the legal entity created to issue a CMO is not taxable. Most CMOs today are created as REMICs. Although it is common to hear market participants refer to a CMO as a REMIC, not all CMOs are REMICs.

STRIPPED MORTGAGE-BACKED SECURITIES

Stripped mortgage-backed securities (MBSs), introduced by Fannie Mae in 1986, are another example of derivative mortgage products. A pass-through divides the cash flow from the underlying pool of mortgages on a pro rata basis across the security holders. A stripped MBS is created by altering the distribution of principal and interest from a pro rata distribution to an unequal distribution. Some of the securities thus created will have a price/yield relationship that is different from the price/yield relationship of the underlying mortgage pool. There are three types of stripped MBS: (1) synthetic-coupon pass-throughs, (2) interest-only/principal-only securities, and (3) CMO strips.

Synthetic-Coupon Pass-Throughs

The first generation of stripped mortgage-backed securities is called synthetic-coupon pass-throughs. This is because the unequal distribution of coupon and principal results in a synthetic coupon rate that is different from that of the underlying collateral.

Interest-Only/Principal-Only Strips

In early 1987, stripped MBS began to be issued where all the interest is allocated to one class (the IO class) and all the principal to the other class (the PO class). The IO class receives no principal payments. IOs and POs are referred to as **mortgage strips.**

The PO security is purchased at a substantial discount from par value. The yield an investor will realize depends on the speed at which prepayments are made. The faster the prepayments, the higher the yield the investor will realize. For example, suppose that there is a pass-through backed by 30-year mortgages with $400 million in par value and that investors can purchase POs backed by this pass-through for $175 million. The dollar return on this investment will be $225 million. How quickly that dollar return is recovered by PO investors determines the yield that will be realized. In the extreme case, if all the homeowners in the underlying mortgage pool decide to prepay their mortgage loans immediately, PO investors will realize the $225 million immediately. At the other extreme, if all homeowners decide to keep their houses for 30 years and make no prepayments, the $225 million will be spread out over 30 years, which will result in a lower yield for PO investors.

Let's look at how the price of the PO can be expected to change as mortgage rates in the market change. When mortgage rates decline below the coupon rate, prepayments are expected to speed up, accelerating payments to the PO holder. Thus, the cash flow of a PO improves (in the sense that principal repayments are received earlier). The cash flow will be discounted at a lower interest rate because the mortgage rate in the market has declined. The result is that the price of a PO will increase when mortgage rates decline. When mortgage rates rise above the coupon rate, prepayments are expected to slow down. The cash flow deteriorates (in the sense of its taking longer to recover principal repayments). Coupled with a higher discount rate, the price of a PO will fall when mortgage rates rise.

When an IO is purchased there is no par value. In contrast to the PO investor, the IO investor wants prepayments to be slow. The reason is that the IO investor receives only interest on the amount of the principal outstanding. As prepayments are made, the outstanding principal declines, and less dollar interest is received. In fact, if prepayments are too fast, the IO investor may not recover the amount paid for the IO.

Let's look at the expected price response of an IO to changes in mortgage rates. If mortgage rates decline below the coupon rate, prepayments are expected to accelerate. This results in a deterioration of the expected cash flow for an IO. Although the cash flow will be discounted at a lower rate, the net effect is typically a decline in the price of an IO. If mortgage rates rise above the coupon rate, the expected cash flow improves but the cash flow is discounted at a higher interest rate. The net effect may be either a rise or a fall for the IO. Thus, we see an interesting characteristic of an IO: Its price tends to move in the same direction as the change in mortgage rates. This effect occurs (1) when mortgage rates fall below the coupon rate, and (2) for some range of mortgage rates above the coupon rate.

An example of this effect can be seen in Exhibit 12-16, which shows for various mortgage rates the price of (1) a 9% pass-through, (2) a PO created from this pass-through, and (3) an IO created from this pass-through. Notice that as mortgage rates decline below 9%, the price of the pass-through does not respond much. This is the

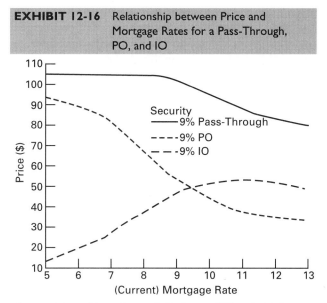

EXHIBIT 12-16   Relationship between Price and Mortgage Rates for a Pass-Through, PO, and IO

Source: Adapted from Steven J. Carlson and Timothy D. Sears, "Stripped Mortgage Pass-Throughs: New Tools for Investors," in Frank J. Fabozzi, ed., *The Handbook of Mortgage-Backed Securities,* rev. ed. (Chicago: Probus Publishing, 1988), p. 564.

negative convexity (or price compression) property of pass-throughs. For the PO security, the price falls monotonically as mortgage rates rise. For the IO security, at mortgage rates above approximately 11%, the price declines as mortgage rates rise; as mortgage rates fall below about 11%, the price of an IO falls as mortgage rates decline. Both POs and IOs exhibit substantial price volatility when mortgage rates change. The greater price volatility of the IO and PO compared with the pass-through from which they were created can be seen by the steepness of a tangent line to the curves at any given mortgage rate.

CMOs that are backed by POs are referred to as **PO-collateralized CMOs.**

CMO Strips   One of the classes in a CMO structure can be a principal-only or an interest-only class. These are called CMO strips. Earlier we discussed how CMO strip tranches can be created.

SUMMARY

Collateralized mortgage obligations are bond classes created by redirecting the cash flows of mortgage-related products (pass-throughs and whole loans). The creation of a CMO cannot eliminate prepayment risk; it can only redistribute the various forms of this risk among different classes of bonds called tranches.

In a CMO there are rules for the distribution of interest and principal from the collateral. The first CMOs were structured so that each class of bond would be retired sequentially, and hence such structures are referred to as sequential-pay CMOs. The average life of the tranches differs from that of the collateral. An accrual tranche allows the creation of even shorter-term and longer-term average life tranches than in a sequential-pay CMO without the inclusion of an accrual tranche. From any of the fixed-rate tranches, a floater and an inverse can be created. Also, an interest-only and a principal-only tranche can be created from a tranche. A notional IO is a tranche created from the difference between the collateral's coupon interest and the total coupon interest paid to the tranches.

Despite the redistribution of prepayment risk with sequential-pay and accrual CMOs, there is still considerable prepayment risk. That is, there is still considerable average life variability for a given tranche. This problem has been mitigated by the creation of a planned amortization class tranche. This type of CMO tranche reduces average life variability. The bonds included in a CMO structure that provide the better protection for PAC tranches are the support or companion tranches. There are various ways in which greater prepayment protection can be provided for some or all of the PAC bonds within a CMO structure. These include a lockout and a reverse PAC structure.

Targeted amortization class bonds are created so as to provide protection against contraction risk but not against extension risk. A reverse TAC also provides one-sided protection: protection against extension risk but not against contraction risk. A very accurately determined maturity bond also provides protection against extension risk.

Support bonds are the riskiest tranche within a CMO structure. From support bonds other types of bonds can be created. For example, a part of the support bonds can be carved up to create support bonds with a principal repayment schedule. Such bonds are referred to as PAC II or level II PAC bonds.

The credit risk exposure depends on whether the issuer is an agency (i.e., the issuer is Ginnie Mae, Fannie Mae, or Freddie Mac) or a nonagency CMO. Agency CMOs are perceived to have no credit risk. Nonagency CMOs can be divided into private-label CMOs in which the underlying collateral is a pool of agency pass-throughs, and whole loan CMOs, in which the underlying collateral is a pool of whole loans. Nonagency CMOs expose investors to credit risk.

A stripped MBS is created by assigning distribution of principal and interest of the underlying pass-through security in unequal portions to two classes of bonds. The result is that the two bonds will have a different price/yield relationship from that of the underlying pass-through. There are three types of stripped MBS: (1) synthetic-coupon pass-throughs, (2) interest-only/principal-only securities, and (3) CMO strips.

Questions

1. How does a CMO alter the cash flow from mortgages so as to shift the prepayment risk across various classes of bondholders?
2. Why is a CMO called a pay-through structure?
3. a. "By creating a CMO, an issuer eliminates the prepayment risk associated with the underlying mortgages." Do you agree with this statement?
   b. Wall Street often refers to CMOs as "customized securities." Explain why.

4. In a discussion of the CMO market, the popular press sometimes refers to this sector of the mortgage-backed securities market as the riskiest sector and the pass-through sector as the safest sector. Comment.

5. Explain the effect on the average lives of sequential-pay structures of including an accrual tranche in a CMO structure.

6. What types of investors would be attracted to an accrual bond?

7. Suppose that a tranche from which an inverse floater is created has an average life of five years. What will the average life of the inverse floater be?

8. This quotation is taken from a 1991 issue of *BondWeek:*

> First Interstate Bank of Texas will look into buying several different types of collateralized mortgage obligation tranches when it starts up its buy program sometime after the second quarter of 1991, according to Jules Pollard, v.p. Pollard said he will consider replacing maturing adjustable-rate mortgage pass-throughs with short companion tranches and planned amortization classes because the ARMS have become rich. . . . Pollard did not provide a dollar figure on the planned investments, which will be made to match fund the bank's liabilities. When he does invest he said he prefers government-guaranteed securities or those with implied guarantees.

   a. Explain the types of securities that Pollard is buying and selling.

   b. Given the preference stated in the last sentence of the quotation, what issuers is he likely to prefer? What issuers would he reject?

9. Describe how the schedule for a PAC tranche is created.

10. Explain the role of a support bond in a CMO structure.

11. What was the motivation for the creation of PAC bonds?

12. Suppose that a savings and loan association has decided to invest in mortgage-backed securities and is considering the following two securities: (i) a Freddie Mac pass-through security with a WAM of 340 months or (ii) a PAC tranche of a Freddie Mac CMO issue with an average life of two years. Which mortgage-backed security would probably be better from an asset/liability perspective?

13. Suppose that a PAC bond is created assuming prepayments speeds of 80 PSA and 350 PSA. If the collateral pays at 100 PSA over its life, what will this PAC tranche's average life be?

14. Suppose that $1 billion of pass-throughs is used to create a CMO structure with a PAC bond with a par value of $700 million and a support bond with a par value of $300 million.

   a. Which of the following will have the greatest average life variability: (i) the collateral, (ii) the PAC bond, or (iii) the support bond? Why?

   b. Which of the following will have the least average life variability: (i) the collateral, (ii) the PAC bond, or (iii) the support bond? Why?

15. Suppose that the $1 billion of collateral in Question 14 was divided into a PAC bond with a par value of $800 million and a support bond with a par value of $200 million. Will the PAC bond in this CMO structure have more or less protection than the PAC bond in Question 14?

16. Suppose that $1 billion of pass-throughs is used to create a CMO structure with a PAC bond with a par value of $700 million (PAC I), a support bond with a schedule (PAC II) with a par value of $100 million, and a support bond without a schedule with a par value of $200 million.

   a. Will the PAC I or PAC II have the smaller average life variability? Why?

   b. Will the support bond without a schedule or the PAC II have the greater average life variability? Why?

17. In a CMO structure with several PAC bonds, explain why, when the support bonds are paid off, the structure will be just like a sequential-pay CMO.

18. Suppose that for the first four years of a CMO, prepayments are well within the initial PAC collar. What will happen to the effective upper collar?

19. The following questions are to be answered by referring to the prospectus supplement that appears on pages 291–316. As indicated on pages of the prospectus (pp. 314–315), the structure and the distribution payments are based on mortgage loans with a 12% mortgage rate and an initial mortgage term of 360 months, and the underlying pass-throughs as having a coupon rate of 10.125% and a remaining term to maturity of 356 months.

   a. How many classes are there in this CMO structure?

   b. (1) Which class is the floating-rate class?
      (2) What benchmark interest rate is used for the floating-rate, and what is the spread to the benchmark?
      (3) What are the cap and the floor on the floating rate after August 24, 1990? How is the floor determined?

   c. (1) Which class is the inverse-floating-rate class?
      (2) What formula is used to determine the coupon rate for the inverse floater?
      (3) What is the coupon leverage?
      (4) What are the cap and the floor on the inverse floater after August 24, 1990?
      (5) How was the cap on the inverse floater determined?
      (6) How was the cap on the floating-rate class determined?

   d. Assuming the initial principal outstanding of both the floating-rate and inverse-floating-rate classes and LIBOR of 9%:
      (1) What dollar coupon interest will be paid to the floating-rate class?
      (2) What dollar coupon interest will be paid to the inverse floater?
      (3) What is the total dollar coupon interest to both classes?
      (4) What is the total dollar coupon interest on the underlying pass-through assuming a coupon rate of 10.125%?

   e. Based on your answer to part (d) what is the weighted-average coupon paid to the sum of the floating- and inverse-floating-rate classes?

   f. Are the floating-rate and inverse-floating-rate classes in this structure PAC or support classes?

   g. (1) How many PAC bonds are in this CMO structure?
      (2) What is the initial PAC collar?

   h. Based on the planned principal balances shown on pages S-16 to S-24:
      (1) When is Class 89-A scheduled to make its first principal payment?
      (2) When is Class 89-A scheduled to make its final principal payment?
      (3) What is the window for Class 89-A?
      (4) When is Class 89-G scheduled to make its first principal payment?
      (5) When is Class 89-G scheduled to make its final principal payment?
      (6) What is the window for Class 89-G?

   i. Which bond is an accrual PAC bond? How did you determine which PAC bond was an accrual PAC bond?

   j. What are the support bonds in this CMO structure?

   k. Based on the percent of original principal balance outstanding reported on pages S-30 to S-34:
      (1) To what extent is Class 89-A subject to extension risk?
      (2) To what extent is Class 89-B subject to contraction risk?
      (3) Explain why the support classes are subject to substantial prepayment risk.

(4) For the PAC bonds, why is the weighted-average life constant between 90% PSA and 275% PSA?

20. Consider the following CMO structure backed by 8% collateral:

Tranche	Par Amount (in millions)	Coupon Rate (%)
A	$300	6.50
B	250	6.75
C	200	7.25
D	250	7.75

Suppose that a client wants a notional IO with a coupon rate of 8%. Calculate the notional amount for this notional IO.

21. An issuer is considering the following two CMO structures:

STRUCTURE I:

Tranche	Par Amount (in millions)	Coupon Rate (%)
A	$150	6.50
B	100	6.75
C	200	7.25
D	150	7.75
E	100	8.00
F	500	8.50

Tranches A to E are a sequence of PAC Is and F is the support bond.

STRUCTURE II:

Tranche	Par Amount (in millions)	Coupon Rate (%)
A	$150	6.50
B	100	6.75
C	200	7.25
D	150	7.75
E	100	8.00
F	200	8.25
G	300	?

Tranches A to E are a sequence of PAC Is, F is a PAC II, and G is a support bond without a PAC schedule.

a. In structure II, tranche G is created from tranche F in structure I. What is the coupon rate for tranche G assuming that the combined coupon rate for tranches F and G in structure II should be 8.5%?

b. What is the effect on the value and average life of tranches A to E by including the PAC II in structure II?

c. What is the difference in the average life variability of tranche G in structure II and tranche F in structure II?

22. a. What is the role of a lockout in a CMO structure?

b. Explain why in a reverse PAC bond structure, the longest average life bond can turn out to be effectively a support bond if all the support bonds in the structure are paid off?

23. What type of prepayment protection is afforded each of the following: (a) a TAC bond; (b) a reverse TAC bond; (c) a VADM?

24. What types of CMO issues require a credit rating?
25. What is a whole loan CMO?
26. What is a REMIC?
27. Indicate why you agree or disagree with the following statement: "All CMOs are REMICs."
28. a. What is a principal-only security? What is an interest-only security?
    b. How is the price of an interest-only security expected to change when interest rates change?
29. Suppose that 8% coupon pass-throughs are stripped into two classes. Class X-1 receives 75% of the principal and 10% of the interest. Class X-2 receives 25% of the principal and 90% of the interest.
    (1) What type of stripped MBS would this be?
    (2) What is the effective coupon rate on Class X-1?
    (3) What is the effective coupon rate on Class X-2?

Prospectus Supplement to Prospectus Dated January 4, 1990
$500,000,000
Federal National Mortgage Association

FannieMae

Guaranteed REMIC Pass-Through Certificates
Fannie Mae REMIC Trust 1990-89

The Guaranteed REMIC Pass-Through Certificates offered hereby (the "REMIC Certificates") represent beneficial ownership interests in one of two trust funds. The REMIC Certificates, other than the Class 89-RL REMIC Certificates, represent beneficial ownership interests in Fannie Mae REMIC Trust 1990-89 (the "Trust"). The assets of the Trust consist of the "regular interests" in a separate trust fund (the "Lower Tier REMIC"), consisting of Fannie Mae Guaranteed Mortgage Pass-Through Certificates (the "MBS Certificates"), each of which represents a beneficial interest in a pool (the "Pool") of first lien, single-family, fixed-rate residential mortgage loans (the "Mortgage Loans") having the characteristics described in this Prospectus Supplement. The Class 89-RL REMIC Certificates will be the "residual interest" in the Lower Tier REMIC. The general characteristics of the REMIC Certificates, including the terms of Fannie Mae's guaranty thereof, are described in the attached Prospectus dated January 4, 1990 (the "REMIC Prospectus"). The general characteristics of the MBS Certificates, including the terms of Fannie Mae's guaranty thereof, are described in the attached MBS Prospectus dated April 1,1990 (the "MBS Prospectus").

(Continued on page 292)

THE OBLIGATIONS OF FANNIE MAE UNDER ITS GUARANTY OF THE REMIC CERTIFICATES ARE OBLIGATIONS OF FANNIE MAE ONLY AND ARE NOT BACKED BY THE FULL FAITH AND CREDIT OF THE UNITED STATES. THE REMIC CERTIFICATES ARE EXEMPT FROM THE REGISTRATION REQUIREMENTS OF THE SECURITIES ACT OF 1933 AND ARE "EXEMPTED SECURITIES" WITHIN THE MEANING OF THE SECURITIES EXCHANGE ACT OF 1934.

	Original Principal Amount	Interest Rate	Final Distribution Date
Class 89-A	$37,101,000	9.00%	March 2000
Class 89-B	31,474,000	9.00%	August 2003
Class 89-X	18,984,000	9.50%	July 2011
Class 89-C	40,000,000	9.50%	March 2014
Class 89-D	40,000,000	9.50%	March 2016
Class 89-E	16,168,000	9.50%	December 2016
Class 89-G	22,028,000	8.75%	October 2017
Class 89-H	15,856,000	8.75%	May 2018
Class 89-J	35,884,000	8.50%	July 2019
Class 89-K	36,683,000	6.50%	July 2020
Class 89-L	209,000	1009.00%	July 2020
Class 89-M	88,649,000	9.50%	July 2020
Class 89-F	9,120,000	(1)	November 2017
Class 89-S	11,400,000	(2)	November 2017
Class 89-N	14,528,000	9.50%	August 2017
Class 89-0	5,991,000	9.50%	November 2017
Class 89-P	51,566,000	9.50%	October 2018
Class 89-Y	7,000,000	9.50%	July 2020
Class 89-Z	6,833,000	9.50%	July 2020
Class 89-R	10,516,000	(3)	July 2020
Class 89-RL	10,000	9.50%	July 2020

(1) During their initial Interest Accrual Period of July 25, 1990 through August 24, 1990, the Class 89-F REMIC Certificates will bear interest at a rate of 8.8125% per annum. During each Interest Accrual Period thereafter, the Class 89-F REMIC Certificates will bear interest, subject to a maximum rate of 11.00% per annum and a minimum rate of 0.50% per annum, at a rate per annum equal to 50 basis points in excess of the London interbank offered rate for one-month U.S. dollar deposits ("LIBOR"), as more fully described herein.

(2) During their initial Interest Accrual Period of July 25, 1990 through August 24, 1990, the Class 89-S REMIC Certificates will bear interest at a rate of 10.05% per annum. During each Interest Accrual Period thereafter, the Class 89-S REMIC Certificates will bear interest, subject to a maximum rate of 16.7% per annum and a minimum rate of 8.3% per annum, at a per annum rate equal to 16.7% - (0.8 X LIBOR).

(3) Holders of the Class 89-R REMIC Certificates will be entitled on each Distribution Date to receive all Surplus Cash. See "Description of the REMIC Certificates—Additional Characteristics of the Class 89-R and Class 89-RL REMIC Certificates" herein.

This Prospectus Supplement does not contain complete information regarding this offering and should be read only in conjunction with the REMIC Prospectus and the MBS Prospectus.

The date of this Prospectus Supplement is June 22, 1990.

Interest on each Class of REMIC Certificates, other than the Class 89-R REMIC Certificates, at the applicable per annum interest rate described on the cover hereof will be distributed on the 25th day of each month (or, if such 25th day is not a business day, on the first business day next succeeding such 25th day), commencing in August 1990 (each, a "Distribution Date"), except for interest distributions on the Class 89-X, Class 89-Y and Class 89-Z REMIC Certificates, which are Accrual Certificates. Interest will accrue on the Accrual Certificates as described under "Description of the REMIC Certificates—Distributions of Interest" herein. Interest to be distributed or added to principal with respect to each REMIC Certificate on a Distribution Date will consist of one month's interest on the outstanding principal amount of such REMIC Certificate immediately prior to such Distribution Date.

The principal distribution on each Distribution Date will be in an amount equal to the sum of the aggregate distributions of principal concurrently made on the MBS Certificates and interest that accrues and is unpaid on the Accrual Certificates. On each Distribution Date, distributions of principal of the REMIC Certificates will be allocated among the Classes of REMIC Certificates in accordance with the priorities described herein.

The Final Distribution Dates of the respective Classes of REMIC Certificates have been determined so that distributions on the underlying MBS Certificates will be sufficient to make timely distributions of interest on the REMIC Certificates and to retire each such Class on or before its Final Distribution Date without the necessity of any call on Fannie Mae under its guaranty of the REMIC Certificates. The rate of distribution of principal of the REMIC Certificates will depend on the rate of payment (including prepayments) of the principal of the Mortgage Loans underlying the MBS Certificates. Both the Trust and the Lower Tier REMIC are subject to early termination only under the limited circumstances described in the REMIC Prospectus under "The Trust Agreement—Termination."

The yields on the REMIC Certificates will be sensitive in varying degrees to the rate of principal payments (including prepayments) of the Mortgage Loans, which generally can be prepaid at any time. An extremely rapid rate of principal payments (including prepayments) may have a negative effect on the yield on the Class 89-L REMIC Certificates, which initially will be offered at a substantial premium to their original principal amount and could result in a failure by investors in the Class 89-L REMIC Certificates to recoup their initial investment. In addition, the Class 89-F and Class 89-S REMIC Certificates will be sensitive to fluctuations in the level of LIBOR. Furthermore, the weighted average life of the Class 89-Y REMIC Certificates may decrease significantly, and the weighted average lives of the Class 89-M, Class 89-F, Class 89-S, Class 89-N, Class 89-0, Class 89-P and Class 89-Z REMIC Certificates may increase in varying degrees, if the prepayment rates of the Mortgage Loans exceed approximately 169% PSA (as defined herein) for any Distribution Date. Such changes in weighted average lives may have a significant effect on the yields on the REMIC Certificates.

The Class 89-R and Class 89-RL REMIC Certificates will be subject to certain transfer restrictions. See "Description of the REMIC Certificates—Additional Characteristics of the Class 89-R and Class 89-RL REMIC Certificates" herein. In addition, any transferee of a Class 89-R or Class 89-RL REMIC Certificate will be required to execute and deliver an affidavit as provided in the REMIC Prospectus. See "Description of the REMIC Certificates—Additional Characteristics of Residual Certificates" and "Certain Federal Income Tax Consequences—Sales of Certificates—*Residual Certificates Transferred to or Held by Disqualified Organizations*" in the REMIC Prospectus.

Elections will be made to treat the Lower Tier REMIC and the Trust as "real estate mortgage investment conduits" ("REMICs") pursuant to the Internal Revenue Code of 1986, as amended (the "Code"). The REMIC Certificates, other than the Class 89-R and Class 89-RL REMIC Certificates, will be designated as "regular interests" in the REMIC constituted by the Trust, and the Class 89-R REMIC Certificates will be designated as the "residual interest" in such REMIC. The interests in the Lower Tier REMIC, with the exception of the Class 89-RL REMIC Certificates (the "Lower Tier Interests"), will be designated as the "regular interests," and the Class 89-RL REMIC Certificates will be designated as the "residual interest," in the Lower Tier REMIC. See "Certain Federal Income Tax Consequences" in the REMIC Prospectus.

THE MBS CERTIFICATES

General

The MBS Certificates underlying the REMIC Certificates are Fannie Mae Guaranteed Mortgage Pass-Through Certificates, which will have an aggregate unpaid principal amount of $500,000,000, Pass-Through Rates of 9.50% and the general characteristics described in the attached MBS Prospectus. The Mortgage Loans that underlie the MBS Certificates are conventional Level Payment Mortgage Loans, each secured by a first mortgage or deed of trust on a one- to four-family ("single-family") residential property, and all of which have an original maturity of up to 30 years, as described under "The Mortgage Pools" and "Yield Considerations" in the MBS Prospectus. The weighted average coupon of the Mortgage Loans in each Pool at the Issue Date of the related MBS Certificate ("WAC") was within the range of 9.75% to 12.00% per annum. The weighted average remaining term to maturity, in months, of the Mortgage Loans in each Pool at the Issue Date of the related MBS Certificate ("WAM"), less the number of months elapsed from such Issue Date through the July 1, 1990 REMIC Issue Date ("Adjusted WAM"), or the current WAM, if available, will not be less than 180 or greater than 360. The weighted average of the Adjusted WAMs (or current WAMs, to the extent available) of all the MBS Certificates underlying the REMIC Certificates is expected to be approximately 356 months. Following the issuance of the REMIC Certificates, Fannie Mae will prepare a Final Data Statement setting forth the Pool number, the WAC at the Issue Date (or current WAC, to the extent available) and the Adjusted WAM (or current WAM, to the extent available) of each MBS Certificate underlying the REMIC Certificates, along with the weighted average of all the WACs (or of any available current WACs) and the weighted average of all the Adjusted WAMs (or of any available current WAMs) based on the current unpaid principal balances of the MBS Certificates as of the REMIC Issue Date. The Final Data Statement will also include the MBS Percentage Schedule as further described herein. Final Data Statements will not accompany Prospectus Supplements but will be made available by Fannie Mae. To request Final Data Statements, telephone Fannie Mae at (202) 752-7585. The contents of the Final Data Statement and other data specific to the REMIC Certificates are available in electronic form by calling Fannie Mae at (202) 782-6000.

Prepayment Considerations and Risks

The rate of principal payments of the MBS Certificates, and therefore of distributions on the REMIC Certificates, is related directly to the rate of payments of principal of the underlying Mortgage Loans, which may be in the form of scheduled amortization or prepayments (for this purpose, the term "prepayment" includes prepayments and liquidations resulting from default, casualty, condemnation and payments made pursuant to any guaranty of payment by, or option to repurchase of, Fannie Mae). In general, when the level of prevailing interest rates declines significantly below the interest rates on fixed-rate mortgage loans, the rate of prepayment is likely to increase, although the prepayment rate is influenced by a number of other factors, including general economic conditions and homeowner mobility. See "Maturity and Prepayment Assumptions" in the MBS Prospectus.

Acceleration of mortgage payments as a result of transfers of the mortgaged property is another factor affecting prepayment rates. The Mortgage Loans underlying the MBS Certificates will generally provide by their terms that, in the event of the transfer or prospective transfer of title to the underlying mortgaged property, the full unpaid principal balance of the Mortgage Loan is due and payable at the option of the holder. As set forth under "Description of Certificates—Collection and Other Servicing Procedures" in the MBS Prospectus, Fannie Mae is required to exercise its right to accelerate the maturity of Mortgage Loans containing enforceable "due-on-sale" provisions upon certain transfers of the mortgaged property.

Prepayments of mortgage loans commonly are measured relative to a prepayment standard or model. The model used in this Prospectus Supplement, the Public Securities Association's standard prepayment model ("PSA"), represents an assumed rate of prepayment each month of the then outstanding principal balance of a pool of new mortgage loans. *PSA does not purport to be either a historical description of the prepayment experience of any pool of mortgage loans or a prediction of the anticipated rate of prepayment of any pool of mortgage loans, including the Mortgage Loans underlying the MBS Certificates backing the PEMIC Certificates.* 100% PSA assumes prepayment rates of 0.2% per annum of the then unpaid principal balance of such mortgage loans in the first month of the life of the mortgage loans and an additional 0.2% per annum in each month thereafter (for example, 0.4% per annum in the second month) until the 30th month. Beginning in the 30th month and in each month thereafter during the life of the mortgage loans, 100% PSA assumes a constant prepayment rate of 6% per annum. Multiples will be calculated from this prepayment rate series; for example, 165% PSA assumes prepayment rates will be 0.33% per annum in month one, 0.66% per annum in month two, reaching 9.9% per annum in month 30 and remaining constant at 9.9% per annum thereafter. 0% PSA assumes no prepayments.

DESCRIPTION OF THE REMIC CERTIFICATES

The following summaries describing certain provisions of the REMIC Certificates do not purport to be complete and are subject to, and are qualified in their entirety by reference to, the REMIC Prospectus and the provisions of the Trust Agreement.

General

Two separate trust funds will be created pursuant to the Trust Agreement, and elections will be made to treat each trust fund as a REMIC for federal income tax purposes.

One trust fund (the "Lower Tier REMIC") will consist of the MBS Certificates. The entire beneficial ownership interest in the Lower Tier REMIC will be evidenced by the Lower Tier Interests and the Class 89-RL REMIC Certificates. Each of the Lower Tier Interests will be designated as a "regular interest" in the REMIC constituted by the Lower Tier REMIC and will bear interest at the rate of 9.50% per annum. The initial aggregate principal amount of the Lower Tier Interests, together with the initial principal amount of the Class 89-RL REMIC Certificates, equals the initial aggregate principal amount of the REMIC Certificates. The Lower Tier Interests, together with the Class 89-RL REMIC Certificates, in the aggregate, will evidence the entire beneficial ownership interest in the distributions of principal and interest on the MBS Certificates. The Class 89-RL REMIC Certificates will be designated as the "residual interest" in the REMIC constituted by the Lower Tier REMIC and will have the characteristics described herein.

The second trust fund (the "Trust") will consist of the Lower Tier Interests. The entire beneficial ownership interest in the Trust will be evidenced by the REMIC Certificates, other than the Class 89-RL REMIC Certificates, as described herein.

Distributions of Interest

The REMIC Certificates, other than the Class 89-R REMIC Certificates, will bear interest at the respective per annum interest rates described on the cover hereof. Interest on the REMIC Certificates is calculated on the basis of a 360-day year consisting of twelve 30-day months and is payable monthly on each Distribution Date, commencing (except in the case of the Class 89-X, Class 89-Y and Class 89-Z REMIC Certificates, which are Accrual Certificates) in August 1990. Interest to be distributed or added to principal of each REMIC Certificate on a Distribution Date will consist of one month's interest on the outstanding principal amount of such REMIC Certificate immediately prior to such Distribution Date. Interest to be distributed or added to principal on a Distribution Date will accrue on the REMIC Certificates, other than the Class 89-F, Class 89-S and Class 89-R REMIC Certificates, during the calendar month preceding the month in which such Distribution Date occurs. In the case of the Class 89-F and Class 89-S REMIC Certificates, such interest will accrue during the one-month period beginning on the 25th day of such preceding month and ending on the 24th day of the month of such Distribution Date (each, an "Interest Accrual Period").

Interest will accrue on the Accrual Certificates at the per annum interest rate of 9.50%; however, such interest will not be distributed to Holders of the Accrual Certificates but rather will be added to the principal balances thereof on each Distribution Date (i) until after the principal balance of the Class 89-B REMIC Certificates has been reduced to zero, in the case of the Class 89-X REMIC Certificates, and (ii) in the case of the Class 89-Y and Class 89-Z REMIC Certificates, for so long as the Class 89-Y and Class 89-Z REMIC Certificates, respectively, are outstanding. Interest so accrued and unpaid on the Accural Certificates will be added to the principal amounts thereof on the applicable Distribution Dates.

Interest will accrue on the Class 89-F REMIC Certificates at the per annum rate of 8.8125% during the initial Interest Accrual Period, and will accrue during each Interest Accrual Period thereafter, subject to a maximum per annum interest rate of 11.00% and a minimum per annum rate of 0.50%, at a variable per annum rate equal to 50 basis points in excess of the London interbank offered rate for one-month U.S. dollar deposits ("LIBOR"). Interest will accrue on the Class 89-S REMIC Certificates at the per annum rate of 10.05% during the initial Interest Accrual Period, and will accrue during each Interest Accrual Period thereafter, subject to a maximum per annum interest rate of 16.7% and a minimum per annum interest rate of 8.3%, at a variable per annum rate equal to 16.7%— (0.8 X LIBOR). In each case, the applicable rate will be determined monthly on the second business day prior to the first day of the related Interest Accrual Period (the "LIBOR Determination Date"). The yields with respect to the Class 89-F and Class 89-S REMIC Certificates will be affected by changes in LIBOR, which may not correlate with changes in mortgage interest rates. It is possible that lower mortgage interest rates could occur concurrently with an increase in the level of LIBOR. Conversely, higher mortgage interest rates could occur concurrently with a decrease in the level of LIBOR.

The effective yield on the REMIC Certificates, other than the Class 89-F, Class 89-S and Class 89-R REMIC Certificates, will be reduced below the yield otherwise produced because interest payable with respect to an Interest Accrual Period will not be distributed until the 25th day following the end of such Interest Accrual Period and will not bear interest during such delay.

Calculation of LIBOR

Commencing on August 23, 1990 and thereafter on each LIBOR Determination Date, until the principal amounts of the Class 89-F and Class 89-S REMIC Certificates have been reduced to zero, Fannie Mae or its agent (initially State Street Bank and Trust Company in Boston, Massachusetts, hereinafter referred to as "State Street") will request each of the designated reference banks meeting the criteria set forth herein (the "Reference Banks") to inform State Street of the quotation offered by its principal London office for making one-month United States dollar deposits in leading banks in the London interbank market, as of 11:00 a.m. (London time) on such LIBOR Determination Date. (For purposes of calculating LIBOR, "business day" means a day on which banks are open for dealing in foreign currency and exchange in London, Boston and New York City.) In lieu of making a request of the Reference Banks, State Street may rely on the quotations for those Reference Banks that appear at such time on the Reuters Screen LIBO Page (as defined in the International Swap Dealers Association, Inc. Code of Standard Wording, Assumptions and Provisions for Swaps, 1986 Edition), to the extent available.

LIBOR will be established by State Street on each LIBOR Determination Date as follows:

(a) If on any LIBOR Determination Date two or more Reference Banks provide such offered quotations, LIBOR for the next Interest Accrual Period shall be the arithmetic mean of such offered quotations (rounded upwards if necessary to the nearest whole multiple of 1/32%).

(b) If on any LIBOR Determination Date only one or none of the Reference Banks provides such offered quotations, LIBOR for the next Interest Accrual Period shall be whichever is the higher of (i) LIBOR as determined on the previous LIBOR Determination Date or (ii) the Reserve Interest Rate. The "Reserve Interest Rate" shall be the rate per annum which State Street determines to be either (i) the arithmetic mean (rounded upwards if necessary to the nearest whole multiple of 1/32%) of the one-month United States dollar lending rates that New York City banks selected by State Street are quoting, on the relevant LIBOR Determination Date, to the principal London offices of at least two of the Reference Banks to which such quotations are, in the opinion of State Street being so made, or (ii) in the event that State Street can determine no such arithmetic mean, the lowest one-month United States dollar lending rate which New York City banks selected by State Street are quoting on such LIBOR Determination Date to leading European banks.

(c) If on the August 23, 1990, LIBOR Determination Date, State Street is required but is unable to determine the Reserve Interest Rate in the manner provided in paragraph (b) above, LIBOR shall be 8.3125%.

Each Reference Bank (i) shall be a leading bank engaged in transactions in Eurodollar deposits in the international Eurocurrency market; (ii) shall not control, be controlled by, or be under common control with Fannie Mae; and (iii) shall have an established place of business in London. If any such Reference Bank should be unwilling or unable to act as such or if Fannie Mae should terminate the appointment of any such Reference Bank, State Street will promptly appoint another leading bank meeting the criteria specified above.

The establishment of LIBOR on each LIBOR Determination Date by State Street and State Street's calculation of the rate of interest applicable to the Class 89-F and Class 89-S REMIC Certificates for the related Interest Accrual Period shall (in the absence of manifest error) be final and binding. Each such rate of interest may be obtained by telephoning State Street at (617) 654-4067 or Fannie Mae at (202) 752-6547.

Distributions of Principal

Principal will be distributed monthly on the Lower Tier Interests and the Class 89-RL REMIC Certificates in an amount equal to the aggregate distributions of principal concurrently made on the MBS Certificates (the "Cash Flow Distribution Amount"). On each Distribution Date, the Class 89-RL REMIC Certificates will receive approximately .002% of the Cash Flow Distribution Amount, which percentage is equal to the proportion that the original principal amount of such Class bears to the aggregate original principal amount of the Lower Tier Interests plus the Class 89-RL REMIC Certificates. The balance of the Cash Flow Distribution Amount (the "Lower Tier Regular Distribution Amount") will be distributed as principal of the Lower Tier Interests held by the Trust.

The principal distribution on the REMIC Certificates, other than the Class 89-RL REMIC Certificates, on each Distribution Date (the "Principal Distribution Amount") will be in an amount equal to the sum of (i) the Lower Tier Regular Distribution Amount and (ii) any interest accrued and added on such Distribution Date to the principal amounts of the Accrual Certificates.

The Class 89-A, Class 89-B, Class 89-X, Class 89-C, Class 89-D, Class 89-E, Class 89-G, Class 89-H, Class 89-J, Class 89-K, Class 89-L and Class 89-R REMIC Certificates are "Planned Principal REMIC Certificates" and the amount necessary to reduce the outstanding principal balances of the Planned Principal REMIC Certificates to their respective Planned Principal Balances on any Distribution Date is referred to herein as the "Planned Principal Amount."

On each Distribution Date, the Principal Distribution Amount will be applied to the distribution of principal of the Classes of REMIC Certificates in the following order of priority:

> (i) to the Classes of Planned Principal REMIC Certificates, in the following order and in the proportions set forth below, in an amount up to the amount necessary to reduce their outstanding principal balances to their respective Planned Principal Balances as set forth in the table beginning on page S-16 for such Distribution Date (which amount will be zero, except in the case of the Class 89-L and Class 89-R REMIC Certificates, until the Distribution Date in June 1992):

	Allocated to	
	Class listed in preceding Column	**Class 89-L**
Class 89-R	99.997507370%	0.002492630%
Class 89-A	99.950000000%	0.050000000%
Class 89-B	99.950000000%	0.050000000%
Class 89-X	100%	
Class 89-C	100%	
Class 89-D	100%	
Class 89-E	100%	
Class 89-G	99.925018745%	0.074981255%
Class 89-H	99.925018745%	0.074981255%
Class 89-J	99.900049975%	0.099950025%
Class 89-K	99.700748129%	0.299251871%

> (ii) on each and every Distribution Date, beginning on the Distribution Date, if any, for which the Cash Flow Distribution Amount is greater than the related MBS Payment Amount (as defined below), to the Class 89-Y REMIC Certificates (the "Class 89-Y Priority Amount"), until the principal balance thereof has been reduced to zero;

(iii) to the Class 89-M REMIC Certificates, in an amount up to the amount necessary to reduce their outstanding principal balance to their Targeted Principal Balance (the "Targeted Principal Amount") as set forth in the table beginning on Page 289 for such Distribution Date;

(iv) concurrently, to the Class 89-F, Class 89-S and Class 89-N REMIC Certificates, in the proportions of 22.2227637126%, 27.7784546407% and 49.9987816467%, respectively, until the principal balance of the Class 89-N REMIC Certificates has been reduced to zero;

(v) concurrently, to the Class 89-F, Class 89-S and Class 89-O REMIC Certificates, in the proportions of 22.2227637126%, 27.7784546407% and 49.9987816467%, respectively, until the principal balances thereof have been reduced to zero;

(vi) to the Class 89-P REMIC Certificates, until the principal balance thereof has been reduced to zero;

(vii) if the Class 89-Y REMIC Certificates are then outstanding, concurrently, to the Class 89-Y and Class 89-Z REMIC Certificates, in proportion to their original principal balances (or approximately 50.6% and 49.4%, respectively), until the principal balance of the Class 89-Y REMIC Certificates has been reduced to zero;

(viii) if the Class 89-Z REMIC Certificates are then outstanding, to the Class 89-Z REMIC Certificates, until the principal balance thereof has been reduced to zero;

(ix) to the Class 89-M REMIC Certificates, without regard to their Targeted Principal Balance and until the principal balance thereof has been reduced to zero; and

(x) to the Planned Principal REMIC Certificates, in the order and in the proportions set forth in clause (i) above, without regard to their respective Planned Principal Balances and until their respective principal balances have been reduced to zero.

Because the timing and amount of distributions of principal of the REMIC Certificates will depend on the rate of principal payments (including prepayments) of the Mortgage Loans underlying the MBS Certificates, there can be no assurance as to the timing of distributions of principal of the REMIC Certificates.

The MBS Payment Amount will equal the product of the corresponding MBS percentage on the MBS Percentage Schedule (as described below) for each Distribution Date multiplied by the aggregate unpaid principal amount of the MBS Certificates (the "MBS Balance") immediately preceding such Distribution Date. An MBS Balance Schedule will be calculated by Fannie Mae based upon the actual characteristics of the MBS Certificates delivered to the Trust (which characteristics will vary from the characteristics assumed herein). Such MBS Balance Schedule will reflect the MBS Balance for each Distribution Date assuming that the Mortgage Loans underlying the MBS Certificates prepay at a constant rate of approximately 169% PSA and that all of the Mortgage Loans underlying each Pool have the same interest rate and remaining term as the WAC (or current WAC, if available) and Adjusted WAM (or current WAM, if available) of the respective Pool. The MBS Percentage Schedule will represent the percentage decrease from one Distribution Date to the next in the MBS Balance Schedule. Consequently, at prepayment levels higher than approximately 169% PSA, the Cash Flow Distribution Amount for each Distribution Date will be greater than the related MBS Payment Amount. The determination by Fannie Mae of the MBS Percentage Schedule will be final and binding and will be included in the Final Data Statement referred to herein under "The MBS Certificates—General." The MBS Balance Schedule will not be included in the Final Data Statement.

PLANNED AND TARGETED PRINCIPAL BALANCES

Distribution Date	Class 89-R Planned Principal Balance	Class 89-A Planned Principal Balance	Class 89-B Planned Principal Balance	Class 89-X Planned Principal Balance	Class 89-C Planned Principal Balance
Initial Balance	$10,516,000.00	$37,101,000.00	$31,474,000.00	$18,984,000.00	$40,000,000.00
August 1990	9,656,730.88	37,101,000.00	31,474,000.00	19,134,290.00	40,000,000.00
September 1990	8,718,585.84	37,101,000.00	31,474,000.00	19,285,769.80	40,000,000.00
October 1990	7,701,706.87	37,101,000.00	31,474,000.00	19,438,448.81	40,000,000.00
November 1990	6,606,271.43	37,101,000.00	31,474,000.00	19,592,336.53	40,000,000.00
December 1990	5,432,492.33	37,101,000.00	31,474,000.00	19,747,442.52	40,000,000.00
January 1991	4,180,617.75	37,101,000.00	31,474,000.00	19,903,776.44	40,000,000.00
February 1991	2,850,931.08	37,101,000.00	31,474,000.00	20,061,348.01	40,000,000.00
March 1991	1,443,750.87	37,101,000.00	31,474,000.00	20,220,167.01	40,000,000.00
April 1991	0.00	37,101,000.00	31,474,000.00	20,380,243.33	40,000,000.00
May 1991	0.00	37,101,000.00	31,474,000.00	20,541,586.93	40,000,000.00
June 1991	0.00	37,101,000.00	31,474,000.00	20,704,207.82	40,000,000.00
July 1991	0.00	37,101,000.00	31,474,000.00	20,868,116.14	40,000,000.00
August 1991	0.00	37,101,000.00	31,474,000.00	21,033,322.06	40,000,000.00
September 199	0.00	37,101,000.00	31,474,000.00	21,199,835.86	40,000,000.00
October 1991.	0.00	37,101,000.00	31,474,000.00	21,367,667.89	40,000,000.00
November 1991	0.00	37,101,000.00	31,474,000.00	21,536,828.59	40,000,000.00
December 1991	0.00	37,101,000.00	31,474,000.00	21,707,328.49	40,000,000.00
January 1992	0.00	37,101,000.00	31,474,000.00	21,879,178.17	40,000,000.00
February 1992	0.00	37,101,000.00	31,474,000.00	22,052,388.33	40,000,000.00
March]992	0.00	37,101,000.00	31,474,000.00	22,226,969.74	40,000,000.00
April 1992	0.00	37,101,000.00	31,474,000.00	22,402,933.26	40,000,000.00
May 1992	0.00	37,101,000.00	31,474,000.00	22,580,289.80	40,000,000.00
June 1992	0.00	34,594,057.88	31,474,000.00	22,759,050.43	40,000,000.00
July 1992.	0.00	32,019,331.02	31,474,000.00	22,939,226.25	40,000,000.00
August 1992	0.00	29,377,691.25	31,474,000.00	23,120,828.45	40,000,000.00
September 1992	0.00	26,670,038.96	31,474,000.00	23,303,868.35	40,000,000.00
October 1992	0.00	23,969,949.25	31,474,000.00	23,488,357.30	40,000,000.00
November 1992	0.00	21,277,352.18	31,474,000.00	23,674,306.80	40,000,000.00
December 1992	0.00	18,592,177.87	31,474,000.00	23,861,728.40	40,000,000.00
January 1993	0.00	15,914,356.46	31,474,000.00	24,050,633.75	40,000,000.00
February 1993	0.00	13,243,818.18	31,474,000.00	24,241,034.60	40,000,000.00
March 1993	0.00	10,580,493.32	31,474,000.00	24,432,942.79	40,000,000.00
April 1993	0.00	7,924,312.18	31,474,000.00	24,626,370.25	40,000,000.00
May 1993	0.00	5,275,205.16	31,474,000.00	24,821,329.01	40,000,000.00
June 1993	0.00	2,633,102.66	31,474,000.00	25,017,831.20	40,000,000.00
July 1993	0.00	0.00	31,471,935.16	25,215,889.03	40,000,000.00
August 1993	0.00	0.00	28,843,633.17	25,415,514.82	40,000,000.00
September 1993	0.00	0.00	26,222,127.22	25,616,720.98	40,000,000.00
October 1993	0.00	0.00	23,607,347.92	25,819,520.02	40,000,000.00
November 1993	0.00	0.00	20,999,225.87	26,023,924.55	40,000,000.00
December 1993	0.00	0.00	18,397,691.74	26,229,947.29	40,000,000.00
January 1994	0.00	0.00	15,802,676.20	26,437,601.04	40,000,000.00
February 1994	0.00	0.00	13,214,109.96	26,646,898.71	40,000,000.00
March 1994	0.00	0.00	10,631,923.77	26,857,853.33	40,000,000.00
April 1994	0.00	0.00	8,056,048.37	27,070,478.00	40,000,000.00
May 1994	.00	0.00	5,486,414.56	27,284,785.95	40,000,000.00
June 1994	0.00	0.00	2,922,953.12	27,500,790.51	40,000,000.00
July 1994	0.00	0.00	365,594.88	27,718,505.10	40,000,000.00
August 1994	0.00	0.00	0.00	25,751,120.52	40,000,000.00
September 1994	0.00	0.00	0.00	23,425,663.23	40,000,000.00
October 1994	0.00	0.00	0.00	21,107,855.58	40,000,000.00
November 1994	0.00	0.00	0.00	18,797,642.23	40,000,000.00
December 1994	0.00	0.00	0.00	16,494,967.99	40,000,000.00

Distribution Date	Class 89-D Planned Principal Balance	Class 89-E Planned Principal Balance	Class 89-G Planned Principal Balance	Class 89-H Planned Principal Balance
Initial Balance	$40,000,000.00	$16,168,000.00	$22,028,000.00	$15,856,000.00
August 1990	40,000,000.00	16,168,000.00	22,028,000.00	15,856,000.00
September 1990	40,000,000.00	16,168,000.00	22,028,000.00	15,856,000.00
October 1990	40,000,000.00	16,168,000.00	22,028,000.00	15,856,000.00
November 1990	40,000,000.00	16,168,000.00	22,028,000.00	15,856,000.00
December 1990	40,000,000.00	16,168,000.00	22,028,000.00	15,856,000.00
January 1991	40,000,000.00	16,168,000.00	22,028,000.00	15,856,000.00
February 1991	40,000,000.00	16,168,000.00	22,028,000.00	15,856,000.00
March 1991	40,000,000.00	16,168,000.00	22,028,000.00	15,856,000.00
April 1991	40,000,000.00	16,168,000.00	22,028,000.00	15,856,000.00
May 1991	40,000,000.00	16,168,000.00	22,028,000.00	15,856,000.00
June 1991	40,000,000.00	16,168,000.00	22,028,000.00	15,856,000.00
July 1991	40,000,000.00	16,168,000.00	22,028,000.00	15,856,000.00
August 1991	40,000,000.00	16,168,000.00	22,028,000.00	15,856,000.00
September 1991	40,000,000.00	16,168,000.00	22,028,000.00	15,856,000.00
October 1991	40,000,000.00	16,168,000.00	22,028,000.00	15,856,000.00
November 1991	40,000,000.00	16,168,000.00	22,028,000.00	15,856,000.00
December 1991	40,000,000.00	16,168,000.00	22,028,000.00	15,856,000.00
January 1992	40,000,000.00	16,168,000.00	22,028,000.00	15,856,000.00
February 1992	40,000,000.00	16,168,000.00	22,028,000.00	15,856,000.00
March 1992	40,000,000.00	16,168,000.00	22,028,000.00	15,856,000.00
April 8 1992	40,000,000.00	16,168,000.00	22,028,000.00	15,856,000.00
May 1992	40,000,000.00	16,168,000.00	22,028,000.00	15,856,000.00
June 1992	40,000,000.00	16,168,000.00	22,028,000.00	15,856,000.00
July 1992	40,000,000.00	16,168,000.00	22,028,000.00	15,856,000.00
August 1992	40,000,000.00	16,168,000.00	22,028,000.00	15,856,000.00
September 1992	40,000,000.00	16,168,000.00	22,028,000.00	15,856,000.00
October 1992	40,000,000.00	16,168,000.00	22,028,000.00	15,856,000.00
November 1992	40,000,000.00	16,168,000.00	22,028,000.00	15,856,000.00
December 1992	40,000,000.00	16,168,000.00	22,028,000.00	15,856,000.00
January 1993	40,000,000.00	16,168,000.00	22,028,000.00	15,856,000.00
February 1993	40,000,000.00	16,168,000.00	22,028,000.00	15,856,000.00
March 1993	40,000,000.00	16,168,000.00	22,028,000.00	15,856,000.00
April 1993	40,000,000.00	16,168,000.00	22,028,000.00	15,856,000.00
May 1993	40,000,000.00	16,168,000.00	22,028,000.00	15,856,000.00
June 1993	40,000,000.00	16,168,000.00	22,028,000.00	15,856,000.00
July 1993	40,000,000.00	16,168,000.00	22,028,000.00	15,856,000.00
August 1993	40,000,000.00	16,168,000.00	22,028,000.00	15,856,000.00
September 1993	40,000,000.00	16,168,000.00	22,028,000.00	15,856,000.00
October 1993	40,000,000.00	16,168,000.00	22,028,000.00	15,856,000.00
November 1993	40,000,000.00	16,168,000.00	22,028,000.00	15,856,000.00
December 1993	40,000,000.00	16,168,000.00	22,028,000.00	15,856,000.00
January 1994	40,000,000.00	16,168,000.00	22,028,000.00	15,856,000.00
February 1994	40,000,000.00	16,168,000.00	22,028,000.00	15,856,000.00
March 1994	40,000,000.00	16,168,000.00	22,028,000.00	15,856,000.00
April 1994	40,000,000.00	16,168,000.00	22,028,000.00	15,856,000.00
May 1994	40,000,000.00	16,168,000.00	22,028,000.00	15,856,000.00
June 1994	40,000,000.00	16,168,000.00	22,028,000.00	15,856,000.00
July 1994	40,000,000.00	16,168,000.00	22,028,000.00	15,856,000.00
August 1994	40,000,000.00	16,168,000.00	22,028,000.00	15,856,000.00
September 1994	40,000,000.00	16,168,000.00	22,028,000.00	15,856,000.00
October 1994	40,000,000.00	16,168,000.00	22,028,000.00	15,856,000.00
November 1994	40,000,000.00	16,168,000.00	22,028,000.00	15,856,000.00
December 1994	40,000,000.00	16,168,000.00	22,028,000.00	15,856,000.00

Distribution Date	Class 89-J Planned Principal Balance	Class 89-K Planned Principal Balance	Class 89-L Planned Principal Balance	Class 89-M Targeted Principal Balance
Initial Balance	$35,884,000.00	$36,683,000.00	$209,000.00	$88,649,000.00
August 1990	35,884,000.00	36,683,000.00	208,978.58	88,433,307.10
September 1990	35,884,000.00	36,683,000.00	208,955.20	88,174,628.99
October 1990	35,884,000.00	36,683,000.00	208,929.85	87,873,135.24
November 1990	35,884,000.00	36,683,000.00	208,902.54	87,529,051.74
December 1990	35,884,000.00	36,683,000.00	208,873.28	87,142,660.69
January 1991	35,884,000.00	36,683,000.00	208,842.08	86,714,300.47
February 1991	35,884,000.00	36,683,000.00	208,808.93	86,244,365.46
March 1991	35,884,000.00	36,683,000.00	208,773.86	85,733,305.69
April 1991	35,884,000.00	36,683,000.00	208,737.87	85,153,938.79
May 1991	35,884,000.00	36,683,000.00	208,737.87	83,496,802.48
June 1991	35,884,000.00	36,683,000.00	208,737.87	81,748,128.50
July 1991	35,884,000.00	36,683,000.00	208,737.87	79,908,896.82
August 1991	35,884,000.00	36,683,000.00	208,737.87	77,980,163.49
September 1991	35,884,000.00	36,683,000.00	208,737.87	75,963,059.54
October 1991	35,884,000.00	36,683,000.00	208,737.87	73,858,789.83
November 1991	35,884,000.00	36,683,000.00	208,737.87	71,668,631.79
December 1991	35,884,000.00	36,683,000.00	208,737.87	69,393,934.01
January 1992	35,884,000.00	36,683,000.00	208,737.87	67,036,114.78
February 1992	35,884,000.00	36,683,000.00	208,737.87	64,596,660.47
March 1992	35,884,000.00	36,683,000.00	208,737.87	62,077,123.88
April 8 1992	35,884,000.00	36,683,000.00	208,737.87	59,479,122.40
May 1992	35,884,000.00	36,683,000.00	208,737.87	56,804,336.19
June 1992	35,884,000.00	36,683,000.00	207,483.77	55,766,253.12
July 1992	35,884,000.00	36,683,000.00	206,195.76	54,701,209.41
August 1992	35,884,000.00	36,683,000.00	204,874.28	53,610,465.91
September 1992	35,884,000.00	36,683,000.00	203,519.78	52,495,318.28
October 1992	35,884,000.00	36,683,000.00	202,169.06	51,397,114.29
November 1992	35,884,000.00	36,683,000.00	200,822.09	50,315,682.15
December 1992	35,884,000.00	36,683,000.00	199,478.83	49,250,851.69
January 1993	35,884,000.00	36,683,000.00	198,139.25	48,202,454.38
February 1993	35,884,000.00	36,683,000.00	196,803.31	47,170,323.27
March 1993	35,884,000.00	36,683,000.00	195,470.98	46,154,293.01
April 1993	35,884,000.00	36,683,000.00	194,142.23	45,154,199.83
May 1993	35,884,000.00	36,683,000.00	192,817.01	44,169,881.52
June 1993	35,884,000.00	36,683,000.00	191,495.30	43,201,177.41
July 1993	35,884,000.00	36,683,000.00	190,177.06	42,247,928.37
August 1993	35,884,000.00	36,683,000.00	188,862.25	41,309,976.79
September 1993	35,884,000.00	36,683,000.00	187,550.84	40,387,166.56
October 1993	35,884,000.00	36,683,000.00	186,242,79	39,479,343.08
November 1993	35,884,000.00	36,683,000.00	184,938.08	38,586,353.19
December 1993	35,884,000.00	36,683,000.00	183,636.66	37,708,045.25
January 1994	35,884,000.00	36,683,000.00	182,338.51	36,844,269.02
February 1994	35,884,000.00	36,683,000.00	181,043.58	35,994,875.74
March 1994	35,884,000.00	36,683,000.00	179,751.84	35,159,718.04
April 1994	35,884,000.00	36,683,000.00	178,463.26	34,338,650.01
May 1994	35,884,000.00	36,683,000.00	177,177.80	33,531,527.09
June 1994	35,884,000.00	36,683,000.00	175,895.42	32,738,206.14
July 1994	35,884,000.00	36,683,000.00	174,616.11	31,958,545.39
August 1994	35,884,000.00	36,683,000.00	174,433.22	31,192,404.42
September 1994	35,884,000.00	36,683,000.00	174,433.22	30,439,644.18
October 1994	35,884,000.00	36,683,000.00	174,433.22	29,700,126.96
November 1994	35,884,000.00	36,683,000.00	174,433.22	28,973,716.35
December 1994	35,884,000.00	36,683,000.00	174,433.22	28,260,277.27

Distribution Date	Class 89-R Planned Principal Balance	Class 89-A Planned Principal Balance	Class 89-B Planned Principal Balance	Class 89-X Planned Principal Balance	Class 89-C Planned Principal Balance
January 1995	$0.00	$0.00	$0.00	$14,199,777.77	$40,000,000.00
February 1995	0.00	0.00	0.00	11,912,016.57	40,000,000.00
March 1995	0.00	0.00	0.00	9,631,629.53	40,000,000.00
April 1995	0.00	0.00	0.00	7,358,561.88	40,000,000.00
May 1995	0.00	0.00	0.00	5,092,758.96	40,000,000.00
June 1995	0.00	0.00	0.00	2,834,166.21	40,000,000.00
July 1995	0.00	0.00	0.00	582,729.17	40,000,000.00
August 1995	0.00	0.00	0.00	0.00	38,338,393.49
September 1995	0.00	0.00	0.00	0.00	36,101,104.92
October 1995	0.00	0.00	0.00	0.00	33,870,809.30
November 1995	0.00	0.00	0.00	0.00	31,647,452.57
December 1995	0.00	0.00	0.00	0.00	29,430,980.75
January 1996	0.00	0.00	0.00	0.00	27,221,339.99
February 1996	0.00	0.00	0.00	0.00	25,018,476.48
March 1996	0.00	0.00	0.00	0.00	22,822,336.55
April 1996	0.00	0.00	0.00	0.00	20,632,866.58
May 1996	0.00	0.00	0.00	0.00	18,450,013.06
June 1996	0.00	0.00	0.00	0.00	16,273,722.55
July 1996	0.00	0.00	0.00	0.00	14,103,941.70
August 1996	0.00	0.00	0.00	0.00	11,940,617.25
September 1996	0.00	0.00	0.00	0.00	9,783,696.00
October 1996	0.00	0.00	0.00	0.00	7,633,124.85
November 1996	0.00	0.00	0.00	0.00	5,488,850.75
December 1996	0.00	0.00	0.00	0.00	3,350,820.76
January 1997	0.00	0.00	0.00	0.00	1,218,981.98
February 1997	0.00	0.00	0.00	0.00	0.00
March 1997	0.00	0.00	0.00	0.00	0.00
April 1997	0.00	0.00	0.00	0.00	0.00
May 1997	0.00	0.00	0.00	0.00	0.00
June 1997	0.00	0.00	0.00	0.00	0.00
July 1997	0.00	0.00	0.00	0.00	0.00
August 1997	0.00	0.00	0.00	0.00	0.00
September 1997	0.00	0.00	0.00	0.00	0.00
October 1997	0.00	0.00	0.00	0.00	0.00
November 1997	0.00	0.00	0.00	0.00	0.00
December 1997	0.00	0.00	0.00	0.00	0.00
January 1998	0.00	0.00	0.00	0.00	0.00
February 1998	0.00	0.00	0.00	0.00	0.00
March 1998	0.00	0.00	0.00	0.00	0.00
April 1998	0.00	0.00	0.00	0.00	0.00
May 1998	0.00	0.00	0.00	0.00	0.00
June 1998	0.00	0.00	0.00	0.00	0.00
July 1998	0.00	0.00	0.00	0.00	0.00
August 1998	0.00	0.00	0.00	0.00	0.00
September 1998	0.00	0.00	0.00	0.00	0.00
October 1998	0.00	0.00	0.00	0.00	0.00
November 1998	0.00	0.00	0.00	0.00	0.00
December 1998	0.00	0.00	0.00	0.00	0.00
January 1999	0.00	0.00	0.00	0.00	0.00
February 1999	0.00	0.00	0.00	0.00	0.00
March 1999	0.00	0.00	0.00	0.00	0.00
April 1999	0.00	0.00	0.00	0.00	0.00
May 1999	0.00	0.00	0.00	0.00	0.00
June 1999 and thereafter	0.00	0.00	0.00	0.00	0.00

Distribution Date	Class 89-D Planned Principal Balance	Class 89-E Planned Principal Balance	Class 89-G Planned Principal Balance	Class 89-H Planned Principal Balance
January 1995	$40,000,000.00	$16,168,000.00	$22,028,000.00	$15,856,000.00
February 1995	40,000,000.00	16,168,000.00	22,028,000.00	15,856,000.00
March 1995	40,000,000.00	16,168,000.00	22,028,000.00	15,856,000.00
April 1995	40,000,000.00	16,168,000.00	22,028,000.00	15,856,000.00
May 1995	40,000,000.00	16,168,000.00	22,028,000.00	15,856,000.00
June 1995	40,000,000.00	16,168,000.00	22,028,000.00	15,856,000.00
July 1995	40,000,000.00	16,168,000.00	22,028,000.00	15,856,000.00
August 1995	40,000,000.00	16,168,000.00	22,028,000.00	15,856,000.00
September 1995	40,000,000.00	16,168,000.00	22,028,000.00	15,856,000.00
October 1995	40,000,000.00	16,168,000.00	22,028,000.00	15,856,000.00
November 1995	40,000,000.00	16,168,000.00	22,028,000.00	15,856,000.00
December 1995	40,000,000.00	16,168,000.00	22,028,000.00	15,856,000.00
January 1996	40,000,000.00	16,168,000.00	22,028,000.00	15,856,000.00
February 1996	40,000,000.00	16,168,000.00	22,028,000.00	15,856,000.00
March 1996	40,000,000.00	16,168,000.00	22,028,000.00	15,856,000.00
April 1996	40,000,000.00	16,168,000.00	22,028,000.00	15,856,000.00
May 1996	40,000,000.00	16,168,000.00	22,028,000.00	15,856,000.00
June 1996	40,000,000.00	16,168,000.00	22,028,000.00	15,856,000.00
July 1996	40,000,000.00	16,168,000.00	22,028,000.00	15,856,000.00
August 1996	40,000,000.00	16,168,000.00	22,028,000.00	15,856,000.00
September 1996	40,000,000.00	16,168,000.00	22,028,000.00	15,856,000.00
October 1996	40,000,000.00	16,168,000.00	22,028,000.00	15,856,000.00
November 1996	40,000,000.00	16,168,000.00	22,028,000.00	15,856,000.00
December 1996	40,000,000.00	16,168,000.00	22,028,000.00	15,856,000.00
January 1997	40,000,000.00	16,168,000.00	22,028,000.00	15,856,000.00
February 1997	39,093,281.60	16,168,000.00	22,028,000.00	15,856,000.00
March 1997	36,973,666.89	16,168,000.00	22,028,000.00	15,856,000.00
April 1997	34,860,085.16	16,168,000.00	22,028,000.00	15,856,000.00
May 1997	32,752,483.80	16,168,000.00	22,028,000.00	15,856,000.00
June 1997	30,650,810.29	16,168,000.00	22,028,000.00	15,856,000.00
July 1997	28,555,012.13	16,168,000.00	22,028,000.00	15,856,000.00
August 1997	26,465,036.91	16,168,000.00	22,028,000.00	15,856,000.00
September 1997	24,380,832.28	16,168,000.00	22,028,000.00	15,856,000.00
October 1997	22,302,345.94	16,168,000.00	22,028,000.00	15,856,000.00
November 1997	20,229,525.65	16,168,000.00	22,028,000.00	15,856,000.00
December 1997	18,162,319.23	16,168,000.00	22,028,000.00	15,856,000.00
January 1998	16,100,674.54	16,168,000.00	22,028,000.00	15,856,000.00
February 1998	14,044,539.51	16,168,000.00	22,028,000.00	15,856,000.00
March 1998	11,993,862.11	16,168,000.00	22,028,000.00	15,856,000.00
April 1998	9,948,590.36	16,168,000.00	22,028,000.00	15,856,000.00
May 1998	7,908,672.33	16,168,000.00	22,028,000.00	15,856,000.00
June 1998	5,874,056.14	16,168,000.00	22,028,000.00	15,856,000.00
July 1998	3,844,689.94	16,168,000.00	22,028,000.00	15,856,000.00
August 1998	1,820,521.94	16,168,000.00	22,028,000.00	15,856,000.00
September 1998	0.00	15,969,S00.37	22,028,000.00	15,856,000.00
October 1998	0.00	13,955,S73.51	22,028,000.00	15,856,000.00
November 1998	0.00	11,962,322.48	22,028,000.00	15,856,000.00
December 1998	0.00	9,999,692.02	22,028,000.00	15,856,000.00
January 1999	0.00	8,067,219.56	22,028,000.00	15,856,000.00
February 1999	0.00	6,164,449.45	22,028,000.00	15,856,000.00
March 1999	0.00	4,290,932.87	22,028,000.00	15,856,000.00
April 1999.	0.00	2,446,227.75	22,028,000.00	15,856,000.00
May 1999	0.00	629,898.63	22,028,000.00	15,856,000.00
June 1999 and thereafter	0.00	0.00	20,870,385.26	15,856,000.00
July 1999			19,110.848.17	15,856,000.00
August 1999			17,378,399.22	15,856,000.00

Distribution Date	Class 89-J Planned Principal Balance	Class 89-K Planned Principal Balance	Class89-L Planned Principal Balance	Class 89-M Targeted Principal Balance
January 1995	$35,884,000.00	$36,683,000.00	$174,433.22	$27,559,675.96
February 1995	35,884,000.00	36,683,000.00	174,433.22	26,871,779.93
March 1995	35,884,000.00	36,683,000.00	174,433.22	26,196,457.96
April 1995	35,884,000.00	36,683,000.00	174,433.22	25,533,580.13
May 1995	35,884,000.00	36,683,000.00	174,433.22	24,883,017.76
June 1995	35,884,000.00	36,683,000.00	174,433.22	24,244,643.40
July 1995	35,884,000.00	36,683,000.00	174,433.22	23,618,330.86
August 1995	35,884,000.00	36,683,000.00	174,433.22	23,003,955.15
September 1995	35,884,000.00	36,683,000.00	174,433.22	22,401,392.51
October 1995	35,884,000.00	36,683,000.00	174,433.22	21,810,520.37
November 1995	35,884,000.00	36,683,000.00	174,433.22	21,231,217.36
December 1995	35,884,000.00	36,683,000.00	174,433.22	20,663,363.26
January 1996	35,884,000.00	36,683,000.00	174,433.22	20,106,839.07
February 1996	35,884,000.00	36,683,000.00	174,433.22	19,561,526.89
March 1996	35,884,000.00	36,683,000.00	174,433.22	19,027,310.02
April 1996	35,884,000.00	36,683,000.00	174,433.22	18,504,072.85
May 1996	35,884,000.00	36,683,000.00	174,433.22	17,991,700.93
June 1996	35,884,000.00	36,683,000.00	174,433.22	17,490,080.92
July 1996	35,884,000.00	36,683,000.00	174,433.22	16,999,100.57
August 1996	35,884,000.00	36,683,000.00	174,433.22	16,518,648.75
September 1996	35,884,000.00	36,683,000.00	174,433.22	16,048,615.40
October 1996	35,884,000.00	36,683,000.00	174,433.22	15,588,891.53
November 1996	35,884,000.00	36,683,000.00	174,433.22	15,139,369.25
December 1996	35,884,000.00	36,683,000.00	174,433.22	14,699,941.68
January 1997	35,884,000.00	36,683,000.00	174,433.22	14,270,503.04
February 1997	35,884,000.00	36,683,000.00	174,433.22	13,850,948.54
March 1997	35,884,000.00	36,683,000.00	174,433.22	13,441,174.45
April 1997	35,884,000.00	36,683,000.00	174,433.22	13,041,078.04
May 1997	35,884,000.00	36,683,000.00	174,433.22	12,650,557.62
June 1997	35,884,000.00	36,683,000.00	174,433.22	12,269,512.46
July 1997	35,884,000.00	36,683,000.00	174,433.22	11,897,842.85
August 1997	35,884,000.00	36,683,000.00	174,433.22	11,535,450.05
September 1997	35,884,000.00	36,683,000.00	174,433.22	11,182,236.31
October 1997	35,884,000.00	36,683,000.00	174,433.22	10,838,104.83
November 1997	35,884,000.00	36,683,000.00	174,433.22	10,502,959.77
December 1997	35,884,000.00	36,683,000.00	174,433.22	10,176,706.24
January 1998	35,884,000.00	36,683,000.00	174,433.22	9,859,250.29
February 1998	35,884,000.00	36,683,000.00	174,433.22	9,550,498.89
March 1998	35,884,000.00	36,683,000.00	174,433.22	9,250,359.95
April 1998	35,884,000.00	36,683,000.00	174,433.22	8,958,742.29
May 1998	35,884,000.00	36,683,000.00	174,433.22	8,675,555.62
June 1998	35,884,000.00	36,683,000.00	174,433.22	8,400,710.56
July 1998	35,884,000.00	36,683,000.00	174,433.22	8,134,118.61
August 1998	35,884,000.00	36,683,000.00	174,433.22	7,875,692.18
September 1998	35,884,000.00	36,683,000.00	174,433.22	7,625,344.51
October 1998	35,884,000.00	36,683,000.00	174,433.22	7,382,989.74
November 1998	35,884,000.00	36,683,000.00	174,433.22	7,137,874.07
December 1998	35,884,000.00	36,683,000.00	174,433.22	6,883,091.18
January 1999	35,884,000.00	36,683,000.00	174,433.22	6,618,838.21
February 1999	35,884,000.00	36,683,000.00	174,433.22	6,345,308.44
March 1999	35,884,000.00	36,683,000.00	174,433.22	6,062,691.30
April 1999	35,884,000.00	36,683,000.00	174,433.22	5,771,172.51
May 1999	35,884,000.00	36,683,000.00	174,433.22	5,470,934.05
June 1999	35,884,000.00	36,683,000.00	173,564.57	5,162,154.28
July 1999	35,884,000.00	36,683,000.00	172,244.26	4,845,008.00
August 1999	35,884,000.00	36,683,000.00	170,944.27	4,519,666.46

Distribution Date	Class 89-G Planned Principal Balance	Class 89-H Planned Principal Balance	Class 89-J Planned Principal Balance
September 1999	$15,672,628.83	$15,856,000.00	$35,884,000.00
October 1999	13,993,133.55	15,856,000.00	35,884,000.00
November 1999	12,339,515.98	15,856,000.00	35,884,000.00
December 1999	10,711,384.71	15,856,000.00	35,884,000.00
January 2000	9,108,354.17	15,856,000.00	35,884,000.00
February 2000	7,530,044.59	15,856,000.00	35,884,000.00
March 2000	5,976,081.92	15,856,000.00	35,884,000.00
April 2000	4,446,097.69	15,856,000.00	35,884,000.00
May 2000	2,939,728.99	15,856,000.00	35,884,000.00
June 2000	1,456,618.33	15,856,000.00	35,884,000.00
July 2000	0.00	15,852,413.61	35,884,000.00
August 2000	0.00	14,414,768.01	35,884,000.00
September 2000	0.00	12,999,339.91	35,884,000.00
October 2000	0.00	11,605,792.83	35,884,000.00
November 2000	0.00	10,233,795.32	35,884,000.00
December 2000	0.00	8,883,020.94	35,884,000.00
January 2001	0.00	7,553,148.12	35,884,000.00
February 2001	0.00	6,243,860.15	35,884,000.00
March 2001	0.00	4,954,845.05	35,884,000.00
April 2001	0.00	3,685,795.54	35,884,000.00
May 2001	0.00	2,436,408.95	35,884,000.00
June 2001	0.00	1,206,387.15	35,884,000.00
July 2001	0.00	0.00	35,879,437.66
August 2001	0.00	0.00	34,687,566.84
September 2001	0.00	0.00	33,514,188.43
October 2001	0.00	0.00	32,359,021.91
November 2001	0.00	0.00	31,221,790.94
December 2001	0.00	0.00	30,102,223.36
January 2002	0.00	0.00	29,000,051.10
February 2002	0.00	0.00	27,915,010.10
March 2002	0.00	0.00	26,846,840.29
April 2002	0.00	0.00	25,795,285.48
May 2002	0.00	0.00	24,760,093.36
June 2002	0.00	0.00	23,741,015.41
July 2002	0.00	0.00	22,737,806.83
August 2002	0.00	0.00	21,750,226.51
September 2002	0.00	0.00	20,778,036.96
October 2002	0.00	0.00	19,821,004.27
November 2002	0.00	0.00	18,878,898.04
December 2002	0.00	0.00	17,951,491.35
January 2003	0.00	0.00	17,038,560.66
February 2003	0.00	0.00	16,139,885.83
March 2003	0.00	0.00	15,255,250.01
April 2003	0.00	0.00	14,384,439.62
May 2003	0.00	0.00	13,527,244.27
June 2003	0.00	0.00	12,683,456.78
July 2003	0.00	0.00	11,852,873.05
August 2003	0.00	0.00	11,035,292.07
September 2003	0.00	0.00	10,230,515.84
October 2003	0.00	0.00	9,438,349.36
November 2003	0.00	0.00	8,658,600.54
December 2003	0.00	0.00	7,891,080.21
January 2004	0.00	0.00	7,135,602.02
February 2004	0.00	0.00	6,391,982.44
March 2004	0.00	0.00	5,660,040.71
April 2004	0.00	0.00	4,939,598.77

Distribution Date	Class 89-K Planned Principal Balance	Class 89-L Planned Principal Balance	Class 89-M Targeted Principal Balance
September 1999	$36,683,000.00	$169,664.30	$4,186,297.47
October 1999	36,683,000.00	168,404.05	3,845,065.40
November 1999	36,683,000.00	167,163.22	3,496,131.30
December 1999	36,683,000.00	165,941.51	3,139,652.90
January 2000	36,683,000.00	164,738.63	2,775,784.67
February 2000	36,683,000.00	163,554.31	2,404,677.90
March 2000	36,683,000.00	162,388.26	2,026,480.75
April 2000	36,683,000.00	161,240.19	1,641,338.24
May 2000	36,683,000.00	160,109.85	1,249,392.39
June 2000	36,683,000.00	158,996.96	850,782.19
July 2000	36,683,000.00	157,901.26	445,643.70
August 2000	36,683,000.00	156,822.49	34,110.07
September 2000	36,683,000.00	155,760.38	0.00
October 2000	36,683,000.00	154,714.70	0.00
November 2000	36,683,000.00	153,685.19	0.00
December 2000	36,683,000.00	152,671.60	0.00
January 2001	36,683,000.00	151,673.70	0.00
February 2001	36,683,000.00	150,691.24	0.00
March 2001	36,683,000.00	149,724.00	0.00
April 2001	36,683,000.00	148,771.73	0.00
May 2001	36,683,000.00	147,834.22	0.00
June 2001	36,683,000.00	146,911.25	0.00
July 2001	36,683,000.00	146,001.44	0.00
August 2001	36,683,000.00	144,808.97	0.00
September 2001	36,683,000.00	143,635.01	0.00
October 2001	36,683,000.00	142,479.26	0.00
November 2001	36,683,000.00	141,341.46	0.00
December 2001	36,683,000.00	140,221.33	0.00
January 2002	36,683,000.00	139,118.61	0.00
February 2002	36,683,000.00	138,033.03	0.00
March 2002	36,683,000.00	136,964.32	0.00
April 2002	36,683,000.00	135,912.24	0.00
May 2002	36,683,000.00	134,876.53	0.00
June 2002	36,683,000.00	133,856.94	0.00
July 2002	36,683,000.00	132,853.23	0.00
August 2002	36,683,000.00	131,865.16	0.00
September 2002	36,683,000.00	130,892.48	0.00
October 2002	36,683,000.00	129,934.97	0.00
November 2002	36,683,000.00	128,992.39	0.00
December 2002	36,683,000.00	128,064.52	0.00
January 2003	36,683,000.00	127,151.14	0.00
February 2003	36,683,000.00	126,252.01	0.00
March 2003	36,683,000.00	125,366.93	0.00
April 2003	36,683,000.00	124,495.69	0.00
May 2003	36,683,000.00	123,638.06	0.00
June 2003	36,683,000.00	122,793.85	0.00
July 2003	36,683,000.00	121,962.85	0.00
August 2003	36,683,000.00	121,144.86	0.00
September 2003	36,683,000.00	120,339.69	0.00
October 2003	36,683,000.00	119,547.12	0.00
November 2003	36,683,000.00	118,766.98	0.00
December 2003	36,683,000.00	117,999.08	0.00
January 2004	36,683,000.00	117,243.22	0.00
February 2004	36,683,000.00	116,499.23	0.00
March 2004	36,683,000.00	115,766.92	0.00
April 2004	36,683,000.00	115,046.12	0.00

Distribution Date	Class 89-G Planned Principal Balance	Class 89-H Planned Principal Balance	Class 89-J Planned Principal Balance	Class 89-K Planned Principal Balance	Class 89-L Planned Principal Balance	Class 89-M Targeted Principal Balance
May 2004	$0.00	$0.00	$4,230,481.27	$36,683,000.00	$114,336.65	$0.00
June 2004	0.00	0.00	3,532,515.47	36,683,000.00	113,638.33	0.00
July 2004	0.00	0.00	2,845,531.26	36,683,000.00	112,951.01	0.00
August 2004	0.00	0.00	2,169,361.07	36,683,000.00	112,274.50	0.00
September 2004	0.00	0.00	1,503,839.87	36,683,000.00	111,608.64	0.00
October 2004	0.00	0.00	848,805.10	36,683,000.00	110,953.28	0.00
November 2004	0.00	0.00	204,096.66	36,683,000.00	110,308.25	0.00
December 2004	0.00	0.00	0.00	36,253,415.61	108,814.65	0.00
January 2005	0.00	0.00	0.00	35,630,135.08	106,943.88	0.00
February 2005	0.00	0.00	0.00	35,016,695.24	105,102.64	0.00
March 2005	0.00	0.00	0.00	34,412,945.72	103,290.48	0.00
April 2005	0.00	0.00	0.00	33,818,738.42	101,506.97	0.00
May 2005	0.00	0.00	0.00	33,233,927.47	99,751.66	0.00
June 2005	0.00	0.00	0.00	32,658,369.21	98,024.12	0.00
July 2005	0.00	0.00	0.00	32,091,922.12	96,323.93	0.00
August 2005	0.00	0.00	0.00	31,534,446.84	94,650.67	0.00
September 2005	0.00	0.00	0.00	30,985,806.11	93,003.92	0.00
October 2005	0.00	0.00	0.00	30,445,864.72	91,383.29	0.00
November 2005	0.00	0.00	0.00	29,914,489.52	89,788.36	0.00
December 2005	0.00	0.00	0.00	29,391,549.35	88,218.76	0.00
January 2006	0.00	0.00	0.00	28,876,915.06	86,674.08	0.00
February 2006	0.00	0.00	0.00	28,370,459.40	85,153.95	0.00
March 2006	0.00	0.00	0.00	27,872,057.08	83,658.00	0.00
April 2006	0.00	0.00	0.00	27,381,584.70	82,185.85	0.00
May 2006	0.00	0.00	0.00	26,898,920.69	80,737.13	0.00
June 2006	0.00	0.00	0.00	26,423,945.34	79,311.49	0.00
July 2006	0.00	0.00	0.00	25,956,540.74	77,908.58	0.00
August 2006	0.00	0.00	0.00	25,496,590.77	76,528.04	0.00
September 2006	0.00	0.00	0.00	25,043,981.06	75,169.53	0.00
October 2006	0.00	0.00	0.00	24,598,598.94	73,832.71	0.00
November 2006	0.00	0.00	0.00	24,160,333.48	72,517.26	0.00
December 2006	0.00	0.00	0.00	23,729,075.40	71,222.84	0.00
January 2007	0.00	0.00	0.00	23,304,717.08	69,949.13	0.00
February 2007	0.00	0.00	0.00	22,887,152.53	68,695.80	0.00
March 2007	0.00	0.00	0.00	22,476,277.36	67,462.56	0.00
April 2007	0.00	0.00	0.00	22,071,988.73	66,249.09	0.00
May 2007	0.00	0.00	0.00	21,674,185.40	65,055.08	0.00
June 2007	0.00	0.00	0.00	21,282,767.63	63,880.24	0.00
July 2007	0.00	0.00	0.00	20,897,637.19	62,724.27	0.00
August 2007	0.00	0.00	0.00	20,518,697.34	61,586.88	0.00
September 2007	0.00	0.00	0.00	20,145,852.80	60,467.79	0.00
October 2007	0.00	0.00	0.00	19,779,009.74	59,366.71	0.00
November 2007	0.00	0.00	0.00	19,418,075.73	58,283.37	0.00
December 2007	0.00	0.00	0.00	19,062,959.76	57,217.49	0.00
January 2008	0.00	0.00	0.00	18,713,572.17	56,168.80	0.00
February 2008	0.00	0.00	0.00	18,369,824.69	55,137.04	0.00
March 2008	0.00	0.00	0.00	18,031,630.35	54,121.95	0.00
April 2008	0.00	0.00	0.00	17,698,903.51	53,123.27	0.00
May 2008	0.00	0.00	0.00	17,371,559.85	52,140.75	0.00
June 2008	0.00	0.00	0.00	17,049,516.29	51,174.14	0.00
July 2008	0.00	0.00	0.00	16,732,691.01	50,223.18	0.00
August 2008	0.00	0.00	0.00	16,421,003.47	49,287.65	0.00
September 2008	0.00	0.00	0.00	16,114,374.29	48,367.31	0.00
October2008	0.00	0.00	0.00	15,812,725.34	47,461.91	0.00
November 2008	0.00	0.00	0.00	15,515,979.64	46,571.22	0.00
December 2008	0.00	0.00	0.00	15,224,061.41	45,695.03	0.00

Distribution Date	Class 89-G Planned Principal Balance	Class 89-H Planned Principal Balance	Class 89-J Planned Principal Balance	Class 89-K Planned Principal Balance	Class 89-L Planned Principal Balance	Class 89-M Targeted Principal Balance
January 2009	$0.00	$0.00	$0.00	$14,936,895.98	$44,833.10	$0.00
February 2009	0.00	0.00	0.00	14,654,409.83	43,985.22	0.00
March 2009	0.00	0.00	0.00	14,376,530.57	43,151.17	0.00
April 2009	0.00	0.00	0.00	14,103,186.88	42,330.73	0.00
May 2009	0.00	0.00	0.00	13,834,308.53	41,523.69	0.00
June 2009	0.00	0.00	0.00	13,569,826.35	40,729.84	0.00
July 2009	0.00	0.00	0.00	13,309,672.24	39,948.99	0.00
August 2009	0.00	0.00	0.00	13,053,779.11	39,180.93	0.00
September 2009	0.00	0.00	0.00	12,802,080.88	38,425.45	0.00
October 2009	0.00	0.00	0.00	12,554,512.51	37,682.38	0.00
November 2009	0.00	0.00	0.00	12,311,009.91	36,961.50	0.00
December 2009	0.00	0.00	0.00	12,071,509.98	36,232.65	0.00
January 2010	0.00	0.00	0.00	11,835,950.56	35,525.61	0.00
February 2010	0.00	0.00	0.00	11,604,270.46	34,830.23	0.00
March 2010	0.00	0.00	0.00	11,376,409.40	34,146.30	0.00
April 2010	0.00	0.00	0.00	11,152,308.02	33,473.66	0.00
May 2010	0.00	0.00	0.00	10,931,907.86	32,812.13	0.00
June 2010	0.00	0.00	0.00	10,715,151.35	32,161.53	0.00
July 2010	0.00	0.00	0.00	10,501,981.78	31,521.71	0.00
August 2010	0.00	0.00	0.00	10,292,343.34	30,892.48	0.00
September 2010	0.00	0.00	0.00	10,086,181.02	30,273.68	0.00
October 2010	0.00	0.00	0.00	9,883,440.67	29,665.15	0.00
November 2010	0.00	0.00	0.00	9,684,068.97	29,066.74	0.00
December 2010	0.00	0.00	0.00	9,488,013.39	28,478.28	0.00
January 2011	0.00	0.00	0.00	9,295,222.22	27,899.62	0.00
February 2011	0.00	0.00	0.00	9,105,644.52	27,330.60	0.00
March 2011	0.00	0.00	0.00	8,919,230.13	26,771.08	0.00
April 2011	0.00	0.00	0.00	8,735,929.65	26,220.90	0.00
May 2011	0.00	0.00	0.00	8,555,694.44	25,679.92	0.00
June 2011	0.00	0.00	0.00	8,378,476.60	25,148.00	0.00
July 2011	0.00	0.00	0.00	8,204,228.94	24,625.00	0.00
August 2011	0.00	0.00	0.00	8,032,905.00	24,110.77	0.00
September 2011	0.00	0.00	0.00	7,864,459.04	23,605.18	0.00
October 2011	0.00	0.00	0.00	7,698,846.00	23,108.09	0.00
November 2011	0.00	0.00	0.00	7,536,021.51	22,619.37	0.00
December 2011	0.00	0.00	0.00	7,375,941.88	22,138.89	0.00
January 2012	0.00	0.00	0.00	7,218,564.08	21,666.52	0.00
February 2012	0.00	0.00	0.00	7,063,845.74	21,202.14	0.00
March 2012	0.00	0.00	0.00	6,911,745.13	20,745.61	0.00
April 2012	0.00	0.00	0.00	6,762,221.17	20,296.81	0.00
May 2012	0.00	0.00	0.00	6,615,233.38	19,855.63	0.00
June 2012	0.00	0.00	0.00	6,470,741.91	19,421.94	0.00
July 2012	0.00	0.00	0.00	6,328,707.55	18,995.62	0.00
August 2012	0.00	0.00	0.00	6,189,091.63	18,576.56	0.00
September 2012	0.00	0.00	0.00	6,051,856.10	18,164.65	0.00
October 2012	0.00	0.00	0.00	5,916,963.51	17,759.77	0.00
November 2012	0.00	0.00	0.00	5,784,376.94	17,361.81	0.00
December 2012	0.00	0.00	0.00	5,654,060.07	16,970.66	0.00
January 2013	0.00	0.00	0.00	5,525,977.10	16,586.22	0.00
February 2013	0.00	0.00	0.00	5,400,092.82	16,208.38	0.00
March 2013	0.00	0.00	0.00	5,276,372.51	15,837.04	0.00
April 2013	0.00	0.00	0.00	5,154,782.01	15,472.08	0.00
May 2013	0.00	0.00	0.00	5,035,287.69	15,113.42	0.00
June 2013	0.00	0.00	0.00	4,917,856.40	14,760.95	0.00
July 2013	0.00	0.00	0.00	4,802,455.53	14,414.57	0.00
August 2013	0.00	0.00	0.00	4,689,052.95	14,074.20	0.00

Distribution Date	Class 89-G Planned Principal Balance	Class 89-H Planned Principal Balance	Class 89-J Planned Principal Balance	Class 89-K Planned Principal Balance	Class 89-L Planned Principal Balance	Class 89-M Targeted Principal Balance
September 2013	$0.00	$0.00	$0.00	$4,577,617.03	$13,739.72	$0.00
October 2013	0.00	0.00	0.00	4,468,116.61	13,411.05	0.00
November 2013	0.00	0.00	0.00	4,360,521.03	13,088.11	0.00
December 2013	0.00	0.00	0.00	4,254,800.08	12,770.78	0.00
January 2014	0.00	0.00	0.00	4,150,924.01	12,459.00	0.00
February 2014	0.00	0.00	0.00	4,048,863.55	12,152.67	0.00
March 2014	0.00	0.00	0.00	3,948,589.85	11,851.69	0.00
April 2014	0.00	0.00	0.00	3,850,074.52	11,556.00	0.00
May 2014	0.00	0.00	0.00	3,753,289.60	11,265.50	0.00
June 2014	0.00	0.00	0.00	3,658,207.56	10,980.11	0.00
July 2014	0.00	0.00	0.00	3,564,801.28	10,699.75	0.00
August 2014	0.00	0.00	0.00	3,473,044.07	10,424.34	0.00
September 2014	0.00	0.00	0.00	3,382,909.65	10,153.81	0.00
October 2014	0.00	0.00	0.00	3,294,372.13	9,888.06	0.00
November 2014	0.00	0.00	0.00	3,207,406.03	9,627.03	0.00
December 2014	0.00	0.00	0.00	3,121,986.26	9,370.64	0.00
January 2015	0.00	0.00	0.00	3,038,088.10	9,118.82	0.00
February 2015	0.00	0.00	0.00	2,955,687.22	8,871.50	0.00
March 2015	0.00	0.00	0.00	2,874,759.68	8,628.59	0.00
April 2015	0.00	0.00	0.00	2,795,281.88	8,390.04	0.00
May 2015	0.00	0.00	0.00	2,717,230.60	8,155.77	0.00
June 2015	0.00	0.00	0.00	2,640,582.97	7,925.71	0.00
July 2015	0.00	0.00	0.00	2,565,316.47	7,699.80	0.00
August 2015	0.00	0.00	0.00	2,491,408.94	7,477.96	0.00
September 2015	0.00	0.00	0.00	2,418,838.54	7,260.14	0.00
October 2015	0.00	0.00	0.00	2,347,583.77	7,046.27	0.00
November 2015	0.00	0.00	0.00	2,277,623.49	6,836.29	0.00
December 2015	0.00	0.00	0.00	2,208,936.85	6,630.12	0.00
January 2016	0.00	0.00	0.00	2,141,503.33	6,427.72	0.00
February 2016	0.00	0.00	0.00	2,075,302.74	6,229.02	0.00
March 2016	0.00	0.00	0.00	2,010,315.18	6,033.96	0.00
April 2016	0.00	0.00	0.00	1,946,521.08	5,842.48	0.00
May 2016	0.00	0.00	0.00	1,883,901.15	5,654.53	0.00
June 2016	0.00	0.00	0.00	1,822,436.41	5,470.04	0.00
July 2016	0.00	0.00	0.00	1,762,108.18	5,288.97	0.00
August 2016	0.00	0.00	0.00	1,702,898.04	5,111.25	0.00
September 2016	0.00	0.00	0.00	1,644,787.88	4,936.83	0.00
October 2016	0.00	0.00	0.00	1,587,759.87	4,765.66	0.00
November 2016	0.00	0.00	0.00	1,531,796.44	4,597.69	0.00
December 2016	0.00	0.00	0.00	1,476,880.30	4,432.86	0.00
January 2017	0.00	0.00	0.00	1,422,994.43	4,271.12	0.00
February 2017	0.00	0.00	0.00	1,370,122.06	4,112.42	0.00
March 2017	0.00	0.00	0.00	1,318,246.70	3,956.72	0.00
April 2017	0.00	0.00	0.00	1,267,352.09	3,803.96	0.00
May 2017	0.00	0.00	0.00	1,217,422.25	3,654.09	0.00
June 2017	0.00	0.00	0.00	1,168,441.42	3,507.08	0.00
July 2017	0.00	0.00	0.00	1,120,394.11	3,362.86	0.00
August 2017	0.00	0.00	0.00	1,073,265.05	3,221.41	0.00
September 2017	0.00	0.00	0.00	1,027,039.21	3,082.66	0.00
October 2017	0.00	0.00	0.00	981,701.79	2,946.58	0.00
November 2017	0.00	0.00	0.00	937,238.24	2,813.12	0.00
December 2017	0.00	0.00	0.00	893,634.22	2,682.24	0.00
January 2018	0.00	0.00	0.00	850,875.61	2,553.90	0.00
February 2018	0.00	0.00	0.00	808,948.51	2,428.06	0.00
March 2018	0.00	0.00	0.00	767,839.24	2,304.67	0.00
April 2018	0.00	0.00	0.00	727,534.33	2,183.69	0.00

Distribution Date	Class 89-G Planned Principal Balance	Class 89-H Planned Principal Balance	Class 89-J Planned Principal Balance	Class 89-K Planned Principal Balance	Class 89-L Planned Principal Balance	Class 89-M Targeted Principal Balance
May 2018	$0.00	$0.00	$0.00	$688,020.53	$2,065.09	$0.00
June 2018	0.00	0.00	0.00	649,284.77	1,948.83	0.00
July 2018	0.00	0.00	0.00	611,314.22	1,834.86	0.00
August 2018	0.00	0.00	0.00	574,096.21	1,723.15	0.00
September 2018	0.00	0.00	0.00	537,618.30	1,613.66	0.00
October 2018	0.00	0.00	0.00	501,868.23	1,506.36	0.00
November 2018	0.00	0.00	0.00	466,833.92	1,401.20	0.00
December 2018	0.00	0.00	0.00	432,503.49	1,298.16	0.00
January 2019	0.00	0.00	0.00	398,865.26	1,197.19	0.00
February 2019	0.00	0.00	0.00	365,907.70	1,098.27	0.00
March 2019	0.00	0.00	0.00	333,619.49	1,001.36	0.00
April 2019	0.00	0.00	0.00	301,989.46	906.42	0.00
May 2019	0.00	0.00	0.00	271,006.63	813.43	0.00
June 2019	0.00	0.00	0.00	240,660.20	722.34	0.00
July 2019	0.00	0.00	0.00	210,939.51	633.13	0.00
August 2019	0.00	0.00	0.00	181,834.10	545.77	0.00
September 2019	0.00	0.00	0.00	153,333.65	460.23	0.00
October 2019	0.00	0.00	0.00	125,428.01	376.47	0.00
November 2019	0.00	0.00	0.00	98,107.19	294.47	0.00
December 2019	0.00	0.00	0.00	71,361.34	214.19	0.0C
January 2020	0.00	0.00	0.00	45,180.80	135.61	0.00
February 2020	0.00	0.00	0.00	19,556.03	58.70	0.00
March 2020 and thereafter	0.00	0.00	0.00	0.00	0.00	0.00

Using the assumptions with respect to the Mortgage Loans specified in the final paragraph of this Prospectus Supplement (other than for O% PSA), the principal balances of the Planned Principal REMIC Certificates will be reduced to their respective Planned Principal Balances for each Distribution Date if prepayments on the Mortgage Loans underlying the MBS Certificates occur at a constant level between approximately 90% PSA and 275% PSA, and the principal balance of the Class 89-M REMIC Certificates will be reduced to their Targeted Principal Balance for each Distribution Date if prepayments occur at a constant level of approximately 165% PSA.

There is no assurance that the principal balances of the Planned Principal REMIC Certificates or the Class 89-M REMIC Certificates will conform on any Distribution Date to the applicable level specified for such Distribution Date in the schedule above. Because any excess of the Principal Distribution Amount over the sum of the Planned and Targeted Principal Amounts for any month will be distributed, the ability to pay the Planned or Targeted Principal Amount for any Distribution Date will not be enhanced by the averaging of high and low principal prepayments, as might be the case if any such excess amounts were held for future applications and not distributed monthly. Moreover, with respect to the Planned Principal REMIC Certificates, the amount of principal available on any Distribution Date may be insufficient to reduce such Classes to their respective Planned Principal Balances for such Distribution Date if prepayments on the Mortgage Loans do not occur at a constant rate, even if such prepayments remain within the range of approximately 90% PSA to 275% PSA. This result could occur, for example, if principal payments on the Mortgage Loans initially occur at a relatively fast rate within such range and subsequently occur at a significantly slower rate within such range. The amount of principal available on any Distribution Date may be insufficient to reduce the principal balance of the Class 89-M REMIC Certificates to their Targeted Principal Balance for such Distribution Date if prepayments on the Mortgage Loans do not occur at a constant rate of approximately 165% PSA. Furthermore, there is no assurance that distributions of principal will begin or end on the Distribution Dates specified in the schedule of Planned and Targeted Principal Balances. See "Final Distribution Dates and Weighted Average Lives of the REMIC Certificates" herein for a further discussion of the effect of prepayments on the Mortgage Loans on the rate of payments of principal and on the weighted average lives of the Classes of REMIC Certificates.

The following table indicates the percentages of the initial principal amount of each Class of REMIC Certificates that would be outstanding after each of the dates shown at various *constant* percentages of PSA and the corresponding weighted average life of each Class of REMIC Certificates. The table has been prepared on the basis of assumptions concerning the characteristics of the Mortgage Loans that will underlie the MBS Certificates, including (i) with respect to the information set forth under 0% PSA, that each Mortgage Loan underlying the MBS Certificates bears an interest rate of 12.00% per annum and has an original and remaining term to maturity of 360 months and (ii) with respect to the remaining information, that each Mortgage Loan underlying the MBS

Percent of Original Principal Balance Outstanding

Date	Class 89-A PSA Prepayment Assumption					Class 89-B PSA Prepayment Assumption					Class 89-X PSA Prepayment Assumption					Class 89-C PSA Prepayment Assumption				
	0%	90%	165%	275%	500%	0%	90%	165%	275%	500%	0%	90%	165%	275%	500%	0%	90%	165%	275%	500%
Initial Percent	100	100	100	100	100	100	100	100	100	100	100	100	100	100	100	100	100	100	100	100
July 1991	100	100	100	100	100	100	100	100	100	100	110	110	110	110	110	100	100	100	100	100
July 1992	100	86	86	86	86	100	100	100	100	100	121	121	121	121	121	100	100	100	100	100
July 1993	83	0	0	0	0	100	100	100	100	19	133	133	133	133	133	100	100	100	100	100
July 1994	64	0	0	0	0	100	1	1	1	0	146	146	146	146	0	100	100	100	100	0
July 1995	43	0	0	0	0	100	0	0	0	0	161	3	3	3	0	100	100	100	100	0
July 1996	20	0	0	0	0	100	0	0	0	0	176	0	0	0	0	100	35	35	35	0
July 1997	0	0	0	0	0	94	0	0	0	0	194	0	0	0	0	100	0	0	0	0
July 1998	0	0	0	0	0	61	0	0	0	0	213	0	0	0	0	100	0	0	0	0
July 1999	0	0	0	0	0	24	0	0	0	0	234	0	0	0	0	100	0	0	0	0
July 2000	0	0	0	0	0	0	0	0	0	0	229	0	0	0	0	100	0	0	0	0
July 2001	0	0	0	0	0	0	0	0	0	0	178	0	0	0	0	100	0	0	0	0
July 2002	0	0	0	0	0	0	0	0	0	0	122	0	0	0	0	100	0	0	0	0
July 2003	0	0	0	0	0	0	0	0	0	0	60	0	0	0	0	100	0	0	0	0
July 2004	0	0	0	0	0	0	0	0	0	0	0	0	0	0	0	95	0	0	0	0
July 2005	0	0	0	0	0	0	0	0	0	0	0	0	0	0	0	58	0	0	0	0
July 2006	0	0	0	0	0	0	0	0	0	0	0	0	0	0	0	17	0	0	0	0
July 2007	0	0	0	0	0	0	0	0	0	0	0	0	0	0	0	0	0	0	0	0
July 2008	0	0	0	0	0	0	0	0	0	0	0	0	0	0	0	0	0	0	0	0
July 2009	0	0	0	0	0	0	0	0	0	0	0	0	0	0	0	0	0	0	0	0
July 2010	0	0	0	0	0	0	0	0	0	0	0	0	0	0	0	0	0	0	0	0
July 2011	0	0	0	0	0	0	0	0	0	0	0	0	0	0	0	0	0	0	0	0
July 2012	0	0	0	0	0	0	0	0	0	0	0	0	0	0	0	0	0	0	0	0
July 2013	0	0	0	0	0	0	0	0	0	0	0	0	0	0	0	0	0	0	0	0
July 2014	0	0	0	0	0	0	0	0	0	0	0	0	0	0	0	0	0	0	0	0
July 2015	0	0	0	0	0	0	0	0	0	0	0	0	0	0	0	0	0	0	0	0
July 2016	0	0	0	0	0	0	0	0	0	0	0	0	0	0	0	0	0	0	0	0
July 2017	0	0	0	0	0	0	0	0	0	0	0	0	0	0	0	0	0	0	0	0
July 2018	0	0	0	0	0	0	0	0	0	0	0	0	0	0	0	0	0	0	0	0
July 2019	0	0	0	0	0	0	0	0	0	0	0	0	0	0	0	0	0	0	0	0
July 2020	0	0	0	0	0	0	0	0	0	0	0	0	0	0	0	0	0	0	0	0
Weighted Average Life (years)**	4.6	2.5	2.5	2.5	2.4	8.3	3.5	3.5	3.5	2.9	11.9	4.6	4.6	4.6	3.3	15.2	5.8	5.8	5.8	3.7

* Indicates an amount above zero and less than 0.5% of the original principal balance is outstanding.

** The weighted average life of a REMIC Certificate is determined by (a) multiplying the amount of the reduction, if any, of the principal amount of such REMIC Certificate from one Distribution Date to the next Distribution Date by the number of years from the date of issuance to the second such Distribution Date, (b) summing the results and (c) dividing the sum by the aggregate amount of the reductions in principal amount of such REMIC Certificate referred to in clause (a).

Certificates bears an interest rate of 10.125% per annum, had an original term to maturity of 360 months and has a remaining term to maturity of 356 months. It is not likely that (i) all of the underlying Mortgage Loans will have the interest rate or remaining term to maturity assumed or (ii) the underlying Mortgage Loans will prepay at a *constant* level of PSA. In addition, the diverse remaining terms to maturity of the Mortgage Loans (which will include recently originated Mortgage Loans) could produce slower or faster principal distributions than indicated in the table at the various *constant* percentages of PSA specified (except 0% PSA), even if the weighted average remaining term to maturity of the Mortgage Loans is 356 months.

Class 89-D					Class 89-E					Class 89-G					Class 89-H				
PSA Prepayment Assumption					PSA Prepayment Assumption					PSA Prepayment Assumption					PSA Prepayment Assumption				
0%	90%	165%	275%	500%	0%	90%	165%	275%	500%	0%	90%	165%	275%	500%	0%	90%	165%	275%	500%
100	100	100	100	100	100	100	100	100	100	100	100	100	100	100	100	100	100	100	100
100	100	100	100	100	100	100	100	100	100	100	100	100	100	100	100	100	100	100	100
100	100	100	100	100	100	100	100	100	100	100	100	100	100	100	100	100	100	100	100
100	100	100	100	100	100	100	100	100	100	100	100	100	100	100	100	100	100	100	100
100	100	100	100	96	100	100	100	100	100	100	100	100	100	100	100	100	100	100	100
100	100	100	100	0	100	100	100	100	26	100	100	100	100	100	100	100	100	100	100
100	100	100	100	0	100	100	100	100	0	100	100	100	100	0	100	100	100	100	43
100	71	71	71	0	100	100	100	100	0	100	100	100	100	0	100	100	100	100	0
100	10	10	10	0	100	100	100	100	0	100	100	100	100	0	100	100	100	100	0
100	0	0	0	0	100	0	0	0	0	100	87	87	87	0	100	100	100	100	^
100	0	0	0	0	100	0	0	0	0	100	0	0	0	0	100	100	100	100	0
100	0	0	0	0	100	0	0	0	0	100	0	0	0	0	100	0	0	0	0
100	0	0	0	0	100	0	0	0	0	100	0	0	0	0	100	0	0	0	0
100	0	0	0	0	100	0	0	0	0	100	0	0	0	0	100	0	0	0	0
100	0	0	0	0	100	0	0	0	0	100	0	0	0	0	100	0	0	0	0
100	0	0	0	0	100	0	0	0	0	100	0	0	0	0	100	0	0	0	0
71	0	0	0	0	100	0	0	0	0	100	0	0	0	0	100	0	0	0	0
19	0	0	0	0	100	0	0	0	0	100	0	0	0	0	100	0	0	0	0
0	0	0	0	0	4	0	0	0	0	100	0	0	0	0	80	0	0	0	0
0	0	0	0	0	0	0	0	0	0	0	0	0	0	0	0	0	0	0	0
0	0	0	0	0	0	0	0	0	0	0	0	0	0	0	0	0	0	0	0
0	0	0	0	0	0	0	0	0	0	0	0	0	0	0	0	0	0	0	0
0	0	0	0	0	0	0	0	0	0	0	0	0	0	0	0	0	0	0	0
0	0	0	0	0	0	0	0	0	0	0	0	0	0	0	0	0	0	0	0
0	0	0	0	0	0	0	0	0	0	0	0	0	0	0	0	0	0	0	0
0	0	0	0	0	0	0	0	0	0	0	0	0	0	0	0	0	0	0	0
0	0	0	0	0	0	0	0	0	0	0	0	0	0	0	0	0	0	0	0
0	0	0	0	0	0	0	0	0	0	0	0	0	0	0	0	0	0	0	0
0	0	0	0	0	0	0	0	0	0	0	0	0	0	0	0	0	0	0	0
0	0	0	0	0	0	0	0	0	0	0	0	0	0	0	0	0	0	0	0
17.4	7.4	7.4	7.4	4.4	18.7	8.5	8.5	8.5	4.9	19.5	9.4	9.4	9.4	5.4	20.2	10.5	10.5	10.5	6.0

Percent of Original Principal Balance Outstanding—(Continued)

Date	Class 89-J					Class 89-K					Class 89-L					Class 89-M						
	PSA Prepayment Assumption					PSA Prepayment Assumption					PSA Prepayment Assumption					PSA Prepayment Assumption						
	0%	90%	165%	275%	500%	0%	90%	165%	275%	500%	0%	90%	165%	275%	500%	0%	90%	165%	169%	170%	275%	500%
Initial Percent	100	100	100	100	100	100	100	100	100	100	100	100	100	100	100	100	100	100	100	100	100	100
July 1991	100	100	100	100	100	100	100	100	100	100	100	100	100	100	100	100	94	90	90	94	90	90
July 1992	100	100	100	100	100	100	100	100	100	100	100	99	99	99	99	100	71	62	62	62	62	55
July 1993	100	100	100	100	100	100	100	100	100	100	98	91	91	91	85	100	71	48	48	48	48	0
July 1994	100	100	100	100	100	100	100	100	100	100	97	84	84	84	83	100	71	36	36	36	36	0
July 1995	100	100	100	100	100	100	100	100	100	100	95	83	83	83	83	100	71	27	27	27	27	0
July 1996	100	100	100	100	100	100	100	100	100	100	93	83	83	83	72	100	71	19	19	19	12	0
July 1997	100	100	100	100	51	100	100	100	100	100	91	83	83	83	61	100	71	13	13	13	4	0
July 1998	100	100	100	100	4	100	100	100	100	100	88	83	83	83	53	100	71	9	9	9	*	0
July 1999	100	100	100	100	0	100	100	100	100	72	85	82	82	82	38	100	69	5	5	5	*	0
July 2000	100	100	100	100	0	100	100	100	100	49	83	76	76	76	26	100	65	1	1	1	*	0
July 2001	100	100	100	100	0	100	100	100	100	34	83	70	70	70	18	100	57	0	0	0	*	0
July 2002	100	63	63	63	0	100	100	100	100	23	83	64	64	64	12	100	47	0	0	0	*	0
July 2003	100	33	33	33	0	100	100	100	100	16	83	58	58	58	8	100	34	0	0	0	*	0
July 2004	100	8	8	8	0	100	100	100	100	11	83	54	54	54	6	100	20	0	0	0	*	0
July 2005	100	0	0	0	0	100	87	87	87	7	83	46	46	46	4	100	4	0	0	0	*	0
July 2006	100	0	0	0	0	100	71	71	71	5	83	37	37	37	3	100	0	0	0	0	*	0
July 2007	100	0	0	0	0	100	57	57	57	3	83	30	30	30	2	100	0	0	0	0	*	0
July 2008	100	0	0	0	0	100	46	46	46	2	83	24	24	24	1	100	0	0	0	0	*	0
July 2009	100	0	0	0	0	100	36	36	36	2	83	19	19	19	1	100	0	0	0	0	*	0
July 2010	100	0	0	0	0	100	29	29	29	1	74	15	15	15	1	100	0	0	0	0	*	0
July 2011	55	0	0	0	0	100	22	22	22	1	62	12	12	12	*	100	0	0	0	0	*	0
July 2012	0	0	0	0	0	66	17	17	17	*	35	9	9	9	*	100	0	0	0	0	*	0
July 2013	0	0	0	0	0	13	13	13	13	*	7	7	7	7	*	81	0	0	0	0	*	0
July 2014	0	0	0	0	0	10	10	10	10	*	5	5	5	5	*	37	0	0	0	0	*	0
July 2015	0	0	0	0	0	7	7	7	7	*	4	4	4	4	*	0	0	0	0	0	*	0
July 2016	0	0	0	0	0	5	5	5	5	*	3	3	3	3	*	0	0	0	0	0	*	0
July 2017	0	0	0	0	0	3	3	3	3	*	2	2	2	2	*	0	0	0	0	0	*	0
July 2018	0	0	0	0	0	2	2	2	2	*	1	1	1	1	*	0	0	0	0	0	*	0
July 2019	0	0	0	0	0	1	1	1	1	*	*	*	*	*	*	0	0	0	0	0	*	0
July 2020	0	0	0	0	0	0	0	0	0	0	0	0	0	0	0	0	0	0	0	0	0	0
Weighted Average Life (years)**	21.1	12.5	12.5	12.5	7.1	22.6	18.6	18.6	18.6	10.8	19.3	13.8	13.8	13.8	8.1	23.7	9.4	3.6	3.6	3.7	3.3	1.9

* Indicates an amount above zero and less than 0.5% of the original principal balance is outstanding.

** The weighted average life of a REMIC Certificate is determined by (a) multiplying the amount of the reduction, if any, of the principal amount of such REMIC Certificate from one Distribution Date to the next Distribution Date by the number of years from the date of issuance to the second such Distribution Date, (b) summing the results and (c) dividing the sum by the aggregate amount of the reductions in principal amount of such REMIC Certificate referred to in clause (a).

Class 89-F and Class 89-S

		PSA Prepayment Assumption				
0%	90%	165%	169%	170%	275%	500%
100	100	100	100	100	100	100
100	100	90	89	100	81	23
100	100	62	58	78	0	0
100	100	47	42	63	0	0
100	100	36	29	52	0	0
100	100	26	18	43	0	0
100	100	19	10	37	0	0
100	100	13	3	34	0	0
100	100	9	0	32	0	0
100	100	5	0	32	0	0
100	100	0	0	31	0	0
100	100	0	0	18	0	0
100	100	0	0	1	0	0
100	100	0	0	0	0	0
100	100	0	0	0	0	0
100	73	0	0	0	0	0
100	34	0	0	0	0	0
100	0	0	0	0	0	0
100	0	0	0	0	0	0
100	0	0	0	0	0	0
72	0	0	0	0	0	0
0	0	0	0	0	0	0
0	0	0	0	0	0	0
0	0	0	0	0	0	0
25.2	16.6	3.6	3.0	5.8	1.4	0.8

Class 89-N

		PSA Prepayment Assumption				
0%	90%	165%	169%	170%	275%	500%
100	100	100	100	100	100	100
100	100	86	85	100	73	0
100	100	46	41	69	0	0
100	100	26	18	48	0	0
100	100	9	0	32	0	0
100	100	0	0	20	0	0
100	100	0	0	12	0	0
100	100	0	0	7	0	0
100	100	0	0	5	0	0
100	100	0	0	4	0	0
100	100	0	0	3	0	0
100	100	0	0	0	0	0
100	62	0	0	0	0	0
100	6	0	0	0	0	0
100	0	0	0	0	0	0
100	0	0	0	0	0	0
100	0	0	0	0	0	0
100	0	0	0	0	0	0
61	0	0	0	0	0	0
0	0	0	0	0	0	0
0	0	0	0	0	0	0
0	0	0	0	0	0	0
25.1	16.2	2.2	2.0	3.5	1.2	0.7

Class 89-O

		PSA Prepayment Assumption				
0%	90%	165%	169%	170%	275%	500%
100	100	100	100	100	100	100
100	100	100	100	100	100	78
100	100	100	100	100	0	0
100	100	90	82	100	0	0
100	100	64	62	100	0	0
100	100	44	33	100	0	0
100	100	30	11	100	0	0
100	100	17	0	100	0	0
100	100	0	0	61	0	0
100	100	0	0	5	0	0
100	100	0	0	0	0	0
100	100	0	0	0	0	0
100	100	0	0	0	0	0
100	0	0	0	0	0	0
100	0	0	0	0	0	0
100	0	0	0	0	0	0
100	0	0	0	0	0	0
100	0	0	0	0	0	0
100	0	0	0	0	0	0
0	0	0	0	0	0	0
0	0	0	0	0	0	0
0	0	0	0	0	0	0
26.5	17.5	7.0	5.5	11.2	1.9	1.1

Class 89-P

		PSA Prepayment Assumption				
0%	90%	165%	169%	170%	275%	500%
100	100	100	100	100	100	100
100	100	100	100	100	100	100
100	100	100	100	100	100	0
100	100	100	100	100	46	0
100	100	100	100	100	7	0
100	100	100	100	100	0	0
100	100	100	100	100	0	0
100	100	100	99	100	0	0
100	100	100	96	100	0	0
100	100	86	78	100	0	0
100	100	69	61	87	0	0
100	100	50	42	72	0	0
100	100	30	22	56	0	0
100	100	8	2	40	0	0
100	100	0	0	24	0	0
100	94	0	0	7	0	0
100	59	0	0	0	0	0
100	22	0	0	0	0	0
100	0	0	0	0	0	0
100	0	0	0	0	0	0
61	0	0	0	0	0	0
0	0	0	0	0	0	0
26.1	19.3	12.9	12.5	15.4	3.0	1.5

Percent of Original Principal Balance Outstanding—(Continued)

Date	Class 86-Y PSA Prepayment Assumptions						Class 86-Z PSA Prepayment Assumptions						Class 86-R PSA Prepayment Assumptions					Class 86-RL PSA Prepayment Assumptions				
	0%	90%	165%	170%	275%	500%	0%	90%	165%	170%	275%	500%	0%	90%	165%	275%	500%	0%	90%	165%	275%	500%
Initial Percent	100	100	100	100	100	100	100	100	100	100	100	100	100	52	0	0	0	100	100	100	100	100
July 1991	110	110	110	100	0	0	110	110	110	110	110	110	0	0	0	0	0	100	98	96	94	89
July 1992	121	121	121	0	0	0	121	121	121	121	110	121	0	0	0	0	0	99	93	88	82	68
July 1993	133	133	133	0	0	0	133	133	133	133	133	133	0	0	0	0	0	99	87	79	68	48
July 1994	146	146	146	0	0	0	146	146	146	146	146	146	0	0	0	0	0	98	82	71	56	33
July 1995	161	161	161	0	0	0	161	161	161	161	161	15	0	0	0	0	0	98	77	63	46	23
July 1996	176	176	176	0	0	0	176	176	176	176	176	0	0	0	0	0	0	97	72	56	38	16
July 1997	194	194	194	0	0	0	194	194	194	194	0	0	0	0	0	0	0	96	67	50	32	11
July 1998	213	213	213	0	0	0	213	213	213	213	0	0	0	0	0	0	0	96	63	45	26	8
July 1999	234	234	234	0	0	0	234	234	234	234	0	0	0	0	0	0	0	94	59	40	22	5
July 2000	258	258	258	0	0	0	258	258	258	258	0	0	0	0	0	0	0	93	55	35	18	4
July 2001	283	283	283	0	0	0	283	283	283	283	0	0	0	0	0	0	0	92	51	31	15	2
July 2002	311	311	311	0	0	0	311	311	311	311	0	0	0	0	0	0	0	91	47	28	12	2
July 2003	342	342	342	0	0	0	342	342	342	342	0	0	0	0	0	0	0	89	44	24	10	1
July 2004	376	376	376	0	0	0	376	376	376	376	0	0	0	0	0	0	0	88	40	21	8	1
July 2005	413	413	413	0	0	0	413	413	413	413	0	0	0	0	0	0	0	86	37	19	6	*
July 2006	454	454	408	0	0	0	454	454	403	380	0	0	0	0	0	0	0	84	34	16	5	*
July 2007	500	500	362	0	0	0	500	500	362	340	0	0	0	0	0	0	0	81	31	14	4	*
July 2008	549	549	303	0	0	0	549	549	322	303	0	0	0	0	0	0	0	78	28	12	3	*
July 2009	604	604	266	0	0	0	604	604	284	266	0	0	0	0	0	0	0	75	25	11	3	*
July 2010	664	664	232	0	0	0	664	664	248	232	0	0	0	0	0	0	0	72	23	9	2	*
July 2011	729	668	200	0	0	0	729	668	214	200	0	0	0	0	0	0	0	68	20	8	2	*
July 2012	802	590	169	0	0	0	802	590	182	169	0	0	0	0	0	0	0	63	18	6	1	*
July 2013	881	512	141	0	0	0	881	512	162	141	0	0	0	0	0	0	0	58	15	5	1	*
July 2014	969	434	115	0	0	0	969	434	124	115	0	0	0	0	0	0	0	53	13	4	1	*
July 2015	1,065	356	90	0	0	0	1,065	356	97	90	0	0	0	0	0	0	0	46	10	3	*	*
July 2016	1,171	279	68	0	0	0	1,171	279	73	68	0	0	0	0	0	0	0	39	8	2	*	*
July 2017	1,111	203	47	0	0	0	1,111	203	51	47	0	0	0	0	0	0	0	31	6	2	*	*
July 2018	785	126	28	0	0	0	785	126	31	28	0	0	0	0	0	0	0	22	4	1	*	*
July 2019	417	51	11	0	0	0	417	51	12	11	0	0	0	0	0	0	0	12	1	*	*	*
July 2020	0	0	0	0	0	0	0	0	0	0	0	0	0	0	0	0	0	0	0	0	0	0
Weighted Average Life (years)**	28.4	25.1	21.5	21.3	0.6	0.3	28.4	25.1	21.5	23.3	4.7	1.9	1.1	0.4	0.4	0.4	0.4	22.5	12.6	8.9	6.1	3.7

* Indicates an amount above zero and less than 0.5% of the original principal balance is outstanding.

** The weighted average life of a REMIC Certificate is determined by (a) multiplying the amount of the reduction, if any, of the principal amount of such REMIC Certificate from one Distribution Date to the next Distribution Date by the number of years from the date of issuance to the second such Distribution Date, (b) summing the results and (c) dividing the sum by the aggregate amount of the reductions in principal amount of such REMIC Certificate referred to in clause (a).

CHAPTER 13

Asset-Backed Securities[*]

Learning Objectives

After reading this chapter you will understand:

- the various types of asset-backed securities
- the cash flow characteristics of asset-backed securities
- the factors considered by rating agencies in assigning ratings to asset-backed securities
- the characteristics of the four major types of asset-backed securities

In Chapters 11 and 12 we discussed securities backed by a pool of standard mortgage loans. By standard loans we mean first-lien mortgage loans. Securities created by pooling loans other than first-lien mortgage loans are referred to as **asset-backed securities.** Although in some countries the term asset-backed securities refers to all types of loans securitized (including first-lien mortgage loans), in the United States the convention is to distinguish between mortgage-backed securities (i.e., securities backed by first-lien mortgage loans) and asset-backed securities (i.e., securities backed by assets other than first-lien mortgage loans). The four largest sectors of the asset-backed securities market in the United States are securities backed by credit card receivables, auto loans, home equity loans, and manufactured housing loans.

In this chapter we will discuss the basic features of asset-backed securities and look at the four major asset-backed security types. Although our focus is on the major types of assets securitized, the list keeps growing. Some of the off-beat receivables that have been securitized are the future publishing royalties of David Bowe, movie royalties, and municipal parking ticket receivables.

CREDIT RISK

Asset-backed securities expose investors to credit risk. The four nationally recognized statistical rating organizations rate asset-backed securities. In analyzing credit risk, the rating companies focus on similar areas of analysis: (1) credit quality of the

---

[*]This chapter is adapted from Chapter 11 in Frank J. Fabozzi, *Fixed Income Securities* (New Hope, PA: Frank J. Fabozzi Associates, 1997).

collateral, (2) the quality of the seller/servicer, (3) cash flow stress and payment structure, and (4) legal structure.[1] We discuss each in the following sections.

Credit Quality of the Collateral

Analysis of the credit quality of the collateral depends on the asset type. The rating companies will look at the borrower's ability to pay and the borrower's equity in the asset. The latter will be a key determinant as to whether the borrower will default or sell the asset and pay off a loan. The rating companies will look at the experience of the originators of the underlying loans and will assess whether the loans underlying a specific transaction have the same characteristics as the experience reported by the issuer.

The concentration of loans is examined. The underlying principle of asset securitization is that the large number of borrowers in a pool will reduce the credit risk via diversification. If there are a few borrowers in the pool that are significant in size relative to the entire pool balance, this diversification benefit can be lost, resulting in a higher level of default risk. This risk is called **concentration risk.** In such instances, rating companies will set concentration limits on the amount or percentage of receivables from any one borrower.

Based on its analysis of the collateral and other factors described next, a rating company will determine the amount of credit enhancement necessary for an issue to receive a particular rating. This is referred to as **sizing** the credit enhancement. All asset-backed securities are credit enhanced. Credit enhancement is used to provide greater protection to investors against losses due to defaults by borrowers. Credit enhancement levels are determined relative to a specific rating desired for a security. Specifically, an investor in a triple A–rated security expects to have "minimal" risk, that is to say, virtually no chance, of losing any principal due to a default.

As with nonagency mortgage-backed securities discussed in Chapter 11, credit enhancement can be either insurance, corporate guarantees, or letters of credit. **Internal credit enhancements** include reserve funds (cash reserves and excess servicing spread), overcollateralization, and senior/subordinated structures. The problem with external credit enhancements is that rating companies take the "weak link" approach to ratings. If the rating of the third-party guarantor is downgraded, the security's rating will be downgraded even if the collateral is performing as expected.

Quality of the Seller/Servicer

Each financial institution or loan originator establishes it own underwriting standards. In many cases the servicer is the seller or originator of the loans used as the collateral. Duff & Phelps, for example, reviews the following when evaluating servicers: (1) servicing history, (2) experience, (3) originations, (4) servicing capabilities, (5) human resources, (6) financial condition, and (6) growth/competition/business environment. Based on its analysis, Duff & Phelps determines whether the servicer is acceptable or unacceptable.[2]

---

[1] Suzanne Michaud, "A Rating Agency Perspective on Asset-Backed Securities," Chapter 16 in Anand K. Bhattacharya and Frank J. Fabozzi, *Asset-Backed Securities* (New Hope, PA: Frank J. Fabozzi Associates, 1997).
[2] Duff & Phelps Corporation, *Servicer Review Policy,* undated.

Cash Flow Stress and Payment Structure

The cash flow of the underlying collateral of an asset-backed security transaction is interest and principal repayment. The cash flow payments that must be made are interest and principal to investors, servicing fees, and any other expenses for which the issuer is liable. The rating companies analyze the structure to test whether the collateral's cash flows match the payments that must be made to satisfy the issuer's obligations. This requires that the rating company make assumptions about losses and delinquencies and consider various interest rate scenarios.

There are different payment or financial structures from which an issuer can choose. By **payment structure** we mean payment priorities, how the bond principal payments should be amortized, and how any excess cash flows should be used. The structure depends on the type of collateral. As with mortgage-backed securities, there are two basic forms: pass-throughs and paythroughs. We will discuss these structures when we describe the four major types of asset-backed securities.

Legal Structure

A corporation using structured financing seeks a rating on the securities it issues that is higher than its own corporate rating. This is done by using the underlying loans as collateral for a debt instrument rather than the general credit of the issuer. Typically, however, the corporate entity (i.e., seller of the collateral) retains some interest in the collateral. For example, the corporate entity can retain a subordinated class. Because the corporate entity retains an interest, rating companies want to be assured that a bankruptcy of that corporate entity will not allow the issuer's creditors assess to the collateral. That is, there is concern that a bankruptcy court could redirect the collateral's cash flows or the collateral itself from the security holders in an asset-backed security deal to the creditors of the corporate entity if it became bankrupt.

To solve this problem, a bankruptcy-remote special purpose vehicle (SPV) is formed. The issuer of the asset-backed security is then the SPV. Legal opinion is needed stating that in the event of bankruptcy of the seller of the collateral, counsel does not believe that a bankruptcy court will consolidate the collateral sold with the assets of the seller.

The SPV is set up as a wholly owned subsidiary of the seller of the collateral. Despite the fact that it is a wholly owned subsidiary, it is established in such a way that it is treated as a third-party entity relative to the seller of the collateral. The collateral is sold to the SPV, which in turn resells the collateral to the trust. The trust holds the collateral on behalf of the investors. It is the SPV that holds the interest retained by the seller of the collateral.

CASH FLOW OF ASSET-BACKED SECURITIES

The collateral for an asset-backed security can be classified as either amortizing or nonamortizing assets. **Amortizing assets** are loans in which the borrower's periodic payment consists of scheduled principal and interest payments over the life of the loan. The schedule for the repayment of the principal is called the **amortization schedule.** The standard residential mortgage loan falls into this category. Auto loans and certain types of home equity loans (specifically, closed-end home equity loans, discussed later in this chapter) are amortizing assets. Any excess payment over the scheduled principal payment is called a prepayment. Prepayments can be made to pay off the entire balance or a partial prepayment, called a curtailment.

In contrast to amortizing assets, nonamortizing assets do not have a schedule for the periodic payments that the borrower must make. Instead, a nonamortizing asset is one in which the borrower must make a minimum periodic payment. If that payment is less than the interest on the outstanding loan balance, the shortfall is added to the outstanding loan balance. If the periodic payment is greater than the interest on the outstanding loan balance, then the difference is applied to the reduction of the outstanding loan balance. There is no schedule of principal payments (i.e., no amortization schedule) for a nonamortizing asset. Consequently, the concept of a prepayment does not apply. Credit card receivables and certain types of home equity loans described later in this chapter are examples of nonamortizing assets.

For an amortizing asset, projection of the cash flows requires projecting prepayments. One factor that may affect prepayments is the prevailing level of interest rates relative to the interest rate on the loan. In projecting prepayments it is critical to determine the extent to which borrowers take advantage of a decline in interest rates below the loan rate in order to refinance the loan.

Modeling defaults for the collateral is critical in estimating the cash flows of an asset-backed security. Proceeds that are recovered in the event of a default of a loan prior to the scheduled principal repayment date of an amortizing asset represent a prepayment. Projecting prepayments for amortizing assets requires an assumption of the default rate and the recovery rate. For a nonamortizing asset, though the concept of a prepayment does not exist, a projection of defaults is still necessary to project how much will be recovered and when.

The analysis of prepayments can be performed on a pool level or a loan level. In pool-level analysis it is assumed that all loans comprising the collateral are identical. For an amortizing asset, the amortization schedule is based on the **gross weighted average coupon (GWAC)** and **weighted average maturity (WAM)** for that single loan. **Pool-level analysis** is appropriate where the underlying loans are homogeneous. **Loan-level analysis** involves amortizing each loan (or group of homogeneous loans).

The maturity of an asset-backed security is not a meaningful parameter. Instead, the average life of the security is calculated. This measure was introduced in Chapter 11 when we discussed agency pass-through securities.

Now that the basics are out of the way, let's look at the four major asset-backed security types: auto loan–backed securities, credit receivable–backed securities, home equity loan–backed securities, and manufactured housing loan–backed securities.

AUTO LOAN–BACKED SECURITIES

Auto loan–backed securities are issued by (1) the financial subsidiaries of auto manufacturers, (2) commercial banks, and (3) independent finance companies and small financial institutions specializing in auto loans. The first group includes the financial subsidiaries of the Big Three (General Motors Acceptance Corporation, Chrysler Financial, and Ford Credit) as well as foreign auto manufacturers (Volvo, Honda, Nissan, and Toyota). The last group includes issuers such as Western Financial, Union Acceptance Corporation, and Olympic Financial.

There are auto loan–backed securities in which the underlying collateral is a pool of recreational vehicle purchase contracts. An example is CIT RV Owner Trust 1995-A, which was issued in June 1995. Asset-backed securities in which the collateral is a pool of auto leases also falls into the category of auto loan–backed securities. An example is Ford Credit Auto Lease Trust 1995-1 issued in May 1995.

Cash Flow

The cash flow for auto loan–backed securities consists of regularly scheduled monthly loan payments (interest and scheduled principal repayments) and any prepayments. The monthly interest rate may be fixed or floating.

Prepayments

For securities backed by auto loans, prepayments result from (1) sales and trade-ins requiring full payoff of the loan, (2) repossession and subsequent resale of the automobile, (3) loss or destruction of the vehicle, (4) payoff of the loan with cash to save on the interest cost, and (5) refinancing of the loan at a lower interest cost.

Prepayments due to repossessions and subsequent resale are sensitive to the economic cycle. In recessionary economic periods, prepayments due to this factor increase. Whereas refinancings may be a major reason for prepayments of mortgage loans, they are of minor importance for automobile loans. Moreover, the interest rates for the automobile loans underlying several issues are substantially below market rates if they are offered by manufacturers as part of a sales promotion.

Prepayments for auto loan–backed securities are measured in terms of the **absolute prepayment rate,** denoted not by APR but by ABS (probably because it was the first prepayment measure used for asset-backed securities). The ABS is the monthly prepayment expressed as a percentage of the *original* collateral amount. Recall that the SMM (monthly CPR) expresses prepayments based on the prior month's balance.

Payment Structure

There are auto loan–backed deals that are pass-through structures and paythrough structures. A typical pass-through structure for an auto loan–backed deal is as follows[3]:

Tranche	Amount ($)	Average Life (Years)	Coupon Rate
A	$187,050,000	1.87	Fixed
B	18,499,000	1.87	Fixed
IO	6,000,000	1.46	Fixed

In this typical pass-through structure there is a senior tranche (A) and a subordinated tranche (B). There is also an interest-only class. While more deals are structured as pass-throughs, this structure is typically used for smaller deals.

---

[3]Thomas Zimmerman and Leo Burrel, "Auto Loan-Backed Securities," Chapter 4 in *Asset-Backed Securities,* Exhibit 7, p. 92. Zimmerman and Burrel obtained this information from Prudential Securities' IMPACT database.

Larger deals usually have a paythrough structure. A typical auto loan–backed paythrough structure is as follows[4]:

Tranche	Amount ($)	Average Life (Years)	Coupon Rate
A1	$250,000,000	0.2	Fixed
A2	545,000,000	0.8	Floating
A3	400,000,000	1.9	Fixed
A4	248,760,000	3.0	Fixed
B	56,240	3.3	Fixed

In this typical paythrough structure, the senior pieces are tranched to create a range of average lives. The subordinated piece is not tranched.

Credit Enhancement

Credit enhancement typically is via a senior/subordinated structure. Usually there is one or more forms of additional enhancement such as cash reserves or overcollateralization. The total support is in the range of 8% to 12%.[5]

CREDIT CARD RECEIVABLE–BACKED SECURITIES

Credit card receivable–backed securities are backed by credit card receivables. Credit cards are originated by banks (e.g., Visa and MasterCard), retailers (e.g., JCPenney and Sears), and travel and entertainment companies (e.g., American Express). For example, consider the following two deals: Sears Credit Account Master Trust II, Series 1995-4, and Standard Credit Card Master Trust I Series 1995-A.

Consider first the Sears deal. Sears offers several open-end revolving credit plans. These plans include the SearsCharge account, the SearsCharge PLUS account, the SearsCharge Modernizing Credit Plan account, and the SearsCharge Home Improvement Plan account. From these various plans, Sears generates a portfolio of receivables. The majority of the portfolio of receivables is from the SearsCharge account. The Sears Credit Account Master Trust II, Series 1995-5, is the sixth of a series issued by Group One of Sears Credit Account Master Trust II. As of July 1995, the master trust was composed of $4 billion of principal receivables. These receivables were randomly selected from the entire portfolio of receivables of Sears Roebuck and Co. About 38% of the accounts have credit limits of $1,999 and about 61% were seasoned at least five years. All series issued from this Master Trust II share in the pool of receivables that were randomly selected. Information about the specific accounts in the pool selected for Master Trust II is not available; however, because of the random selection process, an investor might expect that the composition does not differ significantly from the entire portfolio of receivables. There were two classes of certificates that were offered to the public: Class A Master Trust Certificates and Class B Master

---

[4]Zimmerman and Burrel, "Auto Loan-Backed Securities," p. 92.
[5]Zimmerman and Burrel, "Auto Loan-Backed Securities," p. 91.

Trust Certificates. The principal for the former was $500 million and for the latter $22.5 million.

The Standard Credit Card Master Trust I Series 1995-A is a Citibank deal. This issue is the 22nd in a series issued by Group One of Standard Credit Card Master Trust I and is a Euro issue. The master trust as of May 22, 1995, was composed of 20,092,662 accounts with principal receivables of approximately $24.3 billion and approximately $290.8 million of finance charge receivables. The average credit limit was $3,282 and the average principal balance of the accounts was $1,210. About 69% of the accounts were seasoned more than two years. There was only one certificate offered to the public—$300 million of Floating Rate Class A Credit Card Participation Certificates.

Cash Flow

For credit card receivable–backed securities, the cash flow consists of principal and finance charges collected. Interest to security holders is paid periodically (e.g, monthly, quarterly, or semiannually). The interest may be fixed or floating. For example, the classes of Sears Credit Account Master Trust II, Series 1995-4 have a fixed rate— 6.25% for Class A Master Trust Certificates and 6.35% for Class B Master Trust Certificates. Interest is paid monthly. For Standard Credit Card Master I Trust 1995-A, the Euro issue, the coupon rate is a floating rate and is paid quarterly. The coupon reset formula is three-month LIBOR plus 70 basis points. The coupon rate is uncapped.

In contrast to an auto loan–backed security, the principal repayment of a credit card receivable–backed security is not amortized. Instead, for a specified period of time, referred to as the **lockout period** or **revolving period,** the principal payments made by credit card borrowers constituting the pool are retained by the trustee and reinvested in additional receivables. The lockout period can vary from 18 months to 10 years.

After the lockout period, the principal is no longer reinvested but paid to investors. This period is referred to as the **principal-amortization period,** and the various types of structures are described later.

Early Amortization Triggers   There are provisions in credit card receivable– backed securities that require earlier amortization of the principal if certain events occur. Such provisions, which are referred to as **early** or **rapid amortization,** are included to safeguard the credit quality of the issue. The only way that the cash flows can be altered is by triggering the early amortization provision.

Early amortization is invoked if the trust is not able to generate sufficient income to cover the investor coupon and the servicing fee. For example, in the Sears Credit Account Master Trust II, Series 1995-4, if the net yield provided by the portfolio of receivables is less than the base rate for three monthly periods, early amortization is triggered. Other events that may trigger early amortization are the default of the servicer, credit support decline below a specified level, or the issuer violating agreements regarding pooling and servicing.

Monthly Payment Rate   As noted earlier, the concept of prepayments does not apply to credit card receivable–backed securities because there is no amortization schedule during the lockout period. Instead, for this sector of the asset–backed securities market, participants look at the **monthly payment rate (MPR).** This measure expresses the monthly payment (which includes finance charges collected and any principal) of a credit card receivable portfolio as a percentage of debt outstanding in the previous month. For example, suppose a $500 million credit card receivable portfolio in January realized $50 million of payments in February. The MPR would then be 10% ($50 million divided by $500 million).

For the master trust portfolio for the Sears Credit Account Master Trust II, Series 1995-4, the MPR information provided in the prospectus was as follows:

Seven Months Ended July 31,	1995	1994	1993	1992
Average Monthly Rate (%)	6.64	6.87	7.20	7.31
High Monthly Rate (%)	7.09	7.69	7.85	7.66
Low Monthly Rate (%)	6.22	6.54	6.70	7.06

For the master trust portfolio for the Standard Credit Card Master Trust I Series 1995-A, the MPR information provided in the prospectus was as follows:

Year Ended December 31,	1994	1993	1992	Three Months Ended March 31, 1995
Lowest Month (%)	18.21	15.74	12.58	17.65
Highest Month (%)	21.33	21.97	17.86	20.57
Avg. of Months in Period (%)	19.69	18.22	14.55	19.39

There are two reasons why the MPR is important. First, if the MPR reaches an extremely low level, there is a chance that there will be extension risk with respect to the principal payments. Second, if the MPR is very low, then there is a chance that there will not be sufficient cash flows to pay off principal. Typically, this is one of the events that could trigger early amortization of the principal.

Payment Structure

There are three different amortization structures that have been used in credit card receivable–backed security structures: In a **pass-through structure,** the principal cash flows from the credit card accounts are paid to the security holders on a pro rata basis.[6] In a **controlled-amortization structure,** a scheduled principal amount is established. The scheduled principal amount is sufficiently low so that the obligation can be satisfied even under certain stress scenarios. The investor is paid the lesser of the scheduled principal amount and the pro rata amount. In a **bullet-payment structure,** the investor receives the entire amount in one distribution. Because there is no assurance that the entire amount can be paid in one lump sum, the procedure is for the

---

[6]For a more detailed discussion of these amortization structures, see Robert Karr, Greg Richter, R.J. Shook, and Lirenn Tsai, "Credit-Card Receivables," in *Asset-Backed Securities.*

trustee to place principal monthly into an account that generates sufficient interest to make periodic interest payments and accumulate the principal to be repaid. The time period over which the principal is accumulated is called the **accumulation period.**

The controlled-amortization structure is used in the Sears Credit Account Master Trust II, Series 1995-4. The allocated principal collections were to be paid to investors in the Class A Master Trust Certificates on a monthly basis beginning March 1998. The expectation was that the controlled-amortization period would be 12 months, at which time (February 1999) the Class A certificates would be repaid in full. Investors in the Class B Master Trust Certificates then would begin to receive principal payments with the expectation that they would be repaid in full by March 1999.

In the Standard Credit Card Master Trust I Series 1995-A, the bullet-payment structure is used. During the accumulation period, the investor's share of the principal payments will be placed into a principal funding account and invested monthly in short-term highly rated investments. For the Class A Master Trust Certificates the principal was repaid in full by the end of 1998.

Credit Enhancement

In the earlier credit card structures, the most popular form of credit enhancement was a bank letter of credit. However, as discussed earlier in this chapter and in the previous chapter, the disadvantage of a third-party guarantee is that if the guarantor is downgraded, the structure will be downgraded regardless of how the collateral is performing. With the downgrading of banks that provided letters of credit for earlier credit card deals and the subsequent downgrading of the securities, this form of credit enhancement lost its popularity.

Today the two most popular forms of credit enhancement for credit card deals coupled with any senior/subordinated structure are the cash collateral account and the collateral invested account. Both forms of credit enhancement involve the investment of cash. In the case of the cash collateral account, funds are generally borrowed from a bank and those funds are then invested in commercial paper or other short-debt of the bank. In the collateral invested account, the funds are invested in credit card receivables within the structure rather than commercial paper or other short-term debt.

In the Sears Credit Account Master Trust II, Series 1995-4, there is a senior/subordinated structure. The Class B Master Trust Certificates are subordinated to the Class A Master Trust Certificates. There is also a class not offered to the public, Class C Master Trust Certificates, which provide credit support for the Class A and Class B certificates. At the offering date, the Class B and Class C certificates represented 4% and 7% respectively of the Series 1995-4 invested amount. Therefore, from the perspective of the Class A certificates, the two classes subordinated to it provided an 11% enhancement. Based on the credit enhancement and other factors at the offering date, the Class A certificates were rated triple A by Standard & Poor's, Moody's, and Duff & Phelps.

The only publicly offered certificate for the Standard Credit Card Master Trust I Series 1995-A is the Floating Rate Class A Credit Card Participation Certificates. There was a Class B certificate with a principal amount of $19.15 million that was subordinated to the Class A certificates. Thus, a total of $319 million was invested in receivables ($300 million for the Class A certificates and $19.15 million for the Class B certificates). The Class B certificates therefore provided 6% credit enhancement

($19.15 million divided by $319.15 million). In addition, the Class A certificates had a 5% credit enhancement in the form of a cash collateral account. Consequently, investors in the Class A certificates had an 11% credit enhancement (6% provided by the Class B certificates and 5% provided by the cash collateral account). Based on the credit enhancement and other factors, the Class A certificates were rated triple A by Standard & Poor's, Moody's, and Duff & Phelps.

HOME EQUITY LOAN–BACKED SECURITIES

Home equity loan–backed securities are backed by home equity loans. A **home equity loan (HEL)** is a loan backed by residential property. Typically, the loan is a second lien on property that has already been pledged to secure a first lien. In some cases, the lien may be a third lien. In recent years, some loans have been first liens.

Home equity loans can be closed or open end. A **closed-end HEL** is structured the same way as a fully amortizing residential mortgage loan. That is, it has a fixed maturity and the payments are structured to fully amortize the loan by the maturity date. There are both fixed-rate and variable-rate closed-end HELs. Typically, variable-rate loans have a reference rate of six-month LIBOR and have periodic caps and lifetime caps, just as with adjustable-rate mortgages discussed in Chapter 10. The cash flow of a pool of closed-end HELs is composed of interest, regularly schedule principal repayments, and prepayments, just as with mortgage-backed securities. Thus, it is necessary to have a prepayment model and a default model to forecast cash flows. The prepayment speed is measured in terms of a conditional prepayment rate (CPR).

With an **open-end HEL,** the homeowner is given a credit line and can write checks or use a credit card for up to the amount of the credit line. The amount of the credit line depends on the amount of the equity the borrower has in the property. There is a revolving period over which the homeowner can borrow funds against the line of credit. At the end of the term of the loan, the homeowner either pays off the amount borrowed in one payment or the outstanding balance is amortized.

Originators of HELs look at three key ratios when deciding to underwrite a loan: combined loan-to-value ratio (CLTV), second-lien ratio, and payment-to-income ratio. The CLTV looks at the ratio of all mortgage liens relative to the appraised value of the property. For example, suppose that an applicant seeking a $10,000 second mortgage lien via an HEL on property with an appraised value of $100,000 has a first mortgage-lien on that property of $80,000. Then the CLTV is 90% [($80,000 + $10,000)/$100,000]. The second lien ratio is found by dividing the amount of the second lien sought by the applicant by the combined mortgage liens. In our example, the second lien ratio is 11.11% [$10,000/($80,000 + $10,000)]. In calculating the payment-to-income ratio, the monthly mortgage payment includes all mortgage payments.

Borrowers are segmented into four general credit quality groups, A, B, C, and D. Although there is no industry-wide definition for classifying a borrower, the following definitions based on the borrower's credit history criteria appear to be what some originators use[7]:

---

[7]These definitions are from Joseph C. Hu, "Home Equity Loans (HELs) and HEL-Backed Securities," Chapter 32 in Frank J. Fabozzi *The Handbook of Fixed-Income Securities* (Burr Ridge, IL: Irwin Publishing, 1997). Hu based his definitions on reports by Fitch, Moody's, and Bear Stearns.

- *A/A− (excellent/good credit quality):* (1) no more than two 30-day delinquencies in past 12 months and (2) no prior bankruptcies
- *B and C (satisfactory/fair credit quality):* (1) no more than four 30-day, two 60-day, and one 90-day delinquencies in past 12 months and (2) no bankruptcies in past two to three years
- *D (unsatisfactory/poor credit quality):* (1) more than four 30-day, two 60-day, and 90-day delinquencies in past 12 months and (2) no bankruptcies in past two years

Cash Flow

The monthly cash flow for a home equity loan–backed security backed by closed-end HELs is the same as for mortgage-backed securities. That is, the cash flow consists of (1) net interest, (2) regularly scheduled principal payments, and (3) prepayments. The uncertainty about the cash flows arises from prepayments.

Prepayments

There are differences in the prepayment behavior for HELs and traditional residential mortgage loans. In general it is expected that prepayments due to refinancings would be less important for HELs than for traditional residential mortgage loans because typically the average loan size is less for HELs. In general it is thought that interest rates must fall considerably more for HELs than for traditional residential mortgage loans in order for a borrower to benefit from refinancing.

Wall Street firms involved in the underwriting and market making of home equity loan–backed securities have developed prepayment models for these loans. Several firms have found that the key difference between the prepayment behavior of HELs and traditional residential mortgages is the important role played by the credit characteristics of the borrower.

A study by Bear Stearns strongly suggests that borrower credit quality is the most important determinant of prepayments.[8] The study looked at prepayments for four separate deals. The underlying HELs for each deal had a different level of borrower credit quality (with the credit quality of the loans being classified by the issuer). The four deals whose prepayments were analyzed were FICAL 90-1 (dominated by the highest credit quality borrowers, A++), GE Capital 91-1 (A− borrowers), Fleet Finance 90-1 (B/C borrowers), and Goldome Credit 90-1 (D borrowers). Prepayments were analyzed from the third quarter of 1991 to the third quarter of 1995, a period that encompassed the refinancing wave of 1992 and 1993. The main focus was on how borrower credit quality affected prepayments. The study found that prepayments for the Goldome Credit 90-1 deal (which was composed of D borrowers) were completely uncorrelated to changes in interest rates. The deal with the highest credit quality borrowers, FICAL 90-1, exhibited prepayments similar to that of agency mortgage-backed securities in terms of their sensitivity to interest rates. The correlation between prepayments and interest rates for the deal with A- borrowers (Capital 91-1) was less than for FICAL 90-1 but greater than for the deal with B/C borrowers (Fleet

---

[8]Dale Westhoff and Mark Feldman, "Prepayment Modeling and Valuation of Home Equity Loan Securitizations," Chapter 16 in Frank J. Fabozzi, Chuck Ramsey, Frank Ramirez, and Michael Marz (eds.), *The Handbook of Nonagency Mortgage-Backed Securities* (New Hope, PA: Frank J. Fabozzi Associates, 1997).

Finance 90-1). Consequently, the sensitivity of refinancing to interest rates is reduced the lower the credit quality of the borrower.

Prudential Securities has developed a prepayment benchmark for closed-end, fixed-rate HELs. The benchmark reflects Prudential Securities findings that such loans season much faster than traditional single-family mortgage loans. The benchmark, referred to by Prudential Securities as the **home equity prepayment curve** (or HEP curve), assumes that the loans become seasoned after ten months (as opposed to residential mortgage loans, which are assumed by the PSA prepayment benchmark to season after 30 months). The HEP curve is expressed in terms of the terminal CPR and assumes a linear increase in the CPR each month up to month 10. For example, 10% HEP means a CPR of 1% in month 1 with the CPR for each subsequent month increasing by 1% until month 10 when the CPR is 10%. An 18% HEP means a CPR of 1.8% in month 1 with the CPR for each subsequent month increasing by 1.8% until month 10 when the CPR is 18%.

> Bear Stearns found that seasoning depends on the credit quality of the borrowers and the attributes of the loans. Some loans season in 10 months and some take as long as 30 months. The study by Bear Stearns found that the seasoning process consists of two phases. The first phase exhibits rapid seasoning and an eventual plateau in prepayments. In this phase, all other factors equal, lower credit quality loans tend to season faster and plateau at a higher level than loans of higher credit quality. Bear Stearns found the following pattern in a no-change interest rate scenario[9]:

Borrower Credit Quality	*Seasoning*	*CPR at Plateau*
A	30 months	18% to 20% CPR
B	15 to 18 months	24% CPR
C	12 to 15 months	30% CPR

Bear Stearns hypothesized that the reason for the more rapid seasoning and higher plateau for pools of lower credit quality borrowers is because those borrowers that make timely payments become eligible to move up in credit quality rating and can thereby take advantage of lower loan rates that may be available. Loan originators monitor such loans and solicit loan applications from such potential borrowers. Bear Stearns refers to this as the "credit cure" effect.

In the second phase there is a longer period of steadily declining prepayments. For lower credit quality loans, there is a significant slowdown in prepayments that lasts three to four years. Bear Stearns believes that this is because borrowers who have improved their credit quality refinance in the first phase, which leaves in the remaining pool borrowers who are less able to refinance, as well as those who may exhibit a greater tendency to be delinquent. This phase is referred to as the "credit inertia" effect.

Prospectus Prepayment Curve   Borrower characteristics and the seasoning process must be kept in mind when trying to assess prepayments for a particular deal. In the prospectus of an offering, a base case prepayment assumption is made: The initial

---

[9]Westhoff and Feldman, "Prepayment Modeling and Valuation of Home Equity Loan Securitizations."

speed and the amount of time until the collateral is expected to be seasoned. Thus, the prepayment benchmark is issue specific. Investors are now using the concept of a **prospectus prepayment curve,** or PPC. This is just a multiple of the base case prepayments assumed in the prospectus. For example, in the prospectus for the Contimortgage Home Equity Loan Trust 1996-1, the base case prepayment assumption for the fixed-rate mortgages in the pool is as follows (p. 3–37):

> . . . a 100% Prepayment Assumption assumes conditional prepayment rates of 4% per annum of the then outstanding principal balance of the Home Equity Loans in the Fixed Rate Group in the first month of the life of the mortgage loans and an additional 1.455% (precisely 16/11%) per annum in each month thereafter until the twelfth month. Beginning in the twelfth month and in each month thereafter during the life of the mortgage loans, 100% Prepayment Assumption assumes a conditional prepayment rate of 20% per annum each month.

Therefore, if an investor analyzed the deal based on 200% PPC, this means doubling the CPRs cited in the excerpt and using 12 months for seasoning.

In the Champion Home Equity Loan Trust 1996-1, the base case prepayment assumption is specified in the prospectus as follows (S-28):

> The model used with respect to the Fixed Rate Certificates (the "Prepayment Ramp") assumes that the Home Equity Loans in Loan Group One prepay at a rate of 4% CPR in the first month after origination, and an additional 1.5% each month thereafter until the 14th month. Beginning in the 15th month and each month thereafter, the Prepayment Ramp assumes a prepayment rate of 25% CPR.

Thus, 100% PPC is based on the preceding CPRs assuming seasoning after 14 months.

Payment Structure

Typically, home equity loan–backed securities are securitized by both closed-end fixed-rate and adjustable-rate (or variable-rate) HELs. The securities backed by the latter are called HEL floaters, and most are backed by nonprime HELs. The reference rate of the underlying loans typically is six-month LIBOR. The cash flow of these loans is affected by periodic and lifetime caps on the loan rate. To increase the attractiveness of home equity loan–backed securities to investors, the securities typically have been created in which the reference rate is one-month LIBOR. Because of (1) the mismatch between the reference rate on the underlying loans and that of the HEL floater and (2) the periodic and life caps of the underlying loans, there is a cap on the coupon rate for the HEL floater. Unlike a typical floater, which has a cap that is fixed throughout the security's life, the effective periodic and lifetime cap of a HEL floater is variable. The effective cap, referred to as the **available funds cap,** will depend on the amount of funds generated by the net coupon on the principal, less any fees.[10]

Let's look at one issue, Advanta Mortgage Loan Trust 1995-2 issued in June 1995. At the offering, this issue had approximately $122 million closed-end HELs. There

---

[10]For a further discussion of the determinants of the available funds cap, see Lireen Tsai and Cyrus Mohebbi, "Home-Equity Loan Floaters," Chapter 19 in *Asset-Backed Securities.*

were 1,192 HELs, 727 fixed-rate loans, and 465 variable-rate loans. There were five classes (A-1, A-2, A-3, A-4, and A-5) and a residual. The five classes are summarized below:

Class	Par Amount ($)	Pass-Through Coupon Rate (%)
A-1	9,229,000	7.30
A-2	30,330,000	6.60
A-3	16,455,000	6.85
A-4	9,081,000	floating rate
A-5	56,917,000	floating rate

As explained next, class A-5 had two subclasses, A-5-I and A-5-II.

The collateral is divided into group I and group II. The 727 fixed-rate loans are included in group I and support Classes A-1, A-2, A-3, and A-4. The 465 variable-rate loans are in group II and support Classes A-5-I and A-5-II certificates. All classes receive monthly principal and interest (based on the pass-through coupon rate).

The initial investors in the A-5 floating-rate certificates were given a choice between two subclasses that offered different floating rates. Subclass A-5-I has a pass-through coupon rate equal to the lesser of (1) 12% and (2) one-month LIBOR plus 32 basis points with a cap of 12%. Subclass A-5-II has a pass-through coupon rate equal to the lesser of (1) the interest rate for subclass A-5-I and (2) the group II available funds cap. The available funds cap, also called the net funds cap, is the maximum rate payable on the outstanding Class A-5 certificates principal balance based on the interest due on the variable-rate loans net of fees and minus 50 basis points.

The Class A-4 certificate also has a floating rate. The rate is 7.4% subject to the net funds cap for group I. This is the rate that is paid until the outstanding aggregate loan balances in the trust have declined to 10% or less. At that time, Class A-4 will accrue interest on a payment date that depends on the average net loan rate minus 50 basis points and the net funds cap rate for group I.

Credit Enhancement

All forms of credit enhancement described earlier in this chapter have been used for home equity loan–backed securities.

To illustrate the credit enhancement and structural characteristics, let's return to the Advanta Mortgage Loan Trust 1995-2. All of the classes (A-1 through A-5) received a rating of AAA by Standard & Poor's due to the credit enhancement. All the classes were credit enhanced through excess spread for both group I and group II collateral, and two bond insurance policies issued by MBIA that cover the amount of the certificates. The excess spread was the first layer of credit protection. For the group I loans, the excess spread is the difference between the weighted average loan rate for the fixed-rate loans and the pass-through coupon rate. For group II, the loans are variable rate and the excess spread is the sum of (1) the difference between the floating rate on the loans (which is six-month LIBOR) and the pass-through coupon rate (which is one-month LIBOR) and (2) the weighted average margin on the loans. In determination of the excess spread, it is necessary to assume some prepayment speed. In stress testing the structure, Standard & Poor's used a 23% CPR.

MANUFACTURED HOUSING–BACKED SECURITIES

Manufactured housing–backed securities are backed by loans for manufactured homes. In contrast to site-built homes, manufactured homes are built at a factory and then transported to a manufactured home community or private land. These homes are more popularly referred to as mobile homes. The loan may be either a mortgage loan (for both the land and the mobile home) or a consumer retail installment loan.

Manufactured housing–backed securities are issued by Ginnie Mae and private entities. The former securities are guaranteed by the full faith and credit of the U.S. government. The manufactured housing loans that are collateral for the securities issued and guaranteed by Ginnie Mae are loans guaranteed by the Federal Housing Administration (FHA) or Veterans Administration (VA).

Loans not backed by the FHA or VA are called conventional loans. Manufactured housing–backed securities that are backed by such loans are called conventional manufactured housing–backed securities. These securities are issued by private entities. The largest issuer is Green Tree Financial, which has issued more than 70% of the manufactured housing-backed securities issued. Other issuers include Security Pacific Acceptance Corporation, Vanderbilt Mortgage and Finance, and Oakwood Mortgage Investors. The Resolution Trust Corporation was an issuer of these securities.

Cash Flow

The typical loan for a manufactured home is 15 to 20 years. The loan repayment is structured to fully amortize the amount borrowed. Therefore, as with residential mortgage loans and HELs, the cash flow consists of net interest, regularly scheduled principal, and prepayments. However, prepayments are more stable for manufactured housing–backed securities because they are not sensitive to refinancing.

There are several reasons for this.[11] The loan balances are typically small so that there is no significant dollar savings from refinancing. Second, the rate of depreciation of mobile homes may be such that in the earlier years depreciation is greater than the amount of the loan paid off. This makes it difficult to refinance the loan. Finally, typically borrowers are of lower credit quality and therefore find it difficult to obtain funds to refinance.

As with residential mortgage loans and HELs, prepayments on manufactured housing–backed securities are measured in terms of CPR.

Payment Structure

The payment structure is the same as with home equity loan–backed securities. For example, consider the Green Tree Manufactured Housing Contract Trust 1995-3 issue. There were four classes in this $502.1 million issue: A-1, M-1, B-1, and B-2. Class A-1 is the senior class, Classes M-1, B-1, and B-2 are the subordinated or junior

---

[11]Thomas Zimmerman and Inna Koren, "Manufactured Housing Securities," Chapter 5 in *Asset-Backed Securities.*

classes. The priority of payments is as follows: first payments are made to Class A-1, then to Class M-1, then to Classes B-1, and then finally to Class B-2.

Credit Enhancement

Credit enhancements are the same as with home equity loan–backed securities. In the Green Tree Manufactured Housing Contract Trust 1995-3 issue, there is a senior/subordinated structure and excess spread. The excess spread at the time of issuance was 4% and provided support for all four classes. There was an 18% subordination provided for Class A-1 by the three subordinated classes (M-1, B-1, and B-2). Class A-1 was rated AAA by Standard & Poor's. Class M-1 was supported by a 9% subordination provided by Class B-1 and Class B-2 in addition to the excess servicing spread and was rated AA−. Class B-1 had credit support from Class B-2 (4.5% subordination) and the excess servicing spread, and received a rating of BBB+. Class B-2 was rated BBB based on a guarantee by Green Tree of the timely payment of interest and principal, as well as the excess servicing spread.

SUMMARY

Asset-backed securities are creating by pooling loans and receivables. Traditionally, asset-backed securities differ from mortgage-backed securities in that the latter are backed by first-lien mortgage loans. The four largest sectors of the asset-backed securities market in the United States are securities backed by credit card receivables, auto loans, home equity loans, and manufactured housing loans.

Asset-backed securities expose investors to credit risk. In analyzing credit risk, the rating companies look at basically four elements of a structure: (1) credit quality of the collateral, (2) the quality of the seller/servicer, (3) cash flow stress and payment (financial) structure, and (4) legal structure. Based on its analysis of the four elements, a rating company will determine the amount of credit enhancement needed for an issue to receive a particular rating. Credit enhancement can be either internal (e.g., reserve funds and senior/subordinated structures) or external (e.g. insurance, corporate guarantees, letters of credit, or cash collateral reserves).

All asset-backed securities are credit enhanced to provide greater protection to investors against defaults. There are two general types of credit enhancement structures: external and internal. External credit enhancements come in the form of third-party guarantees that provide for first loss protection against losses up to a specified dollar amount. Internal credit enhancements include reserve funds reserves (cash reserves and excess servicing spread), overcollateralization, and senior/subordinated structures.

The collateral for an asset-backed security can be either amortizing assets (e.g., auto loans and closed-end home equity loans) or nonamortizing assets (e.g., credit card receivables). For an amortizing asset, projection of the cash flow requires projecting prepayments. For nonamortizing assets, the prepayment concept does not apply because there is no schedule of principal repayments.

One factor that may affect prepayments is the prevailing level of interest rates relative to the interest rate on the loan. Because a default is a prepayment, prepayment modeling for an asset-backed security backed by amortizing assets requires a model for projecting the amount that will be recovered and when it will be recovered.

Cash flow analysis can be performed on a pool level or a loan level. The maturity of an asset-backed security is not a meaningful parameter, so the average life of the security is calculated.

Auto loan–backed securities are issued by the financial subsidiaries of auto manufacturers, commercial banks, and independent finance companies and small financial institutions specializing in auto loans. The cash flow for auto loan–backed securities consists of regularly scheduled monthly loan payments (interest and scheduled principal repayments) and any prepayments. Prepayments on auto loans are not sensitive to interest rates. Prepayments on auto loan–backed securities are measured in terms of the absolute prepayment rate (denoted ABS), which measures monthly prepayments relative to the original collateral amount.

Credit card receivable–backed securities are backed by credit card receivables for credit cards issued by banks, retailers, and travel and entertainment companies. For credit card receivable–backed securities, the cash flow consists of finance charges collected (paid monthly, quarterly, or semiannually) and principal. The principal repayment of a credit card receivable–backed security is not amortized; instead, during the lockout period, the principal payments made by credit card borrowers are retained by the trustee and reinvested in additional receivables and after the lockout period (the principal-amortization period), the principal received by the trustee is no longer reinvested but paid to investors. There are provisions in credit card receivable–backed securities that require early amortization of the principal if certain events occur. For credit card receivable–backed securities, the concept of prepayments does not apply, so participants look at the MPR, which expresses the monthly payment (including finance charges collected and any principal) of a credit card receivable portfolio as a percentage of debt outstanding in the previous month.

An HEL is a loan backed by residential property, and the lien is typically a second or third lien on the property. Home equity loans can be either closed end (i.e., structured the same way as a fully amortizing residential mortgage loan) or open end (i.e., homeowner given a credit line). Home equity loan borrowers are segmented into four general credit quality groups, A, B, C, and D, but there is no industry-wide definition for classifying a borrower. The monthly cash flow for a home equity loan–backed security backed by closed-end HELs consists of (1) net interest, (2) regularly scheduled principal payments, and (3) prepayments. In general it is expected that prepayments due to refinancings would be less important for HELs than for traditional residential mortgage loans.

Manufactured housing–backed securities are backed by loans on manufactured homes (i.e., homes built at a factory and then transported to a site). A manufactured housing loan's cash flow consists of net interest, regularly scheduled principal, and prepayments. Prepayments are more stable for manufactured housing–backed securities because they are not sensitive to refinancing.

Questions

1. Why is credit enhancement of an asset-backed security required?
2. Why is an SPV created when issuing an asset-backed security?
3. Why do rating agencies assess the seller/servicer of an asset-backed security?
4. What is the limitation of a third-party guarantee as a form of credit enhancement?

5. An issuer is considering two possible credit enhancement structures backed by a pool of automobile loans. Total principal value underlying the asset-backed security is $300 million.

Principal value for:	Structure I	Structure II
Pool of automobile loans	$304 million	$301 million
Senior class	250	270
Subordinated class	50	30

   a. Which structure would receive a higher credit rating and why?

   b. What forms of credit enhancement are being used in both structures?

6. An asset-backed security has been credit enhanced with a letter of credit from a bank with a single A credit rating. If this is the only form of credit enhancement, explain whether this issue can be assigned a triple A credit rating.

7. a. What is meant by concentration risk?

   b. How do rating agencies seek to limit the exposure of a pool of loans to concentration risk?

8. What is the difference between pool-level and loan-level analysis?

9. The following questions relate to auto loan–backed securities:

   a. What is the cash flow for an auto loan–backed security?

   b. Why are prepayments of minor importance for automobile–loan backed securities?

   c. How are prepayments on pools of auto loans measured?

10. The following questions relate to credit card receivable–backed securities.

    a. What happens to the principal repaid by borrowers in a credit card receivable–backed security during the lockout or revolving period?

    b. What is the role of the early amortization provision in a credit card receivable–backed security structure?

    c. How can the cash flow of a credit card receivable–backed security be altered prior to the principal-amortization period?

    d. What are the three types of principal repayment structures?

    e. Why is the monthly payment rate an important measure to examine when considering investing in a credit card receivable–backed security?

11. The following questions relate to home equity loan–backed securities.

    a. What is the cash flow of a closed-end home equity loan–backed security?

    b. How are prepayment on these securities measured?

    c. What is meant by the prospectus prepayment curve?

    d. What have studies found regarding the relationship between prepayments due to refinancing and the credit quality of the underlying borrowers?

12. What is meant by an available funds cap and how does this cap differ from a typical cap in a floating-rate security?

13. The following questions relate to manufactured housing–backed securities.

    a. What is the cash flow of a manufactured housing–backed security?

    b. How are prepayments measured for manufactured housing–backed securities?

    c. Why are prepayments on manufactured housing–backed securities insensitive to prepayments due to refinancing?

14. The following quotation appeared in an article titled "Burlington Uses New Structure in Lease Deal" that appeared in *BondWeek:*

> Burlington Northern Railroad was expected to hit the market last Friday with the first issue of pass-through securities backed by leases from railroad equipment lease pools, according to Karl Essig, head of asset-backed securities structuring and origination at sole-manager Morgan Stanley.

The pass-through structure made the deal more marketable and channeled cashflow enabled the deal to obtain a higher rating, he noted. "The structure was a very significant advance in obtaining ratings," Essig said.

Most of the leases' average lives were too long to qualify for the target Aa3/A+ rating. By channeling the different cashflows together, Burlington was able to add lease diversity and create an aggregate average life of an acceptable level for the desired rating, said Steven Schiffman, director of corporate finance at Burlington. . . .

The $117 million public offering, Burlington Northern Railroad Pass-through Trust 1990-A, was offered in two pass-through tranches, which had average lives of 8.8 and 16.7 years, respectively. . . . They were backed by seven different leases for automobile racks, new covered hoppers, new gondola cars, box cars, new locomotives and two for remanufactured locomotives, according to Schiffman.

a. At the time of issuance, Burlington Northern Railroad was rated A3/BBB+. Explain how this structure enabled Burlington to issue debt at a lower cost than would be possible by issuing traditional bonds.
b. Why do you think the issue was structured to have two classes of pass-throughs?

CHAPTER 14

Analysis of Bonds with Embedded Options

Learning Objectives

After reading this chapter you will understand:

- the drawbacks of the traditional yield spread analysis

- what static spread is and under what conditions it would differ from the traditional yield spread

- the disadvantages of a callable bond from the investor's perspective

- the yield to worst and the pitfalls of the traditional approach to valuing callable bonds

- the price–yield relationship for a callable bond

- negative convexity and when a callable bond may exhibit it

- how the value of a bond with an embedded option can be decomposed

- the binomial method and how it is used to value a bond with an embedded option

- how a binomial interest-rate tree is constructed to be consistent with the prices for the on-the-run issues of an issuer and a given volatility assumption

- what an option-adjusted spread is and how it is calculated using the binomial method

- the limitations of using modified duration and standard convexity as a measure of the price sensitivity of a bond with an embedded option

- the difference between effective duration and modified duration

- how effective duration and effective convexity are calculated using the binomial method

In earlier chapters we discussed pricing, yield measures, and price volatility for bonds without options. In Chapter 2 we saw that the price of a bond was based on the present value of its cash flow. A bond with an embedded option is one in which either the issuer or the bondholder has the option to alter a bond's cash flows. In this chapter we look at how to analyze bonds with embedded options. Because the most common type of option embedded in a bond is a call option, our primary focus is on callable bonds. We begin by looking at the limitations of traditional yield spread analysis. Although corporate bonds are used in our examples, the analysis presented in this chapter is equally applicable to agency securities and municipal securities. In the next chapter we focus on the analysis of mortgage-backed securities.

DRAWBACKS OF TRADITIONAL YIELD SPREAD ANALYSIS

Traditional analysis of the yield premium for a non-Treasury bond involves calculating the difference between the yield to maturity (or yield to call) of the bond in question and the yield to maturity of a comparable-maturity Treasury. The latter is obtained from the Treasury yield curve. For example, consider two 8.8% coupon 25-year bonds:

Issue	Price	Yield to Maturity (%)
Treasury	$96.6133	9.15
Corporate	87.0798	10.24

The yield spread for these two bonds as traditionally computed is 109 basis points (10.24% minus 9.15%). The drawbacks of this convention, however, are (1) the yield for both bonds fails to take into consideration the term structure of interest rates, and (2) in the case of callable and/or putable bonds, expected interest rate volatility may alter the cash flow of a bond. For now, let's focus only on the first problem: failure to incorporate the term structure of interest rates.

STATIC SPREAD: AN ALTERNATIVE TO YIELD SPREAD

In traditional yield spread analysis, an investor compares the yield to maturity of a bond with the yield to maturity of a similar maturity on-the-run Treasury security. This means that the yield to maturity of a 25-year zero-coupon corporate bond and an 8.8% coupon 25-year corporate coupon bond would both be compared to a benchmark 25-year Treasury security. Such a comparison makes little sense, because the cash flow characteristics of the two corporate bonds will not be the same as that of the benchmark Treasury.

The proper way to compare non-Treasury bonds of the same maturity but with different coupon rates is to compare them with a portfolio of Treasury securities that have the same cash flow. For example, consider the 8.8% 25-year corporate bond selling for 87.0798. The cash flow per $100 par value for this corporate bond, assuming that interest rates do not change (i.e., assuming static interest rates), is 49 six-month payments of $4.40 and a payment in 25 years (50 six-month periods) of $104.40. A portfolio that will replicate this cash flow would include 50 zero-coupon Treasury securities with maturities coinciding with the amount and timing of the cash flows of the corporate bond.

The corporate bond's value is equal to the present value of all the cash flows. The corporate bond's value, assuming that the cash flows are riskless, will equal the present value of the replicating portfolio of Treasury securities. In turn, these cash flows are valued at the Treasury spot rates. Exhibit 14-1 shows how to calculate the price of a risk-free 8.8% 25-year bond assuming the Treasury spot rate curve shown in the exhibit. The price would be $96.6133. The corporate bond's price is $87.0798, less than the package of zero-coupon Treasury securities, because investors in fact require a yield premium for the risk associated with holding a corporate bond rather than a riskless package of Treasury securities.

The **static spread,** also referred to as the **zero-volatility spread,** is a measure of the spread that the investor would realize over the entire Treasury spot rate curve if the bond is held to maturity. It is not a spread off one point on the Treasury yield curve, as is the traditional yield spread. The static spread is calculated as the spread that will make the present value of the cash flows from the corporate bond, when discounted at the Treasury spot rate plus the spread, equal to the corporate bond's price. A trial-and-error procedure is required to determine the static spread.

To illustrate how this is done, let's use the corporate bond in the first illustration. Select a spread, say, 100 basis points. To each Treasury spot rate shown in the third column in Exhibit 14-2, 100 basis points is added. So, for example, the 14-year (period 28) spot rate is 10.0% (9% plus 1%). The spot rate plus 100 basis points is then used to calculate the present value of 88.5473. Because the present value is not equal to the corporate bond's price ($87.0798), the static spread is not 100 basis points. If a spread of 110 basis points is tried, it can be seen from the next-to-last column of Exhibit 14-2 that the present value is $87.8031; again, because this is not equal to the corporate bond's price, 110 basis points is not the static spread. The last column of Exhibit 14-2 shows the present value when a 120-basis-point spread is tried. The present value is equal to the corporate bond price. Therefore, 120 basis points is the static spread, compared to the traditional yield spread of 109 basis points.

Exhibit 14-3 shows the static spread and the traditional yield spread for bonds with various maturities and prices, assuming the Treasury spot rates shown in Exhibit 14-1. Notice that the shorter the maturity of the bond, the less the static spread will differ from the traditional yield spread. The magnitude of the difference between the traditional yield spread and the static spread also depends on the shape of the yield curve. The steeper the yield curve, the more the difference for a given coupon and maturity.

Another reason for the small differences in Exhibit 14-3 is that the corporate bond makes a bullet payment at maturity. The difference between the traditional yield spread and the static spread will be considerably greater for sinking fund bonds and mortgage-backed securities in a steep yield curve environment.

CALLABLE BONDS AND THEIR INVESTMENT CHARACTERISTICS

Now that we know the problems with the traditional yield spread analysis, let's introduce another complexity: the callability of an issue. We begin by examining the characteristics of a callable bond. The holder of a callable bond has given the issuer the right to call the issue prior to the expiration date. The presence of a call option results in two disadvantages to the bondholder.

First, callable bonds expose bondholders to reinvestment risk, because an issuer will call a bond when the yield on bonds in the market is lower than the issue's coupon rate. For example, if the coupon rate on a callable corporate bond is 13% and prevail-

Period	Cash Flow	Treasury Spot Rate (%)	Present Value
1	4.4	7.00000	4.2512
2	4.4	7.04999	4.1055
3	4.4	7.09998	3.9628
4	4.4	7.12498	3.8251
5	4.4	7.13998	3.6922
6	4.4	7.16665	3.5622
7	4.4	7.19997	3.4351
8	4.4	7.26240	3.3077
9	4.4	7.33315	3.1820
10	4.4	7.38977	3.0611
11	4.4	7.44517	2.9434
12	4.4	7.49135	2.8302
13	4.4	7.53810	2.7200
14	4.4	7.57819	2.6141
15	4.4	7.61959	2.5112
16	4.4	7.66205	2.4111
17	4.4	7.70538	2.3139
18	4.4	7.74391	2.2207
19	4.4	7.78888	2.1291
20	4.4	7.83434	2.0404
21	4.4	8.22300	1.8879
22	4.4	8.33333	1.7923
23	4.4	8.40000	1.7080
24	4.4	8.50000	1.6204
25	4.4	8.54230	1.5465
26	4.4	8.72345	1.4500
27	4.4	8.90000	1.3581
28	4.4	9.00000	1.2829
29	4.4	9.01450	1.2252
30	4.4	9.23000	1.1367
31	4.4	9.39000	1.0611
32	4.4	9.44840	1.0045
33	4.4	9.50000	0.9514
34	4.4	9.50000	0.9083
35	4.4	9.50000	0.8671
36	4.4	9.50000	0.8278
37	4.4	9.55000	0.7833
38	4.4	9.56000	0.7462
39	4.4	9.58000	0.7095
40	4.4	9.58000	0.6771
41	4.4	9.60000	0.6436
42	4.4	9.70000	0.6020
43	4.4	9.80000	0.5625
44	4.4	9.90000	0.5251
45	4.4	10.00000	0.4897
46	4.4	10.10000	0.4563
47	4.4	10.30000	0.4154
48	4.4	10.50000	0.3774
49	4.4	10.60000	0.3503
50	104.4	10.80000	7.5278
Theoretical price			96.6133

EXHIBIT 14-2 Calculation of the Static Spread for a 25-Year 8.8% Coupon Corporate Bond

Period	Cash Flow	Treasury Spot Rate (%)	Present Value if Spread Used is:		
			100 BP	110 BP	120 BP
1	4.4	7.00000	4.2308	4.2287	4.2267
2	4.4	7.04999	4.0661	4.0622	4.0583
3	4.4	7.09998	3.9059	3.9003	3.8947
4	4.4	7.12498	3.7521	3.7449	3.7377
5	4.4	7.13998	3.6043	3.5957	3.5871
6	4.4	7.16665	3.4607	3.4508	3.4408
7	4.4	7.19997	3.3212	3.3101	3.2990
8	4.4	7.26240	3.1828	3.1706	3.1584
9	4.4	7.33315	3.0472	3.0340	3.0210
10	4.4	7.38977	2.9174	2.9034	2.8895
11	4.4	7.44517	2.7917	2.7770	2.7624
12	4.4	7.49135	2.6715	2.6562	2.6409
13	4.4	7.53810	2.5552	2.5394	2.5236
14	4.4	7.57819	2.4440	2.4277	2.4115
15	4.4	7.61959	2.3366	2.3198	2.3032
16	4.4	7.66205	2.2327	2.2157	2.1988
17	4.4	7.70538	2.1325	2.1152	2.0981
18	4.4	7.74391	2.0368	2.0193	2.0020
19	4.4	7.78888	1.9435	1.9259	1.9085
20	4.4	7.83434	1.8536	1.8359	1.8184
21	4.4	8.22300	1.7072	1.6902	1.6733
22	4.4	8.33333	1.6131	1.5963	1.5796
23	4.4	8.40000	1.5300	1.5132	1.4967
24	4.4	8.50000	1.4446	1.4282	1.4119
25	4.4	8.54230	1.3722	1.3559	1.3398
26	4.4	8.72345	1.2806	1.2648	1.2492
27	4.4	8.90000	1.1938	1.1785	1.1635
28	4.4	9.00000	1.1224	1.1075	1.0929
29	4.4	9.01450	1.0668	1.0522	1.0378
30	4.4	9.23000	0.9852	0.9712	0.9575
31	4.4	9.39000	0.9154	0.9020	0.8888
32	4.4	9.44840	0.8625	0.8495	0.8367
33	4.4	9.50000	0.8131	0.8004	0.7880
34	4.4	9.50000	0.7725	0.7601	0.7480
35	4.4	9.50000	0.7340	0.7219	0.7100
36	4.4	9.50000	0.6974	0.6855	0.6739
37	4.4	9.55000	0.6568	0.6453	0.6341
38	4.4	9.56000	0.6227	0.6116	0.6007
39	4.4	9.58000	0.5893	0.5785	0.5679
40	4.4	9.58000	0.5597	0.5492	0.5389
41	4.4	9.60000	0.5295	0.5193	0.5093
42	4.4	9.70000	0.4929	0.4832	0.4737
43	4.4	9.80000	0.4585	0.4492	0.4401
44	4.4	9.90000	0.4260	0.4172	0.4086
45	4.4	10.00000	0.3955	0.3871	0.3789
46	4.4	10.10000	0.3668	0.3588	0.3511
47	4.4	10.30000	0.3323	0.3250	0.3179
48	4.4	10.50000	0.3006	0.2939	0.2873
49	4.4	10.60000	0.2778	0.2714	0.2652
50	104.4	10.80000	5.9416	5.8030	5.6677
	Total present value		88.5473	87.8031	87.0798

EXHIBIT 14-3   Comparison of Traditional Yield Spread and Static Spread for Various Bonds[a]

Bond	Price	Yield to Maturity (%)	—Spread (basis points)—		
			Traditional	*Static*	*Difference*
		25-year 8.8% Coupon Bond			
Treasury	96.6133	9.15	—	—	—
A	88.5473	10.06	91	100	9
B	87.8031	10.15	100	110	10
C	87.0798	10.24	109	120	11
		15-year 8.8% Coupon Bond			
Treasury	101.9603	8.57	—	—	—
D	94.1928	9.54	97	100	3
E	93.4639	9.63	106	110	4
F	92.7433	9.73	116	120	4
		10-year 8.8% Coupon Bond			
Treasury	107.4906	7.71	—	—	—
G	100.6137	8.71	100	100	0
H	99.9585	8.81	110	110	0
I	99.3088	8.91	120	120	0
		5-year 8.8% Coupon Bond			
Treasury	105.9555	7.36	—	—	—
J	101.7919	8.35	99	100	1
K	101.3867	8.45	109	110	1
L	100.9836	8.55	119	120	1

[a]Assumes Treasury spot rate curve given in Exhibit 14-1.

ing market yields are 7%, the issuer will find it economical to call the 13% issue and refund it with a 7% issue. From the investor's perspective, the proceeds received will have to be reinvested at a lower interest rate.

Second, as we explain later in this chapter, the price appreciation potential for a callable bond in a declining interest-rate environment is limited. This is because the market will increasingly expect the bond to be redeemed at the call price as interest rates fall. This phenomenon for a callable bond is referred to as **price compression.**

Because of the disadvantages associated with callable bonds, these instruments often feature a period of call protection, an initial period when bonds may not be called. Still, given both price compression and reinvestment risk, why would any investor want to own a callable bond? If the investor receives sufficient potential compensation in the form of a higher potential yield, an investor would be willing to accept call risk.

Traditional Valuation Methodology for Callable Bonds

When a bond is callable, the practice has been to calculate a **yield to worst.** As explained in Chapter 3, the yield to worst is the smallest of the yield to maturity and the yield to call for all possible call dates. The yield to worst is the yield that the traditional approach has investors believing should be used in relative value analysis of callable bonds.

We explained in Chapter 3 the limitations of the **yield to call** as a measure of the potential return of a security. The yield to call does consider all three sources of potential return from owning a bond. However, as in the case of the yield to maturity, it assumes that all cash flows can be reinvested at the computed yield—in this case the yield to call—until the assumed call date. Moreover, the yield to call assumes that (1) the investor will hold the bond to the assumed call date, and (2) the issuer will call the bond on that date.

Often, these underlying assumptions about the yield to call are unrealistic because they do not take into account how an investor will reinvest the proceeds if the issue is called. For example, consider two bonds, M and N. Suppose that the yield to maturity for bond M, a five-year noncallable bond, is 10%, and the yield to call for bond N is 10.5% assuming that the bond will be called in three years. Which bond is better for an investor with a five-year investment horizon? It is not possible to tell for the yields cited. If the investor intends to hold the bond for five years and the issuer calls the bond after three years, the total dollars that will be available at the end of five years will depend on the interest rate that can be earned from investing funds from the call date to the end of the investment horizon.

Price–Yield Relationship for a Callable Bond

As explained in Chapter 4, the price–yield relationship for an option-free bond is convex. Exhibit 14-4 shows the price–yield relationship for both a noncallable bond and the same bond if it is callable. The convex curve a–a′ is the price–yield relationship for the noncallable (option-free) bond. The unusual shaped curve denoted by a–b is the price–yield relationship for the callable bond.

EXHIBIT 14-4 Price-Yield Relationship for a Noncallable and a Callable Bond

The reason for the shape of the price–yield relationship for the callable bond is as follows. When the prevailing market yield for comparable bonds is higher than the coupon interest on the bond, it is unlikely that the issuer will call the bond. For example, if the coupon rate on a bond is 8% and the prevailing yield on comparable bonds is 16%, it is highly improbable that the issuer will call an 8% coupon bond so that it can issue a 16% coupon bond. The bond is unlikely to be called, so the callable bond will have the same convex price–yield relationship as a noncallable bond when yields are greater than y^*. However, even when the coupon rate is just below the market yield, investors may not pay the same price for the callable bond had it been noncallable because there is still the chance the market yield may drop further, making it beneficial for the issuer to call the bond.

As yields in the market decline, the likelihood that yields will decline further so that the issuer will benefit from calling the bond increases. The exact yield level at which investors begin to view the issue likely to be called may not be known, but we do know that there is some level. In Exhibit 14-4, at yield levels below y^*, the price–yield relationship for the callable bond departs from the price–yield relationship for the noncallable bond. Consider a bond that is callable at 104. If market yield would price a comparable noncallable bond at 109, rational investors would not pay 109 for the callable bond. If they did and the bond were called, investors would receive 104 (the call price) for a bond they purchased for 109.

Notice that for a range of yields below y^*, there is price compression—that is, there is limited price appreciation as yields decline. The portion of the callable bond price–yield relationship below y^* is said to be negatively convex.

Negative convexity means that the price appreciation will be less than the price depreciation for a large change in yield of a given number of basis points. For a bond that is option-free and exhibits positive convexity, the price appreciation will be greater than the price depreciation for a large change in yield. The price changes resulting from bonds exhibiting positive convexity and negative convexity are shown in Exhibit 14-5.

It is important to understand that a bond can still trade above its call price even if it is highly likely to be called. For example, consider a callable bond with a 10-year 13% coupon rate that is callable in one year at a call price of 104. Suppose that the yield on 10-year bonds is 6% and that the yield on one-year bonds is 5%. In a 6% interest rate environment for 10-year bonds, investors will expect that the issue will be called in one year. Thus, investors will treat this issue as if it is a one-year bond and price it accordingly. The price must reflect the fact that the investor will receive a 13% coupon rate for one year. The price of this bond would be the present value of the two cash flows, which are (1) $6.5 (per $100 of par value) of coupon interest six months

EXHIBIT 14-5	Price Volatility Implications of Positive and Negative Convexity	
	Absolute Value of Percentage Price Change	
Change in Interest Rates	**Positive Convexity**	**Negative Convexity**
−100 basis points	X%	Less than Y%
+100 basis points	Less than X%	Y%

from now, and (2) $6.50 coupon interest plus the call price of $104 one year from now. Discounting the two cash flows at the 5% prevailing market yield (2.5% every six months) for one-year bonds, the price is

$$\frac{\$6.5}{1.025} + \frac{\$110.5}{(1.025)^2} = \$111.52$$

The price is greater than the call price. Consequently, an investor will be willing to pay a higher price than the call price to purchase this bond.

COMPONENTS OF A BOND WITH AN EMBEDDED OPTION

To develop a framework for analyzing a bond with an embedded option, it is necessary to decompose a bond into its component parts. A **callable bond** is a bond in which the bondholder has sold the issuer an option (more specifically, a call option) that allows the issuer to repurchase the contractual cash flows of the bond from the time the bond is first callable until the maturity date.

Consider the following two bonds: (1) a callable bond with an 8% coupon, 20 years to maturity, and callable in five years at 104, and (2) a 10-year 9% coupon bond callable immediately at par. For the first bond, the bondholder owns a five-year noncallable bond and has sold a call option granting the issuer the right to call away from the bondholder 15 years of cash flows five years from now for a price of 104. The investor who owns the second bond has a 10-year noncallable bond and has sold a call option granting the issuer the right to call immediately the entire 10-year contractual cash flows, or any cash flows remaining at the time the issue is called, for 100.

Effectively, the owner of a callable bond is entering into two separate transactions. First, she buys a noncallable bond from the issuer for which she pays some price. Then, she sells the issuer a call option for which she receives the option price.

In terms of price, a callable bond is therefore equal to the price of the two components parts; that is,

callable bond price = noncallable bond price − call option price

The reason the call option price is subtracted from the price of the noncallable bond is that when the bondholder sells a call option, she receives the option price. Graphically, this can be seen in Exhibit 14-6. The difference between the price of the noncallable bond and the callable bond at any given yield is the price of the embedded call option.[1]

The same logic applies to **putable bonds.** In the case of a putable bond, the bondholder has the right to sell the bond to the issuer at a designated price and time. A putable bond can be broken into two separate transactions. First, the investor buys a

---

[1]Actually, the position is more complicated than we have described. The issuer may be entitled to call the bond at the first call date and anytime thereafter, or at the first call date and any subsequent coupon anniversary. Thus the investor has effectively sold an American-type call option to the issuer, but the call price may vary with the date the call option is exercised. This is because the call schedule for a bond may have a different call price depending on the call date. Moreover, the underlying bond for the call option is the remaining coupon payments that would have been made by the issuer had the bond not been called. For exposition purposes, it is easier to understand the principles associated with the investment characteristics of callable corporate bonds by describing the investor's position as long a noncallable bond and short a call option.

EXHIBIT 14-6   Decomposition of Price of a Callable Bond

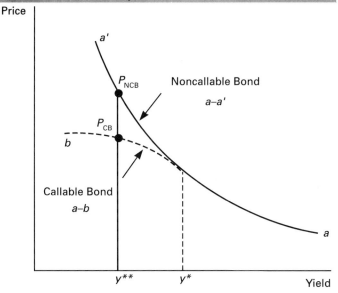

At y^{**} yield level: P_{NCB} = noncallable bond price
P_{CB} = callable bond price
$P_{\text{NCB}} - P_{\text{CB}}$ = call option price

noncallable bond. Second, the investor buys an option from the issuer that allows the investor to sell the bond to the issuer. The price of a putable bond is then

$$\text{putable bond price} = \text{nonputable bond price} + \text{put option price}$$

VALUATION MODEL[2]

Thus far, we described a way to think conceptually about bonds with embedded options. More specifically, the value of a callable bond is equal to the value of a comparable noncallable bond minus the value of the call option. In this section a model for valuing bonds with embedded options is presented.

The valuation principles that we have discussed so far in this book are used here. Specifically, we saw two important things in Chapter 5. First, it is inappropriate to use a single rate to discount all the cash flows of a bond. Second, the correct rate to use to discount each cash flow is the theoretical spot rate. This is equivalent to discounting at a series of forward rates.

What we have to add to the valuation process is how interest-rate volatility affects the value of a bond through its effects on the embedded options. We begin with a review of the valuation technique for bonds without embedded options.

---

[2]This section is adapted from Andrew J. Kalotay, George O. Williams, and Frank J. Fabozzi, "A Model for the Valuation of Bonds and Embedded Options," *Financial Analysts Journal,* May–June 1993, pp. 35–46.

Valuation of Option-Free Bonds

In Chapter 5 we said that the price of an option-free bond is the present value of the cash flows discounted at the spot rates. To illustrate this, let's use the following hypothetical yield curve:

Maturity (years)	Yield to Maturity (%)	Market Value
1	3.50	100
2	4.00	100
3	4.50	100

We will be simplifying the illustration by assuming annual-pay bonds. Using the bootstrapping methodology described in Chapter 5, the spot rates and the one-year forward rates can be obtained.

Year	Spot Rate (%)	One-Year Forward Rate (%)
1	3.500	3.500
2	4.010	4.523
3	4.541	5.580

Now consider an option-free bond with three years remaining to maturity and a coupon rate of 5.25%. The price of this bond can be calculated in one of two ways, both producing the same result. First, the coupon payments can be discounted at the zero-coupon rates:

$$\frac{\$5.25}{(1.035)} + \frac{\$5.25}{(1.0401)^2} + \frac{\$100 + \$5.25}{(1.04541)^3} = 102.075$$

The second way is to discount by the one-year forward rates:

$$\frac{\$5.25}{(1.035)} + \frac{\$5.25}{(1.035)(1.04523)} + \frac{\$100 + \$5.25}{(1.035)(1.04523)(1.05580)} = 102.075$$

Introducing Interest-Rate Volatility

When we allow for embedded options, consideration must be given to interest-rate volatility. This can be done by introducing a **binomial interest-rate tree.** This tree is nothing more than a graphical depiction of the one-period forward rates over time based on some assumption about interest-rate volatility. How this tree is constructed is illustrated next.

Binomial Interest-Rate Tree   Exhibit 14-7 shows an example of a binomial interest-rate tree. In this tree, each node (bold circle) represents a time period that is equal to one year from the node to its left. Each node is labeled with an N,

EXHIBIT 14-7   Three-Year Binomial Interest-Rate Tree

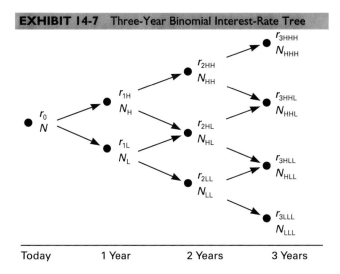

| Today | 1 Year | 2 Years | 3 Years |

representing **node**, and a subscript that indicates the path that one-year forward rates took to get to that node. H represents the *higher* of the two forward rates and L the *lower* of the two forward rates from the preceding year. For example, node N_{HH} means that to get to that node the following path for one-year rates occurred: The one-year rate realized is the higher of the two rates in the first year and then the higher of the one-year rates in the second year.[3]

Look first at the point denoted N in Exhibit 14-7. This is the root of the tree and is nothing more than the current one-year rate, or equivalently, the one-year forward rate, which we denote by r_0. What we have assumed in creating this tree is that the one-year forward rate can take on two possible values in the next period and that the two rates have the same probability of occurring. One rate will be higher than the other. More specifically, it is assumed that the one-year forward rate can evolve over time based on a random process called a **lognormal random walk** with a certain volatility.

We will use the following notation to describe the tree in the first year. Let

σ = assumed volatility of the one-year forward rate

$r_{1,L}$ = the lower one-year rate one year from now

$r_{1,H}$ = the higher one-year rate one year from now

The relationship between $r_{1,L}$ and $r_{1,H}$ is as follows:

$$r_{1,H} = r_{1,L}(e^{2\sigma})$$

where e is the base of the natural logarithm 2.71828. For example, suppose that $r_{1,L}$ is 4.074% and σ is 10% per year; then

$$r_{1,H} = 4.074\%(e^{2\times0.10}) = 4.976\%$$

---

[3]Note that N_{HL} is equivalent to N_{LH} in the second year, and that in the third year N_{HHL} is equivalent to N_{HLH} and N_{LHH} and that N_{HLL} is equivalent to N_{LLH}. We have simply selected one label for a node rather than clutter up the figure with unnecessary information.

In the second year, there are three possible values for the one-year rate, which we will denote as follows:

$r_{2,LL}$ = one-year rate in second year assuming the lower rate in the first year and the lower rate in the second year

$r_{2,HH}$ = one-year rate in second year assuming the higher rate in the first year and the higher rate in the second year

$r_{2,HL}$ = one-year rate in second year assuming the higher rate in the first year and the lower rate in the second year or equivalently the lower rate in the first year and the higher rate in the second year

The relationship between $r_{2,LL}$ and the other two one-year rates is as follows:

$$r_{2,HH} = r_{2,LL}(e^{4\sigma})$$

and

$$r_{2,HL} = r_{2,LL}(e^{2\sigma})$$

So, for example, if $r_{2,LL}$ is 4.53%, then assuming once again that σ is 10%,

$$r_{2,HH} = 4.53\%(e^{4\times0.10}) = 6.757\%$$

and

$$r_{2,HL} = 4.53\%(e^{2\times0.10}) = 5.532\%$$

Exhibit 14-7 shows the notation for the binomial interest-rate tree in the third year. We can simplify the notation by letting r_t be the lower one-year forward rate t years from now because all the other forward rates t years from now depend on that rate. Exhibit 14-8 shows the interest-rate tree using this simplified notation.

EXHIBIT 14-8   Three-Year Binomial Interest-Rate Tree with One-Year Forward Rates

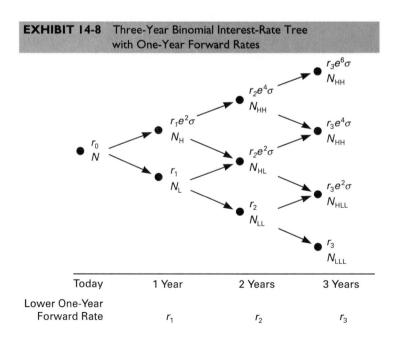

	Today	1 Year	2 Years	3 Years
Lower One-Year Forward Rate		r_1	r_2	r_3

Before we go on to show how to use this binomial interest-rate tree to value bonds, let's focus on two issues here. First, what does the volatility parameter σ in the expression $e^{2\sigma}$ represent? Second, how do we find the value of the bond at each node?

Volatility and the Standard Deviation   It can be shown that the standard deviation of the one-year forward rate is equal to $r_0\sigma$.[4] The standard deviation is a statistical measure of volatility. For now it is important to see that the process that we assumed generates the binomial interest-rate tree (or equivalently, the forward rates) implies that volatility is measured relative to the current level of rates. For example, if σ is 10% and the one-year rate (r_0) is 4%, the standard deviation of the one-year forward rate is 4% $\times$ 10% = 0.4% or 40 basis points. However, if the current one-year rate is 12%, the standard deviation of the one-year forward rate would be 12% $\times$ 10% or 120 basis points.

Determining the Value at a Node   The answer to the second question about how we find the value of the bond at a node is as follows. First calculate the bond's value at the two nodes to the right of the node where we want to obtain the bond's value. For example, in Exhibit 14-8, suppose that we want to determine the bond's value at node N_H. The bond's value at node N_{HH} and N_{HL} must be determined. Hold aside for now how we get these two values because as we will see, the process involves starting from the last year in the tree and working backward to get the final solution we want, so these two values will be known.

Effectively what we are saying is that if we are at some node, the value at that node will depend on the future cash flows. In turn, the future cash flows depend on (1) the bond's value one year from now, and (2) the coupon payment one year from now. The latter is known. The former depends on whether the one-year rate is the higher or lower rate. The bond's value depending on whether the rate is the higher or lower rate is reported at the two nodes to the right of the node that is the focus of our attention. So the cash flow at a node will be either (1) the bond's value if the short rate is the higher rate plus the coupon payment, or (2) the bond's value if the short rate is the lower rate plus the coupon payment. For example, suppose that we are interested in the bond's value at N_H. The cash flow will be either the bond's value at N_{HH} plus the coupon payment or the bond's value at N_{HL} plus the coupon payment.

To get the bond's value at a node we follow the fundamental rule for valuation: The value is the present value of the expected cash flows. The appropriate discount rate to use is the one-year forward rate at the node. Now there are two present values in this case: the present value if the one-year rate is the higher rate and the value if it is the lower rate. Because it is assumed that the probability of both outcomes is equal, an average of the two present values is computed. This is illustrated in Exhibit 14-9 for any node assuming that the one-year forward rate is r_* at the node where the valuation is sought and letting

$$V_H = \text{the bond's value for the higher one-year rate}$$
$$V_L = \text{the bond's value for the lower one-year rate}$$
$$C = \text{coupon payment}$$

---

[4]This can be seen by noting that $e^{2\sigma} \approx 1 + 2\sigma$. Then the standard deviation of one-period forward rates is

$$\frac{re^{2\sigma} - r}{2} \approx \frac{r + 2\sigma r - r}{2} = \sigma r$$

EXHIBIT 14-9 Calculating a Value at a Node

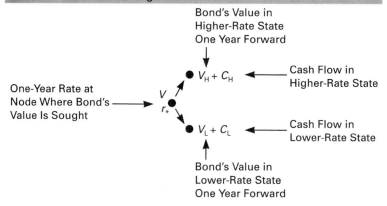

Using our notation, the cash flow at a node is either:

$$V_H + C \text{ for the higher one-year rate, or}$$
$$V_L + C \text{ for the lower one-year rate}$$

The present value of these two cash flows using the one-year rate at the node, r_*, is

$$\frac{V_H + C}{1 + r_*} \qquad \text{present value for the higher one-year rate}$$

$$\frac{V_L + C}{1 + r_*} \qquad \text{present value for the lower one-year rate}$$

Then the value of the bond at the node is found as follows:

$$\text{value at a node} = \frac{1}{2}\left[\frac{V_H + C}{1 + r_*} + \frac{V_L + C}{1 + r_*}\right]$$

Constructing the Binomial Interest-Rate Tree

To see how to construct the binomial interest-rate tree, let's use the assumed current on-the-run yields that we used earlier. We will assume that volatility, σ, is 10% and construct a two-year model using the two-year bond with a coupon rate of 4%.

Exhibit 14-10 shows a more detailed binomial interest-rate tree because at each node the cash flow is shown. We'll see how all the values reported in the exhibit are obtained. The root rate for the tree, r_0, is simply the current one-year rate, 3.5%.

In the first year there are two possible one-year rates, the higher rate and the lower rate. What we want to find is the two forward rates that will be consistent with the volatility assumption, the process that is assumed to generate the forward rates, and the observed market value of the bond. There is no simple formula for this. It must be found by an iterative process (i.e., trial and error). The steps are described and illustrated following.

Step 1: Select a value for r_1. Recall that r_1 is the lower one-year forward rate one year from now. In this first trial we *arbitrarily* selected a value of 4.5%.

EXHIBIT 14-10   Finding the One-Year Forward Rates for Year I Using the Two-Year 4% On-the-Run: First Trial

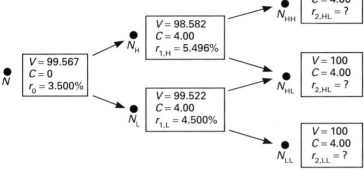

Step 2: Determine the corresponding value for the higher one-year forward rate. As explained earlier, this rate is related to the lower one-year forward rate as follows: $r_1 e^{2\sigma}$. Because r_1 is 4.5%, the higher one-year forward rate is 5.496% ($= 4.5\%\ e^{2\times0.10}$). This value is reported in Exhibit 14-10 at node N_H.

Step 3: Compute the bond's value one year from now. This value is determined as follows:

3a. The bond's value two years from now must be determined. In our example this is simple. We are using a two-year bond, so the bond's value is its maturity value ($100) plus its final coupon payment ($4). Thus, it is $104.

3b. Calculate the present value of the bond's value found in 3a using the higher rate. In our example the appropriate discount rate is the one-year higher forward rate, 5.496%. The present value is $98.582 ($= \$104/1.05496$). This is the value of V_H that we referred to earlier.

3c. Calculate the present value of the bond's value found in 3a using the lower rate. The discount rate used is then the lower one-year forward rate, 4.5%. The value is $99.522 ($= \$104/1.045$) and is the value of V_L.

3d. Add the coupon to V_H and V_L to get the cash flow at N_H and N_L, respectively. In our example we have $102.582 for the higher rate and $103.522 for the lower rate.

3e. Calculate the present value of the two values using the one-year forward rate using r_*. At this point in the valuation, r_* is the root rate, 3.50%. Therefore,

$$\frac{V_H + C}{1 + r_*} = \frac{\$102.582}{1.035} = \$99.113$$

and

$$\frac{V_L + C}{1 + r_*} = \frac{\$103.522}{1.035} = \$100.021$$

Step 4: Calculate the average present value of the two cash flows in step 3. This is the value we referred to earlier as

$$\text{value at a node} = \frac{1}{2}\left[\frac{V_H + C}{1 + r_*} + \frac{V_L + C}{1 + r_*}\right]$$

In our example, we have

$$\text{value at a node} = \frac{1}{2}(\$99.113 + \$100.021) = \$99.567$$

Step 5: Compare the value in step 4 with the bond's market value. If the two values are the same, the r_1 used in this trial is the one we seek. This is the one-year forward rate that would then be used in the binomial interest-rate tree for the lower rate, and the corresponding rate would be for the higher rate. If, instead, the value found in step 4 is not equal to the market value of the bond, this means that the value r_1 in this trial is not the one-period forward rate that is consistent with (1) the volatility assumption of 10%, (2) the process assumed to generate the one-year forward rate, and (3) the observed market value of the bond. In this case the five steps are repeated with a different value for r_1.

In this example, when r_1 is 4.5% we get a value of \$99.567 in step 4, which is less than the observed market value of \$100. Therefore, 4.5% is too large and the five steps must be repeated, trying a lower value for r_1.

Let's jump right to the correct value for r_1 in this example and rework steps 1 through 5. This occurs when r_1 is 4.074%. The corresponding binomial interest-rate tree is shown in Exhibit 14-11.

Step 1: In this trial we select a value of 4.074% for r_1.
Step 2: The corresponding value for the higher one-year forward rate is 4.976%($= 4.074\% \, e^{2\times0.10}$).
Step 3: The bond's value one year from now is determined as follows:
  3a. The bond's value two years from now is \$104, just as in the first trial.

EXHIBIT 14-11 One-Year Forward Rates for Year 1 Using the Two-Year 4% On-the-Run Issue

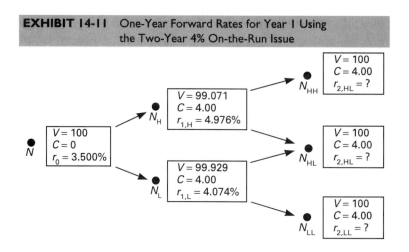

3b. The present value of the bond's value found in 3a for the higher rate, V_H, is $99.071 (= $104/1.04976).

3c. The present value of the bond's value found in 3a for the lower rate, V_L, is $99.929 (= $104/1.04074).

3d. Adding the coupon to V_H and V_L, we get $103.071 as the cash flow for the higher rate and $103.929 as the cash flow for the lower rate.

3e. The present value of the two cash flows using the one-year forward rate at the node to the left, 3.5%, gives

$$\frac{V_H + C}{1 + r_*} = \frac{\$103.071}{1.035} = \$99.586$$

and

$$\frac{V_L + C}{1 + r_*} = \frac{\$103.929}{1.035} = \$100.414$$

Step 4: The average present value is $100, which is the value at the node.

Step 5: Because the average present value is equal to the observed market value of $100, r_1 is 4.074%.

We're not done. Suppose that we want to "grow" this tree for one more year—that is, we want to determine r_2. Now we will use the three-year on-the-run issue, the 4.5% coupon bond, to get r_2. The same five steps are used in an iterative process to find the one-year forward rate two years from now. But now our objective is as follows: Find the value for r_2 that will produce an average present value at node N_H equal to the bond value at that node ($98.074) and will also produce an average present value at node N_L equal to the bond value at that node ($99.926). When this value is found, we know that given the forward rate we found for r_1, the bond's value at the root—the value of ultimate interest to us—will be $100, the observed market price.

It can be demonstrated that the value of r_2 that will produce that desired outcome is 4.530%. Exhibit 14-12 shows the completed binomial interest-rate tree. It is this tree that we can use to value any option-free bond or bond with embedded options.

EXHIBIT 14-12 One-Year Forward Rates for Year 2 Using the Three-Year 4.5% On-the-Run Issue

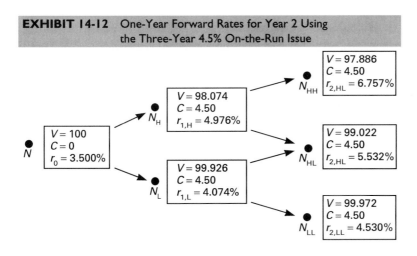

The binomial interest-rate tree constructed is said to be an **arbitrage-free tree.** It is so named because it fairly prices the on-the-run issues.

Application to Valuing an Option-Free Bond

To illustrate how to use the binomial interest-rate tree, consider a 5.25% corporate bond that has two years remaining to maturity and is option-free. Also assume that the issuer's on-the-run yield curve is the one given earlier, and hence the appropriate binomial interest-rate tree is the one in Exhibit 14-12. Exhibit 14-13 shows the various values in the discounting process and produces a bond value of $102.075.

It is important to note that this value is identical to the bond value found earlier when we discounted at either the zero-coupon rates or the one-year forward rates. We should expect to find this result because our bond is option free. This clearly demonstrates that the valuation model is consistent with the standard valuation model for an option-free bond.

Valuing a Callable Corporate Bond

Now we demonstrate how the binomial interest-rate tree can be applied to value a callable corporate bond. The valuation process proceeds in the same fashion as in the case of an option-free bond but with one exception: When the call option may be exercised by the issuer, the bond value at a node must be changed to reflect the lesser of its value if it is not called (i.e., the value obtained by applying the recursive valuation formula described previously) and the call price.

For example, consider a 5.25% corporate bond with three years remaining to maturity that is callable in one year at $100. Exhibit 14-14 shows the values at each node of the binomial interest-rate tree. The discounting process is identical to that shown in Exhibit 14-13 except that at two nodes, N_L and N_{LL}, the values from the recursive valuation formula ($101.001 at N_L and $100.689 at N_{LL}) exceed the call price ($100) and therefore have been struck out and replaced with $100. Each time a value derived from the recursive valuation formula has been replaced, the process for finding the values at that node is reworked starting with the period to the right. The value for this callable bond is $101.432.

EXHIBIT 14-13 Valuing an Option-Free Corporate Bond with Three Years to Maturity and a Coupon Rate of 5.25%

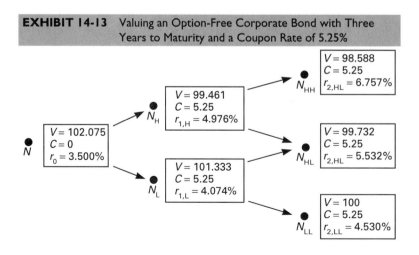

EXHIBIT 14-14   Valuing a Callable Corporate Bond with Three Years to Maturity, a Coupon Rate of 5.25%, and Callable in One Year at 100

The question that we have not addressed in our illustration but which is nonetheless important is the circumstances under which the issuer will call the bond. A discussion of the call rule is beyond the scope of this chapter. Basically, it involves determining when it is economical on an after-tax basis for the issuer to call the bond.

Determining the Call Option Value (or Option Cost)

As explained in Chapter 13, the value of a callable bond is expressed as the difference between the value of a noncallable bond and the value of the call option. This relationship can also be expressed as follows:

value of a call option = value of a noncallable bond − value of a callable bond

But we have just seen how the value of a noncallable bond and the value of a callable bond can be determined. The difference between the two values is therefore the value of the call option. In our illustration, the value of the noncallable bond is $102.075 and the value of the callable bond is $101.432, so the value of the call option is $0.643.

Extension to Other Embedded Options

The bond valuation framework presented here can be used to analyze other embedded options, such as put options, caps and floors on floating-rate notes, and the optional accelerated redemption granted to an issuer in fulfilling its sinking fund requirement.[5] For example, let's consider a putable bond. Suppose that a 5.25% corporate bond with three years remaining to maturity is putable in one year at par ($100). Also assume that the appropriate binomial interest-rate tree for this issuer is the one in Exhibit 14-12. Exhibit 14-15 shows the binomial interest-rate tree with the bond values altered at two nodes (N_{HH} and N_{LH}) because the bond values at these two nodes exceed $100, the value at which the bond can be put. The value of this putable bond is $102.523.

---

[5]Andrew Kalotay and George O. Williams, "The Valuation and Management of Bonds with Sinking Fund Provisions," *Financial Analysts Journal*, March–April 1992, pp. 59–67.

EXHIBIT 14-15 Valuing a Putable Corporate Bond with Three Years to Maturity, a Coupon Rate of 5.25%, and Putable in One Year at 100

Because the value of a nonputable bond can be expressed as the value of a putable bond minus the value of a put option on that bond, this means that

value of a put option = value of a nonputable bond − value of a putable bond

In our example, because the value of the putable bond is $102.523 and the value of the corresponding nonputable bond is $102.075, the value of the put option is −$0.448. The negative sign indicates that the issuer has sold the option, or equivalently, the investor has purchased the option.

The framework can also be used to value a bond with multiple or interrelated embedded options. The bond values at each node are altered based on whether one of the options is exercised.

Incorporating Default Risk

Recently, John Finnerty has extended the basic binomial model explained above to incorporate default risk.[6] The extension involves adjusting the expected cash flows for the probability of a payment default and the expected amount of cash that will be recovered when a default occurs. This extension then requires the manager to estimate (1) the historical default experience of bonds with a similar rating and (2) the expected amount that will be recovered. Empirical data collected by the commercial rating agencies and several well known studies by Edward Altman allow a manager to do a good job of estimating this required data.

An explanation of specifically how the adjustments are made to the model is beyond the scope of this chapter. The article by Finnerty provides not only a detailed discussion of the valuation process but also illustrates how the model was applied to value a pay-in-kind debenture bond of Bucyrus-Erie Company, an issue that was rated non–investment grade at the time of the analysis and had multiple embedded options.

---

[6]John D. Finnerty, "Adjusting the Binomial Model for Default Risk," *Journal of Portfolio Management,* Winter 1999, pp. 93–104.

Modeling Risk

The user of any valuation model is exposed to **modeling risk.** This is the risk that the output of the model is incorrect because the assumptions upon which it is based are incorrect. Consequently, it is imperative that the results of a valuation model be stress-tested for modeling risk by altering the assumptions.

A critical assumption in the valuation model is the volatility assumption. For a callable bond, a higher (lower) volatility assumption lowers (raises) its value. For a putable bond, a higher (lower) volatility assumption raises (lowers) its value.

OPTION-ADJUSTED SPREAD

What an investor seeks to do is to buy securities whose value is greater than their market price. A valuation model such as the one just described allows an investor to estimate the value of a security, which at this point would be sufficient to determine the fairness of the price of the security. That is, the investor can say that this bond is one point cheap or two points cheap, and so on.

A valuation model need not stop here, however. Instead, it can convert the divergence between the price observed in the market for the security and the value derived from the model into a yield spread measure. This step is necessary because most market participants find it more convenient to think about yield spread than about price differences.

The **option-adjusted spread (OAS)** was developed as a measure of the yield spread (in basis points) that can be used to convert dollar differences between value and price. Thus, basically, the OAS is used to reconcile value with market price. But what is it a "spread" over? The OAS is a spread over the spot rate curve or benchmark used in the valuation. The reason that the resulting spread is referred to as *option-adjusted* is because the cash flows of the security whose value we seek are adjusted to reflect the embedded option.

In the case of the binomial method, the OAS is a spread over the binomial interest-rate tree. Some market participants construct the binomial interest-rate tree using the Treasury spot rates. In this case the OAS reflects the richness or cheapness of the security, if any, plus a credit spread. Other market participants construct the binomial interest-rate tree from the issuer's spot rate curve. In this case the credit risk is already incorporated into the analysis, and the OAS therefore reflects the richness or cheapness of a security. Therefore, it is critical to know the on-the-run issues that the modeler used to construct the binomial interest-rate tree.

Translating OAS to Theoretical Value

Although the product of a valuation model is the OAS, the process can be worked in reverse. For a specified OAS, the valuation model can determine the theoretical value of the security that is consistent with that OAS. As with the theoretical value, the OAS is affected by the assumed interest rate volatility. The higher (lower) the expected interest rate volatility, the lower (higher) the OAS.

Determining The Option Value in Spread Terms

Earlier we described how the dollar value of the option is calculated. The option value in spread terms is determined as follows:

$$\text{option value (in basis points)} = \text{static spread} - \text{OAS}$$

EFFECTIVE DURATION AND CONVEXITY

As explained in Chapter 4, money managers also want to know the price sensitivity of a bond when interest rates change. **Modified duration** is a measure of the sensitivity of a bond's price to interest-rate changes, *assuming that the expected cash flow does not change with interest rates.* Consequently, modified duration may not be an appropriate measure for bonds with embedded options because the expected cash flows change as interest rates change. For example, when interest rates fall, the expected cash flow for a callable bond may change. In the case of a putable bond, a rise in interest rates may change the expected cash flow.

Although modified duration may be inappropriate as a measure of a bond's price sensitivity to interest rate changes, there is a duration measure that is more appropriate for bonds with embedded options. Because duration measures price responsiveness to changes in interest rates, the duration for a bond with an embedded option can be estimated by letting interest rates change by a small number of basis points above and below the prevailing yield, and seeing how the prices change. As explained in Chapter 4, in general, the duration for *any* bond can be *approximated* as follows:

$$\text{duration} = \frac{P_- - P_+}{2(P_0)(\Delta y)}$$

where:

P_- = price if yield is decreased by x basis points
P_+ = price if yield is increased by x basis points
P_0 = initial price (per \$100 of par value)
Δy = change in rate used to calculate price (x basis points in decimal form)

In Chapter 4 we showed how the application of this formula to an option-free bond gives the modified duration because the cash flows do not change when yields change.

When the approximate duration formula is applied to a bond with an embedded option, the new prices at the higher and lower yield levels should reflect the value from the valuation model. Duration calculated in this way is called **effective duration** or **option-adjusted duration.**

In general, the relationships among duration, modified duration, and effective duration are as follows. Duration is a generic concept that indicates the responsiveness of a bond to a change in interest rates. Modified duration is a duration measure in which the cash flow is not assumed to change when interest rates change. In contrast, effective duration measures the responsiveness of a bond's price taking into account that the expected cash flow will change as interest rates change due to the embedded option. The difference between modified duration and effective duration for a bond with an embedded option can be quite dramatic. For example, a callable bond could have a modified duration of 5 and an effective duration of 3. For certain highly leveraged mortgage-backed securities, the bond could have a modified duration of 7 and an effective duration of 50! The differences between modified duration and effective duration are summarized in Exhibit 14-16.

Similarly, the standard convexity measure may be inappropriate for a bond with embedded options because it does not consider the effect of a change in interest rates on the bond's cash flow. As explained in Chapter 4, the convexity of any bond can be approximated using the following formula:

EXHIBIT 14-16   Modified Duration versus Effective Duration

$$\frac{P_+ + P_- - 2(P_0)}{(P_0)(\Delta y)^2}$$

When the prices used in this formula assume that the cash flows do not change when yields change, the resulting convexity is a good approximation of the standard convexity for an option-free bond. When the prices used in the formula are derived by changing the cash flows when yields change, the resulting convexity is called **effective convexity.**

Using the binomial method, the procedure for calculating the value of P_+ that should be used to calculate effective duration and effective convexity is as follows:

Step 1: Calculate the OAS for the issue.
Step 2: Shift the on-the-run yield curve up by a small number of basis points.
Step 3: Construct a binomial interest-rate tree based on the new yield curve in step 2.
Step 4: To each of the short rates in the binomial interest-rate tree, add the OAS to obtain an adjusted tree.
Step 5: Use the adjusted tree found in step 4 to determine the value of the security, which is P_+.

To determine the value of P_-, the same five steps are followed except that in step 2 the on-the-run yield curve is shifted down by a small number of basis points.

SUMMARY

The traditional yield spread approach fails to take three factors into account: (1) the term structure of interest rates, (2) the options embedded in the bond, and (3) the expected volatility of interest rates. The static spread measures the spread over the Treasury spot rate curve assuming that interest rates will not change in the future.

The potential investor in a callable bond must be compensated for the risk that the issuer will call the bond prior to the stated maturity date. The two risks faced by a potential investor are reinvestment risk and truncated price appreciation when yields decline (i.e., negative convexity).

The traditional methodology for valuing bonds with embedded options relies on the yield to worst. The limitations of yield numbers are now well recognized. Moreover, the traditional methodology does not consider how future interest-rate volatility will affect the value of the embedded option.

To value a bond with an embedded option, it is necessary to understand that the bond can be decomposed into an option-free component and an option component. The binomial method can be used to value a bond with an embedded option. It involves generating a binomial interest-rate tree based on (1) an issuer's yield curve, (2) an assumed interest-rate generation process, and (3) an assumed interest-rate volatility. The binomial interest-rate tree provides the appropriate volatility-dependent one-period forward rates that should be used to discount the expected cash flows of a bond. Critical to the valuation process is an assumption about expected interest-rate volatility.

The option-adjusted spread (OAS) converts the cheapness or richness of a bond into a spread over the future possible spot rate curves. The spread is option adjusted because it allows for future interest-rate volatility to affect the cash flows.

Modified duration and standard convexity, used to measure the interest-rate sensitivity of an option-free bond, may be inappropriate for a bond with an embedded option because these measures assume that cash flows do not change as interest rates change. The duration and convexity can be approximated for any bond, whether it is option-free or a bond with an embedded option. The approximation involves determining how the price of the bond changes if interest rates go up or down by a small number of basis points. If when interest rates are changed it is assumed that the cash flows do not change, the resulting measures are modified duration and standard convexity. However, when the cash flows are allowed to change when interest rates change, the resulting measures are called effective duration and effective convexity.

Questions

1. What are the two drawbacks of the traditional approach to the valuation of bonds with embedded options?
2. Is the static spread for a three-year 9% coupon corporate bond selling at 105.58, given the following theoretical Treasury spot rate values equal to 50, 100, or 120 basis points?

Month	Spot Rate (%)
1	4.0
2	4.2
3	4.9
4	5.4
5	5.7
6	6.0

3. Under what conditions would the traditional yield spread be close to the static spread?
4. Why is the investor of a callable bond exposed to reinvestment risk?
5. What is negative convexity?
6. Does a callable bond exhibit negative or positive convexity?

7. Suppose that you are given the following information about two callable bonds that can be called immediately:

	Estimated Percentage Change in Price if Interest Rates Change by:	
	−100 basis points	+100 basis points
Bond ABC	+5	−8
Bond XYZ	+22	−16

You are told that both of these bonds have the same maturity and that the coupon rate of one bond is 7% and of the other is 13%. Suppose that the yield curve for both issuers is flat at 8%. Based on this information, which bond is the lower coupon bond and which is the higher coupon bond? Explain why.

8. The theoretical value of a noncallable bond is $103; the theoretical value of a callable bond is $101. Determine the theoretical value of the call option.

9. Explain why you agree or disagree with the following statement: "The value of a putable bond is never greater than the value of an otherwise comparable option-free bond."

10. Explain why you agree or disagree with the following statement: "An investor should be unwilling to pay more than the call price for a bond that is likely to be called."

11. In Robert Litterman, Jose Scheinkman, and Laurence Weiss, "Volatility and the Yield Curve," *Journal of Fixed Income,* Premier Issue, 1991, p. 49, the following statement was made: "Many fixed income securities (e.g., callable bonds) contain embedded options whose prices are sensitive to the level of volatility. Modeling the additional impact of volatility on the value of the coupons allows for a better understanding of the price behavior of these securities." Explain why.

12. If an on-the-run issue for an issuer is evaluated properly using a binomial model, how would the theoretical value compare to the actual market price?

13. The current on-the-run yields for the Ramsey Corporation are as follows:

Maturity (years)	Yield to Maturity (%)	Market Price
1	7.5	100
2	7.6	100
3	7.7	100

Assume that each bond is an annual-pay bond. Each bond is trading at par, so its coupon rate is equal to its yield to maturity.

a. Using the bootstrapping methodology, complete the following table:

Spot Rate Year	One-Year Forward Rate (%)	(%)
1		
2		
3		

b. Using the spot rates, what would be the value of an 8.5% option-free bond of this issuer?

c. Using the one-year forward rates, what would be the value of an 8.5% coupon option-free bond of this issuer?

d. Using the binomial model (which assumes that one-year rates undergo a log-normal random walk with volatility σ), show that if σ is assumed to be 10%, the lower one-year forward rate one year from now *cannot* be 7%.

    e. Demonstrate that if σ is assumed to be 10%, the lower one-year forward rate one year from now is 6.944%.

    f. Demonstrate that if σ is assumed to be 10%, the lower one-year forward rate two years from now is approximately 6.437%.

    g. Show the binomial interest-rate tree that should be used to value any bond of this issuer.

    h. Determine the value of an 8.5% coupon option-free bond for this issuer using the binomial interest-rate tree given in part g.

    i. Determine the value of an 8.5% coupon bond that is callable at par (100) assuming that the issue will be called if the price exceeds par.

14. Explain how an increase in expected interest-rate volatility can decrease the value of a callable bond.

15. How should an interest-rate volatility of 15% be interpreted if the prevailing interest rate is 7%?

16. a. What is meant by the option-adjusted spread?

    b. What is the spread relative to?

17. "The option-adjusted spread measures the yield spread over the Treasury on-the-run yield curve." Explain why you agree or disagree with this statement.

18. What is the effect of greater expected interest-rate volatility on the option-adjusted spread of a security?

19. The following excerpt is taken from an article titled "Call Provisions Drop Off" that appeared in the January 27, 1992, issue of *BondWeek,* p. 2:

> Issuance of callable long-term bonds dropped off further last year as interest rates fell, removing the incentive for many issuers to pay extra for the provision, said Street capital market officials. . . .
>
> The shift toward noncallable issues, which began in the late 1980s, reflects the secular trend of investors unwilling to bear prepayment risk and possibly the cyclical trend that corporations believe that interest rates have hit all time lows. . . .

    a. What "incentive" is this article referring to in the first sentence of the excerpt?

    b. Why would issuers not be willing to pay for this incentive if they feel that interest rates will continue to decline?

20. The following excerpt is taken from an article titled "Eagle Eyes High-Coupon Callable Corporates" that appeared in the January 20, 1992, issue of *BondWeek,* p. 7:

> If the bond market rallies further, Eagle Asset Management may take profits, trading $8 million of seven- to 10-year Treasuries for high-coupon single-A industrials that are callable in two to four years according to Joseph Blanton, senior v.p. He thinks a further rally is unlikely, however. . . .
>
> The corporates have a 95% chance of being called in two to four years and are treated as two- to four-year paper in calculating the duration of the portfolio, Blanton said. . . .

    a. Why is modified duration an inappropriate measure for a high-coupon callable bond?

    b. What would be a better measure than modified duration?

    c. Why would the replacement of 10-year Treasuries with high-coupon callable bonds reduce the portfolio's duration?

21. Suppose that a 7% coupon corporate bond is immediately callable. Also suppose that if this issuer issued new bonds, the coupon rate would be 12%. Why would the modified duration be a good approximation for the effective duration for this bond?

22. The following information was reported in William M. Boyce, Webster Hughes, Peter S. A. Niculescu, and Michael Waldman, "The Implied Volatility of Fixed-Income Markets," in Frank J. Fabozzi (ed.), *Advances and Innovations in the Bond and Mortgage Markets* (Chicago: Probus Publishing, 1989) for two issues of CommonWealth Edison bonds as of December 31, 1987:

Issue	Next Call Date	Call Price	Market Price	Effective Duration[a] (years)
14.375 of 1994	7/15/89	$104.11	$111.30	1.7
10.625 of 1995	9/1/90	102.86	104.12	3.4

[a]Evaluated at 16% volatility.

   a. What is effective duration?
   b. Why is it necessary to make an interest-rate volatility assumption to calculate effective duration?

23. a. Explain how effective duration is calculated using the binomial model.
   b. What is assumed about the OAS in calculating effective duration?

CHAPTER 15

*Analysis of Mortgage-Backed Securities**

Learning Objectives

After reading this chapter you will understand:

- the cash flow yield methodology for analyzing mortgage-backed securities

- the limitations of the cash flow yield methodology

- how the effective duration and convexity are calculated for the cash flow yield methodology

- why the Monte Carlo simulation methodology is used to value mortgage-backed securities

- how interest-rate paths are simulated in a Monte Carlo simulation methodology

- how the Monte Carlo simulation methodology can be used to determine the theoretical value of a mortgage-backed security

- how the option-adjusted spread, effective duration, and effective convexity are computed using the Monte Carlo simulation methodology

- the complexities of modeling collateralized mortgage obligations

- the limitations of option-adjusted spread

- modeling risk and how it can be stress tested

- how the total return is calculated for a mortgage-backed security

- the difficulties of applying the total return framework to mortgage-backed securities

There are two approaches to the analysis of mortgage-backed securities (including pass-throughs, collateralized mortgage obligations, and stripped mortgage-backed securities): (1) the static cash flow yield methodology, and (2) the

---

*This chapter is adapted from Chapters 9 and 10 of Frank J. Fabozzi, Chuck Ramsey, and Frank Ramirez, *Collateralized Mortgage Obligations: Structures and Analysis* (Buckingham, PA: Frank J. Fabozzi Associates, 1994).

366

Monte Carlo simulation methodology. The Monte Carlo simulation methodology provides the theoretical value of a mortgage-backed security. That is, it is a valuation model. A product of this valuation model, as with all valuation models, is the option-adjusted spread (OAS). In this chapter we review the static cash flow yield methodology and its limitations and then focus on the Monte Carlo simulation methodology.

STATIC CASH FLOW YIELD METHODOLOGY

The static cash flow yield methodology is the simplest to use, although we shall see that it offers little insight into the relative value of a mortgage-backed security. It begins with the computation of the cash flow yield measure that we described for pass-throughs in Chapter 11. The cash flow yield is based on some prepayment assumption.

To illustrate the cash flow yield, we'll use one of the CMO structures we developed in Chapter 12, FJF-06. This structure is summarized in Exhibit 12-15. Exhibit 15-1 summarizes cash flow yields according to various PSA prepayment assumptions for the four tranches assuming different purchase prices. Notice that the greater the discount assumed to be paid for the tranche, the more a tranche will benefit from faster prepayments. The converse is true for a tranche for which a premium is paid. The faster the prepayments, the lower the cash flow yield.

Vector Analysis

One practice that market participants use to overcome the drawback of the PSA benchmark is to assume that the PSA speed can change over time. This technique is referred to as **vector analysis.** A **vector** is simply a set of numbers. In the case of prepayments, it is a vector of prepayment speeds. Vector analysis is particularly useful for CMO tranches that are dramatically affected by the initial slowing down of prepayments, and then speeding up of prepayments, or vice versa.

Exhibit 15-2 reports the cash flow yield using vector analysis for the four tranches and collateral of FJF-06. The top panel shows the cash flow yield assuming 165 PSA. Nine vectors are then shown assuming that the PSA is constant from months 1 to 36, and then changes for months 37 through 138, and again changes for months 139 through 357.

Limitations of the Cash Flow Yield

As we have noted several times already, the yield to maturity has two shortcomings as a measure of a bond's potential return: (1) It is assumed that the coupon payments can be reinvested at a rate equal to the yield to maturity, and (2) it is assumed that the bond is held to maturity. These shortcomings are equally present in application of the cash flow yield measure: (1) the projected cash flows are assumed to be reinvested at the cash flow yield, and (2) the mortgage-backed security is assumed to be held until the final payout based on some prepayment assumption. The importance of reinvestment risk, the risk that the cash flow will be reinvested at a rate less than the cash flow yield, is particularly important for many mortgage-backed securities because payments come as frequently as every month. The cash flow yield, moreover, is dependent on realization of the projected cash flow according to some prepayment rate. If

EXHIBIT 15-1 Price/Cash Flow Yield Table for the Four Tranches in FJF-06

Tranche A: Orig. par: $194,500,000; type: sequential; coupon: 6.0% (fixed)

If Price Paid Is:	50.00 PSA	100.00 PSA	165.00 PSA	250.00 PSA	400.00 PSA	500.00 PSA	700.00 PSA	1000.00 PSA
90–24	8.37	9.01	9.76	10.61	11.87	12.59	13.88	15.63
91–24	8.09	8.66	9.32	10.07	11.17	11.81	12.94	14.47
92–24	7.82	8.31	8.88	9.53	10.49	11.03	12.01	13.33
93–24	7.56	7.97	8.45	9.00	9.81	10.27	11.10	12.22
94–24	7.29	7.63	8.03	8.48	9.14	9.52	10.20	11.12
95–24	7.03	7.30	7.61	7.97	8.49	8.79	9.32	10.04
96–24	6.78	6.97	7.20	7.46	7.85	8.06	8.45	8.98
97–24	6.53	6.65	6.80	6.97	7.21	7.35	7.60	7.94
98–24	6.28	6.34	6.40	6.48	6.59	6.65	6.76	6.91
99–24	6.04	6.02	6.01	6.00	5.97	5.96	5.94	5.91
100–24	5.79	5.72	5.62	5.52	5.37	5.28	5.13	4.92
101–24	5.56	5.41	5.24	5.05	4.77	4.61	4.33	3.95
102–24	5.33	5.12	4.87	4.59	4.18	3.95	3.54	2.99
103–24	5.10	4.82	4.50	4.14	3.61	3.30	2.77	2.05
104–24	4.87	4.53	4.14	3.69	3.04	2.66	2.01	1.12
105–24	4.65	4.25	3.78	3.25	2.47	2.03	1.26	0.21
106–24	4.42	3.96	3.42	2.81	1.92	1.41	0.52	−0.68
107–24	4.21	3.69	3.07	2.38	1.37	0.80	−0.21	−1.57
108–24	3.99	3.41	2.73	1.96	0.83	0.20	−0.93	−2.44
109–24	3.78	3.14	2.39	1.54	0.30	−0.40	−1.64	−3.29
Average life:	5.09	3.80	2.93	2.33	1.79	1.58	1.31	1.07
Mod. duration:	4.12	3.22	2.57	2.09	1.64	1.46	1.22	1.00
Exp. maturity:	9.40	7.15	5.40	4.15	3.07	2.65	2.24	1.82

actual prepayments vary from the prepayment rate assumed, the cash flow yield will not be realized.

Yield Spread to Treasuries

It should be clear that at the time of purchase it is not possible to determine an exact yield for a mortgage-backed security; the yield will depend on the actual prepayment experience of the mortgages in the pool. Nevertheless, the convention in all fixed-income markets is to measure the yield on a non-Treasury security to that of a "comparable" Treasury security.

The repayment of principal over time makes it inappropriate to compare the yield of a mortgage-backed security to a Treasury of a stated maturity. Instead, market participants have used two measures: Macaulay duration (as explained in Chapter 4) and average life (as explained in Chapter 11).

Static Spread

As explained in Chapter 14, the practice of spreading the yield to the average life on the interpolated Treasury yield curve is improper for an amortizing bond even in the absence of interest-rate volatility. What should be done instead is to calculate what is

EXHIBIT 15-1 (*cont.*)

Tranche B: Orig. par: $36,000,000; type: sequential; coupon: 6.50% (fixed)

If Price Paid Is:	50.00 PSA	100.00 PSA	165.00 PSA	250.00 PSA	400.00 PSA	500.00 PSA	700.00 PSA	1000.00 PSA
90–31	7.85	8.12	8.49	8.95	9.69	10.13	10.89	11.83
91–31	7.69	7.93	8.25	8.66	9.31	9.70	10.36	11.18
92–31	7.54	7.75	8.02	8.37	8.94	9.27	9.84	10.55
93–31	7.39	7.57	7.80	8.09	8.57	8.85	9.33	9.92
94–31	7.24	7.39	7.58	7.82	8.20	8.43	8.82	9.31
95–31	7.10	7.21	7.35	7.54	7.84	8.02	8.32	8.70
96–31	6.95	7.03	7.14	7.27	7.49	7.61	7.83	8.10
97–31	6.81	6.86	6.92	7.00	7.13	7.21	7.34	7.51
98–31	6.67	6.69	6.71	6.74	6.79	6.82	6.86	6.92
99–31	6.53	6.52	6.50	6.48	6.45	6.42	6.39	6.35
100–31	6.39	6.35	6.29	6.22	6.11	6.04	5.92	5.78
101–31	6.26	6.19	6.09	5.97	5.77	5.66	5.46	5.22
102–31	6.13	6.02	5.89	5.72	5.44	5.28	5.00	4.66
103–31	5.99	5.86	5.69	5.47	5.12	4.91	4.55	4.12
104–31	5.86	5.70	5.49	5.22	4.79	4.54	4.11	3.58
105–31	5.74	5.55	5.30	4.98	4.48	4.18	3.67	3.04
106–31	5.61	5.39	5.10	4.74	4.16	3.82	3.23	2.51
107–31	5.48	5.24	4.91	4.50	3.85	3.46	2.80	1.99
108–31	5.36	5.08	4.72	4.27	3.54	3.11	2.38	1.48
109–31	5.24	4.93	4.54	4.04	3.24	2.76	1.96	0.97
Average life:	10.17	7.76	5.93	4.58	3.35	2.89	2.35	1.90
Mod. duration:	7.23	5.92	4.78	3.84	2.92	2.56	2.11	1.74
Exp. maturity:	10.90	8.40	6.49	4.99	3.65	3.15	2.49	1.99

called the **static spread.** This is the yield spread in a static scenario (i.e., no volatility of interest rates) of the bond over the entire theoretical Treasury spot rate curve, not a single point on the Treasury yield curve.

As explained in Chapter 14, the magnitude of the difference between the traditional yield spread and the static yield spread depends on the steepness of the yield curve: The steeper the curve, the greater the difference between the two values. In a relatively flat interest-rate environment, the difference between the traditional yield spread and the static spread will be small.

There are two ways to compute the static spread for mortgage-backed securities. One way is to use today's yield curve to discount future cash flows and keep the mortgage refinancing rate fixed at today's mortgage rate. Because the mortgage refinancing rate is fixed, the investor can usually specify a reasonable prepayment rate for the life of the security. Using this prepayment rate, the bond's future cash flow can be estimated. Use of this approach to calculate the static spread recognizes different prices today of dollars to be delivered at future dates. This results in the proper discounting of cash flows while keeping the mortgage rate fixed. Effectively, today's prices indicate what the future discount rates will be, but the best estimates of future rates are today's rates.

EXHIBIT 15-1 (*cont.*)

Tranche C: Orig. par: $96,500,000; type: sequential; coupon: 7.00% (fixed)

If Price Paid Is:	50.00 PSA	100.00 PSA	165.00 PSA	250.00 PSA	400.00 PSA	500.00 PSA	700.00 PSA	1000.00 PSA
90–03	8.34	8.53	8.80	9.15	9.77	10.16	10.89	11.85
91–03	8.20	8.37	8.61	8.92	9.47	9.81	10.46	11.31
92–03	8.06	8.21	8.42	8.70	9.17	9.48	10.05	10.79
93–03	7.92	8.06	8.24	8.47	8.88	9.14	9.63	10.27
94–03	7.79	7.90	8.05	8.25	8.60	8.81	9.22	9.76
95–03	7.66	7.75	7.87	8.03	8.31	8.49	8.82	9.25
96–03	7.53	7.60	7.69	7.82	8.03	8.17	8.42	8.76
97–03	7.40	7.45	7.52	7.61	7.76	7.85	8.03	8.26
98–03	7.28	7.31	7.35	7.40	7.48	7.54	7.64	7.78
99–03	7.15	7.16	7.17	7.19	7.21	7.23	7.26	7.30
100–03	7.03	7.02	7.01	6.98	6.95	6.93	6.88	6.83
101–03	6.91	6.88	6.84	6.78	6.69	6.63	6.51	6.36
102–03	6.79	6.74	6.67	6.58	6.43	6.33	6.14	5.90
103–03	6.67	6.61	6.51	6.39	6.17	6.03	5.78	5.45
104–03	6.56	6.47	6.35	6.19	5.92	5.74	5.42	5.00
105–03	6.44	6.34	6.19	6.00	5.67	5.46	5.07	4.56
106–03	6.33	6.21	6.03	5.81	5.42	5.17	4.72	4.12
107–03	6.22	6.08	5.88	5.62	5.18	4.89	4.37	3.69
108–03	6.11	5.95	5.73	5.43	4.94	4.62	4.03	3.26
109–03	6.00	5.82	5.57	5.25	4.70	4.34	3.69	2.84
Average life:	12.77	10.16	7.98	6.24	4.54	3.87	3.04	2.37
Mod. duration:	8.18	7.04	5.92	4.89	3.76	3.28	2.65	2.12
Exp. maturity:	14.57	11.90	9.57	7.65	5.57	4.74	3.65	2.82

The second way to calculate the static spread allows the mortgage rate to go up the curve as implied by the forward interest rates. This procedure is sometimes called the **zero-volatility OAS.** In this case a prepayment model is needed to determine the vector of future prepayment rates implied by the vector of future refinancing rates. A money manager using static spread should determine which approach is used in the calculation.

Effective Duration

Modified duration is a measure of the sensitivity of a bond's price to interest-rate changes, assuming that the expected cash flow does not change with interest rates. Modified duration is consequently not an appropriate measure for mortgage-backed securities, because prepayments do cause the projected cash flow to change as interest rates change. When interest rates fall (rise), prepayments are expected to rise (fall). As a result, when interest rates fall (rise), duration may decrease (increase) rather than increase (decrease). As we explained in Chapter 14, this property is referred to as **negative convexity.**

EXHIBIT 15-1 (*cont.*)

Tranche Z: Orig. par: $73,000,000; type: sequential; coupon: 7.35% (fixed)

If Price Paid Is:	50.00 PSA	100.00 PSA	165.00 PSA	250.00 PSA	400.00 PSA	500.00 PSA	700.00 PSA	1000.00 PSA
90–01	7.87	7.96	8.09	8.27	8.61	8.84	9.33	10.10
91–01	7.82	7.89	8.00	8.16	8.47	8.68	9.11	9.79
92–01	7.76	7.83	7.93	8.07	8.33	8.51	8.89	9.49
93–01	7.71	7.76	7.85	7.97	8.20	8.35	8.68	9.20
94–01	7.65	7.70	7.77	7.87	8.06	8.19	8.47	8.90
95–01	7.60	7.63	7.69	7.77	7.93	8.04	8.26	8.61
96–01	7.54	7.57	7.62	7.68	7.80	7.88	8.05	8.33
97–01	7.49	7.51	7.54	7.59	7.67	7.73	7.85	8.04
98–01	7.44	7.45	7.47	7.49	7.54	7.58	7.65	7.76
99–01	7.38	7.39	7.39	7.40	7.42	7.43	7.45	7.49
100–01	7.33	7.33	7.32	7.31	7.29	7.28	7.26	7.21
101–01	7.28	7.27	7.25	7.22	7.17	7.14	7.06	6.95
102–01	7.23	7.21	7.18	7.13	7.05	6.99	6.87	6.68
103–01	7.18	7.15	7.11	7.05	6.93	6.85	6.68	6.42
104–01	7.13	7.09	7.04	6.96	6.81	6.71	6.49	6.16
105–01	7.08	7.04	6.97	6.88	6.69	6.57	6.31	5.90
106–01	7.04	6.98	6.90	6.79	6.58	6.43	6.13	5.65
107–01	6.99	6.93	6.84	6.71	6.46	6.29	5.94	5.39
108–01	6.94	6.87	6.77	6.62	6.35	6.16	5.77	5.15
109–01	6.89	6.82	6.70	6.54	6.24	6.03	5.59	4.90
Average life:	22.39	19.57	16.21	12.78	9.01	7.46	5.49	3.88
Mod. duration:	19.42	16.68	13.81	11.08	8.06	6.78	5.11	3.67
Exp. maturity:	29.74	29.74	29.74	29.74	29.74	29.74	29.74	24.24

Note: Calculated using SFW Software, copyright © 1989 by Wall Street Analytics, Inc.

Negative convexity has the same impact on the price performance of a mortgage-backed security as it does on the performance of a callable bond (discussed in Chapter 14). When interest rates decline, a bond with an embedded call option, which is what a mortgage-backed security is, will not perform as well as an option-free bond. Although modified duration is an inappropriate measure of interest-rate sensitivity, there is a way to allow for changing prepayment rates on cash flow as interest rates change. This is achieved by calculating the **effective duration,** which allows for changing cash flow when interest rates change.

To illustrate calculation of effective duration for CMO classes, consider FJF-06 once again. The structure is summarized in the top panel of Exhibit 15-3. The second panel provides all the data necessary to calculate modified duration and effective duration of the four tranches and the collateral. This panel shows the assumed cash flow yield and the corresponding initial price for the tranches assuming a prepayment speed of 165 PSA. The two columns following the initial prices give the new prices if the cash flow yield is changed by 25 basis points and assuming no change in the prepayment speed. The last two columns show new prices if the cash flow yield changes

EXHIBIT 15-2 Vector Analysis of Cash Flow Yield for Four Tranches of FRR-06 and Collateral Assumptions:

	Coupon (%)	Price	Cash flow yield at 165 PSA (%)
Tranche A	6.00	99–24	6.00
Tranche B	6.50	99–31	6.50
Tranche C	7.00	100–03	7.00
Tranche Z	7.25	100–01	7.25
Collateral	7.50	100–00	?

		PSA Vector Scenario								
	Months	(1)	(2)	(3)	(4)	(5)	(6)	(7)	(8)	(9)
	1–36	165	165	165	165	165	165	165	165	165
Tranche/	37–138	50	50	300	400	400	400	400	500	600
Parameter	139–357	250	400	400	200	700	500	165	200	1000
Tranche A										
Cash flow yield		6.02	6.02	6.01	6.00	6.00	6.00	6.00	6.00	6.00
Average life		3.51	3.51	2.71	2.63	2.63	2.63	2.63	2.58	2.54
Modified duration		2.97	2.97	2.40	2.34	2.34	2.34	2.34	2.30	2.27
Tranche B										
Cash flow yield		6.52	6.52	6.48	6.48	6.48	6.48	6.48	6.47	6.46
Average life		8.51	8.51	4.82	4.39	4.39	4.39	4.39	4.11	3.91
Modified duration		6.35	6.35	4.02	3.71	3.71	3.71	3.71	3.50	3.36
Tranche C										
Cash flow yield		7.03	7.03	6.98	6.97	6.97	6.97	6.97	6.96	6.95
Average life		11.15	11.07	6.24	5.52	5.52	5.52	5.52	5.04	4.68
Modified duration		7.50	7.47	4.89	4.43	4.43	4.43	4.43	4.11	3.87
Tranche D										
Cash flow yield		7.26	7.25	7.21	7.19	7.19	7.20	7.20	7.17	7.14
Average life		17.08	15.29	11.47	10.49	9.55	11.42	10.65	8.92	7.49
Modified duration		15.44	14.19	10.28	9.19	8.76	9.56	9.26	8.01	6.98
Collateral										
Cash flow yield		7.54	7.53	7.50	7.49	7.49	7.49	7.49	7.48	7.47
Average life		10.90	10.05	6.31	5.68	5.40	5.95	5.72	5.02	4.48
Modified duration		6.47	6.25	4.50	4.14	4.07	4.21	4.16	3.82	3.55

Note: Calculated using SFW Software, copyright © 1989 by Wall Street Analytics, Inc.

by 25 basis points and the prepayment speed is assumed to change; it decreases to 150 PSA if the cash flow yield increases by 25 basis points, and it increases to 200 PSA if the cash flow yield decreases by 25 basis points.

Exhibit 15-3 reports the modified duration and effective duration. To illustrate the calculation, consider tranche C. The data for calculating modified duration using the approximation formula is

$$P_- = 102.1875 \qquad P_+ = 98.4063 \qquad P_0 = 100.2813 \qquad \Delta y = 0.0025$$

Substituting into the duration formula yields

$$\text{modified duration} = \frac{102.1875 - 98.4063}{2(100.2813)(0.0025)} = 7.54$$

The effective duration for the same bond class is calculated as follows:

$$P_- = 101.9063 \text{ (at 200 PSA)} \quad P_+ = 98.3438 \text{ (at 150 PSA)} \quad P_0 = 100.2813 \quad \Delta y = 0.0025$$

Substituting into the formula gives

EXHIBIT 15-3   Calculation of Effective Duration and Convexity for FJF-06

Structure of FRR-06

Class	Par Amount	Coupon Rate (%)
A	$194,500,000	6.00
B	36,000,000	6.50
C	96,500,000	7.00
Z (accrual)	73,000,000	7.25
R	0	0
Collateral	$400,000,000	7.50

Class	Cash Flow Yield (%)	Initial Price	New Price: 165% PSA CFY Change (bp) +25 bp	New Price: 165% PSA CFY Change (bp) −25 bp	New Price: CFY Change (bp)/New PSA +25/150	New Price: CFY Change (bp)/New PSA −25/200
A	6.00	99.7813	99.0625	100.5313	99.0313	100.4375
B	6.50	100.0313	98.6250	101.5000	98.5625	101.2813
C	7.00	100.2813	98.4063	102.1875	98.3438	101.9063
Z	7.25	100.6250	98.0625	103.2500	98.0313	103.0313
Coll.	7.50	100.1250	98.7500	101.5000	98.7188	101.3438

Modified Duration/Convexity and Effective Duration/Convexity

Class	Modified Duration	Effective Duration	Standard Convexity	Effective Convexity
A	2.94	2.82	25.055	−75.164
B	5.75	5.44	49.984	−174.945
C	7.54	7.11	24.930	−249.299
Z	10.31	9.94	49.689	−149.068
Coll.	5.49	5.24	0	−149.813

$$\text{effective duration} = \frac{101.9063 - 98.3438}{2(100.2813)(0.0025)} = 7.11$$

Notice that for all four tranches and the collateral, the effective duration is less than the modified duration.

The divergence between modified duration and effective duration is much more dramatic for bond classes trading at a substantial discount from par or at a substantial premium over par. To demonstrate this, we can create another hypothetical CMO structure, which differs from FJF-06 by including a PO class and an IO class made up from tranche C. Let's look at the duration for the PO class. Assuming that the cash flow yield for the PO class is 7%, based on 165 PSA, the following prices are obtained:

Initial Price	New Price 165 PSA 7.25% CFY	New Price 165 PSA 6.75% CFY	New Price 150 PSA 7.25% CFY	New Price 200 PSA 6.75% CFY
60.3125	59.2500	61.3750	57.6563	64.5938

The modified duration for this PO is 7.05. The effective duration of 23.01 is dramatically different.

Effective Convexity

Exhibit 15-3 reports the standard convexity and the effective convexity for the four tranches in FJF-06 and the collateral. To illustrate the convexity formula, consider once again tranche C in FJF-06. The standard convexity is approximated as follows:

$$\frac{98.4063 + 102.1875 - 2(100.2813)}{(100.2813)(0.0025)^2} = 24.930$$

The effective convexity is

$$\frac{98.3438 + 101.9063 - 2(100.2813)}{(100.2813)(0.0025)^2} = -249.299$$

Note the significant difference in the two convexity measures here and in Exhibit 15-3. The standard convexity indicates that the four tranches have positive convexity, whereas the effective convexity indicates they have negative convexity. The difference is even more dramatic for bonds not trading near par. For a PO created from tranche C, the standard convexity is close to zero whereas the effective convexity is 2,155! This means that if yields change by 100 basis points, the percentage change in price due to convexity would be

$$2,155(0.01)^2(100) = 21.6\%$$

MONTE CARLO SIMULATION METHODOLOGY[1]

For some fixed-income securities and derivative instruments, the periodic cash flows are **path dependent.** This means that the cash flows received in one period is determined not only by the current and future interest rate levels but also by the path that interest rates took to get to the current level.

In the case of mortgage pass-through securities, prepayments are path dependent because this month's prepayment rate depends on whether there have been prior opportunities to refinance since the underlying mortgages were originated. Unlike mortgage loans, the decision as to whether a corporate issuer will elect to refund an issue when the current rate is below the issue's coupon rate is not dependent on how rates evolved over time to the current level.

Moreover, in the case of adjustable-rate pass-throughs (ARMs), prepayments are not only path dependent but the periodic coupon rate depends on the history of the reference rate upon which the coupon rate is determined. This is because ARMs have periodic caps and floors as well as a lifetime cap and floor. For example, an ARM whose coupon rate resets annually could have the following restriction on the coupon rate: (1) The rate cannot change by more than 200 basis points each year, and (2) the rate cannot be more than 500 basis points from the initial coupon rate.

---

[1]Portions of the material in this section and the one to follow are adapted from Frank J. Fabozzi and Scott F. Richard, "Valuation of CMOs," in Frank J. Fabozzi (ed.), *CMO Portfolio Management* (Summit, NJ: Frank J. Fabozzi Associates, 1994).

Pools of pass-throughs are used as collateral for the creation of collateralized mortgage obligations (CMOs). Consequently, for CMOs there are typically two sources of path dependency in a CMO tranche's cash flows. First, the collateral prepayments are path dependent, as discussed previously. Second, the cash flow to be received in the current month by a CMO tranche depends on the outstanding balances of the other tranches in the deal. Thus, we need the history of prepayments to calculate these balances.

Because of the path dependency of a mortgage-backed security's cash flow, the Monte Carlo simulation method is used for these securities rather than the binomial method described in Chapter 14.

Conceptually, the valuation of pass-throughs using the Monte Carlo method is simple. In practice, however, it is very complex. The simulation involves generating a set of cash flows based on simulated future mortgage refinancing rates, which in turn imply simulated prepayment rates.

Valuation modeling for CMOs is similar to valuation modeling for pass-throughs, although the difficulties are amplified because as we explained in Chapter 12, the issuer has sliced and diced both the prepayment risk and the interest-rate risk into smaller pieces called tranches. The sensitivity of the pass-throughs composing the collateral to these two risks is not transmitted equally to every tranche. Some of the tranches wind up more sensitive to prepayment risk and interest-rate risk than the collateral, whereas some of them are much less sensitive.

The objective of the money manager is to figure out how the value of the collateral gets transmitted to the CMO tranches. More specifically, the objective is to find out where the value goes and where the risk goes so that the money manager can identify the tranches with low risk and high value: the ones we want to buy. The good news is that this combination usually exists in every deal. The bad news is that in every deal there are usually tranches with low value and high risk.

Using Simulation to Generate Interest-Rate Paths and Cash Flows

The typical model that Wall Street firms and commercial vendors use to generate random interest-rate paths takes as input today's term structure of interest rates and a volatility assumption. The term structure of interest rates is the theoretical spot rate (or zero-coupon) curve implied by today's Treasury securities. The volatility assumption determines the dispersion of future interest rates in the simulation. The simulations should be normalized so that the average simulated price of a zero-coupon Treasury bond equals today's actual price.

Each model has its own model of the evolution of future interest rates and its own volatility assumptions. Typically, there are no significant differences in the interest-rate models of dealer firms and vendors, although their volatility assumptions can be significantly different.

The random paths of interest rates should be generated from an arbitrage-free model of the future term structure of interest rates. By *arbitrage-free* it is meant that the model replicates today's term structure of interest rates, an input of the model, and that for all future dates there is no possible arbitrage within the model.

The simulation works by generating many scenarios of future interest-rate paths. In each month of the scenario, a monthly interest rate and a mortgage refinancing rate are generated. The monthly interest rates are used to discount the projected cash flows in the scenario. The mortgage refinancing rate is needed to determine the cash flow because it represents the opportunity cost the mortgagor is facing at that time.

If the refinancing rates are high relative to the mortgagor's contract rate, the mortgagor will have less incentive to refinance, or even a positive disincentive (i.e., the homeowner will avoid moving, to avoid refinancing). If the refinancing rate is low relative to the mortgagor's contract rate, the mortgagor has an incentive to refinance.

Prepayments are projected by feeding the refinancing rate and loan characteristics, such as age, into a prepayment model. Given the projected prepayments, the cash flow along an interest-rate path can be determined.

To make this more concrete, consider a newly issued mortgage pass-through security with a maturity of 360 months. Exhibit 15-4 shows N simulated interest-rate path scenarios. Each scenario consists of a path of 360 simulated one-month future interest rates. Just how many paths should be generated is explained later. Exhibit 15-5 shows the paths of simulated mortgage refinancing rate corresponding to the scenarios shown in Exhibit 15-4. Assuming these mortgage refinancing rates, the cash flow for each scenario path is shown in Exhibit 15-6.

Calculating the Present Value for a Scenario Interest-Rate Path

Given the cash flow on an interest-rate path, its present value can be calculated. The discount rate for determining the present value is the simulated spot rate for each month on the interest-rate path plus an appropriate spread. The spot rate on a path can be determined from the simulated future monthly rates. The relationship that holds between the simulated spot rate for month T on path n and the simulated future one-month rates is

$$z_T(n) = \{[1 + f_1(n)][1 + f_2(n)] \cdots [1 + f_T(n)]\}^{1/T} - 1$$

EXHIBIT 15-4 Simulated Paths of One-Month Future Interest Rates

Month	*Interest-Rate Path Number*[a]						
	1	2	3	...	n	...	N
1	$f_1(1)$	$f_1(2)$	$f_1(3)$		$f_1(n)$		$f_1(N)$
2	$f_2(1)$	$f_2(2)$	$f_2(3)$		$f_2(n)$		$f_2(N)$
3	$f_3(1)$	$f_3(2)$	$f_3(3)$		$f_3(n)$		$f_3(N)$
4	$f_4(1)$	$f_4(2)$	$f_4(3)$		$f_4(n)$		$f_4(N)$
.							
.							
.							
t	$f_t(1)$	$f_t(2)$	$f_t(3)$		$f_t(n)$		$f_t(N)$
.							
.							
.							
358	$f_{358}(1)$	$f_{358}(2)$	$f_{358}(3)$		$f_{358}(n)$		$f_{358}(N)$
359	$f_{359}(1)$	$f_{359}(2)$	$f_{359}(3)$		$f_{359}(n)$		$f_{359}(N)$
360	$f_{360}(1)$	$f_{360}(2)$	$f_{360}(3)$		$f_{360}(n)$		$f_{360}(N)$

[a]Notation: $f_t(n)$, one-month future interest rate for month t on path n; N, total number of interest-rate paths.

EXHIBIT 15-5   Simulated Paths of Mortgage Refinancing Rates

Month	Interest-Rate Path Number[a]						
	1	2	3	...	n	...	N
1	$r_1(1)$	$r_1(2)$	$r_1(3)$		$r_1(n)$		$r_1(N)$
2	$r_2(1)$	$r_2(2)$	$r_2(3)$		$r_2(n)$		$r_2(N)$
3	$r_3(1)$	$r_3(2)$	$r_3(3)$		$r_3(n)$		$r_3(N)$
4	$r_4(1)$	$r_4(2)$	$r_4(3)$		$r_4(n)$		$r_4(N)$
.							
.							
.							
t	$r_t(1)$	$r_t(2)$	$r_t(3)$		$r_t(n)$		$r_t(N)$
.							
.							
.							
358	$r_{358}(1)$	$r_{358}(2)$	$r_{358}(3)$		$r_{358}(n)$		$r_{358}(N)$
359	$r_{359}(1)$	$r_{359}(2)$	$r_{359}(3)$		$r_{359}(n)$		$r_{359}(N)$
360	$r_{360}(1)$	$r_{360}(2)$	$r_{360}(3)$		$r_{360}(n)$		$r_{360}(N)$

[a]Notation: $r_t(n)$, mortgage refinancing rate for month t on path n: N, total number of interest-rate paths.

EXHIBIT 15-6   Simulated Cash Flow on Each of the Interest-Rate Paths

Month	Interest-Rate Path Number[a]						
	1	2	3	...	n	...	N
1	$C_1(1)$	$C_1(2)$	$C_1(3)$		$C_1(n)$		$C_1(N)$
2	$C_2(1)$	$C_2(2)$	$C_2(3)$		$C_2(n)$		$C_2(N)$
3	$C_3(1)$	$C_3(2)$	$C_3(3)$		$C_3(n)$		$C_3(N)$
4	$C_4(1)$	$C_4(2)$	$C_4(3)$		$C_4(n)$		$C_4(N)$
.							
.							
.							
t	$C_t(1)$	$C_t(2)$	$C_t(3)$		$C_t(n)$		$C_t(N)$
.							
.							
.							
358	$C_{358}(1)$	$C_{358}(2)$	$C_{358}(3)$		$C_{358}(n)$		$C_{358}(N)$
359	$C_{359}(1)$	$C_{359}(2)$	$C_{359}(3)$		$C_{359}(n)$		$C_{359}(N)$
360	$C_{360}(1)$	$C_{360}(2)$	$C_{360}(3)$		$C_{360}(n)$		$C_{360}(N)$

[a]Notation: $C_t(n)$, cash flow for month t on path n; N, total number of interest-rate paths.

where:

$z_T(n)$ = simulated spot rate for month T on path n

$f_j(n)$ = simulated future one-month rate for month j on path n

Consequently, the interest-rate path for the simulated future one-month rates can be converted to the interest-rate path for the simulated monthly spot rates as shown in Exhibit 15-7.

Therefore, the present value of the cash flow for month T on interest-rate path n discounted at the simulated spot rate for month T plus some spread is

$$PV[C_T(n)] = \frac{C_T(n)}{[1 + z_T(n) + K]^{1/T}}$$

where:

$PV[C_T(n)]$ = present value of cash flow for month T on path n

$C_T(n)$ = cash flow for month T on path n

$z_T(n)$ = spot rate for month T on path n

K = appropriate risk-adjusted spread

The present value for path n is the sum of the present value of the cash flow for each month on path n. That is,

$$PV[\text{path}(n)] = (1/360) \{PV[C_1(n)] + PV[C_2(n)] + \cdots + PV[C_{360}(n)]\}$$

where $PV[\text{path}(n)]$ is the present value of interest-rate path n.

EXHIBIT 15-7 Simulated Paths of Monthly Spot Rates

Month	*Interest-Rate Path*[a]					
	1	*2*	*3*	... *n* ...		*N*
1	$z_1(1)$	$z_1(2)$	$z_1(3)$	$z_1(n)$		$z_1(N)$
2	$z_2(1)$	$z_2(2)$	$z_2(3)$	$z_2(n)$		$z_2(N)$
3	$z_3(1)$	$z_3(2)$	$z_3(3)$	$z_3(n)$		$z_3(N)$
4	$z_4(1)$	$z_4(2)$	$z_4(3)$	$z_4(n)$		$z_4(N)$
.						
.						
.						
t	$z_t(1)$	$z_t(2)$	$z_t(3)$	$z_t(n)$		$z_t(N)$
.						
.						
.						
358	$z_{358}(1)$	$z_{358}(2)$	$z_{358}(3)$	$z_{358}(n)$		$z_{358}(N)$
359	$z_{359}(1)$	$z_{359}(2)$	$z_{359}(3)$	$z_{359}(n)$		$z_{359}(N)$
0						

[a] Notation: $z_t(n)$, spot rate for month t on path n; N, total number of interest-rate paths.

Determining the Theoretical Value

The present value of a given interest-rate path can be thought of as the theoretical value of a pass-through if that path was actually realized. The theoretical value of the pass-through can be determined by calculating the average of the theoretical value of all the interest-rate paths. That is, the theoretical value is equal to

$$\text{theoretical value} = (1/N)\{\text{PV}[\text{path}(1)] + \text{PV}[\text{path}(2)] + \cdots + \text{PV}[\text{path}(N)]\}$$

This procedure for valuing a pass-through is also followed for a CMO tranche. The cash flow for each month on each interest-rate path is found according to the principal repayment and interest distribution rules of the deal. To do this, a CMO structuring model is needed. In any analysis of CMOs, one of the major stumbling blocks is getting a good CMO structuring model.

Looking at the Distribution of the Path Values

The theoretical value generated by the Monte Carlo simulation method is the average of the path values. There is valuable information in the distribution of the path values. For example, consider a well-protected PAC bond. If the theoretical value generated from the Monte Carlo simulation method is 88 and the standard deviation of the path values is 1 point, there is not a great deal of dispersion in the path values. In contrast, suppose that the model indicates that the theoretical value for a support bond is 77 and the standard deviation of the path values is 10 points. Clearly, there is substantial dispersion of the path values and, as a result, the investor is warned about the potential variability of the model's value.[2]

Simulated Average Life

In Chapter 11 the average-life measure for a mortgage-backed security was introduced. The average life reported in a Monte Carlo analysis is the average of the average lives along the interest-rate paths. That is, for each interest-rate path, there is an average life. The average of these average lives is the average life reported. As with the theoretical value, additional information is conveyed by the distribution of the average life. The greater the range and standard deviation of the average life, the more uncertainty there is about the security's average life.

Option-Adjusted Spread

As explained in Chapter 14, the option-adjusted spread is a measure of the yield spread that can be used to convert dollar differences between value and price. It represents a spread over the issuer's spot rate curve or benchmark.

In the Monte Carlo model, the OAS is the spread K that when added to all the spot rates on all interest-rate paths will make the average present value of the paths equal to the observed market price (plus accrued interest). Mathematically, OAS is the spread that will satisfy the following condition:

---

[2]For illustrations, see Robert W. Kopprasch, "A Further Look at Option-Adjusted Spread Analysis," Chapter 30 in Frank J. Fabozzi (ed.), *The Handbook of Mortgage-Backed Securities* (Burr Ridge, IL: Irwin Professional Publishing, 1995).

market price $= (1/N) \{PV[path(1)] + PV[path(2)] + \cdots + PV[path(N)]\}$

where N is the number of interest-rate paths.

Option Cost

The implied cost of the option embedded in any mortgage-backed security can be obtained by calculating the difference between the OAS at the assumed volatility of interest rates and the static spread. That is,

option cost = static spread − option-adjusted spread

The reason that the option cost is measured in this way is as follows. In an environment of no interest-rate changes, the investor would earn the static spread. When future interest rates are uncertain, the spread is less, however, because of the homeowner's option to prepay; the OAS reflects the spread after adjusting for this option. Therefore, the option cost is the difference between the spread that would be earned in a static interest-rate environment (the static spread) and the spread after adjusting for the homeowner's option.

In general, a tranche's option cost is more stable than its OAS in the face of market movements. This interesting feature is useful in reducing the computational costs of calculating the OAS as the market moves. For small market moves, the OAS of a tranche may be approximated by recalculating the static spread (which is relatively cheap and easy to calculate) and subtracting its option cost.

Effective Duration and Convexity

In Chapter 14 we explained how to determine the effective duration and effective convexity for any security. These measures can be calculated using the Monte Carlo method as follows. First, the bond's OAS is found using the current term structure of interest rates. Next, the bond is repriced holding OAS constant but shifting the term structure. Two shifts are used to get the prices needed to apply the effective duration and effective convexity formulas: In one, yields are increased, in the second, they are decreased.

Selecting the Number of Interest-Rate Paths

Let's now address the question of the number of scenario paths or repetitions, N, needed to value a mortgage-backed security. A typical OAS run will be done for 512 to 1,024 interest-rate paths. The scenarios generated using the simulation method look very realistic, and furthermore, reproduce today's Treasury curve. By employing this technique, the money manager is effectively saying that Treasuries are fairly priced today and that the objective is to determine whether a specific mortgage-backed security is rich or cheap relative to Treasuries.

The number of interest-rate paths determines how "good" the estimate is, not relative to the truth but relative to the model. The more paths, the more average spread tends to settle down. It is a statistical sampling problem.

Most Monte Carlo simulation models employ some form of **variance reduction** to cut down on the number of sample paths necessary to get a good statistical sample. Variance reduction techniques allow us to obtain price estimates within a tick. By this we mean that if the model is used to generate more scenarios, price estimates from the model will not change by more than a tick. For example, if 1,024 paths are used to obtain the estimated price for a tranche, there is little more information to be had from the model by generating more than that number of paths. (For some very sensitive CMO tranches, more paths may be needed to estimate prices within one tick.)

Limitations of the OAS Measures

Although the OAS measure is much more useful than the static cash flow yield measure, it still suffers from major pitfalls.[3] These limitations apply not only to the OAS for mortgage-backed securities but also the OAS produced from a binomial model. First, as noted earlier, the OAS is a product of the valuation model. The valuation model may be poorly constructed because it fails to capture the true factors that affect the value of particular securities. Second, in Monte Carlo simulation the interest-rate paths must be adjusted so that on-the-run Treasuries are valued properly. That is, the value of an on-the-run Treasury is equal to its market price or, equivalently, its OAS is zero. The process of adjusting the interest-rate paths to achieve that result is ad hoc.

A third problem with the OAS is that it assumes a constant OAS for each interest-rate path and over time for a given interest-rate path. If there is a term structure to the OAS, this is not captured by having a single OAS number. Finally, the OAS is dependent on the volatility assumption, the prepayment assumption in the case of mortgage-backed securities, and the rules for refunding in the case of corporate bonds.

In addition, there is a problem with calculating an OAS for a portfolio by taking a weighted average of the OAS of the individual portfolio holdings.[4] Instead, if an OAS for a portfolio is sought, it is necessary to obtain the portfolio's cash flow along each interest-rate path. The OAS is then the spread that will make the average portfolio value equal to the portfolio's market value.

Illustration[5]

In this section we use a plain vanilla deal to show how CMOs can be analyzed using the Monte Carlo simulation method. The plain vanilla sequential-pay CMO bond structure in our illustration is FNMA 89-97. A diagram of the principal allocation structure is given in Exhibit 15-8. The structure includes five tranches, A, B, C, D, and

EXHIBIT 15-8   Principal Allocation Structure for FNMA 89-97

---

[3]These pitfalls have been described and documented in David F. Babbel and Stavros A. Zenios, "Pitfalls in the Analysis of Option-Adjusted Spreads," Financial Analysts Journal, July–August 1992, pp. 65–69.
[4]Kopprasch, "A Further Look at Option-Adjusted Spread Analysis."
[5]For additional illustrations, see Fabozzi and Richard, "Valuation of CMOs," pp. 88–100.

EXHIBIT 15-9 Analysis of FNMA 89–97 Classes A, B, C, and Z (as of 4/27/90)

Base Case (Assumes 12% Interest-Rate Volatility)

	Option-Adjusted Spread (basis points)	Option Cost (basis points)
Collateral	70	45
Class		
A	23	29
B	46	41
C	59	36
Z	74	50

Prepayments at 80% and 120% of Prepayment Model (Assumes 12% Interest-Rate Volatility)

	New Option-Adjusted Spread (basis points)		Change in Price per $100 par (holding OAS constant)	
	80%	*120%*	*80%*	*120%*
Collateral	70	71	$0.00	$0.04
Class				
A	8	40	−0.43	0.48
B	31	65	−0.86	1.10
C	53	73	−0.41	0.95
Z	72	93	−0.28	2.70

Interest-Rate Volatility of 8% and 16%

	New Option-Adjusted Spread (basis points)		Change in Price per $100 par (holding OAS constant)	
	8%	*16%*	*8%*	*16%*
Collateral	92	46	$1.03	−$1.01
Class				
A	38	5	0.42	−0.51
B	67	21	1.22	−1.45
C	77	39	1.22	−1.36
Z	99	50	3.55	−3.41

Z, and a residual class. Tranche Z is an accrual bond, and tranche D class is an IOette.[6] The focus of our analysis is on tranches A, B, C, and Z.

The top panel of Exhibit 15-9 shows the OAS and the option cost for the collateral and the five tranches in the CMO structure. The OAS for the collateral is 70 basis points. Because the option cost is 45 basis points, the static spread is 115 basis points (70 basis points plus 45 basis points). The weighted-average OAS of all the classes (including the residual) is equal to the OAS of the collateral.

At the time this analysis was performed, April 27, 1990, the Treasury yield curve was not steep. As we noted earlier, in such a yield curve environment the static spread

---

[6]This is a form of an interest-only tranche that has a nominal par value. Until 1992, all tranches in a CMO structure had to have some par value. As explained in Chapter 12, today, notional IOs are created.

will not differ significantly from the traditionally computed yield spread. Thus, for the four tranches shown in Exhibit 15-9, the static spread is 52 for A, 87 for B, 95 for C, and 124 for D.

Notice that the tranches did not share the OAS equally. The same is true for the option cost. The value tended to go toward the longer tranches, something that occurs in the typical deal. Both the static spread and the option cost increase as the maturity increases. The only tranches where there appears to be a bit of a bargain are B and C. A money manager contemplating the purchase of one of these middle tranches can see that C offers a higher OAS than B and appears to bear less of the risk, as measured by the option cost. The problem a money manager may encounter is that he might not be permitted to extend out as long as the C tranche because of duration, maturity, or average-life constraints.

Now let's look at modeling risk. Examination of the sensitivity of the tranches to changes in prepayments and interest-rate volatility will help us to understand the interaction of the tranches in the structure and who is bearing the risk.

We begin with prepayments. Specifically, we keep the same interest-rate paths as those used to get the OAS in the base case (the top panel of Exhibit 15-9) but reduce the prepayment rate on each interest-rate path to 80% of the projected rate.

As can be seen in the second panel of Exhibit 15-9, slowing down prepayments does not change the OAS for the collateral and its price at all. This is because the collateral is trading close to par. Tranches created by this collateral do not behave the same way, however. The exhibit reports two results of the sensitivity analysis. First, it indicates the change in the OAS. Second, it indicates the change in the price, holding the OAS constant at the base case.

To see how a money manager can use the information in the second panel, consider tranche A. At 80% of the prepayment speed, the OAS for this class declines from 23 basis points to 8 basis points. If the OAS is held constant, the panel indicates that the buyer of tranche A would lose $0.43 per $100 par value.

Notice that for all the tranches reported in Exhibit 15-9 there is a loss. How could all four tranches lose if prepayments are slowed down and the collateral does not lose value? This is because tranche D and the residual (R), which are not reported in the exhibit, got all the benefit of that slowdown. Notice that tranche Z is actually fairly well protected, so it does not lose much value as a result of the slowdown of prepayments. Tranche A by contrast is severely affected.

Also shown in the second panel of the exhibit is the second part of our experiment that tests the sensitivity of prepayments: The prepayment rate is assumed to be 120% of the base case. Once again, as the collateral is trading at close to par, its price does not move very much, about four cents per $100 of par value. In fact, because the collateral is trading slightly below par, the speeding up of prepayments will make the collateral look better while the OAS increases by only one basis point.

Now look at the four tranches. They all benefited. The results reported in the exhibit indicate that a money manager who is willing to go out to the long end of the curve, such as tranche Z, would realize most of the benefits of that speedup of prepayments. Because the four tranches benefited and the benefit to the collateral was minor, tranche D, the IOette, and the residual were affected adversely. In general, IO types of tranches will be affected adversely by a speedup.

Now let's look at the sensitivity to the interest-rate volatility assumption, 12% in the base case. Two experiments are performed: reducing the volatility assumption to 8% and increasing it to 16%. These results are reported in the third panel of Exhibit 15-9.

Reducing the volatility to 8% increases the dollar price of the collateral by $1 and increases the OAS from 70 in the base case to 92. This $1 increase in the price of the collateral is not equally distributed, however, among the four tranches. Most of the increase in value is realized by the longer tranches. The OAS gain for each of the tranches follows more or less the OAS durations of those tranches. This makes sense, because the longer the duration, the greater the risk, and when volatility declines, the reward is greater for the risk accepted.

At the higher level of assumed interest-rate volatility of 16%, the collateral is affected severely. The collateral's loss is distributed among the tranches in the expected manner: The longer the duration, the greater the loss. In this case tranche D and the residual are the least affected.

Using the OAS from the Monte Carlo simulation methodology, a fair conclusion can be made about this simple plain vanilla structure: What you see is what you get. The only surprise in this structure seems to be tranches B and C. In general, however, a money manager willing to extend duration gets paid for that risk.

TOTAL RETURN ANALYSIS

Neither the static cash flow methodology nor the Monte Carlo simulation methodology will tell a money manager whether investment objectives can be satisfied. The performance evaluation of an individual mortgage-backed security requires specification of an investment horizon, whose length for most financial institutions is dictated by the nature of its liabilities.

The measure that should be used to assess the performance of a security or a portfolio over some investment horizon is the total return that we discussed in Chapter 3. The total dollars received from investing in a mortgage-backed security consist of

1. The projected cash flow from the projected interest payments and the projected principal repayment (scheduled plus prepayments).
2. The interest earned on reinvestment of the projected interest payments and the projected principal prepayments.
3. The projected price of the mortgage-backed security at the end of the investment horizon.

To obtain the cash flow, a prepayment rate over the investment horizon must be assumed. The second step requires assumption of a reinvestment rate. Finally, either of the methodologies described in this chapter—cash flow yield or Monte Carlo simulation—can be used to calculate the price at the end of the investment horizon under a particular set of assumptions. Either approach requires assumption of the prepayment rate and the Treasury rates (i.e., the yield curve) at the end of the investment horizon. The cash flow yield methodology uses an assumed spread to a comparable Treasury to determine the required cash flow yield, which is then used to compute the projected price. The Monte Carlo simulation methodology requires an assumed OAS at the investment horizon. From this assumption, the OAS methodology can produce the horizon price.

To test the sensitivity of total return to various alternative assumptions scenario analysis is helpful. Its limitation is that only a small number of potential scenarios can be considered, and it fails to take into consideration the dynamics of changes in the yield curve and the dynamics of the deal structure.

Horizon Price for CMO Tranches

The most difficult part of estimating total return is projecting the price at the horizon date. In the case of a CMO tranche the price depends on the characteristics of the tranche and the spread to Treasuries *at the termination date*. The key determinants are the "quality" of the tranche, its average life (or duration), and its convexity.

Quality refers to the type of CMO tranche. Consider, for example, that an investor can purchase a CMO tranche that is a PAC bond but as a result of projected prepayments could become a sequential-pay tranche. As another example, suppose that a PAC bond is the longest-average-life tranche in a reverse PAC structure. Projected prepayments in this case might occur in an amount to change the class from a long-average-life PAC tranche to a support tranche. The converse is that the quality of a tranche may improve as well as deteriorate. For example, the effective collar for a PAC tranche could widen at the horizon date when prepayment circumstances increase the par amount of support tranches outstanding as a proportion of the deal.

OAS–Total Return

The total return and OAS frameworks can be combined to determine the projected price at the horizon date. At the end of the investment horizon, it is necessary to specify how the OAS is expected to change. The horizon price can be "backed out" of the Monte Carlo simulation model.

Assumptions about the OAS value at the investment horizon reflect the expectations of the money manager. It is common to assume that the OAS at the horizon date will be the same as the OAS at the time of purchase. A total return calculated using this assumption is sometimes referred to as a **constant-OAS total return.** Alternatively, active total return managers will make bets on how the OAS will change—either widening or tightening. The total return framework can be used to assess how sensitive the performance of a mortgage-backed security is to changes in the OAS.

SUMMARY

There are two methodologies commonly used to analyze mortgage-backed securities: cash flow yield methodology and Monte Carlo simulation methodology. The cash flow yield is the interest rate that will make the present value of the projected cash flow from a mortgage-backed security equal to its market price. The cash flow yield assumes that (1) all the cash flows can be reinvested at a rate equal to the cash flow yield, (2) the mortgage-backed security is held to the maturity date, and (3) the prepayment speed used to project the cash flow will be realized. In addition, the cash flow yield methodology fails to recognize that future interest-rate changes will affect the cash flow.

Modified duration is not a good measure of price volatility for mortgage-backed securities because it assumes that the cash flow does not change as yield changes. Effective duration does take into consideration how yield changes will affect prepayments and therefore cash flow.

A mortgage-backed security is a security whose cash flow is path dependent. This means that cash flow received in one period is determined not only by the current and future interest-rate levels, but also by the path that interest rates took to get to the current level. A methodology used to analyze path dependent cash flow securities is Monte Carlo simulation. This methodology involves randomly generating many scenarios of future interest-rate paths, where the interest-rate paths are generated based on some volatility assumption for interest rates.

The random paths of interest rates should be generated from an arbitrage-free model of the future term structure of interest rates. The Monte Carlo simulation methodology applied to mortgage-backed securities involves randomly generating a set of cash flows based on simulated future mortgage refinancing rates. The theoretical value of a security on any interest-rate path is the present value of the cash flow on that path, where the spot rates are those on the corresponding interest-rate path. The theoretical value of a security is the average of the theoretical values over all the interest-rate paths. Information about the distribution of the path values is useful in understanding the variability around the theoretical value. The average life reported is the average of the average lives from all the interest-rate paths and information about the distribution of the average life is useful.

In the Monte Carlo simulation methodology, the option-adjusted spread is the spread that when added to all the spot rates on all interest-rate paths will make the average present value of the paths equal to the observed market price (plus accrued interest). The effective duration and effective convexity are calculated using the Monte Carlo simulation methodology by holding the OAS constant and shifting the term structure up and down.

Total return is the correct measure for assessing the potential performance of CMO tranches over a specified investment horizon. The static cash flow yield or Monte Carlo simulation methodology can be incorporated into a total return framework to calculate the mortgage-backed security's price at the horizon date. Scenario analysis is one way to evaluate the risk associated with investing in a mortgage-backed security.

Questions

1. Suppose you are told that the cash flow yield of a pass-through security is 9% and that you are seeking to invest in a security with a yield greater than 8.8%.
   a. What additional information would you need to know before you might invest in this pass-through security?
   b. What are the limitations of the cash flow yield for assessing the potential return from investing in a mortgage-backed security?

2. Using the cash flow yield methodology, a spread is calculated over a comparable Treasury security. How is a comparable Treasury determined?
3. What is vector analysis?
4. In the calculation of effective duration and effective convexity, why is a prepayment model needed?
5. The following excerpt is taken from an article titled "Fidelity Eyes $250 Million Move into Premium PACs and I-Os" that appeared in the January 27, 1992, issue of *BondWeek,* pp. 1 and 21:

> Three Fidelity investment mortgage funds are considering investing this quarter a total of $250 million in premium planned amortization classes of collateralized mortgage obligations and some interest-only strips, said Jim Wolfson, portfolio manager. . . . Wolfson . . . will look mainly at PACs backed by 9–10% Federal Home Loan Mortgage Corp. and Federal National Mortgage Association pass-throughs. These have higher option-adjusted spreads than regular agency pass-throughs, or similar premium Government National Mortgage Association-backed, PACs, he said. He expects I-Os will start to perform better as prepayments start to slow later in this quarter.
>
> The higher yields on I-Os and premium PACs compensate for their higher prepayment risk, said Wolfson. "You get paid in yield to take on negative convexity," he said. He does not feel prepayments will accelerate. . . .

   a. Why would premium PACs and interest-only strips offer higher yields if the market expects that prepayments will accelerate or are highly uncertain?

   b. What does Wolfson mean when he says: "You get paid in yield to take on negative convexity"?

   c. What measure is Wolfson using to assess the risks associated with prepayments?

6. In an article titled "CUNA Mutual Looks for Noncallable Corporates" that appeared in the November 4, 1991, issue of *BondWeek,* p. 6, Joe Goglia, a portfolio manager for CUNA Mutual Insurance Group, stated that he invests in "planned amortization class tranches, which have less exposure to prepayment risk and are more positively convex than other mortgage-backeds." Is this true?
7. What is a path-dependent cash flow security?
8. Why is a pass-through security a path-dependent cash flow security?
9. Give two reasons why a CMO tranche is a path-dependent cash flow security.
10. Explain how given the cash flow on the simulated interest-rate paths the theoretical value of a mortgage-backed security is determined.
11. Explain how given the cash flow on the simulated interest-rate paths the average life of a mortgage-backed security is determined.
12. Suppose that a support bond is being analyzed using the Monte Carlo simulation methodology. The theoretical value using 1,500 interest-rate paths is 88. The range for the path present values is a low of 50 and a high of 115. The standard deviation is 15 points. How much confidence would you place on the theoretical value of 88?
13. In a well-protected PAC structure, what would you expect the distribution of the path present values and average lives to be compared to a support bond from the same CMO structure?
14. An analysis of a CMO structure using the Monte Carlo method indicated the following assuming 12% volatility:

	OAS (basis points)	Static Spread (basis points)
Collateral	80	120
Tranche		
PAC I A	40	60
PAC I B	55	80
PAC I C	65	95
PAC II	95	125
Support	75	250

   a. Calculate the option cost for each tranche.

   b. Which tranche is clearly too rich?

   c. What would happen to the static spread for each tranche if a 15% volatility is assumed?

   d. What would happen to the OAS for each tranche if a 15% volatility is assumed?

15. Why would the option-adjusted spread vary across dealer firms?

16. Explain how the number of interest-rate paths used in the Monte Carlo simulation methodology is determined.

17. Explain why you agree or disagree with the following statement: "When the Monte Carlo simulation methodology is used to value a mortgage-backed security, a PSA assumption is employed for all interest-rate paths."

18. What assumption is made about the OAS in calculating the effective duration and effective convexity of a mortgage-backed security?

19. What are the limitations of the option-adjusted spread measure?

20. What assumptions are required to assess the potential total return of a mortgage-backed security?

21. What are the complications of assessing the potential total return of a CMO tranched using the total return framework?

CHAPTER 16

Analysis of Convertible Bonds

Learning Objectives

After reading this chapter you will understand:

- what a convertible bond is

- what an exchangeable bond is

- the basic features of a convertible security

- conversion value, market conversion price, conversion premium per share, conversion premium ratio, and premium over straight value of a convertible bond

- the investment features of a convertible security

- what the minimum value of a convertible bond is

- the premium payback period

- the downside risk associated with a convertible bond

- the pros and cons of investing in a convertible bond

- the options approach to valuing a convertible bond

- why an option pricing approach is needed to value convertible securities properly

In Chapter 7 we described convertible bonds. In this chapter we explain methodologies for analyzing them, beginning with a review of the basic provisions of convertible bonds.

CONVERTIBLE BOND PROVISIONS

The conversion provision in a corporate bond issue grants the bondholder the right to convert the bond into a predetermined number of shares of common stock of the issuer. A convertible bond is therefore a corporate bond with a call option to buy the common stock of the issuer.

Exchangeable bonds grant the bondholder the right to exchange the bonds for the common stock of a firm *other* than the issuer of the bond. For example, Dart & Kraft has an outstanding bond issue that is exchangeable for the common stock of Minnesota Mining and Manufacturing. (Dart & Kraft obtained the 3M common stock in exchange for the sale of Riker Laboratories.) Some Ford Motor Credit bonds are exchangeable for the common stock of the parent company, Ford Motor Company. A few issues are exchangeable into more than one security. General Cinema, for example, has an outstanding issue that is convertible into the common stock of R.J. Reynolds and Sea-Land Corporation.

The number of shares of common stock that the bondholder will receive from exercising the call option of a convertible bond or an exchangeable bond is called the **conversion ratio.** The conversion privilege may extend for all or only some portion of the bond's life, and the stated conversion ratio may fall over time. It is always adjusted proportionately for stock splits and stock dividends.

At the time of issuance of a convertible bond, the issuer has effectively granted the bondholder the right to purchase the common stock at a price equal to

$$\frac{\text{par value of convertible bond}}{\text{conversion ratio}}$$

Along with the conversion privilege granted to the bondholder, most convertible bonds are callable at the option of the issuer. Some convertible bonds are putable. Put options can be classified as hard puts and soft puts. A **hard put** is one in which the convertible security must be redeemed by the issuer only for cash. In the case of a **soft put,** the issuer has the option to redeem the convertible security for cash, common stock, subordinated notes, or a combination of the three. In our initial analysis, we ignore any call or put options.

Illustration

To illustrate how to analyze a convertible bond, we use the same hypothetical bond throughout the chapter, XYZ bond:

$$\text{maturity} = 10 \text{ years}$$
$$\text{coupon rate} = 10\%$$
$$\text{conversion ratio} = 50$$
$$\text{par value} = \$1,000$$
$$\text{current market price of XYZ bond} = \$950$$
$$\text{current market price of XYZ common stock} = \$17$$
$$\text{dividends per share} = \$1$$

The conversion price for XYZ bond is

$$\text{conversion price} = \frac{\$1,000}{50} = \$20$$

MINIMUM VALUE OF A CONVERTIBLE BOND

The **conversion value** of a convertible bond is the value of the bond if it is converted immediately.[1] That is,

$$\text{conversion value} = \text{market price of common stock} \times \text{conversion ratio}$$

---

[1]Technically, the standard textbook definition of conversion value given here is theoretically incorrect because as bondholders convert, the price of the stock will decline. The theoretically correct definition for the conversion value is that it is the product of the conversion ratio and the stock price *after* conversion.

The minimum price of a convertible bond is the greater of

1. Its conversion value, or
2. Its value as a corporate bond without the conversion option—that is, based on the convertible bond's cash flows if not converted (i.e., a plain vanilla bond). This value is called its **straight value.**

To estimate the straight value, we must determine the required yield on a nonconvertible bond with the same quality rating and similar investment characteristics. Given this estimated required yield, the straight value is then the present value of the bond's cash flows using this yield to discount the cash flows.

If the convertible bond does not sell for the greater of these two values, arbitrage profits could be realized. For example, suppose that the conversion value is greater than the straight value and the bond trades at its straight value. An investor can buy the convertible bond at the straight value and convert it. By doing so, the investor realizes a gain equal to the difference between the conversion value and the straight value. Suppose, instead, that the straight value is greater than the conversion value, and the bond trades at its conversion value. By buying the convertible at the conversion value, the investor will realize a higher yield than a comparable straight bond.

Illustration

For the XYZ convertible bond, the conversion value is equal to

$$\text{conversion value} = \$17 \times 50 = \$850$$

To determine the straight value, it is necessary to determine what comparable bonds are trading for in the market. Suppose that comparable bonds are trading to yield 14%. The straight value is then the price of a 10% 10-year bond selling to yield 14%. The price for such a bond would be $788.[2]

Given a conversion value of $850 and a straight value of $788, the minimum price for the XYZ bond is $850. To see this, note that if the bond is selling at its straight value rather than its conversion value, an investor could buy the bond for $788 and simultaneously sell 50 shares of XYZ stock at $17 per share. When the short sale of the stock is covered when the bond is converted, the transaction would produce an arbitrage profit of $62 per XYZ bond purchased. The only way to eliminate this arbitrage profit is for the XYZ bond to sell for $850, its conversion value.

Suppose, instead, that comparable nonconvertible bonds are trading to yield 11.8%. Then the straight value of XYZ bond would be $896. The minimum price for the XYZ bond must be its straight value in this case, because that is a value higher than the conversion value of $850. To see this, suppose that the market price of the XYZ bond is $850. At this price, the yield would be about 12.7%, 90 basis points greater than comparable nonconvertible bonds. Investors would find the bond attractive. As investors buy the bond, they will bid up its price to where the new yield is 11.8%.

---

[2]Actually, it is $788.10, but $788 will be used in our illustrations.

MARKET CONVERSION PRICE

The price that an investor effectively pays for the common stock if the convertible bond is purchased and then converted into the common stock is called the **market conversion price.**[3] It is found as follows:

$$\text{market conversion price} = \frac{\text{market price of convertible bond}}{\text{conversion ratio}}$$

The market conversion price is a useful benchmark because when the actual market price of the stock rises above the market conversion price, any further stock price increase is certain to increase the value of the convertible bond by at least the same percentage. Therefore, the market conversion price can be viewed as a break-even point.

An investor who purchases a convertible bond rather than the underlying stock typically pays a premium over the current market price of the stock. This premium per share is equal to the difference between the market conversion price and the current market price of the common stock. That is,

market conversion premium per share = market conversion price − current market price

The market conversion premium per share is usually expressed as a percentage of the current market price as follows:

$$\text{market conversion premium ratio} = \frac{\text{conversion premium per share}}{\text{market price of common stock}}$$

Why would someone be willing to pay a premium to buy this stock? Recall that the minimum price of a convertible bond is the greater of its conversion value or its straight value. Thus, as the stock price declines, the price of the convertible bond will not fall below its straight value. The straight value therefore acts as a floor for the convertible bond price.

Viewed in this context, the market conversion premium per share can be seen as the price of a call option. As explained in Chapter 22, the buyer of a call option limits the downside risk to the option price. In the case of a convertible bond, for a premium, the bondholder limits the downside risk to the straight value of the bond. The difference between the buyer of a call option and the buyer of a convertible bond is that the former knows precisely the dollar amount of the downside risk, whereas the latter knows only that the most that can be lost is the difference between the convertible bond price and the straight value. The straight value at some future date, however, is not known; the value will change as the interest rate changes.

Illustration

At a market price of $950, a stock price of $17, and a conversion ratio of 50, the market conversion price, market conversion premium per share, and market conversion premium ratio of the XYZ convertible bond are calculated as follows:

---

[3] The market conversion price is also called the **conversion parity price.**

$$\text{market conversion price} = \frac{\$950}{50} = \$19$$

$$\text{market conversion premium per share} = \$19 - \$17 = \$2$$

$$\text{market conversion premium ratio} = \frac{\$2}{\$17} = 0.118 \text{ or } 11.8\%$$

CURRENT INCOME OF CONVERTIBLE BOND VERSUS STOCK

As an offset to the market conversion premium per share, investing in the convertible bond rather than buying the stock directly generally means that the investor realizes higher current income from the coupon interest paid on the convertible bond than would be received as dividends paid on the number of shares equal to the conversion ratio. Analysts evaluating a convertible bond typically compute the time it takes to recover the premium per share by computing the **premium payback period** (which is also known as the **break-even time**). This is computed as follows:

$$\frac{\text{market conversion premium per share}}{\text{favorable income differential per share}}$$

where the favorable income differential per share is equal to[4]

$$\frac{\text{coupon interest from bond} - (\text{conversion ratio} \times \text{dividend per share})}{\text{conversion ratio}}$$

Notice that the premium payback period does **not** take into account the time value of money.

Illustration

For the XYZ convertible bond, the market conversion premium per share is $2. The favorable income differential per share is found as follows:

$$\text{coupon interest from bond} = 0.10 \times \$1,000 = \$100$$

$$\text{conversion ratio} \times \text{dividend per share} = 50 \times \$1 = \$50$$

Therefore,

$$\text{favorable income differential per share} = \frac{\$100 - \$50}{50} = \$1$$

and

$$\text{premium payback period} = \frac{\$2}{\$1} = 2 \text{ years}$$

Without considering the time value of money, the investor would recover the market conversion premium per share in two years.

---

[4]A more precise methodology for calculating the favorable income from holding the convertible is recommended in Luke Knecht and Mike McCowin, "Valuing Convertible Securities," in Frank J. Fabozzi (ed.), *Advances and Innovations in Bond and Mortgage Markets* (Chicago: Probus Publishing, 1989). In most cases the conventional formula presented in the text is sufficient.

DOWNSIDE RISK WITH A CONVERTIBLE BOND

Investors usually use the straight value of the bond as a measure of the downside risk of a convertible bond, because the price of the convertible bond cannot fall below this value. Thus, the straight value acts as the *current* floor for the price of the convertible bond. The downside risk is measured as a percentage of the straight value and computed as follows:

$$\text{premium over straight value} = \frac{\text{market price of the convertible bond}}{\text{straight value}} - 1$$

The higher the premium over straight value, all other factors constant, the less attractive the convertible bond.

Despite its use in practice, this measure of downside risk is flawed because the straight value (the floor) changes as interest rates change. If interest rates rise (fall), the straight value falls (rises) making the floor fall (rise). Therefore, the downside risk changes as interest rates change.

Illustration

Earlier we said that if comparable nonconvertible bonds are trading to yield 14%, the straight value of the XYZ bond would be $788. The premium over straight value is then

$$\text{premium over straight value} = \frac{\$950}{\$788} - 1 = 0.21 \text{ or } 21\%$$

If the yield on a comparable nonconvertible bond is 11.8% instead of 14%, the straight value would be $896 and the premium over straight value would be

$$\text{premium over straight value} = \frac{\$950}{\$896} - 1 = 0.06 \text{ or } 6\%$$

INVESTMENT CHARACTERISTICS OF A CONVERTIBLE BOND

The investment characteristics of a convertible bond depend on the stock price. If the price of the stock is low, so that the straight value is considerably higher than the conversion value, the bond will trade much like a straight bond. The convertible bond in such instances is referred to as a **bond equivalent** or a **busted convertible.**

When the price of the stock is such that the conversion value is considerably higher than the straight value, the convertible bond will trade as if it were an equity instrument; in this case it is said to be an **equity equivalent.** In such cases the market conversion premium per share will be small.

Between these two cases, bond equivalent and equity equivalent, the convertible bond trades as a **hybrid security,** having the characteristics of both a bond and an equity instrument.

PROS AND CONS OF INVESTING IN A CONVERTIBLE BOND

So far we have presented several measures that can be used to analyze convertible bonds. Let's use the XYZ convertible bond to drive home the pros and cons of investing in a convertible bond.

Suppose that an investor is considering purchase of a stock or a convertible bond. The stock can be purchased in the market for $17. By buying the convertible bond, the investor is effectively purchasing the stock for $19 (the market conversion price per share).

Look at the outcome one month from now, assuming that XYZ stock rises to $34. An investor buying the stock would realize a gain of $17 ($34 − $17) on a $17 investment, or a 100% return. In contrast, the conversion value for the bond would be $1,700 ($34 × 50). Because the price of XYZ bond is $950, the investor would realize a return of about 79%. The return would in fact probably be slightly higher because the convertible bond would trade at a slight premium to its conversion value. The reason for the lower return by buying the convertible bond rather than the stock directly is that the investor has effectively paid $2 per share more for the stock. Thus, the investor realizes a gain based on a stock price of $19 rather than $17.

So far, we've illustrated the advantage of owning the stock rather than the bond when the price of the stock rises. Let's look at the situation where the stock declines in value to $7. The investor who buys the stock now realizes a loss of $10 per share for a return of −59%. The conversion value of the XYZ bond likewise drops, to $350 ($7 × 50). Its price, however, will not fall to that level. Recall from our earlier discussion that the minimum price of a convertible bond will be the greater of its conversion value or its straight value. Assuming that the straight value is $788, and it does not change over the one-month period, the value of XYZ bond will fall to only $788. This means that the investor realizes a loss of only 17%. The loss would be even less in fact because the convertible bond would trade at a premium to its straight value.

The critical assumption in this analysis is that the straight value does not change, although it can change for any of the reasons cited in Chapter 2. More specifically, if interest rates rise in the economy, the straight value will decline. Even if interest rates do not rise, the perceived creditworthiness of the issuer may deteriorate, causing investors to demand a higher yield. In fact, the stock price and the yield required by investors are not independent. When the price of the stock drops precipitously, as in our $17 to $7 illustration, the perceived creditworthiness of the issuer may decline, causing a decline in the straight value. In any event, although the straight value may decline, it still is a floor (albeit a moving floor) for the convertible bond price. In our illustration, the straight value would have to fall about $390 (59% loss on $950), to equal the loss on the stock purchase.

The illustration clearly demonstrates that there are benefits and drawbacks of investing in convertible bonds. The disadvantage is the upside potential given up because a premium per share must be paid. An advantage is the reduction in downside risk (as determined by the straight value), with the opportunity to recoup the premium per share through the higher current income from owning the convertible bond.

Call Risk

Convertible issues are callable by the issuer. This is a valuable feature for issuers, who deem the current market price of their stock undervalued enough so that selling stock directly would dilute the equity of current stockholders. The firm would prefer to raise equity funds over incurring debt, so it issues a convertible setting the conversion ratio on the basis of a stock price it regards as acceptable. When the market price reaches the conversion point, the firm will want to see the conversion happen in view of the risk that the price may drop in the future. This gives the firm an interest in forcing conversion, even though this is not in the interest of the owners of the security whose price is likely to be adversely affected by the call.

Takeover Risk

Corporate takeovers represent another risk to investing in convertible bonds. If an issuer is acquired by another company or by its own management (as in the case of a management-led leveraged buyout), the stock price may not appreciate sufficiently for the holders of the convertible bond to benefit from the conversion feature. As the stock of the acquired company may no longer trade after a takeover, the investor can be left with a bond that pays a lower coupon rate than comparable-risk corporate bonds.

OPTIONS APPROACH

In our discussion of convertible bonds, we did not address the following questions:

1. What is a fair value for the conversion premium per share?
2. How do we handle convertible bonds with call and/or put options?
3. How does a change in interest rates affect the stock price?

The option pricing approach to valuation described in Chapter 14 can help us answer these questions. Consider first a noncallable/nonputable convertible bond. The investor who purchases this bond would be entering into two separate transactions: (1) buying a noncallable/nonputable straight bond, and (2) buying a call option (or warrant) on the stock, where the number of shares that can be purchased with the call option is equal to the conversion ratio.

The question is: What is the fair value for the call option? The fair value depends on the factors (discussed in Chapter 22) that affect the price of a call option. One key factor is the expected price volatility of the stock: the more the expected price volatility, the greater the value of the call option. The theoretical value of a call option can be valued using the Black–Scholes option pricing model[5] or the binomial option pricing model.[6] As a first approximation to the value of a convertible bond, the formula would be

convertible bond value = straight value + price of the call option on the stock

The price of the call option is added to the straight value because the investor has purchased a call option on the stock.

Now let's add in a common feature of a convertible bond: the issuer's right to call the bond. The issuer can force conversion by calling the bond. For example, suppose that the call price is $1,030 per $1,000 par and the conversion value is $1,700. If the issuer calls the bonds, the optimal strategy for the investor is to convert the bond and

---

[5]Fischer Black and Myron Scholes, "The Pricing of Corporate Liabilities," *Journal of Political Economy,* May–June 1973, pp. 637–659.

[6]John C. Cox, Stephen A. Ross, and Mark Rubinstein, "Option Pricing: A Simplified Approach," *Journal of Financial Economics,* September 1979, pp. 229–263; Richard J. Rendleman and Brit J. Bartter, "Two-State Option Pricing," *Journal of Finance,* December 1979, pp. 1093–1110; and William F. Sharpe, *Investments* (Englewood Cliffs, NJ: Prentice Hall, 1981), Chap. 16.

receive shares worth $1,700.[7] The investor, however, loses any premium over the conversion value that is reflected in the market price. Therefore, the analysis of convertible bonds must take into account the value of the issuer's right to call the bond. This depends, in turn, on (1) future interest rate volatility, and (2) economic factors that determine whether it is optimal for the issuer to call the bond.

The Black–Scholes option pricing model cannot handle this situation. Instead, the binomial option pricing model can be used simultaneously to value the bondholder's call option on the stock and the issuer's right to call the bonds. The bondholder's put option can also be accommodated. To link interest rates and stock prices together (the third question we raised previously), statistical analysis of historical movements of these two variables must be estimated and incorporated into the model.

The option pricing approach offers a great deal of promise and models have been proposed as far back as 1977.[8] In the experience of the author, the most complicated model employed by practitioners uses the Black–Scholes model and tests the sensitivity of the factors that affect any other embedded options.[9]

SUMMARY

In this chapter we have discussed the basic provisions of convertible bonds and explored a framework for evaluating these bonds. Analysis of a convertible bond requires calculation of the conversion value, straight value, market conversion price, market conversion premium ratio, and premium payback period.

The downside risk of a convertible bond usually is estimated by calculating the premium over straight value. The limitation of this measure is that the straight value (the floor) changes as interest rates change. Convertible bond investors are also subject to call risk and takeover risk.

The option pricing approach can be used to determine the fair value of the embedded call option. The value of the call option following this approach is estimated using some equity option pricing model such as the Black–Scholes model.

Questions

1. In the October 26, 1992, prospectus summary of the Staples 5% convertible subordinated debentures due 1999, the offering stated: "Convertible into Common Stock at a conversion price of $45 per share. . . ." If the par value is $1,000, what is the conversion ratio?

---

[7] Actually, the conversion value would be less than $1,700, because the per share value after conversion would decline.

[8] See, for example, Michael Brennan and Eduardo Schwartz, "Convertible Bonds: Valuation and Optimal Strategies for Call and Conversion," *Journal of Finance,* December 1977, pp. 1699–1715; Jonathan Ingersoll, "A Contingent-Claims Valuation of Convertible Securities," *Journal of Financial Economics,* May 1977, pp. 289–322; Michael Brennan and Eduardo Schwartz, "Analyzing Convertible Bonds," *Journal of Financial and Quantitative Analysis,* November 1980, pp. 907–929; and George Constantinides, "Warrant Exercise and Bond Conversion in Competitive Markets," *Journal of Financial Economics,* September 1984, pp. 371–398.

[9] See, for example, Mihir Bhattacharya and Yu Zhu, "Valuation and Analysis of Convertible Securities," Chapter 36 in Frank J. Fabozzi and T. Dessa Fabozzi (eds.), *The Handbook of Fixed Income Securities* (Burr Ridge, IL: Irwin Professional Publishing, 1995); and Frank J. Fabozzi, *Valuation of Fixed Income Securities and Derivatives* (New Hope, PA: Frank J. Fabozzi Associates, 1995), Chapter 9.

2. What is the difference between a soft put and a hard put?
3. This excerpt is taken from an article titled "Caywood Looks for Convertibles," which appeared in the January 13, 1992, issue of *BondWeek,* p. 7:

   > Caywood Christian Capital Management will invest new money in its $400 million high-yield portfolio in "busted convertibles," double- and triple-B rated convertible bonds of companies. . . . , said James Caywood, ceo. Caywood likes these convertibles as they trade at discounts and are unlikely to be called, he said.

   a. What is a busted convertible?
   b. What is the premium over straight value at which these bonds would trade?
   c. Why does Mr. Caywood seek convertibles with higher investment-grade ratings?
   d. Why is Mr. Caywood interested in call protection?
4. Explain the limitation of using premium over straight value as a measure of the downside risk of a convertible bond.
5. This excerpt comes from an article titled "Bartlett Likes Convertibles" in the October 7, 1991, issue of *BondWeek,* p. 7:

   > Bartlett & Co. is selectively looking for opportunities in convertible bonds that are trading cheaply because the equity of the issuer has dropped in value, according to Dale Rabiner, director of fixed income at the $800 million Cincinnati-based fund. Rabiner said he looks for five-year convertibles trading at yields comparable to straight bonds of companies he believes will rebound.

   Discuss this strategy for investing in convertible bonds.
6. Consider a convertible bond as follows:

$$\text{par value} = \$1,000$$
$$\text{coupon rate} = 9.5\%$$
$$\text{market price of convertible bond} = \$1,000$$
$$\text{conversion ratio} = 37.383$$
$$\text{estimated straight value of bond} = \$510$$
$$\text{yield to maturity of straight bond} = 18.7\%$$

Assume that the price of the common stock is $23 and that the dividend per share is $0.75 per year.
   a. Calculate each of the following:
      (1) Conversion value
      (2) Market conversion price
      (3) Conversion premium per share
      (4) Conversion premium ratio
      (5) Premium over straight value
      (6) Favorable income differential per share
      (7) Premium payback period
   b. Suppose that the price of the common stock increases from $23 to $46.
      (1) What will be the approximate return realized from investing in the convertible bond?
      (2) What would be the return realized if $23 had been invested in the common stock?
      (3) Why would the return on investing in the common stock directly be higher than investing in the convertible bond?
   c. Suppose that the price of the common stock declines from $23 to $8.

(1) What will be the approximate return realized from investing in the convertible bond?

(2) What would be the return realized if $23 had been invested in the common stock?

(3) Why would the return on investing in the convertible bond be higher than investing in the common stock directly?

7. A Merrill Lynch note structure called a *liquid yield option note* (LYON) is a zero-coupon instrument that is convertible into the common stock of the issuer. The conversion ratio is fixed for the entire life of the note. If investors wish to convert to the shares of the issuer, they must exchange the LYON for the stock. As a result, the conversion price increases over time. Why?

8. (This question is from CFA Examination III, June 1, 1991, Afternoon Session, Question 13.) Simon Evans, CFA, is researching SOC Corporation, a company that has issued both convertible and straight bonds. A major broker/dealer makes an over-the-counter market in options on SOC's common stock. Evans is considering two possible portfolios:

- Portfolio X: five SOC convertible bonds (total par value $5,000) with a conversion ratio of 20
- Portfolio Y: five SOC straight bonds (total par value $5,000) and a call option for 100 SOC shares

Evans believes that portfolios X and Y are similar in some ways, because each portfolio holds SOC bonds and rights to own SOC stock.

In preparing to make a portfolio decision, Evans obtained the current information presented in the following table:

SOC Bonds Data	Convertible	Straight
Coupon	5.5%	10.5%
Maturity	5 years	5 years
Conversion ratio	20.0	—
Market price	93.75	100.00
Yield to maturity	7.0%	10.5%

SOC call/option data (American style):

$$\text{strike price} = \$50.00$$
$$\text{expiration date} = 5 \text{ years}$$
$$\text{call premium} = \$7.50$$

a. Certain steps are required to change each portfolio from SOC bonds to SOC common stock. Using *only* the information provided here, compare portfolios X and Y with respect to *each* of the following:

- Transactions required to change holdings from bonds to stocks
- Parties involved in the transactions
- Potential risks or costs associated with the changes

b. Complete the following table. (Use 8.5302 as the present value of an ordinary annuity of $1 paid semiannually for five years discounted at a 6% risk-free annual discount rate.)

	Straight SOC Bonds	*Convertible SOC Bonds*	*Difference*
Cost of five bonds	————	————	————
Dollar amount of semiannual coupon for five bonds	————	————	————
Present value of cash flow differences	————	————	————

c. Recommend and justify the purchase of either portfolio X or portfolio Y, using your analysis in parts a and b.

CHAPTER 17

Active Bond Portfolio Management Strategies

Learning Objectives

After reading this chapter you will understand:

- the five basic steps involved in the investment management process

- the difference between active and passive strategies

- the importance of knowing the market consensus before implementing an active strategy

- the different types of active bond portfolio strategies: interest-rate expectations strategies, yield curve strategies, yield spread strategies, option-adjusted spread-based strategies, and individual security selection strategies

- bullet, barbell, and ladder yield curve strategies

- the limitations of using duration and convexity to assess the potential performance of bond portfolio strategies

- why it is necessary to use the dollar duration when implementing a yield spread strategy

- how to assess the allocation of funds within the corporate bond sector

- why leveraging is used by managers and traders and the risks and rewards associated with leveraging

- how to leverage using the repo market

This chapter and the two that follow discuss bond portfolio management strategies. We begin with an overview of the investment management process and the factors to consider in the selection of a portfolio strategy, distinguishing between active portfolio strategies and structured portfolio strategies. Active strategies are discussed in this chapter, and structured portfolio strategies are the subject of the next two chapters.

OVERVIEW OF THE INVESTMENT MANAGEMENT PROCESS

Regardless of the type of financial institution, the investment management process involves the following five steps:

1. Setting investment objectives
2. Establishing investment policy
3. Selecting a portfolio strategy
4. Selecting assets
5. Measuring and evaluating performance

Setting Investment Objectives

The first step in the investment management process is setting investment objectives. The investment objective will vary by type of financial institution. For institutions such as pension funds, the investment objective is to generate sufficient cash flow from investments to satisfy pension obligations. For life insurance companies, the basic objective is to satisfy obligations stipulated in insurance policies and generate a profit. Most insurance products guarantee a dollar payment or a stream of dollar payments at some time in the future. The premium that the life insurance company charges a policyholder for one of its products will depend on the interest rate that the company can earn on its investments. To realize a profit, the life insurance company must earn a higher return on the premium it invests than the implicit (or explicit) interest rate it has guaranteed policyholders.

For institutions such as banks and thrifts, funds are obtained from the issuance of certificates of deposit, short-term money market instruments, or floating-rate notes. These funds are then invested in loans and marketable securities. The objective in this case is to earn a return on invested funds that is higher than the cost of acquiring those funds. For these sorts of institutions, investment objectives are dictated essentially by the nature of their liabilities—obligations to pension recipients, policyholders, and depositors. For investment companies (mutual funds), the investment objectives will be as set forth in a prospectus. With the exception of mutual funds that have a specified termination date (called **target term trusts**), there are no specific liabilities that must be met. Typically, the fund establishes a target dividend payout. Because of the importance of the nature of the liabilities in determining investment objectives, in Chapter 19 we examine this topic more closely.

Establishing Investment Policy

The second step in investment management is establishing policy guidelines for meeting the investment objectives. Setting policy begins with the asset allocation decision; that is, there must be a decision as to how the funds of the institution should be distributed among the major classes of investments (cash equivalents, equities, fixed-income securities, real estate, and foreign securities).

Client and regulatory constraints are considerations in establishing an investment policy. Examples of constraints that the sponsor of a pension fund might impose are the following: No funds may be invested in a bond of an issuer whose credit rating is below a specified level; no more than a predetermined percentage of the fund's assets may be invested in a particular industry; and options and futures may be used only to protect asset values, not for speculative purposes. Regulators of state-regulated institutions such as insurance companies (both life and property and casualty companies) may restrict the amount of funds allocated to certain major asset classes. Even the amount allocated within a major asset class may be restricted, depending on the characteristics of the particular asset. In the case of investment companies, restrictions on asset allocation are set forth in the prospectus when the fund is launched and may be changed only with approval of the fund's board of directors.

Tax and financial reporting implications must also be considered in adopting investment policies. For example, life insurance companies enjoy certain tax advantages that make investing in tax-exempt municipal securities generally unappealing. Because pension funds too are exempt from taxes, they also are not particularly interested in tax-exempt municipal securities.

Institutional investors must prepare periodic financial statements. These financial statements must be prepared in accordance with "generally accepted accounting principles" (GAAPs). Thus, the assets and liabilities reported are based on GAAP accounting. The accounting treatment for assets is governed by a relatively new accounting requirement, Statement of Financial Accounting Standards No. 115, more popularly referred to as FASB 115.[1] Financial Accounting Standards Board Statements Nos. 87 and 88 and the Omnibus Budget Reconciliation Act of 1987 affect the ways in which pension funds establish investment policies.

It is unfortunate but true that financial reporting considerations can cause institutions to establish investment policies that may not be in the best interest of the institution in the long run. Basically, financial reporting considerations prior to the adoption of FASB 115 were due to use of accounting for assets at cost rather than market value (i.e., marking assets to market). FASB 115 limited the use of reporting assets at cost.

Selecting a Portfolio Strategy

Selecting a portfolio strategy that is consistent with the objectives and policy guidelines of the client or institution is the third step in the investment management process. Portfolio strategies can be classified as either **active strategies** or **passive strategies.** Essential to all active strategies is specification of expectations about the factors that influence the performance of an asset class. In the case of active equity strategies, this may include forecasts of future earnings, dividends, or price/earnings ratios. In the case of active bond management, this may involve forecasts of future interest rates, future interest-rate volatility, or future yield spreads. Active portfolio strategies involving foreign securities will require forecasts of future exchange rates.

Passive strategies involve minimal expectational input. One popular type of passive strategy is indexing, whose objective is to replicate the performance of a predetermined index. Although indexing has been employed extensively in the management of equity portfolios, the use of indexing for managing bond portfolios is a relatively new practice.

Between the extremes of active and passive strategies have sprung up strategies that have elements of both. For example, the core of a portfolio may be indexed, with the balance managed actively. Or a portfolio may be primarily indexed but employ

---

[1] FASB 115 was issued in May 1993 and became effective with fiscal years beginning after December 15, 1993.

low-risk strategies to enhance the indexed portfolio's return. This strategy is commonly referred to as **enhanced indexing** or **indexing plus.**

In the bond area, several strategies classified as **structured portfolio strategies** have commonly been used. A structured portfolio strategy calls for design of a portfolio to achieve the performance of a predetermined benchmark. Such strategies are frequently followed when funding liabilities. When the predetermined benchmark is the generation of sufficient funds to satisfy a single liability, regardless of the course of future interest rates, a strategy known as **immunization** is often used. When the predetermined benchmark requires funding multiple future liabilities regardless of how interest rates change, strategies such as immunization, **cash flow matching** (or **dedication**), or **horizon matching** can be employed.

As part of the immunization and cash flow matching strategies, low-risk active management strategies can be employed. For example, contingent immunization strategy allows the portfolio manager to manage a portfolio actively until certain parameters are violated. If and when those parameters are violated, the portfolio is then immunized.

Indexing can also be considered a structured portfolio strategy, because the benchmark is to achieve the performance of a predetermined index.[2] In Chapters 18 and 19 we describe structured portfolio strategies: Chapter 18 focuses on indexing, and Chapter 19 on immunization and cash flow matching/dedication.

Given the choice among active, structured, or passive management, which should be selected? The answer depends on (1) the client or money manager's view of the pricing efficiency of the market, and (2) the nature of the liabilities to be satisfied. First let's consider the pricing efficiency of a market.

Pricing efficiency is taken to describe a market where prices at all times fully reflect all available information that is relevant to the valuation of securities. When a market is price-efficient, active strategies will not consistently produce superior returns after adjusting for (1) risk and (2) transactions costs.

What strategy should be pursued by an investor who believes that the market is sufficiently efficient that superior risk-adjusted returns cannot be realized consistently after accounting for transactions costs? Capital market theory argues that indexing is the strategy of choice.

But pricing efficiency is not the sole determinant of the type of investment strategy that should be employed. The nature of the liabilities is also of paramount importance. Although indexing may be a reasonable strategy for an institution that does not have a future liability stream to be satisfied, consider the circumstances in which pension funds operate. If a pension fund indexes its portfolio, the fund's return will be roughly the same as the index return. Yet the index may not provide a return that is sufficient to satisfy the fund's obligations. Consequently, for some institutions,

---

[2] Portfolio insurance strategies—strategies commonly used in the equity area to reproduce the payoff of a put option—where the objective is to ensure that the value of the portfolio does not fall below a predetermined level, are also viewed as structured portfolio strategies. However, portfolio insurance strategies are rarely used in the fixed-income area. For an illustration of the application of portfolio insurance strategies in the fixed-income area, see Colin Negrych and Dexter Senft, "Portfolio Insurance Using Synthetic Puts: The Reasons, Rewards and Risks," in Frank J. Fabozzi (ed.), *Handbook of Fixed-Income Options* (Chicago: Probus Publishing, 1989).

such as pension funds and life insurance companies, structured portfolio strategies such as immunization or dedication may be more appropriate to achieve investment objectives. Within the context of these strategies, an active or enhanced return strategy may be followed.

Selecting Assets

After a portfolio strategy is specified, the next step is to select the specific assets to be included in the portfolio, which requires an evaluation of individual securities. In an active strategy, this means identifying mispriced securities. In the case of bonds, the characteristics of a bond (i.e., coupon, maturity, credit quality, and options granted to either the issuer or bondholder) must be examined carefully to determine how these characteristics will influence the performance of the bond over some investment horizon.

It is in this phase that the investment manager attempts to construct an efficient portfolio. An efficient portfolio is one that provides the greatest expected return for a given level of risk, or, equivalently, the lowest risk for a given expected return.

Measuring and Evaluating Performance

The measurement and evaluation of investment performance is the last step in the investment management process. (Actually, it is technically not the "last" step because investment management is an ongoing process.) This step involves measuring the performance of the portfolio, then evaluating that performance relative to some benchmark. The benchmark selected for evaluating performance is called a **benchmark** or **normal portfolio.**

The benchmark portfolio may be a popular index such as the S&P 500 for equity portfolios or one of the bond indexes discussed in Chapter 18. Pension sponsors have worked with money managers and pension consultants to establish customized benchmark portfolios. Evaluating the performance of a money manager is not simple. Clients typically rely on the services of a firm that specializes in evaluating money managers.

Although the performance of a money manager according to some benchmark portfolio may seem superior, this does not necessarily mean that the portfolio satisfies its investment objective. For example, suppose that a life insurance company establishes as its objective the maximization of portfolio return and allocates 75% of the fund to stocks and the balance to bonds. Suppose further that the money manager responsible for the equity portfolio of this pension fund earns a return over a one-year horizon that is 200 basis points higher than the benchmark portfolio, which had a return of 2%. Assuming that the risk of the portfolio is similar to that of the benchmark portfolio, it would appear that the money manager outperformed the benchmark portfolio. Despite this performance, however, suppose that the life insurance company cannot meet its liabilities because the rate it must pay to policyholders is 7%. Then the failure is in establishing the investment objectives and setting policy, not in the money manager's performance.

ACTIVE PORTFOLIO STRATEGIES

The starting point in our discussion of active strategies is an investigation of the various sources of return from holding a fixed-income portfolio. As we explain in Chapter 3, the three sources of return are coupon income, any capital gain (or loss), and reinvestment income. Here we explore the factors that affect one or more of these sources. In general, the following factors affect a portfolio's return:

1. Changes in the level of interest rates
2. Changes in the shape of the yield curve
3. Changes in yield spreads among bond sectors
4. Changes in the option-adjusted spread
5. Changes in the yield spread (risk premium) for a particular bond
6. Changes in asset allocation within a bond sector

Manager Expectations versus the Market Consensus

A money manager who pursues an active strategy will position a portfolio to capitalize on expectations about future interest rates. But the potential outcome (as measured by total return) must be assessed before an active strategy is implemented. The primary reason for this is that the market (collectively) has certain expectations for future interest rates and these expectations are embodied into the market price of bonds. One lesson we learned in Chapter 5 when we discussed forward rates is that the outcome of a strategy will depend on how a manager's expectation differs from that of the market. Moreover, it does not make a difference if the market's expectation is correct. What is relevant is that the price of a bond embodies those expectations. The same is true for the strategies we discuss in this chapter.

Consequently, though some managers might refer to an "optimal strategy" that should be pursued given certain expectations, that is insufficient information in making an investment decision. If the market's expectations are the same as the manager's, bond prices reflect these expectations. For this reason we emphasize the use of the total return framework for evaluating active strategies rather than the blind pursuit of a strategy based merely on general statements such as "if you expect . . . , you should pursue . . . strategy."

Interest-Rate Expectations Strategies

A money manager who believes that he or she can accurately forecast the future level of interest rates will alter the portfolio's sensitivity to interest-rate changes. As duration is a measure of interest-rate sensitivity, this involves increasing a portfolio's duration if interest rates are expected to fall and reducing duration if interest rates are expected to rise. For those managers whose benchmark is a bond index, this means increasing the portfolio duration relative to the benchmark index if interest rates are expected to fall and reducing it if interest rates are expected to rise. The degree to which the duration of the managed portfolio is permitted to diverge from that of the benchmark index may be limited by the client.

A portfolio's duration may be altered by swapping (or exchanging) bonds in the portfolio for new bonds that will achieve the target portfolio duration. Such swaps are commonly referred to as **rate anticipation swaps.** Alternatively, a more efficient means for altering the duration of a bond portfolio is to use interest-rate futures contracts. As we explain in Chapter 21, buying futures increases a portfolio's duration, whereas selling futures decreases it.

The key to this active strategy is, of course, an ability to forecast the direction of future interest rates. The academic literature, however, does not support the view that interest rates can be forecasted so that risk-adjusted excess returns can be realized consistently. It is doubtful whether betting on future interest rates will provide a consistently superior return.

Although a manager may not pursue an active strategy based strictly on future interest-rate movements, there can be a tendency to make an interest-rate bet to cover inferior performance relative to a benchmark index. For example, suppose that a manager holds himself or herself out to a client as pursuing one of the active strategies discussed later in this chapter. Suppose further that the manager is evaluated over a one-year investment horizon and that three months before the end of the investment horizon, the manager is performing below the client-specified benchmark index. If the manager believes the account will be lost because of underperformance, there is an incentive to bet on interest-rate movements. If the manager is correct, the account will be saved, although an incorrect bet will result in underperforming the benchmark index by a greater amount. A client can prevent this type of gaming by a manager by imposing constraints on the degree that the portfolio's duration can vary from that of the benchmark index. Also, in the performance-evaluation stage of the investment management process described in Chapter 20, decomposing the portfolio's return into the factors that generated the return will highlight the extent to which a portfolio's return is attributable to changes in the level of interest rates.

There are other active strategies that rely on forecasts of future interest-rate levels. Future interest rates, for instance, affect the value of options embedded in callable bonds and the value of prepayment options embedded in mortgage-backed securities. Callable corporate and municipal bonds with coupon rates above the expected future interest rate will underperform relative to noncallable bonds or low-coupon bonds. This is because of the negative convexity feature of callable bonds. For the wide range of mortgage-backed securities described in Chapters 11 and 12, the effect of interest rates on prepayments cause some to benefit from higher future interest rates and others to benefit from lower future interest rates.

Yield Curve Strategies

As we explain in Chapter 5, the yield curve for U.S. Treasury securities shows the relationship between their maturities and yields. The shape of this yield curve changes over time. **Yield curve strategies** involve positioning a portfolio to capitalize on expected changes in the shape of the Treasury yield curve. In this section we describe various ways in which the Treasury yield curve has shifted, the different types of yield curve strategies, the usefulness of duration as a measure of the price sensitivity of a bond or portfolio when the yield curve shifts, and how to assess the potential outcome of yield curve strategies.

Types of Shifts in the Yield Curve and Impact on Historical Returns   A shift in the yield curve refers to the relative change in the yield for each Treasury maturity. A

parallel shift in the yield curve is a shift in which the change in the yield on all maturities is the same. A **nonparallel shift in the yield curve** indicates that the yield for maturities does not change by the same number of basis points.

Historically, two types of nonparallel yield curve shifts have been observed: a twist in the slope of the yield curve and a change in the humpedness of the yield curve. All of these shifts are portrayed graphically in Exhibit 17-1. A twist in the slope of the yield curve refers to a flattening or steepening of the yield curve. In practice, the slope of the yield curve is measured by the spread between some long-term Treasury yield and some short-term Treasury yield. For example, some practitioners refer to the slope as the difference between the 30-year Treasury yield and the one-year Treasury yield. Others refer to it as the spread between the 20-year Treasury yield and the two-year Treasury yield. Regardless of how it is defined, a **flattening of the yield curve** indicates that the yield spread between the yield on a long-term and a short-term Treasury has

EXHIBIT 17-1 Types of Yield Curve Shifts

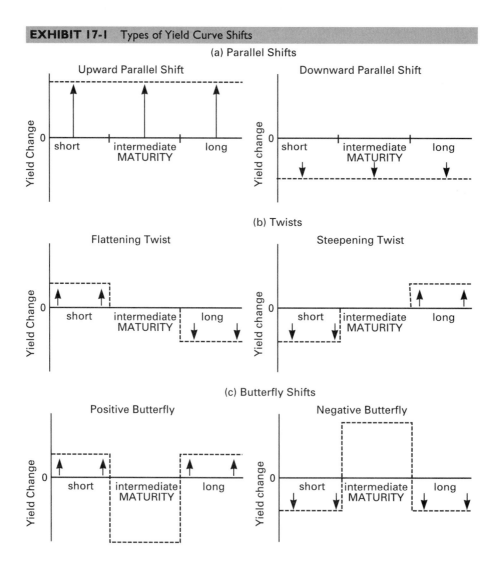

decreased; a **steepening of the yield curve** indicates that the yield spread between a long-term and a short-term Treasury has increased. The other type of nonparallel shift, a change in the humpedness of the yield curve, is referred to as a **butterfly shift.**

Frank Jones analyzed the types of yield curve shifts that occurred between 1979 and 1990.[3] He found that the three types of yield curve shifts are not independent, with the two most common types of yield curve shifts being (1) a downward shift in the yield curve combined with a steepening of the yield curve, and (2) an upward shift in the yield curve combined with a flattening of the yield curve. These two types of shifts in the yield curve are depicted in Exhibit 17-2. For example, his statistical analysis indicated that an upward parallel shift in the Treasury yield curve and a flattening of the

EXHIBIT 17-2 Combinations of Yield Curve Shifts

Upward Shift/Flattening/Positive Butterfly

Downward Shift/Steepening/Negative Butterfly

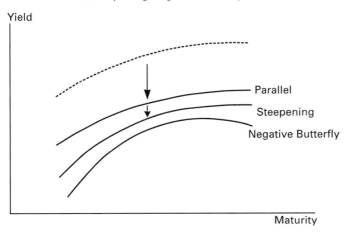

[3]Frank J. Jones, "Yield Curve Strategies," *Journal of Fixed Income,* September 1991, pp. 43–48.

yield curve have a correlation of 0.41. This suggests that an upward shift of the yield curve by 10 basis points is consistent with a 2.5-basis-point flattening of the yield curve. Moreover, he finds that an upward shift and flattening of the yield curve is correlated with a positive butterfly (less humpedness), whereas a downward shift and steepening of the yield curve is correlated with a negative butterfly (more humpedness).

Jones also provides empirical evidence of the importance of changes in the yield curve in determining returns of Treasury securities for various maturity sectors from 1979 to 1990. He finds that parallel shifts and twists in the yield curve are responsible for 91.6% of Treasury returns, and 3.4% of the return is attributable to butterfly shifts and the balance, 5%, to unexplained factor shifts.[4] This discussion indicates that yield curve strategies require a forecast of the direction of the shift and a forecast of the type of twist.

Yield Curve Strategies In portfolio strategies that seek to capitalize on expectations based on short-term movements in yields, the dominant source of return is the impact on the price of the securities in the portfolio. This means that the maturity of the securities in the portfolio will have an important impact on the portfolio's return. For example, a total return over a one-year investment horizon for a portfolio consisting of securities all maturing in one year will not be sensitive to changes in how the yield curve shifts one year from now. In contrast, the total return over a one-year investment horizon for a portfolio consisting of securities all maturing in 30 years will be sensitive to how the yield curve shifts because one year from now the value of the portfolio will depend on the yield offered on 29-year securities. As we know from Chapter 3, long maturity bonds have substantial price volatility when yields change.

When the yield curve shifts, a portfolio consisting of equal proportions of securities maturing in one year and securities maturing in 30 years will have quite a different total return over a one-year investment horizon than the two portfolios we described previously. The price of the one-year securities in the portfolio will not be sensitive to how the one-year yield has changed, but the price of the 30-year securities will be highly sensitive to how long-term yields have changed.

The key point is that for short-term investment horizons, the spacing of the maturity of bonds in the portfolio will have a significant impact on the total return. Consequently, yield curve strategies involve positioning a portfolio with respect to the maturities of the securities across the maturity spectrum included in the portfolio. There are three yield curve strategies: (1) bullet strategies, (2) barbell strategies, and (3) ladder strategies. Each of these strategies is depicted in Exhibit 17-3.

In a **bullet strategy,** the portfolio is constructed so that the maturity of the securities in the portfolio are highly concentrated at one point on the yield curve. In a **barbell strategy,** the maturity of the securities included in the portfolio are concentrated at two extreme maturities. Actually, in practice when managers refer to a barbell strategy it is relative to a bullet strategy. For example, a bullet strategy might be to create a portfolio with maturities concentrated around 10 years, whereas a corresponding barbell strategy might be a portfolio with five- and 20-year maturities. In a **ladder strategy** the portfolio is constructed to have approximately equal amounts of each maturity. So, for example, a portfolio might have equal amounts of securities with one year to maturity, two years to maturity, and so on.

---

[4]These findings are consistent with those reported in Robert Litterman and Jose Scheinkman, "Common Factors Affecting Bond Returns," *Journal of Fixed Income,* June 1991, pp. 54–61.

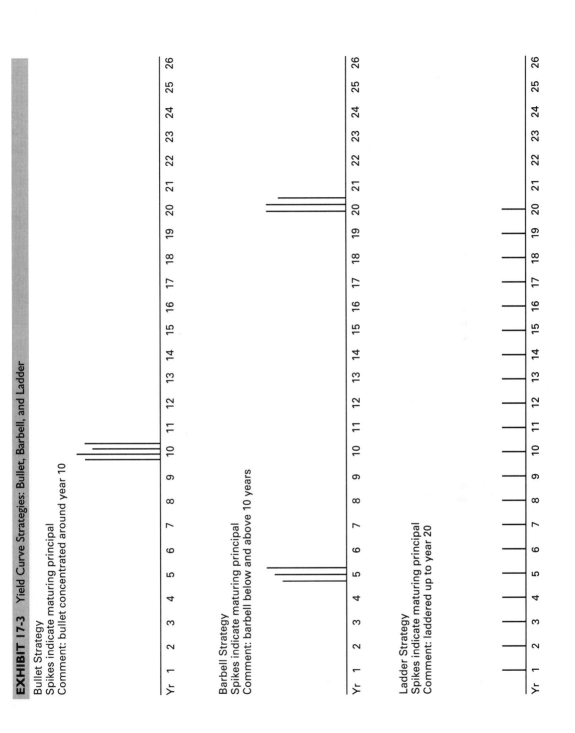

EXHIBIT 17-3 Yield Curve Strategies: Bullet, Barbell, and Ladder

Bullet Strategy
Spikes indicate maturing principal
Comment: bullet concentrated around year 10

Barbell Strategy
Spikes indicate maturing principal
Comment: barbell below and above 10 years

Ladder Strategy
Spikes indicate maturing principal
Comment: laddered up to year 20

Each of these strategies will result in different performance when the yield curve shifts. The actual performance will depend on both the type of shift and the magnitude of the shift. Thus no general statements can be made about the optimal yield curve strategy. The framework for analyzing a yield curve strategy will be discussed later.

Duration and Yield Curve Shifts   Before discussing how to analyze yield curve strategies, let's reconsider the concept of duration and its role in approximating the price volatility of a bond portfolio when the yield curve shifts. In Chapter 4 we explained how duration is a measure of the sensitivity of the price of a bond or the value of a bond portfolio to changes in market yields. Thus a portfolio with a duration of 4 means that if market yields change by 100 basis points, the portfolio will change by approximately 4%.

In explaining the limitations of duration, we indicated that there is an assumption made about how market yields change. Specifically, if a portfolio of bonds consists of five-year bonds, 10-year bonds, and 20-year bonds, and the portfolio's duration is 4, what market yield is assumed to change when we say that this portfolio will change in value by 4% if yields change by 100 basis points? Is it the five-year yield, the 10-year yield, or the 20-year yield? In fact, the assumption made when using duration as a measure of how the value of a portfolio will change if market yields change is that the yield on *all* maturities will change by the same number of basis points. Thus if our three-bond portfolio has a duration of 4, the statement that the portfolio's value will change by 4% for a 100-basis-point change in yields actually should be stated as follows: The portfolio's value will change by 4% if the yield on five-, 10-, and 20-year bonds all change by 100 basis points. That is, it is assumed that there is a parallel yield curve shift.

An illustration of what happens to a bond portfolio when the yield curve shift is not parallel is demonstrated in the next section. The key point of the illustration is that two portfolios with the same duration may perform quite differently when the yield curve shifts.

Analyzing Expected Yield Curve Strategies   The proper way to analyze any portfolio strategy is to look at its potential total return. We indicated this at the outset of this chapter. If a manager wants to assess the outcome of a portfolio for any assumed shift in the Treasury yield curve, this should be done by calculating the potential total return if that shift actually occurs.

We illustrate this by looking at the performance of two hypothetical portfolios of Treasury securities assuming different shifts in the Treasury yield curve. The three hypothetical Treasury securities shown in Exhibit 17-4 are considered for inclusion in

EXHIBIT 17-4   Three Hypothetical Treasury Securities

Bond	Coupon (%)	Maturity (years)	Price plus Accrued	Yield to Maturity (%)	Dollar Duration	Dollar Convexity
A	8.50	5	100	8.50	4.005	19.8164
B	9.50	20	100	9.50	8.882	124.1702
C	9.25	10	100	9.25	6.434	55.4506

our two portfolios.[5] Thus, for our illustration, the Treasury yield curve consists of these three Treasury securities: a short-term security (A, the five-year security), an intermediate-term security (C, the 10-year security), and a long-term security (B, the 20-year security).

Consider the following two yield curve strategies: a bullet strategy and a barbell strategy. We will label the portfolios created based on these two strategies as the "bullet portfolio" and the "barbell portfolio" and they comprise the following:

- *Bullet portfolio:* 100% bond C
- *Barbell portfolio:* 50.2% bond A and 49.8% bond B

The bullet portfolio consists of only bond C, the 10-year bond. In our hypothetical portfolio, all the principal is received when bond C matures in 10 years. The barbell portfolio consists of almost an equal amount of the short- and long-term securities. It is the result of a barbell strategy because principal will be received at two ends of the maturity spectrum. Specifically, relative to the bullet portfolio, which in our illustration has all its principal being returned in 10 years, for the barbell portfolio the principal is being returned at shorter (five years) and longer (20 years) dates.

As we explained in Chapter 4, dollar duration is a measure of the dollar price sensitivity of a bond or a portfolio. As indicated in Exhibit 17-4, the dollar duration for the bullet portfolio per 100-basis-point change in yield is 6.434. For the barbell portfolio, the dollar duration is just the weighted average of the dollar duration of the two bonds. Therefore,

dollar duration of barbell portfolio = 0.502(4.005) + 0.498(8.882) = 6.434

The dollar duration of the barbell portfolio is the same as that of the bullet portfolio. (In fact, the barbell portfolio was designed to produce this result.)

As we explained in Chapter 4, duration is just a first approximation of the change in price resulting from a change in interest rates. Convexity provides a second approximation. Although we did not discuss **dollar convexity,** it has a meaning similar to *convexity,* in that it provides a second approximation to the dollar price change. For two portfolios with the same dollar duration, the greater the convexity, the better the performance of a bond or a portfolio when yields change. What is necessary to understand for this illustration is that the larger the dollar convexity, the greater the dollar price change due to a portfolio's convexity. As shown in Exhibit 17-4, the dollar convexity of the bullet portfolio is 55.4506. The dollar convexity for the barbell portfolio is a weighted average of the dollar convexity of the two bonds. That is,

dollar convexity of barbell portfolio = 0.502(19.8164) + 0.498(124.1702) = 71.7846

Therefore, the dollar convexity of the barbell portfolio is greater than that of the barbell portfolio.

Similarly, the yield for the two portfolios is not the same. The yield for the bullet portfolio is simply the yield to maturity of bond C, 9.25%. The traditional yield calculation for the barbell portfolio, which is found by taking a weighted average of the yield to maturity of the two bonds included in the portfolio, is 8.998%:

---

[5]This illustration is adapted from Ravi E. Dattatreya and Frank J. Fabozzi, *Active Total Return Management of Fixed Income Portfolios* (Chicago: Probus Publishing, 1989).

portfolio yield for barbell portfolio = 0.502(8.50%) + 0.498(9.50%) = 8.998%

This approach suggests that the yield of the bullet portfolio is 25.2 basis points greater than that of the barbell portfolio (9.25% − 8.998%). Although both portfolios have the same dollar duration, the yield of the bullet portfolio is greater than the yield of the barbell portfolio. However, the dollar convexity of the barbell portfolio is greater than that of the bullet portfolio. The difference in the two yields is sometimes referred to as the **cost of convexity** (i.e., giving up yield to get better convexity).

Now, suppose that a portfolio manager with a six-month investment horizon has a choice of investing in the bullet portfolio or the barbell portfolio. Which one should he choose? The manager knows that (1) the two portfolios have the same dollar duration, (2) the yield for the bullet portfolio is greater than that of the barbell portfolio, and (3) the dollar convexity of the barbell portfolio is greater than that of the bullet portfolio. Actually, this information is not adequate in making the decision. What is necessary is to assess the potential total return when the yield curve shifts.

Exhibit 17-5 provides an analysis of the six-month total return of the two portfolios when the yield curve shifts.[6] The numbers reported in the exhibit are the difference in the total return for the two portfolios. Specifically, the following is shown:

$$\text{difference in dollar return} = \text{bullet portfolio's total return} \\ - \text{barbell portfolio's total return}$$

Thus a positive value means that the bullet portfolio outperformed the barbell portfolio, and a negative sign means that the barbell portfolio outperformed the bullet portfolio.

Let's focus on the second column of Exhibit 17-5, which is labeled "parallel shift." This is the relative total return of the two portfolios over the six-month investment horizon assuming that the yield curve shifts in a parallel fashion. In this case parallel movement of the yield curve means that the yields for the short-term bond (A), the intermediate-term bond (C), and the long-term bond (B) change by the same number of basis points, shown in the "yield change" column of the table.

Which portfolio is the better investment alternative if the yield curve shifts in a parallel fashion and the investment horizon is six months? The answer depends on the amount by which yields change. Notice that when yields change by less than 100 basis points, the bullet portfolio outperforms the barbell portfolio. The reverse is true if yields change by more than 100 basis points.

This illustration makes two key points. First, even if the yield curve shifts in a parallel fashion, two portfolios with the same dollar duration will not give the same performance. The reason is that the two portfolios do not have the same dollar convexity. The second point is that although with all other things equal it is better to have more convexity than less, the market charges for convexity in the form of a higher price or a lower yield. But the benefit of the greater convexity depends on how much yields change. As can be seen from the second column of Exhibit 17-5, if market yields change by less than 100 basis points (up or down), the bullet portfolio, which has less convexity, will provide a better total return.

---

[6]Note that no assumption is needed for the reinvestment rate because the three bonds shown in Exhibit 17-4 are assumed to be trading right after a coupon payment has been made, and therefore there is no accrued interest.

EXHIBIT 17-5 Relative Performance of Bullet Portfolio and Barbell Portfolio over a Six-Month Investment Horizon[a]

Yield Change	Parallel Shift	Nonparallel Shift[b]	Nonparallel Shift[c] (%)
−5.000	−7.19	−10.69	−3.89
−4.750	−6.28	−9.61	−3.12
−4.500	−5.44	−8.62	−2.44
−4.250	−4.68	−7.71	−1.82
−4.000	−4.00	−6.88	−1.27
−3.750	−3.38	−6.13	−0.78
−3.500	−2.82	−5.44	−0.35
−3.250	−2.32	−4.82	0.03
−3.000	−1.88	−4.26	0.36
−2.750	−1.49	−3.75	0.65
−2.500	−1.15	−3.30	0.89
−2.250	−0.85	−2.90	1.09
−2.000	−0.59	−2.55	1.25
−1.750	−0.38	−2.24	1.37
−1.500	−0.20	−1.97	1.47
−1.250	−0.05	−1.74	1.53
−1.000	0.06	−1.54	1.57
−0.750	0.15	−1.38	1.58
−0.500	0.21	−1.24	1.57
−0.250	0.24	−1.14	1.53
0.000	0.25	−1.06	1.48
0.250	0.24	−1.01	1.41
0.500	0.21	−0.98	1.32
0.750	0.16	−0.97	1.21
1.000	0.09	−0.98	1.09
1.250	0.01	−1.00	0.96
1.500	−0.08	−1.05	0.81
1.750	−0.19	−1.10	0.66
2.000	−0.31	−1.18	0.49
2.250	−0.44	−1.26	0.32
2.500	−0.58	−1.36	0.14
2.750	−0.73	−1.46	−0.05
3.000	−0.88	−1.58	−0.24
3.250	−1.05	−1.70	−0.44
3.500	−1.21	−1.84	−0.64
3.750	−1.39	−1.98	−0.85
4.000	−1.57	−2.12	−1.06
4.250	−1.75	−2.27	−1.27
4.500	−1.93	−2.43	−1.48
4.750	−2.12	−2.58	−1.70
5.000	−2.31	−2.75	−1.92

[a]Performance is based on the difference in total return over a six-month investment horizon. Specifically,

bullet portfolio's total return − barbell portfolio's total return

Therefore a negative value means that the barbell portfolio outperformed the bullet portfolio.
[b]Change in yield for bond C. Nonparallel shift as follows (flattening of yield curve):

yield change bond A = yield change bond C + 25 basis points

yield change bond B = yield change bond C − 25 basis points
[c]Change in yield for bond C. Nonparallel shift as follows (steepening of yield curve):

yield change bond A = yield change bond C − 25 basis points

yield change bond B = yield change bond C + 25 basis points

Now let's look at what happens if the yield curve does not shift in a parallel fashion. The last two columns of Exhibit 17-5 show the relative performance of the two portfolios for a nonparallel shift of the yield curve. Specifically, the first nonparallel shift column assumes that if the yield on bond C (the intermediate-term bond) changes by the amount shown in the first column, bond A (the short-term bond) will change by the same amount plus 25 basis points, whereas bond B (the long-term bond) will change by the same amount shown in the first column less 25 basis points. Measuring the steepness of the yield curve as the spread between the long-term yield (yield on bond B) and the short-term yield (yield on Bond A), the spread has decreased by 50 basis points. As we noted earlier, such a nonparallel shift means a flattening of the yield curve. As can be seen in Exhibit 17-5, for this assumed yield curve shift, the barbell outperforms the bullet.

In the last column, the nonparallel shift assumes that for a change in bond C's yield, the yield on bond A will change by the same amount less 25 basis points, whereas that on bond B will change by the same amount plus 25 points. Thus the spread between the long-term yield and the short-term yield has increased by 50 basis points, and therefore the yield curve has steepened. In this case the bullet portfolio outperforms the barbell portfolio as long as the yield on bond C does not rise by more than 250 basis points or fall by more than 325 basis points.

The key point here is that looking at measures such as yield (yield to maturity or some type of portfolio yield measure), duration, or convexity tells us little about performance over some investment horizon, because performance depends on the magnitude of the change in yields and how the yield curve shifts. Therefore, when a manager wants to position a portfolio based on expectations as to how he might expect the yield curve to shift, it is imperative to perform total return analysis. For example, in a steepening yield curve environment, it is often stated that a bullet portfolio would be better than a barbell portfolio. As can be seen from Exhibit 17-5, it is not the case that a bullet portfolio would outperform a barbell portfolio. Whether the bullet portfolio outperforms the barbell depends on how much the yield curve steepens. An analysis similar to that in Exhibit 17-5 based on total return for different degrees of steepening of the yield curve clearly demonstrates to a manager whether a particular yield curve strategy will be superior to another. The same analysis can be performed to assess the potential outcome of a ladder strategy.

Yield Spread Strategies

As discussed in Chapter 5, the bond market is classified into sectors in several ways: by type of issuer (Treasury, agencies, corporates, and mortgage-backeds), quality or credit (risk-free Treasuries, triple A, double A, and so on), coupon (high-coupon/premium bonds, current-coupon/par bonds, and low-coupon/discount bonds), and maturity (short, intermediate, or long term). Yield spreads between maturity sectors involve changes in the yield curve as discussed in the preceding section.

Yield spread strategies involve positioning a portfolio to capitalize on expected changes in yield spreads between sectors of the bond market. Swapping (or exchanging) one bond for another when the manager believes that the prevailing yield spread between the two bonds in the market is out of line with their historical yield spread, and that the yield spread will realign by the end of the investment horizon, are called **intermarket spread swaps.**

Credit Spreads   Credit or quality spreads change because of expected changes in economic prospects. Credit spreads between Treasury and non-Treasury issues widen in a declining or contracting economy and narrow during economic expansion. The economic rationale is that in a declining or contracting economy, corporations experience a decline in revenue and reduced cash flow, making it difficult for corporate issuers to service their contractual debt obligations. To induce investors to hold non-Treasury securities of lower-quality issuers, the yield spread relative to Treasury securities must widen. The converse is that during economic expansion and brisk economic activity, revenue and cash flow pick up, increasing the likelihood that corporate issuers will have the capacity to service their contractual debt obligations. Yield spreads between Treasury and federal agency securities will vary depending on investor expectations about the prospects that an implicit government guarantee will be honored.

Yield spreads are also related to the level of interest rates. For example, in 1957, when the yield on Treasuries was 3%, the yield spread between a triple B–rated utility bond and Treasuries was 40 basis points. This represented a relative yield spread of 13% (0.4% divided by 3%). When the yield on Treasuries exceeded 10% in 1985, however, a yield spread of 40 basis points would have meant only a relative yield spread of 4%.[7] Consequently, the yield spread measured in basis points had to be greater than 40 basis points to produce a similar relative yield. Exhibit 17-6 suggests that the relative yield spread—as measured by the ratio of the yield spread to the level of Treasury yields—and the yield ratio—the ratio of non-Treasury and Treasury yields—tends to be relatively stable over time.

Spreads between Callable and Noncallable Securities   Spreads attributable to differences in callable and noncallable bonds and differences in coupons of callable bonds will change as a result of expected changes in (1) the direction of the change in interest rates, and (2) interest-rate volatility. An expected drop in the level of interest

EXHIBIT 17-6 Relative Yield Spreads				
Period	*Average 10-year Treasury Yield*	*Average BBB Utility Yield*	*Average Spread (%)*	*Relative Yield (%)*	*Yield Ratio*
1955–1959	3.46	4.21	75	22	1.217
1960–1964	4.03	4.79	76	19	1.189
1965–1969	5.32	6.22	95	17	1.169
1970–1974	6.82	8.75	197	28	1.283
1975–1979	8.17	10.04	191	23	1.229
1980–1984	12.30	15.18	276	23	1.234
1985–1989	8.81	10.92	209	24	1.240

Source: Chris P. Dialynas and David H. Edington, "Bond Yield Spreads—A Postmodern View," *Journal of Portfolio Management*, Fall 1992. This copyrighted material is reprinted with permission from Institutional Investor, Inc./*The Journal of Portfolio Management*, 488 Madison Avenue, New York, NY 10022.

---

[7]Chris P. Dialynas and David H. Edington, "Bond Yield Spreads—A Postmodern View," *Journal of Portfolio Management*, Fall 1992. This copyrighted material is reprinted with permission from Institutional Investor, Inc./Journal of Portfolio Management, 488 Madison Avenue, New York, NY 10022.

rates will widen the yield spread between callable bonds and noncallable bonds as the prospects that the issuer will exercise the call option increase. The reverse is true: The yield spread narrows if interest rates are expected to rise. As we explain in Chapter 14, an increase in interest-rate volatility increases the value of the embedded call option and thereby increases the yield spread between callable bonds and noncallable bonds. Expectations about the direction of the change in interest rates and interest-rate volatility will affect the yield spread between Treasury and mortgage pass-through securities and the yield spread between low-coupon and high-coupon pass-throughs in the same way as it affects the yield spreads for corporates.

Importance of Dollar Duration Weighting of Yield Spread Strategies What is critical in assessing yield spread strategies is to compare positions that have the same dollar duration. To understand why, consider two bonds, X and Y. Suppose that the price of bond X is 80 with a modified duration of 5, and bond Y has a price of 90 with a modified duration of 4. Because modified duration is the approximate percentage change per 100-basis-point change in yield, a 100-basis-point change in yield for bond X would change its price by about 5%. Based on a price of 80, its price will change by about $4 per $80 of market value. Thus its dollar duration for a 100-basis-point change in yield is $4 per $80 of market value. Similarly, for bond Y, its dollar duration for a 100-basis-point change in yield per $90 of market value can be determined. In this case it is $3.6. So if bonds X and Y are being considered as alternative investments in a strategy other than one based on anticipating interest-rate movements, the amount of each bond in the strategy should be such that they will both have the same dollar duration.

To illustrate this, suppose that a portfolio manager owns $10 million of par value of bond X, which has a market value of $8 million. The dollar duration of bond X per 100-basis-point change in yield for the $8 million market value is $400,000. Suppose further that this portfolio manager is considering exchanging bond X that it owns in its portfolio for bond Y. If the portfolio manager wants to have the same interest-rate exposure (i.e., dollar duration) for bond Y that she currently has for bond X, she will buy a market value amount of bond Y with the same dollar duration. If the portfolio manager purchased $10 million of *par value* of bond Y and therefore $9 million of *market value* of bond Y, the dollar price change per 100-basis-point change in yield would be only $360,000. If, instead, the portfolio manager purchased $10 million of *market value* of bond Y, the dollar duration per 100-basis-point change in yield would be $400,000. Because bond Y is trading at 90, $11.11 million of par value of bond Y must be purchased to keep the dollar duration of the position from bond Y the same as for bond X.

Mathematically, this problem can be expressed as follows:

Let

$\$D_X$ = dollar duration per 100-basis-point change in yield for bond X for the market value of bond X held

MD_Y = modified duration for bond Y

MV_Y = market value of bond Y needed to obtain the same dollar duration as bond X

Then the following equation sets the dollar duration for bond X equal to the dollar duration for bond Y:

$$\$D_X = \frac{\text{MD}_Y}{100} \text{MV}_Y$$

Solving for MV_Y yields

$$\text{MV}_Y = \frac{\$D_X}{\dfrac{\text{MD}_Y}{100}}$$

Dividing by the price per \$1 of par value of bond Y gives the par value of Y that has an approximately equivalent dollar duration as bond X.

In our illustration, $\$D_X$ is \$400,000 and MD_Y is 4; then

$$\text{MV}_Y = \frac{\$400,000}{\dfrac{4}{100}} = \$10,000,000$$

The market value of bond Y is 90 per \$100 of par value, so the price per \$1 of par value is 0.9. Dividing \$10 million by 0.9 indicates that the par value of bond Y that should be purchased is \$11.11 million.

Failure to adjust a portfolio repositioning based on some expected change in yield spread so as to hold the dollar duration the same means that the outcome of the port-folio will be affected not only by the expected change in the yield spread but also by a change in the yield level. Thus a manager would be making a conscious yield spread bet and possibly an undesired bet on the level of interest rates.

Option-Adjusted Spread-Based Strategies

As we have indicated in Chapters 14 and 15, the practice today is to measure the yield spread on bonds with embedded options in terms of their option-adjusted spread. Money managers can position a portfolio to take advantage of expectations as to how the option-adjusted spread will change over an investment horizon.

There have been several empirical tests of the performance of option-adjusted spread-based trading strategies for mortgage-backed securities. One is an examina-tion by Lakhbir Hayre and Kenneth Lauterbach of the six-month performance of GNMA pass-throughs and similar-duration Treasuries using an option-adjusted spread-based trading strategy for the period from mid-1985 to 1988.[8] They find the relative performance of GNMA pass-throughs to be closely related to the option-ad-justed spread at the beginning of the six-month investment horizon. For the period in-vestigated, when the option-adjusted spread at the beginning of the period was less than 100 basis points, the GNMA pass-throughs were outperformed by similar-dura-tion Treasuries more than 68% of the time. When the option-adjusted spread ex-ceeded 100 basis points, however, GNMA pass-throughs were the better-performing security class more than 75% of the time.

Hayre and Lauterbach also find an option-adjusted spread-based trading strategy to be superior to a strategy based on the traditional cash flow yield spread described in Chapter 15.[9] Specifically, they report that the correlation between the option-

---

[8]Lakhbir S. Hayre and Kenneth Lauterbach, "Stochastic Valuation of Debt Securities," in Frank J. Fabozzi (ed.), *Managing Institutional Assets* (New York: Harper & Row, 1990).
[9]Hayre and Lauterbach refer to the cash flow yield spread in their study as the "regular yield spread."

adjusted spread at the beginning of the six-month investment horizon and the subsequent six-month total return was 68%, whereas the corresponding correlation between the traditional cash flow yield spread and the subsequent six-month total return was only 53%.

One other test performed by Hayre and Lauterbach is noteworthy. They calculate the six-month total return for the following two strategies:

Strategy A: Purchase at the beginning of each month a GNMA with the highest cash flow yield spread, and finance the acquisition by shorting a comparable-duration Treasury.

Strategy B: Purchase at the beginning of each month a GNMA with the highest option-adjusted spread, and finance the acquisition by shorting a comparable-duration Treasury.

They find that strategy A produced positive returns in 62% of the cases, whereas strategy B produced positive returns in 81% of the cases. The average return for strategy A was only 84 basis points, smaller than that for strategy B, which was 258 basis points. Moreover, in only 8% of the cases did strategy A outperform strategy B. These results support the view that an option-adjusted spread-based trading strategy may not only lead to enhanced returns but also be superior to a trading strategy based on traditional yield spreads. These results are similar to those reported by researchers at Morgan Stanley in 1988.[10]

Individual Security Selection Strategies

There are several active strategies that money managers pursue to identify mispriced securities. The most common strategy identifies an issue as undervalued because either (1) its yield is higher than that of comparably rated issues, or (2) its yield is expected to decline (and price therefore rise) because credit analysis indicates that its rating will improve.

A swap in which a money manager exchanges one bond for another bond that is similar in terms of coupon, maturity, and credit quality, but offers a higher yield, is called a **substitution swap.** This swap depends on a capital market imperfection. Such situations sometimes exist in the bond market owing to temporary market imbalances and the fragmented nature of the non-Treasury bond market. The risk the money manager faces in making a substitution swap is that the bond purchased may not be truly identical to the bond for which it is exchanged. Moreover, typically, bonds will have similar but not identical maturities and coupon. This could lead to differences in the convexity of the two bonds, and any yield spread may reflect the cost of convexity.

An active strategy used in the mortgage-backed securities market is to identify individual issues of pass-throughs, CMO classes, or stripped MBS that are mispriced, given the assumed prepayment speed to price the security. Another active strategy commonly used in the mortgage-backed securities market is to create a package of securities that will have a better return profile for a wide range of interest-rate and yield curve scenarios than similar duration securities available in the market. Because of

---

[10]See David P. Jacob, Gary D. Latainer, and Alden Toevs, "Value and Performance of Mortgage-Backed Securities," Chapter 27 in Frank J. Fabozzi (ed.), *The Handbook of Mortgage-Backed Securities,* rev. ed. (Chicago: Probus Publishing, 1988).

the fragmented nature of the mortgage-backed securities market and the complexity of the structures, such opportunities are not unusual.

Strategies for Asset Allocation within Bond Sectors

The ability to outperform a benchmark index will depend on the how the manager allocates funds within a bond sector relative to the composition of the benchmark index. As explained in the next chapter, the three major sectors of the broad-based bond market indexes are government/agencies, corporates, and mortgage-backed securities. Within the corporate sector, for example, the manager must decide how to allocate funds among the different credit ratings. (Only investment grade ratings are included in the broad-based bond market indexes.) In the case of mortgage-backed securities where only pass-through securities are included with different coupon rates, there is the decision of how to allocate funds among the different coupon issues. This is important because prepayment rates and the performance of pass-throughs will depend on the coupon issues selected by the manager.

We already discussed strategies that will affect the allocation decision among the bond sectors. Expected changes in the level of interest rates will affect the allocation of funds within the corporate and mortgage-backed securities sectors because the more attractive the call feature of a security, the worse it may perform in a declining interest rate environment due to negative convexity. Yield curve strategies would affect the maturity selection within sectors. While our focus above was on strategies involving anticipated changes in credit spreads or OAS between sectors in the bond market, the same strategies are used in making intersector asset allocation decisions.

Below we look at a framework for guiding and assessing the allocation of funds among the credit sectors within the corporate bond sector. This strategy was first suggest by Leland Crabbe.[11]

The framework relies on the historical experience of credit quality changes. This information is captured in a table referred to as a *rating transition matrix* and shows on a percentage basis how ratings on issues change over time. Exhibit 17-7 shows a one-year rating transition matrix (table) based on a Moody's study for the period 1970–1993. Here is how to interpret the table. The rows indicate the rating at the beginning of a year. The columns show the rating at the end of the year. For example, look at the second row. This row shows the transition for double-A rated bonds at the beginning of a year. The number 91.26 in the second row means that on average 91.26% of double-A rated bonds at the beginning of the year remained double-A rated at year end. The value of 1.13 means that on average 1.13% of double-A rated bonds at the beginning of the year were upgraded to triple A. The value of 0.31 means that on average 0.31% of double-A rated bonds at the beginning of the year were downgraded to a triple B rating.

From Exhibit 17-7 it should be clear that the probability of a downgrade is much higher than for an upgrade for investment grade bonds. While the historical rating transition matrix is a useful starting point since it represents an average over the study period (the 1970–1993 period in the exhibit), a manager must modify the matrix based

---

[11]Leland E. Crabbe, "A Framework for Corporate Bond Strategy," *Journal of Fixed Income,* June 1995, pp. 15–25.

EXHIBIT 17-7 One Year Rating Transition Probabilities (%)

	Aaa	*Aa*	*A*	*Baa*	*Ba*	*Bb*	*C or D*	*Total*
Aaa	91.90	7.38	0.72	0.00	0.00	0.00	0.00	100.00
Aa	1.13	91.26	7.09	0.31	0.21	0.00	0.00	100.00
A	0.10	2.56	91.20	5.33	0.61	0.20	0.00	100.00
Baa	0.00	0.21	5.36	87.94	5.46	0.82	0.21	100.00

Source: Exhibit 1 of Leland E. Crabbe, "A Framework for Corporate Bond Strategy," *Journal of Fixed Income,* June 1995, p. 16. Reprinted by permission of Institutional Investor.

on expectations of upgrades and downgrades given current and anticipated economic conditions.

Given the rating transition matrix that the manager expects, an *expected incremental return* can be calculated for each credit quality sector. This involves four steps. First, estimate what the spread over Treasuries will be for all ratings at the end of the investment horizon. Second, estimate the price change for upgraded and downgraded bonds based on the new spreads. Third, compute the return for upgraded and downgraded bonds based on the price change calculated in the first step and the coupon interest. Finally, calculate the expected incremental return for the credit quality sector by weighting the returns by the probabilities as given in the manager's rating transition matrix.

To illustrate this, suppose that the manager's rating transition matrix is the one shown in Exhibit 17-7. Second, suppose that the manager expects that the spreads will not change over the one year investment horizon. Consider the double-A rated sector. Exhibit 17-8 shows the expected incremental return estimates for a portfolio consisting of only three-year double-A rated bonds. The first column shows the initial spread. The second column is the rating at the end of the investment horizon. The horizon spread is the spread over Treasuries at the end of the investment horizon for each of the credit quality sectors for the three-year maturity sector shown in the second column. For example, if there is no change in the rating, the

EXHIBIT 17-8 Expected Incremental Return Estimates for Three-Year AA-Rated Bonds Over a One-Year Horizon

Initial Spread	*Horizon Rating*	*Horizon Spread*	*Return over Treasuries (bp)*	×	*Transition Probability (%)*	=	*Contribution to Incremental Return (bp)*
30	Aaa	25	38		1.13		0.43
30	Aa	30	30		91.26		27.38
30	A	35	21		7.09		1.49
30	Baa	60	−24		0.31		−0.07
30	Ba	130	−147		0.21		−0.31

Portfolio Incremental Return over Treasuries = 28.90

Source: Exhibit 2 of Leland E. Crabbe, "A Framework for Corporate Bond Strategy," *Journal of Fixed Income,* June 1995, p. 17. Reprinted by permission of Institutional Investor.

horizon spread is the same as the initial spread of 30 basis points. An upgrade reduces the spread, a downgrade increases it. The assumption in our illustration is that the horizon spread is the same as currently observed. The fourth column shows the horizon return over Treasuries based on price change and coupon interest. The next to the last column gives the probabilities from the rating transition matrix (i.e., the second row of Exhibit 17-7). The sum of the product of the fourth and fifth columns gives the expected incremental return over Treasuries of 28.9 basis points.

There are two reasons why the expected incremental return over Treasuries of 28.9 basis points is less than the initial spread of 30 basis points. First, the probability of an upgrade is significantly less than for a downgrade. Second, the steepness of the credit spread curve at the end of the investment horizon penalizes downgrades.

From this illustration it can be seen that the incremental return over Treasuries depends on the initial spread, the change in the spread, and the probability of a rating change.

The framework can be extended to any maturity sector. Exhibit 17-9 shows expected incremental returns over Treasuries assuming the rating transition matrix given in Exhibit 17-7 and assuming that the horizon spreads are the same as the initial spreads. For example, the first box in Exhibit 17-9 shows that the expected incremental return in the three-year maturity sector of the corporate bond market is 28.9 basis points for Aa rated bonds and 46.3 basis points for triple-B rated bonds.

The exhibit provides a guide for assessing relative value within each maturity sector. Notice that for all rating sectors and maturity sectors, expected incremental returns are less than the initial spread. For the three-year and five-year maturity sectors, the ranking by expected incremental return is the same as for the ranking by initial spread. However, this is not true for the ten-year and 30-year maturity sectors. This is because of the significant influence of the duration of the bonds in these sectors and the steepness of the credit quality spread. Exhibit 17-9 can also be used to assess relative value among maturity sectors for a given rating sector.

While the illustrations assumed the rating transmission matrix in Exhibit 17-7 and that the spread over Treasuries at the end of the investment horizon would be unchanged from the initial spread, this will not be the case in practice. The manager will modify both assumptions based on prevailing and expected market conditions.

EXHIBIT 17-9   Expected Incremental Returns Over Treasuries When Rating Transitions Match Historical Experience (One-Year Horizon; bp)

	Initial Spread	Incremental Return	Initial Spread	Incremental Return	Initial Spread	Incremental Return	Initial Spread	Incremental Return
Aaa	25	24.2	30	28.4	35	31.7	45	34.6
Aa	30	28.9	35	31.4	40	30.3	55	34.8
A	35	31.1	45	37.3	55	37.9	75	42.7
Baa	60	46.3	70	39.9	85	21.9	115	27.4

Source: Exhibit 3 of Leland E. Crabbe, "A Framework for Corporate Bond Strategy," *Journal of Fixed Income,* June 1995, p. 18. Reprinted by permission of Institutional Investor.

THE USE OF LEVERAGE

If permitted by investment guidelines a manager may use leverage in an attempt to enhance portfolio returns. A portfolio manager can create leverage by borrowing funds in order to acquire a position in the market that is greater than if only cash were invested. For example, a manager may have cash to invest in the bond market of $50 million but wants an exposure of $200 million.

The funds available to invest without borrowing are referred to as the "equity." In our example, the equity is $50. A portfolio that does not contain any leverage is called an **unlevered portfolio.** A **levered portfolio** is a portfolio in which a manager has created leverage. The levered portfolio in this example is $200 million.

In this section we'll take a look at leverage. First, we'll look at why a manager uses leverage and the measurement of the duration of a portfolio that uses leverage. Then we will look at how a manager can create leverage using the repo market.

Motivation for Leverage

The basic principle in using leverage is that a manager wants to earn a return on the borrowed funds that is greater than the cost of the borrowed funds. The return from borrowing funds is produced from a higher income and/or greater price appreciation relative to a scenario in which no funds are borrowed.

Let's first look at the higher income that may be generated from a levered portfolio relative to an unlevered portfolio. If a manager can invest $50 million earning 5% for a year but borrow funds at a cost of 4.5% for a year, then the manager can generate for the year 50 basis points in income over its funding cost. By borrowing greater amounts, the manager can magnify the 50 basis points. This is a benefit of leveraging. The risk of leveraging is that the return generated from the borrowed funds will be less than the funding cost. In our example, the risk is that if the return from investing the amount borrowed is less than 4.5%, then there will be negative return on the funds borrowed.

The return from investing the funds comes from two sources. The first is the interest income and the second is the change in the value of the security (or securities) at the end of the borrowing period. For example, suppose our manager invests all the funds borrowed in a security that matures in one year, is selling at par, and has a coupon rate of 5%. At the end of one year (the time period we assumed in our example that the manager borrowed the funds), the return is 5% if the issuer of the security pays off the bond at par. Suppose instead that the bond is a 10-year bond that can be purchased at par and has a coupon rate of 5%. Then the return over the one-year period for which the funds are borrowed will be 5% in interest income adjusted for how the price of the bond changes at the end of one year. At the end of one year, the 10-year bond is a nine-year bond and its price will be greater than or less than par depending on market rates at the end of one year. The risk, of course, is that the change in the value of the security will decline such that the return will be negative.

There are some managers who use leverage in the hopes of benefiting primarily from price changes. Small price changes will be magnified by using leveraging. For example, if a manager expects interest rates to fall, the manager can borrow funds to increase price exposure to the market. Effectively, the manager is increasing the duration of the portfolio, a point that we will return to later.

Thus, the risk associated with borrowing funds is that the security (or securities) in which the borrowed funds are invested may earn less than the cost of the borrowed funds due to failure to generate interest income plus capital appreciation as expected when the funds were borrowed.

Leveraging is a necessity for depository institutions (such as banks and savings and loan associations) because the spread over the cost of borrowed funds is typically small. The magnitude of the borrowing (i.e., the degree of leverage) is what produces an acceptable return for the institution. For traders, individual trades typically produce small spreads over funding costs. It is the leveraging of those trades that will generate a return needed to make them attractive to traders.

Duration of a Leveraged Portfolio

Now let's look at how to calculate the duration of a fund that has borrowed money. This can be done by using an example to understand the general principle.

Suppose that a portfolio has a market value of $100 million and the manager invests the proceeds in a bond with a duration of 3. This means that the manager would expect that for a 100-basis-point change in interest rates, the portfolio's value would change by approximately $3 million. For this unlevered fund, the duration of the portfolio is 3.

Suppose now that the manager of this portfolio can borrow an additional $300 million. This means that the levered fund will have $400 million to invest, consisting of $100 million that the manager has available before borrowing (i.e., the equity) and $300 million borrowed. All of the funds are invested in a bond with a duration of 3. Now let's look at what happens if interest rates change by 100 basis points. The levered portfolio's value will change by $12 million (3% times $400 million). This means that on an investment of $100 million, the portfolio's value changes by $12 million. The proper way to measure the portfolio's duration is relative to the unlevered amount or equity because the manager is concerned with the risk exposure relative to equity. Thus, the duration for the portfolio is 12 because a duration of 12 will change the portfolio's equity value of $100 million by 12% or $12 million for a 100 basis point change in rates.

In general, the procedure for calculating the duration of a portfolio that uses leverage is as follows:

Step 1: Calculate the duration of the levered portfolio.

Step 2: Determine the dollar duration of the portfolio of the levered portfolio for a change in interest rates.

Step 3: Compute the ratio of the dollar duration of the levered portfolio to the value of the initial unlevered portfolio (i.e., initial equity).

Step 4: The duration of the unlevered portfolio is then found as follows:

$$\text{Ratio computed in Step 3} \times \frac{100}{\text{Rate change used in Step 2 in bps}} \times 100$$

To illustrate the procedure, suppose that the initial value of the unlevered portfolio is $100 million and the leveraged portfolio is $400 million ($100 million equity plus $300 million borrowed).

Step 1: Assume that calculation of the duration of the levered portfolio finds that the duration is 3.

Step 2: Let's use a 50 basis point change in interest rates to compute the dollar duration. If the duration of the levered portfolio is 3, then the dollar duration for a 50 basis point change in interest rates is $6 million (1.5% change for a 50 basis point move times $400 million).

Step 3: The ratio of the dollar duration for a 50 basis point change in interest rates to the $100 million initial market value of the unlevered portfolio is 0.06 ($6 million divided by $100 million).

Step 4: The duration of the unlevered portfolio is:

$$0.06 \times \frac{100}{50} \times 100 = 12$$

How to Create Leverage via the Repo Market[12]

A manager can create leverage in one of two ways. One way is through the use of derivative instruments. As is explained in Chapters 21–23, interest rate derivatives instruments can produce the same effect as leverage. The second way is to borrow funds via a collateralized loan arrangement. The two most common ways a money manager can borrow via a collateralized loan arrangement is through a reverse repurchase agreement or margin buying. The former is the most common transaction used by institutional money managers, so we discuss it next.

Repurchase Agreement   A **repurchase agreement** is the sale of a security with a commitment by the seller to buy the same security back from the purchaser at a specified price at a designated future date. The price at which the seller must subsequently repurchase the security for is called the **repurchase price,** and the date that the security must be repurchased is called the **repurchase date.** Basically, a repurchase agreement is a collateralized loan, where the collateral is the security sold and subsequently repurchased. The agreement is best explained with an illustration.

Suppose a government securities dealer has purchased $10 million of a particular Treasury security. The dealer uses the repurchase agreement or "repo" market to obtain financing. In the repo market the dealer can use the $10 million of the Treasury security as collateral for a loan. The term of the loan and the interest rate that the dealer agrees to pay are specified. The interest rate is called the **repo rate.** When the term of the loan is one day, it is called an **overnight repo;** a loan for more than one day is called a **term repo.** The transaction is referred to as a repurchase agreement because it calls for the sale of the security and its repurchase at a future date. Both the sale price and the purchase price are specified in the agreement. The difference between the purchase (repurchase) price and the sale price is the dollar interest cost of the loan.

Back to the dealer who needs to finance $10 million of a Treasury security that it purchased and plans to hold overnight. Suppose that a customer of the dealer has excess funds of $10 million. (The customer might be a municipality with tax receipts that it has just collected and no immediate need to disburse the funds.) The dealer would agree to deliver ("sell") $10 million of the Treasury security to the customer for an amount determined by the repo rate and buy ("repurchase") the same Treasury secu-

---

[12]This section draws from Chapter 13 in Frank J. Fabozzi, *Fixed Income Securities* (New Hope, PA: Frank J. Fabozzi Associates, 1997).

rity from the customer for $10 million the next day. Suppose that the overnight repo rate is 6.5%. Then, as is explained subsequently, the dealer would agree to deliver the Treasury securities for $9,998,195 and repurchase the same securities for $10 million the next day. The $1,805 difference between the "sale" price of $9,998,195 and the repurchase price of $10 million is the dollar interest on the financing.

The following formula is used to calculate the dollar interest on a repo transaction:

Dollar interest = (Dollar amount borrowed) × (Repo rate) × Repo term/360

Notice that the interest is computed on a 360-day basis.

In our example, at a repo rate of 6.5% and a repo term of one day (overnight), the dollar interest is $1,805 as shown here:

$$\$9,998,195 \times 0.065 \times 1/360 = \$1,805$$

The advantage to the dealer of using the repo market for borrowing on a short-term basis is that the rate is lower than the cost of bank financing. (The reason for this is explained later.) From the customer's perspective, the repo market offers an attractive yield on a short-term secured transaction that is highly liquid.

Although the example illustrates financing a dealer's long position in the repo market, dealers can also use the market to cover a short position. For example, suppose a government dealer sold $10 million of Treasury securities two weeks ago and must now cover the position—that is, deliver the securities. The dealer can do a **reverse repo** (agree to buy the securities and sell them back). Of course, the dealer eventually would have to buy the Treasury security in the market in order to cover its short position. In this case, the dealer is actually making a collateralized loan to its customer. The customer may be using the funds obtained from the collateralized loan to create leverage.

There is a good deal of Wall Street jargon describing repo transactions. To understand it, remember that one party is lending money and accepting a security as collateral for the loan; the other party is borrowing money and providing collateral to borrow the money. When someone lends securities in order to receive cash (i.e., borrow money), that party is said to be "reversing out" securities. A party that lends money with the security as collateral is said to be "reversing in" securities. The expressions "to repo securities" and "to do repo" are also used. The former means that someone is going to finance securities using the security as collateral; the latter means that the party is going to invest in a repo. Finally, the expressions "selling collateral" and "buying collateral" are used to describe a party financing a security with a repo on the one hand and lending on the basis of collateral on the other.

Rather than using industry jargon, investment guidelines should be clear as to what a manager is permitted to do. For example, a client may have no objections to its money manager using a repo as a short-term investment; that is, the money manager may lend funds on a short-term basis. The investment guidelines will set forth how the loan arrangement should be structured to protect against credit risk. We'll discuss this next. However, if a client does not want a money manager to use the repo agreement as a vehicle for borrowing funds in order to create leverage, it should state so.

Although in our illustration we used Treasury securities as the collateral, the collateral in a repo is not limited to government securities. Money market instruments, federal agency securities, and mortgage-backed securities[13] are also used. In some specialized markets, whole loans are used as collateral.

Credit Risks   Despite the fact that there may be high-quality collateral underlying a repo transaction, both parties to the transaction are exposed to credit risk. Why does credit risk occur in a repo transaction? Consider our initial example in which the dealer uses $10 million of government securities as collateral to borrow. If the dealer cannot repurchase the government securities, the customer may keep the collateral; if interest rates on government securities increase subsequent to the repo transaction, however, the market value of the government securities will decline, and the customer will own securities with a market value less than the amount it lent to the dealer. If the market value of the security rises instead, the dealer will be concerned with the return of the collateral, which then has a market value higher than the loan.

Repos should be carefully structured to reduce credit risk exposure. The amount lent should be less than the market value of the security used as collateral, thereby providing the lender with some cushion should the market value of the security decline. The amount by which the market value of the security used as collateral exceeds the value of the loan is called **repo margin** or simply **margin.** Margin is also referred to as the "haircut." Repo margin is generally between 1% and 3%. For borrowers of lower credit worthiness and/or when less liquid securities are used as collateral, the repo margin can be 10% or more.

Another practice to limit credit risk is to mark the collateral to market on a regular basis. (Marking a position to market means recording the value of a position at its market value.) When market value changes by a certain percentage, the repo position is adjusted accordingly.

One concern in structuring a repo is delivery of the collateral to the lender. The most obvious procedure is for the borrower to deliver the collateral to the lender or to the lender's clearing agent. In such instances, the collateral is said to be "delivered out." At the end of the repo term, the lender returns the collateral to the borrower in exchange for the principal and interest payment. This procedure may be too expensive, though, particularly for short-term repos, because of costs associated with delivering the collateral. The cost of delivery would be factored into the transaction by a lower repo rate that the borrower would be willing to pay. The risk of the lender not taking possession of the collateral is that the borrower may sell the security or use the same security as collateral for a repo with another party.

As an alternative to delivering out the collateral, the lender may agree to allow the borrower to hold the security in a segregated customer account. Of course, the lender still faces the risk that the borrower may use the collateral fraudulently by offering it as collateral for another repo transaction. If the borrower of the cash does not deliver out the collateral, but instead holds it, then the transaction is called a **hold-in-custody repo (HIC repo).** Despite the credit risk associated with a HIC repo, it is used in some transactions when the collateral is difficult to deliver (such as in whole loans) or the transaction amount is small and the lender of funds is comfortable with the reputation of the borrower of the cash.

---

[13]A special repo called a "dollar roll" is available when the security used as collateral is a mortgage pass-through security.

Another method is for the borrower to deliver the collateral to the lender's custodial account at the borrower's clearing bank. The custodian then has possession of the collateral that it holds on behalf of the lender. This practice reduces the cost of delivery because it is merely a transfer within the borrower's clearing bank. If, for example, a dealer enters into an overnight repo with Customer A, the next day the collateral is transferred back to the dealer. The dealer can then enter into a repo with Customer B for, say, five days without having to redeliver the collateral. The clearing bank simply establishes a custodian account for Customer B and holds the collateral in that account. This specialized type of repo arrangement is called a **tri-party repo.**

Determinants of the Repo Rate   There is not one repo rate. The rate varies from transaction to transaction depending on a variety of factors: quality of collateral, term of the repo, delivery requirement, availability of collateral, and the prevailing federal funds rate.

The higher the credit quality and liquidity of the collateral, the lower the repo rate. The effect of the term of the repo on the rate depends on the shape of the yield curve. As noted earlier, if delivery of the collateral to the lender is required, the repo rate will be lower. If the collateral can be deposited with the bank of the borrower, a higher repo rate is paid.

The more difficult it is to obtain the collateral, the lower the repo rate. To understand why this is so, remember that the borrower (or equivalently the seller of the collateral) has a security that lenders of cash want, for whatever reason. Such collateral is referred to as **hot** or **special collateral.** (Collateral that does not have this characteristic is referred to as **general collateral.**) The party that needs the hot collateral will be willing to lend funds at a lower repo rate in order to obtain the collateral.

Whereas these factors determine the repo rate on a particular transaction, the federal funds rate determines the general level of repo rates. The repo rate generally will be a rate lower than the federal funds rate, because a repo involves collateralized borrowing, whereas a federal funds transaction is unsecured borrowing.

SUMMARY

There are five basic steps in investment management. The first and principal step in the investment management process is setting investment objectives. The second step is establishing policy guidelines to satisfy the investment objectives; it begins with the asset allocation decision. The third step is selecting a portfolio strategy that is consistent with the objectives and policy guidelines of the client or institution. The fourth step is selecting the specific assets to be included in the portfolio. The measurement and evaluation of investment performance is the final step in the ongoing investment management process.

Active bond portfolio strategies seek to capitalize on expectations about changes in factors that will affect the price and therefore the performance of an issue over some investment horizon. The factors that affect a portfolio's return are (1) changes in the level of interest rates, (2) changes in the shape of the yield curve, (3) changes in yield spreads among bond sectors, (4) changes in the option-adjusted spread, and (5) changes in the yield spread for a particular bond. The total return framework should be used to assess how changes in these factors will affect the performance of a strategy over some investment horizon.

The performance of an actively managed portfolio will also be affected by how the manager allocates funds among the various sectors within a bond sector. In the case of the corporate bond sector, a framework that estimates the expected incremental return over Treasuries using a rating transition matrix can be used.

Leveraging involves creating an exposure to a market in excess of the exposure that can be obtained without borrowing funds. The objective is to earn a return in excess of the cost of the borrowed funds. The risk is that the manager will earn a return less than the cost of the borrowed funds. The return on the borrowed funds is realized from the interest earned plus the change in the value of the securities acquired. The duration of a portfolio is magnified by leveraging a portfolio.

The most common way in which a manager can borrow funds is via a repurchase agreement. This is a collateralized loan arrangement in which the manager borrows funds from a dealer. (It is called a reverse repo agreement, and the phrase *repo agreement* is reserved for when a dealer borrows funds.) There is credit risk in a repo agreement, and there are mechanisms for mitigating this risk.

Questions

1. Why might the investment objective of a portfolio manager of a life insurance company be different from that of a mutual fund manager?
2. Explain how it can be possible for a portfolio manager to outperform a benchmark but still fail to meet the investment objective of a client.
3. What is the essential ingredient in all active portfolio strategies?
4. a. What is an active portfolio strategy?
   b. What will determine whether an active or a passive portfolio strategy will be pursued?
5. What are the limitations of using duration and convexity measures in active portfolio strategies?
6. Below are two portfolios with a market value of $500 million. The bonds in both portfolios are trading at par value. The dollar duration of the two portfolios is the same.

Bonds Included in Portfolio I

Issue	Years to Maturity	ParValue (in millions)
A	2.0	$120
B	2.5	130
C	20.0	150
D	20.5	100

Bonds Included in Portfolio II

Issue	Years to Maturity	ParValue (in millions)
E	9.7	$200
F	10.0	230
G	10.2	70

   a. Which portfolio can be characterized as a bullet portfolio?
   b. Which portfolio can be characterized as a barbell portfolio?
   c. The two portfolios have the same dollar duration; explain whether their performance will be the same if interest rates change.

d. If they will not perform the same, how would you go about determining which would perform best assuming that you have a six-month investment horizon?

7. Explain why you agree or disagree with the following statements:

   a. "It is always better to have a portfolio with more convexity than one with less convexity."

   b. "A bullet portfolio will always outperform a barbell portfolio with the same dollar duration if the yield curve steepens."

8. What is a laddered portfolio?

9. A portfolio manager owns $5 million par value of bond ABC. The bond is trading at 70 and has a modified duration of 6. The portfolio manager is considering swapping out of bond ABC and into bond XYZ. The price of this bond is 85 and it has a modified duration of 3.5.

   a. What is the dollar duration of bond ABC per 100-basis-point change in yield?

   b. What is the dollar duration for the $5 million position of bond ABC?

   c. How much in market value of bond XYZ should be purchased so that the dollar duration of bond XYZ will be approximately the same as that for bond ABC?

   d. How much in par value of bond XYZ should be purchased so that the dollar duration of bond XYZ will be approximately the same as that for bond ABC?

10. Explain why in implementing a yield spread strategy it is necessary to keep the dollar duration constant.

11. The excerpt that follows is taken from an article titled "Smith Plans to Shorten," which appeared in the January 27, 1992, issue of *BondWeek*, p. 6:

    > When the economy begins to rebound and interest rates start to move up, Smith Affiliated Capital will swap 30-year Treasuries for 10-year Treasuries and those with average remaining lives of nine years, according to Bob Smith, executive v.p. The New York firm doesn't expect this to occur until the end of this year or early next, however, and sees the yield on the 30-year Treasury first falling below 7%. Any new cash that comes in now will be put into 30-year Treasuries, Smith added.

    What type of portfolio strategy is Smith Affiliated Capital pursuing?

12. The following excerpt is taken from an article titled "MERUS to Boost Corporates," which appeared in the January 27, 1992, issue of *BondWeek*, p. 6:

    > MERUS Capital Management will increase the allocation to corporates in its $790 million long investment-grade fixed-income portfolio by $39.5 million over the next six months to a year, according to George Wood, managing director. MERUS will add corporates rated single A or higher in the expectation that spreads will tighten as the economy recovers and that some credits may be upgraded.

    What types of active portfolio strategies is MERUS Capital Management pursuing?

13. This excerpt comes from an article titled "Eagle Eyes High-Coupon Callable Corporates" in the January 20, 1992, issue of *BondWeek*, p. 7:

    > If the bond market rallies further, Eagle Asset Management may take profits, trading $8 million of seven- to 10-year Treasuries for high-coupon single-A industrials that are callable in two to four years according to Joseph Blanton, senior v.p. He thinks a further rally is unlikely, however.
    >   Eagle has already sold seven- to 10-year Treasuries to buy $25 million of high-coupon, single-A nonbank financial credits. It made the move to cut the duration of its $160 million fixed income portfolio from 3.7 to 2.5 years, substantially lower than the 3.3-year duration of its bogey . . . because it thinks the bond rally has run its course. . . .

> Blanton said he likes single-A industrials and financials with 9½–10% coupons because these are selling at wide spreads of about 100–150 basis points off Treasuries.

What types of active portfolio strategies are being pursued by Eagle Asset Management?

14. The following excerpt is taken from an article titled "W.R. Lazard Buys Triple Bs," which appeared in the November 18, 1991, issue of *BondWeek*, p. 7:

> W.R. Lazard & Co. is buying some corporate bonds rated triple B that it believes will be upgraded and some single As that the market perceives as risky but Lazard does not, according to William Schultz, v.p. The firm, which generally buys corporates rated single A or higher, is making the move to pick up yield, Schultz said.

What types of active portfolio strategies are being followed by W.R. Lazard & Co.?

15. In an article titled "Signet to Add Pass-Throughs," which appeared in the October 14, 1991, issue of *BondWeek*, p. 5, it was reported that Christian Goetz, assistant vice president of Signet Asset Management, "expects current coupons to outperform premium pass-throughs as the Fed lowers rates because mortgage holders will refinance premium mortgages." If Goetz pursues a strategy based on this, what type of active strategy is it?

16. The following excerpt comes from an article titled "Securities Counselors Eyes Cutting Duration" in the February 17, 1992, issue of *BondWeek*, p. 5:

> Securities Counselors of Iowa will shorten the 5.3 year duration on its $250 million fixed-income portfolio once it is convinced interest rates are moving up and the economy is improving. . . . It will shorten by holding in cash equivalents the proceeds from the sale of an undetermined amount of 10-year Treasuries and adding a small amount of high-grade electric utility bonds that have short-maturities if their spreads widen out at least 100 basis points. . . .
>
> The portfolio is currently allocated 85% to Treasuries and 15% to agencies. It has not held corporate bonds since 1985, when it perceived as risky the barrage of hostile corporate takeovers. . . .

  a. Why would Securities Counselors want to shorten duration if it believes that interest rates will rise?

  b. How does the purchase of cash equivalents and short-maturity high-grade utilities accomplish the goal of shortening the duration?

  c. What risk is Securities Counselors indicating in the last sentence of the excerpt that it is seeking to avoid by not buying corporate bonds?

17. The next excerpt is taken from an article titled "Wood Struthers to Add High-Grade Corporates," which appeared in the February 17, 1992, issue of *BondWeek*, p. 5:

> Wood Struthers & Winthrop is poised to add a wide range of high-grade corporates to its $600 million fixed-income portfolio. . . . It will increase its 25% corporate allocation to about 30% after the economy shows signs of improving. . . . It will sell Treasuries and agencies of undetermined maturities to make the purchase. . . .
>
> Its duration is 4½–5 years and is not expected to change significantly. . . .

Comment on this portfolio strategy.

18. a. What is a rating transition matrix?

b. Explain how a rating transition matrix can be used as a starting point in assessing how a manager may want to allocate funds to the different credit sectors of the corporate bond market.

19. What is the risk associated with the use of leverage?

20. Suppose that the initial value of an unlevered portfolio of Treasury securities is $200 million and the duration is 7. Suppose further that the manager can borrow $800 million and invest it in the identical Treasury securities so that the levered portfolio has a value of $1 billion. What is the duration of this levered portfolio?

21. Suppose a manager wants to borrow $50 million of a Treasury security that it plans to purchase and hold for 20 days. The manager can enter into a reverse repo agreement with a dealer firm that would provide financing at a 4.2% repo rate and a 2% margin requirement. What is the dollar interest cost that the manager will have to pay for the borrowed funds?

22. Two trustees of a pension fund are discussing repurchase agreements. Trustee A told Trustee B that she feels it is a safe short-term investment for the fund. Trustee B told Trustee A that repurchase agreements are highly speculative vehicles because they are leveraged instruments. You've been called in by the trustees to clarify the investment characteristics of repurchase agreements. What would you say to the trustees?

23. Suppose that a manager buys an adjustable-rate pass-through security backed by Freddie Mac or Fannie Mae, two government-sponsored enterprises. Suppose that the coupon rate is reset monthly based on the following coupon formula:

$$1\text{-month LIBOR} + 80 \text{ basis points}$$

with a cap of 9% (i.e., maximum coupon rate of 9%).

Suppose that the manager can use these securities in a repo transaction in which (1) a repo margin of 5% is required, (2) the term of the repo is one month, and (3) the repo rate is one-month LIBOR plus 10 basis points. Also assume that the manager wishes to invest $1 million of his client's funds in these securities. The manager can purchase $20 million in par value of these securities because only $1 million is required. The amount borrowed would be $19 million. Thus, the manager realizes a spread of 70 basis points on the $19 million borrowed because LIBOR plus 80 basis points is earned in interest each month (coupon rate) and LIBOR plus 10 basis point is paid each month (repo rate).

What are the risks associated with this strategy?

24. Why is there credit risk in a repo transaction?

CHAPTER 18

Indexing

Learning Objectives

After reading this chapter you will understand:

- the objectives and motivation for bond indexing
- the advantages and disadvantages of bond indexing
- the different types of bond indexes: broad-based markets indexes and specialized market indexes
- the characteristics of the broad-based indexes
- how the diversification of bonds varies with portfolio size
- the methodologies for constructing an indexed portfolio
- the difficulties associated with implementing a bond indexing strategy
- what enhanced bond indexing is

In this chapter and the next we describe several structured portfolio strategies. Structured strategies generally do not rely on expectations of interest-rate movements or changes in yield spread relationships. Their objective, instead, is to design a portfolio that will achieve the performance of some predetermined benchmark. The target to achieve may be (1) the return on a specific benchmark index, (2) sufficient dollars to satisfy a future single liability, or (3) sufficient dollars to satisfy each liability of a future liability stream. The structured bond portfolio strategy used when the target to be achieved is replication of a predetermined benchmark index is called an indexing strategy. When the target objective is, instead, to generate sufficient funds to pay off predetermined future liabilities, the strategy is called a liability funding strategy. Indexing is discussed in this chapter; liability funding is discussed in Chapter 19.

OBJECTIVE OF AND MOTIVATION FOR BOND INDEXING

Bond indexing means designing a portfolio so that its performance will match the performance of some bond index. In indexing, performance is measured in terms of total rate of return achieved (or simply, total return) over some investment horizon. Total return over some investment horizon incorporates all three sources of return from holding a portfolio of bonds.

Indexing an equity portfolio is commonplace. On the bond side, indexing is a relatively recent phenomenon. Several factors explain the recent popularity and phenomenal rate of growth of bond indexing.[1] First, the empirical evidence suggests that historically the overall performance of active bond managers has been poor. Second is the reduced advisory management fees charged for an indexed portfolio compared to active management advisory fees. Advisory fees charged by active managers typically range from 15 to 50 basis points. The range for indexed portfolios, in contrast, is 1 to 20 basis points, with the upper range representing the fees for enhanced and customized benchmark funds, discussed later in this chapter. Some pension funds have decided to do away with advisory fees and to manage some or all of their funds inhouse following an indexing strategy.

Lower nonadvisory fees, such as custodial fees, is the third explanation for the popularity of indexing. Finally, sponsors have greater control over external managers when an indexing strategy is selected. For example, in an actively managed portfolio, a sponsor who specifies a restriction on the portfolio's duration still gives the manager ample leeway to pursue strategies that may significantly underperform the index selected as a benchmark. In contrast, requiring an investment advisor to match an index gives little leeway to the manager and, as a result, should result in performance that does not significantly diverge from a benchmark.

Critics of indexing point out that although an indexing strategy matches the performance of some index, the performance of that index does not necessarily represent optimal performance. Moreover, matching an index does not mean that the manager will satisfy a client's return requirement objective. For example, if the objective of a life insurance company or a pension fund is to have sufficient funds to satisfy a predetermined liability, indexing only reduces the likelihood that performance will not be materially worse than the index. The index's return is not necessarily related to the sponsor's liability. Finally, matching an index means that a money manager is restricted to the sectors of the bond market that are in the index, even though there may be attractive opportunities in market sectors excluded from the index. While the broad-based bond market indexes typically include agency pass-through securities, other mortgage-backed securities such as nonagency mortgage-backed securities and collateralized mortgage obligations are generally not included. Yet it is in these newer markets that attractive returns to enhance performance may be available.

At the theoretical level, the index fund approach is supported by the work of Markowitz[2] on the construction of efficient portfolios and by capital market theory as developed by Sharpe,[3] Lintner,[4] and Mossin.[5] Markowitz demonstrates how portfolios can be constructed so as to maximize return for a given level of risk. Such portfolios are referred to as efficient portfolios.

[1]Sharmin Mossavar-Rahmani, *Bond Index Funds* (Chicago: Probus Publishing, 1991), p. 212.

[2]Harry M. Markowitz, "Portfolio Selection," *Journal of Finance,* March 1952, pp. 71–91, and *Portfolio Selection: Efficient Diversification of Investment* (New York: Wiley, 1959).

[3]William F. Sharpe, "Capital Asset Prices: A Theory of Market Equilibrium under Conditions of Risk," *Journal of Finance,* September 1964, pp. 425–442.

[4]John Lintner, "Security Prices, Risk, and Maximal Gains from Diversification," *Journal of Finance,* December 1965, pp. 587–616.

[5]Jan Mossin, "Equilibrium in a Capital Asset Market," *Econometrica,* October 1966, pp. 76–83.

The Sharpe–Lintner–Mossin analysis demonstrates that a "market" portfolio offers the highest level of return per unit of risk in an efficient market. An efficient market is one in which market participants cannot consistently earn abnormal risk-adjusted returns after considering transactions costs. A combination of securities in a portfolio with characteristics similar to the market is able to capture the efficiency of the market. The theoretical market portfolio consists of all risky assets. The weight of each risky asset in the market portfolio is equal to the ratio of its market value to the aggregate market value of all risky assets. That is, the market portfolio is a capitalization-weighted (value-weighted) portfolio of all risky assets.[6] Exhibit 18-1 summarizes the advantages and disadvantages of bond indexing.

FACTORS TO CONSIDER IN SELECTING AN INDEX

A money manager who wishes to pursue an indexing strategy must determine which bond index to replicate. There are a number of bond indexes from which to select, and several factors influence the decision. The first is the investor's risk tolerance. Selection of an index that includes corporate bonds will expose the investor to credit risk. If this risk is unacceptable, an investor should avoid an index that includes this sector.

The second factor influencing the selection of an index is the investor's objective. For example, although the total return of the various indexes tends to be highly positively correlated, the variability of total returns has been quite different. Therefore, an investor whose objective may be to minimize the variability of total returns will be biased toward one that has had, and expects to continue to have, low variability (i.e., a shorter duration relative to other indexes). Moreover, variability of total return may not be symmetric in rising and falling markets. Investors who have expectations about the future direction of interest rates will favor the index that is expected to perform better given their expectations.

BOND INDEXES

The wide range of bond market indexes available can be classified as broad-based market indexes and specialized market indexes. Why have broker/dealer firms developed and aggressively marketed their bond indexes? Enhancing the firm's image is

EXHIBIT 18-1 Advantages and Disadvantages of Bond Indexing

Advantages	Disadvantages
No dependence on expectations and little risk of underperforming the index	Bond indexes do not reflect optimal performance
Reduced advisory and nonadvisory fees	Bond index may not match the sponsor's liabilities
Greater sponsor control	Restrictions on fund; management ignores opportunities

---

[6]Granito argues that although the theoretical arguments are appropriate for indexing a common stock portfolio, they are inappropriate for justifying indexing of a bond portfolio. See Michael R. Granito, "The Problem with Bond Index Funds," *Journal of Portfolio Management,* Summer 1987, pp. 41–48.

only a minor reason. The key motivation lies in the potential profit that the firm will make by executing trades to set up an indexed portfolio and rebalance it. Typically, a broker/dealer charges a money manager who wants to set up or rebalance an index a nominal amount for providing the necessary data but expects that the bulk of the trades will be executed through its trading desks. Also, by keeping the makeup of the index proprietary, those firms attempt to lock in customers to using their index.

The three broad-based market indexes most commonly used by institutional investors are the Lehman Brothers Aggregate Index, the Salomon Brothers Broad Investment-Grade Bond Index, and the Merrill Lynch Domestic Market Index. The bond market sectors covered by these three indexes are the Treasury, agency, investment-grade corporate, mortgage-backed, and Yankee markets. Yankee issues are included in the corporate sector. Asset-backed securities are included as a sector in the Lehman Brothers index.

There are more than 5,000 issues in each index.[7] All three indexes exclude issues that are non–investment grade (i.e., below BBB) and issues that have a maturity of one year or less. To be included in the Lehman Brothers index, the size of the issue must be more than $100 million; for the Merrill Lynch and Salomon Brothers indexes, the issue size need only be $50 million. Convertible corporate issues are included in all three indexes; floating-rate securities are included in the Lehman Brothers and Salomon Brothers indexes.

The three broad-based indexes are computed daily and are market value weighted. The securities in the Salomon Brothers Index are all trader priced. For the two other indexes, the securities are either trader priced or model priced. Each index has a different way in which it handles intra-month cash flows that must be reinvested. For the Salomon Brothers index, these cash flows are assumed to be reinvested at the one-month Treasury bill rate, whereas for the Merrill Lynch index, they are assumed to be reinvested in specific bonds. There is no reinvestment of intra-month cash flows for the Lehman Brothers index.

The specialized market indexes focus on only one sector of the bond market or a subsector of the bond market. Indexes on sectors of the market are published by the three investment banking firms that produce the broad-based market indexes. For example, Lehman Brothers produces a Government Bond Index, a Government/Corporate Bond Index, a Corporate Bond Index, a Mortgage Backed Securities Index, and a Yankee Bond Index. Salomon Brothers produces a World Government Bond Index, a High-Yield Market Index, a Eurodollar Bond Index, and Brady Bond Index.

Firms that do not produce one of the three broad-based market indexes have provided specialized indexes. Some examples are the Morgan Stanley Actively Traded MBS Index, the Donaldson Lufkin & Jenrette High Yield Index, the First Boston High Yield Index, the Goldman, Sachs Convertible 100, and the Ryan Labs Treasury Index. The Ryan index has been a popular index followed by institutional investors. The index consists of seven Treasury issues, equally weighted and priced based on actual market prices.

---

[7]Information about the broad-based indexes described here is based on the data reported in Exhibit 7-1 in Frank K. Reilly and David J. Wright, "Bond Market Indexes," Chapter 7 in Frank J. Fabozzi (ed.), *The Handbook of Fixed Income Securities* (Burr Ridge, IL: Irwin Professional Publishing, 1997), p. 132 and Table I in Frank K. Reilly, G. Wenchi Kao, and David J. Wright, "Alternative Bond Market Indexes," *Financial Analysts Journal,* May–June 1992, p. 47.

In recent years, money managers in consultation with their clients have been moving in the direction of **customized benchmarks,** which are benchmarks designed to meet a client's requirements and long-term objectives.[8] For example, in December 1986, Salomon Brothers Inc. introduced its Large Pension Fund Baseline Bond Index as a standardized customized benchmark tailor-made for large pension funds "seeking to establish long-term core portfolios that more closely match the longer durations of their nominal dollar liabilities."[9]

Historical Performance Characteristics of the Bond Indexes

Reilly, Kao, and Wright have performed extensive statistical analysis on the broad-based indexes and several specialized market indexes.[10] The bottom panel of Exhibit 18-2 shows the 15 bond indexes they analyzed. Exhibit 18-2 shows the annual percentage rates of return and standard deviations for the years 1976 through 1990. Because of the large number of issues in each index, unique risks have been eliminated and the standard deviation is a good measure of systematic risk. Notice that the bond indexes that include only government bonds have the lowest average returns, followed by corporates. The bond indexes that have only mortgage-backed securities have the highest average returns but also have the highest standard deviation.

Reilly, Kao, and Wright found the correlation of annual returns between the three broad-based indexes to be around 98%. There were also correlations in excess of 90% for the specialized sectors covered by the three dealer firms. Although over long time periods the correlations are high, the authors of the study found that there were month-to-month differences in performance.

DIVERSIFICATION AND PORTFOLIO SIZE

One of the key considerations in an indexing strategy is how many bond issues are necessary to obtain adequate diversification. A study by McEnally and Boardman examined how diversification of bonds varies with portfolio size.[11] Their sample consisted of 515 corporate bonds with quality ratings ranging from Aaa to Baa. For all the bonds in their sample and for each quality rating, they constructed 1,000 randomly selected portfolios for a given number of issues. They then computed the variance of monthly returns. The results of the McEnally–Boardman study are summarized in Exhibit 18-3.

The first row of the exhibit shows the average variance of returns for the 515 issues. The last row presents the variance of returns for a portfolio consisting of all bond issues. The body of the exhibit shows the average variance for the 1,000 randomly constructed portfolios as the number of issues in the portfolio increases. As can be seen, as the number of issues in the portfolio increases, the average variance of the portfolio return decreases and approaches the variance of returns of the portfolio

---

[8]For a discussion of customized benchmarks and the reasons for the growing interest in them, see Sharmin Mossavar-Rahmani, "Customized Benchmarks in Structured Management," *Journal of Portfolio Management,* Summer 1987, pp. 65–68.

[9]Martin L. Leibowitz, Thomas Klaffky and Steven Mandel, *Introducing the Salomon Brothers Large Pension Fund Baseline Bond Index* (New York: Salomon Brothers Inc., December 1986), p. 1.

[10]Frank K. Reilly, G. Wenchi Kao, and David J. Wright, "Alternative Bond Market Indexes," *Financial Analysts Journal,* May–June 1992, pp. 44–58.

[11]Richard W. McEnally and Calvin M. Boardman, "Aspects of Corporate Bond Portfolio Diversification," *Journal of Financial Research,* Spring 1979, pp. 27–36.

EXHIBIT 18-2 Annual Percentage Rates of Return and Standard Deviations, 1976–1990

	Lehman Brothers						Merrill Lynch					Salomon Brothers				S&P 500
	Govt./Corp.	Govt.	Corp.	Mort.	Yank.	Agg.	Govt./Corp.	Govt.	Corp.	Dom.	Mort.	Broad	Govt.	Corp.	Mort.	
1976	15.58	12.36	19.34	16.31	15.08	15.60	14.76	11.90	18.81	14.80	15.22					23.84
1977	2.98	2.80	3.16	1.89	5.22	3.03	3.10	2.59	3.81	3.02	1.87					-7.18
1978	1.19	1.80	0.35	2.41	2.92	1.40	1.24	1.83	0.34	1.30	2.00					6.56
1979	2.29	5.41	-2.10	0.13	-0.43	1.93	2.27	5.34	2.21	2.10	0.54					18.44
1980	3.06	5.19	-0.29	0.65	1.92	2.71	3.35	5.06	0.54	2.99	0.47	2.73	5.38	-0.32	0.50	32.42
1981	7.26	9.36	2.95	0.07	3.48	6.25	7.00	9.55	2.30	6.43	2.34	6.70	9.76	2.75	1.18	-4.91
1982	31.10	27.75	39.20	43.04	35.82	32.62	29.83	26.90	35.53	30.91	40.15	31.78	26.90	37.12	41.34	21.41
1983	7.99	7.39	9.27	10.13	9.43	8.35	7.78	6.84	9.32	8.03	9.51	8.21	7.19	8.95	10.83	22.51
1984	15.02	14.50	16.62	15.79	16.38	15.15	15.12	14.83	16.21	15.20	15.83	14.98	14.35	16.04	15.77	6.27
1985	21.30	20.43	24.06	25.21	26.00	22.10	21.82	20.64	25.36	22.40	25.45	22.23	20.45	24.93	25.68	32.16
1986	15.62	15.31	16.53	13.43	16.27	15.26	15.63	15.38	16.30	15.22	13.14	15.44	15.48	17.03	13.44	18.47
1987	2.29	2.20	2.56	4.29	1.89	2.76	2.10	2.17	1.84	2.40	3.53	2.60	2.13	2.06	4.06	5.23
1988	7.58	7.03	9.22	8.72	8.81	7.89	7.72	7.11	9.76	8.04	9.15	7.98	7.09	9.47	8.80	16.81
1989	14.24	14.23	14.09	15.35	15.42	14.53	14.13	14.13	14.12	14.18	14.60	14.44	14.23	13.97	15.18	31.49
1990	8.28	8.72	7.05	10.72	7.05	8.96	8.50	8.83	7.37	9.10	10.84	9.09	8.77	7.28	10.90	-3.15
Arithmetic mean																
1976–1990	10.39	10.30	10.80	11.21	11.02	10.57	10.29	10.21	10.63	10.41	10.98					14.69
1980–1990	12.16	12.01	12.84	13.40	12.95	12.42	12.09	11.95	12.60	12.26	13.18	12.38	11.98	12.66	13.42	16.25
Standard deviation (annual returns)																
1976–1990	8.41	7.25	11.14	11.51	10.03	8.76	8.20	7.17	10.55	8.44	10.82					13.45
1980–1990	8.51	7.41	11.34	12.21	10.58	8.93	8.30	7.30	10.64	8.57	11.38	8.73	7.21	11.01	11.73	13.65
Geometric mean																
1976–1990	10.10	10.08	10.31	10.70	10.62	10.26	10.02	10.00	10.18	10.12	10.52					13.93
1980–1990	11.88	11.79	12.36	12.85	12.52	12.11	11.82	11.74	12.17	11.98	12.70	12.08	11.77	12.20	12.91	15.50
Standard deviation (monthly returns)																
1976–1990	2.08	1.86	2.59	2.79	2.51	2.16	2.09	1.89	2.51	2.13	2.75					4.57
1980–1990	2.27	2.04	2.81	3.10	2.78	2.36	2.28	2.08	2.76	2.35	3.06	2.32	2.01	2.75	3.03	4.79

Source: Frank K. Reilly, G. Wenchi Kao, and David J. Wright, "Alternative Bond Market Indexes," *Financial Analysts Journal,* May–June 1992, p. 48. Reprinted with permission from *Financial Analysts Journal,* May/June 1992. Copyright 1992. Association for Investment Management Research, Charlottesville, VA. All rights reserved.

EXHIBIT 18-3 Monthly Return Variance of Corporate Bond Portfolios, January 1973 to June 1976 ($\times 10^4$)[a]

	All Issues	Aaa	Aa	A	Baa
All bonds in universe, individually [Var(P_1)]	9.257	7.756	8.419	9.912	10.977
Random portfolios of bonds [Var(P_n)][b]					
1 bond	9.367 (1.85)[c]	7.737 (1.21)	8.308 (1.47)	9.721 (2.10)	10.974 (2.52)
2 bonds	7.469 (1.48)	7.175 (1.20)	7.234 (1.28)	7.316 (1.58)	7.557 (1.73)
4 bonds	6.004 (1.19)	6.777 (1.06)	6.298 (1.11)	5.827 (1.26)	6.100 (1.40)
6 bonds	5.782 (1.15)	6.630 (1.03)	6.096 (1.08)	5.503 (1.19)	5.446 (1.25)
8 bonds	5.591 (1.11)	6.644 (1.04)	6.075 (1.07)	5.309 (1.15)	5.229 (1.20)
10 bonds	5.376 (1.07)	6.482 (1.01)	5.965 (1.05)	5.133 (1.11)	4.982 (1.14)
12 bonds	5.401 (1.07)	6.537 (1.02)	5.894 (1.04)	5.050 (1.09)	4.912 (1.13)
14 bonds	5.341 (1.06)	6.549 (1.02)	5.871 (1.04)	5.003 (1.08)	4.845 (1.11)
16 bonds	5.299 (1.05)	6.484 (1.02)	5.876 (1.04)	4.940 (1.07)	4.768 (1.09)
18 bonds	5.266 (1.05)	6.524 (1.02)	5.784 (1.02)	4.917 (1.06)	4.760 (1.09)
20 bonds	5.274 (1.05)	6.410 (1.00)	5.809 (1.03)	4.928 (1.06)	4.699 (1.07)
40 bonds	5.155 (1.02)	6.449 (1.00)	5.767 (1.02)	4.776 (1.03)	4.513 (1.03)
All bond portfolio [Var(M)]	5.039	6.416	5.661	4.633	4.362

[a]Var(P_1), mean variance of individual issues: Var(P_n), mean variance of portfolios constructed by investing $1/n$ of the portfolio in each of n randomly selected securities: Var(M), mean systematic or market-related variance for the universe.
[b]Based on 1,000 portfolios in each cell.
[c]Var(P_n)/Var(M) = ratio of mean variance of portfolio to mean market-related variance. (Computed by author)

Source: Richard W. McEnally and Calvin M. Boardman, "Aspects of Corporate Bond Portfolio Diversification," *Journal of Financial Research*, Spring 1979, p. 31. Reprinted by permission of Institutional Investor.

consisting of all issues. Also shown in Exhibit 18-3 is the nondiversifiable return variation (i.e., the variance of the return for the all-bond portfolio) as a proportion of the total return variation (i.e., the average variation of return) for the random portfolios.

Viewing the entire sample of bonds as the universe of all fixed-income securities and the quality ratings as a sector, the McEnally–Boardman results have several interesting implications for indexing strategies.

First, the following theoretical relationship between portfolio size and the variance of return of a portfolio consisting of n issues is supported by their analysis:

$$\text{Var}(P_n) = \text{Var}(M) + \frac{1}{n}\text{Var}(R_1)$$

where:

n = number of securities in the portfolio

Var(P_n) = expected value of the variance of returns of portfolios constructed by investing $1/n$ of the portfolio in each of n randomly selected securities

Var(M) = average systematic or market related variance of returns from the universe from which the n securities are drawn

Var(R_1) = average nonsystematic (diversifiable or residual) variance of the one-security portfolios from which the n securities are drawn

Thus, as an additional security is added to the portfolio, the variance of the portfolio can be expected to decrease by $1/n$ times the average nonsystematic risk of the one-security portfolios. This can be seen in Exhibit 18-4, which repeats the results for all corporate bonds in Exhibit 18-3 and shows the theoretical expected value of the variance for a portfolio of size n. There is no statistically significant difference between the theoretical expected value and the average value observed for the variance for any of the portfolios.

Second, it appears that the effect of portfolio size on diversification closely parallels the relationship found in common stocks.[12] This suggests that when a desired target is selected, it can be replicated with a manageable number of securities, probably fewer than 40 issues.

Finally, when portfolios are constructed from different segments of the market, the number of securities necessary to diversify away nonsystematic risk in that segment may differ. For the segments represented by the quality rating of the issue, for example, the results in Exhibit 18-4 indicate that it takes fewer issues to eliminate systematic risk for higher-quality bonds than for lower-quality bonds. For example, a four-bond portfolio consisting of Aaa issues had a 6% greater average variance than that of a completely diversified portfolio of Aaa issues. On the other hand, a four-

EXHIBIT 18-4	Monthly Return Variance of Randomly Generated Portfolios of Corporate Bonds of All Quality Classes, January 1973 to June 1976 ($\times 10^4$)	
Number of Bonds in Portfolio	*Mean Var(P_n)^a*	*Theoretical Var(P_n)*
1	9.367	9.257
2	7.469	7.148
4	6.004	6.094
6	5.782	5.742
8	5.591	5.566
10	5.376	5.461
12	5.401	5.391
14	5.341	5.340
16	5.299	5.303
18	5.266	5.273
20	5.274	5.250
40	5.155	5.144

^{a}Var(P_n), mean (expected value in case of theoretical) variance of portfolios constructed by investing $1/n$ of the portfolio in each of n randomly selected securities.

Source: Richard W. McEnally and Calvin M. Boardman, "Aspects of Corporate Bond Portfolio Diversification," *Journal of Financial Research,* Spring 1979, p. 34. Reprinted by permission of Institutional Investor.

---

[12]See John L. Evans and Stephen H. Archer, "Diversification and the Reduction of Dispersion: An Empirical Analysis," *Journal of Finance,* December 1968, pp. 761–767.

bond portfolio consisting of Baa issues had a 40% larger average variance than that of a completely diversified portfolio of Baa issues.

INDEXING METHODOLOGIES

After a money manager has decided to pursue an indexing strategy and has selected an index (broad-based bond market index, specialized market index, or customized benchmark), the next step is to construct a portfolio that will track the index. Any discrepancy between the performance of the indexed portfolio and the index (whether positive or negative) is referred to as **tracking error.** Tracking error has three sources: (1) transaction costs in constructing the indexed portfolio, (2) differences in the composition of the indexed portfolio and the index itself, and (3) discrepancies between prices used by the organization constructing the index and transaction prices paid by the indexer.

One approach in constructing the indexed portfolio is for the money manager to purchase all the issues in the index according to their weight in the benchmark index. However, substantial tracking error will result from the transactions costs (and other fees) associated with purchasing all the issues and reinvesting cash flow (maturing principal and coupon interest). A broad-based market index could include more than 5,000 issues, so large transactions costs may make this approach impractical. In addition, some issues in the index may not be available at the prices used in constructing the index.

Instead of purchasing all issues in the index, the money manager may purchase just a sample of issues. Although this approach reduces tracking error resulting from high transaction costs, it increases tracking error resulting from the mismatch of the indexed portfolio and the index.

Generally speaking, the fewer the number of issues used to replicate the index, the smaller the tracking error due to transactions costs but the greater the tracking error risk due to the mismatch of the characteristics of the indexed portfolio and the index. In contrast, the more issues purchased to replicate the index, the greater the tracking error due to transactions costs and the smaller the tracking error risk due to the mismatch of the indexed portfolio and the index. Obviously, then, there is a trade-off between tracking error and the number of issues used to construct the indexed portfolio.

There are three methodologies for designing a portfolio to replicate an index: (1) the stratified sampling or cell approach, (2) the optimization approach, and (3) the variance minimization approach. For each of these approaches, the initial question that the indexer must ask is: What factors affect a bond index's performance? Each approach assumes that the performance of an individual bond depends on a number of systematic factors that affect the performance of all bonds and on a factor unique to the individual issue. This last risk is diversifiable risk. The objective of the three approaches is to construct an indexed portfolio that eliminates this diversifiable risk.

Stratified Sampling or Cell Approach

Under the **stratified sampling approach to indexing,** the index is divided into cells, each cell representing a different characteristic of the index. The most common characteristics used to break down an index are (1) duration, (2) coupon, (3) maturity,

(4) market sectors (Treasury, corporate, mortgage-backed), (5) credit rating, (6) call factors, and (7) sinking fund features. The last two factors are particularly important because the call and sinking fund features of an issue will affect its performance.

For example, suppose that a manager selects the following characteristics to partition a Treasury/agency/corporate bond index:

Characteristic 1: effective duration range: (1) less than or equal to five years, and (2) greater than five years;

Characteristic 2: maturity range: (1) less than five years, (2) between five and 15 years, and (3) greater than or equal to 15 years;

Characteristic 3: market sectors: (1) Treasury, (2) agencies, and (3) corporates;

Characteristic 4: credit rating: (1) triple A, (2) double A, (3) single A, and (4) triple B.

The total number of cells would be equal to 72 ($= 2 \times 3 \times 3 \times 4$).

The objective, then, is to select from all the issues in the index one or more issues in each cell that can be used to represent the entire cell. The total dollar amount purchased of the issues from each cell will be based on the percentage of the index's total market value that the cell represents. For example, if 40% of the market value of all the issues in the index is made up of corporate bonds, 40% of the market value of the indexed portfolio should be composed of corporate bond issues.

The number of cells that the indexer uses will depend on the dollar amount of the portfolio to be indexed. In indexing a portfolio of less than $50 million, for example, using a large number of cells would require purchasing odd lots of issues. This increases the cost of buying the issues to represent a cell and thus would increase the tracking error. Reducing the number of cells to overcome this problem increases tracking error risk of index mismatch because the characteristics of the indexed portfolio may differ materially from those of the index.

Optimization Approach

In the **optimization approach to indexing,** the money manager seeks to design an indexed portfolio that will match the cell breakdown as just described, and satisfy other constraints, but also optimize some objective. An objective might be to maximize the portfolio yield, to maximize convexity, or to maximize expected total returns.[13] Constraints other than matching the cell breakdown might include not purchasing more than a specified amount of one issuer or group of issuers, or overweighing certain sectors for enhanced indexing (discussed later).

The computational technique used to derive the optimal solution to the indexing problem in this approach is mathematical programming. When the objective function that the indexer seeks to optimize is a linear function, linear programming (a specific form of mathematical programming) is used. If the objective function is quadratic, the particular mathematical programming technique used is quadratic programming.

---

[13]For a mathematical presentation of this approach as well as the variance minimization approach, see Christina Seix and Ravi Akoury, "Bond Indexation: The Optimal Quantitative Approach," *Journal of Portfolio Management,* Spring 1986, pp. 50–53. For an illustration, see Philip Galdi, "Indexing Fixed Income Portfolios," in Fabozzi and Garlicki (eds.), *Advances in Bond Analysis and Portfolio Strategies.*

Variance Minimization Approach

The **variance minimization approach to indexing** is by far the most complex of the methodologies. This approach requires using historical data to estimate the variance of the tracking error. This is done by estimating a price function for every issue in the index. The price function is estimated on the basis of two sets of factors: (1) the cash flows from the issue discounted at the theoretical spot rates, and (2) other factors, such as the duration or sector characteristics discussed earlier. Using a large universe of issues and statistical techniques, the price function is estimated from historical data. When the price function for each issue is obtained, a variance equation for the tracking error can be constructed. The objective then is to minimize the variance of the tracking error in constructing the indexed portfolio. As the variance is a quadratic function (the difference between the benchmark return and the indexed portfolio's return, squared), quadratic programming is used to find the optimal indexed portfolio in terms of minimized tracking error. The biggest problem with this approach is that estimating the price function from historical data is very difficult in the Treasury market, let alone the corporate market or the new issue market. Also, the price function may not be stable.

Although the stratified sampling (or cell) approach seems to be the easiest to use, it is extremely difficult to implement when large, diversified portfolios are taken as the benchmark. In this case, many cells are required, and the problem becomes complex. Also, because the handpicking of issues to match each cell is subjective, tracking error may result. Mathematical programming reduces the complexity of the problem when well-defined constraints are employed, allowing the indexer to analyze large quantities of data optimally.

LOGISTICAL PROBLEMS IN IMPLEMENTING AN INDEXING STRATEGY[14]

An indexer faces several logistical problems in constructing an indexed portfolio. First, the prices for each issue used by the organization that publishes the index may not be execution prices available to the indexer. In fact, they may be materially different from the prices offered by some dealers. In addition, the prices used by organizations reporting the value of indexes are based on bid prices. Dealer ask prices, however, are the ones that the money manager would have to transact at when constructing or rebalancing the indexed portfolio. Thus there will be a bias between the performance of the index and the indexed portfolio that is equal to the bid–ask spread.

Furthermore, there are logistical problems unique to certain sectors in the bond market. Consider first the corporate bond market. There are typically about 3,500 issues in the corporate bond sector of a broad-based index. Because of the illiquidity of this sector of the bond market, not only may the prices used by the organization that publishes the index be unreliable, but many of the issues may not even be available. Next, consider the mortgage-backed securities market. There are more than 300,000 agency pass-through issues. The organizations that publish indexes lump all these issues into a few hundred generic issues. The indexer is then faced with the difficult task of finding pass-through securities with the same risk–return profiles of these hypothetical issues.

---

[14]For a more detailed discussion, see Mossavar-Rahmani, *Bond Indexing*.

Finally, recall that the total return depends on the reinvestment rate available on coupon interest. If the organization publishing the index regularly overestimates the reinvestment rate, the indexed portfolio could underperform the index by 10 to 15 basis points a year.[15]

ENHANCED INDEXING

So far we have discussed straight or "plain vanilla" indexing. The objective of an **enhanced indexing strategy** is to replicate the total return performance of some predetermined index. In enhanced indexing (also called "indexing plus"), the objective is consistently to exceed the total return performance of the index by an amount sufficient to justify a higher management advisory fee and a higher level of risk of underperforming the index. The total return on the index becomes the minimum total return objective rather than the target total return. Thus enhanced indexing brings active strategies back into the portfolio management process, although they are assumed to employ only low-risk strategies.

Exhibit 18-5 summarizes the bond management risk spectrum versus a benchmark—indexing, enhanced indexing, and active strategies. Basically, any departure of a portfolio's composition from that of the benchmark represents the risk exposure of a portfolio. In plain vanilla indexing, the portfolio manager attempts to replicate the benchmark index as best as possible subject to the limitations discussed earlier regarding implementation. In enhanced indexing, there is a controlled departure of the portfolio's composition from that of the benchmark index. As the departure from the benchmark index becomes greater, the portfolio manager crosses over into the area of active management. Just where that crossover occurs differs from manager to manager.

EXHIBIT 18-5 Bond Management Risk Spectrum

Source: Kenneth E. Volpert, "Managing Indexed and Enhanced Indexed Portfolios," Chap. 12 in *Managing Fixed Income Portfolios*, ed. Frank J. Fabozzi (New Hope, PA: Frank J. Fabozzi Associates, 1997), p. 192, Exhibit 1.

---

[15]Fran Hawthorne, "The Battle of the Bond Indexes," *Institutional Investor,* April 1986, p. 122.

What are some of the strategies employed in enhanced indexing? We discussed most of them in Chapter 17. Any of the strategies employed would involve only those issues in the index. Another strategy for enhancing total return is to use securities not included in the index. For example, the broad-based indexes do not include derivative mortgage-backed securities such as collateralized mortgage obligations. If money managers pursuing enhanced index strategies believe that derivative mortgage-backed securities will outperform the agency pass-through securities in the index, they can substitute the former securities for the latter. Or the money manager may be able to create synthetic agency pass-through securities by using stripped mortgage-backed securities (interest-only and principal-only securities) that would exhibit better performance in certain interest-rate environments.

SUMMARY

Indexing a portfolio means designing a portfolio so that its total return will match the performance of some predetermined index. The indexing approach has been motivated by the poor historical performance of money managers and the lower management fees.

The three broad-based market indexes most commonly used by institutional investors are the Lehman Brothers Aggregate Index, the Salomon Brothers Broad-Based Investment-Grade Bond Index, and the Merrill Lynch Domestic Market Index. The performance of these broad-based indexes is highly correlated. Lehman Brothers, Salomon Brothers, and Merrill Lynch, as well as other firms, also produce specialized indexes.

Indexing requires selecting a bond index to be replicated and constructing a portfolio so as to minimize tracking error. The methodologies used to construct an indexed portfolio include the stratified sampling or cell approach, the optimization approach, and the variance minimization approach. In an enhanced indexing strategy, the performance of the index becomes the minimum return objective that the portfolio manager attempts to achieve.

Questions

1. What factors led to the use of bond indexing?
2. Is there any problem with a commercial bank using an indexing strategy to invest one-year funds on which the bank has agreed to pay a fixed rate?
3. What are the three most commonly used broad-based bond market indexes used by institutional investors?
4. What are the major sectors covered by the broad-based market indexes?
5. What types of mortgage-backed securities are included in a broad-based market index?
6. Why is a reinvestment rate assumption needed in order to calculate the monthly total return of an index?
7. What is a customized index?
8. What are the major findings of the McEnally–Boardman study on how diversification of bonds varies with portfolio size?
9. Why does tracking error occur in a bond indexing strategy?
10. What is the stratified sampling or cell approach to indexing?
11. What are the various types of enhanced bond indexing strategies?

CHAPTER 19

Liability Funding Strategies

Learning Objectives

After reading this chapter you will understand:

- the types of liabilities that an institution may face

- the two important dimensions of a liability: the amount and timing of the payment

- why the same factors that affect the risk of financial assets also affect liabilities

- the goals of asset/liability management

- the difference between an institution's accounting surplus, regulatory surplus, and economic surplus

- how assets are handled for accounting purposes

- how to use the duration of assets and liabilities to calculate the sensitivity of the economic surplus of an institution when interest rates change

- what a liability funding strategy is

- the risks associated with mismatching portfolio assets and liabilities

- what immunizing a portfolio is

- the basic principles of an immunization strategy and the role of duration in an immunization strategy

- the risks associated with immunizing a portfolio

- what a contingent immunization strategy is and the key factors in implementing such a strategy

- the two liability funding strategies when there are multiple liabilities: multiperiod liability immunization and cash flow matching

- the advantages and disadvantages of a multiple liability immunization strategy versus a cash flow matching strategy

- how liability funding strategies can be extended to cases in which the liabilities are not known with certainty

- what an active/immunization combination strategy is

In our discussion of the investment management process in Chapter 17, we explained that an investor must set objectives. For institutional investors, objectives are influenced by the nature of the institution's liabilities. Although investors are exposed to the same types of risks when they invest in financial assets, the nature of liabilities varies from institution to institution and is therefore the key factor in a portfolio manager's selection of the asset classes to include in a portfolio.

In this chapter we begin with the basic principles underlying the management of assets relative to liabilities, popularly referred to as **asset/liability management.** *We then describe several structured portfolio strategies, strategies that seek to match the performance of a predetermined benchmark. Bond portfolio indexing, discussed in Chapter 18, is an example of such a strategy. There, the benchmark is based on a bond index but may not actually satisfy the needs of the sponsoring institution. In this chapter we discuss* **liability funding strategies** *that select assets so that cash flows will equal or exceed the client's obligations. The client's liabilities, then, serve as the benchmark for portfolio performance. Specifically, when the liability is a single liability, an immunization strategy is employed. When there are multiple liabilities, there are two strategies to choose from: multiperiod immunization and cash flow matching.*

GENERAL PRINCIPLES OF ASSET/LIABILITY MANAGEMENT

The nature of an institutional investor's liabilities will dictate the investment strategy it will request its money manager to pursue. Depository institutions, for example, seek to generate income by the spread between the return that they earn on their assets and the cost of their funds. Consequently, banking is referred to as **spread banking.** Life insurance companies are in the spread business. Pension funds are not in the spread business, in that they themselves do not raise funds in the market. Sponsors of defined benefit pension plans seek to cover the cost of pension obligations at a minimum cost that is borne by the sponsor of the pension plan. Most investment companies face no explicit costs for the funds they acquire and must satisfy no specific liability obligations.

Classification of Liabilities

A **liability** is a cash outlay that must be made at a specific time to satisfy the contractual terms of an issued obligation. An institutional investor is concerned with both the amount and timing of liabilities, because its assets must produce the cash to meet any payments it has promised to make in a timely way. In fact, liabilities are classified according to the degree of certainty of their amount and timing, as shown in Exhibit 19-1. The classification assumes that the holder of the obligation will not cancel it prior to an actual or projected payout date.

The descriptions of cash outlays as either known or uncertain are undoubtedly broad. When we refer to a cash outlay as being uncertain, we do not mean that it cannot be predicted. There are some liabilities for which "law of large numbers" makes it easier to predict the timing and/or amount of cash outlays. This work is typically done

EXHIBIT 19-1	Classification of Liabilities of Institutional Investors	
Liability Type	*Amount of Cash Outlay*	*Timing of Cash Outlay*
I	Known	Known
II	Known	Uncertain
III	Uncertain	Known
IV	Uncertain	Uncertain

by actuaries, but even actuaries have difficulty predicting natural catastrophes such as floods and earthquakes.

Next we illustrate each type of risk category. The important thing to note is that just like assets, there are risks associated with liabilities. Some of these risks are affected by the same factors that affect asset risks.

Type I Liabilities   A type I liability is one for which both the amount and timing of the liabilities are known with certainty. An example is a liability in which an institution knows that it must pay $50,000 six months from now. Banks and thrifts know the amount that they are committed to pay (principal plus interest) on the maturity date of a fixed-rate deposit, assuming that the depositor does not withdraw funds prior to the maturity date.

Type I liabilities, however, are not limited to depository institutions. A major product sold by life insurance companies is a **guaranteed investment contract,** popularly referred to as a **GIC.** The obligation of the life insurance company under this contract is that for a sum of money (called a **premium**), it will guarantee an interest rate up to some specified maturity date. For example, suppose that a life insurance company, for a premium of $10 million, issues a five-year GIC agreeing to pay 10% compounded annually. The life insurance company knows that it must pay $16.11 million to the GIC policyholder in five years.[1]

Type II Liabilities   A type II liability is one for which the amount of cash outlay is known but the timing of the cash outlay is uncertain. The most obvious example of a type II liability is a life insurance policy. There are many types of life insurance policies, but the most basic type provides that for an annual premium, a life insurance company agrees to make a specified dollar payment to policy beneficiaries upon the death of the insured. Naturally, the timing of the insured's death is uncertain.

Type III Liabilities   A type III liability is one for which the timing of the cash outlay is known but the amount is uncertain. A two-year floating-rate CD in which the interest rate resets quarterly based on a market interest rate is an example. Not surprisingly, there are also floating-rate GICs; these also fall into the type III liabilities category.

Type IV Liabilities   A type IV liability is one in which there is uncertainty as to both the amount and timing of the cash outlay. There are numerous insurance products and pension obligations in this category. Probably the most obvious

---

[1] This amount is determined as follows: $\$10,000,000 \times (1.10)^5$.

examples are automobile and home insurance policies issued by property and casualty insurance companies. When, and if, a payment will have to be made to the policyholder is uncertain. Whenever damage is done to an insured asset, the amount of the payment that must be made is uncertain.

The liabilities of pension plans can also be type IV liabilities. In defined benefit plans, retirement benefits depend on the participant's income for a specified number of years before retirement and the total number of years the participant worked. This will affect the amount of the cash outlay. The timing of the cash outlay depends on when the employee elects to retire and whether the employee remains with the sponsoring plan until retirement. Moreover, both the amount and the timing will depend on how the employee elects to have payments made—over only the employee's life or those of the employee and spouse.

Liquidity Concerns

Because of uncertainty about the timing and/or the amount of the cash outlays, an institution must be prepared to have sufficient cash to satisfy its obligations. Also keep in mind that the entity that holds the obligation against the institution may have the right to change the nature of the obligation, perhaps incurring a penalty. For example, in the case of a CD, the depositor may request the withdrawal of funds prior to the maturity date. Typically, the deposit-accepting institution will grant this request but assess an early withdrawal penalty. In the case of certain types of investment companies, shareholders have the right to redeem their shares at any time. These rights add to the uncertainty of the liability from the point of view of the financial institution.

Similarly, some life insurance products have a cash surrender value. This means that at specified dates, the policyholder can exchange the policy for a lump-sum payment. Typically, the lump-sum payment will penalize the policyholder for turning in the policy. Some life insurance products have a loan value, which means that the policyholder has the right to borrow against the cash value of the policy. Both factors increase the uncertainty of the insurance company's liabilities.

In addition to uncertainty about the timing and amount of the cash outlays and the potential for the depositor or policyholder to withdraw cash early or borrow against a policy, an institution has to be concerned with possible reduction in cash inflows. In the case of a depository institution, this means the inability to obtain deposits. For insurance companies, it means reduced premiums because of the cancellation of policies. For certain types of investment companies, it means not being able to find new buyers for shares.

Surplus Management

The two goals of a financial institution are (1) to earn an adequate return on funds invested, and (2) to maintain a comfortable surplus of assets beyond liabilities. The task of managing funds of a financial institution to accomplish these goals is referred to as **asset/liability management** or **surplus management.** This task involves a trade-off between controlling the risk of a decline in the surplus and taking on acceptable risks in order to earn an adequate return on the funds invested. With respect to the risks, the manager must consider the risks of both the assets and the liabilities.

Institutions may calculate three types of surpluses: economic, accounting, and regulatory. The method of valuing assets and liabilities greatly affects the apparent health of a financial institution. Unrealistic valuation, although allowable under accounting procedures and regulations, is not sound investment practice.

Economic Surplus   The **economic surplus** of any entity is the difference between the market value of all its assets and the market value of its liabilities; that is,

economic surplus = market value of assets − market value of liabilities

Although the concept of a market value of assets may not seem unusual, one might ask: What is the market value of liabilities? This value is simply the present value of the liabilities, in which the liabilities are discounted at an appropriate interest rate. A rise in interest rates will therefore decrease the present value or market value of the liabilities; a decrease in interest rates will increase the present value or market value of liabilities. Thus the economic surplus can be expressed as

economic surplus = market value of assets − present value of liabilities

For example, consider an institution that has a portfolio consisting only of bonds and liabilities. Let's look at what happens to the economic surplus if interest rates rise. This will cause the bonds to decline in value, but it will also cause the liabilities to decline in value. Both the assets and liabilities decline, so the economic surplus can either increase, decrease, or not change. The net effect depends on the relative interest-rate sensitivity of the assets compared to the liabilities. Because duration is a measure of the responsiveness of cash flows to changes in interest rates, a duration can be calculated for liabilities in the same way in which it is calculated for assets. Thus the duration of liabilities measures their responsiveness to a change in interest rates.

If the duration of the assets is greater than the duration of the liabilities, the economic surplus will increase if interest rates fall. For example, suppose that the current market value of a portfolio of assets is equal to $100 million and the present value of liabilities is $90 million. Then the economic surplus is $10 million. Suppose that the duration of the assets is 5 and the duration of the liabilities is 3. Consider the following two scenarios:

Scenario 1: *Interest rates decline by 100 basis points.* Because the duration of the assets is 5, the market value of the assets will increase by approximately 5% or $5 million (5% × $100 million) to $105 million. The liabilities will also increase. If the duration of the liabilities is assumed to be 3, the present value of the liabilities will increase by $2.7 million (3% × $90 million) to $92.7 million. Thus the surplus increased from $10 million to $12.3 million.

Scenario 2: *Interest rates rise by 100 basis points.* Because the duration of the assets is 5, the market value of the assets will decrease by approximately 5%, to $95 million. The liabilities will also decrease. If the duration of the liabilities is 3, the present value of the liabilities will decrease by $2.7 million to $87.3 million. The surplus is then reduced to $7.7 million from $10 million.

The net effect on the surplus depends on the duration or interest-rate sensitivity of the assets and liabilities, so it is imperative that portfolio managers be able to measure this sensitivity for all assets and liabilities accurately.

Accounting Surplus   Institutional investors must prepare periodic financial statements. These financial statements must be prepared in accordance with **generally**

accepted accounting principles (GAAP). Thus the assets and liabilities reported are based on GAAP accounting. The accounting treatment for assets is governed by a relatively new accounting requirement, Statement of Financial Accounting Standards No. 115, more popularly referred to as FASB 115.[2] However, it does not deal with the accounting treatment for liabilities.

With respect to the financial reporting of assets, there are three possible methods for reporting: (1) amortized cost or historical cost, (2) market value, or (3) the lower of cost or market value. Despite the fact that the real cash flow is the same regardless of the accounting treatment, there can be substantial differences in the financial statements using these three methods.

In the **amortized cost method,** the value reported in the balance sheet reflects an adjustment to the acquisition cost for debt securities purchased at a discount or premium from their maturity value. This method is sometimes referred to as **book value accounting.** In the **market value accounting method,** the balance sheet reported value of an asset is its market value. When an asset is reported in the financial statements of an institution at its market value, it is said to be "marked to market." Finally, the **lower of cost** or **market method** requires comparison of market value to the amortized cost, with the lower of these two values reported in the balance sheet. The value reported cannot exceed the amortized cost.

FASB 115 specifies which of these three methods must be followed for assets. Specifically, the accounting treatment required for a security depends on how the security is classified. There are three classifications of investment accounts: (1) held to maturity, (2) available for sale, and (3) trading. The definition of each account is set forth in FASB 115 and we summarize each next.

The **held-to-maturity account** includes assets that the institution plans to hold until they mature. Obviously, the assets classified in this account cannot be common stock because they have no maturity. For all assets in the held-to-maturity account, the amortized cost method must be used.

An asset is classified as in the **available-for-sale account** if the institution does not have the ability to hold the asset to maturity or intends to sell it. An asset that is acquired for the purpose of earning a short-term trading profit from market movements is classified in the **trading account.** For all assets in the available-for-sale and trading accounts, market value accounting is used. Thus these two accounts more accurately reflect the economic condition of the assets held by the institution. Exhibit 19-2 summarizes the accounting treatment of assets as set forth by FASB 115.

EXHIBIT 19-2 Summary of Key Provisions of FASB 115

Account Classification	Accounting Method for Assets	Will Affect Surplus	Will Affect Reported Earnings
Held to maturity	Amortized cost	No	No
Available for sale	Market value	Yes	No
Trading	Market value	Yes	Yes

[2]FASB 115 was issued in May 1993 and became effective with fiscal years beginning after December 15, 1993.

When financial statements are prepared, the change in the value of assets must be accounted for. An unrealized gain or loss occurs when the asset's value has changed but the gain or loss is not realized because the asset is not sold. For example, if an asset has a market value of $100 at the beginning of an accounting period and is held in the portfolio at the end of the account period with a market value of $110, the unrealized gain is $10.

Any unrealized gain or loss affects the accounting surplus. Specifically, an unrealized gain increases the surplus and an unrealized loss reduces the accounting surplus. The unrealized gain or loss may or may not affect the reported earnings.

Under FASB 115, the accounting treatment for any unrealized gain or loss depends on the account in which the asset is classified. Specifically, any unrealized gain or loss is ignored for assets in the held-to-maturity account. Thus for assets in this account there is no affect on reported earnings or the accounting surplus. For the other two accounts, any unrealized gain or loss affects the accounting surplus as described previously. However, there is a difference as to how reported earnings are affected. For assets classified in the available-for-sale account, unrealized gains or losses are not included in reported earnings; in contrast, for assets classified in the trading account, any gains or losses are included in reported earnings. These provisions are summarized in Exhibit 19-2.

Regulatory Surplus Institutional investors that are regulated at the state or federal levels must provide financial reports to regulators based on regulatory accounting principles (RAP). RAP accounting for a regulated institution need not use the same rules as set forth by FASB 115 (i.e., GAAP accounting). Liabilities may or may not be reported at their present value, depending on the type of institution and the type of liability. The surplus as measured using RAP accounting, called **regulatory surplus,** may, as in the case of accounting surplus, differ materially from economic surplus.

IMMUNIZATION OF A PORTFOLIO TO SATISFY A SINGLE LIABILITY

In the balance of this chapter we focus on liability funding strategies. Tens of billions of dollars in pension monies went into these liability funding strategies in the early and mid-1980s when interest rates were high because of the strong incentive to reduce pension costs by locking in these rates. The insurance industry has also made widespread use of these strategies for their fixed-liability insurance products.

We begin with a strategy referred to as an **immunization strategy.** The person generally credited with pioneering this strategy, F. M. Reddington, defined immunization in 1952 as "the investment of the assets in such a way that the existing business is immune to a general change in the rate of interest."[3]

To comprehend the basic principles underlying the immunization of a portfolio against interest-rate changes so as to satisfy a single liability, consider the situation faced by a life insurance company that sells a guaranteed investment contract (GIC). Under this policy, for a lump-sum payment a life insurance company guarantees that

---

[3]The theory of immunization was first set forth in F. M. Reddington, "Review of the Principle of Life Office Valuation," *Journal of the Institute of Actuaries,* 1952, pp. 286–340.

specified dollars will be paid to the policyholder at a specified future date. Or, equivalently, the life insurance company guarantees a specified rate of return on the payment. For example, suppose that a life insurance company sells a GIC that guarantees an interest rate of 6.25% every six months (12.5% on a bond-equivalent yield basis) for 5.5 years (11 six-month periods). Also suppose that the payment made by the policyholder is $8,820,262. Then the value that the life insurance company has guaranteed the policyholder 5.5 years from now is

$$\$8,820,262(1.0625)^{11} = \$17,183,033$$

When investing the $8,820,262, the target accumulated value for the portfolio manager of the life insurance company is $17,183,033 after 5.5 years, which is the same as a target yield of 12.5% on a bond-equivalent basis.[4]

Suppose that the portfolio manager buys $8,820,262 par value of a bond selling at par with a 12.5% yield to maturity that matures in 5.5 years. Will the portfolio manager be assured of realizing the target yield of 12.5% or, equivalently, a target accumulated value of $17,183,033? As we explain in Chapter 3, the portfolio manager will realize a 12.5% yield only if the coupon interest payments can be reinvested at 6.25% every six months. That is, the accumulated value will depend on the reinvestment rate.

To demonstrate this, we will suppose that immediately after investing the $8,820,262 in the 12.5% coupon 5.5-year maturity bond, yields in the market change and stay at the new level for the remainder of the 5.5 years. Exhibit 19-3 illustrates what happens at the end of 5.5 years. The first column shows the new yield level. The second column shows the total coupon interest payments (which remains constant). The third column gives the interest on interest over the entire 5.5 years if the coupon interest payments are reinvested at the new yield level shown in the first column. The price of the bond at the end of 5.5 years shown in the fourth column is the par value. The fifth column is the accumulated value from all three sources: coupon interest, interest on interest, and bond price. The total return on a bond-equivalent yield basis is shown in the last column, according to the formula[5]

$$2\left[\left(\frac{\text{accumulated value}}{\$8,820,262}\right)^{1/11} - 1\right]$$

If yields do not change, so that the coupon payments can be reinvested at 12.5% (6.25% every six months), the portfolio manager will achieve the target accumulated value. If market yields rise, an accumulated value (total return) higher than the target accumulated value (target yield) will be achieved. This is because the coupon interest payments can be reinvested at a higher rate than the initial yield to maturity. Contrast this with what happens when the yield declines. The accumulated value (total return) will be less than the target accumulated value (target yield). *Therefore, investing in a coupon bond with a yield to maturity equal to the target yield and a maturity equal to the investment horizon does not assure that the target accumulated value will be achieved.*

---

[4]Actually, the life insurance company will not guarantee the interest rate that it expects to earn, but a lower rate. The spread between the interest rate earned and the interest rate it guarantees is the return for the risk of not achieving the target return.

[5]The procedure for calculating the total return is given in Chapter 3.

EXHIBIT 19-3   Accumulated Value and Total Return after 5.5 Years: 5.5-Year 12.5% Bond Selling to Yield 12.5%

Investment horizon (years): 5.5
Coupon rate: 0.125
Maturity (years): 5.5
Yield to maturity: 0.125
Price: 100
Par value purchased: $8,820,262
Purchase price: $8,820,262
Target accumulated value: $17,183,033

	After 5.5 Years				
New Yield[a]	*Coupon Interest*	*Interest on Interest*	*Price of Bond[b]*	*Accumulated Value*	*Total Return*
0.160	$6,063,930	$3,112,167	$8,820,262	$17,996,360	0.1340
0.155	6,063,930	2,990,716	8,820,262	17,874,908	0.1326
0.145	6,063,930	2,753,177	8,820,262	17,637,369	0.1300
0.140	6,063,930	2,647,037	8,820,262	17,521,230	0.1288
0.135	6,063,930	2,522,618	8,820,262	17,406,810	0.1275
0.130	6,063,930	2,409,984	8,820,262	17,294,086	0.1262
0.125	6,063,930	2,298,840	8,820,262	17,183,033	0.1250
0.120	6,063,930	2,189,433	8,820,262	17,073,625	0.1238
0.115	6,063,930	2,081,648	8,820,262	16,965,840	0.1225
0.110	6,063,930	1,975,462	8,820,262	16,859,654	0.1213
0.105	6,063,930	1,870,852	8,820,262	16,755,044	0.1201
0.100	6,063,930	1,767,794	8,820,262	16,651,986	0.1189
0.095	6,063,930	1,666,266	8,820,262	16,550,458	0.1178
0.090	6,063,930	1,566,246	8,820,262	16,450,438	0.1166
0.085	6,063,930	1,467,712	8,820,262	16,351,904	0.1154
0.080	6,063,930	1,370,642	8,820,262	16,254,834	0.1143
0.075	6,063,930	1,275,014	8,820,262	16,159,206	0.1132
0.070	6,063,930	1,180,808	8,820,262	16,065,000	0.1120
0.065	6,063,930	1,088,003	8,820,262	15,972,195	0.1109
0.060	6,063,930	996,577	8,820,262	15,880,769	0.1098
0.055	6,063,930	906,511	8,820,262	15,790,703	0.1087
0.050	6,063,930	817,785	8,820,262	15,701,977	0.1077

[a]Immediate change in yield.
[b]Maturity value.

Suppose that instead of investing in a bond maturing in 5.5 years the portfolio manager invests in a 15-year bond with a coupon rate of 12.5% that is selling at par to yield 12.5%. Exhibit 19-4 presents the accumulated value and total return if the market yield changes immediately after the bond is purchased and remains at the new yield level. The fourth column of the table is the market price of a 12.5% coupon 9.5-year bond (because 5.5 years have passed), assuming the market yields shown in the first column. If the market yield increases, the portfolio will fail to achieve the target

EXHIBIT 19-4 Accumulated Value and Total Return after 5.5 Years: 15-Year 12.5% Bond Selling to Yield 12.5%

Investment horizon (years): 5.5
Coupon rate: 0.1250
Maturity (years): 15
Yield to maturity: 0.1250
Price: 100
Par value purchased: $8,820,262
Purchase price: $8,820,262
Target accumulated value: $17,183,033

After 5.5 Years

New Yield[a]	Coupon Interest	Interest on Interest	Price of Bond	Accumulated Value	Total Return
0.160	$6,063,930	$3,112,167	$ 7,337,902	$16,514,000	0.1173
0.155	6,063,930	2,990,716	7,526,488	16,581,134	0.1181
0.145	6,063,930	2,753,177	7,925,481	16,742,587	0.1200
0.140	6,063,930	2,637,037	8,136,542	16,837,510	0.1211
0.135	6,063,930	2,522,618	8,355,777	16,942,325	0.1223
0.130	6,063,930	2,409,984	8,583,555	17,057,379	0.1236
0.125	6,063,930	2,298,840	8,820,262	17,183,033	0.1250
0.120	6,063,930	2,189,433	9,066,306	17,319,699	0.1265
0.115	6,063,930	2,081,648	9,322,113	17,467,691	0.1282
0.110	6,063,930	1,975,462	9,588,131	17,627,523	0.1299
0.105	6,063,930	1,870,852	9,864,831	17,799,613	0.1318
0.100	6,063,930	1,767,794	10,152,708	17,984,432	0.1338
0.095	6,063,930	1,666,266	10,452,281	18,182,477	0.1359
0.090	6,063,930	1,566,246	10,764,095	18,394,271	0.1382
0.085	6,063,930	1,467,712	11,088,723	18,620,366	0.1406
0.080	6,063,930	1,370,642	11,462,770	18,861,342	0.1431
0.075	6,063,930	1,275,014	11,778,867	19,117,812	0.1457
0.070	6,063,930	1,180,808	12,145,682	19,390,420	0.1485
0.065	6,063,930	1,088,003	12,527,914	19,679,847	0.1514
0.060	6,063,930	996,577	12,926,301	19,986,808	0.1544
0.055	6,063,930	906,511	13,341,617	20,312,058	0.1576
0.050	6,063,930	817,785	13,774,677	20,656,393	0.1609

[a]Immediate change in yield.

accumulated value; the opposite will be true if the market yield decreases: The accumulated value (total return) will exceed the target accumulated value (target yield).

The reason for this result can be seen in Exhibit 19-5, which summarizes the change in interest on interest and the change in price resulting from a change in the market yield. For example, if the market yield rises instantaneously by 200 basis points, from 12.5% to 14.5%, interest on interest will be $454,336 greater; however, the market price of the bond will decrease by $894,781. The net effect is that the accumulated value will be $440,445 less than the target accumulated value. The reverse

EXHIBIT 19-5   Change in Interest on Interest and Price Due to Interest Rate Change after 5.5 Years: 15-Year 12.5% Bond Selling to Yield 12.5%

New Yield	Change in Interest on Interest	Change in Price	Total Change in Accumulated Value
0.160	$ 813,327	−$1,482,360	−$ 669,033
0.155	692,875	−1,293,774	−601,898
0.145	454,336	−894,781	−440,445
0.140	338,197	−683,720	−345,523
0.135	223,778	−464,485	−240,707
0.130	111,054	−236,707	−125,654
0.125	0	0	0
0.120	−109,407	246,044	136,636
0.115	−217,192	501,851	284,659
0.110	−323,378	767,869	444,491
0.105	−427,989	1,044,569	616,581
0.100	−531,046	1,332,446	801,400
0.095	−632,574	1,632,019	999,445
0.090	−732,594	1,943,833	1,211,239
0.085	−831,128	2,268,461	1,437,333
0.080	−928,198	2,606,508	1,678,309
0.075	−1,023,826	2,958,605	1,934,779
0.070	−1,118,032	3,325,420	2,207,388
0.065	−1,210,838	3,707,652	2,496,814
0.060	−1,302,263	4,106,039	2,803,776
0.055	−1,392,329	4,521,355	3,129,026
0.050	−1,481,055	4,954,415	3,473,360

will be true if the market yield decreases. The change in the price of the bond will more than offset the decline in the interest on interest, resulting in an accumulated value that exceeds the target accumulated value.

Now we can see what is happening to the accumulated value. There is a trade-off between interest rate (or price) risk and reinvestment risk. For this 15-year bond, the target accumulated value will be realized only if the market yield does not increase.

Because neither a coupon bond with the same maturity nor a bond with a longer maturity ensures realization of the target accumulated value, perhaps a bond with a maturity shorter than 5.5 years will. Consider a 12.5% bond with six months remaining to maturity selling at par. Exhibit 19-6 shows the accumulated value and total return over the 5.5-year investment horizon. The second column shows the accumulated value after six months. The third column shows the value that is accumulated after 5.5 years by reinvesting the value accumulated after six months at the yield shown in the first column; that is,

$$\$9,371,528\left(1 + \frac{\text{new yield}}{2}\right)^2$$

EXHIBIT 19-6 Accumulated Value and Total Return: Six-Month, 12.5% Bond Selling to Yield 12.5%

Investment horizon (years): 5.5
Coupon rate: 0.125
Maturity (years): 0.5
Yield to maturity: 0.125
Price: 100
Par value purchased: $8,820,262
Purchase price: $8,820,262
Target accumulated value: $17,183,033

		After 5.5 Years	
New Yield[a]	After 6 Months	Accumulated Value	Total Return
0.160	$9,371,528	$20,232,427	0.1568
0.155	9,371,528	19,768,932	0.1523
0.145	9,371,528	18,870,501	0.1432
0.140	9,371,528	18,435,215	0.1386
0.135	9,371,528	18,008,986	0.1341
0.130	9,371,528	17,591,647	0.1295
0.125	9,371,528	17,183,033	0.1250
0.120	9,371,528	16,782,980	0.1205
0.115	9,371,528	16,391,330	0.1159
0.110	9,371,528	16,007,924	0.1114
0.105	9,371,528	15,632,609	0.1068
0.100	9,371,528	15,265,232	0.1023
0.095	9,371,528	14,905,644	0.0977
0.090	9,371,528	14,553,697	0.0932
0.085	9,371,528	14,209,247	0.0886
0.080	9,371,528	13,872,151	0.0841
0.075	9,371,528	13,542,270	0.0795
0.070	9,371,528	13,219,466	0.0749
0.065	9,371,528	12,903,604	0.0704
0.060	9,371,528	12,594,550	0.0658
0.055	9,371,528	12,292,175	0.0613
0.050	9,371,528	11,996,349	0.0567

[a]Immediate change in yield.

By investing in this six-month bond, the portfolio manager incurs no interest-rate risk, although there is reinvestment risk. The target accumulated value will be achieved only if the market yield remains at 12.5% or rises. Once again, the portfolio manager is not assured of achieving the target accumulated value.

If we assume there is a one-time instantaneous change in the market yield, is there a coupon bond that the portfolio manager can purchase to assure the target accumulated value whether the market yield rises or falls? The portfolio manager should look for a coupon bond so that however the market yield changes, the change in the interest on interest will be offset by the change in the price.

Consider, for example, an eight-year 10.125% coupon bond selling at 88.20262 to yield 12.5%. Suppose that $10,000,000 of par value of this bond is purchased for $8,820,262. Exhibit 19-7 provides the same information for this bond as Exhibits 19-3 and 19-4 did for the previous bonds. Looking at the last two columns, we see that the accumulated value and the total return are never less than the target accumulated value and the target yield. Thus the target accumulated value is assured regardless of

EXHIBIT 19-7 Accumulated Value and Total Return: Eight-Year 10.125% Bond Selling to Yield 12.5%

Investment horizon (years): 5.5
Coupon rate: 0.10125
Maturity (years): 8
Yield to maturity: 0.125
Price: 88.20262
Par value purchased: $10,000,000
Purchase price: $8,820,262
Target accumulated value: $17,183,033

	After 5.5 Years				
New Yield[a]	Coupon Interest	Interest on Interest	Price of Bond	Accumulated Value	Total Return
0.160	$5,568,750	$2,858,028	$ 8,827,141	$17,253,919	0.1258
0.155	5,568,750	2,746,494	8,919,852	17,235,096	0.1256
0.145	5,568,750	2,528,352	9,109,054	17,206,156	0.1253
0.140	5,568,750	2,421,697	9,205,587	17,196,034	0.1251
0.135	5,568,750	2,316,621	9,303,435	17,188,807	0.1251
0.130	5,568,750	2,213,102	9,402,621	17,184,473	0.1250
0.125	5,568,750	2,111,117	9,503,166	17,183,033	0.1250
0.120	5,568,750	2,010,644	9,605,091	17,184,485	0.1250
0.115	5,568,750	1,911,661	9,708,420	17,188,831	0.1251
0.110	5,568,750	1,814,146	9,813,175	17,196,071	0.1251
0.105	5,568,750	1,718,078	9,919,380	17,206,208	0.1253
0.100	5,568,750	1,623,436	10,027,059	17,219,245	0.1254
0.095	5,568,750	1,530,199	10,136,236	17,235,185	0.1256
0.090	5,568,750	1,438,347	10,246,936	17,254,033	0.1258
0.085	5,568,750	1,347,859	10,359,184	17,275,793	0.1260
0.080	5,568,750	1,258,715	10,473,006	17,300,472	0.1263
0.075	5,568,750	1,170,897	10,588,428	17,328,075	0.1266
0.070	5,568,750	1,084,383	10,705,477	17,358,610	0.1270
0.065	5,568,750	999,156	10,824,180	17,392,086	0.1273
0.060	5,568,750	915,197	10,944,565	17,428,511	0.1277
0.055	5,568,750	832,486	11,066,660	17,467,895	0.1282
0.050	5,568,750	751,005	11,190,494	17,510,248	0.1268

[a]Immediate change in yield.

EXHIBIT 19-8 Change in Interest on Interest and Price Due to Interest Rate Change after 5.5 Years: Eight-Year 10.125% Bond Selling to Yield 12.5%

New Yield	Change in Interest on Interest	Change in Price	Total Change in Accumulated Value
0.160	$ 746,911	−$ 676,024	$ 70,887
0.155	635,377	−583,314	52,063
0.145	417,235	−394,112	23,123
0.140	310,580	−297,579	13,001
0.135	205,504	−199,730	5,774
0.130	101,985	−100,544	1,441
0.125	0	0	0
0.120	−100,473	101,925	1,452
0.115	−199,456	205,254	5,798
0.110	−296,971	310,010	13,038
0.105	−393,039	416,215	23,176
0.100	−487,681	523,894	36,212
0.095	−580,918	633,071	52,153
0.090	−672,770	743,771	71,000
0.085	−763,258	856,019	92,760
0.080	−852,402	969,841	117,439
0.075	−940,221	1,085,263	145,042
0.070	−1,026,734	1,202,311	175,578
0.065	−1,111,961	1,321,014	209,053
0.060	−1,195,921	1,441,399	245,478
0.055	−1,278,632	1,563,494	284,862
0.050	−1,360,112	1,687,328	327,216

what happens to the market yield. Exhibit 19-8 shows why. When the market yield rises, the change in the interest on interest more than offsets the decline in price. When the market yield declines, the increase in price exceeds the decline in interest on interest.

Let's look at the characteristic of this bond that seems to assure that the target accumulated value will be realized regardless of how the market yield changes. The duration for each of the four bonds we have considered is shown in Exhibit 19-9. Recall from our earlier discussion of duration in this book that there is modified duration

EXHIBIT 19-9 Modified Durations of Selected Bonds

Bond	Modified Duration
5.5-year 12.5% coupon, selling at par	3.90
15-year 12.5% coupon, selling at par	6.70
6-month 12.5% coupon, selling at par	0.48
8-year 10.125% coupon, selling for 88.20262	5.18

and effective duration. Because the bonds in our illustration are all assumed to be option-free bonds, modified duration is used. However, when portfolios include securities with embedded options, the effective duration is used. Throughout the remainder of the discussion in this chapter, when we refer to *duration* we mean the appropriate measure of duration given the types of securities in the portfolio. For most institutional portfolios, this will typically be effective duration.

Given the duration for each bond as shown in Exhibit 19-9, let's compare them to the duration of the liability. This is a simple liability because there is only one cash payment at the maturity date and it is assumed that there is no embedded option in the liability. For an asset or a liability with only one cash flow, the duration is equal to the number of years to maturity divided by one plus one-half the yield. If the number of years to maturity is 5.5 years and the yield for a 5.5-year liability is 12.5%, then the duration is 5.5 divided by one plus 0.0625, or 5.18. We can see from Exhibit 19-9 that the duration of the eight-year 10.125% coupon issue has the same duration as the liability. This is the bond that assured immunization in our illustration.

This equality of the duration of the asset and the duration of the liability is the key to immunization. Generalizing this observation to bond portfolios from individual bonds, the key is: *To immunize a portfolio's target accumulated value (target yield), a portfolio manager must construct a bond portfolio such that (1) the duration of the portfolio is equal to the duration of the liability, and (2) the present value of the cash flow from the portfolio equals to the present value of the future liability.*

Often in discussions of immunization, the condition for immunization is cast in terms of Macaulay duration, a concept discussed in Chapter 4. The reason for the focus on Macaulay duration is that the bonds and liabilities are assumed to be option-free so that modified duration is appropriate and therefore from the relationship between modified duration and Macaulay duration, the analysis can be cast in terms of the latter.

Rebalancing an Immunized Portfolio

Our illustrations of the principles underlying immunization assume a one-time instantaneous change in the market yield. In practice, the market yield will fluctuate over the investment horizon. As a result, the duration of the portfolio will change as the market yield changes. In addition, the duration will change simply because of the passage of time.

Even in the face of changing market yields, a portfolio can be immunized if it is rebalanced so that its duration is equal to the duration of the liability's remaining time. For example, if the liability is initially 5.5 years, the initial portfolio should have a duration of 5.5 years. After six months the liability will be five years, but the duration of the portfolio will probably be different from five years. This is because duration depends on the remaining time to maturity and the new level of yields, and there is no reason why the change in these two values should reduce the duration by exactly six months. Thus the portfolio must be rebalanced so that its duration is five years. Six months later the portfolio must be rebalanced again so that its duration will equal 4.5 years. And so on.

How often should the portfolio be rebalanced to adjust its duration? On the one hand, the more frequent rebalancing increases transactions costs, thereby reducing the likelihood of achieving the target yield. On the other hand, less frequent rebalancing will result in the duration wandering from the target duration, which will also reduce the likelihood of achieving the target yield. Thus the portfolio manager faces a trade-off: Some transactions costs must be accepted to prevent the duration from wandering too far from its target, but some maladjustment in the duration must be accepted or transactions costs will become prohibitively high.

Immunization Risk

The sufficient condition for the immunization of a single liability is that the duration of the portfolio be equal to the duration of the liability. However, a portfolio will be immunized against interest-rate changes only if the yield curve is flat and any changes in the yield curve are parallel changes (i.e., interest rates move either up or down by the same number of basis points for all maturities). Recall from Chapter 4 that duration is a measure of price volatility for parallel shifts in the yield curve. If there is a change in interest rates that does not correspond to this shape-preserving shift, matching the portfolio's duration to the liability's duration will not assure immunization. That is, the target yield will no longer be the minimum total return for the portfolio.

As there are many duration-matched portfolios that can be constructed to immunize a liability, is it possible to construct one that has the lowest risk of not realizing the target yield? That is, in light of the uncertain way in which the yield curve may shift, is it possible to develop a criterion for minimizing the risk that a duration-matched portfolio will not be immunized? Fong and Vasicek[6] and Bierwag, Kaufman, and Toevs[7] explore this question. Exhibit 19-10 illustrates how to minimize immunization risk.

The spikes in the two panels of Exhibit 19-10 represent actual portfolio cash flows. The taller spikes depict the actual cash flows generated by securities that have matured, and the smaller spikes represent coupon payments. Portfolios A and B are both composed of two bonds with a portfolio's duration equal to the liability's duration. Portfolio A is, in effect, a barbell portfolio, one composed of short and long maturities and interim coupon payments. For portfolio B the two bonds mature very close to the date the liability is due, and the coupon payments are nominal over the investment horizon. Portfolio B is, in effect, a bullet portfolio.

We can now see why the barbell portfolio should be riskier than the bullet portfolio. Assume that both portfolios have durations equal to the liability's duration, so that each is immune to parallel changes in the yield curve. Suppose that the yield curve changes in a nonparallel way so that short-term interest rates decline while long-term interest rates increase. Both portfolios would then produce an accumulated value at the liability due date that is below the target accumulated value, because they would experience a capital loss owing to the higher long-term interest rate and less interest on interest resulting from the lower reinvestment rate when the short-term interest rate declines.

The accumulated value for the barbell portfolio at the liability due date, however, would miss the target accumulated value by more than the bullet portfolio. There are

[6]H. Gifford Fong and Oldrich Vasicek, "A Risk Minimizing Strategy for Multiple Liability Immunization," *Journal of Finance*, December 1984, pp. 1541–1546.
[7]G. O. Bierwag, George K. Kaufman, and Alden Toevs, "Bond Immunization and Stochastic Process Risk," working paper, Center for Capital Market Research, University of Oregon, July 1981.

EXHIBIT 19-10   Immunization Risk Measure

(a) Portfolio A: High-Risk Immunized Portfolio

Portfolio cash flow

$T = 0$
Current date

$T = H$
Liablity due date

Time

Note:
  Portfolio duration matches liability duration.
  Portfolio's cash flow dispersed around the liability due date.

(b) Portfolio B: Low-Risk Immunized Portfolio

Portfolio cash flow

$T = 0$
Current date

$T = H$
Liablity due date

Time

Note:
  Portfolio duration matches liability duration.
  Portfolio's cash flow concentrated around liability due date.

two reasons for this. First, the lower reinvestment rates are experienced on the barbell portfolio for larger interim cash flows over a longer time period than on the bullet portfolio. Second, the portion of the barbell portfolio still outstanding at the end of the liability due date is much longer than the maturity of the bullet portfolio, resulting in a greater capital loss for the barbell than for the bullet. Thus the bullet portfolio has less risk exposure than the barbell portfolio to any changes in the interest-rate structure that might occur.

What should be evident from this analysis is that immunization risk is the risk of reinvestment. The portfolio that has the least reinvestment risk will have the least immunization risk. When there is a high dispersion of cash flows around the liability due date, the portfolio is exposed to high reinvestment risk. When the cash flows are concentrated around the liability due date, as in the case of the bullet portfolio, the portfolio is subject to low reinvestment risk.

Fong and Vasicek have developed a measure of immunization risk. They have demonstrated that if the yield curve shifts in any arbitrary way, the relative change in the portfolio value will depend on the product of two terms. The first term depends solely on the characteristics of the investment portfolio. The second term is a function of interest-rate movement only. The second term characterizes the nature of the change in the shape of the yield curve. Because that change will be impossible to predict a priori, it is not possible to control for it. The first term, however, can be controlled for when constructing the immunized portfolio, because it depends solely on the composition of the portfolio. This first term, then, is a measure of risk for immunized portfolios and is equal to

$$\frac{CF_1(1 - H)^2}{1 + y} + \frac{CF_2(2 - H)^2}{(1 + y)^2} + \cdots + \frac{CF_n(n - H)^2}{(1 + y)^n}$$

where:

CF_t = cash flow of the portfolio at time period t
H = length (in years) of the investment horizon or liability due date
y = yield for the portfolio
n = time to receipt of the last cash flow

The immunization risk measure agrees with our earlier graphic analysis of the relative risk associated with a barbell and a bullet portfolio. For the barbell portfolio (portfolio A in Exhibit 19-10), the portfolio's cash flow payments are widely dispersed in time and the immunization risk measure would be high. The portfolio cash flow payments for the bullet portfolio (portfolio B in Exhibit 19-10) are close to the liability due date, so the immunization risk measure is low.

Notice that if all the cash flows are received at the liability due date, the immunization risk measure is zero. In such a case the portfolio is equivalent to a pure discount security (zero-coupon security) that matures on the liability due date. If a portfolio can be constructed that replicates a pure discount security maturing on the liability due date, that portfolio will be the one with the lowest immunization risk. Typically, however, it is not possible to construct such an ideal portfolio.

The objective in constructing an immunized portfolio, then, is to match the portfolio's duration to the liability's duration and select the portfolio that minimizes the immunization risk. The immunization risk measure can be used to construct approximate confidence intervals for the target yield and the target accumulated value.

Zero-Coupon Bonds and Immunization

So far we have dealt with coupon bonds. An alternative approach to immunizing a portfolio against changes in the market yield is to invest in zero-coupon bonds with a maturity equal to the investment horizon. This is consistent with the basic principle of immunization, because the duration of a zero-coupon bond is equal to the liability's duration. However, in practice, the yield on zero-coupon bonds is typically lower than the yield on coupon bonds. Thus using zero-coupon bonds to fund a bullet liability requires more funds, because a lower target yield (equal to the yield on the zero-coupon bond) is being locked in.

Suppose, for example, that a portfolio manager must invest funds to satisfy a known liability of $20 million five years from now. If a target yield of 10% on a bond-equivalent basis (5% every six months) can be locked in using zero-coupon Treasury bonds, the funds necessary to satisfy the $20 million liability will be $12,278,260, the present value of $20 million using a discount rate of 10% (5% semiannually).

Suppose, instead, that by using coupon Treasury securities, a target yield of 10.3% on a bond-equivalent basis (5.15% every six months) is possible. Then the funds needed to satisfy the $20 million liability will be $12,104,240, the present value of $20 million discounted at 10.3% (5.15% semiannually). Thus a target yield higher by 30 basis points would reduce the cost of funding the $20 million by $174,020

($12,278,260 − $12,104,240). But the reduced cost comes at a price—the risk that the target yield will not be achieved.

Credit Risk and the Target Yield

The target yield may not be achieved if any of the bonds in the portfolio default or decrease in value because of credit quality deterioration. Restricting the universe of bonds that may be used in constructing an immunized portfolio to Treasury securities eliminates credit risk. The target yield that can be achieved, however, will be lower than that for bonds with credit risk, so that the cost of funding a liability would be increased.

In most immunization applications, the client specifies an acceptable level of credit risk. Issues selected for the immunized portfolio are then restricted to those with that quality rating or higher. The more credit risk the client is willing to accept, the higher the achievable target yield, but the greater the risk that the immunized portfolio will fail to meet that target yield because of defaulted or downgraded issues. After the minimum credit risk is specified and the immunized portfolio is constructed, the portfolio manager must then monitor the individual issues for possible decreases in credit quality. Should an issue be downgraded below the minimum quality rating, that issue must be sold or the acceptable level of credit risk changed.

Call Risk

When the universe of acceptable issues includes corporate bonds, the target yield may be jeopardized if a callable issue is included that is subsequently called. Call risk can be avoided by restricting the universe of acceptable bonds to noncallable bonds and deep-discount callable bonds. This strategy does not come without a cost. Because noncallable and deep-discount bonds offer lower yields in a low-interest-rate environment, restricting the universe to these securities reduces the achievable target yield and therefore increases the cost of funding a liability. Also, it may be difficult to find acceptable noncallable bonds.

An immunized portfolio that includes callable bond issues must be carefully monitored so that issues likely to be called are sold and replaced with bond issues that have a lower probability of being called.

Constructing the Immunized Portfolio

When the universe of acceptable issues is established and any constraints are imposed, the portfolio manager has a large number of possible securities from which to construct an initial immunized portfolio and from which to select to rebalance an immunized portfolio. An objective function can be specified, and a portfolio that optimizes the objective function using mathematical programming tools can be determined. A common objective function, given the risk of immunization discussed earlier, is to minimize the immunization risk measure.[8]

---

[8]For a discussion of alternative objective functions, see H. Gifford Fong and Frank J. Fabozzi, *Fixed Income Portfolio Management* (Homewood, IL: Dow Jones–Irwin, 1985), Chapter 6; Peter C. Christensen and Frank J. Fabozzi, "Bond Immunization: An Asset Liability Optimization Strategy," Chapter 31 in Frank J. Fabozzi and Irving M. Pollack (eds.), *The Handbook of Fixed Income Securities,* (Homewood, IL: Dow Jones–Irwin, 1987); and Peter C. Christensen and Frank J. Fabozzi, "Dedicated Bond Portfolios," Chapter 32 in Frank J. Fabozzi (ed.), *The Handbook of Fixed Income Securities,* 3rd ed. (Homewood, IL: Business One-Irwin, 1991).

Contingent Immunization

Contingent immunization is a strategy that consists of identifying both the available immunization target rate and a lower safety net level return with which the investor would be minimally satisfied.[9] The money manager pursues an active portfolio strategy until an adverse investment experience drives the then-available potential return—the combined active return from actual past experience and immunized return from expected future experience—down to the safety net level. When that point is reached, the money manager is obligated to immunize the portfolio completely and lock in the safety net level return. As long as the safety net is not violated, the money manager can continue to manage the portfolio actively. When the immunization mode is activated because the safety net is violated, the manager can no longer return to the active mode, unless, of course, the contingent immunization plan is abandoned.

To illustrate this strategy, suppose that a client investing $50 million is willing to accept a 10% rate of return over a four-year investment horizon at a time when a possible immunized rate of return is 12%. The 10% return is called the **safety net return.** The difference between the immunized return and the safety net return is called the **safety cushion.** In our example, the safety cushion is 200 basis points (12% minus 10%).

Because the initial portfolio value is $50 million, the minimum target value at the end of four years, based on semiannual compounding, is $73,872,772 [$= \$50,000,000(1.05)^8$]. The rate of return at the time is 12%, so the assets required at this time to achieve the minimum target value of $73,872,772 represent the present value of $73,872,772 discounted at 12% on a semiannual basis, which is $43,348,691 [$= \$73,872,772/(1.06)^8$]. Therefore, the safety cushion of 200 basis points translates into an initial *dollar safety margin* of $6,651,309 ($50,000,000 − $43,348,691). Had the safety net of return been 11% instead of 10%, the safety cushion would have been 100 basis points and the initial dollar safety margin, $1,855,935. In other words, the smaller the safety cushion, the smaller the dollar safety margin. Exhibit 19-11 illustrates the contingency immunization strategy by showing the portfolio's initial value and for two scenarios six months later.

Initially, the money manager pursues an active portfolio strategy within the contingent immunization strategy. Suppose that the money manager puts all the funds into a 20-year 12% coupon bond selling at par to yield 12%. Let's look at what happens if the market yield falls to 9% at the end of six months. The value of the portfolio at the end of six months would consist of (1) the value of the 19.5-year 12% coupon bond at a 9% market yield and (2) six months of coupon interest. The price of the bond would increase from 100 to 127.34, so that the price of $50 million of these bonds would rise to $63.67 million. Coupon interest is $3 million (0.50 × 0.12 × $50 million). Thus the portfolio value at the end of six months is $66.67 million.

How much would be necessary to achieve the minimum target return of $73,872,772 if a portfolio can be immunized at the current interest rate of 9%? The required dollar value is found by computing the present value of the minimum target return at 9% for 3.5 years. The required dollar amount is $54,283,888 [$= \$73,872,772/(1.045)^7$].

The portfolio value of $66.67 million is greater than the required portfolio value of $54,283,888. The money manager can therefore continue to manage the portfolio

---

[9]Martin L. Leibowitz, "The Uses of Contingent Immunization," *Journal of Portfolio Management,* Fall 1981, pp. 51–55.

EXHIBIT 19-11   Contingency Immunization: Two Scenarios

Initial conditions:

$50 million investment

Achievable immunization rate: 12%   Initial investment:

Safety net return: 10%   20-year 12% coupon bond, selling at

Planning horizon: 4 years   par to yield 12%

	Interest Rates		
Scenario	Initial Rate 12%	Drops to 9% in 6 Months	Rises to 14.26% in 6 Months
Minimum target value to horizon	$73,872,772	$73,872,772	$73,872,772
Current portfolio value	50,000,000	66,670,000	45,615,776
Present value of minimum target	43,348,691	54,283,888	45,614,893
Dollar safety margin (current value − present value of minimum target)	6,651,309	12,386,112	883
Management strategy	Active	Active	Immunize

actively. The dollar safety margin is now $12,386,112 ($66,670,000 − $54,283,888). As long as the dollar safety margin is positive (i.e., the portfolio value is greater than the required portfolio value to achieve the minimum target value at the prevailing interest rate), the portfolio is actively managed.

Suppose that instead of declining to 9% in six months, interest rates rose to 14.26%. The market value of the bond would decline to $42,615,776. The portfolio value would then equal $45,615,776 (the market value of the bonds plus $3 million of coupon interest). The required dollar amount to achieve the minimum target value of $73,872,772 at the current interest rate (14.26%) would be $45,614,893 [= $73,872,772/(1.0713)^7]. The required dollar amount is approximately equal to the portfolio value (i.e., the dollar safety margin is almost zero). Thus the money manager would be required to immunize the portfolio to achieve the minimum target value (safety net return) over the investment horizon.

The three key factors in implementing a contingent immunization strategy are (1) establishing accurate immunized initial and ongoing available target returns, (2) identifying a suitable and immunizable safety net return, and (3) designing an effective monitoring procedure to ensure that the safety net return is not violated.

STRUCTURING A PORTFOLIO TO SATISFY MULTIPLE LIABILITIES

Thus far we have discussed immunizing a single liability. For pension funds, there are multiple liabilities that must be satisfied—payments to the beneficiaries of the pension fund. A stream of liabilities must also be satisfied for a life insurance company that sells an insurance policy requiring multiple payments to policyholders, such as an annuity policy. There are two strategies that can be used to satisfy a liability stream: (1) multiperiod immunization, and (2) cash flow matching.

Multiperiod Immunization

Multiperiod immunization is a portfolio strategy in which a portfolio is created that will be capable of satisfying more than one predetermined future liability regardless if interest rates change. Even if there is a parallel shift in the yield curve, Bierwag, Kaufman, and Toevs demonstrate that matching the duration of the portfolio to the duration of the liabilities is not a sufficient condition to immunize a portfolio seeking to satisfy a liability stream.[10] Instead, it is necessary to decompose the portfolio payment stream in such a way that each liability is immunized by one of the component streams. The key to understanding this approach is recognizing that the payment stream on the portfolio, not the portfolio itself, must be decomposed in this manner. There may be no actual bonds that would give the component payment stream.

In the special case of a parallel shift of the yield curve, Fong and Vasicek demonstrate the necessary and sufficient conditions that must be satisfied to assure the immunization of multiple liabilities[11]:

1. The portfolio's duration must equal the duration of the liabilities.
2. The distribution of durations of individual portfolio assets must have a wider range than the distribution of the liabilities.[12]
3. The present value of the cash flows from the bond portfolio must equal the present value of the liability stream.

However, these conditions will immunize only in the case of a parallel shift in the yield curve. To cope with the problem of failure to immunize because of nonparallel shifts in the yield curve, Fong and Vasicek generalize the immunization risk measure for a single liability discussed earlier in this chapter to the multiple liability case. An optimal immunization strategy is to minimize this immunization risk measure subject to the three constraints above (duration, dispersion of assets and liabilities, and equality of present value of asset cash flow and liability stream), as well as any other constraints that a client may impose.

In a series of articles, Reitano has explored the limitations of the parallel shift assumption.[13] He has also developed models that generalize the immunization of multiple liabilities to arbitrary yield curve shifts. His research makes it clear that classical multiple-period immunization can disguise the risks associated with nonparallel yield curve shifts and that a model that protects against one type of yield curve shift may allow a great deal of exposure and vulnerability to other types of shifts.

---

[10]G. O. Bierwag, George K. Kaufman, and Alden Toevs, "Immunization Strategies for Funding Multiple Liabilities," *Journal of Financial and Quantitative Analysis,* March 1983, pp. 113–124.

[11]Fong and Vasicek, "A Risk Minimizing Strategy for Multiple Liability Immunization."

[12]The reason for the second condition can be illustrated using an example. Suppose that a liability stream with 10 payments of $5 million each year is funded with a zero-coupon bond with a maturity (duration) equal to the duration of the liability stream. Suppose also that when the first $5 million payment is due, interest rates rise so that the value of the zero-coupon bond falls. Even though interest rates have increased, there is no offset to reinvestment income because the bond is a zero-coupon bond. Thus there is no assurance that the portfolio will generate sufficient cash flow to satisfy the remaining liabilities. In the case of a single liability, the second condition is satisfied automatically.

[13]Robert R. Reitano, "A Multivariate Approach to Immunization Theory," *Actuarial Research Clearing House,* Vol. 2, 1990; and "Multivariate Immunization Theory," *Transactions of the Society of Actuaries,* Vol. XLIII, 1991. For a detailed illustration of the relationship between the underlying yield curve shift and immunizations, see Robert R. Reitano, "Non-Parallel Yield Curve Shifts and Immunization," *Journal of Portfolio Management,* Spring 1992, pp. 36–43.

Cash Flow Matching

An alternative to multiperiod immunization is **cash flow matching.** This approach, also referred to as **dedicating a portfolio,** can be summarized as follows. A bond is selected with a maturity that matches the last liability stream. An amount of principal plus final coupon equal to the amount of the last liability stream is then invested in this bond. The remaining elements of the liability stream are then reduced by the coupon payments on this bond, and another bond is chosen for the new, reduced amount of the next-to-last liability. Going backward in time, this cash flow matching process is continued until all liabilities have been matched by the payment of the securities in the portfolio.

Exhibit 19-12 provides a simple illustration of this process for a five-year liability stream. Mathematical programming techniques can be employed to construct a least-cost cash flow matching portfolio from an acceptable universe of bonds.

The differences between the cash flow matching and multiperiod immunization strategies should be understood. First, unlike the immunization approach, the cash flow matching approach has no duration requirements. Second, with immunization, rebalancing is required even if interest rates do not change. In contrast, no rebalancing is necessary for cash flow matching except to delete and replace any issue whose quality rating has declined below an acceptable level. Third, there is no risk that the liabilities will not be satisfied (barring any defaults) with a cash flow–matched portfolio. For a portfolio constructed using multiperiod immunization, there is immunization risk due to reinvestment risk.

The differences just cited may seem to favor the use of cash flow matching. However, what we have ignored is the relative cost of the two strategies. Using the cost of the initial portfolio as an evaluation measure, Gifford Fong Associates has found that cash flow–matched portfolios, using a universe of corporate bonds rated at least double A, cost from 3% to 7% more in dollar terms than do multiperiod immunized portfolios. The reason cash flow matching is more expensive is that, typically, the matching of cash flows to liabilities is not perfect. This means that more funds than necessary must be set aside to match the liabilities. Optimization techniques used to design cash flow–matched portfolios assume that excess funds are reinvested at a conservative reinvestment rate. With multiperiod immunization, all reinvestment returns are assumed to be locked in at a higher target rate of return. Therefore, money managers face a trade-off in deciding between the two strategies: avoidance of the risk of not satisfying the liability stream under cash flow matching versus the lower cost attainable with multiperiod immunization.

In the basic cash flow–matching technique, only asset cash flows occurring prior to a liability date can be used to satisfy the liability. The technique has been extended to handle situations in which cash flows occurring both before and after the liability date can be used to meet a liability.[14] This technique, called **symmetric cash matching,** allows for the short-term borrowing of funds to satisfy a liability prior to the liability due date. The opportunity to borrow short term so that symmetric cash matching can be employed results in a reduction in the cost of funding a liability.

A popular variation of multiperiod immunization and cash flow matching to fund liabilities is one that combines the two strategies. This strategy, referred to as **combi-**

---

[14]T. Dessa Fabozzi, Tom Tong, and Yu Zhu, "Extensions of Dedicated Bond Portfolio Techniques," Chapter 44 in *The Handbook of Fixed Income Securities,* 3rd ed.

EXHIBIT 19-12 Cash Flow Matching Process

Assume: 5-year liability stream.
   Cash flow from bonds are annual.

Step 1:
Cash flow from bond A selected to satisfy L_5
   Coupons $= A_s$; Principal $= A_p$ and $A_s + A_p = L_5$
Unfunded liabilities remaining:

Step 2:
Cash flow from bond B selected to satisfy L_4
   Unfunded liability $= L_4 - A_s$
   Coupons $= B_s$; Principal $= B_p$ and $B_s + B_p = L_4 - A_s$
Unfunded liabilities remaining:

Step 3:
Cash flow from bond C selected to satisfy L_3
   Unfunded liability $= L_3 - A_s - B_s$
   Coupons $= C_s$; Principal $= C_p$ and $C_s + C_p = L_3 - A_s - B_s - C_s$
Unfunded liabilities remaining:

$L_1 - A_s - B_s - C_s \qquad L_2 - A_s - B_s - C_s$ Unfunded
                                                    Liability
                                                    ─────────
                                                      Time

```
├──────────┼──────────┤
0          1          2
```

Step 4:
Cash flow from bond D selected to satisfy L_2
   Unfunded liability $= L_2 - A_s - B_s - C_s$
   Coupons $= D_s$; Principal $= D_p$ and $D_s + D_p = L_2 - A_s - B_s - C_s$
Unfunded liabilities remaining:

$L_1 - A_s - B_s - C_s - D_s$ Unfunded
                              Liability
                              ─────────
                                Time

```
├──────────┤
0          1
```

Step 5:
Select bond E with a cash flow of $L_1 - A_s - B_s - C_s - D_s$

nation matching or **horizon matching,** creates a portfolio that is duration matched with the added constraint that it be cash matched in the first few years, usually five years. The advantage of combination matching over multiperiod immunization is that liquidity needs are provided for in the initial cash flow–matched period. Cash flow matching the initial portion of the liability stream reduces the risk associated with nonparallel shifts of the yield curve. The disadvantage of combination matching over multiperiod immunization is that the cost is slightly greater.

Within the immunization and dedicated cash flow strategies, some portfolio managers are permitted to manage the portfolio actively by entering into bond swaps to enhance portfolio performance. Obviously, only small bets can be made, to minimize the likelihood that the liability payments will not be satisfied.

EXTENSIONS OF LIABILITY FUNDING STRATEGIES

As we explained at the outset of this chapter, liabilities may be uncertain with respect to both timing and amount of the payment. In the techniques we have discussed in this chapter, we have assumed that the timing and the amount of the cash payment of liabilities are known with certainty. That is, we assume that the liabilities are deterministic.

We assume, moreover, that the cash flows from the assets are known with certainty, although you have learned that most non-Treasury securities have embedded options that permit the borrower or the investor to alter the cash flows. Thus the models presented in this chapter are referred to as **deterministic models,** because they assume that the liability payments and the asset cash flows are known with certainty.

Since the mid-1980s, a good number of models have been developed to handle real-world situations in which liability payments and/or asset cash flows are uncertain. Such models are called **stochastic models.**[15] Such models require that the portfolio manager incorporate an interest-rate model, that is, a model that describes the probability distribution for interest rates. Optimal portfolios then are solved for using a mathematical programming technique known as **stochastic programming.**

The complexity of stochastic models, however, has limited their application in practice. Nevertheless, they are gaining in popularity as more portfolio managers become comfortable with their sophistication. There is increasing awareness that stochastic models reduce the likelihood that the liability objective will not be satisfied and that transactions costs can be reduced through less frequent rebalancing of a portfolio derived from these models.

COMBINING ACTIVE AND IMMUNIZATION STRATEGIES

In our discussion of contingent immunization, the money manager is permitted to manage the portfolio actively until the safety net is violated. However, contingent immunization is not a combination or mixture strategy. The money manager is either in the immunization mode by choice or because the safety net is violated or in the active management mode. In contrast to an immunization strategy, an active/immunization combination strategy is a mixture of two strategies that are pursued by the money manager at the same point in time.

---

[15]For a review of such models, see Randall S. Hiller and Christian Schaack, "A Classification of Structured Bond Portfolio Modeling Techniques," *Journal of Portfolio Management,* Fall 1990, pp. 37–48.

The immunization component of this strategy could be either a single-liability immunization or a multiple-liability immunization using the techniques discussed earlier in this chapter. In the single-liability immunization case, an assured return would be established so as to serve to stabilize the portfolio's total return. In the multiple-liability immunization case, the component to be immunized would be immunized now, with new requirements, as they become known, taken care of through reimmunization. This would be an adaptive strategy in that the immunization component would be based on an initial set of liabilities and modified over time to changes in future liabilities (e.g., for actuarial changes for the liabilities in the case of a pension fund). The active portion would continue to be free to maximize expected return, given some acceptable risk level.

The following formula suggested by Gifford Fong Associates can be used to determine the portion of the initial portfolio to be managed actively, with the balance immunized[16]:

active component

$$= \frac{\text{immunization target rate } - \text{ minimum return established by client}}{\text{immunization target rate } - \text{expected worst case active return}}$$

In the formula it is assumed that the immunization target return is greater than either the minimum return established by the client or the expected worst-case return from the actively managed portion of the portfolio.

As an illustration, assume that the available immunization target return is 7% per year, the minimum return acceptable to the client is 5%, and the expected worst-case return for the actively managed portion of the portfolio is 2%. Then the percentage in the active portion of the portfolio would be

$$\text{active component} = \frac{0.07 - 0.05}{0.07 - 0.02} = 0.40 \text{ or } 40\%$$

Notice from the formula for determining the active component that for any given immunization target return, the smaller the minimum acceptable return to the client and the larger the expected worst-case active return, the larger will be the percentage allocated to active management. Since the return values in the formula change over time, the money manager must monitor these values constantly, adjusting and rebalancing the allocation between the immunized and active components as appropriate. As long as the worst-case scenario is not violated—that is, as long as the actual return experienced does not drop below the expected worst-case active return—the minimum return for the portfolio established by the client will be achieved.

SUMMARY

The nature of their liabilities, as well as regulatory considerations, determines the investment strategy pursued by all institutional investors. By nature, liabilities vary with respect to the amount and timing of their payment. The liabilities will generally fall into one of the four types shown in Exhibit 19-1.

Surplus management is a more appropriate description of the activity of asset/liability management of an institution. The economic surplus of any entity is the differ-

---

[16]*The Costs of Cash Flow Matching* (Santa Monica, CA: Gifford Fong Associates, 1981).

ence between the market value of all its assets and the present value of its liabilities. Institutional investors will pursue a strategy either to maximize economic surplus or to hedge economic surplus against any adverse change in market conditions. In addition to economic surplus, there are accounting surplus and regulatory surplus. The former is based on GAAP accounting, specifically, FASB 115, and the latter on RAP accounting. To the extent that these two surplus measures may not reflect the true financial condition of an institution, future financial problems may arise.

Liability funding strategies involve designing a portfolio to produce sufficient funds to satisfy liabilities whether or not interest rates change. When there is only one future liability to be funded, an immunization strategy can be used. An immunization strategy is designed so that as interest rates change, interest-rate risk and reinvestment risk will offset each other in such a way that the minimum accumulated value (or minimum rate of return) becomes the target accumulated value (or target yield). An immunization strategy requires that a money manager create a bond portfolio with a duration equal to the duration of the liability. Because immunization theory is based on parallel shifts in the yield curve, the risk is that a portfolio will not be immunized even if the duration-matching condition is satisfied. Immunization risk can be quantified so that a portfolio that minimizes this risk can be constructed.

When there are multiple liabilities to be satisfied, either multiperiod immunization or cash flow matching can be used. Multiperiod immunization is a duration-matching strategy that exposes the portfolio to immunization risk. The cash flow–matching strategy does not impose any duration requirement. Although the only risk that the liabilities will not be satisfied is that issues will be called or will default, the dollar cost of a cash flow–matched portfolio may be higher than that of a portfolio constructed using a multiperiod immunization strategy.

Liability funding strategies in which the liability payments and the asset cash flows are known with certainty are deterministic models. In a stochastic model, either the liability payments or the asset cash flows, or both, are uncertain. Stochastic models require specification of a probability distribution for the process that generates interest rates.

A combination of active and immunization strategies can be pursued. Allocation of the portion of the portfolio to be actively managed is based on the immunization target rate, the minimum return acceptable to the client, and the expected worst-case return from the actively managed portfolio. In a contingent immunization strategy, a money manager is either actively managing the portfolio or immunizing it. Because both strategies are not pursued at the same time, contingent immunization is not a combination or mixture strategy.

Questions

1. What are the two dimensions of a liability?
2. Why is it not always simple to estimate the liability of an institution?
3. Why is asset/liability management best described as surplus management?
4. a. What is the economic surplus of an institution?
   b. What is the accounting surplus of an institution?
   c. What is the regulatory surplus of an institution?
   d. Which surplus best reflects the economic well-being of an institution?
   e. Under what circumstances are all three surplus measures the same?

5. Suppose that the present value of the liabilities of some financial institution is $600 million and the surplus $800 million. The duration of the liabilities is equal to 5. Suppose further that the portfolio of this financial institution includes only bonds and the duration for the portfolio is 6.
   a. What is the market value of the portfolio of bonds?
   b. What does a duration of 6 mean for the portfolio of assets?
   c. What does a duration of 5 mean for the liabilities?
   d. Suppose that interest rates increase by 50 basis points; what will be the approximate new value for the surplus?
   e. Suppose that interest rates decrease by 50 basis points; what will be the approximate new value for the surplus?

6. a. Why is the interest-rate sensitivity of an institution's assets and liabilities important?
   b. In 1986, Martin Leibowitz of Salomon Brothers Inc. wrote a paper titled "Total Portfolio Duration: A New Perspective on Asset Allocation." What do you think a total portfolio duration means?

7. If an institution has liabilities that are interest-rate sensitive and invests in a portfolio of common stocks, can you determine what will happen to the institution's economic surplus if interest rates change?

8. The following quotes are taken from Phillip D. Parker (Associate General Counsel of the SEC), "Market Value Accounting—An Idea Whose Time Has Come?" in Elliot P. Williams (ed.), *Managing Asset/Liability Portfolios* (Charlottesville, VA: Association for Investment Management and Research, 1991), published prior to the passage of FASB 115: "The use of market value accounting would eliminate any incentive to sell or retain investment securities for reasons of accounting treatment rather than business utility." Explain why this statement is correct. (Note that in historical accounting a loss is recognized only when a security is sold.)

9. Indicate why you agree or disagree with the following statements.
   a. "Under FASB 115 all assets must be marked to market."
   b. "The greater the price volatility of assets classified in the held-to-maturity account, the greater the volatility of the accounting surplus and reported earnings."

10. What is meant by immunizing a bond portfolio?

11. a. What is the basic underlying principle in an immunization strategy?
    b. Why may the matching of the maturity of a coupon bond to the remaining time to maturity of a liability fail to immunize a portfolio?

12. Why must an immunized portfolio be rebalanced periodically?

13. What are the risks associated with a bond immunization strategy?

14. "I can immunize a portfolio simply by investing in zero-coupon Treasury bonds." Comment on this statement.

15. Three portfolio managers are discussing a strategy for immunizing a portfolio so as to achieve a target yield. Manager A, whose portfolio consists of Treasury securities and option-free corporates, stated that the duration of the portfolio should be constructed so that the Macaulay duration of the portfolio is equal to the number of years until the liability must be paid. Manager B, with the same types of securities in his portfolio as Manager A, feels that Manager A is wrong because the portfolio should be constructed so that the modified duration of the portfolio is equal to the modified duration of the liabilities. Manager C believes Manager B is correct. However, unlike the portfolios of Managers A and B, Manager C invests in mortgage-backed securities and callable corporate bonds.
    Discuss the position taken by each manager and explain why they are correct.

16. Why is there greater risk in a multiperiod immunization strategy than a cash flow–matching strategy?
17. a. What is a contingent immunization strategy?
    b. What is the safety net cushion in a contingent immunization strategy?
    c. Is it proper to classify a contingent immunization as a combination active/immunization strategy?
18. What is a combination matching strategy?
19. In a stochastic liability funding strategy, why is an interest-rate model needed?
20. Suppose that a client has granted a money manager permission to pursue an active/immunized combination strategy. Suppose further that the minimum return expected by the client is 9% and that the money manager believes that an achievable immunized target return is 4% and the worst possible return from the actively managed portion of the portfolio is 1%. Approximately how much should be allocated to the active component of the portfolio?
21. One of your clients, a newcomer to the life insurance business, questioned you about the following excerpt from Peter E. Christensen, Frank J. Fabozzi, and Anthony Lo-Faso, "Dedicated Bond Portfolios," Chapter 43 in Frank J. Fabozzi (ed.), *The Handbook of Fixed Income Securities* (Homewood, IL: Richard D. Irwin, 1991):

> For financial intermediaries such as banks and insurance companies, there is a well-recognized need for a complete funding perspective. This need is best illustrated by the significant interest-rate risk assumed by many insurance carriers in the early years of their Guaranteed Investment Contract (GIC) products. A large volume of compound interest (zero coupon) and simple interest (annual pay) GICs were issued in three- through seven-year maturities in the positively sloped yield-curve environment of the mid-1970s. Proceeds from hundreds of the GIC issues were reinvested at higher rates in the longer 10- to 30-year private placement, commercial mortgage, and public bond instruments. At the time, industry expectations were that the GIC product would be very profitable because of the large positive spread between the higher "earned" rate on the longer assets and the lower "credited" rate on the GIC contracts.
>
> By pricing GICs on a spread basis and investing the proceeds on a mismatched basis, companies gave little consideration to the rollover risk they were assuming in volatile markets. As rates rose dramatically in the late 1970s and early 1980s, carriers were exposed to disintermediation as GIC liabilities matured and the corresponding assets had 20 years remaining to maturity and were valued at only a fraction of their original cost.

Answer the following questions posed to you by your client.
  a. "It is not clear to me what risk an issuer of a GIC is facing. A carrier can invest the proceeds in assets offering a higher yield than they are guaranteeing to GIC policyholders, so what's the problem? Isn't it just default risk that can be controlled by setting tight credit standards?"
  b. "I understand that disintermediation means that when a policy matures, the funds are withdrawn from the insurance company by the policyholder. But why would a rise in interest rates cause GIC policyholders to withdraw their funds? The insurance company can simply guarantee a higher interest rate."
  c. "What do the authors mean by 'pricing GICs on a spread basis and investing the proceeds on a mismatched basis,' and what is this 'rollover risk' they are referring to?"

22. Suppose that a life insurance company sells a five-year guaranteed investment contract that guarantees an interest rate of 7.5% per year on a bond-equivalent yield basis (or equivalently, 3.75% every six months for the next 10 six-month periods). Also suppose that the payment made by the policyholder is $9,642,899. Consider the following three investments that can be made by the portfolio manager:

Bond X: Buy $9,642,899 par value of an option-free bond selling at par with a 7.5% yield to maturity that matures in five years.

Bond Y: Buy $9,642,899 par value of an option-free bond selling at par with a 7.5% yield to maturity that matures in 12 years.

Bond Z: Buy $10,000,000 par value of a six-year 6.75% coupon option-free bond selling at 96.42899 to yield 7.5%.

a. Holding aside the spread that the insurance company seeks to make on the invested funds, demonstrate that the target accumulated value to meet the GIC obligation five years from now is $13,934,413.

b. Complete Table A assuming that the manager invests in bond X and immediately following the purchase, yields change and stay the same for the five-year investment horizon.

c. Based on Table A, under what circumstances will the investment in bond X fail to satisfy the target accumulated value?

TABLE A Accumulated Value and Total Return after Five Years: Five-Year 7.5% Bond Selling to Yield 7.5%

Investment horizon (years): 5
Coupon rate: 7.50%
Maturity (years): 5
Yield to maturity: 7.50%
Price: 100.00000
Par value purchased: $9,642,899
Purchase price: $9,642,899
Target accumulated value: $13,934,413

New Yield (%)	Coupon	*After Five Years* Interest on Interest	Price of Bond	Accumulated Value	Total Return (%)
11.00	$3,616,087	$1,039,753	$9,642,899	$14,298,739	8.04
10.00	3,616,087				
9.00	3,616,087				
8.00	3,616,087				
7.50	3,616,087				
7.00	3,616,087				
6.00	3,616,087				
5.00	3,616,087				
4.00	3,616,087	343,427	9,642,899	13,602,414	7.00

d. Complete Table B, assuming that the manager invests in bond Y and immediately following the purchase, yields change and stay the same for the five-year investment horizon.

e. Based on Table B, under what circumstances will the investment in bond Y fail to satisfy the target accumulated value?

f. Complete Table C, assuming that the manager invests in bond Z and immediately following the purchase, yields change and stay the same for the five-year investment horizon.

g. Based on Table C, under what circumstances will the investment in bond Z fail to satisfy the target accumulated value?

h. What is the modified duration of the liability?

i. Complete the following table for the three bonds assuming that each bond is trading to yield 7.5%:

Bond	Modified Duration
Five-year, 7.5% coupon, selling at par	
12-year, 7.5% coupon, selling at par	
Six-year, 6.75% coupon, selling for 96.42899	

j. For which bond is the modified duration equal to the duration of the liability?

k. Why in this example can one focus on modified duration rather than effective duration?

TABLE B Accumulated Value and Total Return after Five Years: 12-Year 7.5% Bond Selling to Yield 7.5%

Investment horizon (years): 5
Coupon rate: 7.5%
Maturity (years): 12
Yield to maturity: 7.5%
Price: 100.00000
Par value purchased: $9,642,899
Purchase price: $9,642,899
Target accumulated value: $13,934,413

	After Five Years				
New Yield (%)	Coupon	Interest on Interest	Price of Bond	Accumulated Value	Total Return (%)
11.00	$3,616,087	$1,039,753	$ 8,204,639	$12,680,479	5.55
10.00	3,616,087				
9.00	3,616,087				
8.00	3,616,087				
7.50	3,616,087				
7.00	3,616,087				
6.00	3,616,087				
5.00	3,616,087				
4.00	3,616,087	343,427	11,685,837	15,645,352	9.92

TABLE C Accumulated Value and Total Return after Five Years:
Six-Year 6.75% Bond Selling to Yield 7.5%

Investment horizon (years): 5
Coupon rate: 6.75%
Maturity (years): 6
Yield to maturity: 7.5%
Price: 96.42899
Par value purchased: $10,000,000
Purchase price: $9,642,899
Target accumulated value: $13,934,413

	After Five Years				
New Yield (%)	*Coupon*	*Interest on Interest*	*Price of Bond*	*Accumulated Value*	*Total Return (%)*
11.00	$3,375,000	$970,432	$ 9,607,657	$13,953,089	7.53
10.00	3,375,000				
9.00	3,375,000				
8.00	3,375,000				
7.50	3,375,000				
7.00	3,375,000				
6.00	3,375,000				
5.00	3,375,000				
4.00	3,375,000	320,531	10,266,965	13,962,495	7.54

CHAPTER 20

Bond Performance Measurement and Evaluation

Learning Objectives

After reading this chapter you will understand:

- the difference between performance measurement and performance evaluation

- the various methods for calculating the rate of return over some evaluation period: the arithmetic average rate of return, the time-weighted rate of return, and the dollar-weighted rate of return

- the impact of client contributions and withdrawals on the calculated return

- the method of calculating return that minimizes the effect of client contributions and withdrawals

- the objectives of the Association for Investment Management and Research's Performance Presentation Standards, the key requirements and mandatory disclosures to be in compliance with the standards, and some key guidelines and disclosures recommended in the standards

- why it is necessary to establish a benchmark

- how normal portfolios are created and the difficulties of creating them

- what a fixed-income performance attribution model is and why it is useful in assessing the performance of a money manager

In this chapter we will see how to measure and evaluate the investment performance of a fixed-income portfolio manager. Performance measurement *involves the calculation of the return realized by a portfolio manager over some time interval, which we call the* evaluation period. Performance evaluation *is concerned with two issues. The first is to determine whether the manager added value by outperforming the established benchmark. The second is to determine how the manager achieved the calculated return. For example, as explained in Chapter 17, there are several active strategies that a fixed-income manager can employ. The decomposition of the performance results to explain the reasons why those results were achieved is called performance or return attribution analysis.*

REQUIREMENTS FOR A BOND PERFORMANCE AND ATTRIBUTION ANALYSIS PROCESS

There are three desired requirements of a bond performance and attribution analysis process. The first is that the process be accurate. For example, as we will explain, there are several ways of measuring portfolio return. The return should recognize the time when each cash flow actually occurs, resulting in a much more accurate measure of the actual portfolio performance. The second requirement is that the process be informative. It should be capable of evaluating the managerial skills that go into fixed-income portfolio management. To be informative, the process must effectively address the key management skills and explain how these can be expressed in terms of realized performance. The final requirement is that the process be simple. Whatever the output of the process, it should be understood by the manager and client, or others who may be concerned with the performance of the portfolio. As we explain the process for analyzing bond performance in this chapter these requirements should be kept in mind.

PERFORMANCE MEASUREMENT

The starting point for evaluating the performance of a manager is measuring return. As we will see, there are several important issues that must be addressed in developing a methodology for calculating a portfolio's return. Because different methodologies are available and these methodologies can lead to quite disparate results, it is difficult to compare the performances of managers. Consequently, there is a great deal of confusion concerning the meaning of the data provided by managers to their clients and their prospective clients. This has led to abuses by some managers in reporting performance results that are better than actual performance. To mitigate this problem the Committee for Performance Standards of the Association of Investment Management and Research has established standards for calculating performance results and how to present those results.

Alternative Return Measures

Let's begin with the basic concept. The dollar return realized on a portfolio for any evaluation period (i.e., a year, month, or week) is equal to the sum of (1) the difference between the market value of the portfolio at the end of the evaluation period and the market value at the beginning of the evaluation period, and (2) any distributions made from the portfolio. It is important that any capital or income distributions from the portfolio to a client or beneficiary of the portfolio be included.

The rate of return, or simply return, expresses the dollar return in terms of the amount of the market value at the beginning of the evaluation period. Thus, the return can be viewed as the amount (expressed as a fraction of the initial portfolio value) that can be withdrawn at the end of the evaluation period while maintaining the initial market value of the portfolio intact.

In equation form, the portfolio's return can be expressed as follows:

$$R_P = \frac{MV_1 - MV_0 + D}{MV_0} \qquad (20.1)$$

where:

R_P = return on the portfolio
MV_1 = portfolio market value at the end of the evaluation period
MV_0 = portfolio market value at the beginning of the evaluation period
D = cash distributions from the portfolio to the client during the evaluation period

To illustrate the calculation of a return, assume the following information for an external manager for a pension plan sponsor: The portfolio's market value at the beginning and end of the evaluation period is $25 million and $28 million, respectively, and during the evaluation period $1 million is distributed to the plan sponsor from investment income. Thus

$$MV_1 = \$28,000,000$$
$$MV_0 = \$25,000,000$$
$$D = \$1,000,000$$

Then

$$R_p = \frac{\$28,000,000 - \$25,000,000 + \$1,000,000}{\$25,000,000}$$
$$= 0.16 = 16\%$$

There are three assumptions in measuring return as given by equation (20.1). First, it assumes that cash inflows into the portfolio from interest income that occur during the evaluation period but are not distributed are reinvested in the portfolio. For example, suppose that during the evaluation period $2 million is received from interest income. This amount is reflected in the market value of the portfolio at the end of the period.

The second assumption is that if there are distributions from the portfolio, they occur at the end of the evaluation period or are held in the form of cash until the end of the evaluation period. In our example, $1 million is distributed to the plan sponsor. But when did that distribution actually occur? To understand why the timing of the distribution is important, consider two extreme cases: (1) the distribution is made at the end of the evaluation period, as assumed by equation (20.1), and (2) the distribution is made at the beginning of the evaluation period. In the first case, the manager had the use of the $1 million to invest for the entire evaluation period. By contrast, in the second case, the manager loses the opportunity to invest the funds until the end of the evaluation period. Consequently, the timing of the distribution will affect the return, but this is not considered in equation (20.1).

The third assumption is that there is no cash paid into the portfolio by the client. For example, suppose that sometime during the evaluation period, the plan sponsor gives an additional $1.5 million to the external manager to invest. Consequently, the market value of the portfolio at the end of the evaluation period, $28 million in our example, would reflect the contribution of $1.5 million. Equation (20.1) does not reflect that the ending market value of the portfolio is affected by the cash paid in by the sponsor. Moreover, the timing of this cash inflow will affect the calculated return.

Thus, while the return calculation for a portfolio using equation (20.1) can be determined for an evaluation period of any length of time, such as one day, one month, or five years, from a practical point of view the assumptions discussed above limit its application. The longer the evaluation period, the more likely the assumptions will be violated. For example, it is highly likely that there may be more than one distribution to the client and more than one contribution from the client if the evaluation period is five years. Thus a return calculation made over a long period of time, if longer than a few months, would not be very reliable because of the assumption underlying the calculations that all cash payments and inflows are made and received at the end of the period.

Not only does the violation of the assumptions make it difficult to compare the returns of two managers over some evaluation period, but it is also not useful for evaluating performance over different periods. For example, equation (20.1) will not give reliable information to compare the performance of a one-month evaluation period and a three-year evaluation period. To make such a comparison, the return must be expressed per unit of time, for example, per year.

The way to handle these practical issues is to calculate the return for a short unit of time such as a month or a quarter. We call the return so calculated the **subperiod return.** To get the return for the evaluation period, the subperiod returns are then averaged. So, for example, if the evaluation period is one year and 12 monthly returns are calculated, the monthly returns are the subperiod returns and they are averaged to get the one-year return. If a three-year return is sought and 12-quarterly returns can be calculated, quarterly returns are the subperiod returns and they are averaged to get the three-year return. The three-year return can then be converted into an annual return by the straightforward procedure described later.

There are three methodologies that have been used in practice to calculate the average of the subperiod returns: (1) the arithmetic average rate of return, (2) the time-weighted rate of return (also called the geometric rate of return), and (3) the dollar-weighted return.

Arithmetic Average Rate of Return   The **arithmetic average rate of return** is an unweighted average of the subperiod returns. The general formula is

$$R_A = \frac{R_{P1} + R_{P2} + \cdots + R_{PN}}{N}$$

where:

R_A = arithmetic average rate of return
R_{Pk} = portfolio return for subperiod k as measured by equation (20.1), $k = 1, \ldots, N$
N = number of subperiods in the evaluation period

For example, if the portfolio returns [as measured by equation (20.1)] were $-10\%, 20\%$, and 5% in July, August, and September, respectively, the arithmetic average monthly return is 5%:

$$N = 3 \qquad R_{P1} = -0.10 \qquad R_{P2} = 0.20 \qquad R_{P3} = 0.05$$
$$R_A = \frac{-0.10 + 0.20 + 0.05}{3} = 0.05 = 5\%$$

There is a major problem with using the arithmetic average rate of return. To see this problem, suppose that the initial market value of a portfolio is $28 million and the market values at the end of the next two months are $58 million and $28 million, and assume that there are no distributions or cash inflows from the client for either month. Then using equation (20.1) the subperiod return for the first month (R_{P1}) is 100% and the subperiod return for the second month (R_{P2}) is −50%. The arithmetic average rate of return is then 25%. Not a bad return! But think about this number. The portfolio's initial market value was $28 million. Its market value at the end of two months is $28 million. The return over this two-month evaluation period is zero. Yet the arithmetic average rate of return says that it is a whopping 25%.

Thus it is improper to interpret the arithmetic average rate of return as a measure of the average return over an evaluation period. The proper interpretation is as follows: It is the average value of the withdrawals (expressed as a fraction of the initial portfolio market value) that can be made at the end of each subperiod while keeping the initial portfolio market value intact. In our first example in which the average monthly return is 5%, the investor must add 10% of the initial portfolio market value at the end of the first month, can withdraw 20% of the initial portfolio market value at the end of the second month, and can withdraw 5% of the initial portfolio market value at the end of the third month. In our second example, the average monthly return of 25% means that 100% of the initial portfolio market value ($28 million) can be withdrawn at the end of the first month and 50% must be added at the end of the second month.

Time-Weighted Rate of Return   The **time-weighted rate of return** measures the compounded rate of growth of the initial portfolio market value during the evaluation period, assuming that all cash distributions are reinvested in the portfolio. It is also commonly referred to as the **geometric rate of return** because it is computed by taking the geometric average of the portfolio subperiod returns computed from equation (20.1). The general formula is

$$R_T = [(1 + R_{P1})(1 + R_{P2}) \cdots (1 + R_{PN})]^{1/N} - 1$$

where R_T is the time-weighted rate of return and R_{Pk} and N are as defined earlier. For example, let us assume that the portfolio returns were −10%, 20%, and 5% in July, August, and September, as in the first example, the time-weighted rate of return is

$$R_T = \{[1 + (-0.10)](1 + 0.20)(1 + 0.05)\}^{1/3} - 1$$
$$= [(0.90)(1.20)(1.05)]^{1/3} - 1 = 0.043$$

If the time-weighted rate of return is 4.3% per month, one dollar invested in the portfolio at the beginning of July would have grown at a rate of 4.3% per month during the three-month evaluation period.

The time-weighted rate of return in the second example is 0%, as expected:

$$R_T = \{(1 + 1.00)[1 + (-0.50)]\}^{1/2} - 1$$
$$= [(2.00)(0.50)]^{1/2} - 1 = 0\%$$

In general, the arithmetic and time-weighted average returns will give different values for the portfolio return over some evaluation period. This is because in computing the arithmetic average rate of return, the amount invested is assumed to be maintained (through additions or withdrawals) at its initial portfolio market value. The time-weighted return, on the other hand, is the return on a portfolio that varies in size because of the assumption that all proceeds are reinvested.

In general, the arithmetic average rate of return will exceed the time-weighted average rate of return. The exception is in the special situation where all the subperiod returns are the same, in which case the averages are identical. The magnitude of the difference between the two averages is smaller the less the variation in the subperiod returns over the evaluation period. For example, suppose that the evaluation period is four months and that the four monthly returns are as follows:

$$R_{P1} = 0.04 \qquad R_{P2} = 0.06 \qquad R_{P3} = 0.02 \qquad R_{P4} = -0.02$$

The average arithmetic rate of return is 2.5% and the time-weighted average rate of return is 2.46%. Not much of a difference. In our earlier example in which we calculated an average rate of return of 25% but a time-weighted average rate of return of 0%, the large discrepancy is due to the substantial variation in the two monthly returns.

Dollar-Weighted Rate of Return   The **dollar-weighted rate of return** is computed by finding the interest rate that will make the present value of the cash flows from all the subperiods in the evaluation period plus the terminal market value of the portfolio equal to the initial market value of the portfolio. The cash flow for each subperiod reflects the difference between the cash inflows due to investment income (i.e., coupon interest) and contribution made by the client to the portfolio, and the cash outflows reflecting distributions to the client. Notice that it is not necessary to know the market value of the portfolio for each subperiod to determine the dollar-weighted rate of return.

The dollar-weighted rate of return is simply an internal rate-of-return calculation and hence it is also called the **internal rate of return.** The general formula for the dollar-weighted return is

$$V_0 = \frac{C_1}{1 + R_D} + \frac{C_2}{(1 + R_D)^2} + \cdots + \frac{C_N + V_N}{(1 + R_D)^n}$$

where:

R_D = dollar-weighted rate of return
V_0 = initial market value of the portfolio
V_N = terminal market value of the portfolio
C_k = cash flow for the portfolio (cash inflows minus cash outflows) for subperiod
    $k, k = 1, 2, \ldots, N$

For example, consider a portfolio with a market value of $100,000 at the beginning of July, capital withdrawals of $5,000 at the end of months July, August, and September, no cash inflows from the client in any month, and a market value at the end of September of $110,000. Then $V_0 = \$100,000$, $N = 3$, $C_1 = C_2 = C_3 = \$5,000$, $V_3 = \$110,000$, and R_D is the interest rate that satisfies the following equation:

$$\$100,000 = \frac{\$5,000}{1 + R_D} + \frac{\$5,000}{(1 + R_D)^2} + \frac{\$5,000 + \$110,000}{(1 + R_D)^3}$$

It can be verified that the interest rate that satisfies the expression above is 8.1%. This, then, is the dollar-weighted return.

The dollar-weighted rate of return and the time-weighted rate of return will produce the same result if no withdrawals or contributions occur over the evaluation period and all investment income is reinvested. The problem with the dollar-weighted rate of return is that it is affected by factors that are beyond the control of the manager. Specifically, any contributions made by the client or withdrawals that the client requires will affect the calculated return. This makes it difficult to compare the performance of two managers.

To see this, suppose that a pension plan sponsor engaged two managers, A and B, with $10 million given to A to manage and $200 million to B. Suppose that (1) both managers invest in identical portfolios (i.e., the two portfolios have the same securities and are held in the same proportion), (2) for the following two months the rate of return on the two portfolios is 20% for month 1 and 50% for month 2, and (3) the amount received in investment income is in cash. Also assume that the plan sponsor does not make an additional contribution to the portfolio of either manager. Under these assumptions, it is clear that the performance of both managers would be identical. Suppose, however, that the plan sponsor withdraws $4 million from A at the beginning of month 2. This means that A could not invest the entire amount at the end of month 1 and capture the 50% increase in the portfolio value. A's net cash flow would be as follows: (1) in month 1 the net cash flow is $-$2 million because $2 million is realized in investment income and $4 million is withdrawn by the plan sponsor. The dollar-weighted rate of return is then calculated as follows:

$$\$10 = \frac{-\$2}{1 + R_D} + \frac{\$12}{(1 + R_D)^2} \rightarrow R_D = 0\%$$

For B, the cash inflow for month 1 is $40 million ($200 million times 20%) and the portfolio value at the end of month 2 is $360 million ($240 million times 1.5). The dollar-weighted rate of return is

$$\$200 = \frac{\$40}{1 + R_D} + \frac{\$330}{(1 + R_D)^2} \rightarrow R_D = 38.8\%$$

These are quite different results for two managers who we agreed had identical performance. The withdrawal by the plan sponsor and the size of the withdrawal relative to the portfolio value had a significant impact on the calculated return. Notice also that even if the plan sponsor had withdrawn $4 million from B at the beginning of month 2, this would not have had as significant an impact. The problem would also have occurred if we assumed that the return in month 2 is -50% and that instead of A realizing a withdrawal of $4 million, the plan sponsor contributed $4 million.

Despite this limitation, the dollar-weighted rate of return does provide information. It indicates information about the growth of the fund that a client will find useful. This growth, however, is not attributable to the performance of the manager because of contributions and withdrawals.

Annualizing Returns

The evaluation period may be less than or greater than one year. Typically, return measures are reported as an average annual return. This requires the annualization of the subperiod returns. The subperiod returns are typically calculated for a period of less than one year for the reasons described earlier. The subperiod returns are then annualized using the following formula:

$$\text{annual return} = (1 + \text{average period return})^{\text{number of periods in year}} - 1$$

For example, suppose that the evaluation period is three years and a monthly period return is calculated. Suppose further that the average monthly return is 2%. Then the annual return would be

$$\text{annual return} = (1.02)^{12} - 1 = 26.8\%$$

Suppose instead that the period used to calculate returns is quarterly and the average quarterly return is 3%. Then the annual return is

$$\text{annual return} = (1.03)^{4} - 1 = 12.6\%$$

AIMR Performance Presentation Standards

As explained previously, there are subtle issues in calculating the return over the evaluation period. There are also industry concerns as to how managers should present results to clients and how managers should disclose performance data and records to prospects from whom they are seeking to obtain funds to manage. According to Claude N. Rosenberg, Jr., Chairman of the Committee for Performance Presentation Standards (CPPS) of the Association for Investment Management and Research (AIMR):

> There is little consistency within the investment management industry in the presentation of performance data and records. There certainly has been a great deal of confusion about what should be reported to clients and prospects. The investment management industry has pretty much operated on an honor system, and although there is a great deal of honor in our industry, there are too many approaches that make this whole subject a real hornet's nest. Because there has been confusion, there has been misuse, and some of the misuse must, bluntly, be recognized as deception, and in some cases—we hope not too many—misuse has been motivated by outright dishonesty.[1]

Although the Securities and Exchange Commission has established standards for reporting performance results, they are not very specific. Accordingly, the CPPS was charged with developing standards for disclosure. The standards adopted by the AIMR went into effect in 1993 and "are a set of guiding ethical principles intended to promote full disclosure and fair representation by investment managers in reporting their investment results."[2] A secondary objective of the standards is to ensure uniformity in the presentation of results so that it is easier for clients to compare the performance of managers. It is important to emphasize that the AIMR standards deal with the presentation of the data and what must be disclosed, not with how the manager should be evaluated. In developing these standards, the CPPS recognized that in practice there is no single ideal set of performance presentation standards that are applicable to all users. There are provisions in the standards to prevent certain abusive practices. Rather than mandating other practices, the standards provide guidelines and recommendations for reporting. Thus the standards can be broken down into (1) the require-

---

[1]Claude N. Rosenberg, Jr., panel discussion, as reported in *Performance Measurement: Setting Standards, Interpreting the Numbers* (Charlottesville, VA: Institute for Chartered Financial Analysts, 1989), p. 15.
[2]*Performance Presentation Standards: 1993* (Charlottesville, VA: Association for Investment Management and Research, 1993).

ments and mandatory disclosures for compliance, and (2) practices recommended. In the following sections we highlight some of the standards.

Requirements and Mandatory Disclosures   To be considered in compliance with the standards, the following practices and disclosures *must* be followed:

- Calculate performance on a total return basis.
- Employ accrual accounting rather than cash accounting in calculating return.
- Calculate return using the time-weighted rate of return methodology, with valuation on at least a quarterly basis and geometric linking of period returns.
- Include all actual fee-paying, discretionary portfolios in one composite or aggregate measure. This prevents a manager from showing only the performance of selective accounts that have performed well to a client it is soliciting. The number of portfolios and amount of assets in the composite and the percentage of the firm's total assets the composite represents must be disclosed. The firm must also disclose the existence of any minimum size below which portfolios are excluded from a composite and the inclusion of any non–fee-paying portfolios in the composite.
- Do not link the results of simulated and model portfolios with actual portfolio performance. That is, only actual portfolio performance, not the performance that would have been realized if a certain strategy had been employed, can be reported.
- Deduct all trading costs in calculating the return.
- Disclose whether the performance results are calculated gross or net of management fees. If net results are reported, the average weighted management fee must be disclosed.
- Disclose the tax-rate assumption if the results are reported after taxes.
- Present at least a 10-year performance record. If the firm has been in existence for less than 10 years, the performance since inception must be reported.
- Present annual returns for all years.
- Provide a complete list and description of all the firm's composites.

There are other required practices and disclosures dealing with the reporting of results of accounts that have been terminated, the treatment of new portfolios added to a composite, and special requirements for international and real estate portfolios.

Recommended Guidelines and Disclosures   Some of the practices that AIMR encourages are as follows:

- Revalue a portfolio whenever cash flows in or out of the portfolio and market action combine to distort performance. We focus on this in the next section when we discuss the return calculation under the standards.
- Present performance gross of management fees in one-on-one presentation to clients.[3] The results should be presented before taxes.
- Treat convertible and other hybrid securities consistently across and within composites.

---

[3]This is also acceptable to the SEC for one-on-one presentations with clients. If a manager distributes the information to more than one client, the SEC requires that the returns be reported after deducting management fees.

- Disclose external risk measures such as standard deviation of composite returns across time.
- Disclose benchmarks that parallel the risk or investment style the client is expected to track. We discuss benchmarks later in this chapter.
- For leveraged portfolios, disclose the results on an unleveraged basis where possible.

There are specific recommended guidelines and disclosures for international portfolios.

Calculating Returns under the Standards   In our illustrations of the various ways to measure portfolio return, we used the same length of time for the subperiod (e.g., a month or a quarter). The subperiod returns were averaged, with the preferred method being geometric averaging. The AIMR standards require that the return measure minimize the effect of contributions and withdrawals so that cash flow beyond the control of the manager is minimized. If the subperiod return is calculated daily, the impact of contributions and withdrawals will be minimized. The time-weighted return measure can then be calculated from the daily returns.

From a practical point of view, the problem is that calculating a daily return requires that the market value of the portfolio be determined at the end of each day. Although this does not present a problem for a mutual fund that must calculate the net asset value of the portfolio each business day, it is a time-consuming administrative problem for other managers. Moreover, there are asset classes in which the determination of daily prices would be difficult (e.g., certain fixed-income securities, securities in emerging markets, and real estate).

An alternative to the time-weighted rate of return has been suggested. This is the dollar-weighted rate of return, which as we noted earlier is less desirable in comparing the performance of managers because of the effect of withdrawals and contributions beyond the control of the manager. The advantage of this method from an operational perspective is that market values do not have to be calculated daily. The effect of withdrawals and contributions is minimized if they are small relative to the length of the subperiod. However, if the cash flow is over 10% at any time, the AIMR standards require that the portfolio be revalued on that date.[4]

After the subperiod returns in an evaluation period are calculated, they are compounded. The AIMR standards specify that for evaluation periods of less than one year returns should *not* be annualized. Thus if the evaluation period is seven months and the subperiod returns are calculated monthly, the seven-month return should be reported by calculating the compounded seven-month return instead.

PERFORMANCE ATTRIBUTION ANALYSIS

In the preceding section, we concentrated on performance measurement and the AIMR performance reporting standards. Our focus in this section is on how to evaluate the performance of a manager to determine if the manager added value beyond

---

[4]For a further discussion of the implementation of the AIMR Standards, see Deborah H. Miller, "How to Calculate the Numbers According to the Standards," in *Performance Reporting for Investment Managers: Applying the AIMR Performance Presentation Standards* (Charlottesville, VA: Association for Investment Management and Research, 1991).

what could have been achieved by a passive strategy in a benchmark portfolio and whether that performance was due to skill or luck.

Bond attribution models seek to identify the active management decisions that contributed to the performance of a portfolio and give a quantitative assessment of the contribution of these decisions. In Chapter 17 we explained active strategies in managing a fixed-income portfolio: interest-rate expectation strategies, yield curve expectations strategies, yield spread strategies, and individual security selection strategies. The performance of a portfolio can be decomposed in terms of these four strategies.

Benchmark Portfolios

To evaluate the performance of a manager, a client must specify a benchmark against which the manager will be measured. There are two types of benchmarks that have been used in evaluating fixed-income portfolio managers: (1) market indexes published by dealer firms and vendors, and (2) normal portfolios. We discussed the various types of market indexes in Chapter 18. The other types of benchmarks are discussed next.

A **normal portfolio** is a customized benchmark that includes "a set of securities that contains all of the securities from which a manager normally chooses, weighted as the manager would weight them in a portfolio."[5] Thus, a normal portfolio is a specialized index. It is argued that normal portfolios are more appropriate benchmarks than market indexes because they control for investment management style, thereby representing a passive portfolio against which a manager can be evaluated.

The construction of a normal portfolio for a particular manager is no simple task.[6] The principle is to construct a portfolio that, given the historical portfolios held by the manager, will reflect that manager's style in terms of assets and the weighting of those assets. The construction of a normal portfolio for a manager requires (1) defining the universe of fixed-income securities to be included in the normal portfolio, and (2) determining how these securities should be weighted (i.e., equally weighted or capitalization weighted).

Defining the set of securities to be included in the normal portfolio begins with discussions between the client and the manager to determine the manager's investment style. Based on these discussions, the universe of all publicly traded securities is reduced to a subset that includes those securities that the manager considers eligible given his or her investment style.

Given these securities, the next question is how they should be weighted in the normal portfolio. The two choices are equal weighting or capitalization weighting of each security. Various methodologies can be used to determine the weights. These methodologies typically involve a statistical analysis of the historical holdings of a manager and the risk exposure contained in those holdings.

Plan sponsors work with pension consultants to develop normal portfolios for a manager. The consultants use vendor systems that have been developed for performing the needed statistical analysis and the necessary optimization program to create a

---

[5]Jon Christopherson, "Normal Portfolios: Construction of Customized Benchmarks," Chapter 6 in Frank J. Fabozzi (ed.), *Active Equity Portfolio Management* (New Hope, PA: Frank J. Fabozzi Associates, 1998), p. 92.
[6]See Mark Kritzman, "How to Build a Normal Portfolio in Three Easy Steps," *Journal of Portfolio Management*, Spring 1987, pp. 21–23.

portfolio exhibiting similar factor positions to replicate the "normal" position of a manager. A plan sponsor must recognize that there is a cost to developing and updating the normal portfolio.

There are some who advocate the responsibility of developing normal portfolios should be left to the manager. However, many clients are reluctant to let their managers control the construction of normal portfolios because they believe that the managers will produce easily beaten, or "slow rabbit," benchmarks. Bailey and Tierney demonstrate that under reasonable conditions there is no long-term benefit for the manager to construct a "slow rabbit" benchmark and explain the disadvantage of a manager pursuing such a strategy.[7] In addition, they recommend that clients let managers control the benchmarks. Clients should, instead, focus their efforts on monitoring the quality of the benchmarks and the effectiveness of the managers' active management strategies.

Performance Attribution Analysis Model[8]

There are several vendors of performance attribution models. The performance attribution model described here is that of Gifford Fong Associates of Lafayette, California. The particular system that monitors and evaluates the performance of a fixed-income portfolio as well as the individual securities held in the portfolio is called **BONDPAR.** BONDPAR decomposes the return into those elements beyond the manager's control, such as the interest-rate environment and client-imposed-duration policy constraints, and those that the management process contributes to, such as interest-rate management, sector/quality allocations, and individual bond selection.

BONDPAR answers the following six questions: (1) How does each element of the manager's return compare with the same elements of return of the benchmark? (2) What is the cost of being in the bond market? (3) What effect do client policies have on portfolio returns? (4) Has the manager successfully anticipated interest-rate changes? (5) Has the manager been successful at selecting the issuing sector and quality groups that enhance the portfolio's performance? and (6) Has the manager improved returns by selecting individual bonds because of company fundamentals?

An explanation of the technology for decomposing the portfolio's return so that these questions can be answered is beyond the scope of this chapter.[9] Instead, we illustrate the product of the system with a hypothetical portfolio for the period February 28, 1990 to March 31, 1990 and how it answers the six questions. Exhibit 20-1 shows the holdings of the portfolio and the transactions during the period. Also shown for each security are the beginning and ending par amount, proceeds, accrued value, interest paid during the evaluation period, and capital gain or loss.

Exhibit 20-2 shows the results of the performance attribution analysis for the portfolio in Exhibit 20-1. Let's look first at the three columns in the exhibit. The "evaluation period return" column is the return and components of return for the portfolio over the evaluation period. The "bond equivalent annualized return" column

---

[7]Jeffery V. Bailey and David E. Tierney, "Gaming Manager Benchmarks," *Journal of Portfolio Management,* Summer 1993, pp. 37–40.

[8]This section is adapted from Chapter 12 in Frank J. Fabozzi and H. Gifford Fong, *Advanced Fixed Income Portfolio Management* (Chicago: Probus Publishing, 1994).

[9]An explanation of the technology is provided in Fabozzi and Fong, *Advanced Fixed Income Portfolio Management.*

EXHIBIT 20-1   Bond Performance Analysis: Individual Security Listing and Transactions

Individual Security Listing[a]

Cusip	Bond Description	Initial/ Last Date	Beg/End Par ($000)	Beg/ End Prc (%)	Beg/ End Acc ($000)	Interest Paid ($000)	Capital Gain/ Loss ($000)
041033BM							
ARKANSAS POWER & LIGHT CO							
1 14.125%	11/1/14 E4	2/28/90	24500.000	98.689	1124.70		
		3/31/90	20000.000	98.765	1177.08	0.00	17.99
161610BA							
CHASE MANHATTAN CORP							
2 9.750%	9/15/99 F3	2/28/90	25000.000	99.969	1103.65		
		3/31/90	30000.000	100.080	130.00	1462.50	69.05
172921CT							
CITICORP MORTGAGES SECS INC							
3 9.500%	1/1/19 PS	2/28/90	76151.720	86.250	542.58		
		3/31/90	76151.720	85.031	602.87	602.87	−928.29
3024519X							
FHA INSURED PROJECT MORTGAGE							
4 7.400%	2/1/21 PS	2/28/90	73071.970	84.438	405.55		
		3/31/90	73071.970	83.875	450.61	450.61	−411.40
313400KK							
FEDERAL HOME LOAN MTG CORP							
5 12.250%	3/15/95 AG	2/28/90	30600.000	106.250	1718.93		
		3/31/90	30600.000	105.813	162.98	1874.25	−133.72
4581829H							
INTER-AMERICAN DEVELOPMENT							
6 11.000%	12/11/92 XI	2/28/90	5600.000	103.313	131.76		
		3/31/90	5600.000	102.813	188.22	0.00	−28.00
674599AW							
OCCIDENTAL PETROLEUM CORP							
7 11.750%	3/15/11 04	2/28/90	34000.000	102.875	1808.85		
		3/31/90	34000.000	102.500	177.56	1997.50	−127.50
912827TQ							
UNITED STATES TREASURY NOTES							
8 7.375%	5/15/96 TR	2/28/90	93500.000	94.156	2000.11		
		3/31/90	93500.000	93.594	2590.62	0.00	−525.47
912827WN							
UNITED STATES TREASURY NOTES							
9 9.250%	8/15/98 TR	3/13/90	92000.000	102.531	658.23		
		3/31/90	92000.000	102.969	1034.36	0.00	402.96
912827XM							
UNITED STATES TREASURY NOTES							
10 9.000%	5/15/92 TR	2/28/90	85900.000	101.031	2242.42		
		3/10/90	0.000	100.750	2498.69	0.00	−241.38

[a]The Individual Security Listing is an optional report that is used to review the beginning and ending holdings, price, and accrued interest for all individual securities held during the evaluation period. This report also displays the amount of interest paid for individual securities during the evaluation period.

EXHIBIT 20-1 (*cont.*)

Transactions Report[b]

Cusip	Bond Description	Type of/ Transact	Trade Date	Settle Date	Par ($000)	Acc ($000)	Prc (%)	Cost/ Proceeds ($000)
041033BM								
ARKANSAS POWER & LIGHT CO								
1 14.125%	11/1/14 E4	Sale	3/5/90	3/12/90	4500.000	231.30	98.751	4675.1
161610BA								
CHASE MANHATTAN CORP								
2 9.750%	9/15/99 F3	Purchase	3/6/90	3/13/90	5000.000	241.04	99.254	5203.7
912827XM								
UNITED STATES TREASURY NOTES								
10 9.000%	5/15/92 TR	Termsale	3/10/90	3/12/90	85900.000	2498.69	100.750	89042.9
912827WN								
UNITED STATES TREASURY NOTES								
9 9.250%	8/15/98 TR	Purchase	3/13/90	3/15/90	92000.000	658.23	102.531	94986.8

[b]The Transactions Report can be used to review the total cost and proceeds of all purchase and sale transactions during the evaluation period. This report displays the type of transaction, the trade and settlement date, the par amount in ($000), the price of the transaction, and the accrued interest calculated by the BONDPAR system.

is the annualized return and components of return for the portfolio over the evaluation period. The "Salomon B.I.G. Index" column shows the evaluation period return of a market index (benchmark).

The decomposition of the evaluation period return is shown in the sections labeled I, II, III, and IV. Section I, "interest-rate effect," is the return over the evaluation period of the full Treasury index. The values in this section are interpreted as follows. The subtotal 0.09 means that the actual monthly return on Treasuries was 9 basis points. The value of 0.66 indicates that the expected monthly return from investing in Treasury bonds over this period was 66 basis points. From where does this value come? Recall from Chapter 5 that we demonstrated that forward rates can be calculated from the Treasury yield curve. These rates are taken as the market's consensus of rates that can be earned. It is the forward rate that is the expected return that is reported in the row "expected." The unexpected return is the difference between the actual return of 9 basis points and the expected return of 66 basis points.

The results reported in the section "interest-rate effect" can be interpreted as the cost of being in the bond market. That is, if any investor wanted to invest in default-free bonds (i.e., Treasury securities) and simply bought a portfolio of Treasury securities, the return would have been 9 basis points. Therefore, this component of return is considered out of the manager's control because such a return would have been realized by anyone who decided to commit funds to the bond market.

Row II shows the **policy effect.** This information provides the necessary information to analyze the duration policy constraint specified by the manager's client. BONDPAR calculates the portion of the total return due to the policy constraint and

EXHIBIT 20-2 Performance Attribution Analysis for a Portfolio with BONDPAR

	Eval. Period Return (%)	Bond Equiv. Annualized Return (%)	Salomon B.I.G. Index Eval. Period Return (%)
I. Interest rate effect (SAL Treasury Index)			
1. Expected	0.66	7.93	0.66
2. Unexpected	−0.57	−6.87	−0.57
Subtotal	0.09	1.06	0.09
II. Policy effect			
3. Portfolio duration reqt.	0.01	0.07	0.01
(4.60 years)			
III. Interest rate management effect			
4. Duration	0.06	0.69	0.00
5. Convexity	−0.07	−0.84	−0.10
6. Yield curve shape change	−0.15	−1.78	0.10
Subtotal (options adjusted)	−0.16	−1.93	0.00
IV. Other management effects			
7. Sector/quality	0.18	2.15	0.10
8. Bond selectivity	0.32	3.79	0.00
9. Transactions cost	−0.03	−0.38	0.00
Subtotal	0.47	5.56	0.10
V. Total return	0.41	4.76	0.20
VI. Sources of return			
1. Capital gains	−0.44	−5.20	
2. Interest income	0.85	9.96	
Total return	0.41	4.76	

separates it from the interest-rate management effect. This effect, shown in section III, shows the option-adjusted default-free return for the portfolio. This component of return shows whether the manager has successfully anticipated interest-rate changes. The interest-rate management effect is broken into three subcomponents: (1) the duration effect, which is the effect on the return due to the magnitude of the yield curve shift;[10] (2) the convexity effect, which is the return component of managing the convexity of the portfolio; and (3) the yield curveshape change effect, which is the return due to the change in the shape of the yield curve (i.e., the residual return component not measured by duration and convexity).

Other management effects are shown in Section IV. These are divided into three effects. The **sector/quality effect** is the return component that shows whether the manager successfully selected the sector and quality groups that performed better over the evaluation period. The **bond selectivity effect** is the return component due to the selection of individual bonds in the portfolio. **Transactions cost** refers to the hypothetical effect of transactions on the portfolios return.

---

[10]Consistent with the concept of using the Treasury index to measure the unmanaged interest-rate effect, this component is measured relative to the duration of the Treasury index.

EXHIBIT 20-3 Performance Attribution Analysis for Each Security with BONDPAR[a]

Init. Face Value ($000) Bond Description	Initial Date	Last Date	Market Perf.			Portfolio Management			= Total Return %	Return Source	
			Market Expect. +	Rate Change +	Int. Rate +	Sector /Qual. +	Selectivity +	Trans. Cost	=	= Capit. Gains +	Inter. Income
1 24500.0 ARKANSAS POWER & LIGHT CO 14.125% 11/14 E4 041033BM	2/28/90	3/31/90	0.66	−0.57	0.37	0.69	0.25	−.07	1.33	0.07	1.25
2 25000.0 CHASE MANHATTAN CORP 9.750% 9/15/99 F3 161610BA	2/28/90	3/31/90	0.66	−0.57	−0.19	0.01	1.12	−.04	0.98	0.11	0.88
3 76151.7 CITICORP MORTGAGE SECS INC 9.500% 1/1/19 PS 172921CT	2/28/90	3/31/90	0.66	−0.57	−0.04	0.25	−0.70	00.00	−0.40	−1.31	0.91
4 73072.0 FHA INSURED PROJECT MORTGAG 7.400% 2/1/21 PS 3024519X	2/28/90	3/31/90	0.66	−0.57	−0.55	0.70	−0.10	00.00	0.14	−0.59	0.73
5 30600.0 FEDERAL HOME LOAN MTG CORP 12.250% 3/15/95 AG 313400KK	2/28/90	3/31/90	0.66	−0.57	−0.08	0.06	0.50	00.00	0.57	−0.39	0.96
6 5600.0 INTER-AMERICAN DEVELOPMENT 11.000% 12/11/92 XI 4581829H	2/28/90	3/31/90	0.66	−0.57	0.05	−0.03	0.37	00.00	0.48	−0.47	0.95
7 34000.0 OCCIDENTAL PETROLEUM CORP 11.750% 3/15/11 04 674599AW	2/28/90	3/31/90	0.66	−0.57	−0.31	0.05	0.84	00.00	0.68	−0.35	1.02
8 93500.0 UNITED STATES TREASURY NOTE 7.375% 5/15/96 TR 912827TQ	2/28/90	3/31/90	0.66	−0.57	−0.19	0.00	0.17	00.00	0.07	−0.58	0.66
9 92000.0 UNITED STATES TREASURY NOTE 9.250% 8/15/98 TR 912827WN	3/13/90	3/13/90	0.39	−0.33	−0.15	0.00	0.99	−0.06	0.82	0.42	0.40
10 85900.0 UNITED STATES TREASURY NOTE 9.000% 5/15/96 TR 912827XM	2/28/90	3/10/90	0.21	−0.18	0.13	00.00	−0.08	−0.06	0.02	−0.27	0.29

[a]The *individual security performance* report lists the return components for all individual securities held during the evaluation period. *Initial face value* indicates in ($000) the beginning holding position for the bond. *Bond description* displays the security's portfolio bond number, cusip number, coupon, maturity date, and sector/quality. *Initial date* and *last date* display the evaluation period for the security being analyzed. The remaining columns break down the components of return for the individual security over the evaluation period.

The last two sections, V and VI, provide summary information. **Total return** is the time-weighted total return for the evaluation period. This is the sum of the interest-rate effect, policy effect, interest-rate management effect, and other management effects. The "sources of return" section separates the return into capital gains (the change in price) and interest income.

Exhibit 20-2 shows the decomposition of return for the entire portfolio; the same analysis can be done for each security, as shown in Exhibit 20-3.

SUMMARY

Performance measurement involves calculation of the return realized by a money manager over some evaluation period. Performance evaluation is concerned with determining whether the money manager added value by outperforming the established benchmark and how the money manager achieved the calculated return.

The rate of return expresses the dollar return in terms of the amount of the initial investment (i.e., the initial market value of the portfolio). Three methodologies have been used in practice to calculate the average of the subperiod returns: (1) the arithmetic average rate of return, (2) the time-weighted (or geometric) rate of return, and (3) the dollar-weighted return. The arithmetic average rate of return is the average value of the withdrawals (expressed as a fraction of the initial portfolio market value) that can be made at the end of each period while keeping the initial portfolio market value intact. The time-weighted rate of return measures the compounded rate of growth of the initial portfolio over the evaluation period, assuming that all cash distributions are reinvested in the portfolio. The time-weighted return is the return on a portfolio that varies in size because of the assumption that all proceeds are reinvested. In general, the arithmetic average rate of return will exceed the time-weighted average rate of return. The magnitude of the difference between the two averages is smaller the less the variation in the subperiod returns over the evaluation period.

The dollar-weighted rate of return is computed by finding the interest rate that will make the present value of the cash flows from all the subperiods in the evaluation period plus the terminal market value of the portfolio equal to the initial market value of the portfolio. The dollar-weighted rate of return is an internal rate-of-return calculation and will produce the same result as the time-weighted rate of return if (1) no withdrawals or contributions occur over the evaluation period and (2) all dividends are reinvested. The problem with using the dollar-weighted rate of return to evaluate the performance of money managers is that it is affected by factors that are beyond the control of the money manager. Specifically, any contributions made by the client or withdrawals that the client requires will affect the calculated return, making it difficult to compare the performance of two money managers.

The AIMR has adopted standards for the presentation and disclosure of performance results. In developing them, the CPPS of the AIMR recognized that in practice there is no single ideal set of performance presentation standards that are applicable to all users. There are provisions in the standards to prevent certain abusive practices. Rather than mandating other practices, the standards provide guidelines and recommendations for reporting.

The role of performance evaluation is to determine if a money manager added value beyond what could have been achieved by a passive strategy in a benchmark portfolio.

The analysis requires the establishment of a benchmark. One such benchmark is a normal portfolio. This is a customized benchmark that includes a set of securities that contains the universe of securities that a manager normally selects from and weighted as the manager would weight them in a portfolio. Advocates claim that normal portfolios are more appropriate benchmarks than market indexes because they control for investment management style, thereby representing a passive portfolio against which a manager can be evaluated. It is neither an easy nor a costless process to construct normal portfolios.

In the fixed-income area, returns are attributed to those elements beyond the manager's control, such as the interest-rate environment and duration policy constraints imposed by a client, and those that the management process contributes to, such as interest-rate management, sector/quality allocations, and individual bond selection.

Questions

1. What is the difference between performance measurement and performance evaluation?
2. Suppose that the monthly return for two bond managers is as follows:

Month	Manager I	Manager II
1	9%	25%
2	13%	13%
3	22%	22%
4	−18%	−24%

   What is the arithmetic average monthly rate of return for the two managers?
3. What is the time-weighted average monthly rate of return for the two managers in Question 2?
4. Why does the arithmetic average monthly rate of return diverge more from the time-weighted monthly rate of return for manager II than for manager I in Question 2?
5. Smith & Jones is a money management firm specializing in fixed-income securities. One of its clients gave the firm $100 million to manage. The market value for the portfolio for the four months after receiving the funds was as follows:

End of Month	Market Value (in millions)
1	$ 50
2	150
3	75
4	100

   a. Calculate the rate of return for each month.
   b. Smith & Jones reported to the client that over the four-month period the average monthly rate of return was 33.33%. How was that value obtained?
   c. Is the average monthly rate of return of 33.33% indicative of the performance of Smith & Jones? If not, what would be a more appropriate measure?
6. The Mercury Company is a fixed-income management firm that manages the funds of pension plan sponsors. For one of its clients it manages $200 million. The cash flow for this particular client's portfolio for the past three months was $20 million, −$8 million, and $4 million. The market value of the portfolio at the end of three months was $208 million.

a. What is the dollar-weighted rate of return for this client's portfolio over the three-month period?

b. Suppose that the $8 million cash outflow in the second month was a result of withdrawals by the plan sponsor and that the cash flow after adjusting for this withdrawal is therefore zero. What would the dollar-weighted rate of return then be for this client's portfolio?

7. If the average monthly return for a portfolio is 1.23%, what is the annualized return?

8. If the average quarterly return for a portfolio is 1.78%, what is the annualized return?

9. The High Quality Corporation is a money management firm that was started five years ago. The firm has 20 discretionary, fee-paying accounts with an aggregate amount under management of $500 million. In preparing a report for a client that it is prospecting for funds, it has done the following: (1) presented the return for the past three years for five representative portfolios; (2) calculated the arithmetic average annual return over the past three years where the return subperiod was measured each year; (3) disclosed what the return would have been for the past ten years based on the actual performance for the past three years and simulated returns for the seven prior years using the same strategy that it employed for the actual portfolio; and (4) calculated the return before transaction costs and management fees. Based on this information, explain whether High Quality Corporation is in compliance with the AIMR standards.

10. In *Performance Measurement: Setting the Standards, Interpreting the Numbers,* John Sherrerd, a member of the Performance Presentation Standards Committee of the AIMR, stated:

> It is important to keep in mind that the objective of these performance statistics is to measure the capabilities of the manager, not the cash flows. It is not an attempt to measure how many dollars the client has earned over a period of time. If the performance of the manager is being measured, those results should not be influenced by whether the client is taking money out and spending it, the way most endowments might, or leaving it in, as many corporations do.

a. Why is the dollar-weighted rate of return affected by contributions and withdrawals by the client?

b. What rate-of-return methodology does the AIMR standards require?

11. In the calculation of return, the AIMR standards recommend the use of a daily return.

a. Explain why it would be ideal to calculate daily returns.

b. Why is it difficult to calculate daily returns?

12. What are the difficulties of constructing a normal portfolio?

13. The following is a statement from John H. Watts, Chairman of Fischer Francis Trees & Watts, as published in *Performance Reporting for Investment Managers: Applying the AIMR Performance Presentation Standards* (Charlottesville, VA: Association for Investment Management and Research, 1991), p. 57:

> Results are often analyzed, for either comparison or evaluation purposes, over an arbitrary specified number of years. The period we see used most often is five years. Particularly for fixed-income portfolios, an arbitrarily chosen period can lead to an unintended, if not perverse, conclusion. For

example, if a five-year reporting period happens to fall within a bull market, a manager that has a long-term bond bias will look strong, and vice versa.

a. Why is this statement true for fixed-income portfolios if comparisons are based on actual returns?

b. How does performance attribution analysis reduce the risk of distorting performance results for a fixed-income portfolio?

CHAPTER 21

Interest-Rate Futures Contracts

Learning Objectives

After reading this chapter you will understand:

- what a futures contract is

- the differences between a futures and a forward contract

- the basic features of various interest-rate futures contracts

- for a Treasury bond futures contract what the cheapest-to-deliver issue is and how it is determined

- how the theoretical price of a futures contract is determined

- how the theoretical price of a Treasury bond futures contract is affected by the delivery options

- how futures contracts can be used in bond portfolio management: speculation, changing duration, yield enhancement, and hedging

- how to calculate the hedge ratio and the number of contracts to short when hedging with Treasury bond futures contracts

A futures contract is an agreement that requires a party to the agreement either to buy or sell something at a designated future date at a predetermined price. In this chapter we describe interest-rate futures contracts. Interest-rate options and options on futures are covered in Chapter 22. Interest-rate swaps and agreements are the subject of Chapter 23.

With the advent of interest-rate futures, options, swaps, caps, and floors, proactive portfolio risk management, in its broadest sense, assumes a new dimension. Money managers can achieve new degrees of freedom. It is now possible to alter the interest-rate sensitivity of a bond portfolio or an asset/liability position economically and quickly. These derivative contracts, so called because they derive their value from an underlying asset, offer money managers risk and return patterns that previously were either unavailable or too costly to create.

MECHANICS OF FUTURES TRADING

A **futures contract** is a firm legal agreement between a buyer (seller) and an established exchange or its clearinghouse in which the buyer (seller) agrees to take (make) delivery of something at a specified price at the end of a designated period of time. The price at which the parties agree to transact in the future is called the futures price. The designated date at which the parties must transact is called the **settlement** or **delivery date.**

To illustrate, suppose that there is a futures contract traded on an exchange where the something to be bought or sold is bond XYZ, and the settlement is three months from now. Assume further that Bob buys this futures contract, and Sally sells this futures contract, and the price at which they agree to transact in the future is $100. Then $100 is the **futures price.** At the settlement date, Sally will deliver bond XYZ to Bob. Bob will give Sally $100, the futures price.

Most financial futures contracts have settlement dates in the months of March, June, September, or December. This means that at a predetermined time in the contract settlement month the contract stops trading, and a price is determined by the exchange for settlement of the contract. The contract with the nearest settlement date is called the **nearby futures contract.** The next futures contract is the one that settles just after the nearby contract. The contract furthest away in time from settlement is called the **most distant futures contract.**

Opening Position

When an investor takes a position in the market by buying a futures contract, the investor is said to be in a **long position** or to be **long futures.** If, instead, the investor's opening position is the sale of a futures contract, the investor is said to be in a **short position** or **short futures.**

Liquidating a Position

A party to a futures contract has two choices on liquidation of the position. First, the position can be liquidated prior to the settlement date. For this purpose, the party must take an offsetting position in the same contract. For the buyer of a futures contract, this means selling the same number of identical futures contracts; for the seller of a futures contract, this means buying the same number of identical futures contracts.

The alternative is to wait until the settlement date. At that time the party purchasing a futures contract accepts delivery of the underlying asset at the agreed-upon price; the party that sells a futures contract liquidates the position by delivering the underlying asset at the agreed-upon price. For some futures contracts that we describe in this chapter, settlement is made in cash only. Such contracts are referred to as **cash-settlement contracts.**

Role of the Clearinghouse

Associated with every futures exchange is a clearinghouse, which performs several functions. One of these functions is guaranteeing that the two parties to the transaction will perform. To see the importance of this function, consider potential problems in the futures transaction described earlier from the perspective of the two parties:

Bob the buyer and Sally the seller. Each must be concerned with the other's ability to fulfill the obligation at the settlement date. Suppose that at the settlement date the price of bond XYZ in the cash market is $70. Sally can buy bond XYZ for $70 and deliver it to Bob, who, in turn, must pay her $100. If Bob does not have the capacity to pay $100 or refuses to pay, however, Sally has lost the opportunity to realize a profit of $30. Suppose, instead, that the price of bond XYZ in the cash market is $150 at the settlement date. In this case Bob is ready and willing to accept delivery of bond XYZ and pay the agreed-upon price of $100. If Sally does not have the ability or refuses to deliver bond XYZ, Bob has lost the opportunity to realize a profit of $50.

The clearinghouse exists to meet this problem. When an investor takes a position in the futures market, the clearinghouse takes the opposite position and agrees to satisfy the terms set forth in the contract. Because the clearinghouse exists, the investor need not worry about the financial strength and integrity of the party taking the opposite side of the contract. After initial execution of an order, the relationship between the two parties ends. The clearinghouse interposes itself as the buyer for every sale and the seller for every purchase. Thus investors are free to liquidate their positions without involving the other party in the original contract and without worry that the other party may default. This is the reason why we define a futures contract as an agreement between a party and a clearinghouse associated with an exchange.

Besides its guarantee function, the clearinghouse makes it simple for parties to a futures contract to unwind their positions prior to the settlement date. Suppose that Bob wants to get out of his futures position. He will not have to seek out Sally and work out an agreement with her to terminate the original agreement. Instead, Bob can unwind his position by selling an identical futures contract. As far as the clearinghouse is concerned, its records will show that Bob has bought and sold an identical futures contract. At the settlement date, Sally will not deliver bond XYZ to Bob but will be instructed by the clearinghouse to deliver to someone who bought and still has an open futures position. In the same way, if Sally wants to unwind her position prior to the settlement date, she can buy an identical futures contract.

Margin Requirements

When a position is first taken in a futures contract, the investor must deposit a minimum dollar amount per contract as specified by the exchange. This amount, called the **initial margin,** is required as deposit for the contract.[1] The initial margin may be in the form of an interest-bearing security such as a Treasury bill. As the price of the futures contract fluctuates, the value of the investor's equity in the position changes. At the end of each trading day, the exchange determines the settlement price for the futures contract. This price is used to mark to market the investor's position, so that any gain or loss from the position is reflected in the investor's equity account.

The **maintenance margin** is the minimum level (specified by the exchange) by which an investor's equity position may fall as a result of an unfavorable price movement before the investor is required to deposit additional margin. The additional margin deposited, called the **variation margin,** is the amount necessary to bring the equity in the account back to its initial margin level. Unlike initial margin, variation

---

[1]Individual brokerage firms are free to set margin requirements above the minimum established by the exchange.

margin must be in cash, not in interest-bearing instruments. Any excess margin in the account may be withdrawn by the investor. If a party to a futures contract who is required to deposit variation margin fails to do so within 24 hours, the futures position is closed out.

Although there are initial and maintenance margin requirements for buying securities on margin, the concept of margin differs for securities and futures. When securities are acquired on margin, the difference between the price of the security and the initial margin is borrowed from the broker. The security purchased serves as collateral for the loan, and the investor pays interest. For futures contracts, the initial margin, in effect, serves as "good faith" money, an indication that the investor will satisfy the obligation of the contract. Normally, no money is borrowed by the investor.

Commissions

Commissions on futures contracts are fully negotiable. They are usually quoted on the basis of a **round turn,** a price that includes the opening and closing out of the futures contract. In most cases the commission is the same regardless of the maturity date or type of the underlying instrument. Commissions for institutional accounts vary enormously, ranging from a low of about $11 to a high of about $30 per contract.

FUTURES VERSUS FORWARD CONTRACTS

Just like a futures contract, a **forward contract** is an agreement for the future delivery of the underlying at a specified price at the end of a designated period of time. Futures contracts are standardized agreements as to the delivery date (or month) and quality of the deliverable and are traded on organized exchanges. A forward contract differs in that it is usually nonstandardized (i.e., the terms of each contract are negotiated individually between buyer and seller), there is no clearinghouse, and secondary markets are often nonexistent or extremely thin. Unlike a futures contract, which is an exchange-traded product, a forward contract is an over-the-counter instrument.

Because there is no clearinghouse that guarantees the performance of a counterparty in a forward contract, the parties to a forward contract are exposed to **counterparty risk.** Counterparty risk is the risk that the other party to the transaction will fail to perform. That is, a party to a forward contract is exposed to credit or default risk.

Although both futures and forward contracts set forth terms of delivery, futures contracts are not intended to be settled by delivery. In fact, generally less than 2% of outstanding contracts are settled by delivery. Forward contracts, in contrast, are intended for delivery.

A futures contract is marked to market at the end of each trading day, whereas a forward contract may or may not be marked to market. Just how much variation margin may be required by one or both parties of a forward contract depends on the terms negotiated. Therefore, although a futures contract is subject to interim cash flows as additional margin may be required in the case of adverse price movements, or as cash is withdrawn in the case of favorable price movements, variation margin may or may not result from a forward contract.

Finally, the parties in a forward contract are exposed to credit risk because either party may default on the obligation. Credit risk is minimal in the case of futures contracts because the clearinghouse associated with the exchange guarantees the other side of the transaction. Other than these differences, most of what we say about futures contracts applies to forward contracts.

RISK AND RETURN CHARACTERISTICS OF FUTURES CONTRACTS

The buyer of a futures contract will realize a profit if the futures price increases; the seller of a futures contract will realize a profit if the futures price decreases. For example, suppose that one month after Bob and Sally take their positions in the futures contract, the futures price of bond XYZ increases to $120. Bob, the buyer of the futures contract, could then sell the futures contract and realize a profit of $20. Effectively, at the settlement date he has agreed to buy bond XYZ for $100 and agreed to sell bond XYZ for $120. Sally, the seller of the futures contract, will realize a loss of $20.

If the futures price falls to $40 and Sally buys the contract, she realizes a profit of $60 because she agreed to sell bond XYZ for $100 and now can buy it for $40. Bob would realize a loss of $60. Thus if the futures price decreases, the buyer of a futures contract realizes a loss while the seller of a futures contract realizes a profit.

Leveraging Aspect of Futures

When a position is taken in a futures contract, the party need not put up the entire amount of the investment. Instead, only initial margin must be put up. If Bob has $100 and wants to invest in bond XYZ because he believes its price will appreciate as a result of a decline in interest rates, he can buy one bond if bond XYZ is selling for $100. If the exchange where the futures contract for bond XYZ is traded requires an initial margin of $5, however, Bob can purchase 20 contracts with his $100 investment. (This example ignores the fact that Bob may need funds for variation margin.) His payoff will then depend on the price action of 20 XYZ bonds, not the one he could buy with $100. Thus he can leverage the use of his funds. Although the degree of leverage available in the futures market varies from contract to contract, the leverage attainable is considerably greater than in the cash market.

At first, the leverage available in the futures market may suggest that the market benefits only those who want to speculate on price movements. This is not true. Futures markets can be used to reduce price risk. Without the leverage possible in futures transactions, the cost of reducing price risk using futures would be too high for many market participants.

CURRENTLY TRADED INTEREST-RATE FUTURES CONTRACTS

The more actively traded interest-rate futures contracts in the United States are described in the following sections. Most major financial markets outside the United States have similar futures contracts in which the underlying security is a fixed-income security issued by the central government.

Treasury Bill Futures

Treasury bill futures, as well as the Eurodollar futures contracts described next, are futures contracts whose underlying instrument is a short-term debt obligation. The Treasury bill futures contract, which is traded on the IMM, is based on a 13-week (three-month) Treasury bill with a face value of $1 million. More specifically, the seller of a

Treasury bill futures contract agrees to deliver to the buyer at the settlement date a Treasury bill with 13 weeks remaining to maturity and a face value of $1 million. The Treasury bill delivered can be newly issued or seasoned. The futures price is the price at which the Treasury bill will be sold by the short and purchased by the long. For example, a Treasury bill futures contract that settles in nine months requires that nine months from now the short deliver to the long $1 million face value of a Treasury bill with 13 weeks remaining to maturity. The Treasury bill could be a newly issued 13-week Treasury bill or a Treasury bill that was issued one year prior to the settlement date and therefore at the settlement has only 13 weeks remaining to maturity.

As explained in Chapter 6, Treasury bills are quoted in the cash market in terms of the annualized yield on a bank discount basis, where

$$Y_d = \frac{D}{F} \times \frac{360}{t}$$

where:

Y_d = annualized yield on a bank discount basis (expressed as a decimal)
D = dollar discount, which is equal to the difference between the face value and the price of a bill maturing in t days
F = face value
t = number of days remaining to maturity.

The dollar discount (D) is found by

$$D = Y_d \times F \times \frac{t}{360}$$

In contrast, the Treasury bill futures contract is quoted not directly in terms of yield but instead on an index basis that is related to the yield on a bank discount basis as follows:

$$\text{index price} = 100 - (Y_d \times 100)$$

For example, if Y_d is 8%, the index price is

$$100 - (0.08 \times 100) = 92$$

Given the price of the futures contract, the yield on a bank discount basis for the futures contract is determined as follows:

$$Y_d = \frac{100 - \text{index price}}{100}$$

To see how this works, suppose that the index price for a Treasury bill futures contract is 92.52. The yield on a bank discount basis for this Treasury bill futures contract is

$$Y_d = \frac{100 - 92.52}{100} = 0.0748 \text{ or } 7.48\%$$

The invoice price that the buyer of $1 million face value of 13-week Treasury bills must pay at settlement is found by first computing the dollar discount, as follows:

$$D = Y_d \times \$1,000,000 \times \frac{t}{360}$$

where t is either 90 or 91 days.

Typically, the number of days to maturity of a 13-week Treasury bill is 91 days. The invoice price is then

$$\text{invoice price} = \$1,000,000 - D$$

For example, for the Treasury bill futures contract with an index price of 92.52 (and a yield on a bank discount basis of 7.48%), the dollar discount for the 13-week Treasury bill to be delivered with 91 days to maturity is

$$D = 0.0748 \times \$1,000,000 \times \frac{91}{360}$$

$$= \$18,907.78$$

The invoice price is

$$\text{invoice price} = \$1,000,000 - \$18,907.78 = \$981,092.22$$

The minimum index price fluctuation or "tick" for this futures contract is 0.01. A change of 0.01 for the minimum index price translates into a change in the yield on a bank discount basis of one basis point (0.0001). A change of one basis point will change the dollar discount, and therefore the invoice price, by

$$0.0001 \times \$1,000,000 \times \frac{t}{360}$$

For a 13-week Treasury bill with 91 days to maturity, the change in the dollar discount is

$$0.0001 \times \$1,000,000 \times \frac{91}{360} = \$25.28$$

For a 13-week Treasury bill with 90 days to maturity, the change in the dollar discount would be $25. Despite the fact that a 13-week Treasury bill typically has 91 days to maturity, market participants commonly refer to the value of a basis point for this futures contract as $25.

Eurodollar CD Futures

Eurodollar certificates of deposit (CDs) are denominated in dollars but represent the liabilities of banks outside the United States. The contracts are traded on both the International Monetary Market of the Chicago Mercantile Exchange and the London International Financial Futures Exchange. The rate paid on Eurodollar CDs is the London interbank offered rate (LIBOR).

The three-month Eurodollar CD is the underlying instrument for the Eurodollar CD futures contract. As with the Treasury bill futures contract, this contract is for $1 million of face value and is traded on an index price basis. The index price basis in which the contract is quoted is equal to 100 minus the annualized futures LIBOR. For example, a Eurodollar CD futures price of 94.00 means a futures three-month LIBOR of 6%.

The minimum price fluctuation (tick) for this contract is 0.01 (or 0.0001 in terms of LIBOR). This means that the price value of a basis point for this contract is $25, found as follows. The simple interest on $1 million for 90 days is equal to

$$\$1,000,000 \times (\text{LIBOR} \times 90/360)$$

If LIBOR changes by 1 basis point (0.0001), then

$$\$1,000,000 \times (0.0001 \times 90/360) = \$25$$

The Eurodollar CD futures contract is a cash settlement contract. That is, the parties settle in cash for the value of a Eurodollar CD based on LIBOR at the settlement date. The Eurodollar CD futures contract is one of the most heavily traded futures contracts in the world. It is frequently used to trade the short end of the yield curve, and many hedgers have found this contract to be the best hedging vehicle for a wide range of hedging situations.

Treasury Bond Futures

The Treasury bond futures contract is traded on the Chicago Board of Trade (CBT). The underlying instrument for a Treasury bond futures contract is $100,000 par value of a hypothetical 20-year 8% coupon bond.* The futures price is quoted in terms of par being 100. Quotes are in 32nds of 1%. Thus a quote for a Treasury bond futures contract of 97-16 means 97 and 16/32nds, or 97.50. So if a buyer and seller agree on a futures price of 97-16, this means that the buyer agrees to accept delivery of the hypothetical underlying Treasury bond and pay 97.50% of par value and the seller agrees to accept 97.50% of par value. Because the par value is $100,000, the futures price that the buyer and seller agree to transact for this hypothetical Treasury bond is $97,500.

The minimum price fluctuation for the Treasury bond futures contract is a 32nd of 1%. The dollar value of a 32nd for a $100,000 par value (the par value for the underlying Treasury bond) is $31.25. Thus the minimum price fluctuation is $31.25 for this contract.

We have been referring to the underlying as a hypothetical Treasury bond. Does this mean that the contract is a cash settlement contract, as is the case with the Eurodollar CD futures contract? The answer is no. The seller of a Treasury bond futures who decides to make delivery rather than liquidate his position by buying back the contract prior to the settlement date must deliver some Treasury bond. But what Treasury bond? The CBT allows the seller to deliver one of several Treasury bonds that the CBT declares is acceptable for delivery. The specific bonds that the seller may deliver are published by the CBT prior to the initial trading of a futures contract with a specific settlement date. Exhibit 21-1 shows the Treasury issues that the seller can select from to deliver to the buyer of the June 1997 futures contract. The CBT makes its determination of the Treasury issues that are acceptable for delivery from all outstanding Treasury issues that meet the following criteria: An issue must have at least 15 years to maturity from the date of delivery if not callable; in the case of callable Treasury bonds, the issue must not be callable for at least 15 years from the first day of the delivery month.

The delivery process for the Treasury bond futures contract makes the contract interesting. At the settlement date, the seller of a futures contract (the short) is required to deliver the buyer (the long) $100,000 par value of an 8% 20-year Treasury bond. Because no such bond exists, the seller must choose from one of the acceptable deliverable Treasury bonds that the CBT exchange has specified. Suppose that the

---

*As this book goes to press, the CBT has approved a change in the coupon for the hypothetical Treasury bond from 8% to 6%. The principles discussed below still apply.

EXHIBIT 21-1	Treasury Bond Issues Acceptable for Delivery to Satisfy the June 1997 Futures Contract	

Issue

Coupon (%)	Maturity	Conversion Factor
6.625	2/15/27	0.8451
6.500	11/15/26	0.8312
6.750	8/15/26	0.8598
6.000	2/15/26	0.7767
6.875	8/15/25	0.8750
7.625	2/15/25	0.9585
7.500	11/15/24	0.9447
6.250	8/15/23	0.8097
7.125	2/15/23	0.9054
7.625	11/15/22	0.9594
7.250	8/15/22	0.9194
8.000	11/15/22	0.9998
8.125	8/15/21	1.0132
8.125	5/15/21	1.0130
7.875	2/15/21	0.9868
8.750	8/15/20	1.0783
8.750	5/15/20	1.0778
8.500	2/15/20	1.0518
8.125	8/15/19	1.0128
8.875	2/15/19	1.0891
9.000	11/15/19	1.1012
9.125	5/15/18	1.1128
9.875	8/15/17	1.0866
8.750	5/15/17	1.0736
7.500	11/15/16	0.9511
7.250	5/15/16	0.9276
9.250	2/15/16	1.1196
9.875	11/15/15	1.1781
10.625	8/15/15	1.2482
11.250	2/15/15	1.3033

seller is entitled to deliver $100,000 of a 6% 20-year Treasury bond to settle the futures contract. The value of this bond of course is less than the value of an 8% 20-year bond. If the seller delivers the 6% 20-year bond, this would be unfair to the buyer of the futures contract who contracted to receive $100,000 of an 8% 20-year Treasury bond. Alternatively, suppose that the seller delivers $100,000 of a 10% 20-year Treasury bond. The value of a 10% 20-year Treasury bond is greater than that of an 8% 20-year bond, so this would be a disadvantage to the seller.

How can this problem be resolved? To make delivery equitable to both parties, the CBT has introduced **conversion factors** for determining the invoice price of each acceptable deliverable Treasury issue against the Treasury bond futures contract. The conversion factor is determined by the CBT before a contract with a specific settlement date begins trading. Exhibit 21-1 shows for each of the acceptable Treasury issues the corresponding conversion factor.[2] The conversion factor is constant throughout the trading period of the futures contract. The short must notify the long of the actual bond that will be delivered one day before the delivery date.

The price that the buyer must pay the seller when a Treasury bond is delivered is called the **invoice price.** The invoice price is the settlement futures price plus accrued interest on the bonds delivered. However, as just noted, the seller can deliver one of several acceptable Treasury issues and to make delivery fair to both parties, the invoice price must be adjusted based on the actual Treasury issue delivered. It is the conversion factors that are used to adjust the invoice price. The invoice price is

$$\text{invoice price} = \text{contract size} \times \text{futures contract settlement price}$$
$$\times \text{ conversion factor} + \text{accrued interest}$$

Suppose that the Treasury bond futures contract settles at 94-08 and that the short elects to deliver a Treasury bond issue with a conversion factor of 1.20. The futures contract settlement price of 94-08 means 94.25% of par value. As the contract size is $100,000, the invoice price the buyer pays the seller is

$$\$100,000 \times 0.9425 \times 1.20 + \text{accrued interest} = \$113,100 + \text{accrued interest}$$

In selecting the issue to be delivered, the short will select from all the deliverable issues the one that is cheapest to deliver. This issue is referred to as the **cheapest-to-deliver issue;** it plays a key role in the pricing of this futures contract. The cheapest-to-deliver issue is determined by participants in the market as follows. For each of the acceptable Treasury issues from which the seller can select, the seller calculates that return that can be earned by buying that issue and delivering it at the settlement date. Note that the seller can calculate the return because he knows the price of the Treasury issue now and the futures price that he agrees to deliver the issue. The return so calculated is called the **implied repo rate.** The cheapest-to-deliver issue is then the one issue among all acceptable Treasury issues with the highest implied repo rate because it is the issue that would give the seller of the futures contract the highest return by buying and then delivering the issue. This is depicted in Exhibit 21-2.

In addition to the choice of which acceptable Treasury issue to deliver—sometimes referred to as the **quality option** or **swap option**—the short position has two more options granted under CBT delivery guidelines. The short position is permitted to decide when in the delivery month delivery actually will take place. This is called the **timing option.** The other option is the right of the short position to give notice of intent to deliver up to 8:00 P.M. Chicago time after the closing of the exchange (3:15 P.M. Chicago time) on the date when the futures settlement price has been fixed. This option is referred to as the **wild card option.** The quality option, the timing option, and the wild card option (in sum referred to as the **delivery options**) mean that the long position can never be sure of which Treasury bond will be delivered or when it will be delivered. The delivery options are summarized in Exhibit 21-3.

---

[2] The conversion factor is based on the price that a deliverable bond would sell for at the beginning of the delivery month if it were to yield 8%.

EXHIBIT 21-2 Determination of Cheapest-to-Deliver Issue Based on the Implied Repo Rate

Implied repo rate: Rate of return by buying an acceptable Treasury issue, shorting the Treasury bond futures, and delivering the issue at the settlement date.

Buy this issue	Deliver this issue at futures price	Calculate return (implied repo rate)
Acceptable Treasury issue #1	Deliver issue #1	Implied repo rate #1
Acceptable Treasury issue #2	Deliver issue #2	Implied repo rate #2
Acceptable Treasury issue #3	Deliver issue #3	Implied repo rate #3
. . .	. . .	. . .
Acceptable Treasury issue #N	Deliver issue #N	Implied repo rate #N

Cheapest to deliver is issue that produces maximum implied repo rate.

Treasury Note Futures

There are three Treasury note futures contracts: 10-year, five-year, and two-year. All three contracts are modeled after the Treasury bond futures contract and are traded on the CBT. The underlying instrument for the 10-year Treasury note futures contract is $100,000 par value of a hypothetical 10-year 8% Treasury note. There are several acceptable Treasury issues that may be delivered by the short. An issue is acceptable if the maturity is not less than 6.5 years and not greater than 10 years from the first day of the delivery month. The delivery options granted to the short position and the minimum price fluctuation are the same as for the Treasury bond futures contract.

For the five-year Treasury note futures contract, the underlying is $100,000 par value of a U.S. Treasury note that satisfies the following conditions: (1) an original maturity of not more than five years and three months, (2) a remaining maturity no

EXHIBIT 21-3 Delivery Options Granted to the Short (Seller) of a CBT Treasury Bond Futures Contract

Delivery Option	*Description*
Quality or swap option	Choice of which acceptable Treasury issue to deliver
Timing option	Choice of when in delivery month to deliver
Wild card option	Choice to deliver after the closing price of the futures contract is determined

greater than five years and three months, and (3) a remaining maturity not less than four years and three months.

The underlying for the two-year Treasury note futures contract is $200,000 par value of a U.S. Treasury note with a remaining maturity of not more than two years and not less than one year and nine months. Moreover, the original maturity of the note delivered to satisfy the two-year futures cannot be more than five years and two months.

Bond Buyer's Municipal Bond Index Futures

Traded on the CBT, the underlying product for this contract is a basket, or index, of 40 municipal bonds. The Bond Buyer, publisher of the **Bond Buyer** (a trade publication of the municipal bond industry), serves as the index manager for the contract and prices each bond in the index based on prices received between 1:30 and 2:00 P.M. (Central Standard Time) from five municipal bond brokers. It is necessary to obtain several independent prices from brokers because municipal bonds trade in the over-the-counter market.

After the prices are received from the five pricing brokers for a given issue, the lowest and highest prices are dropped. The remaining three prices are averaged, and the resulting value is referred to as the **appraisal value.** The appraisal value for each issue is then divided by a conversion factor that equates the bond to an 8% issue. This gives a converted price for each issue. The converted prices are then summed and divided by 40, for an average converted price on the index. The index is revised bimonthly, when newer issues are added and older issues or issues that no longer meet the criteria for inclusion in the index are dropped.[3] A smoothing coefficient is calculated on the index revision date so that the index will not change merely because of changes in the composition of the index. The average converted dollar price for the index is multiplied by this coefficient to get the index value for a particular date.

As delivery on all 40 bonds in the index is not possible, the contract is a cash settlement contract, with settlement price based on the value of the index on the delivery date. The contract is quoted in points and 32nds of a point. For example, suppose that the settlement price for the contract is 93-21. This translates into a price of 93 and 21/32, or 93.65635. The dollar value of a contract is equal to $1,000 times the Bond Buyer Municipal Bond Index. For example, the dollar value based on the settlement price is

$$\$1,000 \times 93.65635 = \$93,656.35$$

PRICING AND ARBITRAGE IN THE INTEREST-RATE FUTURES MARKET

One of the primary concerns that most traders and investors have when taking a position in futures contracts is whether the futures price at which they transact will be a "fair" price. Buyers are concerned that the price may be too high and that they

---

[3]The inclusion criteria, as well as the revision process and pricing of the index, are spelled out in a publication titled "The Chicago Board of Trade's Bond Futures Contract," 1987.

will be picked off by more experienced futures traders waiting to profit from the mistakes of the uninitiated. Sellers worry that the price is artificially low and that savvy traders may have manipulated the markets so that they can buy at bargain-basement prices. Furthermore, prospective participants frequently find no rational explanation for the sometimes violent ups and downs that occur in the futures markets. Theories about efficient markets give little comfort to anyone who knows of or has experienced the sudden losses that can occur in the highly leveraged futures markets.

Fortunately, the futures markets are not as irrational as they may at first seem; if they were, they would not have become so successful. The interest-rate futures markets are not perfectly efficient markets, but they probably come about as close as any market. Furthermore, there are both very clear reasons why futures prices are what they are and methods by which traders, investors, and borrowers can and will quickly eliminate any discrepancy between futures prices and their fair levels.

There are several different ways to price futures contracts. Fortunately, all lead to the same fair price for a given contract. Each approach relies on the "law of one price." This law states that a given financial asset (or liability) must have the same price regardless of the means by which it is created. We explain here one way in which futures contracts can be combined with cash market instruments to create cash flows that are identical to other cash securities.[4] The law of one price implies that the synthetically created cash securities must have the same price as the actual cash securities. Similarly, cash instruments can be combined to create cash flows that are identical to futures contracts. By the law of one price the futures contract must have the same price as the synthetic futures created from cash instruments.

Pricing of Futures Contracts

To understand how futures contracts should be priced, consider the following example. Suppose that a 20-year 100-par-value bond with a coupon rate of 12% is selling at par. Also suppose that this bond is the deliverable for a futures contract that settles in three months. If the current three-month interest rate at which funds can be loaned or borrowed is 8% per year, what should be the price of this futures contract?

Suppose that the price of the futures contract is 107. Consider the following strategy:

- Sell the futures contract at 107.
- Purchase the bond for 100.
- Borrow 100 for three months at 8% per year.

The borrowed funds are used to purchase the bond, resulting in no initial cash outlay for this strategy. Three months from now, the bond must be delivered to settle the futures contract and the loan must be repaid. These trades will produce the following cash flows:

---

[4]For the other ways to price futures contracts, see Chapter 5 in Mark Pitts and Frank J. Fabozzi, *Interest Rate Futures and Options* (Chicago: Probus Publishing, 1990).

From Settlement of the Futures Contract:	
Flat price of bond	107
Accrued interest (12% for 3 months)	3
Total proceeds	110
From the Loan:	
Repayment of principal of loan	100
Interest on loan (8% for 3 months)	2
Total outlay	102
Profit	8

This strategy will guarantee a profit of 8. Moreover, the profit is generated with no initial outlay because the funds used to purchase the bond are borrowed. The profit will be realized *regardless of the futures price at the settlement date*. Obviously, in a well-functioning market, arbitrageurs would buy the bond and sell the futures, forcing the futures price down and bidding up the bond price so as to eliminate this profit.

In contrast, suppose that the futures price is 92 instead of 107. Consider the following strategy:

- Buy the futures contract at 92.
- Sell (short) the bond for 100.
- Invest (lend) 100 for 3 months at 8% per year.

Once again, there is no initial cash outlay. Three months from now a bond will be purchased to settle the long position in the futures contract. That bond will then be used to cover the short position (i.e., to cover the short sale in the cash market). The outcome in three months would be as follows:

From Settlement of the Futures Contract:	
Flat price of bond	92
Accrued interest (12% for 3 months)	3
Total outlay	95
From the Loan:	
Principal received from maturing investment	100
Interest earned from the 3-month investment (8% for 3 months)	2
Total outlay	102
Profit	7

The profit of 7 is a pure arbitrage profit. It requires no initial cash outlay and will be realized *regardless of the futures price at the settlement date*.

There is a futures price that will eliminate the arbitrage profit, however. There will be no arbitrage if the futures price is 99. Let's look at what would happen if the two previous strategies are followed and the futures price is 99. First, consider the following strategy:

- Sell the futures contract at 99.
- Purchase the bond for 100.
- Borrow 100 for three months at 8% per year.

In three months, the outcome would be as follows:

From Settlement of the Futures Contract:	
Flat price of bond	99
Accrued interest (12% for 3 months)	3
Total proceeds	102
From the Loan:	
Repayment of principal of loan	100
Interest on loan (8% for 3 months)	2
Total outlay	102
Profit	0

There is no arbitrage profit in this case.

Next consider the following strategy:

- Buy the futures contract at 99.
- Sell (short) the bond for 100.
- Invest (lend) 100 for three months at 8% per year.

The outcome in three months would be as follows:

From Settlement of the Futures Contract:	
Flat price of bond	99
Accrued interest (12% for 3 months)	3
Total outlay	102
From the Loan:	
Principal received from maturing investment	100
Interest earned from the 3-month investment (8% for 3 months)	2
Total proceeds	102
Profit	0

Thus neither strategy results in a profit. Hence the futures price of 99 is the theoretical futures price, because any higher or lower futures price will permit arbitrage profits.

Theoretical Futures Price Based on Arbitrage Model

Considering the arbitrage arguments just presented, the theoretical futures price can be determined on the basis of the following information:

1. The price of the bond in the cash market.
2. The coupon rate on the bond. In our example, the coupon rate is 12% per year.
3. The interest rate for borrowing and lending until the settlement date. The borrowing and lending rate is referred to as the **financing rate.** In our example, the financing rate is 8% per year.

We will let

r = financing rate
c = current yield, or coupon rate divided by the cash market price
P = cash market price
F = futures price
t = time, in years, to the futures delivery date

and then consider the following strategy that is initiated on a coupon date:s

- Sell the futures contract at F.
- Purchase the bond for P.
- Borrow P until the settlement date at r.

The outcome at the settlement date is

From Settlement of the Futures Contract:	
Flat price of bond	F
Accrued interest	ctP
Total proceeds	$F + ctP$
From the Loan:	
Repayment of principal of loan	P
Interest on loan	rtP
Total outlay	$P + rtP$

The profit will be

$$\text{profit} = \text{total proceeds} - \text{total outlay}$$
$$= F + ctP - (P + rtP)$$

In equilibrium the theoretical futures price occurs where the profit from this trade is zero. Thus to have equilibrium, the following must hold:

$$0 = F + ctP - (P + rtP)$$

Solving for the theoretical futures price, we have

$$F = P[1 + t(r - c)] \tag{21.1}$$

Alternatively, consider the following strategy:

- Buy the futures contract at F.
- Sell (short) the bond for P.
- Invest (lend) P at r until the settlement date.

The outcome at the settlement date would be

From Settlement of the Futures Contract:	
Flat price of bond	F
Accrued interest	ctP
Total outlay	$F + ctP$
From the Loan:	
Proceeds received from maturing of investment	P
Interest earned	rtP
Total proceeds	$P + rtP$

The profit will be

$$\text{profit} = \text{total proceeds} - \text{total outlay}$$
$$= P + rtP - (F + ctP)$$

Setting the profit equal to zero so that there will be no arbitrage profit and solving for the futures price, we obtain the same equation for the futures price as equation (21.1).

Let's apply equation (21.1) to our preceding example, in which

$r = 0.08$
$c = 0.12$
$P = 100$
$t = 0.25$

Then the theoretical futures price is

$$F = 100[1 + 0.25(0.08 - 0.12)] = 99$$

This agrees with the theoretical futures price that we derived earlier.

The theoretical futures price may be at a premium to the cash market price (higher than the cash market price) or at a discount from the cash market price (lower than the cash market price), depending on $(r - c)$. The term $r - c$ is called the **net financing cost** because it adjusts the financing rate for the coupon interest earned. The net financing cost is more commonly called the **cost of carry,** or simply **carry. Positive carry** means that the current yield earned is greater than the financing cost; **negative carry** means that the financing cost exceeds the current yield. The relationships can be expressed as follows:

Carry	*Futures Price*
Positive $(c > r)$	Will sell at a discount to cash price $(F < P)$
Negative $(c > r)$	Will sell at a premium to cash price $(F > P)$
Zero $(c > r)$	Will be equal to cash price $(F = P)$

In the case of interest-rate futures, carry (the relationship between the short-term financing rate and the current yield on the bond) depends on the shape of the yield curve. When the yield curve is upward-sloping, the short-term financing rate will generally be less than the current yield on the bond, resulting in positive carry. The futures price will then sell at a discount to the cash price for the bond. The opposite will hold true when the yield curve is inverted.

Closer Look at the Theoretical Futures Price

To derive the theoretical futures price using the arbitrage argument, we made several assumptions, which have certain implications.

Interim Cash Flows   No interim cash flows due to variation margin or coupon interest payments were assumed in the model. However, we know that interim cash flows can occur for both of these reasons. Because we assumed no variation margin, the price derived is technically the theoretical price for a forward contract (which is not marked to market at the end of each trading day). If interest rates rise, the short position in futures will receive margin as the futures price decreases; the margin can then be reinvested at a higher interest rate. In contrast, if interest rates fall, there will be variation margin that must be financed by the short position; however, because interest rates have declined, financing will be possible at a lower cost. Thus, whichever way rates move, those who are short futures gain relative to those who are short forwards. Conversely, those who are long futures lose relative to those who are long forwards. These facts account for the difference between futures and forward prices.

Incorporating interim coupon payments into the pricing model is not difficult. However, the value of the coupon payments at the settlement date will depend on the interest rate at which they can be reinvested. The shorter the maturity of the futures contract and the lower the coupon rate, the less important the reinvestment income is in determining the futures price.

Short-Term Interest Rate (Financing Rate)   In deriving the theoretical futures price it is assumed that the borrowing and lending rates are equal. Typically, however, the borrowing rate is higher than the lending rate. We will let

r_B = borrowing rate
r_L = lending rate

Consider the following strategy:

- Sell the futures contract at F.
- Purchase the bond for P.
- Borrow P until the settlement date at r_B.

The futures price that would produce no arbitrage profit is

$$F = P[1 + t(r_B - c)] \tag{21.2}$$

Now consider the following strategy:

- Buy the futures contract at F.
- Sell (short) the bond for P.
- Invest (lend) P at r_L until the settlement date.

The futures price that would produce no profit is

$$F = P[1 + t(r_L - c)] \tag{21.3}$$

Equations (21.2) and (21.3) together provide boundaries for the theoretical futures price. Equation (21.2) provides the upper boundary and equation (21.3) the lower boundary. For example, assume that the borrowing rate is 8% per year and the lending rate is 6% per year. Then using equation (21.2) and the preceding example, the upper boundary is

$$F(\text{upper boundary}) = \$100[1 + 0.25\,(0.08 - 0.12)]$$
$$= \$99$$

The lower boundary using equation (21.3) is

$$F(\text{lower boundary}) = \$100[1 + 0.25\,(0.06 - 0.12)]$$
$$= \$98.50$$

In calculating these boundaries, we assume that no transaction costs are involved in taking the position. In actuality, the transaction costs of entering into and closing the cash position as well as the round-trip transaction costs for the futures contract must be considered and do affect the boundaries for the futures contract.

Deliverable Bond Is Not Known   The arbitrage arguments used to derive equation (21.1) assumed that only one instrument is deliverable. But the futures contracts on Treasury bonds and Treasury notes are designed to allow the short the choice of delivering one of a number of deliverable issues (the quality or swap option). Because there may be more than one deliverable, market participants track the price of each deliverable bond and determine which bond is the cheapest to deliver. The futures price will then trade in relation to the cheapest-to-deliver issue.

There is the risk that though an issue may be the cheapest to deliver at the time a position in the futures contract is taken, it may not be the cheapest to deliver after that time. A change in the cheapest-to-deliver issue can dramatically alter the futures price.

What are the implications of the quality (swap) option on the futures price? Because the swap option is an option granted by the long to the short, the long will want to pay less for the futures contract than indicated by equation (21.1). Therefore, as a result of the quality option, the theoretical futures price as given by equation (21.1) must be adjusted as follows:

$$F = P[1 + t(r - c)] - \text{value of quality option} \tag{21.4}$$

Market participants have employed theoretical models in attempting to estimate the fair value of the quality option. These models are beyond the scope of this chapter.[5]

---

[5] Several studies have investigated the magnitude of the mispricing caused by the delivery option. See, for example, Gerald D. Gay and Steven Manaster, "The Quality Option Implicit in Futures Contracts," *Journal of Financial Economics,* September 1984, pp. 353–370; Gerald D. Gay and Steven Manaster, "Implicit Delivery Options and Optimal Delivery Strategies for Financial Futures Contracts," *Journal of Financial Economics,* May 1986, pp. 41–72; Alex Kane and Alan Marcus, "The Quality Option in the Treasury Bond Futures Market: An Empirical Assessment," *Journal of Futures Markets,* Summer 1986, pp. 231–248; Alex Kane and Alan Marcus, "Valuation and Optimal Exercise of the Wild Card Option in the Treasury Bond Futures Market," *Journal of Finance,* March 1986, pp. 195–207; and Michael J. Hemler, "The Quality Delivery Option in Treasury Bond Futures Contracts," doctoral dissertation, Graduate School of Business, University of Chicago, March 1988.

Delivery Date Is Not Known   In the pricing model based on arbitrage arguments, a known delivery date is assumed. For Treasury bond and note futures contracts, the short has a timing and wild card option, so the long does not know when the securities will be delivered. The effect of the timing and wild card options on the theoretical futures price is the same as with the quality option. These delivery options should result in a theoretical futures price that is lower than the one suggested in equation (21.1), as shown here:

$$F = P[1 + t(r - c)] - \text{value of quality option} \\ - \text{value of timing option} - \text{value of wildcard option} \tag{21.5}$$

or alternatively,

$$F = P[1 + t(r - c)] - \text{delivery options} \tag{21.6}$$

Market participants attempt to value the delivery option in order to apply equation (21.6).

Deliverable Is Not a Basket of Securities   The municipal index futures contract is a cash settlement contract based on a basket of securities. The difficulty in arbitraging this futures contract is that it is too expensive to buy or sell every bond included in the index. Instead, a portfolio including a smaller number of bonds may be constructed to "track" the index. The arbitrage, however, is no longer risk-free because there is tracking error risk.

BOND PORTFOLIO MANAGEMENT APPLICATIONS

There are various ways in which a money manager can use interest-rate futures contracts.

Speculating on the Movement of Interest Rates

The price of a futures contract moves in the opposite direction from interest rates: When rates rise, the futures price will fall; when rates fall, the futures price will rise. A portfolio manager who wants to speculate that interest rates will rise (fall) can sell (buy) interest-rate futures. Before interest-rate futures were available, investors who wanted to speculate on interest rates did so with the long-term Treasury bond; they shorted the bond if they expected interest rates to rise, and they bought it if they expected interest rates to fall. Using interest-rate futures instead of the cash markets (instead of trading long-term Treasuries themselves) has three advantages. First, transactions costs for trading futures are lower than trading in the cash market. Second, margin requirements are lower for futures than for Treasury securities; using futures thus permits greater leverage. Finally, it is easier to sell short in the futures market than in the Treasury market. The leverage advantages in trading futures may encourage speculation on interest-rate movements; making speculation easier for investors is not the function of interest-rate futures contracts.

Controlling the Interest-Rate Risk of a Portfolio

Interest-rate futures can be used to alter the interest-rate sensitivity of a portfolio. Money managers with strong expectations about the direction of the future course of interest rates will adjust the durations of their portfolios so as to capitalize on their expectations. Specifically, if a manager expects rates to increase, the duration will be shortened; if interest rates are expected to decrease, the duration will be lengthened.

Although money managers can alter the durations of their portfolios with cash market instruments, a quick and inexpensive means for doing so (on either a temporary or permanent basis) is to use futures contracts.

In addition to adjusting a portfolio based on anticipated interest-rate movements, futures contracts can be used in constructing a portfolio with a longer duration than is available with cash market securities. As an example of the latter, suppose that in a certain interest-rate environment a pension fund manager must structure a portfolio to have a duration of 15 years to accomplish a particular investment objective. Bonds with such a long duration may not be available. By buying the appropriate number and kind of interest-rate futures contracts, a pension fund manager can increase the portfolio's duration to the target level of 15.

A formula to approximate the number of futures contracts necessary to adjust the portfolio duration to a new level is

$$\text{approximate number of contracts} = \frac{(D_T - D_I)P_I}{D_F P_F}$$

where:

D_T = target effective duration for the portfolio
D_I = initial effective duration for the portfolio
P_I = initial market value of the portfolio
D_F = effective duration for the futures contact
P_F = market value of the futures contract

Notice that if the money manager wishes to increase the duration, D_T will be greater than D_I, and the equation will have a positive sign. This means that futures contracts will be purchased. The opposite is true if the objective is to shorten the portfolio duration.

Creating Synthetic Securities for Yield Enhancement

A cash market security can be created synthetically by taking a position in the futures contract together with the deliverable instrument. If the yield on the synthetic security is the same as the yield on the cash market security, there will be no arbitrage opportunity. Any difference between the two yields can be exploited so as to enhance the yield on the portfolio.

To see how, consider an investor who owns a 20-year Treasury bond and sells Treasury futures that call for the delivery of that particular bond three months from now. Although the maturity of the Treasury bond is 20 years, the investor has effectively shortened the maturity of the bond to three months.

Consequently, the long position in the 20-year bond and the short futures position are equivalent to a long position in a three-month riskless security. The position is riskless because the investor is locking in the price to be received three months from now— the futures price. By being long the bond and short the futures, the investor has synthetically created a three-month Treasury bill. The return the investor should expect to earn from this synthetic position should be the yield on a three-month Treasury bill. If the yield on the synthetic three-month Treasury bill is greater than the yield on the cash market Treasury bill, the investor can realize an enhanced yield by creating the synthetic short-term security. The fundamental relationship for creating synthetic securities is

$$RSP = CBP - FBP \tag{21.7}$$

where:

RSP = riskless short-term security position
CBP = cash bond position
FBP = bond futures position

A negative sign before a position means a short position. In terms of our previous example, CBP is the long cash bond position, the negative sign before FBP refers to the short futures position, and RSP is the riskless synthetic three-month security or Treasury bill.

Equation (21.7) states that an investor who is long the cash market security and short the futures contract should expect to earn the rate of return on a risk-free security with the same maturity as the futures delivery date. Solving equation (21.7) for the long bond position, we have

$$\text{CBP} = \text{RSP} + \text{FBP} \tag{21.8}$$

Equation (21.8) states that a cash bond position equals a short-term riskless security position plus a long bond futures position. Thus a cash market bond can be created synthetically by buying a futures contract and investing in a Treasury bill.

Solving equation (21.8) for the bond futures position, we have

$$\text{FBP} = \text{CBP} - \text{RSP} \tag{21.9}$$

Equation (21.9) tells us that a long position in the futures contract can be created synthetically by taking a long position in the cash market bond and shorting the short-term riskless security. But shorting the short-term riskless security is equivalent to borrowing money. Notice that it was equation (21.9) that we used in deriving the theoretical futures price when the futures contract was underpriced. Recall that when the actual futures price is greater than the theoretical futures price, the strategy to obtain an arbitrage profit is to sell the futures contract and create a synthetic long futures position by buying the asset with borrowed funds. This is precisely what equation (21.9) states. In this case, instead of creating a synthetic cash market instrument as we did with equations (21.7) and (21.8), we have created a synthetic futures contract. The fact that the synthetic long futures position is cheaper than the actual long futures position provides an arbitrage opportunity. If we reverse the sign of both sides of equation (21.9), we can see how a short futures position can be created synthetically.

In an efficient market the opportunities for yield enhancement should not exist very long. But even in the absence of yield enhancement, money managers can use synthetic securities to hedge a portfolio position that they find difficult to hedge in the cash market either because of lack of liquidity or because of other constraints.

Hedging

Hedging with futures calls for taking a futures position as a temporary substitute for transactions to be made in the cash market at a later date. If cash and futures prices move together, any loss realized by the hedger from one position (whether cash or futures) will be offset by a profit on the other position. When the net profit or loss from the positions is exactly as anticipated, the hedge is referred to as a **perfect hedge.**

In practice, hedging is not that simple. The amount of net profit will not necessarily be as anticipated. The outcome of a hedge will depend on the relationship between the cash price and the futures price both when a hedge is placed and when it is lifted. The difference between the cash price and the futures price is the **basis.** The risk that the basis will change in an unpredictable way is called **basis risk.**

In bond portfolio management, typically, the bond to be hedged is not identical to the bond underlying the futures contract. This type of hedging is referred to as **cross hedging.** There may be substantial basis risk in cross hedging. An unhedged position is exposed to price risk, the risk that the cash market price will move adversely. A hedged position substitutes basis risk for price risk.

A **short** (or **sell**) **hedge** is used to protect against a decline in the cash price of a bond. To execute a short hedge, futures contracts are sold. By establishing a short hedge, the hedger has fixed the future cash price and transferred the price risk of ownership to the buyer of the futures contract. To understand why a short hedge might be executed, suppose that a pension fund manager knows that bonds must be liquidated in 40 days to make a $5 million payment to the beneficiaries of the pension fund. If interest rates rise during the 40-day period, more bonds will have to be liquidated to realize $5 million. To guard against this possibility, the manager can sell bonds in the futures market to lock in a selling price.

A **long** (or **buy**) **hedge** is undertaken to protect against an increase in the cash price of a bond. In a long hedge, the hedger buys a futures contract to lock in a purchase price. A pension fund manager might use a long hedge when substantial cash contributions are expected, and the manager is concerned that interest rates will fall. Also, a money manager who knows that bonds are maturing in the near future and expects that interest rates will fall can employ a long hedge to lock in a rate for the proceeds to be reinvested.

Conceptually, cross hedging is somewhat more complicated than hedging deliverable securities, because it involves two relationships. First, there is the relationship between the cheapest-to-deliver security and the futures contract. Second, there is the relationship between the security to be hedged and the cheapest-to-deliver security.

The Hedge Ratio   The key to minimizing risk in a cross hedge is to choose the right hedge ratio. The hedge ratio depends on volatility weighting, or weighting by relative changes in value. The purpose of a hedge is to use gains or losses from a futures position to offset any difference between the target sale price and the actual sale price of the asset. Accordingly, the hedge ratio is chosen with the intention of matching the volatility (i.e., the dollar change) of the futures contract to the volatility of the asset. Consequently, the hedge ratio is given by

$$\text{hedge ratio} = \frac{\text{volatility of bond to be hedged}}{\text{volatility of hedging instrument}} \tag{21.10}$$

As equation (21.10) shows, if the bond to be hedged is more volatile than the hedging instrument, more of the hedging instrument will be needed.

Although it might be fairly clear why volatility is the key variable in determining the hedge ratio, *volatility* has many definitions. For hedging purposes we are concerned with volatility in absolute dollar terms. To calculate the dollar volatility of a bond, one must know the precise point in time that volatility is to be calculated (because volatility generally declines as a bond seasons) as well as the price or yield at which to calculate volatility (because higher yields generally reduce dollar volatility for a given yield change). The relevant point in the life of the bond for calculating volatility is the point at which the hedge will be lifted. Volatility at any other point is essentially irrelevant because the goal is to lock in a price or rate only on that particular day. Similarly, the relevant yield at which to calculate volatility initially is the target yield. Consequently, the "volatility of the bond to be hedged" referred to in equation (21.10) is the price value of a basis point for the bond on the date the hedge is expected to be delivered.[6]

An example shows why volatility weighting leads to the correct hedge ratio.[7] Suppose that on April 19, 1985, an investor owned the Southern Bell 11¾% bonds of 2023 and sold June 1985 Treasury bond futures to hedge a future sale of the bonds. This is an example of a cross hedge. Suppose that (1) the Treasury 7⅝s of 2007 were the cheapest-to-deliver issue on the contract and that they were trading at 11.50%, (2) the Southern Bell bonds were at 12.40%, and (3) the Treasury bond futures were at a price of 70. To simplify, assume also that the yield spread between the two bonds remains at 0.90% (i.e., 90 basis points) and that the anticipated sale date was the last business day in June 1985.

Because the conversion factor for the deliverable 7⅝s for the June 1985 contract was 0.9660, the target price for hedging the 7⅝s would be 67.62 (from 70 × 0.9660), and the target yield would be 11.789% (the yield at a price of 67.62). The yield on the telephone bonds is assumed to stay at 0.90% above the yield on the 7⅝s, so the target yield for the Southern Bell bonds would be 12.689%, with a corresponding price of 92.628. At these target levels, the price value of a basis point (PVBP) for the 7⅝s and telephone bonds are, respectively, 0.056332 and 0.072564. As indicated earlier, all these calculations are made using a settlement date equal to the anticipated sale date, in this case the end of June 1985. Thus the relative price volatilities of the bonds to be hedged and the deliverable security are easily obtained from the assumed sale date and target prices.

However, to calculate the hedge ratio [equation (21.10)] we need the volatility not of the cheapest-to-deliver issue, but of the hedging instrument, that is, of the futures contract. Fortunately, knowing the volatility of the bond to be hedged relative to the cheapest-to-deliver issue and the volatility of the cheapest-to-deliver bond relative to the futures contract, we can easily obtain the relative volatilities that define the hedge ratio:

$$\text{hedge ratio} = \frac{\text{volatility of bond to be hedged}}{\text{volatility of CTD}}$$
$$\times \frac{\text{volatility of CTD}}{\text{volatility of hedging instrument}} \tag{21.11}$$

where CTD is the cheapest-to-deliver issue. The second ratio can be shown to equal the conversion factor for the CTD. Assuming a fixed yield spread between the bond to be hedged and the cheapest-to-deliver issue, equation (21.11) can be rewritten as

---

[6]The yield that is to be used on this date in order to determine the price value of a basis point is the forward rate. We discussed forward rates in Chapter 5.

[7]This example is adapted from Mark Pitts and Frank J. Fabozzi, *Interest Rate Futures and Options* (Chicago: Probus Publishing, 1989).

$$\text{hedge ratio} = \frac{\text{PVBP of bond to be hedged}}{\text{PVBP of CTD}} \times \text{conversion factor for CTD} \qquad (21.12)$$

The hedge ratio at hand is therefore approximately 1.24 [from $(0.072564/0.056332) \times 0.9660$].

Given the hedge ratio, the number of contracts that must be short is determined as follows:

$$\text{number of contracts} = \text{hedge ratio} \times \frac{\text{par value to be hedged}}{\text{par value of contract}} \qquad (21.13)$$

Because the amount to be hedged is $10 million and each Treasury bond futures contract is for $100,000, this means that the number of futures contracts that must be sold is

$$\text{number of contracts} = \text{hedge ratio} \times \frac{\$10,000,000}{\$100,000}$$

$$= 1.24 \times 100 = 124 \text{ contracts}$$

Exhibit 21-4 shows that if the simplifying assumptions hold, a futures hedge using the recommended hedge ratio very nearly locks in the target price for $10 million face value of the telephone bonds.[8]

Another refinement in the hedging strategy is usually necessary for hedging non-deliverable securities. This refinement concerns the assumption about the relative yield spread between the cheapest-to-deliver bond and the bond to be hedged. In the prior discussion, we assumed that the yield spread was constant over time. Yield spreads, however, are not constant over time. They vary with the maturity of the instruments in question and the level of rates, as well as with many unpredictable and nonsystematic factors.

Regression analysis allows the hedger to capture the relationship between yield levels and yield spreads and use it to advantage. For hedging purposes, the variables are the yield on the bond to be hedged and the yield on the cheapest-to-deliver bond. The regression equation takes the form

$$\text{yield on bond to be hedged} = a + b \times \text{yield on CTD} + \text{error} \qquad (21.14)$$

The regression procedure provides an estimate of b (the **yield beta**), which is the expected relative change in the two bonds. Our example that used constant spreads implicitly assumes that the yield beta, b in equation (21.14), equals 1.0 and that a equals 0.90 (because 0.90 is the assumed spread).

For the two issues in question, that is, the Southern Bell 11¾s and the Treasury 7⅝s, the estimated yield beta was 1.05. Thus yields on the corporate issue are expected to move 5% more than yields on the Treasury issue. To calculate the relative volatility of the two issues correctly, this fact must be taken into account; thus the hedge ratio derived in our earlier example is multiplied by the factor 1.05. Consequently, instead of shorting 124 Treasury bond futures contracts to hedge $10 million of telephone bonds, the investor would short 130 contracts.

---

[8]In practice, most of the remaining error could be eliminated by frequent adjustments to the hedge ratio to account for the fact that the price value of a basis point changes as rates move up or down.

EXHIBIT 21-4 Hedging a Nondeliverable Bond to a Delivery Date with Futures

Instrument to be hedged: Southern Bell 11¾% of 4/19/23
Hedge ratio: 1.24
Price of futures contract when sold: 70
Target price for Southern Bell bonds: 92.628

Actual Sale Price of Telephone Bonds	Yield at Sale	Yield on Treas. 7⅝%[a]	Price of Treas. 7⅝	Futures Price[b]	Gain (Loss) on 124 Contracts ($10/0.01/Contract)	Effective Sale Price[c]
$ 7,600,000	15.468%	14.568%	54.590	56.511	$1,672,636	$9,272,636
7,800,000	15.072	14.172	56.167	58.144	1,470,144	9,270,144
8,000,000	14.696	13.769	57.741	59.773	1,268,148	9,268,148
8,200,000	14.338	13.438	59.313	61.401	1,066,276	9,266,276
8,400,000	13.996	13.096	60.887	63.030	864,280	9,264,280
8,600,000	13.671	12,771	62.451	64.649	663,524	9,263,524
8,800,000	13.359	12.459	64.018	66.271	462,396	9,262,396
9,000,000	13.061	12.161	65.580	67.888	261,888	9,261,888
9,200,000	12.776	11.876	67.134	69.497	62,372	9,262,372
9,400,000	12.503	11.603	68.683	71.100	(136,400)	9,263,600
9,600,000	12.240	11.340	70.233	72.705	(335,420)	9,264,580
9,800,000	11.988	11.088	71.773	74.299	(533,076)	9,266,924
10,000,000	11.745	10.845	73.312	75.892	(730,608)	9,269,392
10,200,000	11.512	10.612	74.839	77.473	(926,652)	9,273,348
10,400,000	11.287	10.387	76.364	79.052	(1,122,448)	9,277,552
10,600,000	11.070	10.170	77.884	80.625	(1,317,500)	9,282,500
10,800,000	10.861	9.961	79.394	82.188	(1,511,312)	9,288,688
11,000,000	10.659	9.759	80.889	83.746	(1,704,504)	9,295,496
11,200,000	10.463	9.563	82.403	85.303	(1,897,572)	9,302,428

[a]By assumption, the yield on the 7⅝s of 2007 is 90 basis points lower than the yield on the Southern Bell bond.
[b]By convergence, the futures price equals the price of the 7⅝s of 2007 divided by 0.9660 (the conversion factor).
[c]Transaction costs and the financing of margin flows are ignored.

The formula for the hedge ratio, equation (21.12), is revised as follows to incorporate the impact of the yield beta:

$$\text{hedge ratio} = \frac{\text{PVBP of bond to be hedged}}{\text{PVBP of CTD}} \quad (21.15)$$

$$\times \text{ conversion factor for CTD} \times \text{yield beta}$$

where the yield beta is derived from the yield of the bond to be hedged regressed on the yield of the cheapest-to-deliver issue. As before, PVBP stands for the change in price for a one-basis-point change in yield.

The effect of a change in the cheapest-to-deliver issue and the yield spread can be assessed a priori. An exhibit similar to that of Exhibit 21-4 can be constructed under a wide range of assumptions. For example, at different yield levels at the date the hedge is to be lifted (the second column in Exhibit 21-4), a different yield spread may be appropriate and a different acceptable issue will be the CTD. The money manager can determine what this will do to the outcome of the hedge.

Allocating Funds between Stocks and Bonds

A pension sponsor may wish to alter the composition of the pension's funds between stocks and bonds, that is, change its asset allocation. Suppose that a pension sponsor wants to shift a $1 billion fund from its current allocation of $500 million in stocks and $500 million in bonds to $300 million in stocks and $700 million in bonds. This can be done directly by selling $200 million of stocks and buying a similar amount of bonds. The costs associated with shifting funds in this manner are (1) the transactions costs with respect to commissions and bid–ask spreads, (2) the market impact costs, and (3) the disruption of the activities of the money managers employed by the pension sponsor.

An alternative course of action is to use interest-rate futures and stock index futures. Assume that the pension sponsor wants to shift $200 million from stocks to bonds. Buying an appropriate number of interest-rate futures and selling an appropriate number of stock index futures can achieve the desired exposure to stocks and bonds. Futures positions can be maintained or slowly liquidated as funds invested in the cash markets are actually shifted. The advantages of using financial futures contracts are as follows: (1) Transactions costs are lower, (2) market impact costs are avoided or reduced by allowing the sponsor time to buy and sell securities in the cash market, and (3) activities of the money managers employed by the pension sponsor are not disrupted.[9]

To determine the approximate number of interest-rate futures contracts needed to change the market value of the portfolio allocated to bonds, assuming that the duration of the portfolio is to remain constant, we can use the formula

$$\text{approximate number of contracts} = \frac{(P_T - P_I)D_I}{D_F P_F}$$

where P_T is the target market value allocated to bonds and the other terms are the same as in the formula given earlier to approximate the number of contracts to adjust a portfolio's duration. Notice that if the market value of the portfolio allocated to bonds is to be increased, the numerator of the equation will be positive. This means that futures contracts will be purchased. If funds are to be reallocated to stocks and withdrawn from bonds, the numerator of the equation will be negative, which means that interest-rate futures contracts will be sold.

SUMMARY

A futures contract is a firm legal agreement between a buyer (seller) and an established exchange or its clearinghouse in which the buyer (seller) agrees to take (make) delivery of something at a specified price (called the futures price) at the end of a designated period of time (called the settlement or delivery date). Associated with every

---

[9]See Roger Clarke, "Asset Allocation Using Futures," Chapter 16 in Robert Arnott and Frank J. Fabozzi (eds.), *Asset Allocation* (Chicago: Probus Publishing, 1988), and Mark Zurak and Ravi Dattatreya, "Asset Allocation Using Futures Contracts," Chapter 20 in Frank J. Fabozzi and Gregory Kipnis (eds.), *The Handbook of Stock Index Futures and Options* (Homewood, IL: Probus Publishing, 1988).

futures exchange is a clearinghouse, which guarantees that the two parties to the transaction will perform and allows parties to unwind their position without the need to deal with the counterparty to the initial transaction. A party to a futures contract must comply with margin requirements (initial, maintenance, and variation margin). A forward contract differs from a futures contract in that it is usually nonstandardized (i.e., the terms of each contract are negotiated individually between buyer and seller), there is no clearinghouse, and secondary markets are often nonexistent or extremely thin.

Currently traded interest-rate futures contracts include Treasury bill futures, Eurodollar CD futures, Treasury bond and note futures, and the Bond Buyer municipal index futures. Interest-rate futures are also traded on foreign exchanges, where the underlying fixed-income security is foreign debt.

The theoretical price of a futures contract is equal to the cash or spot price plus the cost of carry. The cost of carry is equal to the cost of financing the position less the cash yield on the underlying security. The shape of the yield curve will affect the cost of carry. There are several reasons why the actual futures price will depart from the theoretical futures price. In the case of the Treasury bond futures contracts, the delivery options granted to the seller reduce the actual futures price below the theoretical futures price suggested by the standard arbitrage model.

Interest-rate futures contracts can be used by money managers to speculate on the movement of interest rates, to control the interest-rate risk of a portfolio, to allocate funds between stocks and bonds, and to enhance returns when futures are mispriced.

Questions

1. Explain the differences between a futures contract and a forward contract.
2. a. What is counterparty risk?
   b. Why do both the buyer and seller of a forward contract face counterparty risk?
3. What does it mean if the cost of carry is positive for a Treasury bond futures contract?
4. If the Eurodollar CD futures contract is quoted at 91.75, what is the annualized futures three-month LIBOR?
5. How do you think the cost of carry will affect the decision of the short as to when in the delivery month the short will elect to deliver?
6. Explain the asymmetric effect on the variation margin and cash flow for the short and long in an interest-rate futures contract when interest rates change.
7. What are the delivery options granted to the seller of the Treasury bond futures contract?
8. How is the theoretical futures price of a Treasury bond futures contract affected by the delivery options granted to the short?
9. Explain how the shape of the yield curve influences the theoretical price of a Treasury bond futures contract.
10. Suppose that the conversion factor for a particular Treasury bond that is acceptable for delivery in a Treasury bond futures contract is 0.85 and that the futures price settles at 105. Assume also that the accrued interest for this Treasury bond is 4. What is the invoice price if the seller delivers this Treasury bond at the settlement date?
11. Suppose that bond ABC is the underlying asset for a futures contract with settlement six months from now. You know the following about bond ABC and the fu-

tures contract: (1) In the cash market ABC is selling for $80 (par value is $100); (2) ABC pays $8 in coupon interest per year in two semiannual payments of $4, and the next semiannual payment is due exactly six months from now; and (3) the current six-month interest rate at which funds can be loaned or borrowed is 6%.

a. What is the theoretical futures price?

b. What action would you take if the futures price is $83?

c. What action would you take if the futures price is $76?

d. Suppose that bond ABC pays interest quarterly instead of semiannually. If you know that you can reinvest any funds you receive three months from now at 1% for three months, what would the theoretical futures price for six-month settlement be?

e. Suppose that the borrowing rate and lending rate are not equal. Instead, suppose that the current six-month borrowing rate is 8% and the six-month lending rate is 6%. What is the boundary for the theoretical futures price?

12. What is the implied repo rate?

13. Explain why the implied repo rate is important in determining the cheapest-to-deliver issue.

14. A manager wishes to hedge a bond with a par value of $20 million by selling Treasury bond futures. Suppose that (1) the conversion factor for the cheapest-to-deliver issue is 0.91, (2) the price value of a basis point of the cheapest-to-deliver issue at the settlement date is 0.06895, and (3) the price value of a basis point of the bond to be hedged is 0.05954.

a. What is the hedge ratio?

b. How many Treasury bond futures contracts should be sold to hedge the bond?

15. Suppose that a manager wants to reduce the duration of a portfolio. Explain how this can be done using Treasury bond futures contracts.

16. What risks are associated with hedging?

17. How could a money manager use a Treasury bond futures contract to hedge against increased interest rates over the next quarter?

18. Suppose that an institutional investor wants to hedge a portfolio of mortgage pass-through securities using Treasury bond futures contracts. What are the risks associated with such a hedge?

19. The following excerpt appeared in the following article, "Duration," in the November 16, 1992, issue of *Derivatives Week,* p. 9: "TSA Capital Management in Los Angeles must determine duration of the futures contract it uses in order to match it with the dollar duration of the underlying, explains David Depew, principal and head of trading at the firm. Futures duration will be based on the duration of the underlying bond most likely to be delivered against the contract. . . ."

a. Explain why it is necessary to know the dollar duration of the underlying in order to hedge.

b. Why can the price value of basis point be used instead of the dollar duration?

20. You work for a conservative investment management firm. You recently asked one of the senior partners for permission to open up a futures account so that you could trade interest-rate futures as well as cash instruments. He replied, "Are you crazy? I might as well write you a check, wish you good luck, and put you on a bus to Las Vegas. The futures markets are nothing more than a respectable game of craps. Don't you think you're taking enough risk trading bonds?" How would you try to persuade the senior partner to allow you to use futures?

CHAPTER 22

Interest-Rate Options

Learning Objectives

After reading this chapter you will understand:

- the basic features of interest-rate options contracts

- why over-the-counter interest-rate options are used by institutional investors

- what futures options are, their trading mechanics, and the reasons for their popularity

- the differences between options and futures

- the basic option positions

- the factors that affect the value of an option

- what the intrinsic value and time value of an option are

- the relationship between the price of a put and a call option

- the limitations of applying the Black–Scholes option pricing model to options on fixed-income securities

- how the arbitrage-free binomial model can be used to value options on fixed-income securities

- how the Black model is used to value an option on an interest rate futures contract

- measures to estimate the sensitivity of the option price to the factors that determine the price

- what implied volatility is

- how to calculate the duration of an option

- how futures options can be used to hedge

In this chapter we explain the various types of interest-rate options, their applications to money management, and how they are priced.

OPTIONS DEFINED

An **option** is a contract in which the writer of the option grants the buyer of the option the right to purchase from or sell to the writer a designated instrument at a specified price within a specified period of time. The writer, also referred to as the seller, grants this right to the buyer in exchange for a certain sum of money called the **option price** or **option premium.** The price at which the instrument may be bought or sold is called the **strike** or **exercise price.** The date after which an option is void is called the **expiration date.** An **American option** may be exercised at any time up to and including the expiration date. A **European option** may be exercised only on the expiration date.

When an option grants the buyer the right to purchase the designated instrument from the writer, it is called a **call option.** When the option buyer has the right to sell the designated instrument to the writer (seller), the option is called a **put option.** The buyer of any option is said to be **long the option;** the writer (seller) is said to be **short the option.**

The maximum amount that an option buyer can lose in such a transaction is the option price. The maximum profit that the option writer (seller) can realize likewise is the option price. The option buyer has substantial upside return potential, whereas the option writer has substantial downside risk. We will investigate the risk/reward relationship for option positions later in this chapter.

Differences between an Option and a Futures Contract

Notice that options differ from futures contracts, in that the buyer of an option has the right but not the obligation to perform, whereas the option seller (writer) has the obligation to perform. In the case of a futures contract, both the buyer and the seller are obligated to perform. Also notice that in a futures contract, the buyer does not pay the seller to accept the obligation; in the case of an option, the buyer pays the seller the option price.

Consequently, the risk/reward characteristics of the two contracts are also different. In a futures contract the long position realizes a dollar-for-dollar gain when the price of the futures increases and suffers a dollar-for-dollar loss when the price of the futures decreases. The opposite occurs for the short position. Options do not provide such a symmetric risk/reward relationship. The most that a long may lose is the option price; yet the long retains all the upside potential, although the gain is always reduced by the option price. The maximum profit that the short may realize is the option price, but this position has substantial downside risk.

TYPES OF INTEREST-RATE OPTIONS

Interest-rate options can be written on cash instruments or futures. At one time, there were several exchange-traded option contracts whose underlying instrument was a debt instrument. These contracts are referred to as **options on physicals.** The most liquid exchange-traded option on a fixed-income security at the time of this writing is an option on Treasury bonds traded on the Chicago Board Options Exchange. For reasons to be explained later, options on futures have been far more popular than options on physicals. In recent years, market participants have made increasingly greater use of over-the-counter options on Treasury and mortgage-backed securities.

Certain institutional investors who want to purchase an option on a specific Treasury security or a Ginnie Mae pass-through can do so on an over-the-counter basis.[1] There are government and mortgage-backed securities dealers who make a market in options on specific securities. Over-the-counter (or dealer) options typically are purchased by institutional investors who want to hedge the risk associated with a specific security. For example, a thrift may be interested in hedging its position in a specific mortgage pass-through security. Typically, the maturity of the option coincides with the time period over which the buyer of the option wants to hedge, so the buyer is usually not concerned with the option's liquidity. Besides options on fixed-income securities, there are over-the-counter options on the shape of the yield curve[2] or the yield spread between two securities (such as the spread between mortgage pass-through securities and Treasuries, or between double A corporates and Treasuries).

EXCHANGE-TRADED FUTURES OPTIONS

An option on a futures contract, commonly referred to as a **futures option,** gives the buyer the right to buy from or sell to the writer a designated futures contract at a designated price at any time during the life of the option. If the futures option is a call option, the buyer has the right to purchase one designated futures contract at the exercise price. That is, the buyer has the right to acquire a long futures position in the designated futures contract. If the buyer exercises the call option, the writer (seller) acquires a corresponding short position in the futures contract.

A put option on a futures contract grants the buyer the right to sell one designated futures contract to the writer at the exercise price. That is, the option buyer has the right to acquire a short position in the designated futures contract. If the put option is exercised, the writer acquires a corresponding long position in the designated futures contract.

Mechanics of Trading Futures Options

Exercising a Futures Option   As the parties to the futures option will realize a position in a futures contract when the option is exercised, the question is: What will the futures price be? That is, at what price will the long be required to pay for the instrument underlying the futures contract, and at what price will the short be required to sell the instrument underlying the futures contract?

Upon exercise, the futures price for the futures contract will be set equal to the exercise price. The position of the two parties is then immediately marked to market in terms of the then-current futures price. Thus the futures position of the two parties will be at the prevailing futures price. At the same time, the option buyer will receive from the option seller the economic benefit from exercising. In the case of a call futures option, the option writer must pay the difference between the current futures price and the exercise price to the buyer of the option. In the case of a put futures op-

---

[1] For a more detailed discussion of over-the-counter options, see Mark Pitts and Frank J. Fabozzi, *Interest Rate Futures and Options* (Chicago: Probus Publishing, 1989), Chapter 2.

[2] For example, Goldman, Sachs offers an option on the slope of the yield curve which it calls SYCURVE. The option represents the right to buy (in the case of a call option) or sell (in the case of a put option) specific segments of the yield curve.

tion, the option writer must pay the option buyer the difference between the exercise price and the current futures price.

For example, suppose that an investor buys a call option on some futures contract in which the exercise price is 85. Assume also that the futures price is 95 and that the buyer exercises the call option. Upon exercise, the call buyer is given a long position in the futures contract at 85 and the call writer is assigned the corresponding short position in the futures contract at 85. The futures positions of the buyer and the writer are immediately marked to market by the exchange. Because the prevailing futures price is 95 and the exercise price is 85, the long futures position (the position of the call buyer) realizes a gain of 10, while the short futures position (the position of the call writer) realizes a loss of 10. The call writer pays the exchange 10 and the call buyer receives from the exchange 10. The call buyer, who now has a long futures position at 95, can either liquidate the futures position at 95 or maintain a long futures position. If the former course of action is taken, the call buyer sells a futures contract at the prevailing futures price of 95. There is no gain or loss from liquidating the position. Overall, the call buyer realizes a gain of 10. The call buyer who elects to hold the long futures position will face the same risk and reward of holding such a position, but still has realized a gain of 10 from the exercise of the call option.

Suppose instead that the futures option is a put rather than a call, and the current futures price is 60 rather than 95. Then if the buyer of this put option exercises it, the buyer would have a short position in the futures contract at 85; the option writer would have a long position in the futures contract at 85. The exchange then marks the position to market at the then-current futures price of 60, resulting in a gain to the put buyer of 25 and a loss to the put writer of the same amount. The put buyer who now has a short futures position at 60 can either liquidate the short futures position by buying a futures contract at the prevailing futures price of 60 or maintain the short futures position. In either case the put buyer realizes a gain of 25 from exercising the put option.

Margin Requirements   There are no margin requirements for the buyer of a futures option after the option price has been paid in full. Because the option price is the maximum amount that the buyer can lose, regardless of how adverse the price movement of the underlying instrument, there is no need for margin.

Because the writer (seller) of an option has agreed to accept all of the risk (and none of the reward) of the position in the underlying instrument, the writer (seller) is required to deposit not only the margin required on the interest rate futures contract position if that is the underlying instrument, but also (with certain exceptions) the option price that is received for writing the option. In addition, as prices adversely affect the writer's position, the writer would be required to deposit variation margin as it is marked to market.

Reasons for the Popularity of Futures Options

There are three reasons why futures options on fixed-income securities have largely supplanted options on physicals as the options vehicle of choice for institutional investors. First, unlike options on fixed-income securities, options on Treasury coupon futures do not require payments for accrued interest to be made. Consequently, when a futures option is exercised, the call buyer and the put writer need not compensate the other party for accrued interest.

Second, futures options are believed to be "cleaner" instruments because of the reduced likelihood of delivery squeezes. Market participants who must deliver an instrument are concerned that at the time of delivery the instrument to be delivered will be in short supply, resulting in a higher price to acquire the instrument. As the deliverable supply of futures contracts is more than adequate for futures options currently traded, there is no concern about a delivery squeeze. Finally, in order to price any option, it is imperative to know at all times the price of the underlying instrument. In the bond market, current prices are not as easily available as price information on the futures contract.

Specifications for the Actively Traded Futures Options

There are options on all of the futures contracts described in Chapter 21. Options on Treasury bond and note futures are traded on the Chicago Board of Trade (CBT) and options on the Eurodollar CD futures are traded on the International Monetary Market (IMM). All futures options are of the American type. If the option buyer elects to exercise early, he or she must notify the clearing corporation which then randomly selects a clearing member that must select a short from amongst its customers.

The CBT's Treasury bond futures contracts have delivery months of March, June, September, and December. In Chapter 21 we described the delivery process and the choices granted to the short. There are futures options that expire in the next three regular quarterly expiration months. Trading of futures options on Treasury bonds stops in the month prior to the underlying futures contract's delivery month. The day in that month in which the futures options stop trading is the first Friday preceding, by at least five days, the first notice day for the Treasury bond futures contract. The CBT also lists futures options for the current front month.

In an attempt to compete with the OTC option market, the CBT introduced in 1994 the **flexible Treasury futures options.** These futures options allow counterparties to customize options within certain limits. Specifically, the strike price, expiration date, and type of exercise (American or European) can be customized subject to CBT constraints. One key constraint is that the expiration date of a flexible contract cannot exceed that of the longest standard option traded on the CBT. Unlike an OTC option, where the option buyer is exposed to counterparty risk, a flexible Treasury futures option is guaranteed by the clearing house. The minimum size requirement for the launching of a flexible futures option is 100 contracts.

INTRINSIC VALUE AND TIME VALUE OF AN OPTION

The cost to the buyer of an option is primarily a reflection of the option's intrinsic value and any additional amount over that value. The premium over intrinsic value is often referred to as **time value.**

Intrinsic Value of an Option

The intrinsic value of an option is the economic value of the option if it is exercised immediately. Because the buyer of an option need not exercise the option, and, in fact, will not do so if no economic gain will result from exercising it, the intrinsic value cannot be less than zero.

Call Options   The intrinsic value of a call option on a bond is the difference between the bond price and the strike price. For example, if the strike price for a call option is $100 and the current bond price is $105, the intrinsic value is $5. That is, if the option buyer exercises the option and sells the bond simultaneously, the option buyer would realize $105 from the sale of the bond, which would be covered by acquiring the bond from the option writer for $100, thereby netting a $5 gain.

When a call option has intrinsic value, it is said to be **in-the-money.** Our call option with a strike price of $100 is in-the-money when the price of the underlying bond is greater than $100. When the strike price of a call option exceeds the bond price, the call option is said to be **out-of-the-money** and has no intrinsic value. An option for which the strike price is equal to the current bond price is said to be **at-the-money.** Both at-the-money and out-of-the-money options have an intrinsic value of zero because it is not profitable to exercise the option.

Put Options   For a put option, the intrinsic value is equal to the amount by which the bond price is below the strike price. For example, if the strike price of a put option is $100 and the current bond price is $92, the intrinsic value is $8. That is, the buyer of the put option who exercises the put option and buys the bond simultaneously will net $8 because the bond will be sold to the writer for $100 and purchased in the market for $92.

When the put option has intrinsic value, the option is said to be in-the-money. For our put option with a strike price of $100, the option will be in-the-money when the bond price is less than $100. A put option is out-of-the-money when the current bond price exceeds the strike price. A put option is at-the-money when the strike price is equal to the bond price.

Time Value of an Option

The time value of an option is the amount by which the option price exceeds the intrinsic value. The option buyer hopes that at some time prior to expiration, changes in the market yield will increase the value of the rights conveyed by the option. For this prospect, the option buyer is willing to pay a premium above the intrinsic value. For example, if the price of a call option with a strike price of $100 is $9 when the current bond price is $105, the time value of this option is $4 ($9 minus the intrinsic value of $5). If the current bond price is $90 instead of $105, the time value of this option is $9 because the option has no intrinsic value.

There are two ways in which an option buyer may realize the value of a position taken in the option. First, the investor may exercise the option. In the case of a futures option, by exercising the buyer will be assigned a position in the underlying futures contract at the current futures price and be paid by the writer any difference between the current futures price and the strike price. The investor can sell the futures contract at the current price. For example, for our hypothetical call option with a strike price of $100 and an option price of $9, in which the current futures price is $105, the option buyer can exercise the option. This will produce a long position in the futures contract currently at $105. The call writer will pay the buyer $5 (the difference between the current futures price of $105 and the strike price of $100). By simultaneously selling the underlying futures for $105, the option buyer will realize $5.

The second way of realizing the value of an option position is by selling the call option for $9. Obviously, this is the preferable alternative because the exercise of an option will cause the immediate loss of any time value (in this case, $4).

Whether any option will be exercised prior to the expiration date depends on whether the total proceeds at the expiration date would be greater by holding the option or by exercising and reinvesting any cash proceeds received until the expiration date.

PROFIT AND LOSS PROFILES FOR SIMPLE NAKED OPTION STRATEGIES

To appreciate the opportunities available with interest-rate options, the profit and loss profiles for various option strategies must be understood. We begin with simple strategies in only one option on a bond, which are referred to as **naked option strategies.** That is, no other position is taken in another option or bond. *The profit and loss profiles that we present assume that each option position is held to the expiration date and not exercised earlier.* Also, to simplify the illustrations, we assume that there are no transactions costs to implement the strategies.

The four naked option strategies that we illustrate are (1) long call strategy (buying call options); (2) short call strategy (selling or writing call options); (3) long put strategy (buying put options); and (4) short put strategy (selling or writing put options).

Long Call Strategy (Buying Call Options)

The most straightforward option strategy for participating in an anticipated decrease in interest rates (increase in the price of bonds) is to buy a call option on a debt instrument. This is called a **long call strategy.** To illustrate this strategy, assume that there is a call option on a particular 8% coupon bond with a par value of $100 and 20 years and one month to maturity. The call option expires in one month and the strike price is $100. The option price is $3. Although this option is an option on a cash market security, the principles apply equally to futures options.

Suppose that the current price of the bond is $100 (i.e., the bond is selling at par), which means that the yield on this bond is currently 8%. As the strike price is equal to the current price of the bond, this option is at-the-money. What would the profit or loss be for the investor who purchases this call option and holds it to the expiration date?

The profit and loss from the strategy will depend on the price of the bond at the expiration date. The price, in turn, will depend on the yield on 20-year bonds with an 8% coupon, because in one month the bond will have only 20 years to maturity. Exhibit 22-1 shows the price of a 20-year 8% coupon bond for interest rates ranging from 4 to 12%. Five outcomes are possible:

1. If the price of the bond at the expiration date is less than $100 (which means that the market yield is greater than 8%), the investor would not exercise the option. (Why bother exercising the option and paying the option writer $100 when the same bond can be purchased in the market at a lower price?) In this case the option buyer will lose the entire option price of $3. Notice, however, that this is the maximum loss that the option buyer will realize, no matter how far the price of the bond declines.

EXHIBIT 22-1	Price/Yield Relationship for a 20-Year 8% Coupon Bond		
Yield	*Price*	*Yield*	*Price*
4.0	154.71	8.1	99.02
4.2	151.08	8.2	98.05
4.4	147.56	8.3	97.10
4.6	144.15	8.4	96.16
4.8	140.85	8.5	95.23
5.0	137.65	8.6	94.32
5.2	134.56	8.7	93.42
5.4	131.56	8.8	92.53
5.6	128.66	8.9	91.66
5.8	125.84	9.0	90.80
6.0	123.11	9.1	89.95
6.1	121.78	9.2	89.11
6.2	120.47	9.3	88.29
6.3	119.18	9.4	87.48
6.4	117.91	9.5	86.68
6.5	116.66	9.6	85.89
6.6	115.42	9.7	85.11
6.7	114.21	9.8	84.34
6.8	113.01	9.9	83.59
6.9	111.84	10.0	82.84
7.0	110.68	10.2	81.38
7.1	109.54	10.4	79.96
7.2	108.41	10.6	78.58
7.3	107.30	10.8	77.24
7.4	106.21	11.0	75.93
7.5	105.14	11.2	74.66
7.6	104.08	11.4	73.42
7.7	103.04	11.6	72.22
7.8	102.01	11.8	71.05
7.9	101.00	12.0	69.91
8.0	100.00		

2. If the price of the bond is equal to $100 (which means that the market yield is unchanged at 8%), no economic value will result from exercising the option. As in the outcome when the price of the bond is less than $100, the buyer of this call option will lose the entire option price, $3.

3. If the price of the bond is greater than $100 but less than $103 (which means that the market yield is less than 8% but greater than 7.70%—see Exhibit 22-1), the option buyer will exercise the option. By exercising, the option buyer purchases the bond for $100 (the strike price) and can sell it in the market for a higher price. Suppose, for example, that the market yield is 7.8%, so that the price of the bond is about $102 at the expiration date. The buyer of this call option will realize a $2 gain by exercising the option, offset

by the $3 cost of purchasing the call option. Hence $1 is the total loss on this strategy. If the investor fails to exercise the option, the $3 is lost.

4. If the price of the bond at the expiration date is equal to $103 (a market yield of about 7.70%), the investor will exercise the option. In this case, the investor breaks even, realizing a gain of $3 on the bond, which offsets the cost of the option, $3. Although there is no net gain, the price of the option is recouped.

5. If the price of the bond at the expiration date is greater than $103 (a market yield of less than 7.70%), the investor will exercise the option and realize a profit. For example, if the price of the bond is $113 because the market yield has declined from 8% to 6.8%, exercising the option will generate a profit on the bond of $13. Reducing this gain by the cost of the option ($3) means that the investor realizes a net profit of $10 on this strategy.

Exhibit 22-2 shows the profit/loss in tabular form for the buyer of the hypothetical call option, and Exhibit 22-3 portrays it graphically. Although the break-even point and the loss will depend on the option price and the strike price, the shape shown in Exhibit 22-3 will hold for all buyers of call options. That shape indicates that the maximum loss is the option price, yet there is substantial upside potential.

It is worthwhile to compare the profit and loss profile of a call option buyer to a long bond strategy in the same bond. The payoff from the strategy depends on the price of the bond at the expiration date, which, in turn, depends on the market yield at the expiration date. Consider again the five price outcomes given previously:

1. If the price of the bond at the expiration date is less than $100 (market yield rises above 8%), the investor would lose the entire option price of $3. In contrast, a long bond position will have one of three possible outcomes:
   (a) If the price of the bond is lower than $100 (market yield greater than 8%) but higher than $97 (market yield less than about 8.3%), the loss on the long bond position will be less than $3.
   (b) If the price of the bond is $97 (market yield of about 8.3%), the loss on the long bond position will be $3.
   (c) If the price of the bond is lower than $97, the loss on the long bond position will be more than $3. For example, if the price at the expiration date is $80 because the market yield has risen to 10.4%, the long bond position will result in a loss of $20.

2. If the price of the bond is equal to $100 because the market yield is unchanged, the buyer of the call option will realize a loss of $3 (the cost of the option). There will be no gain or loss on the long bond position.

3. If the price of the bond is higher than $100 because the market yield has fallen below 8% but lower than $103 (market yield above 7.70%), the option buyer will realize a loss of less than $3, while the long bond position will realize a profit.

4. If the market yield falls to about 7.70% so that the price of the bond at the expiration date is equal to $103, there will be no loss or gain from buying the call option. The long bond position will produce a gain of $3.

5. If the price of the bond at the expiration date is higher than $103 because the market yield has fallen below 7.7%, both the call option purchase and the

EXHIBIT 22-2   Profit/Loss Profile for a Long Call Strategy

Assumptions:
  Call option price: 3
  Strike price: 100
  Time to expiration: 1 month

At Expiration Date:			At Expiration Date:		
Market Yield	*Price of Bond*	*Net Profit*	*Market Yield*	*Price of Bond*	*Net Profit*
4.0	154.71	51.71	8.1	99.02	−3.00
4.2	151.08	48.08	8.2	98.05	−3.00
4.4	147.56	44.56	8.3	97.10	−3.00
4.6	144.15	41.15	8.4	96.16	−3.00
4.8	140.85	37.85	8.5	95.23	−3.00
5.0	137.65	34.65	8.6	94.32	−3.00
5.2	134.56	31.56	8.7	93.42	−3.00
5.4	131.56	28.56	8.8	92.53	−3.00
5.6	128.66	25.66	8.9	91.66	−3.00
5.8	125.84	22.84	9.0	90.80	−3.00
6.0	123.11	20.11	9.1	89.95	−3.00
6.1	121.78	18.78	9.2	89.11	−3.00
6.2	120.47	17.47	9.3	88.29	−3.00
6.3	119.18	16.18	9.4	87.48	−3.00
6.4	117.91	14.91	9.5	86.68	−3.00
6.5	116.66	13.66	9.6	85.89	−3.00
6.6	115.42	12.42	9.7	85.11	−3.00
6.7	114.21	11.21	9.8	84.34	−3.00
6.8	113.01	10.01	9.9	83.59	−3.00
6.9	111.84	8.84	10.0	82.84	−3.00
7.0	110.68	7.68	10.2	81.38	−3.00
7.1	109.54	6.54	10.4	79.96	−3.00
7.2	108.41	5.41	10.6	78.58	−3.00
7.3	107.30	4.30	10.8	77.24	−3.00
7.4	106.21	3.21	11.0	75.93	−3.00
7.5	105.14	2.14	11.2	74.66	−3.00
7.6	104.08	1.08	11.4	73.42	−3.00
7.7	103.04	0.04	11.6	72.22	−3.00
7.8	102.01	−0.99	11.8	71.05	−3.00
7.9	101.00	−2.00	12.0	69.91	−3.00
8.0	100.00	−3.00			

long bond position will result in a profit. However, the profit for the buyer of the call option will be $3 less than that on the long bond position. For example, if the market yield falls to 6.8% so that the price of the bond is $113, the profit from the long call position is $10 and the profit from the long bond position is $13.

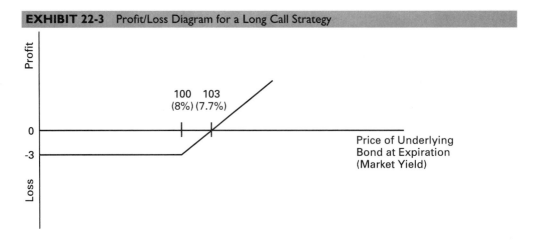

EXHIBIT 22-3 Profit/Loss Diagram for a Long Call Strategy

Exhibit 22-4 compares the long call strategy and the long bond strategy. This comparison clearly demonstrates the way in which an option can change the risk/return profile available to investors. An investor who takes a long position in the bond realizes a profit of $1 for every $1 increase in the price of the bond as the market yield falls. However, as the market yield rises, this investor loses dollar for dollar. So if the price decreases by more than $3, this strategy will result in a loss of more than $3. The long call strategy, in contrast, limits the loss to only the option price of $3, but retains the upside potential, which will be $3 less than for the long bond position.

We can use this hypothetical call option to demonstrate the speculative appeal of options. Suppose that an investor has strong expectations that market yields will fall in one month. With an option price of $3, the speculator can purchase 33.33 call options for each $100 invested. Thus if the market yield declines, the investor realizes the price appreciation associated with 33.33 bonds of $100 par each (or $3,333 par). With the same $100, the investor could buy only one $100 par value bond and realize the appreciation associated with that one bond if the market yield declines. Now, suppose that in one month the market yield declines to 6% so that the price of the bond increases to $123.11. The long call strategy will result in a profit of $670.26 ($23.11 × 33.33 − $100), a return of 670% on the $100 investment in the call options. The long bond strategy results merely in a profit of $23.11, a 23% return on $100.

It is this greater leverage that an option buyer can achieve that attracts investors to options when they wish to speculate on interest-rate movements. It does not come without drawbacks, however. Suppose that the market yield is unchanged at the expiration date so that the price of the bond is $100. The long call strategy will result in the loss of the entire investment of $100, whereas the long bond strategy will produce neither a gain nor a loss.

Short Call Strategy (Selling or Writing Call Options)

An investor who believes that interest rates will rise or change very little can, if those expectations prove correct, realize income by writing (selling) a call option. This strategy is called a **short call strategy.**

EXHIBIT 22-4 Comparison of a Long Call Strategy and a Long Bond Strategy

Assumptions:
  Current price of bond: 100
  Call option price: 3
  Strike price: 100
  Time to expiration: 1 month

Market Yield	Price of Bond	Long Call	Long Bond	Market Yield	Price of Bond	Long Call	Long Bond
4.0	154.71	51.71	54.71	8.1	99.02	−3.00	−0.98
4.2	151.08	48.08	51.08	8.2	98.05	−3.00	−1.95
4.4	147.56	44.56	47.56	8.3	97.10	−3.00	−2.90
4.6	144.15	41.15	44.15	8.4	96.16	−3.00	−3.84
4.8	140.85	37.85	40.85	8.5	95.23	−3.00	−4.77
5.0	137.65	34.65	37.65	8.6	94.32	−3.00	−5.68
5.2	134.56	31.56	34.56	8.7	93.42	−3.00	−6.58
5.4	131.56	28.56	31.56	8.8	92.53	−3.00	−7.47
5.6	128.66	25.66	28.66	8.9	91.66	−3.00	−8.34
5.8	125.84	22.84	25.84	9.0	90.80	−3.00	−9.20
6.0	123.11	20.11	23.11	9.1	89.95	−3.00	−10.05
6.1	121.78	18.78	21.78	9.2	89.11	−3.00	−10.89
6.2	120.47	17.47	20.47	9.3	88.29	−3.00	−11.71
6.3	119.18	16.18	19.18	9.4	87.48	−3.00	−12.52
6.4	117.91	14.91	17.91	9.5	86.68	−3.00	−13.32
6.5	116.66	13.66	16.66	9.6	85.89	−3.00	−14.11
6.6	115.42	12.42	15.42	9.7	85.11	−3.00	−14.89
6.7	114.21	11.21	14.21	9.8	84.34	−3.00	−15.66
6.8	113.01	10.01	13.01	9.9	83.59	−3.00	−16.41
6.9	111.84	8.84	11.84	10.0	82.84	−3.00	−17.16
7.0	110.68	7.68	10.68	10.2	81.38	−3.00	−18.62
7.1	109.54	6.54	9.54	10.4	79.96	−3.00	−20.04
7.2	108.41	5.41	8.41	10.6	78.58	−3.00	−21.42
7.3	107.30	4.30	7.30	10.8	77.24	−3.00	−22.76
7.4	106.21	3.21	6.21	11.0	75.93	−3.00	−24.07
7.5	105.14	2.14	5.14	11.2	74.66	−3.00	−25.34
7.6	104.08	1.08	4.08	11.4	73.42	−3.00	−26.58
7.7	103.04	0.04	3.04	11.6	72.22	−3.00	−27.78
7.8	102.01	−0.99	2.01	11.8	71.05	−3.00	−28.95
7.9	101.00	−2.00	1.00	12.0	69.91	−3.00	−30.09
8.0	100.00	−3.00	0.00				

At Expiration Date: — *Profit* (Long Call / Long Bond) columns repeated for each half.

To illustrate this option strategy, we use the same call option we used to demonstrate the long call strategy. The profit and loss profile of the short call strategy (the position of the call option writer) is the mirror image of the profit and loss profile of the long call strategy (the position of the call option buyer). That is, the profit (loss) of the short call position for any given price of the bond at the expiration date is the same as the loss (profit) of the long call position. Consequently, the maximum profit that the short call strategy can produce is the option price. But the maximum loss is limited only by how high the price of the bond can increase (i.e., how low the market yield can fall) by the expiration date, less the option price. Exhibit 22-5 diagrams the profit and loss profile for a short call strategy.

Long Put Strategy (Buying Put Options)

The most straightforward option strategy for benefiting from an expected increase in interest rates is to buy a put option. This strategy is called a long put strategy.

To illustrate this strategy, we'll assume a hypothetical put option for an 8% coupon bond with a par value of $100, 20 years and one month to maturity, and a strike price of $100 that is selling for $2. The current price of the bond is $100 (yield of 8%); hence the put option is at-the-money. The profit or loss for this strategy at the expiration date depends on the market yield at the time. The following outcomes are possible:

1. If the price of the bond is higher than $100 because the market yield has fallen below 8%, the buyer of the put option will not exercise it because exercising would mean selling the bond to the writer for a price that is lower than the current market price. Consequently, a loss of $2 (the option price) will result from the long put strategy. Once again, the option price represents the maximum loss to which the buyer of the put option is exposed.
2. If the price of the bond at expiration is equal to $100 because the market yield has remained at 8%, the put will not be exercised, leaving the long put position with a loss equal to the option price of $2.
3. Any price for the bond that is lower than $100 because the market yield has risen above 8% but higher than $98 (market yield of approximately 8.2%) will result in a loss; exercising the put option, however, limits the loss to less than the option price of $2. For example, suppose that the market yield rises to 8.6%, resulting in a price of $99.03 for the bond at the expiration date. By

EXHIBIT 22-5   Profit/Loss Profile Diagram for a Short Call Strategy exercising the option, the option buyer will realize a loss of $1.03. This is because the buyer of the put option can sell the bond, purchased in the market for $99.03, to the writer for $100, realizing a gain of $0.97. Deducting the $2 cost of the option results in a loss of $1.03.

4. At a $98 price for the bond (a market yield of roughly 8.2%) at the expiration date, the long put strategy will break even: The investor will realize a gain of $2 by selling the bond to the writer of the option for $100, offsetting the cost of the option ($2).

5. If the market yield rises above 8.2% so that the price of the bond is below $98 at the expiration date, the long put position will realize a profit. For example, if the market yield rises 260 basis points (from 8% to 10.6%), the price of the bond at expiration will be $78.58. The long put strategy will produce a profit of $19.42: a gain of $21.42 on the bond less the $2 option price.

The profit and loss profile for the long put strategy is shown in tabular form in Exhibit 22-6 and in graphic form in Exhibit 22-7. As with all long option positions, the loss is limited to the option price. However, the profit potential is substantial, the theoretical maximum profit being generated if the bond price falls to zero.

Once again, we can see how an option alters the risk/return profile for an investor by comparing it with a position in the bond. In the case of a long put position, it would be compared with a short bond position, because both strategies realize profits if market yields rise (the price falls). Suppose that an investor sells the bond short for $100. The short bond position would produce the following profit or loss as compared with the long put position:

1. If the price of the bond increases above $100 because the market yield declines, the long put option will result in a loss of $2, but the short bond position will realize one of the following:
   (a) If the price of the bond is lower than $102 because the market yield has fallen to below 7.80%, there will be a loss of less than $2.
   (b) If the price of the bond is equal to $102, the loss will be $2, the same as for the long put strategy.
   (c) If the price of the bond is higher than $102, the loss will be more than $2. For example, if the price is $125.84, because market yields declined to 5.8%, the short bond position will realize a loss of $25.84, because the short seller must now pay $125.84, for a bond sold short at $100.

2. If the price of the bond at expiration is equal to $100 because the market yield is unchanged, the long put strategy will realize a $2 loss, and there will be no profit or loss on the short bond strategy.

3. Any price for the bond that is lower than $100 but higher than $98 (market yield of about 8.2%) will result in a loss of less than $2 for the long put strategy but a profit for the short bond strategy. For example, a price of $99.02 (market yield of 8.1%) at the expiration date will result in a loss of $1.02 for the long put strategy but a profit of $.98 for the short bond strategy.

4. At a $98 price for the bond at the expiration date, the long put strategy will break even, but the short bond strategy will generate a $2 profit.

EXHIBIT 22-6 Profit/Loss Profile for a Long Put Strategy

Assumptions:
  Put option price: 2
  Strike price: 100
  Time to expiration: 1 month

At Expiration Date:			At Expiration Date:		
Market Yield	*Price of Bond*	*Net Profit*	*Market Yield*	*Price of Bond*	*Net Profit*
4.0	154.71	−2.00	8.1	99.02	−1.92
4.2	151.08	−2.00	8.2	98.05	−0.05
4.4	147.56	−2.00	8.3	97.10	0.90
4.6	144.15	−2.00	8.4	96.16	1.84
4.8	140.85	−2.00	8.5	95.23	2.77
5.0	137.65	−2.00	8.6	94.32	3.68
5.2	134.56	−2.00	8.7	93.42	4.58
5.4	131.56	−2.00	8.8	92.53	5.47
5.6	128.66	−2.00	8.9	91.66	6.34
5.8	125.84	−2.00	9.0	90.80	7.20
6.0	123.11	−2.00	9.1	89.95	8.05
6.1	121.78	−2.00	9.2	89.11	8.89
6.2	120.47	−2.00	9.3	88.29	9.71
6.3	119.18	−2.00	9.4	87.48	10.52
6.4	117.91	−2.00	9.5	86.68	11.32
6.5	116.66	−2.00	9.6	85.89	12.11
6.6	115.42	−2.00	9.7	85.11	12.89
6.7	114.21	−2.00	9.8	84.34	13.66
6.8	113.01	−2.00	9.9	83.59	14.41
6.9	111.84	−2.00	10.0	82.84	15.16
7.0	110.68	−2.00	10.2	81.38	16.62
7.1	109.54	−2.00	10.4	79.96	18.04
7.2	108.41	−2.00	10.6	78.58	19.42
7.3	107.30	−2.00	10.8	77.24	20.76
7.4	106.21	−2.00	11.0	75.93	22.07
7.5	105.14	−2.00	11.2	74.66	23.34
7.6	104.08	−2.00	11.4	73.42	24.58
7.7	103.04	−2.00	11.6	72.22	25.78
7.8	102.01	−2.00	11.8	71.05	26.95
7.9	101.00	−2.00	12.0	69.91	28.09
8.0	100.00	−2.00			

5. At a price below $98 (market yield greater than 8.2%) both strategies will generate a profit. However, the profit will always be $2 less for the long put strategy.

Exhibit 22-8 is a tabular comparison of the profit and loss profile for the long put and short bond strategies. Whereas the investor who pursues a short bond strategy

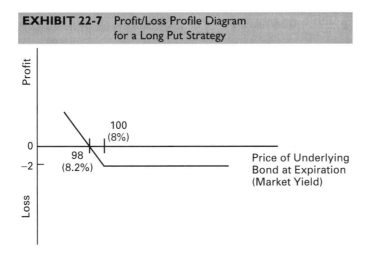

EXHIBIT 22-7   Profit/Loss Profile Diagram
for a Long Put Strategy

participates in all the upside potential and faces all the downside risk, the long put strategy allows the investor to limit the downside risk to the option price while still maintaining upside potential. However, the upside potential is less than that for a short put position by an amount equal to the option price.

Short Put Strategy (Selling or Writing Put Options)

The last naked option position that we shall consider is the short put strategy. The **short put strategy** involves the selling (writing) of put options. This strategy is employed if the investor expects interest rates to fall or stay flat so that the price of the bond will increase or stay the same. The profit and loss profile for a short put option is the mirror image of that for the long put option. The maximum loss is limited only by how low the price of the bond can fall by the expiration date less the option price received for writing the option. Exhibit 22-9 graphically depicts this profit and loss profile.

To summarize, long calls and short puts allow the investor to gain if bond prices rise (interest rates fall). Short calls and long puts allow the investor to gain if bond prices fall (interest rates rise). An investor would want to use each strategy under the following circumstances:

Circumstance	Strategy
Very bullish	Buy call
Slightly bullish	Write put
Slightly bearish	Write call
Very bearish	Buy put

Considering the Time Value of Money

Our illustrations of the four naked option positions do not reflect the time value of money. Specifically, the buyer of an option must pay the seller the option price at the time the option is purchased. Thus the buyer must either finance the purchase price of

EXHIBIT 22-8 Comparison of a Long Put Strategy and a Short Bond Strategy

Assumptions:
  Current price of bond: 100
  Put option price: 2
  Strike price: 100
  Time to expiration: 1 month

At Expiration Date:		*Profit*		*At Expiration Date:*		*Profit*	
Market Yield	*Price of Bond*	*Long Put*	*Short Bond*	*Market Yield*	*Price of Bond*	*Long Put*	*Short Bond*
4.0	154.71	−2.00	−54.71	8.1	99.02	−1.02	0.98
4.2	151.08	−2.00	−51.08	8.2	98.05	−0.05	1.95
4.4	147.56	−2.00	−47.56	8.3	97.10	0.90	2.90
4.6	144.15	−2.00	−44.15	8.4	96.16	1.84	3.84
4.8	140.85	−2.00	−40.85	8.5	95.23	2.77	4.77
5.0	137.65	−2.00	−37.65	8.6	94.32	3.68	5.68
5.2	134.56	−2.00	−34.56	8.7	93.42	4.58	6.58
5.4	131.56	−2.00	−31.56	8.8	92.53	5.47	7.47
5.6	128.66	−2.00	−28.66	8.9	91.66	6.34	8.34
5.8	125.84	−2.00	−25.84	9.0	90.80	7.20	9.20
6.0	123.11	−2.00	−23.11	9.1	89.95	8.05	10.05
6.1	121.78	−2.00	−21.78	9.2	89.11	8.89	10.89
6.2	120.47	−2.00	−20.47	9.3	88.29	9.71	11.71
6.3	119.18	−2.00	−19.18	9.4	87.48	10.52	12.52
6.4	117.91	−2.00	−17.91	9.5	86.68	11.32	13.32
6.5	116.66	−2.00	−16.66	9.6	85.89	12.11	14.11
6.6	115.42	−2.00	−15.42	9.7	85.11	12.89	14.89
6.7	114.21	−2.00	−14.21	9.8	84.34	13.66	15.66
6.8	113.01	−2.00	−13.01	9.9	83.59	14.41	16.41
6.9	111.84	−2.00	−11.84	10.0	82.84	15.16	17.16
7.0	110.68	−2.00	−10.68	10.2	81.38	16.62	18.62
7.1	109.54	−2.00	−9.54	10.4	79.96	18.04	20.04
7.2	108.41	−2.00	−8.41	10.6	78.58	19.42	21.42
7.3	107.30	−2.00	−7.30	10.8	77.24	20.76	22.76
7.4	106.21	−2.00	−6.21	11.0	75.93	22.07	24.07
7.5	105.14	−2.00	−5.14	11.2	74.66	23.34	25.34
7.6	104.08	−2.00	−4.08	11.4	73.42	24.58	26.58
7.7	103.04	−2.00	−3.04	11.6	72.22	25.78	27.78
7.8	102.01	−2.00	−2.01	11.8	71.05	26.95	28.95
7.9	101.00	−2.00	−1.00	12.0	69.91	28.09	30.09
8.0	100.00	−2.00	0.00				

the option or, if the proceeds do not have to be borrowed, lose the interest that could be earned by investing the option price until the expiration of the option. The seller, in contrast, assuming that the option price does not have to be used as margin for the short position, has the opportunity to invest this option price.

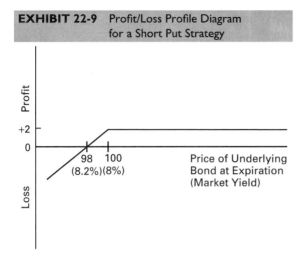

EXHIBIT 22-9   Profit/Loss Profile Diagram for a Short Put Strategy

The profit profiles of the naked option positions change when the time value of money is taken into consideration. The break-even price for the buyer and the seller of an option will not be the same as in our illustrations. The break-even price for the underlying instrument at the expiration date is higher for the buyer of the option; for the seller, it is lower.

We also ignored the time value of money in comparing the option strategies with positions in the underlying instrument. In this case, we did not consider the fact that when the underlying instrument is a cash market coupon security, coupon payments may be made between the time the option is purchased and the option's expiration date. When these coupon payments are received, they can be reinvested. Thus reinvestment income must be factored into the analysis of an option position. Also, the effects of financing costs and opportunity costs on the long or short bond positions, respectively, must be factored into the analysis. For the sake of simplicity, however, we shall ignore the time value of money throughout the remainder of this chapter.

PUT–CALL PARITY RELATIONSHIP AND EQUIVALENT POSITIONS

Is there a relationship between the price of a call option and the price of a put option on the same underlying instrument, with the same strike price and the same expiration date? There is. To see this relationship, which is commonly referred to as the **put–call parity relationship,** let's use an example.

Previous illustrations have used a put and a call option on the same underlying instrument (a bond currently with 20 years and one month to maturity), both options having a strike price of $100 and one month to expiration. The price of the underlying bond is assumed to be $100. The call price and put price are assumed to be $3 and $2, respectively. Consider the following strategy:

- Buy the bond at a price of $100.
- Sell a call option at a price of $3.
- Buy a put option at a price of $2.

This strategy therefore involves the following:

- Long the bond.
- Short the call option.
- Long the put option.

Exhibit 22-10 shows the profit and loss profile at the expiration date for this strategy. Notice that no matter what the price of the underlying bond at expiration date, the strategy produces a profit of $1. Ignoring the cost of financing the long position and the long put position, this situation cannot exist in an efficient market. The actions of market participants in implementing this strategy to capture the $1 profit will result in one or more of the following consequences, which will tend to eliminate the $1 profit: (1) an increase in the price of the bond, (2) a decrease in the call option price, and/or (3) an increase in the put option price.

In our example, assuming that the bond price does not change, this means that the call price and the put price must be equal. But this is true only when we ignore the time value of money (financing cost, opportunity cost, coupon income, and reinvestment income). Also, in the illustration we did not consider the possibility of early exercise of the options. Thus we have been considering a put–call parity relationship only for European options. Ignoring the time value of money and considering European options, the outcome from the following position must be one of no arbitrage profits:

$$\text{long the bond} + \text{short call option} + \text{long put option} = 0 \qquad (22.1)$$

EXHIBIT 22-10 Profit/Loss Profile for a Strategy Involving a Long Bond Position, Short Call Option Position, and Long Put Option Position

Assumptions:

Current price of bond: 100	Price of put option: 2
Price of call option: 3	Put strike price: 100
Call strike price: 100	Time to expiration: 1 month

At Expiration Date:

Market Yield	Price of Bond	Profit from Long Bond	Price Received for Call	Price Paid for Put	Overall Profit
5.0	137.65	0*	3	−2	1
6.0	123.11	0*	3	−2	1
7.0	110.68	0*	3	−2	1
7.9	101.00	0*	3	−2	1
8.0	100.00	0	3	−2	1
8.1	99.02	0‡	3	−2	1
9.0	90.80	0‡	3	−2	1
10.0	82.84	0‡	3	−2	1
11.0	75.93	0‡	3	−2	1

*If the price of the bond is more than the strike price, the buyer of the call option will exercise the option.
‡If the price of the bond is lower than the strike price, the investor will exercise the put option.

In terms of price, it can be shown that there will be no arbitrage profits at any time (not just expiration) if

$$P_{po} = P_{co} + S - P_b \tag{22.2}$$

where:

P_{po} = price of put option
P_{co} = price of call option
   S = strike price of option
P_b = current price of the underlying bond

and the strike price and expiration date are the same for both options. This relationship is one form of the put–call parity relationship for European options when the time value of money is ignored. It is approximately true for American options. Considering the time value of money, the put–call parity relationship for coupon bonds is

$$P_{po} = P_{co} + PV(S) + PV(coupon) - P_b \tag{22.3}$$

where:

   $PV(S)$ = present value of the strike price
$PV(coupon)$ = present value of the coupon payments

Equivalent Positions

Working with equation (22.1), we can identify equivalent positions, that is, positions that will provide the same profit profile. For example, subtracting the long put position from both sides of equation (22.1), we have

$$\text{long the bond} + \text{short call option} = -\text{long put option} \tag{22.4}$$

But the position on the right-hand side of equation (22.4) is the same as a short put position. Therefore,

$$\text{long the bond} + \text{short call option} = \text{short put option} \tag{22.5}$$

We will see later in this chapter that a covered call position, which is a long bond position plus a short call option position on the same bond, has the same profit profile as a short put option position. This is what equation (22.5) states. Owning callable securities is equivalent to a long bond position plus a short call position. Thus these securities will have a payoff similar to a short put position. But remember, the equivalent position holds only for European options, and a more precise relationship requires that the time value of money be considered.

Manipulating equation (22.1) gives us the following equivalent positions:

$$\text{short the bond} + \text{short put} = \text{short call}$$
$$\text{long the bond} + \text{long put} = \text{long call}$$
$$\text{short the bond} + \text{long call} = \text{long put}$$
$$\text{long call} + \text{short put} = \text{long the bond}$$
$$\text{long put} + \text{short call} = \text{short the bond}$$

Thus an investor can synthetically create any of the positions on the right-hand side of these equations by taking the two positions indicated on the left-hand side.

OPTION PRICE

Six factors will influence the option price:

1. Current price of the underlying instrument
2. Strike price
3. Time to expiration
4. Short-term risk-free interest rate over the life of the option
5. Coupon rate on the bond
6. Expected volatility of yields (or prices) over the life of the option

The impact of each of these factors may depend on whether (1) the option is a call or a put, (2) the option is an American option or a European option, and (3) the underlying instrument is a bond or a futures contract on a bond.[3]

Current Price of the Underlying Instrument   For a call option, as the current price of the underlying instrument increases (decreases), the option price increases (decreases). For a put option, as the current price of the underlying instrument decreases (increases), the option price increases (decreases).

Strike Price   All other factors being constant, the higher the strike price, the lower the price of a call option. For a put option, the opposite is true: The higher the strike price, the higher the price of a put option.

Time to Expiration   For American options (both puts and calls), all other factors held constant, the longer the time to expiration, the higher the option price. No general statement can be made for European options. The impact of the time to expiration on European options will depend on whether the option is a put or a call.

Short-Term Risk-Free Interest Rate over the Life of the Option   Holding all other factors constant, the price of a call option on a bond will increase as the short-term risk-free interest rate rises. For a put option, the opposite is true: An increase in the short-term risk-free interest rate will decrease the price of a put option. In contrast, for a futures option, the price of both a call and a put option will decrease if the short-term risk-free interest rate rises.[4]

Coupon Rate   For options on bonds, coupons tend to reduce the price of a call option because the coupons make it more attractive to hold the bond than the option. Thus call options on coupon-bearing bonds will tend to be priced lower than similar call options on non–coupon-bearing bonds. Conversely, coupons tend to increase the price of put options.

Expected Volatility of Yields over the Life of the Option   As the expected volatility of yields over the life of the option increases, the price of the option will also increase. The reason is that the greater the expected volatility, as measured by the standard deviation or variance of yields, the greater the probability that the price of

---

[3]For a more detailed discussion of the impact of these factors, see Pitts and Fabozzi, *Interest Rate Futures and Options.*
[4]Ibid.

the underlying bond or futures contract will move in the direction that will benefit the option buyer.

MODELS FOR PRICING OPTIONS

Several models have been developed for determining the theoretical value of an option. These models, referred to as option pricing models. There are models for valuing options on bonds and options on bond futures. We discuss the various models below.

Models for Valuing Options on Bonds

First we will discuss models for valuing options on bonds (i.e., options on physicals). In the equity options area, the most popular model is the Black–Scholes option pricing model.[5] This model, however, is limited in pricing options on bonds, as we shall see next. A more appropriate model that takes into account the yield curve builds on the valuation procedure described in Chapter 14, where we introduced a binomial interest-rate tree.

Black–Scholes Option Pricing Model   By imposing certain assumptions (to be discussed later) and using arbitrage arguments, the **Black–Scholes option pricing model** computes the fair (or theoretical) price of a European call option on a non–dividend-paying stock with the following formula:

$$C = SN(d_1) - Xe^{-rt} N(d_2) \tag{22.6}$$

where

$$d_1 = \frac{\ln(S/X) + (r + 0.5s^2)t}{s\sqrt{t}} \tag{22.7}$$

$$d_2 = d_1 - s\sqrt{t} \tag{22.8}$$

where:

- $\ln$ = natural logarithm
- C = call option price
- S = current stock price
- X = strike price
- r = short-term risk-free interest rate
- e = 2.718 (natural antilog of 1)
- t = time remaining to the expiration date (measured as a fraction of a year)
- s = standard deviation of the stock price
- $N(\cdot)$ = cumulative probability density [the value of $N(\cdot)$ is obtained from a normal distribution function that is tabulated in most statistics textbooks]

With the exception of the cash payments, notice that the factors that we said earlier influence the price of an option are included in the formula. Cash payments are not included because the model is for a non–dividend-paying stock.

The option price derived from the Black–Scholes option pricing model is "fair" in the sense that if any other price existed, it would be possible to earn riskless arbitrage

---

[5]Fischer Black and Myron Scholes, "The Pricing of Corporate Liabilities," *Journal of Political Economy,* May–June 1973, pp. 637–659.

profits by taking an offsetting position in the underlying stock. That is, if the price of the call option in the market is higher than that derived from the Black–Scholes option pricing model, an investor could sell the call option and buy a certain number of shares in the underlying stock. If the reverse is true, that is, the market price of the call option is less than the "fair" price derived from the model, the investor could buy the call option and sell short a certain number of shares in the underlying stock. This process of hedging by taking a position in the underlying stock allows the investor to lock in the riskless arbitrage profit. The number of shares necessary to hedge the position changes as the factors that affect the option price change, so the hedged position must be changed constantly.

Computing the Price of a Call Option on a Zero-Coupon Bond   Because the basic Black–Scholes formula as given by equation (22.6) is for a non–cash-paying security, let's apply it to a zero-coupon bond with three years to maturity. Assume the following values:

$$\text{Strike price} = \$88.00$$
$$\text{Time remaining to expiration} = 2 \text{ years}$$
$$\text{Current price} = \$83.96$$
$$\text{Expected price volatility} = \text{standard deviation} = 10\%$$
$$\text{Risk-free rate} = 6\%$$

Note that the current price is $83.96, which is the present value of the maturity value of $100 discounted at 6% (assuming a flat yield curve).

In terms of the values in the formula,

$$S = 83.96$$
$$X = 88.00$$
$$t = 2$$
$$s = 0.10$$
$$r = 0.06$$

Substituting these values into equations (22.7) and (22.8) yields

$$d_1 = \frac{\ln(83.96/88) + [0.06 + 0.5(0.10)^2]2}{0.10\sqrt{2}} = 0.5869$$

$$d_2 = 0.5869 - 0.10\sqrt{2} = 0.4455$$

From a normal distribution table,

$$N(0.5869) = 0.7214 \quad \text{and} \quad N(0.4455) = 0.6720$$

Then, from equation (22.6),

$$C = 83.96(0.7214) - 88\left[e^{-(0.06)(2)}(0.6720)\right] = \$8.116$$

There is no reason to suspect that this estimated value is unreasonable. However, let's change the problem slightly. Instead of a strike price of $88, let's make the strike price $100.25. Substituting the new strike price into equations (22.7) and (22.8):

$$d_1 = \frac{\ln(83.96/100.25) + [0.06 + 0.5(0.10)^2]2}{0.10\sqrt{2}} = -0.3346$$

$$d_2 = -0.3346 - 0.10\sqrt{2} = -0.4761$$

From a normal distribution table,

$$N(-0.3346) = 0.3689 \quad \text{and} \quad N(-0.4761) = 0.3170$$

Then, from equation (22.6),

$$C = 83.96(0.3689) - 100.25[e^{-(0.06)(2)}(0.3170)] = \$2.79$$

Thus the Black–Scholes option pricing model tells us that this call option has a fair value of $2.79. Is there any reason to believe that this is unreasonable? Well, consider that this is a call option on a zero-coupon bond that will *never* have a value greater than its maturity value of $100. Consequently, a call option struck at $100.25 must have a value of zero. Yet the Black–Scholes option pricing model tells us that the value is $2.79! In fact, with a higher volatility assumption, the model would give an even greater value for the call option.

Why is the Black–Scholes model off by so much in our previous illustration? The answer lies in its underlying assumptions. There are three assumptions underlying the Black–Scholes model that limit its use in pricing options on interest-rate instruments. First, the probability distribution for the prices assumed by the Black–Scholes option pricing model permits some probability—no matter how small—that the price cannot take on any positive value. But in the case of a zero-coupon bond, the price can take on a value above $100. In the case of a coupon bond, we know that the price cannot exceed the sum of the coupon payments plus the maturity value. For example, for a five-year 10% coupon bond with a maturity value of $100, the price cannot be greater than $150 (five coupon payments of $10 plus the maturity value of $100). Thus, unlike stock prices, bond prices have a maximum value. The only way that a bond's price can exceed the maximum value is if negative interest rates are permitted. This is not likely to occur, so any probability distribution for prices assumed by an option pricing model that permits bond prices to be higher than the maximum bond value could generate nonsensical option prices. The Black–Scholes model does allow bond prices to exceed the maximum bond value (or, equivalently, allows negative interest rates). That is one of the reasons why we can get a senseless option price for the three-month European call option on the three-year zero-coupon bond.

The second assumption of the Black–Scholes option pricing model is that the short-term interest rate is constant over the life of the option. Yet the price of an interest-rate option will change as interest rates change. A change in the short-term interest rate changes the rates along the yield curve. Therefore, to assume that the short-term rate will be constant is inappropriate for interest-rate options. The third assumption is that the variance of prices is constant over the life of the option. Recall from Chapter 4 that as a bond moves closer to maturity its price volatility declines. Therefore, the assumption that price variance is constant over the life of the option is inappropriate.

We have illustrated the problem of using the Black–Scholes model to price interest-rate options; we can also show that the binomial option pricing model based on the price distribution of the underlying bond suffers from the same problems.

Arbitrage-Free Binomial Model   The proper way to value options on interest-rate instruments is to use an arbitrage-free model that takes into account the yield curve. These models can incorporate different volatility assumptions along the yield curve.

The most popular model employed by dealer firms is the Black–Derman–Toy model.[6]

We have already developed the basic principles for employing this model. In Chapter 14 we explained how to construct a binomial interest-rate tree such that the tree would be arbitrage free. We used the interest-rate tree to value bonds (both option-free and bonds with embedded options). But the same tree can be used to value a stand-alone European option on a bond.

To illustrate how this is done, let's consider a two-year European call option on a 5.25% three-year Treasury bond with a strike price of 99.25. We will assume that the yield for the on-the-run Treasuries is the one in Chapter 14 and that the volatility assumption is 10% per year. Exhibit 14-13 shows the binomial interest-rate tree along with the value of the Treasury bond at each node. It is a portion of that exhibit we use to value the call option. Specifically, Exhibit 22-11 shows the value of our Treasury bond (excluding coupon interest) at each node at the end of year 2. There are three values shown: 98.5884, 99.7328, and 100.6888. Given these three values, the value of a call option struck at 99.25 can be determined at each node. For example, if in two years the price of this Treasury bond is 98.5884, then because the strike price is 99.25, the value of the call option would be zero. In the other two cases, because the price two years from now is greater than the strike price, the value of the call option is the difference between the price of the bond and 99.25.

Exhibit 22-11 shows the value of the call option two years from now (the option expiration date) for each of the three nodes. Given these values, the binomial interest-rate tree is used to find the present value of the call option. The backward induction procedure is used. The discount rates are those from the binomial interest-rate tree. For years 0 and 1, the discount rate is the second number shown at each node. The first number at each node for year 1 is the average present value found by discounting the call option value of the two nodes to the right using the discount rate at the node. The value of the call option is the first number shown at the root, $0.55707.

The same procedure is used to value a European put option. This is illustrated in Exhibit 22-12 assuming that the put option has two years to expiration and that the strike price is 99.25. The value of the put option two years from now is shown at each of the three nodes in year 2.

To demonstrate that the arbitrage-free binomial model satisfies the put–call parity relationship for European options given by equation (22.3), let's use the values from our illustration. We just found that

$$P_{po} = 0.55707$$
$$P_{co} = 0.15224$$

In Chapter 14 we showed that the theoretical price for the 5.25% three-year option-free bond is 102.075. Therefore,

$$P_b = 102.075$$

Also in Chapter 14, we showed the spot rates for each year. The spot rate for year 2 is 4.01%. Therefore, the present value of the strike price of 99.25 is

---

[6]Fischer Black, Emanuel Derman, and William Toy, "A One-Factor Model of Interest Rates and Its Application to Treasury Bond Options," *Financial Analysts Journal,* January–February 1990, pp. 24–32.

EXHIBIT 22-11 Valuing a European Call Option Using the Binomial Method

Underlying: 3-year, 5.25% Treasury

Call Option:
expiration: 2 years
strike price: 99.25
current price: 102.075
volatility assumption: 10%

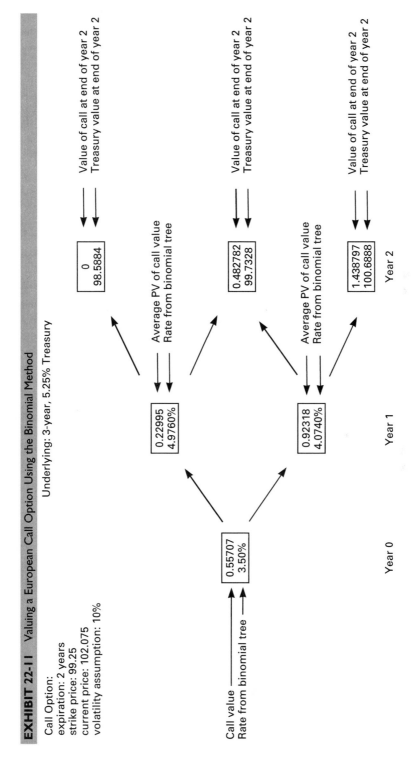

553

EXHIBIT 22-12 Valuing a European Put Option Using the Binomial Method

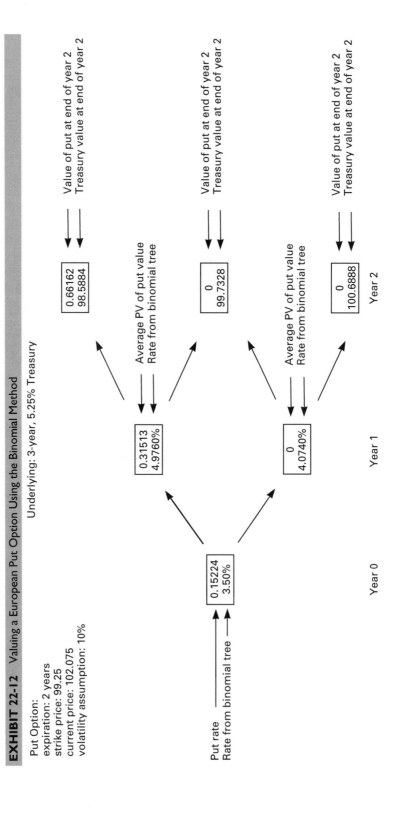

Put Option:
expiration: 2 years
strike price: 99.25
current price: 102.075
volatility assumption: 10%

Underlying: 3-year, 5.25% Treasury

Put rate
Rate from binomial tree

| 0.15224 |
| 3.50% |

| 0.31513 |
| 4.9760% |

Average PV of put value
Rate from binomial tree

| 0.66162 |
| 98.5884 |

Value of put at end of year 2
Treasury value at end of year 2

| 0 |
| 99.7328 |

Value of put at end of year 2
Treasury value at end of year 2

| 0 |
| 4.0740% |

Average PV of put value
Rate from binomial tree

| 0 |
| 100.6888 |

Value of put at end of year 2
Treasury value at end of year 2

Year 0   Year 1   Year 2

$$PV(S) = \frac{99.25}{(1.0401)^2} = 91.7446$$

The present value of the coupon payments are found by discounting the two coupon payments of 5.25 by the spot rates. As just noted, the spot rate for year 2 is 4.01%; the spot rate for year 1 is 3.5%. Therefore,

$$PV(\text{coupon}) = \frac{5.25}{1.035} + \frac{5.25}{(1.0401)^2} = 9.9255$$

The put–call parity relationship as given by equation (22.3) is repeated as follows:

$$P_{po} = P_{co} + PV(S) + PV(\text{coupon}) - P_b$$

Substituting the values into the right-hand side of the relationship, we find that

$$0.55707 + 91.7446 + 9.9255 - 102.075 = 0.15217$$

The put value that we found is 0.15224. The discrepancy is due simply to rounding error. Therefore, put–call parity holds.

Implied Volatility   Option pricing models provide a theoretical option price depending on the six factors earlier. The only one of these factors that is not known and must be estimated is the expected volatility of yield or price over the life of the option. A popular methodology to assess whether an option is fairly priced is to assume that the option is priced correctly and then, using an option pricing model, estimate the volatility that is implied by that model, given the observed option price and the other five factors that determine the price of an option. The estimated volatility computed in this manner is called the **implied volatility.**

For example, suppose that a money manager using some option pricing model, the current price of the option, and the five other factors that determine the price of an option computes an implied yield volatility of 12%. If the money manager expects that the volatility of yields over the life of the option will be greater than the implied volatility of 12%, the option is considered to be undervalued. In contrast, if the money manager's expected volatility of yields over the life of the option is less than the implied volatility, the option is considered to be overvalued. Although we have focused on the option price, the key to understanding the options market is knowing that trading and investment strategies in this market involve buying and selling volatility. Estimating the implied volatility and comparing it with the trader's or money manager's expectations of future volatility is just another way of evaluating options. If an investor uses expected volatility to compute the fair value of the option, the option will appear cheap or expensive in exactly the same cases.

Models for Valuing Options on Bond Futures

The most commonly used model for futures options was developed by Fischer Black.[7] The model was initially developed for valuing European options on forward contracts. The value of a call and put based on the Black model is:

$$C = e^{-rt}[FN(d_1) - XN(d_2)]$$
$$P = e^{-rt}[XN(-d_2) - FN(-d_1)]$$

---

[7]Fischer Black, "The Pricing of Commodity Contracts," *Journal of Financial Economics,* March 1976, pp. 161–179.

where:

$$d_1 = \frac{\ln(F/X) + 0.5s^2t}{s\sqrt{t}}$$

$d_2 = d_1 - s\sqrt{t}$

ln = natural logarithm

C = call option price

P = put option price

F = futures price

X = strike price

r = short-term risk-free interest rate

e = 2.718 (natural antilog of 1)

t = time remaining to the expiration date (measured as a fraction of a year)

s = standard deviation of the price

$N(\cdot)$ = the cumulative probability density. The value for $N(\cdot)$ is obtained from a normal distribution function

There are two problems with this model. First, the Black model does not overcome the problems cited earlier for the Black–Scholes model. Failing to recognize the yield curve means that there will not be a consistency between pricing Treasury futures and options on Treasury futures. Second, the Black model was developed for pricing European options on futures contracts. Treasury futures options, however, are American options.

The second problem can be overcome. The Black model was extended by Barone-Adesi and Whaley to American options on futures contracts.[8] This is the model used by the Chicago Board of Trade to settle the flexible Treasury futures options. However, this model was also developed for equities and is subject to the first problem noted above. Despite its limitations, the Black model is the most popular option pricing model for options on Treasury futures.

SENSITIVITY OF OPTION PRICE TO CHANGE IN FACTORS

In employing options in an investment strategy, a money manager would like to know how sensitive the price of an option is to a change in any one of the factors that affect its price. Here we look at the sensitivity of a call option's price to changes in the price of the underlying bond, the time to expiration, and expected volatility.

Call Option Price and Price of the Underlying Bond

Exhibit 22-13 shows the theoretical price of a call option based on the price of the underlying bond. The horizontal axis is the price of the underlying bond at any point in time. The vertical axis is the call option price. The shape of the curve representing the theoretical price of a call option, given the price of the underlying bond, would be the same regardless of the actual option pricing model used. In particular, the relationship

---

[8]Giovanni Barone-Adesi and Robert E. Whaley, "Efficient Analytic Approximation of American Option Values," *Journal of Finance*, June 1987, pp. 301–320.

EXHIBIT 22-13   Theoretical Call Price and the Price of the Underlying Bond

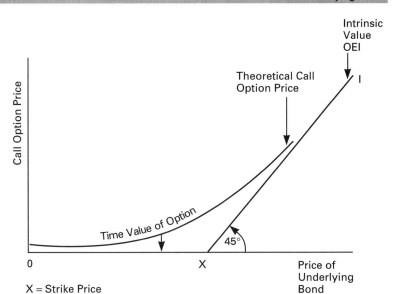

X = Strike Price

between the price of the underlying bond and the theoretical call option price is convex. Thus option prices also exhibit convexity.

The line from the origin to the strike price on the horizontal axis in Exhibit 22-13 is the intrinsic value of the call option when the price of the underlying bond is less than the strike price, because the intrinsic value is zero. The 45-degree line extending from the horizontal axis is the intrinsic value of the call option once the price of the underlying bond exceeds the strike price. The reason is that the intrinsic value of the call option will increase by the same dollar amount as the increase in the price of the underlying bond. For example, if the strike price is $100 and the price of the underlying bond increases from $100 to $101, the intrinsic value will increase by $1. If the price of the bond increases from $101 to $110, the intrinsic value of the option will increase from $1 to $10. Thus the slope of the line representing the intrinsic value after the strike price is reached is 1.

Because the theoretical call option price is shown by the convex line, the difference between the theoretical call option price and the intrinsic value at any given price for the underlying bond is the time value of the option.

Exhibit 22-14 shows the theoretical call option price but with a tangent line drawn at the price of p^*. The tangent line in the figure can be used to estimate what the new option price will be (and therefore what the change in the option price will be) if the price of the underlying bond changes. Because of the convexity of the relationship between the option price and the price of the underlying bond, the tangent line closely approximates the new option price for a small change in the price of the underlying bond. For large changes, however, the tangent line does not provide as good an approximation of the new option price.

EXHIBIT 22-14 Estimating the Theoretical Option Price with a Tangent Line

The slope of the tangent line shows how the theoretical call option price will change for small changes in the price of the underlying bond. The slope is popularly referred to as the **delta** of the option. Specifically,

$$\text{delta} = \frac{\text{change in price of call option}}{\text{change in price of underlying bond}}$$

For example, a delta of 0.4 means that a $1 change in the price of the underlying bond will change the price of the call option by approximately $0.40.

Exhibit 22-15 shows the curve of the theoretical call option price with three tangent lines drawn. The steeper the slope of the tangent line, the greater the delta. When an option is deep out of the money (i.e., the price of the underlying bond is substantially below the strike price), the tangent line is nearly flat (see line 1 in Exhibit 22-15). This means that delta is close to zero. To understand why, consider a call option with a strike price of $100 and two months to expiration. If the price of the underlying bond is $20, its price would not increase by much, if anything, should the price of the underlying bond increase by $1, from $20 to $21.

For a call option that is deep in the money, the delta will be close to 1. That is, the call option price will increase almost dollar for dollar with an increase in the price of the underlying bond. In terms of Exhibit 22-15, the slope of the tangent line approaches the slope of the intrinsic value line after the strike price. As we stated earlier, the slope of that line is 1.

Thus the delta for a call option varies from zero (for call options deep out of the money) to 1 (for call options deep in the money). The delta for a call option at the money is approximately 0.5.

EXHIBIT 22-15 Theoretical Option Price with Three Tangents

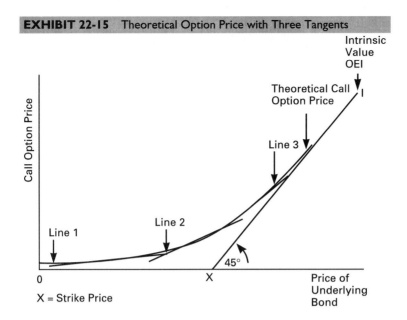

The curvature of the convex relationship can also be approximated. This is the rate of change of delta as the price of the underlying bond changes. The measure is commonly referred to as **gamma** and is defined as follows:

$$\text{gamma} = \frac{\text{change in delta}}{\text{change in price of underlying bond}}$$

Call Option Price and Time to Expiration

All other factors constant, the longer the time to expiration, the greater the option price. Because each day the option moves closer to the expiration date, the time to expiration decreases. The **theta** of an option measures the change in the option price as the time to expiration decreases, or equivalently, it is a measure of **time decay.** Theta is measured as follows:

$$\text{theta} = \frac{\text{change in price of option}}{\text{decrease in time to expiration}}$$

Assuming that the price of the underlying bond does not change (which means that the intrinsic value of the option does not change), theta measures how quickly the time value of the option changes as the option moves towards expiration. Buyers of options prefer a low theta so that the option price does not decline quickly as it moves toward the expiration date. An option writer benefits from an option that has a high theta.

Call Option Price and Expected Interest Rate Volatility

All other factors constant, a change in the expected interest rate volatility will change the option price. The **kappa** of an option measures the dollar price change in the price of the option for a 1% change in the expected price volatility. That is,

$$\text{kappa} = \frac{\text{change in option price}}{1\% \text{ change in expected price volatility}}$$

Duration of an Option

The modified duration of an option measures the price sensitivity of the option to changes in interest rates. The modified duration of an option can be shown to be equal to

$$\text{modified duration for an option} = \begin{array}{c}\text{modified duration}\\ \text{of underlying}\\ \text{instrument}\end{array} \times \text{delta}$$

$$\times \frac{\text{price of underlying instrument}}{\text{price of option}}$$

As expected, the modified duration of an option depends on the modified duration of the underlying bond. It also depends on the price responsiveness of the option to a change in the underlying instrument, as measured by the option's delta. The leverage created by a position in an option comes from the last ratio in the formula. The higher the price of the underlying instrument relative to the price of the option, the greater the leverage (i.e., the more exposure to interest rates for a given dollar investment).

It is the interaction of all three factors that affects the modified duration of an option. For example, a deep-out-of-the-money option offers higher leverage than a deep-in-the-money option, but the delta of the former is less than that of the latter.

Because the delta of a call option is positive, the modified duration of an interest rate call option will be positive. Thus when interest rates decline, the value of an interest rate call option will rise. A put option, however, has a delta that is negative. Thus the modified duration is negative. Consequently, when interest rates rise, the value of a put option rises.

HEDGE STRATEGIES

Hedge strategies involve taking a position in an option and a position in the underlying bond in such a way that changes in the value of one position will offset any unfavorable price (interest rate) movement in the other position. We discuss two popular hedge strategies here: (1) the protective put buying strategy, and (2) the covered call writing strategy. In this section we demonstrate these two strategies using futures options. The exercise is worthwhile because it shows how complicated hedging with futures options is and the key parameters involved in the process. We also compare the outcome of hedging with futures and hedging with futures options.[9]

---

[9]The illustrations in this section are taken from Chapter 10 of Pitts and Fabozzi, *Interest Rate Futures and Options.*

Hedging Long-Term Bonds with Puts on Futures

Investors often want to hedge their bond positions against a possible increase in interest rates. Buying puts on futures is one of the easiest ways to purchase protection against rising rates. To illustrate this strategy, we can use the same utility bond example that we used in Chapter 21 to demonstrate how to hedge with Treasury bond futures. In that example, an investor held 11¾% bonds of 2023 and used futures to lock in a sale price for those bonds on a futures delivery date. Now we want to show how the hedger could have used futures options instead of futures to protect against rising rates.

In the example (summarized at the top of Exhibit 22-16), rates were already fairly high; the hedged bonds were selling at a yield of 12.40%, the Treasury 7⅝% of 2007 (the cheapest to deliver issue at the time) were at 11.50%. For simplicity, we assumed

EXHIBIT 22-16   Hedging a Nondeliverable Bond to a Delivery Date with Puts on Futures

Instrument to be hedged: 11¾% of 4/19/23
Hedge ratio: 1.24
Strike price for puts on futures: 66-0
Target minimum price for hedged bonds: 87.203
Put option price per contract: $375

Actual Sale Price of Hedged Bonds	Futures Price[a]	Value of 124 Put Options[b]	Cost of 124 Put Options	Effective Sale Price[c]
$ 7,600,000	56.511	$1,176,636	$46,500	$ 8,730,136
7,800,000	58.144	974,144	46,500	8,727,644
8,000,000	59.773	772,148	46,500	8,725,648
8,200,000	61.401	570,276	46,500	8,723,776
8,400,000	63.030	368,280	46,500	8,721,780
8,600,000	64.649	167,524	46,500	8,721,024
8,800,000	66.271	0	46,500	8,753,500
9,000,000	67.888	0	46,500	8,953,500
9,200,000	69.497	0	46,500	9,153,500
9,400,000	71.100	0	46,500	9,353,500
9,600,000	72.705	0	46,500	9,553,500
9,800,000	74.299	0	46,500	9,753,500
10,000,000	75.892	0	46,500	9,953,500
10,200,000	77.473	0	46,500	10,153,500
10,400,000	79.052	0	46,500	10,353,500
10,600,000	80.625	0	46,500	10,553,500
10,800,000	82.188	0	46,500	10,753,500
11,000,000	83.746	0	46,500	10,953,500
11,200,000	85.303	0	46,500	11,153,500

[a]These numbers are approximate because futures trade in even 32nds.
[b]From 124 × $1,000 × Max{(66 − futures price), 0}.

that this yield spread would remain at 90 basis points. In terms of a yield regression, this would be equivalent to a regression in which the beta equals 1.0 and the intercept term is 0.90%.

The hedger must determine the minimum price that she wants to establish for the hedged bonds. In our illustration it is assumed that the minimum price is 87.668. This is equivalent to saying that the hedger wants to establish a strike price for a put option on the hedged bonds of 87.668. But the hedger is not buying a put option on the utility bonds. She is buying a put option on a Treasury bond futures contract. Therefore, the hedger must determine the strike price for a put option on a Treasury bond futures contract that is equivalent to a strike price of 87.668 for the utility bonds.

This can be done with the help of Exhibit 22-17. We begin at the top left-hand box of the exhibit. Because the minimum price is 87.668 for the utility bonds, this means that the hedger is attempting to establish a maximum yield of 13.41%. This is found from the relationship between price and yield: Given a price of 87.668 for the utility bond, this is equivalent to a yield of 13.41%. (This gets us to the lower left-hand box in Exhibit 22-17.) From our assumption that the spread between the utility bonds and the cheapest-to-deliver issue is a constant 90 basis points, setting a maximum yield of 13.41% for the utility bond is equivalent to setting a maximum yield of 12.51% for the cheapest-to-deliver issue. (Now we are at the lower box in the middle column of Exhibit 22-17.) Given the yield of 12.51% for the cheapest-to-deliver issue, the minimum price can be determined (the top box in the middle column of the figure). A 12.51% yield for the Treasury 7⅝% of 2007 (the cheapest-to-deliver issue at the time) is 63.756. The corresponding futures price is found by dividing the price of the cheapest-to-deliver by the conversion factor. This gets us to the box in the right-hand column of Exhibit 22-17. Because the conversion factor is 0.9660, the futures price is about 66 (63.7567 divided by 0.9660). This means that a strike price of 66 for a put option on a Treasury bond futures contract is roughly equivalent to a put option on the utility bonds with a strike price of 87.668.

The foregoing steps are always necessary to obtain the appropriate strike price on a put futures option. The process is not complicated. It involves simply (1) the rela-

EXHIBIT 22-17   Calculating Equivalent Prices and Yields for Hedging with Futures Options

tionship between price and yield, (2) the assumed relationship between the yield spread between the hedged bonds and the cheapest-to-deliver issue, and (3) the conversion factor for the cheapest-to-deliver issue. As with hedging employing futures illustrated earlier in Chapter 21, the success of the hedging strategy will depend on (1) whether the cheapest-to-deliver issue changes, and (2) the yield spread between the hedged bonds and the cheapest-to-deliver issue.

The hedge ratio is determined using equation (21.12) of Chapter 21 because we will assume a constant yield spread between the security to be hedged and the cheapest-to-deliver issue. For increased accuracy, we calculate the price values of a basis point at the option expiration date (assumed to be June 28, 1985) and at the yields corresponding to the futures strike price of 66 (12.51% for the cheapest-to-deliver issue and 13.41% for the hedged bonds). The respective price values of a basis point are 0.065214 and 0.050969. This results in a hedge ratio of 1.236 for the options hedge, or 1.24 with rounding.

To create a table for the protective put hedge, we can use some of the numbers from Exhibit 21-4 of Chapter 21. Everything will be the same except the last two columns. For the put option hedge we have to insert the value of the 124 futures put options in place of the 124 futures contracts in the next-to-last column. This is easy because the value of each option at expiration is just the strike price of the futures option (66) minus the futures price (or zero if that difference is negative), all multiplied by $1,000. The effective sale price for the hedged bonds is then just the actual market price for the hedged bonds, plus the value of the options at expiration, minus the cost of the options.

Suppose that the price of the put futures option with a strike price of 66 is 24. An option price of 24 means 24/64 of 1% of par value, or $375. With a total of 124 options, the cost of the protection would have been $46,500 (124 × $375, not including financing costs and commissions). This cost, together with the final value of the options, is combined with the actual sale price of the hedged bonds to arrive at the effective sale price for the hedged bonds. These final prices are shown in the last column of Exhibit 22-16. This effective sale price is never less than 87.203. This equals the price of the hedged bonds equivalent to the futures strike price of 66 (i.e., 87.668), minus the cost of the puts (i.e., 0.4650 = 1.24 × 24/64). This minimum effective sale price is something that can be calculated before the hedge is ever initiated. (As prices decline, the effective sale price actually exceeds the projected effective minimum sale price of 87.203 by a small amount. This is due only to rounding and the fact that the hedge ratio is left unaltered, although the relative price values of a basis point that go into the hedge ratio calculation change as yields change.) As prices increase, however, the effective sale price of the hedged bonds increase as well; unlike the futures hedge shown in Exhibit 21-4, the options hedge using puts protects the investor if rates rise but allows the investor to profit if rates fall.

Covered Call Writing with Futures Options

Unlike the protective put strategy, covered call writing is not entered into with the sole purpose of protecting a portfolio against rising rates. The covered call writer, believing that the market will not trade much higher or much lower than its present level, sells out of the money calls against an existing bond portfolio. The sale of the calls brings in premium income that provides partial protection in case rates increase.

The premium received does not, of course, provide the kind of protection that a long put position provides, but it does provide some additional income that can be used to offset declining prices. If, on the other hand, rates fall, portfolio appreciation is limited because the short call position constitutes a liability for the seller, and this liability increases as rates go down. Consequently, there is limited upside potential for the covered call writer. Of course, this is not so bad if prices are essentially going nowhere; the added income from the sale of options is obtained without sacrificing any gains.

To see how covered call writing with futures options works for the bond used in the protective put example, we construct a table much as we did before. With futures selling around 71-24 on the hedge initiation date, a sale of a 78 call option on futures might be appropriate. As before, it is assumed that the hedged bond will remain at a 90 basis point spread off the cheapest-to-deliver Treasury bond, the 7⅝% of 2007. We also assume for simplicity that the price of the 78 calls is 24/64. The number of options contracts sold will be the same, namely 124 contracts for $10 million face value of underlying bonds. Exhibit 22-18 shows the results of the covered call writing strategy given these assumptions.

To calculate the effective sale price of the bonds in the covered call writing strategy, the premium received from the sale of calls is added to the actual sale price of the bonds, and the liability associated with the short call position is subtracted from the actual sale price. The liability associated with each call is the futures price minus the strike price of 78 (or zero if this difference is negative), all multiplied by $1,000. The middle column in the table is just this value multiplied by 124, the number of options sold.

Just as the minimum effective sale price could be calculated beforehand for the protective put strategy, the maximum effective sale price can be calculated beforehand for the covered call writing strategy. The maximum effective sale price will be the price of the hedged security corresponding to the strike price of the option sold, plus the premium received. In this case the strike price on the futures call option was 76. A futures price of 76 corresponds to a price of 75.348 (from 76 times the conversion factor), and a corresponding yield of 10.536% for the cheapest-to-deliver bond, the 7⅝% of 2007. The equivalent yield for the hedged bond is 90 basis points higher, or 11.436%, for a corresponding price of 102.666. Adding on the premium received, 0.465 point, the final maximum effective sale price will be about 103.131. As Exhibit 22-18 shows, if the hedged bond does trade at 90 basis points over the cheapest-to-deliver issue as assumed, the maximum effective sale price for the hedged bond is, in fact, slightly over 103. The discrepancies shown in the table are due to rounding and the fact that the position is not adjusted even though the relative price values of a basis point change as yields change.

Comparing Alternative Strategies

In Chapter 21 and this chapter we reviewed three basic hedging strategies for hedging a bond position: (1) hedging with futures, (2) hedging with out-of-the-money protective puts, and (3) covered call writing with out-of-the-money calls. Similar but opposite strategies exist for those whose risks are that rates will decrease. As might be expected, there is no "best" strategy. Each strategy has advantages and disadvantages, and we never get something for nothing. To get anything of value, something else of value must be forfeited.

EXHIBIT 22-18   Hedging a Nondeliverable Bond to a Delivery Date with Calls on Futures

Instrument to be hedged: 11¾% of 4/19/23
Hedge ratio: 1.24
Strike price for calls on futures: 78-0
Expected maximum price for hedged bonds: 103.131
Call option price per contract: $375

Actual Sale Price of Hedged Bonds	Futures Price[a]	Liability of 124 Call Options[b]	Premium from 124 Call Options	Effective Sale Price[c]
$ 7,600,000	56.511	0	$46,500	$ 7,646,500
7,800,000	58.144	0	46.500	7,846,500
8,000,000	59.773	0	46,500	8,046,500
8,200,000	61.401	0	46,500	8,246,500
8,400,000	63.030	0	46,500	8,446,500
8,600,000	64.649	0	46,500	8,646,500
8,800,000	66.271	0	46,500	8,846,500
9,000,000	67.888	0	46,500	9,046,500
9,200,000	69.497	0	46,500	9,246,500
9,400,000	71.100	0	46,500	9,446,500
9,600,000	72.705	0	46,500	9,646,500
9,800,000	74.299	0	46,500	9,846,500
10,000,000	75.892	0	46,500	10,046,500
10,200,000	77.473	0	46,500	10,246,500
10,400,000	79.052	130,448	46,500	10,316,052
10,600,000	80.625	325,500	46,500	10,321,000
10,800,000	82.188	519,312	46,500	10,327,188
11,000,000	83.746	712,504	46,500	10,333,996
11,200,000	85.303	905,572	46,500	10,340,928

[a]These numbers are approximate because futures trade in even 32nds.
[b]From 124 × $1,000 × Max{(futures price − 76), 0}.
[c]Does not include transaction costs or the financing of the options position.

To make a choice among strategies, it helps to lay the alternatives side by side. Using the futures and futures options examples from this chapter, Exhibit 22-19 shows the final values of the portfolio for the various alternatives. It is easy to see from Exhibit 22-19 that if one alternative is superior to another alternative at one level of rates, it will be inferior at some other level of rates.

Consequently, we cannot conclude that one strategy is the best strategy. The manager who makes the strategy decision makes a choice among probability distributions, not usually among specific outcomes. Except for the perfect hedge, there is always some range of possible final values of the portfolio. Of course, exactly what that range is, and the probabilities associated with each possible outcome, is a matter of opinion.

EXHIBIT 22-19 Alternative Hedging Strategies Compared

Actual Sale Price of Bonds	Effective Sale Price with Futures Hedge	Effective Sale Price with Protective Puts	Effective Sale Price with Covered Calls
$ 7,600,000	$9,272,636	$ 8,730,136	$ 7,646,500
7,800,000	9,270,144	8,727,644	7,846,500
8,000,000	9,268,148	8,725,648	8,046,500
8,200,000	9,266,276	8,723,776	8,246,500
8,400,000	9,264,280	8,721,780	8,446,500
8,600,000	9,263,524	8,721,024	8,646,500
8,800,000	9,262,396	8,753,500	8,846,500
9,000,000	9,261,888	8,953,500	9,046,500
9,200,000	9,262,372	9,153,500	9,246,500
9,400,000	9,263,600	9,353,500	9,446,500
9,600,000	9,264,580	9,553,500	9,646,500
9,800,000	9,266,924	9,753,500	9,846,500
10,000,000	9,269,392	9,953,500	10,046,500
10,200,000	9,273,348	10,153,500	10,246,500
10,400,000	9,277,552	10,353,500	10,316,052
10,600,000	9,282,500	10,553,500	10,321,000
10,800,000	9,288,688	10,753,500	10,327,188
11,000,000	9,295,496	10,953,500	10,333,996
11,200,000	9,302,428	11,153,500	10,340,928

SUMMARY

An option grants the buyer of the option the right either to buy (in the case of a call option) or to sell (in the case of a put option) the underlying asset to the seller (writer) of the option at a stated price called the strike (exercise) price by a stated date called the expiration date. The price that the option buyer pays to the writer of the option is called the option price or option premium. An American option allows the option buyer to exercise the option at any time up to and including the expiration date; a European option may be exercised only at the expiration date.

Interest-rate options include options on fixed-income securities and options on interest-rate futures contracts. The latter, more commonly called futures options, are the preferred vehicle for implementing investment strategies. Because of the difficulties of hedging particular bond issues or pass-through securities, many institutions find over-the-counter options more useful; these contracts can be customized to meet specific investment goals.

The buyer of an option cannot realize a loss greater than the option price and has all the upside potential. By contrast, the maximum gain that the writer (seller) of an option can realize is the option price; the writer is exposed to all the downside risk.

The option price consists of two components: the intrinsic value and the time value. The intrinsic value is the economic value of the option if it is exercised immediately (except that if there is no positive economic value that will result from exercising immediately, the intrinsic value is zero). The time value is the amount by which the option price exceeds the intrinsic value. Six factors influence the option price: (1) the current price of the underlying bond, (2) the strike price of the option, (3) the time remaining to the expiration of the option, (4) the expected price volatility of the underlying bond (i.e., expected interest-rate volatility), (5) the short-term risk-free interest rate over the life of the option, and (6) coupon payments.

An option pricing model determines the theoretical or fair value of an option. There are option pricing models for options on bonds (i.e., options on physcials) and options on bond futures. The two models used to value options on bonds are the Black–Scholes option pricing model and the arbitrage-free binomial option pricing model. The limitations of the former when applied to options on bonds are that it fails to incorporate the yield curve in the model and does not recognize that there is a maximum price that a bond can reach. The most common model to value an option on a bond futures contract is the Black model. The two popular strategies using options are protective put buying and covered call writing.

Questions

1. An investor owns a call option on bond X with a strike price of 100. The coupon rate on bond X is 9% and has 10 years to maturity. The call option expires today at a time when bond X is selling to yield 8%. Should the investor exercise the call option?

2. When the buyer of a put option on a futures contract exercises, explain the resulting position for the buyer and the writer.

3. An investor wants to protect against a rise in the market yield on a Treasury bond. Should the investor purchase a put option or a call option to obtain protection?

4. What is the intrinsic value and time value of a call option on bond W given the following information?

$$\text{strike price of call option} = 97$$
$$\text{current price of bond W} = 102$$
$$\text{call option price} = 9$$

5. "There's no real difference between options and futures. Both are hedging tools, and both are derivative products. It's just that with options you have to pay an option premium, whereas futures require no upfront payment except for a 'good faith' margin. I can't understand why anyone would use options." Do you agree with this statement?

6. What arguments would be given by those who feel that the Black–Scholes model does not apply in pricing interest-rate options?

7. Here are some excerpts from an article titled "It's Boom Time for Bond Options as Interest-Rate Hedges Bloom," published in the November 8, 1990, issue of *The Wall Street Journal*:

   a. "The threat of a large interest-rate swing in either direction is driving people to options to hedge their portfolios of long-term Treasury bonds and medium-term Treasury notes, said Steven Northern, who manages fixed-income mutual funds for Massachusetts Financial Services Co. in Boston." Why would a large interest rate swing in either direction encourage people to hedge?

   b. "If the market moves against an option purchaser, the option expires worthless, and all the investor has lost is the relatively low purchase price, or 'premium,' of the option." Comment on the accuracy of this statement.
   c. "Futures contracts also can be used to hedge portfolios, but they cost more, and there isn't any limit on the amount of losses they could produce before an investor bails out." Comment on the accuracy of this statement.
   d. "Mr. Northern said Massachusetts Financial has been trading actively in bond and note put options. 'The concept is simple,' he said. 'If you're concerned about interest rates but don't want to alter the nature of what you own in a fixed-income portfolio, you can just buy puts.' " Why might put options be a preferable means of altering the nature of a fixed-income portfolio?

8. What are the differences between an option on a bond and an option on a bond futures contract?
9. What is the motivation for the purchase of an over-the-counter option?
10. Does it make sense for an investor who wants to speculate on interest-rate movements to purchase an over-the-counter option?
11. "I don't understand how money managers can calculate the duration of an interest-rate option. Don't they mean the amount of time remaining to the expiration date?" Respond to this question.
12. a. What factors affect the modified duration of an interest-rate option?
    b. Deep-in-the-money option always provides a higher modified duration for an option than a deep-out-of-the-money option. Comment.
    c. The modified duration of all options is positive. Is this statement correct?
13. How is the implied volatility of an option determined?
14. What are the delta and gamma of an option?
15. Explain why the writer of an option would prefer an option with a high theta (all other factors equal).
16. In implementing a protective put buying strategy, explain the trade-off between the cost of the strategy and the strike price selected.
17. Here is an excerpt from an article titled "Dominguez Barry Looks at Covered Calls," appearing in the July 20, 1992, issue of *Derivatives Week,* p. 7:

> SBC Dominguez Barry Funds Management in Sydney, with A\$5.5 billion under management, is considering writing covered calls on its Australian bond portfolio to take advantage of very high implied volatilities, according to Carl Hanich, portfolio manager. The implied price volatility on at-the-money calls is 9.8%, as high as Hanich can ever remember. . . .
>
> In response to rising volatility, Hanich is thinking about selling calls with a strike of 8.5%, generating premium income. "I'd be happy to lose bonds at 8.5%, given our market's at 8.87% now," he said.
>
> Explain the strategy that Mr. Hanich is considering.

18. Determine the price of a European call option on a 6.5% four-year Treasury bond with a strike price of 100.25 and two years to expiration assuming: (1) the arbitrage-free binomial interest-rate tree shown in Exhibit A (based on a 10% volatility assumption), and (2) the price of the Treasury bond two years from now shown at each node.
19. Determine the price of a European put option on a 6.5% four-year Treasury bond with a strike price of 100.25 and two years to expiration assuming the same information as in Exhibit A.

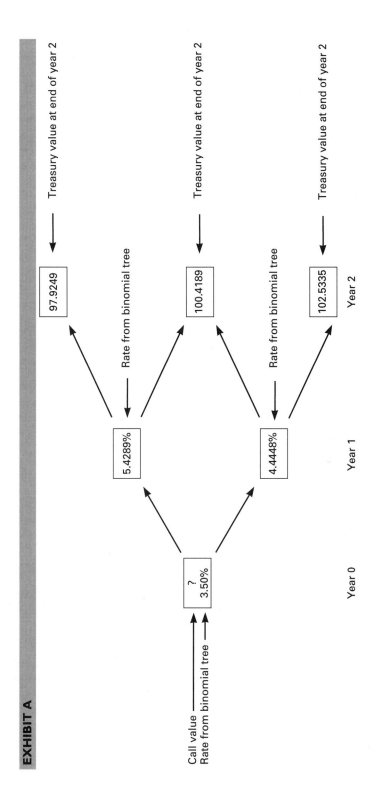

EXHIBIT A

Treasury value at end of year 2

Treasury value at end of year 2

Treasury value at end of year 2

97.9249

100.4189

102.5335

Rate from binomial tree

Rate from binomial tree

5.4289%

4.4448%

?
3.50%

Call value ——
Rate from binomial tree ——

Year 0

Year 1

Year 2

CHAPTER 23

Interest-Rate Swaps and Agreements

Learning Objectives

After reading this chapter you will understand:

- what an interest-rate swap is

- the relationship between an interest-rate swap and forward contracts

- how interest-rate swap terms are quoted in the market

- how the swap rate is calculated

- how the value of a swap is determined

- the primary determinants of the swap rate

- how a swap can be used by institutional investors for asset/liability management

- how a structured note is created using an interest-rate swap

- what an option on an interest-rate swap is, and how it can be used by institutional investors

- what a rate cap and floor are, and how these agreements can be used by institutional investors

- the relationship between a cap and floor and options

- how an interest-rate collar can be created

In Chapters 21 and 22 we discussed how interest-rate futures and options can be used to control interest-rate risk. There are other contracts useful for controlling such risk that commercial banks and investment banks can customize for their clients. These include (1) interest-rate swaps and options on swaps, and (2) interest-rate agreements (caps and floors) and options on these agreements. These contracts are relatively new. In this chapter we review each of them and explain how they can be used by institutional investors.

INTEREST-RATE SWAPS

In an *interest-rate swap,* two parties (called *counterparties*) agree to exchange periodic interest payments. The dollar amount of the interest payments exchanged is based on a predetermined dollar principal, which is called the *notional principal amount.* The dollar amount that each counterparty pays to the other is the agreed-upon periodic interest rate times the notional principal amount. The only dollars that are exchanged between the parties are the interest payments, not the notional principal amount. In the most common type of swap, one party agrees to pay the other party fixed-interest payments at designated dates for the life of the contract. This party is referred to as the *fixed-rate payer.* The other party, who agrees to make interest rate payments that float with some reference rate, is referred to as the *floating-rate payer.* The frequency with which the interest rate that the floating-rate payer must pay is called the *reset frequency.*

The reference rates that have been used for the floating rate in an interest-rate swap are those on various money market instruments: Treasury bills, the London Interbank Offered Rate, commercial paper, banker's acceptances, certificates of deposit, the federal funds rate, and the prime rate. The most common is the London Interbank Offered Rate (LIBOR). LIBOR is the rate at which prime banks offer to pay on Eurodollar deposits available to other prime banks for a given maturity. Basically, it is viewed as the global cost of bank borrowing. There is not just one rate but a rate for different maturities. For example, there is a one-month LIBOR, three-month LIBOR, and six-month LIBOR.

To illustrate an interest-rate swap, suppose that for the next five years party X agrees to pay party Y 10% per year, while party Y agrees to pay party X six-month LIBOR (the reference rate). Party X is a fixed-rate payer/floating-rate receiver, while party Y is a floating-rate payer/fixed-rate receiver. Assume that the notional principal amount is $50 million and that payments are exchanged every six months for the next five years. This means that every six months, party X (the fixed-rate payer/floating-rate receiver) will pay party Y $2.5 million (10% times $50 million divided by 2). The amount that party Y (the floating-rate payer/fixed-rate receiver) will pay party X will be six-month LIBOR times $50 million divided by 2. If six-month LIBOR is 7%, party Y will pay party X $1.75 million (7% times $50 million divided by 2). Note that we divide by two because one-half year's interest is being paid.

Later we will illustrate how market participants can use an interest-rate swap to alter the cash flow character of assets or liabilities from a fixed-rate basis to a floating-rate basis, or vice versa.

Entering into a Swap and Counterparty Risk

Interest-rate swaps are over-the-counter instruments. This means that they are not traded on an exchange. An institutional investor wishing to enter into a swap transaction can do so through either a securities firm or a commercial bank that transacts in swaps.[1] These entities can do one of the following. First, they can

---

[1]Don't get confused here about the role of commercial banks. A bank can use a swap in its asset/liability management; or a bank can transact (buy and sell) swaps to clients to generate fee income. It is in the latter sense that we are discussing the role of a commercial bank in the swap market here.

arrange or broker a swap between two parties that want to enter into an interest-rate swap. In this case, the securities firm or commercial bank is acting in a brokerage capacity.

The second way in which a securities firm or commercial bank can get an institutional investor into a swap position is by taking the other side of the swap. This means that the securities firm or the commercial bank is a dealer rather than a broker in the transaction. Acting as a dealer, the securities firm or the commercial bank must hedge its swap position in the same way that it hedges its position in other securities that it holds. Also it means that the dealer (which we refer to as a **swap dealer**) is the counterparty to the transaction. Goldman, Sachs, for example, is a swap dealer. If an institutional investor entered into a swap with Goldman, Sachs, the institutional investor will look to Goldman, Sachs to satisfy the obligations of the swap; similarly, Goldman, Sachs looks to the institutional investor to fulfill its obligations as set forth in the swap. Today, swaps are typically transacted using a swap dealer.

The risks that the two parties take on when they enter into a swap is that the other party will fail to fulfill its obligations as set forth in the swap agreement. That is, each party faces default risk. The default risk in a swap agreement is called **counterparty risk.** In fact, counterparty risk is more general than the default risk for only a swap agreement. In any agreement between two parties that must perform according to the terms of a contract, counterparty risk is the risk that the other party will default. With futures and exchange-traded options, the counterparty risk is the risk that the clearinghouse established to guarantee performance of the contracts will default. Market participants view this risk as small. In contrast, counterparty risk in a swap can be significant.

Because of counterparty risk, not all securities firms and commercial banks can be swap dealers. Several securities firms have actually established subsidiaries that are separately capitalized so that they have a high credit rating, which permits them to enter into swap transactions as a dealer. Thus it is imperative to keep in mind that any party who enters into a swap is subject to counterparty risk.

Interpreting a Swap Position

There are two ways that a swap position can be interpreted: (1) as a package of forward/ futures contracts, and (2) as a package of cash flows from buying and selling cash market instruments.

Package of Forward Contracts   Consider the hypothetical interest-rate swap described earlier to illustrate a swap. Let's look at party X's position. Party X has agreed to pay 10% and receive six-month LIBOR. More specifically, assuming a $50 million notional principal amount, X has agreed to buy a commodity called six-month LIBOR for $2.5 million. This is effectively a six-month forward contract in which X agrees to pay $2.5 million in exchange for delivery of six-month LIBOR. If interest rates increase to 11%, the price of that commodity (six-month LIBOR) is higher, resulting in a gain for the fixed-rate payer, who is effectively long a six-month forward contract on six-month LIBOR. The floating-rate payer is effectively short a six-month forward contract on six-month LIBOR. There is therefore an implicit forward contract corresponding to each exchange date.

Consequently, interest-rate swaps can be viewed as a package of more basic interest-rate control tools, such as forwards. The pricing of an interest-rate swap will then depend on the price of a package of forward contracts with the same settlement dates in which the underlying for the forward contract is the same index.

Although an interest-rate swap may be nothing more than a package of forward contracts, it is not a redundant contract, for several reasons. First, maturities for forward or futures contracts do not extend out as far as those of an interest-rate swap; an interest-rate swap with a term of 15 years or longer can be obtained. Second, an interest-rate swap is a more transactionally efficient instrument. By this we mean that in one transaction an entity can effectively establish a payoff equivalent to a package of forward contracts. The forward contracts would each have to be negotiated separately. Third, the interest-rate swap market has grown in liquidity since its establishment in 1981; interest-rate swaps now provide more liquidity than forward contracts, particularly long-dated (i.e., long-term) forward contracts.

Package of Cash Market Instruments   To understand why a swap can also be interpreted as a package of cash market instruments, consider an investor who enters into the following transaction:

- Buy a $50 million par of a five-year floating-rate bond that pays six-month LIBOR every six months.
- Finance the purchase by borrowing $50 million for five years on terms requiring 10% annual interest rate paid every six months.

The cash flows for this transaction are shown in Exhibit 23-1. The second column of the table shows the cash flow from purchasing the five-year floating-rate bond. There is a $50 million cash outlay and then 10 cash inflows. The amount of the cash inflows is uncertain because they depend on future LIBOR. The next column shows the cash flow from borrowing $50 million on a fixed-rate basis. The last column shows the net cash flow from the entire transaction. As the last column indicates, there is no initial cash flow (no cash inflow or cash outlay). In all 10 six-month periods, the net position results in a cash inflow of LIBOR and a cash outlay of $2.5 million. This net position, however, is identical to the position of a fixed-rate payer/floating-rate receiver.

It can be seen from the net cash flow in Exhibit 23-1 that a fixed-rate payer has a cash market position that is equivalent to a long position in a floating-rate bond and a short position in a fixed-rate bond—the short position being the equivalent of borrowing by issuing a fixed-rate bond.

What about the position of a floating-rate payer? It can be easily demonstrated that the position of a floating-rate payer is equivalent to purchasing a fixed-rate bond and financing that purchase at a floating-rate, where the floating rate is the reference interest rate for the swap. That is, the position of a floating-rate payer is equivalent to a long position in a fixed-rate bond and a short position in a floating-rate bond.

EXHIBIT 23-1 Cash Flow for the Purchase of a Five-Year Floating-Rate Bond Financed by Borrowing on a Fixed-Rate Basis

Transaction: Purchase for $50 million a five-year floating-rate bond: floating rate = LIBOR, seminannual pay; borrow $50 million for five years: fixed rate = 10%, semiannual payments

	Cash Flow (millions of dollars) from:		
Six-month Period	**Floating-Rate Bond**[a]	**Borrowing Cost**	**Net**
0	− $50	+ $50.0	$0
1	+ (LIBOR$_1$/2) × 50	− 2.5	+ (LIBOR$_1$/2) × 50 − 2.5
2	+ (LIBOR$_2$/2) × 50	− 2.5	+ (LIBOR$_2$/2) × 50 − 2.5
3	+ (LIBOR$_3$/2) × 50	− 2.5	+ (LIBOR$_3$/2) × 50 − 2.5
4	+ (LIBOR$_4$/2) × 50	− 2.5	+ (LIBOR$_4$/2) × 50 − 2.5
5	+ (LIBOR$_5$/2) × 50	− 2.5	+ (LIBOR$_5$/2) × 50 − 2.5
6	+ (LIBOR$_6$/2) × 50	− 2.5	+ (LIBOR$_6$/2) × 50 − 2.5
7	+ (LIBOR$_7$/2) × 50	− 2.5	+ (LIBOR$_7$/2) × 50 − 2.5
8	+ (LIBOR$_8$/2) × 50	− 2.5	+ (LIBOR$_8$/2) × 50 − 2.5
9	+ (LIBOR$_9$/2) × 50	− 2.5	+ (LIBOR$_9$/2) × 50 − 2.5
10	+ (LIBOR$_{10}$/2) × 50 + 50	− 52.5	+ (LIBOR$_{10}$/2) × 50 − 2.5

[a]The subscript for LIBOR indicates the six-month LIBOR as per the terms of the floating-rate bond at time *t*.

Terminology, Conventions, and Market Quotes

Here we review some of the terminology used in the swaps market and explain how swaps are quoted. The date that the counterparties commit to the swap is called the **trade date.** The date that the swap begins accruing interest is called the **effective date,** and the date that the swap stops accruing interest is called the **maturity date.**

Although our illustrations assume that the timing of the cash flows for both the fixed-rate payer and floating-rate payer will be the same, this is rarely the case in a swap. In fact, an agreement may call for the fixed-rate payer to make payments annually but the floating-rate payer to make payments more frequently (semiannually or quarterly). Also, the way in which interest accrues on each leg of the transaction differs, because there are several day-count conventions in the fixed-income markets.

The terminology used to describe the position of a party in the swap markets combines cash market jargon and futures jargon, given that a swap position can be interpreted as a position in a package of cash market instruments or a package of futures/forward positions. As we have said, the counterparty to an interest-rate swap is either a fixed-rate payer or floating-rate payer. Exhibit 23-2 describes these positions in several ways.

The first two expressions in Exhibit 23-2 to describe the position of a fixed-rate payer and floating-rate payer are self-explanatory. To understand why the fixed-rate payer is viewed as short the bond market and the floating-rate payer is viewed as long the bond market, consider what happens when interest rates change. Those who borrow on a fixed-rate basis will benefit if interest rates rise because they have locked in a lower interest rate. But those who have a short bond position will also benefit if interest rates rise. Thus a fixed-rate payer can be said to be short the bond market. A float-

EXHIBIT 23-2 Describing the Counterparties to a Swap

Fixed-Rate Payer	*Floating-Rate Payer*
Pays fixed rate in the swap	Pays floating rate in the swap
Receives floating in the swap	Receives fixed in the swap
Is short the bond market	Is long the bond market
Has bought a swap	Has sold a swap
Is long a swap	Is short a swap
Has established the price sensitivities of a longer-term liability and a floating-rate asset	Has established the price sensitivities of a longer-term asset and a floating-rate liability

Source: Robert F. Kopprasch, John Macfarlane, Daniel R. Ross, and Janet Showers, "The Interest Rate Swap Market: Yield Mathematics, Terminology, and Conventions," Chapter 58 in Frank J. Fabozzi and Irving M. Pollack (eds.), *The Handbook of Fixed Income Securities* (Homewood, IL: Dow Jones–Irwin, 1987).

ing-rate payer benefits if interest rates fall. A long position in a bond also benefits if interest rates fall, so terminology describing a floating-rate payer as long the bond market is not surprising. From our discussion of the interpretation of a swap as a package of cash market instruments, describing a swap in terms of the sensitivities of long and short cash positions follows naturally.

The convention that has evolved for quoting swaps levels is that a swap dealer sets the floating rate equal to the index and then quotes the fixed rate that will apply. To illustrate this convention, consider a 10-year swap offered by a dealer to market participants shown in Exhibit 23-3.

The offer price that the dealer would quote the fixed-rate payer would be to pay 8.85% and receive LIBOR "flat" ("flat" meaning with no spread to LIBOR). The bid price that the dealer would quote the floating-rate payer would be to pay LIBOR flat and receive 8.75%. The bid–offer spread is 10 basis points.

The fixed rate is some spread above the Treasury yield curve with the same term to maturity as the swap. In our illustration, suppose that the 10-year Treasury yield is 8.35%. Then the offer price that the dealer would quote to the fixed-rate payer is the 10-year Treasury rate plus 50 basis points versus receiving LIBOR flat. For the floating-rate payer, the bid price quoted would be LIBOR flat versus the 10-year Treasury rate plus 40 basis points. The dealer would quote such a swap as 40–50, meaning that the dealer is willing to enter into a swap to receive LIBOR and pay a fixed rate equal to the 10-year Treasury rate plus 40 basis points; and it would be willing to enter into a swap to pay LIBOR and receive a fixed rate equal to the 10-year Treasury rate plus 50 basis points. The difference between the Treasury rate paid and received is the bid–offer spread.

EXHIBIT 23-3 Meaning of a "40–50" Quote for a 10-Year Swap When Treasuries Yield 8.35% (Bid–Offer Spread of 10 Basis Points)

	Floating-Rate Payer	*Fixed-Rate Payer*
Pay	Floating rate of six-month LIBOR	Fixed rate of 8.85%
Receive	Fixed rate of 8.75%	Floating rate of six-month LIBOR

Calculation of the Swap Rate

At the initiation of an interest-rate swap, the counterparties are agreeing to exchange future interest-rate payments and no upfront payments by either party are made. This means that the swap terms must be such that the present value of the cash flows for the payments to be made by the counterparties must be equal. This is equivalent to saying that the present value of the cash flows of payments to be received by the counterparties must be equal. The equivalence of the cash flows is the principle in calculating the swap rate.

For the fixed-rate side, when a swap rate is determined, the payments of the fixed-rate payer are known. However, the floating-rate payments are not known because they depend on the value of the reference rate at the reset dates. For a LIBOR-based swap, the Eurodollar CD futures contract (discussed in Chapter 21) can be used to establish the forward (or future) rate for three-month LIBOR. Given the cash flow based on the forward rate for three-month LIBOR, the swap rate is the interest rate that will make the present value of the payments on the fixed-rate side equal to the payments on the floating-rate side.

The next question is: What interest rate should be used to discount the payments? As explained in Chapter 5, the appropriate rate to discount any cash flow is the theoretical spot rate. Each cash flow should be discounted at a unique discount rate. Where do we get the theoretical spot rates? Recall from Chapter 5 that spot rates can be obtained from forward rates. It is the same three-month LIBOR forward rates derived from the Eurodollar CD futures contract that can be used to obtain the theoretical spot rates.

Let's illustrate the procedure with an example. Consider the following hypothetical swap:

- *Swap term:* three-year swap
- *Notional amount:* $100 million
- *Fixed receiver:* actual/360-day count basis and quarterly payments
- *Floating receiver:* three-month LIBOR, actual/360-day count basis, quarterly payments, and quarterly reset

Our worktable for calculating the swap rate is Exhibit 23-4. The first column just lists the quarterly periods. There is a Eurodollar CD futures contract with a settlement date that corresponds to each period. The second column shows the number of days in the period for each Eurodollar CD futures contract. The third column shows the futures price for each contract. We know from Chapter 21 that the future three-month LIBOR is found by subtracting the futures price from 100. This is shown in column (4), representing the forward rate.[2]

It is from the forward rates that the discount rates that will be used to discount the cash flows (payments) will be calculated. The discount factor (i.e., the present value of $1 based on the spot rate) is found as follows[3]:

$$\frac{\text{discount factor in the previous period}}{1 + (\text{forward rate in preceding period} \times \text{no. days in period}/360)}$$

---

[2]In practice, the forward rate is adjusted for the convexity of the Eurodollar CD futures contract.

[3]The formulas presented below are taken from Chapter 6 of Ravi E. Dattatreya, Raj E. S. Venkatesh, and Vijaya E. Venkatesh, *Interest Rate and Currency Swaps* (Chicago: Probus Publishing, 1994).

EXHIBIT 23-4 Determining the Swap Rate[a]

Goal: Determination of swap rate
  Three-year swap
  Notional amount: $100 million

Fixed receiver:
  Actual/360-day count basis
  Quarterly payments

Floating receiver:
  Three-month LIBOR
  Actual/360-day count basis
  Quarterly payments and reset

Swap rate is the rate that will produce a fixed cash flow whose present value will equal the present value of the floating cash flow; in the illustration the swap rate is 4.987551%.

(1) Period	(2) Day Count	(3) Futures Price	(4) Fwd Rate	(5) Discount Factor	(6) Floating Cash Flow	(7) PV of Floating CF	(8) Fixed Cash Flow	(9) PV of Fixed CF
1	91		4.05	1.00000				
2	90	95.85	4.15	0.98998	1,012,500	1,002,351	1,246,888	1,234,390
3	91	95.45	4.55	0.97970	1,049,028	1,027,732	1,260,742	1,235,148
4	91	95.28	4.72	0.96856	1,150,139	1,113,978	1,260,742	1,221,104
5	91	95.10	4.90	0.95714	1,193,111	1,141,974	1,260,742	1,206,706
6	94	94.97	5.03	0.94505	1,279,444	1,209,137	1,302,305	1,230,741
7	91	94.85	5.15	0.93318	1,271,472	1,186,516	1,260,742	1,176,503
8	90	94.75	5.25	0.92132	1,287,500	1,186,201	1,246,888	1,148,784
9	91	94.60	5.40	0.90925	1,327,083	1,206,657	1,260,742	1,146,335
10	91	94.50	5.50	0.89701	1,365,000	1,224,419	1,260,742	1,130,899
11	91	94.35	5.65	0.88471	1,390,278	1,229,993	1,260,742	1,115,392
12	93	94.24	5.76	0.87198	1,459,583	1,272,732	1,288,451	1,123,507
13	91	94.10	5.79	0.85947	1,456,000	1,251,387	1,260,742	1,083,569
Total						14,053,077		14,053,078

[a]Explanation of columns:

Column (2): The day count refers to the number of days in the period.

Column (3): The Eurodollar CD futures price.

Column (4): Fwd rate = forward rate. The forward rate for LIBOR found from the futures price of the Eurodollar CD futures contract as follows: 100.00 − future price

Column (5): The discount factor is found as follows:

$$\frac{\text{discount factor in the previous period}}{1 + (\text{forward rate in previous period} \times \text{no. days in period}/360)}$$

The number of days in the period is found in column (2).

Column (6): The floating cash flow is found by multiplying the forward rate and the notional amount, adjusted for the number of days in the payment period; that is,

$$\frac{\text{forward rate in previous period} \times \text{no. days in period}}{360} \times \text{notional amount}$$

Column (7): Present value of floating cash flow, found as follows: column (5) × column (6).

Column (8): This column is found by trial and error, based on a guess of the swap rate. In determining the fixed cash flow, the cash flow must be adjusted for the day count, as follows:

$$\frac{\text{assumed swap rate} \times \text{no. days in period}}{360} \times \text{notional amount}$$

Column (9): Present value of fixed cash flow, found as follows: column (5) × column (7).

The discount factors are shown in column (5).

The floating cash flow is found by multiplying the forward rate and the notional amount. However, the forward rate must be adjusted for the number of days in the payment period. The formula to do so is

$$\frac{\text{forward rate previous period} \times \text{no. days in period}}{360} \times \text{notional amount}$$

These values represent the payments by the floating-rate payer and the receipts of the fixed-rate receiver. The values are shown in column (6). The present value of each of these cash flows is shown in column (7) using the discount factor shown in column (5). The present value of the floating cash flow is $14,053,077.

In order for no other payments to be exchanged between the counterparties other than the interest payments, the swap rate must be set such that the present value of the fixed cash flows is equal to the same value, $14,053,077. This can only be found by trial and error. For our hypothetical swap, when a swap rate of 4.987551% is tried, the cash flow is as shown in column (8). In determining the fixed cash flows, each cash flow must be adjusted for the day count, as follows:

$$\frac{\text{assumed swap rate} \times \text{no. days in period}}{360} \times \text{notional amount}$$

Using the discount factors in column (5), the present value of the fixed cash flows is equal to $14,053,078. Therefore, the swap rate is 4.987551%, because it is this rate that equates the present value of the floating and fixed cash flows.

Given the swap rate, the swap spread can be determined. For example, because this is a three-year swap, the three-year on-the-run Treasury rate would be used as the benchmark. If the yield on that issue is 4.587551%, the swap spread is then 40 basis points.

The calculation of the swap rate for all swaps follows the same principle: equating the present value of the cash flows.[4] Later in this section the economic determinants of the swap rate are discussed.

Valuing a Swap

When the swap transaction is completed, changes in market interest rates will change the cash flow of the floating-rate side of the swap. The value of an interest-rate swap is the difference between the present value of the cash flow of the two sides of the swap. The three-month LIBOR forward rates from the current Eurodollar CD futures contracts are used to (1) calculate the floating cash flows, and (2) determine the discount factors at which to calculate the present value of the cash flows.

To illustrate this, consider the three-year swap used to demonstrate how to calculate the swap rate. Suppose that one year later, interest rates change such that column (3) in Exhibit 23-5 shows the prevailing futures price for the Eurodollar CD futures contract. Columns (4) and (5) then show the corresponding forward rates and discount factors. Column (6) shows the floating cash flow based on the forward rates in column (4) and column (7) shows the present value of the floating cash flow using the discount

---

[4]For a more detailed explanation of how this is done with more complicated swaps, see Chapter 6 of Datta-treya, Venkatesh, and Venkatesh, *Interest Rate and Currency Swaps*.

EXHIBIT 23-5   Determining the Value of a Swap

Goal: Determination of swap
   value after one year
   Two-year swap
   Notional amount: $100 million

Floating receiver:
   Three-month LIBOR
   Actual/360-day count basis
   Quarterly payments and reset

Fixed receiver:
   Swap rate 4.987551%
   Actual/360-day count basis
   Quarterly payments

(1) Period	(2) Day Count	(3) Futures Price	(4) Fwd Rate	(5) Discount Factor	(6) Floating Cash Flow	(7) PV of Floating CF	(8) Fixed Cash Flow	(9) PV of Fixed CF
1	91		5.25	1.000000				
2	94	94.27	5.73	0.987045	1,370,833	1,353,074	1,302,305	1,285,434
3	91	94.22	5.78	0.972953	1,448,417	1,409,241	1,260,742	1,226,642
4	90	94.00	6.00	0.958942	1,445,000	1,385,671	1,246,888	1,195,693
5	91	93.85	6.15	0.944615	1,516,667	1,432,667	1,260,742	1,190,916
6	91	93.75	6.25	0.929686	1,554,583	1,445,274	1,260,742	1,172,094
7	91	93.54	6.46	0.915227	1,579,861	1,445,931	1,260,742	1,153,865
8	93	93.25	6.75	0.900681	1,668,833	1,503,086	1,288,451	1,160,483
9	91	93.15	6.85	0.885571	1,706,250	1,511,005	1,260,742	1,116,476
						11,485,949		9,501,603

PV of floating cash flow $11,485,949
PV of fixed cash flow $ 9,501,603
Value of swap $ 1,984,346

factors in column (5). The present value of the floating cash flow is $11,485,949. This means that the floating-rate payer has agreed to make payments with a value of $11,485,949 and the fixed-rate payer will receive a cash flow with this value.

Now let's look at the fixed-rate side. The swap rate is fixed over the life of the swap. The fixed cash flow is given in column (8) and the present value based on the discount factors in column (5) is shown in column (9). The present value of the fixed cash flows is $9,501,601. This means that the fixed-rate payer has agreed to make payments with a value of $9,501,603, and the floating-rate payer will receive a cash flow with this value.

From the fixed-rate payer's perspective, a floating cash flow with a present value of $11,485,949 is going to be received and a fixed cash flow with a present value of $9,501,601 is going to be paid out. The difference between these two present values, $1,984,346, is the value of the swap. It is a positive value for the fixed-rate payer because the present value of what is to be received exceeds the present value of what is to be paid out.

From the floating-rate payer's perspective, a floating cash flow with a present value of $11,485,949 is going to be paid out and a fixed cash flow with a present value of $9,501,601 is going to be received. Once again, the difference between these two present values, $1,984,346, is the value of the swap. It is a negative value for the floating-rate payer because the present value of what is to be received is less than the present value of what is to be paid out.

Duration of a Swap

As with any fixed-income contract, the value of a swap will change as interest rates change. Dollar duration is a measure of the interest-rate sensitivity of a fixed-income contract. From the perspective of the party who pays floating and receives fixed, the interest-rate swap position can be viewed as follows: long a fixed-rate bond + short a floating-rate bond. This means that the dollar duration of an interest-rate swap from the perspective of a floating-rate payer is simply the difference between the dollar duration of the two bond positions that make up the swap; that is,

$$\text{dollar duration of a swap} = \text{dollar duration of a fixed-rate bond}$$
$$- \text{dollar duration of a floating-rate bond}$$

Most of the dollar price sensitivity of a swap due to interest-rate changes will result from the dollar duration of the fixed-rate bond because the dollar duration of the floating-rate bond will be small. The closer the swap is to the date that the coupon rate is reset, the smaller the dollar duration of a floating-rate bond.

Application of a Swap to Asset/Liability Management

So far we have merely described an interest-rate swap and looked at its characteristics. Here we illustrate how they can be used in asset/liability management. Other types of interest-rate swaps have been developed that go beyond the generic or "plain vanilla" swap described and we describe these later.

An interest-rate swap can be used to alter the cash flow characteristics of an institution's assets so as to provide a better match between assets and liabilities. The two institutions we use for illustration are a commercial bank and a life insurance company.

Suppose that a bank has a portfolio consisting of five-year term commercial loans with a fixed interest rate. The principal value of the portfolio is $50 million, and the interest rate on all the loans in the portfolio is 10%. The loans are interest-only loans; interest is paid semiannually, and the principal is paid at the end of five years. That is, assuming no default on the loans, the cash flow from the loan portfolio is $2.5 million every six months for the next five years and $50 million at the end of five years. To fund its loan portfolio, assume that the bank is relying on the issuance of six-month certificates of deposit. The interest rate that the bank plans to pay on its six-month CDs is six-month LIBOR plus 40 basis points.

The risk that the bank faces is that six-month LIBOR will be 9.6% or greater. To understand why, remember that the bank is earning 10% annually on its commercial loan portfolio. If six-month LIBOR is 9.6%, it will have to pay 9.6% plus 40 basis points, or 10%, to depositors for six-month funds and there will be no spread income. Worse, if six-month LIBOR rises above 9.6%, there will be a loss; that is, the cost of funds will exceed the interest rate earned on the loan portfolio. The bank's objective is to lock in a spread over the cost of its funds.

The other party in the interest-rate-swap illustration is a life insurance company that has committed itself to pay a 9% rate for the next five years on a guaranteed investment contract (GIC) it has issued. The amount of the GIC is $50 million. Suppose that the life insurance company has the opportunity to invest $50 million in what it considers an attractive five-year floating-rate instrument in a private placement transaction. The interest rate on this instrument is six-month LIBOR plus 160 basis points.

The coupon rate is set every six months. The risk that the life insurance company faces in this instance is that six-month LIBOR will fall so that the company will not earn enough to realize a spread over the 9% rate that it has guaranteed to the GIC holders. If six-month LIBOR falls to 7.4% or less, no spread income will be generated. To understand why, suppose that six-month LIBOR at the date the floating-rate instrument resets its coupon is 7.4%. Then the coupon rate for the next six months will be 9% (7.4% plus 160 basis points). Because the life insurance company has agreed to pay 9% on the GIC policy, there will be no spread income. Should six-month LIBOR fall below 7.4%, there will be a loss.

We can summarize the asset/liability problems of the bank and the life insurance company as follows.

BANK:
1. Has lent long term and borrowed short term.
2. If six-month LIBOR rises, spread income declines.

LIFE INSURANCE COMPANY:
1. Has lent short term and borrowed long term.
2. If six-month LIBOR falls, spread income declines.

Now let's suppose the market has available a five-year interest-rate swap with a notional principal amount of $50 million. The swap terms available to the bank are as follows:

1. Every six months the bank will pay 8.45% (annual rate).
2. Every six months the bank will receive LIBOR.

The swap terms available to the insurance company are as follows:

1. Every six months the life insurance company will pay LIBOR.
2. Every six months the life insurance company will receive 8.40%.

What has this interest-rate contract done for the bank and the life insurance company? Consider first the bank. For every six-month period for the life of the swap agreement, the interest-rate spread will be as follows:

Annual Interest Rate Received:	
From commercial loan portfolio	10.00%
From interest-rate swap	six-month LIBOR
Total	10.00% + six-month LIBOR

Annual Interest Rate Paid:	
To CD depositors	six-month LIBOR
On interest-rate swap	8.45%
Total	8.45% + six-month LIBOR

Outcome:	
To be received	10.00% + six-month LIBOR
To be paid	8.45% + six-month LIBOR
Spread income	1.55% or 155 basis points

Thus, whatever happens to six-month LIBOR, the bank locks in a spread of 155 basis points.

Now let's look at the effect of the interest-rate swap on the life insurance company:

Annual Interest Rate Received:	
From floating-rate instrument	1.6% + six-month LIBOR
From interest-rate swap	8.40%
Total	10.00% + six-month LIBOR
Annual Interest Rate Paid:	
To GIC policyholders	9.00%
On interest-rate swap	six-month LIBOR
Total	9.00% + six-month LIBOR
Outcome:	
To be received	10.00% + six-month LIBOR
To be paid	9.00% + six-month LIBOR
Spread income	1.0% or 100 basis points

Regardless of what happens to six-month LIBOR, the life insurance company locks in a spread of 100 basis points.

The interest-rate swap has allowed each party to accomplish its asset/liability objective of locking in a spread.[5] It permits the two financial institutions to alter the cash flow characteristics of its assets: from fixed to floating in the case of the bank, and from floating to fixed in the case of the life insurance company. This type of transaction is referred to as an **asset swap.** Another way the bank and the life insurance company could use the swap market would be to change the cash flow nature of their liabilities. Such a swap is called a **liability swap.**

Of course, there are other ways that two such institutions can accomplish the same objectives. The bank might refuse to make fixed-rate commercial loans. However, if borrowers can find someplace else willing to lend on a fixed-rate basis, the bank has lost these customers. The life insurance company might refuse to purchase a floating-rate instrument. But suppose that the terms on a private placement instrument offered to the life insurance company were more attractive than those available on a comparable credit-risk floating-rate instrument, and that by using the swap market the life insurance company can earn more than it could by investing directly in a five-year fixed-rate bond. For example, suppose that the life insurance company can invest in a comparable credit risk five-year fixed-rate bond with a yield of 9.8%. Assuming that it commits itself to a GIC with a 9% rate, this would result in spread income of 80 basis points, less than the 100-basis-point spread income it achieves by purchasing the floating-rate instrument and entering into the swap.

---

[5]Whether the size of the spread is adequate is not an issue for us in this illustration.

Consequently, not only can an interest-rate swap be used to change the risk of a transaction by changing the cash flow characteristics of assets or liabilities, but under certain circumstances, it can also be used to enhance returns. Obviously, this depends on the existence of market imperfections.

Creation of Structured Notes Using Swaps

As explained in Chapter 7, corporations can customize medium-term notes for institutional investors who want to make a market play on interest rate, currency, and/or stock market movements. That is, the coupon rate on the issue will be based on the movements of these financial variables. A corporation can do so in such a way that it can still synthetically fix the coupon rate. This can be accomplished by issuing an MTN and entering into a swap simultaneously. MTNs created in this way are called **structured MTNs.**

The following illustration demonstrates how an interest-rate swap can be used to create a structured note in which the coupon rate floats inversely with LIBOR, that is, an inverse floater. As we explained in Chapter 8, an inverse floater can be created from a fixed-rate security by creating a corresponding floater. By using an interest-rate swap, it is not necessary to create the floater.

To see how this can be done using an interest-rate swap, let's assume the following. The Arbour Corporation wants to issue $100 million of a five-year fixed-rate MTN. The firm's banker indicates that the yield it would have to offer is 6.10%. However, it recommends that the corporation issue an inverse-floating-rate MTN and proposes the following two transactions:

Transaction 1: Issue $100 million of a five-year inverse-floating-rate MTN with a coupon payment that resets every six months based on the following formula: 13% − LIBOR.

Transaction 2: Enter into a five-year interest-rate swap with its banker with a notional principal amount of $100 million in which semiannual payments are exchanged as follows:

Arbour Corporation pays LIBOR.

Arbour Corporation receives 7%.

Notice that Arbour Corporation's MTN is an inverse-floating-rate note because as LIBOR increases, the coupon rate decreases. However, although the MTN may have an inverse floating rate, the combination of the two transactions results in a fixed-rate financing for Arbour Corporation, as follows:

Arbour Corporation Receives:	
From its banker for swap	7%

Arbour Corporation Pays:	
To MTN holders	13% − LIBOR
To its banker for swap	LIBOR
Net payments:	(13% − LIBOR) + LIBOR − 7% = 6%

The advantage of this structured MTN is that the issuer was able to obtain a funding cost of 6% rather than 6.1% if it issued a fixed-rate MTN. By using other types of swaps (equity and currency), any type of coupon rate can be created.

Primary Determinants of Swap Spreads

Earlier we provided two interpretations of a swap: (1) a package of futures/forward contracts, and (2) a package of cash market instruments. The swap spread is determined by the same factors that influence the spread over Treasuries on financial instruments (futures/forward contracts or cash) that produce a similar return or funding profile. As we explain subsequently, the key determinant of the swap spread for swaps with maturities of five years or less is the cost of hedging in the Eurodollar CD futures market. For longer maturity swaps, the key determinant of the swap spread is the credit spreads in the corporate bond market.

Given that a swap is a package of futures/forward contracts, the swap spread can be determined by looking for futures/forward contracts with the same risk/return profile. A Eurodollar CD futures contract is a swap where a fixed dollar payment (i.e., the futures price) is exchanged for three-month LIBOR. There are available Eurodollar CD futures contracts that have maturities every three months for five years. A market participant can synthesize a (synthetic) fixed-rate security or a fixed-rate funding vehicle of up to five years by taking a position in a strip of Eurodollar CD futures contracts (i.e., a position in every three-month Eurodollar CD up to the desired maturity date).

For example, consider a financial institution that has fixed-rate assets and floating-rate liabilities. Both the assets and liabilities have a maturity of three years. The interest rate on the liabilities resets every three months based on three-month LIBOR. This financial institution can hedge this mismatched asset/liability position by buying a three-year strip of Eurodollar CD futures contracts. By doing so, the financial institution is receiving LIBOR over the three-year period and paying a fixed dollar amount (i.e., the futures price). The financial institution is now hedged because the assets are fixed rate, and the strip of long Eurodollar CDs futures synthetically creates a fixed-rate funding arrangement. From the fixed dollar amount over the three years, an effective fixed interest rate that the financial institution pays can be calculated. Alternatively, the financial institution can synthetically create a fixed-rate funding arrangement by entering into a three-year swap in which it pays fixed and receives three-month LIBOR. The financial institution will use the vehicle that gives the lowest cost of hedging the mismatched position. This will drive the synthetic fixed rate in the swap market to that available by hedging in the Eurodollar CD futures market.

For swaps with maturities longer than five years, the spread is determined primarily by the credit spreads in the corporate bond market. Because a swap can be interpreted as a package of long and short positions in a fixed-rate bond and a floating-rate bond, it is the credit spreads in those two market sectors that will be the key determinant of the swap spread. Boundary conditions for swap spreads based on prices for fixed-rate and floating-rate corporate bonds can be determined.[6] Several technical fac-

---

[6]These boundary conditions are derived in the appendix to Ellen Evans and Gioia Parente Bales, "What Drives Interest Rate Swap Spreads?" Chapter 13 in Carl R. Beidleman (ed.), *Interest Rate Swaps* (Homewood, IL: Richard D. Irwin, 1991).

tors, such as the relative supply of fixed-rate and floating-rate corporate bonds and the cost to dealers of hedging their inventory position of swaps, influence where between the boundaries the actual swap spread will be.[7]

Development of the Interest-Rate-Swap Market

The interest-rate swap was developed in late 1981. By 1987, the market had grown to more than $500 billion (in terms of notional principal amount). What is behind this rapid growth? As our asset/liability application earlier demonstrated, an interest-rate swap is a quick way for institutional investors to change the nature of assets and liabilities or to exploit any perceived capital market imperfection. The same applies to borrowers such as corporations, sovereigns, and supranationals.

In fact, the initial motivation for the interest-rate-swap market was borrower exploitation of what were perceived to be "credit arbitrage" opportunities because of differences between the quality spread between lower- and higher-rated credits in the U.S. and Eurodollar bond fixed-rate market and the same spread in these two floating-rate markets. Basically, the argument for swaps was based on a well-known economic principle of comparative advantage in international economics. The argument in the case of swaps is that even though a high credit-rated issuer could borrow at a lower cost in both the fixed- and floating-rate markets (i.e., have an absolute advantage in both), it will have a comparative advantage relative to a lower credit-rated issuer in one of the markets (and a comparative disadvantage in the other). Under these conditions, each borrower could benefit from issuing securities in the market in which it has a comparative advantage and then swapping obligations for the desired type of financing. The swap market was the vehicle for swapping obligations.

Despite arguments that credit arbitrage opportunities are rare in reasonably efficient international capital markets, and that even if they did exist, they would be eliminated quickly by arbitrage, the number of interest-rate-swap transactions has grown substantially. Another explanation is suggested in a May 1984 contribution sponsored by Citicorp that appeared in *Euromoney:*

> The nature of swaps is that they arbitrage market imperfections. As with any arbitrage opportunity, the more it is exploited, the smaller it becomes. . . .
>
> But some of the causes of market imperfections are unlikely to disappear quickly. For example, insurance companies in many countries are constrained to invest mainly in instruments that are domestic in that country. That requirement will tend to favour domestic issuers artificially, and is unlikely to be changed overnight. And even in the world's most liquid markets there are arbitrage opportunities. They are small and exist only briefly. But they exist nevertheless.[8]

As this opinion demonstrates, as early as 1984 it was argued that the difference in quality spreads in the two markets may be attributable to differences in regulations in

---

[7]For a discussion of these other factors, see Evans and Bales, "What Drives Interest Rate Swap Spreads?" pp. 293–301.

[8]"Swap Financing Techniques: A Citicorp Guide," Special Sponsored Section, *Euromoney,* May 1984, pp. S1–S7.

two countries. Similarly, differences in tax treatment across countries also create market imperfections that can be exploited using swaps. Thus swaps can be used for regulatory or tax arbitrage.

Rather than relying exclusively on an arbitrage argument, one study suggests that the swaps market grew because it allowed borrowers to raise a type of financing that was not possible prior to the introduction of interest-rate swaps.[9]

Finally, another argument suggested for the growth of the interest-rate-swap market is the increased volatility of interest rates that has led borrowers and lenders to hedge or manage their exposure. Even though risk/return characteristics can be replicated by a package of forward contracts, interest-rate forward contracts are not as liquid as interest-rate swaps. And entering into or liquidating swap transactions has been facilitated by the standardization of documentation published by the International Swap Dealers Association in early 1987.

Role of the Intermediary   The role of the intermediary in an interest-rate swap sheds some light on the evolution of the market. Intermediaries in these transactions have been commercial banks and investment banks, who in the early stages of the market sought out end users of swaps. That is, they found in their client bases those entities that needed the swap to accomplish a funding or investing objective, and they matched the two entities. In essence, the intermediary in this type of transaction performed the function of a broker.

The only time that the intermediary would take the opposite side of a swap (i.e., would act as a principal) was to balance out the transaction. For example, if an intermediary had two clients that were willing to do a swap but one wanted the notional principal amount to be $100 million and the other wanted it to be $85 million, the intermediary might become the counterparty to the extent of $15 million. That is, the intermediary would warehouse or take a position as a principal to the transaction to make up the $15 million difference between client objectives. To protect itself against an adverse interest-rate movement, the intermediary would hedge its position.

There is another problem in an interest-rate swap that we have yet to address. The parties to swaps have to be concerned that the other party might default on its obligation. Although a default would not mean any principal was lost because the notional principal amount had not been exchanged, it would mean that the objective for which the swap was entered into would be impaired. As the early transactions involved a higher- and a lower-credit-rated entity, the former would be concerned with the potential for default of the latter. To reduce the risk of default, many early swap transactions required that the lower-credit-rated entity obtain a guarantee from a highly rated commercial bank.

As the frequency and the size of the transactions increased, many intermediaries became comfortable with the transactions and became principals instead of acting as brokers. As long as an intermediary had one entity willing to do a swap, the intermediary was willing to be the counterparty. Consequently, interest-rate swaps became part of an intermediary's inventory of product positions. Advances in quantitative techniques and futures products for hedging complex positions such as swaps made the protection of large inventory positions feasible.

---

[9]Marcelle Arak, Arturo Estrella, Laurie Goodman, and Andrew Silver, "Interest Rate Swaps: An Alternative Explanation," *Financial Management,* Summer 1988, pp. 12–18.

Yet another reason encouraged intermediaries to become principals rather than brokers in swaps. As more intermediaries entered the swap market, bid–ask spreads on swaps declined sharply. To make money in the swaps market, intermediaries had to do a sufficient volume of business, which could be done only if an intermediary had (1) an extensive client base willing to use swaps, and (2) a large inventory of swaps. This necessitated that intermediaries act as principals.

Consequently, the development of the swap market can be described as one that originated to exploit real or perceived imperfections in the capital market, but that evolved into a transactionally efficient market for accomplishing asset/liability objectives.

Secondary Market Swap Transactions

There are three general types of transactions in the secondary market for swaps. These include (1) a swap reversal, (2) a swap sale (or assignment), and (3) a swap buy-back (or close-out or cancellation). Exhibit 23-6 summarizes the secondary market for swaps.

In a **swap reversal,** the party that wants out of the transaction will arrange for a swap in which (1) the maturity on the new swap is equal to the time remaining for the original swap, (2) the index is the same, and (3) the notional principal amount is the same. For example, suppose that party X enters into a five-year swap with a notional principal amount of $50 million in which it pays 10% and receives LIBOR, but that two years later, X wants out of the swap. In a swap reversal, X would enter into a three-year interest-rate swap, with a counterparty different from the original counterparty, let's say Z, in which the notional principal amount is $50 million, and X pays LIBOR and receives a fixed rate. The fixed rate that X receives from Z will depend on prevailing swap terms for floating-rate receivers at the initiation of the three-year swap.

Although party X has effectively terminated the original swap in economic terms, there is a major drawback to this approach: Party X is still liable to the original counterparty Y, as well as to the new counterparty, Z. That is, party X now has two offsetting interest-rate swaps on its books instead of one, and as a result it has increased its counterparty risk exposure.

EXHIBIT 23-6	Types of Secondary Market Swap Transactions		
	Swap Reversal	*Swap Sale*	*Swap Buy-Back*
Purpose	Counterbalance a swap until maturity	End the party's obligation	End the party's obligation
Strategy	Take the opposite side of a swap with equivalent maturity, reference rate, and notional principal	Seek another party to accept the obligation	Sell the swap back to the original counterparty
Drawbacks	Having two swaps increases counterparty risk	Counterparty must be willing to accept the credit of the new party	

The **swap sale** or **swap assignment** overcomes this drawback. In this secondary market transaction, the party that wishes to close out the original swap finds another party that is willing to accept its obligations under the swap. In our illustration, this means that X finds another party, say, A, that will agree to pay 10% to Y and receive LIBOR from Y for the next three years. A will have to be compensated to accept the position of X, or A will have to be willing to compensate X. The compensation depends on the value of the swap. If from X's perspective the swap has a positive value, that is the value A must pay to X. If, on the other hand, the value of the swap from X's perspective is negative, X must compensate A.

When the transaction is completed, it is then A not X that is obligated to perform under the swap terms. (Of course an intermediary could act as principal and become party A to help its client X.) In order to accomplish a swap sale, the original counterparty, Y in our example, must agree to the sale. A key factor in whether Y will agree is whether it is willing to accept the credit of A. For example, if A's credit rating is double-B and X's is double-A, Y would be unlikely to accept A as a counterparty.

A swap buy-back (or **close-out sale** or **cancellation**) involves the sale of the swap to the original counterparty. As in the case of a swap sale, one party might have to compensate the other, depending on how interest rates and credit spreads have changed since the inception of the swap. These methods for getting out of or into a swap leave much to be desired for market participants. It is this illiquidity in the secondary market that will hamper swap market growth. There have been proposals to create a swap clearing corporation, similar to the clearing corporations for futures and options, in which case swaps could be marked-to-market and credit exposure to a swap reduced.

Beyond the "Plain Vanilla" Swap

Thus far we have described the "plain vanilla" or generic interest-rate swap. Non-generic or individualized swaps have evolved as a result of the asset/liability needs of borrowers and lenders, and some are described in the following sections.

Amortizing, Accreting, and Roller Coaster Swaps   In a generic swap, the notional principal amount does not vary over the life of the swap. Thus, it is sometimes referred to as a **bullet swap.** In contrast, for amortizing, accreting, and roller coaster swaps, the notional principal amount varies over the life of the swap.

To explain an **amortizing swap,** we can use our earlier illustration of the interest-rate swap between the commercial bank and the life insurance company. Recall that it was the fixed-rate commercial loans that were generating the cash flow that the bank was using to make the fixed-rate payment on the interest-rate swap. We assumed that the loans were interest-only loans and that the principal would be repaid at the end of five years. Suppose, instead, that the loan was a level-payment, fully amortized one, meaning that the principal outstanding would decline over the five years, and therefore the interest would decline over time. In such an instance, the amount received every six months from the commercial loans would be less than the fixed-rate payments to be made on the interest-rate swap, if interest rates decline. This is because the principal repaid every six months would have to be reinvested at an interest rate less than 10% (the interest on the original loan balance).

An amortizing swap can be used to solve this problem. An amortizing swap is one in which the notional principal amount decreases in a predetermined way over the life of the swap. In situations in which a liability to be funded increases over time, an accreting swap can be employed. An **accreting swap** is one in which the notional principal amount increases at a predetermined way over time. An accreting swap could be used by a lending institution that has committed to lend increasing amounts to a customer for a long-term project.

In a **roller coaster swap,** the notional principal amount can rise or fall from period to period according to an institution's liability structure.

Zero-Coupon Swaps   In a **zero-coupon swap,** the fixed-rate payer does not make any payments until the maturity date of the swap but receives floating-rate payments at regular payment dates. This type of swap exposes the floating-rate payer to significant credit risk because this party makes regular payments but does not receive any payments until the maturity date of the swap.

Basis Rate Swap   The terms of a typical interest-rate swap call for the exchange of fixed- and floating-rate payments. In a **basis rate swap,** both parties exchange floating-rate payments based on a different money market index. As an example, assume a commercial bank has a portfolio of loans in which the lending rate is based on the prime rate, but the bank's cost of funds is based on LIBOR. The risk the bank faces is that the spread between the prime rate and LIBOR will change. This is referred to as basis risk. The bank can use a basis rate swap to make floating-rate payments based on the prime rate and receive floating-rate payments based on LIBOR.

Forward Rate Swaps   A forward swap is simply a forward contract on an interest-rate swap. The terms of the swap are set today, but the parties agree that the swap will begin at a specified date in the future.

Options on Swaps

The second generation of products in the interest-rate swap market are options on interest-rate swaps, which are referred to as **swaptions.** The buyer of a swaption has the right to enter into an interest-rate swap agreement by some specified date in the future. The swaption agreement will specify whether the buyer of the swaption will be a fixed-rate receiver or a fixed-rate payer. The writer of the swaption becomes the counterparty to the swap if the buyer exercises.

If the buyer of the swaption has the right to enter into a swap as a fixed-rate payer, it is called a **put swaption.** The writer therefore becomes the fixed-rate receiver/floating-rate payer. If the buyer of the swaption has the right to enter into a swap as a floating-rate payer, it is called a **call swaption.** The writer of the swaption therefore becomes the floating-rate receiver/fixed-rate payer.

The strike rate of the swaption indicates the fixed rate that will be swapped versus the floating rate. The swaption will also specify the maturity date of the swap. A swaption may be European or American. Of course, as in all options, the buyer of a swaption pays the writer a premium, although the premium can be structured into the swap terms so that no upfront fee has to be paid.

A swaption can be used to hedge a portfolio strategy that uses an interest-rate swap but where the cash flow of the underlying asset or liability is uncertain. The cash flow of the asset would be uncertain if it (1) is callable, as in the case of a callable corporate bond, a mortgage loan, a pass-through security, or a loan that can be prepaid; and/or (2) exposes the investor/lender to default risk.[10]

To illustrate the use of a swaption, suppose that a savings and loan association enters into a four-year swap in which it agrees to pay 9% fixed and receive LIBOR. The fixed-rate payments will come from a portfolio of mortgage pass-through securities with a coupon rate of 9%. Suppose that one year after the swap begins, mortgage rates decline to 6%, resulting in large prepayments. The prepayments received will have to be reinvested at a rate lower than 9%, but the S&L must still pay 9% under the terms of the swap. As the S&L is paying fixed and receiving floating, it would seek to use a swaption that allows it to unwind the original swap by receiving fixed and paying floating. More specifically, the S&L will enter into a swaption that will allow it to receive 9% and pay LIBOR. The purchase of a put swaption with a strike rate of 9% (and a LIBOR floating rate) would be the appropriate swaption to terminate the original swap.

INTEREST-RATE AGREEMENTS (CAPS AND FLOORS)

An **interest-rate agreement** is an agreement between two parties whereby one party, for an upfront premium, agrees to compensate the other at specific time periods if a designated interest rate, called the **reference rate,** is different from a predetermined level. When one party agrees to pay the other when the reference rate exceeds a predetermined level, the agreement is referred to as an **interest-rate cap** or **ceiling.** The agreement is referred to as an **interest-rate floor** when one party agrees to pay the other when the reference rate falls below a predetermined level. The predetermined interest-rate level is called the **strike rate.**

The terms of an interest-rate agreement include

1. The reference rate
2. The strike rate that sets the ceiling or floor
3. The length of the agreement
4. The frequency of settlement
5. The notional principal amount

Suppose that C buys an interest-rate cap from D with terms as follows:

1. The reference rate is six-month LIBOR
2. The strike rate is 8%
3. The agreement is for seven years
4. Settlement is every six months
5. The notional principal amount is $20 million

Under this agreement, every six months for the next seven years, D will pay C whenever six-month LIBOR exceeds 8%. The payment will equal the dollar value of the difference between six-month LIBOR and 8% times the notional principal

---

[10]For an explanation of how swaptions can be used to manage a portfolio of callable bonds, see Robert M. Stavis and Victor J. Haghani, "Putable Swaps: Tools for Managing Callable Assets," Chapter 20 in Frank J. Fabozzi (ed.), *The Handbook of Fixed Income Options* (Chicago: Probus Publishing, 1989).

amount divided by 2. For example, if six months from now six-month LIBOR is 11%, D will pay C 3% (11% minus 8%) times $20 million divided by 2, or $300,000. If six-month LIBOR is 8% or less, D does not have to pay anything to C.

In the case of an interest-rate floor, assume the same terms as those for the interest-rate cap we just illustrated. In this case, if six-month LIBOR is 11%, C receives nothing from D, but if six-month LIBOR is less than 8%, D compensates C for the difference. For example, if six-month LIBOR is 7%, D will pay C $100,000 (8% minus 7% times $20 million divided by 2).

Interest-rate caps and floors can be combined to create an interest-rate collar. This is done by buying an interest-rate cap and selling an interest-rate floor. Some commercial banks and investment banking firms write options on interest-rate agreements for customers. Options on caps are **captions;** options on floors are called **flotions.**

Risk/Return Characteristics

In an interest-rate agreement, the buyer pays an upfront fee, which represents the maximum amount that the buyer can lose and the maximum amount that the writer of the agreement can gain. The only party that is required to perform is the writer of the interest-rate agreement. The buyer of an interest-rate cap benefits if the underlying interest rate rises above the strike rate because the seller (writer) must compensate the buyer. The buyer of an interest rate floor benefits if the interest rate falls below the strike rate, because the seller (writer) must compensate the buyer.

To better understand interest-rate caps and floors, we can look at them as in essence equivalent to a package of interest-rate options. Because the buyer benefits if the interest rate rises above the strike rate, an interest-rate cap is similar to purchasing a package of call options on an interest rate or purchasing a put option on a bond. The seller of an interest-rate cap has effectively sold a package of call options on an interest rate or sold a package of put options on a bond. The buyer of an interest-rate floor benefits from a decline in the interest rate below the strike rate. Therefore, the buyer of an interest-rate floor has effectively bought a package of put options on an interest rate or a package of call options on a bond from the writer of the option.

Once again, a complex contract can be seen to be a package of basic contracts, or options in the case of interest-rate agreements. Captions and flotions can be viewed as options on a package of options.

Applications

To see how interest-rate agreements can be used for asset/liability management, consider the problems faced by the commercial bank and the life insurance company we discussed in demonstrating the use of an interest-rate swap.[11] Recall that the bank's objective is to lock in an interest-rate spread over its cost of funds. Yet because it borrows short term, its cost of funds is uncertain. The bank may be able to purchase a cap, however, so that the cap rate plus the cost of purchasing the cap is less than the rate it is earning on its fixed-rate commercial loans. If short-term rates decline, the bank does not benefit from the cap, but its cost of funds declines. The cap therefore

---

[11]For additional applications in the insurance industry, see David F. Babbel, Peter Bouyoucos, and Robert Stricker, "Capping the Interest Rate Risk in Insurance Products," Chapter 21 in Frank J. Fabozzi (ed.), *Fixed Income Portfolio Strategies* (Chicago: Probus Publishing, 1989).

allows the bank to impose a ceiling on its cost of funds while retaining the opportunity to benefit from a decline in rates.

The bank can reduce the cost of purchasing the cap by selling a floor. In this case the bank agrees to pay the buyer of the floor if the reference rate falls below the strike rate. The bank receives a fee for selling the floor, but it has sold off its opportunity to benefit from a decline in rates below the strike rate. By buying a cap and selling a floor, the bank has created a predetermined range for its cost of funds (i.e., a collar).

Recall the problem of the life insurance company that guarantees a 9% rate on a GIC for the next five years and is considering the purchase of an attractive floating-rate instrument in a private placement transaction. The risk that the company faces is that interest rates will fall so that it will not earn enough to realize the 9% guaranteed rate plus a spread. The life insurance company may be able to purchase a floor to set a lower bound on its investment return, yet retain the opportunity to benefit should rates increase. To reduce the cost of purchasing the floor, the life insurance company can sell an interest-rate cap. By doing so, however, it gives up the opportunity of benefiting from an increase in six-month LIBOR above the strike rate of the interest-rate cap.

SUMMARY

An interest-rate swap is an agreement specifying that the parties exchange interest payments at designated times. In a typical swap, one party will make fixed-rate payments, and the other will make floating-rate payments, with payments based on the notional principal amount. Participants in financial markets use interest-rate swaps to alter the cash flow characteristics of their assets or liabilities, or to capitalize on perceived capital market inefficiencies.

A swap position can be interpreted as either a package of forward/futures contracts or a package of cash flows from buying and selling cash market instruments. The swap rate is determined by finding the rate that will make the present value of the cash flow of both sides of the swap equal. The value of an existing swap is equal to the difference in the present value of the two payments. The interest-rate sensitivity or duration of a swap from the perspective of a floating-rate payer is just the difference between the duration of the fixed-rate bond and duration of the floating-rate bond that compose the swap. Most of the interest-rate sensitivity of a swap will result from the duration of the fixed-rate bond since the duration of the floating-rate bond will be small.

There are three general types of transactions in the secondary market for swaps: (1) a swap reversal, (2) a swap sale (or assignment), and (3) a swap buy-back (or close-out or cancellation). A number of types of swaps have been developed to satisfy various needs of market participants. These include swaps in which the notional principal amount varies over the life of the swap (amortizing, accreting, and roller coaster swaps), zero-coupon swaps, and basis rate swaps. The second generation of swaps is options on swaps: put and call swaptions.

An interest-rate agreement allows one party for an upfront premium the right to receive compensation from the writer of the agreement if a designated interest rate is different from a predetermined level. An interest-rate cap calls for one party to receive a payment if a designated interest rate is above the strike rate. An interest-rate floor lets one party receive a payment if a designated interest rate is below the strike rate. An interest-rate cap can be used to establish a ceiling on the cost of funding; an interest-rate floor can be used to establish a floor return. Buying a cap and selling a floor creates a collar.

Questions

1. Consider an interest-rate swap with these features: maturity is five years, notional principal is $100 million, payments occur every six months, the fixed-rate payer pays a rate of 9.05% and receives LIBOR, while the floating-rate payer pays LIBOR and receives 9%. Now suppose that at a payment date, LIBOR is at 6.5%. What is each party's payment and receipt at that date?
2. Suppose that a dealer quotes these terms on a five-year swap: fixed-rate payer to pay 9.5% for LIBOR and floating-rate payer to pay LIBOR for 9.2%.
   a. What is the dealer's bid–asked spread?
   b. How would the dealer quote the terms by reference to the yield on five-year Treasury notes?
3. Give two interpretations of an interest-rate swap.
4. In determining the cash flow for the floating-rate side of a LIBOR swap, explain how the cash flow is determined.
5. How is the swap rate calculated?
6. How is the value of a swap determined?
7. What factors affect the swap rate?
8. Describe the role of an intermediary in a swap.
9. What types of transactions occur in the secondary market for an interest-rate swap?
10. Suppose that a life insurance company has issued a three-year GIC with a fixed rate of 10%. Under what circumstances might it be feasible for the life insurance company to invest the funds in a floating-rate security and enter into a three-year interest-rate swap in which it pays a floating rate and receives a fixed rate?
11. The following excerpt is taken from an article titled "IRS Rule to Open Swaps to Pension Funds," which appeared in the November 18, 1991, issue of *BondWeek,* pp. 1–2:

> A proposed Internal Revenue Service rule that gives tax-free status to income earned on swaps by pension funds and other tax-exempt institutions is expected to spur pension fund use of these products, say swap and pension fund professionals. . . .
>
> UBS Asset Management has received permission from most of its pension fund clients to use interest rate and currency swaps in its fixed-income portfolios and is awaiting the IRS regulation before stepping into the market, says Kenneth Choie, v.p. and head of research and product development. . . . "The IRS' proposed rule is great news for pension fund managers," as the use of swaps can enhance returns and lower transaction costs, Choie says. . . .
>
> While some pension funds are exploring the swap market, pension fund consultants underscore that the funds' entrance into the market is likely to be slow. Counterparty risk has been a more formidable obstacle than the ambiguity of the tax status of income from interest-rate and currency swaps, says Paul Burik, director of research at Ennis, Knupp & Associates, a pension fund consulting firm.

[The rule referred to has been adopted.]

a. In the article, Choie indicates that one "possible application that UBS is considering is to switch between fixed- and floating-rate income streams without incurring the transaction costs of trading chunks of securities." Explain how an interest-rate swap can be used for this application.

b. What is counterparty risk?

c. How can counterparty risk be reduced?

12. What is a swaption?

13. Consider the three-year swap shown in Exhibit 23-4. Suppose that one year later the Eurodollar CD futures prices are as follows:

Period	Day Count	Futures Price
1	91	
2	94	96.70
3	91	96.70
4	90	96.66
5	91	96.60
6	91	96.55
7	91	96.52
8	93	96.47
9	91	96.40

What is the value of the swap?

14. The following table shows information for a three-year swap.

(1) Period	(2) Day Count	(3) Futures Price	(4) Fwd Rate	(5) Discount Factor	(6) Floating Cash flow
1	90		5.65	1.00000	
2	91	94.25	5.75	0.98592	1,428,194
3	90	94.15	5.85	0.97195	1,437,500
4	90	94.05	5.95	0.95794	1,462,500
5	91	93.88	6.12	0.94374	1,504,028
6	90	93.80	6.20	0.92952	1,530,000
7	91	93.74	6.26	0.91518	1,567,222
8	90	93.65	6.35	0.90108	1,565,000
9	91	93.50	6.50	0.88684	1,605,139
10	91	93.45	6.55	0.87251	1,643,056
11	91	93.38	6.62	0.85830	1,655,694
12	90	93.28	6.72	0.84432	1,655,000
13	91	93.20	6.80	0.83022	1,698,667

Demonstrate that the swap rate is 6.192181%.

15. Suppose that a savings and loan association buys an interest-rate cap that has these terms: The reference rate is the six-month Treasury bill rate; the cap will last for five years; payment is semiannual; the strike rate is 5.5%; and the notional principal is $10 million. Suppose further that at the end of a six-month period, the six-month Treasury bill rate is 6.1%.

a. What is the amount of the payment that the savings and loan association will receive?

b. What would the writer of this cap pay if the six-month Treasury rate were 5.45% instead of 6.1%?

16. What is the relationship between an interest-rate agreement and an option on an interest rate?

17. How can an interest-rate collar be created?

Index